The Tutorverse
MAKING THE UNIVERSE BRIGHTER, ONE STUDENT AT A TIME

The New SAT®:
1,500+ Practice Questions

The New SAT®: 1,500+ Practice Questions

Published in the United States of America by:

The Tutorverse, LLC

222 Broadway, 19th Floor

New York, NY 10038

Web: www.thetutorverse.com

Email: help@thetutorverse.com

For information about buying this title in bulk or to place a special order, please contact us at help@thetutorverse.com.

ISBN-13: 978-1530731510
ISBN-10: 1530731518

SAT® is a trademark registered and/or owned by the College Board, which was not involved in the production of, and does not endorse, this book.

Neither the author nor publisher claim any responsibility for the accuracy and appropriateness of the content in this book, nor do they claim any responsibility over the outcome of students who use these materials.

The views and opinions expressed in this book do not necessarily reflect the official policy, position, or point of view of the author or publisher. Such views and opinions do not constitute an endorsement to perform, attempt to perform, or otherwise emulate any procedures, experiments, etc. described in any of the passages, excerpts, adaptations, cited materials, or similar information. Such information is included only to facilitate the development of questions, answer choices, and answer explanations for purposes of preparing for the SAT®.

Contents

The New SAT®:
1,500+ Practice Questions

Welcome

Dear Students, Parents, and Educators,

We believe that a postsecondary education has many benefits. Students who study at postsecondary institutions receive an education that can open many doors and pave the way to many opportunities. At school, students often forge enduring friendships and discover lifelong interests. Indeed, time spent at a postsecondary institution can be so formative and impactful that it is difficult to overstate its influence on a person's life.

Of course, before one can reap the benefits of a postsecondary education, one must work hard for the opportunity. One of the first steps to take is to prepare for a standardized, postsecondary entrance exam, like the SAT.

Preparing for the SAT can be challenging. Students often juggle academic, extracurricular, and even formal job responsibilities in the last several years of secondary school. Finding the time to study for the SAT is a difficult – but often necessary – step. This need to carve out time for study is especially important given the content on the SAT, some of which can be infrequently taught in classrooms.

Because the SAT is a knowledge-based test, tips and tricks – though helpful – may not compensate for a lack of preparation and a command of the content. The purpose of this book is to introduce students to the format and content of the SAT and to reinforce knowledge and understanding through practice.

Best wishes, good luck, and welcome to The Tutorverse!

Regards,

The Team at The Tutorverse

The Tutorverse

How to Use This Book

Test Overview

The SAT, created and administered by the College Board, is a complicated test with a complicated scoring system. The purpose of this section is to provide readers with easy-to-understand, high-value, and concise information about the SAT that has a direct bearing on preparing for the test. Understanding the information in this section is critical; without a solid understanding of these basics, it will be very difficult to properly prepare for the test.

Content

The SAT is comprised of three required tests and one optional test. These tests have the following question counts and time limits:

Test	Questions	Time Limit (minutes)
Reading	52	65
Writing & Language	44	35
Math	58	80
Required Sections	154	180
Essay (Optional)	1	50
Total (Including Essay)	155	230

Reading (Required)
Everyone who takes the SAT must complete the Reading Test. On the Reading Test, students must read passages and answer questions about those passages. Some questions assess the student's ability to critically read and comprehend the passage. These questions ask students to determine what is stated explicitly in and what is suggested implicitly by the passage. Other questions ask the student to analyze the actual writing itself, such as the sentence structure, organization, and style of the passage.

There are four stand-alone passages on the Reading Test as well as one paired passage, for a total of five passages. On average, each passage is 625 words in length. The passages vary in difficulty, ranging from early secondary (high school) to early postsecondary (college/university) levels. The passages also vary in purpose, as some are narratives that relate a story, experience, event, etc., while others are expository or persuasive passages that seek to provide information or convince the reader of a point of view. The passages consist of excerpts or adaptations from the following types of published works:

- One literary work of fiction (such as a short story or novel)
- One social science-related work (such as those related to the fields of economics, sociology, and political science)
- One historical, civics/politics-related document (such as The Federalist Papers in the U.S. or a similarly significant document from around the world)

The Tutorverse

🐢 Two science-related works (such as ideas and events related to the earth science, biology, chemistry, or physics fields)

Some passages are accompanied by charts, tables, and other graphical information. This supplemental information is related to the written passage and is the subject of certain questions.

There are 10 -11 questions related to each passage. Discussed in greater detail in the *Part One: Reading* section of this workbook, these questions fall into the following categories:

- 🐢 Information & Ideas
    - 🐢 Close Reading
    - 🐢 Textual Evidence
    - 🐢 Main Ideas
    - 🐢 Summarizing
    - 🐢 Relationships
    - 🐢 Words/Phrases in Context
- 🐢 Rhetoric
    - 🐢 Word Choice
    - 🐢 Text Structure
    - 🐢 Point of View
    - 🐢 Purpose
    - 🐢 Arguments
- 🐢 Synthesis
    - 🐢 Multiple Texts
    - 🐢 Quantitative Information

These questions count toward the section score for Reading and Writing & Language (200-800), the total score of the SAT (400-1600), the test score of the Reading Test (1-40), and the Command of Evidence and Words in Context subscores (1-15 each). Some of these questions also count toward the Analysis in Science and Analysis in Social Studies cross-test scores (1-40 each). Refer to the *Scoring & Reporting* section below for additional information.

Writing & Language (Required)

As with the Reading Test, the Writing & Language Test is required for all SAT test takers. On the Writing & Language Test, students need to read passages and suggest revisions and edits to the passage in order to improve the written expression of ideas and to correct for errors in writing convention.

There are four stand-alone passages on the Writing & Language Test. On average, each passage is 425 words in length. Like the Reading Test, passages on the Writing & Language Test vary in difficulty, ranging from early secondary (high school) to early postsecondary (college/university) levels. The passages also vary in purpose. Where the narrative passage in the Reading Test is fictional, the narrative passage on the Writing & Language Test relates historical or scientific information. The remaining passages are expository or persuasive passages, seeking to provide information or convince the reader of a point of view. The passages consist of the following types of original works:

- 🐢 One career-related topic (concerning trends, issues, and debates in major industries)
- 🐢 One humanities-related topic (concerning arts, art, film, music, and literature)
- 🐢 One history/social studies-related topic (concerning history, anthropology, archaeology, economics, and psychology)
- 🐢 One science-related topic (concerning basic concepts and advances in earth science, biology, chemistry, astronomy, and physics)

The Tutorverse

Some passages are accompanied by charts, tables, and other graphical information. This supplemental information is related to the written passage and is the subject of certain questions.

There are 11 questions related to each passage. Discussed in greater detail in the *Part Two: Writing & Language Test* section of this workbook, these questions generally fall into the following categories:

- Improving Expression
- Standard English Conventions

These questions count toward the section score for Reading and Writing & Language (200-800), the total score of the SAT (400-1600), and the test score of the Writing & Language Test (1-40). These questions will also count toward the Command of Evidence, Words in Context, Expression of Ideas, and Standard English Conventions subscores (1-15 each). Some of these questions will also count toward the Analysis in Science and Analysis in Social Studies cross-test scores (1-40 each). Refer to the *Scoring & Reporting* section below for additional information.

Math (Required)

The Math Test is also a required test on the SAT. The Math Test contains questions that are framed in everyday contexts. There are two parts to the Math Test: questions that permit the use of a calculator, and questions that do not permit the use of a calculator. The Math test features both multiple choice questions as well as student-produced response questions where students fill in the correct answer.

Math questions will generally be framed in the following contexts:

- Science
- Social Science
- Career Scenarios

Discussed in greater detail in the *Part Three: Math* section of this workbook, these questions can generally be categorized as follows:

- Algebra (including linear equations and systems of equations)
- Data Analysis (including ratios, percentages, and graphical/statistical interpretation)
- Advanced Math (geometry, polynomials, function notation, and other more complex topics)
- Additional Math Topics (complex and imaginary numbers, trigonometry)

These questions count toward the section score for Math (200-800), the total score of the SAT (400-1600), and the test score of the Math Test (1-40). These questions will also count toward the subscores of Algebra, Data Analysis, and Advanced Math (1-15 each). Some of these questions will also count toward the Analysis in Science and Analysis in Social Studies cross-test scores (1-40 each). Refer to the *Scoring & Reporting* section below for additional information.

Essay (Optional)

The Essay is the only optional part of the SAT, and is administered at the end of the three mandatory tests. The essay prompt is always the same: analyze the argument presented in a passage and explain how an argument is constructed in order to persuade the reader.

While the prompt is always the same, the passage provided changes from one administration of the test to another. This passage is on average 700 words in length. Additional information about the Essay can be found in the *Part Four: Essay* section of this workbook.

Note that opting to take the Essay portion of the test is a personal decision, as certain postsecondary institutions require the Essay, while others do not.

The Tutorverse

Tips & Tricks

Because every student is unique, there is no one-size-fits-all approach to taking the SAT. Nevertheless, there are certain strategies that will benefit all test-takers:

- *Read each question and answer choice carefully.*
  Don't rush through the exam, since some answer choices are designed to look correct at first glance.
- *Skip and make note of questions that can't be answered quickly and confidently.*
  Come back to questions that are difficult to answer. Students may wish to "bank" as many points as possible by first answering questions they find to be relatively "easy."
- *Never leave a question blank.*
  There is no penalty for guessing on the SAT, so venture a guess on very difficult questions (or, if running out of time). If there is time remaining at the end of a section, review any guesswork.

Scoring & Reporting

There are several different scores reported for the SAT.

The Reading and Writing & Language Tests are combined, scored, and reported together on a scale ranging from 200-800. The Math Test is reported on a similar scale: from 200-800. These two separate scores represent section scores. The Essay is scored separately and does not contribute to the scores of any other section. The total score is the sum of both section scores, and ranges from 400-1600.

In addition to the section and total scores, several additional scores are reported as well. These additional scores are not a component of the section or total scores (i.e. they do not add up to the section or total scores). Instead, they are separate scores that evaluate the student's performance in more specific areas. Each of the three required tests (Reading, Writing & Language, and Math) will receive a score from 10-40. These three scores are known as test scores. These scores are based primarily on the number of questions answered correctly (commonly known as the raw score). The raw score is converted to a scaled score between 10-40.

As described in the *Content* section above, there are several sub-topics within each of the three required tests. Performance on each of these sub-topics are reported on a scale of 1-15, and are known as subscores. Each of the following seven subsections will receive a score between 1-15:

- (Reading and Writing & Language) Command of Evidence
- (Reading and Writing & Language) Words in Context
- (Writing & Language) Expression of Ideas
- (Writing & Language) Standard English Conventions
- (Math) Algebra
- (Math) Data Analysis
- (Math) Advanced Math

Finally, each of the three required tests (Reading, Writing & Language, and Math) contain questions pertaining to science and history/social studies. Like a "test within a test," performance on these types of questions are reported on a scale of 10-40 and are known as cross-test scores. Two scores between 10-40 are reported: one for science, and one for history/social studies.

The Essay is reported separately in three separate scores: Reading, Analysis, and Writing. The Reading score is based on the student's understanding of the passage as demonstrated by the incorporation of evidence from the passage in the essay itself. The Analysis score is based on the accuracy of the student's accounting of the passage's argument, including the judicious use of relevant evidence from the passage. The Writing score is based on the quality of the essay itself, which should be free of grammatical errors, focused, cohesive, and well-organized.

The Tutorverse

The different types of scores and score ranges are summarized on the below chart. *Note that the test, subscore, and cross-test scores do not add up to the section or total scores.*

Score Type	Lowest Possible Score	Highest Possible Score
Section Scores		
Math	200	800
Reading and Writing & Language	200	800
Total Score	400	1600
Test Score		
Reading	10	40
Writing & Language	10	40
Math	10	40
Subscore		
Reading and Writing & Language		
Command of Evidence	1	15
Words in Context	1	15
Writing & Language		
Expression of Ideas	1	15
Standard English Conventions	1	15
Math		
Algebra	1	15
Data Analysis	1	15
Advanced Math	1	15
Cross-test Score		
Analysis in Science	10	40
Analysis in History/Social Studies	10	40
Essay		
Reading	2	8
Analysis	2	8
Writing	2	8

Additional Information

Sometimes, too much information is a bad thing. Extraneous information can be confusing and can detract from the most important information. That's why the information presented in this section is not exhaustive. We have deliberately omitted certain information – such as when or where to take the SAT, or certain score reporting services offered by the College Board – in order to focus on the information most pertinent to preparing for the test: the content and scoring of the SAT.

To find out more about what the College Board offers, as well as when and where the SAT is administered, consider consulting the College Board's official resources online or in print.

The Tutorverse

In This Workbook

There are over 1,500 practice questions in this workbook. The purpose of this section is to explain how these questions are structured and to describe the organization of the workbook.

Organization & Question Types

This workbook is organized into five parts. Each of the four tests (three required and one optional) are assigned a part in this workbook. The last part of the workbook is a full-length practice test.

With the exception of the practice test, each part of this workbook begins with an Overview describing the content and format of the questions found in that particular test. The Overview contains very important information and is more detailed than the *Content* section of this workbook. It is important for students to read the Overview before proceeding to practice questions.

After the Overview are Tips & Strategies, which range from general best practices to specific recommendations.

What we call *Guided Practice* questions are the first set of questions in each part of the workbook. *Guided Practice* questions are designed to allow students the opportunity to focus on specific types of questions. *Guided Practice* questions zero in on different types of questions, and grouping them together so that the student can master – through practice – different or new content.

For example, there are questions that pertain to Standard English Conventions on the Writing & Language Test. However, within Standard English Conventions are a number of different units. Learning the concepts underlying these units will help students master the entire Writing & Language Test. The Overview of Writing & Language will highlight the different units found on the Writing & Language Test. For the Standard English Conventions component of the Writing & Language Test, one unit pertains to the concept of Pronoun Clarity. *Guided Practice* questions will help students focus on pronoun clarity as a concept by providing questions that pertain to pronoun clarity.

There are *Guided Practice* questions for each topic and unit of each of the three required tests.

At the end of the Reading, Writing & Language, and Math parts of the workbook are what we call *Mixed Practice* (Math) and *Passage-Based Practice* (Reading & Writing). These questions aggregate various units together as they might appear on the actual test. Where *Guided Practice* separates questions by unit, *Mixed Practice* and *Passage-Based Practice* includes questions of different types and units in order to simulate a more realistic test-taking scenario.

Taking a practice test can be very helpful for students. The last part of this workbook includes a full-length practice test. Once completed, students should evaluate their performance and revisit *Guided Practice*, *Mixed Practice*, or *Passage-Based Practice* as needed.

Additional Resources

It's important to practice for the SAT. Becoming familiar with the instructions, types of questions, content, and time constraints of the test will help students to perform their best on test day.

We encourage all students to reach out to trusted educators for help preparing for the SAT. These teachers and tutors can help students carve out time to study, identify concepts requiring additional focus, and help build mastery over time.

The Tutorverse

Part One: Reading

Overview

The first part of the SAT is the Reading Test, which requires that students read passages and answer questions related to those passages. These passages cover a number of different topics (literature, social studies, and science) and styles (persuasive, expository, and narrative), and are on average 625 words in length.

On the Actual Test

Students will have 65 minutes to answer 52 total questions addressing 5 total passages. 4 of the 5 passages will be stand-alone passages; 1 of the 5 passages will consist of a pair of shorter, related passages. Some of these passages will be accompanied by information graphics, such as charts, graphs, and tables. Following each passage (or pair of passages) will be a question set of 10 or 11 questions.

2 of the 5 total passages will pertain to social studies (i.e. an excerpt from a notable U.S. founding document or other civics related document, plus a passage relating to a topic in the social studies), another 2 will pertain to the sciences, and the remaining passage will pertain to literature (i.e. a literary excerpt or narrative that tells a story).

It won't be possible to know in advance which topic will be covered by a pair of passages, nor will it be possible to know in advance the style in which each passage will be written. Similarly, it won't be possible to know in advance which passages will be accompanied by an information graphic.

Types of Questions

The Reading Test of the SAT draws from a bank of 13 question categories. Therefore, because there are only 10 or 11 questions per passage, not every question set following a passage will include a question from every question category. In fact, a question set may contain multiple instances of a question category. Furthermore, each category of question can be represented in a number of different ways. A summary of each of these 13 categories is provided below.

- *Summarizing.* Choose the best summary of the entire passage or a specific part of a passage. The words "summary" or "summarize" frequently (but not always) identify these questions.
- *Text Structure.* Classify the general organization of the whole passage or determine how a particular part of a passage relates to the whole passage.
- *Arguments.* Identify claims, assertions, reasons, and supporting information and how specific information might relate to these elements of an argument. The words "evidence," "claim," and "reason" are frequently used to identify these questions.
- *Main Ideas.* Identify a concise and accurate interpretation of the passage's (or part of the passage's) main point, claim, or theme (in the case of a literary passage). Such points, claims, or themes may be explicitly or implicitly stated.
- *Purpose.* Categorize the reason why some part of a passage is included. This differs from Summarizing or Main Ideas in that the question asks about the function of the excerpt in terms of the broader passage.
- *Point of View.* Identify the point of view of a given party as it relates to the passage. Such parties are often the author or narrator, or another character or perspective represented in the passage.
- *Relationships.* Determine how different aspects of a passage relate to each other. Such questions might be straight forward, asking the sequential order of events, for example. Or, they may be more nuanced, asking how two things are alike or not alike or how one thing led to another.
- *Close Reading.* Identify or interpret something explicitly or implicitly stated in the passage. These "things" can be ideas, statements, suggestions, questions, claims, supporting detail, or any number of other elements that are pertinent to the passage. The words "imply," "indicate," etc., often (but not always) identify these questions.

The Tutorverse

- *Textual Evidence*. Cite a specific part of the passage (generally provided in the form of line-numbered quotations) that supports a statement provided by the question or that supports the answer to another question. The words "evidence for" or "support for" often (but not always) identify these questions.
- *Word Choice*. Determine the impact of or reason for using a particular word, phrase, or sentence. Such words, phrases, or sentences will often help to strengthen an argument, describe a circumstance, or convey a mood. This is different from asking for the contextual meaning or definition of a word or phrase.
- *Words/Phrases in Context*. Infer the meaning of a word or phrase based on the rest of the sentence, paragraph, or passage. Such words and phrases can often have multiple definitions, so choosing the correct answer will require contextual understanding.
- *Quantitative Information*. Understand the information presented in a graphic and how it relates to the passage or part of a passage. Such questions are only relevant when there is an information graphic (such as a chart, table, or graph) included at the end of the passage.
- *Multiple Texts*. Draw connections between two related (paired) passages. Such questions will address one of the two passages individually or will address both passages collectively (to see how both passages are similar or different or how one passage might respond to the other).

Understanding each of the above question categories is essential.

How to Use This Section

The goal of this section is to help familiarize students with both the type of passages that may be encountered on the SAT as well as the type of questions that may be asked on the SAT. To accomplish this goal, each passage in this section contains 13 questions instead of the 10-11 found on the actual exam. The reason for this is to ensure that students have as much exposure to each category of question as possible. Some passages are followed by each of the 13 question categories, while others are not. This variation is by design, as not all question categories are relevant to every passage – a question without an information graphic, for example, will naturally not have a question that asks about interpreting an information graphic. Similarly, a stand-alone passage will not be followed by a question that asks about the relationship between a pair of passages.

This section is split into two units: *Guided Practice* and *Passage-Based Practice*.

In the *Guided Practice* unit, each question is labeled with the question category to which it belongs. This is intended to help students to become familiar with and start to recognize the different question categories that may appear on the actual test. Take as much time as needed in this unit.

In the *Passage-Based Practice* unit, question category labels have been removed. The only significant difference between the question sets found in this unit and those found on the actual test are the number of questions (13 in the former, and 10-11 in the latter). The best way to prepare for the actual test is for students to give themselves approximately 16 minutes to finish each passage and question set in this unit – this is 1.25 minutes per question, including time spent reading the passage (this is the same time allotment per question as on the actual test).

We recommend that students practice at least 5 question sets per week in preparing for the exam (though this number should, of course, be tailored to fit a student's individual study plan).

Over the course of their studies, students should not be surprised to encounter words that are unfamiliar to them.

In fact, we encourage students to make a list of unfamiliar or difficult words, whether they appear in passages, questions, answer choices, or answer explanations. This is a natural way to build not only vocabulary, but also the ability to infer a words meaning through context (and is, in fact, a worthwhile habit to carry into everyday reading and writing). Consider writing down the definition of each word as well as a sentence using the word. Students may also want to consider writing down whether the word has a positive or negative association, and any root words that can help them to remember the word.

The Tutorverse

Tutorverse Tips & Strategies

In addition to tips and strategies outlined in the *Test Overview* section of this workbook, consider employing the following Reading Test-specific suggestions:

🐢 *Learn the Reading Test question categories.*
  The stronger a student's command of the Reading Test's question categories, the better he or she will be able to recognize important information when reading a passage the first time around – even before looking at the questions themselves. This will save the student precious time on the actual exam.

🐢 *Read the passage in its entirety and take notes along the way.*
  Students are allowed to make notes and otherwise mark up their test booklet (though only answers included on the answer sheet will be scored). As students read through the passage, they should think about and make note of (underline or circle) important information that is relevant to the categories of questions commonly found on the Reading Test. For example, identifying a passage's main claim or idea is a question generally found at least once on the test.

🐢 *When answering questions, refer back to notes taken.*

🐢 *Know that more general questions relating to the passage in its entirety appear toward the beginning of a question set.*
  Questions relating to specific parts of the passage appear after the more general questions, usually in order of how it appears in the passage. Questions that pertain to graphics or paired passages generally appear toward the end of the question set.

Guided Practice

Directions: The following passages are followed by 13 questions. After reading each passage or pair of passages, select the best answer to each question based on the information implied or stated in the passage and provided in any graphics (such as charts, tables, or graphs). Take as much time as you need.

Passage AA *(Answers & explanations on page 334).*

The following passage is an excerpt from activist Upton Sinclair's *The Jungle*, published in 1906. Jurgis is a recent immigrant struggling to make a life in the United States.

When Jurgis got up again he went quietly enough. He was exhausted and half dazed, and besides he saw the blue uniforms of the policemen. He drove in a patrol wagon with half a dozen of
5 them watching him; keeping as far away as possible, however, on account of the fertilizer. Then he stood before the sergeant's desk and gave his name and address, and saw a charge of assault and battery entered against him. On his way to his
10 cell a burly policeman cursed him because he started down the wrong corridor, and then added a kick when he was not quick enough; nevertheless, Jurgis did not even lift his eyes — he had lived two years and a half in Packingtown, and he knew
15 what the police were. It was as much as a man's very life was worth to anger them, here in their inmost lair; like as not a dozen would pile on to him at once, and pound his face into a pulp. It would be nothing unusual if he got his skull
20 cracked in the melee — in which case they would report that he had been drunk and had fallen down, and there would be no one to know the difference or to care.

So a barred door clanged upon Jurgis and he
25 sat down upon a bench and buried his face in his hands. He was alone; he had the afternoon and all of the night to himself.

At first he was like a wild beast that has glutted itself; he was in a dull stupor of
30 satisfaction. He had done up the scoundrel pretty well — not as well as he would have if they had given him a minute more, but pretty well, all the same; the ends of his fingers were still tingling from their contact with the fellow's throat. But
35 then, little by little, as his strength came back and his senses cleared, he began to see beyond his

momentary gratification; that he had nearly killed the boss would not help Ona — not the horrors that she had borne, nor the memory that would
40 haunt her all her days. It would not help to feed her and her child; she would certainly lose her place, while he — what was to happen to him God only knew.

Half the night he paced the floor, wrestling
45 with this nightmare; and when he was exhausted he lay down, trying to sleep, but finding instead, for the first time in his life, that his brain was too much for him. In the cell next to him was a drunken wife-beater and in the one beyond a
50 yelling maniac. At midnight they opened the stationhouse to the homeless wanderers who were crowded about the door, shivering in the winter blast, and they thronged into the corridor outside of the cells. Some of them stretched themselves
55 out on the bare stone floor and fell to snoring; others sat up, laughing and talking, cursing and quarrelling. The air was fetid with their breath, yet in spite of this some of them smelt Jurgis and called down the torments of hell upon him, while
60 he lay in a far corner of his cell, counting the throbbings of the blood in his forehead.

They had brought him his supper, which was "duffers and dope" — being hunks of dry bread on a tin plate, and coffee, called "dope" because it
65 was drugged to keep the prisoners quiet. Jurgis had not known this, or he would have swallowed the stuff in desperation; as it was, every nerve of him was a-quiver with shame and rage. Toward morning the place fell silent, and he got up and
70 began to pace his cell; and then within the soul of him there rose up a fiend, red-eyed and cruel, and tore out the strings of his heart.

The Tutorverse

1 *[Summarizing]*
Which of the following choices best summarizes the passage?
A) A man spends the night in jail.
B) A man angers policemen and is injured in the process.
C) A man regrets his actions.
D) A man copes with the consequences of his actions.

2 *[Text Structure]*
From the first paragraph to the third paragraph, the focus of the passage shifts from
A) a description of inner thoughts to the telling of events.
B) the telling of events to description of inner thoughts.
C) the sharing of an opinion to a declaration of fact.
D) the argument of a point to questions raised in response.

3 *[Close Reading]*
The passage indicates that Jurgis is in a(n)
A) jail.
B) asylum.
C) slaughterhouse.
D) fertilizer manufacturing plant.

4 *[Arguments]*
The author most likely includes the narrator's account of potential injury in police custody in lines 9-22 ("On his...care") in order to
A) incite outrage in the reader and generate sympathy for Jurgis.
B) explain draconian punishments and generate apathy for Jurgis.
C) describe and generate empathy for the police's point of view.
D) provide an example of the consequences to Jurgis' actions.

5 *[Main Ideas]*
The second paragraph is primarily concerned with
A) describing a character's motivations.
B) demonstrating a character's emotions.
C) describing the setting of the rest of the passage.
D) comparing one setting with another.

6 *[Word Choice]*
Which choice most closely captures the meaning of the simile in lines 28-29 ("At first...itself")?
A) Jurgis was regretful of his actions.
B) Jurgis behaved poorly when confined with other people.
C) Jurgis was confused by his own sense of gratification.
D) Jurgis was filled with a deep sense of gratification.

7 *[Close Reading]*
The narrator implies that Ona is
A) directly responsible for his punishment.
B) ungrateful for Jurgis' help.
C) independent and does not need Jurgis.
D) someone Jurgis cares deeply about.

8 *[Relationships]*
The narrator indicates that Jurgis is being punished because
A) he stole fertilizer.
B) he was homeless.
C) he disrespected a policeman.
D) he tried to help Ona.

9 *[Point of View]*
According to the passage, how might Jurgis view his punishment?
A) Jurgis might suggest that he does not belong with real criminals, drunks, and homeless people.
B) Jurgis might assent as to the reasonableness of his punishment, given his crime.
C) Jurgis might have no opinion of the matter, having been drugged after drinking his coffee.
D) Jurgis might be ambivalent toward his punishment, having accomplished his goal.

10 *[Close Reading]*
Based on the information in the passage, it can be reasonably inferred that the smell of fertilizer referred to in line 6 emanates from
A) the police.
B) Jurgis himself.
C) the other men in the patrol wagon.
D) the patrol wagon itself.

The Tutorverse

11 *[Textual Evidence]*
Which choice best supports the answer in the previous question?
A)   Lines 24-26 ("So a…hands")
B)   Lines 50-55 ("At midnight…snoring")
C)   Lines 57-61 ("The air…forehead")
D)   Lines 65-67 ("Jurgis had…desperation")

12 *[Words/Phrases in Context]*
The word "fetid," as used in line 57, most nearly means
A)   foul.
B)   heavy.
C)   filled.
D)   fragrant.

13 *[Purpose]*
The author includes the final sentence in lines 68-72 ("Toward morning…heart") in order to emphasize Jurgis'
A)   remorse and spite.
B)   anxiety and regret.
C)   restlessness and myopia.
D)   selfishness and contrition.

The Tutorverse

Passage BB *(Answers & explanations on page 335).*

Passage 1

Eighteenth-century European scientists largely subscribed to a worldview heavily influenced by
5 the Christian Bible. According to this worldview, the earth and the life that calls it home is static and relatively young – merely thousands of years old. As plant and animal life becomes extinct, new species take their places through divine
10 intervention. At the time, the scientific community had so tied together religion and science that it was difficult to distinguish between the two.

There were, however, a number of scientists who began to question the biblical worldview of
15 science – questions fueled in part by fossil discoveries that contradicted commonly accepted knowledge about the earth. One of the first scientists to propose a non-biblical view of the earth's history was a French naturalist named
20 Georges-Louis Leclerc. Leclerc believed that, under certain circumstances, life begins spontaneously. However, part of Leclerc's theory had to do with how animals changed, which he believed must have been related to the changing
25 climate. As animals migrated to find their ideal climates, he surmised, they changed as a result of their environments. Leclerc's theory was, at the time, supported by the fossils of elephants uncovered in Siberia and North America; at the
30 time, living elephants were only found in Africa and Asia. Clearly, animal migration was real; the fact that the Siberian and North American fossils were similar but not identical to the skeletons of African and Asian elephants suggested that the
35 animals changed over time.

Jean-Baptiste Lamarck drew heavily from Leclerc's work and agreed that life was spontaneously created. However, Lamarck took this a step further. He studied plants and a wide
40 range of animals. He found the organisms he studied had many profound similarities, and theorized that life was not static. Lamarck observed that when environments changed, animals changed their behavior in response in
45 order to survive and reproduce. Lamarck cited the giraffe as an example. By stretching its neck, he believed, early giraffes could better reach the leaves on top of trees. Lamarck thought a "nervous fluid" would flow into the giraffe's neck, thereby
50 causing it to grow longer. When the giraffe bore offspring, it would pass this trait on to the next generation. After generations of this process, the giraffe came to possess a long neck.

Perhaps one of the most well-known thinkers
55 who worked to separate science from religion was Charles Darwin. A student of Lamarck's theories, Darwin worked closely with respected British scientists Adam Sedgwick and John Henslow, both of whom also questioned the established biblical
60 view of the origins of life. Together, they produced a theory of life that would turn the world upside down and sparked a hitherto unseen scientific controversy.

65 Passage 2

Shortly after Christmas 1831, 22-year-old Charles Darwin boarded the *HMS Beagle* to work as a naturalist. The ship's captain, Robert Fitzroy,
70 was interested in science – especially geology – and brought a large library with him on the trip. Darwin, having access to these books, read extensively during the journey. Darwin was particularly interested in books that discussed how
75 life on earth changed with changing geology.

Darwin studied the birds of the Galapagos Islands and discovered that the various species of birds there had slight differences from each other. The key differences between the finches he
80 cataloged were in the size and shape of their beaks. These differences generally corresponded to the kind of food the birds ate, which was influenced by the microenvironment on each island. The environments across the Galapagos islands were as
85 varied as the bird species – some parts were dry, while others were more humid; some birds were smaller and others were larger. Darwin saw that each bird species was uniquely suited to its environment. Over many generations, he
90 concluded, the birds changed in ways that allowed them to better survive their specific environments. Darwin sketched out his theory in the form of a tree showing how an ancestral species branched out and evolved into multiple descendent species
95 that later adapted to different ecological niches. Darwin came to believe that within a population of species, there were individuals with slight differences from each other. Those individuals

having advantages suited to a particular
100 environment tended to stay alive longer and passed
on their advantageous traits to the next generation
more frequently. This process became known as
natural selection.

Darwin's observation of the Galapagos finches
105 could be applied to other species. Darwin argued

that species adapted over time and those that didn't
went extinct; species were not spontaneously
generated, as was thought at the time, but instead
evolved from an older species. Though the idea
110 was controversial in its day, Darwin's ideas are
now widely accepted by the scientific community.

---

1   *[Summarizing]*
Which of the following choices best summarizes
Passage 1?
A) A traditional point of view is upheld.
B) A traditional point of view is challenged.
C) A new theory is proven incontrovertible.
D) A new theory mirrors a traditional theory.

2   *[Point of View]*
In Passage 1, the author's point of view is best
described as that of a(n)
A) impassioned advocate trying to discredit
outdated scientific ideas.
B) experienced scientist explaining scientific
concepts to other scientists.
C) impartial reporter describing historical
understanding of scientific concepts.
D) opinionated scientist trying to prove a
scientific point.

3   *[Text Structure]*
The author of Passage 1 refers to elephant fossils
(lines 27-35) primarily to
A) develop Leclerc's argument regarding
climate change.
B) show how fossil evidence supported
Leclerc's ideas
C) show how fossil evidence refuted
Leclerc's ideas.
D) contrast Leclerc's ideas with the biblical
view of the day.

4   *[Purpose]*
The most likely reason the author of Passage 1
mentions giraffes in the third paragraph is to
A) provide an example of how Lamarck's
theory applied to the natural world.
B) discredit Lamarck's theory as illogical and
ridiculous.
C) emphasize how Lamarck's ideas were
similar to Darwin's.
D) contrast Lamarck's ideas with Leclerc's.

5   *[Close Reading]*
The author of Passage 1 suggests that Leclerc's
and Lamarck's ideas about earth's history were
A) no more accurate than the biblical view.
B) easily disproved with fossil evidence.
C) important contributions to Darwin's work.
D) the first accurate view of the earth's
history.

6   *[Main Ideas]*
The central idea of Passage 2 is that
A) Darwin was an avid sailor and traveler.
B) Darwin was a student of birds and other
animals.
C) Darwin's theories are incomplete and
largely debunked.
D) Darwin's observations produced an
influential new theory.

The Tutorverse

7 *[Word Choice]*

In the context of Passage 2, the author's use of the phrase "uniquely suited" (line 88) is primarily meant to convey that

A) large groups of animals behave in predictable ways.

B) special characteristics help an animal survive.

C) each species of finch has a different coloring.

D) individuals within a species tend to have similar traits.

8 *[Words/Phrases in Context]*

As used in line 99, "advantages" most nearly means

A) good opportunities.

B) desirable circumstances.

C) strong positions.

D) favorable features.

9 *[Relationships]*

According to Passage 2, Darwin recognized that the finches on the Galapagos islands differed slightly from island to island, which led him to conclude that

A) the finches spontaneously changed to adapt to their environment.

B) the finches were descended from different ancestral species.

C) the finches gained advantageous traits over several generations.

D) some finches previously thought to be extinct were rediscovered.

10 *[Main Ideas]*

With which of the following statements would the authors of both passages likely agree?

A) Darwin succeeded in coming up with a theory of evolution after Lamarck and Leclerc failed.

B) The theory of evolution was the result of contributions from several generations of scientists.

C) Scientists have not established a theory of evolution that satisfactorily explains life on earth.

D) Fossils offer circumstantial evidence to support the theories of Lamarck, Leclerc, and Darwin.

11 *[Multiple Texts]*

Is the main conclusion presented by the author of Passage 2 consistent with the conclusion about early scientific views of the origins of life shown in Passage 1?

A) Yes, because Leclerc's and Darwin's observations were similar.

B) Yes, because both show scientists who proposed non-biblical views of the world.

C) No, because Darwin's work completely refuted the work of the earlier scientists.

D) No, because none of the theories presented are widely held.

12 *[Arguments]*

Lamarck, of Passage 1, would most likely respond to the discussion of finch beak shape in lines 79-83, Passage 2, by stating that

A) life is static, and only changes in response to climate change.

B) like elephants, finch beak shape changes spontaneously.

C) Darwin's analysis on the passing of traits across generations seems reasonable.

D) Darwin's analysis of changes to early finch beak shapes is accurate.

13 *[Textual Evidence]*

Which choice provides the best evidence for the answer to the previous question?

A) Lines 10-12 ("At the…two")

B) Lines 25-27 ("As animals…environments")

C) Lines 46–48 ("By stretching…trees")

D) Lines 50–53 ("When the…neck")

Passage CC *(Answers & explanations on page 336).*

Infrastructure refers to basic facilities and structures that allow for the operation of a society. These facilities – roads, bridges, airports, power plants, railways, and ports, to name just a few –
5 are critical to the functioning of a modern society. The development and investment in such infrastructure has long been seen as an economic necessity. Lately, however, such investment has – as a percentage of the country's productivity –
10 begun to decline as infrastructure spending has become a contentious subject of political debate. This political stagnation is coming at an inopportune time: as recently as 2013, the American Society of Civil Engineers gave
15 American infrastructure a grade of D (where A was the best possible grade, and F was the worst possible grade). In February of 2014, Thomas Donohue, President & CEO of the Chamber of Commerce, a business-friendly organization, and
20 Richard Trumka, President of the AFL-CIO, the largest labor union in the country, appeared before a Senate Environment & Public Works Committee hearing and pressed members of Congress to pass a long-term funding bill for infrastructure projects.
25 Their plea reflects the importance of investing in infrastructure for the overall welfare of a country: that developing infrastructure creates jobs, stimulates the economy, and benefits commerce.

Paving roads, expanding the power grid, and
30 otherwise investing in infrastructure can create thousands upon thousands of well-paying jobs. Infrastructure development can create opportunities in a wide range of industries, including engineering, construction, equipment
35 manufacturing and maintenance, energy, raw materials, and even accounting. The U.S. Department of Transportation has estimated that every $1 billion invested in infrastructure could create some 35,000 new jobs. Linked to job
40 creation is what economists call the multiplier effect. A dollar spent on infrastructure development leads to a return of more than two dollars. For example, building a power plant creates many new jobs. The people who work on
45 the power plant need places to live, food to eat, and things to do. As a result, investments in the local community begin to grow as people spend money on homes, transportation, food, and entertainment. In addition to providing people with
50 electricity, the power plant becomes a catalyst for new growth for a range of businesses and services.

According to a study conducted by the National Economic Council (NEC), after housing expenses, Americans spend the most money on
55 transportation. The same study says that "reducing fuel consumption, decreasing the need for car maintenance due to poor road conditions, and increasing the availability of affordable and accessible public transportation systems would
60 allow Americans to spend less money on transportation." A joint study between the NEC and the President's Council of Economic Advisers found that "the average motorist in the U.S. pays $377 each year in additional vehicle operating
65 costs as a result of driving on roads in need of repair." Improved infrastructure could give individuals and families an opportunity to save time and money. If families spend less time and money on transportation, they will be able to
70 spend more of their time and money on other things, like recreational activities, travel, and family needs.

In addition to individuals and families, businesses also benefit from infrastructure
75 investments. Upgrading our aging transportation network would allow businesses to transport goods in a more cost-effective way. A strong network of roads, for example, would provide businesses with more efficient access to suppliers and markets. For
80 example, a new bridge or highway might be able to provide businesses with faster routes, which could lead to productivity gains and could increase the number of deliveries made in a given period of time.

85 In his 1955 State of the Union Address, President Dwight Eisenhower said, "A modern, efficient highway system is essential to meet the needs of our growing population, our expanding economy, and our national security." The
90 following year, he signed The Federal-Aid Highway Act of 1956, the largest public works program at the time. For the good of their constituents – and of the country as a whole, politicians should set aside party differences and
95 come to an agreement on infrastructure investment.

Total Public Spending for Transportation and Water Infrastructure in Constant Dollars and as a Share of GDP, 1956 to 2007

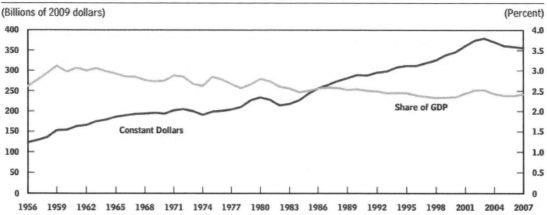

Source: Congressional Budget Office.

Note 1: GDP is a measure of economic productivity.
Note 2: Constant dollars refers to inflation-adjusted values.

1 *[Summarizing]*
Which answer choice best summarizes the passage?
A) Because infrastructure is critical to a society, it is worthy of continued investment.
B) Government must constantly monitor the infrastructure to ensure the public safety
C) Infrastructure in the U.S. is among the worst in the world, and something must be done to improve it.
D) A relic of the mid-20th century, the notion of investing in infrastructure is outdated and irrelevant.

2 *[Main Ideas]*
The passage most clearly suggests that infrastructure development is important because
A) it allows for faster transportation, improving businesses and saving time.
B) it allows business interests to prevail over those of individuals and families.
C) it gives politicians control over the country's most important assets.
D) it stimulates the economy in numerous ways.

3 *[Purpose]*
The main purpose of lines 17-24 ("In February...projects") is to
A) enumerate, with various examples, the different ways that infrastructure development can be funded.
B) describe the steps politicians are taking to rectify the problem of an aging infrastructure.
C) illustrate that businesses and labor can work together to achieve a common goal: improving infrastructure.
D) demonstrate, through example, the urgency and importance of infrastructure development for businesses and workers.

4 *[Quantitative Information]*
Data in the graph provides the most direct support for which idea in the passage?
A) Infrastructure spending is politically contentious.
B) Infrastructure spending helps to boost the economy and improve economic output.
C) Infrastructure spending as a share of the country's economic output has declined.
D) Investing in infrastructure is important to the future.

The Tutorverse

5   *[Close Reading]*

The second paragraph most strongly suggests that

A) investing in infrastructure can help lower the unemployment rate.

B) better infrastructure means that people will spend less on transportation.

C) community infrastructure is more important than national infrastructure.

D) the multiplier effect leads to luxury time.

6   *[Word Choice]*

The use of the phrase "even accounting" in line 36 is used in order to

A) emphasize the far-reaching power of infrastructure development to create jobs.

B) diminish the importance and relevance of accountants to infrastructure.

C) explain how accountants work together with engineers and construction workers.

D) underscore the importance of fair and balanced bookkeeping.

7   *[Words/Phrases in Context]*

In line 50, the word "catalyst" most nearly means

A) compound.

B) substance.

C) vehicle.

D) incentive.

8   *[Arguments]*

The focus on family in the third paragraph helps the author

A) illustrate how infrastructure development can promote job growth in communities.

B) establish a connection with the reader by linking infrastructure to relatable benefits.

C) contest the view that infrastructure development only benefits businesses.

D) persuade the reader to connect personally with infrastructure development.

9   *[Textual Evidence]*

Which choice best provides evidence for the answer to the previous question?

A) Lines 32-36 ("Infrastructure development…accounting")

B) Lines 46-49 ("As a…entertainment")

C) Lines 73-75 ("In addition…investments")

D) Lines 75-77 ("Upgrading our…way")

10   *[Relationships]*

According to the author, how might the construction of a new port benefit a city?

A) It might revitalize a depressed part of town and increase property values.

B) It might foster investment in the city, increasing the multiplier effect.

C) It might lead to a wider variety of products available for consumers to purchase.

D) It might increase the profitability of businesses, leading to more tax revenue.

11   *[Text Structure]*

The examples in lines 36-39 ("The U.S. Department…jobs") and lines 61-66 ("A joint…repair") are used primarily to

A) connect infrastructure development to possible projects.

B) explain the government's point of view on infrastructure.

C) support the argument presented by the author with research.

D) draw a correlation between jobs created and vehicle operating cost savings.

12   *[Purpose]*

What is the purpose of referencing the events of 1955 and 1956 in the final paragraph?

A) To draw parallels between past successes and the argument advanced in the passage.

B) To mark a contrast between circumstances then and now that would affect infrastructure development.

C) To show that even political leaders understand the importance of infrastructure in economic terms.

D) To convince the reader that history always repeats itself, and that programs from the past can work again today.

13   *[Point of View]*

In context of the passage, President Eisenhower would most likely agree with which choice?

A) Infrastructure is important, but it is not the highest priority on the national agenda.

B) A sound infrastructure will strengthen the country in many ways.

C) Because of benefits to business, government must support infrastructure.

D) Investing in infrastructure is a matter that is best left to Congress to legislate.

The Tutorverse

Passage DD *(Answers & explanations on page 337).*

This passage is adapted from President Ronald Reagan's 1987 remarks on East-West relations at the Brandenburg Gate in West Berlin. Many Berliners attended. The city of Berlin was, from 1949 to 1990, split in half politically: West Berlin was supported by democratic states, while East Berlin was supported by communist states.

Behind me stands a wall that encircles the free sectors of this city, part of a vast system of barriers that divides the entire continent of Europe. From the Baltic, south, those barriers cut across
5   Germany in a gash of barbed wire, concrete, dog runs, and guard towers. Farther south, there may be no visible, no obvious wall. But there remain armed guards and checkpoints all the same – still a restriction on the right to travel, still an instrument
10 to impose upon ordinary men and women the will of a totalitarian state. Yet it is here in Berlin where the wall emerges most clearly; here, cutting across your city, where the news photo and the television screen have imprinted this brutal division of a
15 continent upon the mind of the world. Standing before the Brandenburg Gate, every man is a German, separated from his fellow men. Every man is a Berliner, forced to look upon a scar.

President von Weizsacker has said: "The
20 German question is open as long as the Brandenburg Gate is closed." Today I say: As long as this gate is closed, as long as this scar of a wall is permitted to stand, it is not the German question alone that remains open, but the question of
25 freedom for all mankind. Yet I do not come here to lament. For I find in Berlin a message of hope, even in the shadow of this wall, a message of triumph...

In West Germany and here in Berlin, there
30 took place an economic miracle, the Wirtschaftswunder. Adenauer, Erhard, Reuter, and other leaders understood the practical importance of liberty – that just as truth can flourish only when the journalist is given freedom of speech, so
35 prosperity can come about only when the farmer and businessman enjoy economic freedom. The German leaders reduced tariffs, expanded free trade, lowered taxes. From 1950 to 1960 alone, the standard of living in West Germany and Berlin
40 doubled.

Where four decades ago there was rubble, today in West Berlin there is the greatest industrial output of any city in Germany – busy office blocks, fine homes and apartments, proud avenues,
45 and the spreading lawns of park land. Where a city's culture seemed to have been destroyed, today there are two great universities, orchestras and an opera, countless theaters, and museums. Where there was want, today there's abundance – food,
50 clothing, automobiles-the wonderful goods of the Ku'damm[1]. From devastation, from utter ruin, you Berliners have, in freedom, rebuilt a city that once again ranks as one of the greatest on Earth. The Soviets may have had other plants. But, my
55 friends, there were a few things the Soviets didn't count on – *Berliner herz, Berliner humor, ja, und Berliner schnauze*[2].

In the 1950's, Khrushchev[3] predicted: "We will bury you." But in the West today, we see a
60 free world that has achieved a level of prosperity and well-being unprecedented in all human history. In the Communist world, we see failure, technological backwardness, declining standards of health, even want of the most basic kind – too
65 little food. Even today, the Soviet Union still cannot feed itself. After these four decades, then, there stands before the entire world one great and inescapable conclusion: Freedom leads to prosperity. Freedom replaces the ancient hatreds
70 among the nations with comity and peace. Freedom is the victor.

And now the Soviets themselves may, in a limited way, be coming to understand the importance of freedom. We hear much from
75 Moscow about a new policy of reform and openness. Some political prisoners have been released. Certain foreign news broadcasts are no longer being jammed. Some economic enterprises have been permitted to operate with greater
80 freedom from state control. Are these the

[1] A famous shopping and cultural avenue in Berlin.
[2] "Berliner hearts, Berliner humor, and yes, the [famous] Berliner big-city attitude." The crowd then laughs.

[3] First leader of the Communist Party of the Soviet Union, from 1958-1964.

The Tutorverse

beginnings of profound changes in the Soviet
state? Or are they token gestures, intended to raise
false hopes in the West, or to strengthen the Soviet
system without changing it? We welcome change
85 and openness; for we believe that freedom and
security go together, that the advance of human
liberty can only strengthen the cause of world
peace.

There is one sign the Soviets can make that
90 would be unmistakable, that would advance
dramatically the cause of freedom and peace.
General Secretary Gorbachev[4], if you seek peace,
if you seek prosperity for the Soviet Union and
Eastern Europe, if you seek liberalization: Come
95 here to this gate! Mr. Gorbachev, open this gate!
Mr. Gorbachev, tear down this wall!

---

1   *[Text Structure]*
Which choice most accurately captures the
change in focus throughout the passage?
A)   A call-to-action is issued, historical
problems are highlighted, and a theory is
detailed.
B)   A problem is enumerated, a call-to-action
is issued, and a theory is explained.
C)   A problem is enumerated, a theory
supported by examples, and a call-to-
action is issued.
D)   A theory is explained, a call-to-action is
issued, and potential problems are
highlighted.

2   *[Summarizing]*
Which statement best describes what takes place
in the passage?
A)   A challenge is issued to a political foe.
B)   A city's cultural and political history is
discussed.
C)   Different political ideologies are compared
using a specific example.
D)   The sayings of famous politicians are
analyzed.

3   *[Word Choice]*
Reagan's repeated references to the Berlin Wall
as "a scar" (lines 18, 22) serves mainly to
A)   describe the damage done to Berlin.
B)   liken the wall to a reminder of an injury.
C)   remind people that some scars do not fade
over time.
D)   show why the wall is difficult to
dismantled.

4   *[Arguments]*
Reagan suggests that Wirtschaftswunder was due
primarily to
A)   economic freedom.
B)   freedom of speech.
C)   a resilient population.
D)   the division of East and West Berlin.

5   *[Close Reading]*
According to Reagan, West Berlin was able to
rebuild because of
A)   President von Weizsacker.
B)   liberal economic, social, and political
policies.
C)   support from the United States and other
democracies.
D)   their unity against the forces of
communism.

6   *[Textual Evidence]*
Which of the following choices best supports the
answer to the previous question?
A)   Lines 15-18 ("Standing before…scar")
B)   Lines 19-21 ("President von…closed")
C)   Lines 51-53 ("From devastation…Earth")
D)   Lines 72-74 ("And now…freedom")

7   *[Purpose]*
Reagan's telling of a joke in German (lines 56-
57) primarily serves to
A)   highlight the Soviets' strategic errors.
B)   defuse tensions with the Soviet Union.
C)   poke fun at Berliners' speech and
appearance.
D)   demonstrate his solidarity and respect for
the Berliners.

---

[4] Eighth leader of the Communist Party of the Soviet
Union, from 1985-1991.

The Tutorverse

8 *[Purpose]*

In context of the paragraph, Reagan quotes Khrushchev in lines 58-59 in order to

A) demonstrate the violent nature of a famous communist.

B) discredit the latter's leadership abilities.

C) emphasize how communism has failed.

D) explain the reason for Berlin's earlier destruction.

9 *[Point of View]*

Khrushchev, mentioned in line 58, would most likely attribute the success of West Berlin to

A) communism.

B) democracy.

C) freedom.

D) luck.

10 *[Relationships]*

The author most likely uses the examples of "technological backwardness…too little food" (lines 63-65) in order to

A) commend communism on their progress.

B) congratulate the West Berliners on winning an ideological battle.

C) illustrate the negative impact of a lack of freedom.

D) stoke tensions between East and West Berlin.

11 *[Textual Evidence]*

Of the following choices, which best supports the answer to the previous question?

A) Lines 41-43 ("Where four…Germany")

B) Lines 68-71 ("Freedom leads…victor")

C) Lines 72-74 ("And now…freedom")

D) Lines 95-96 ("Mr. Gorbachev…wall")

12 *[Words/Phrases in Context]*

As used in line 82, the word "token" most nearly means

A) adequate.

B) misleading.

C) perfunctory.

D) vacuous.

13 *[Main Ideas]*

The central idea of the last paragraph is that

A) Berlin and the Soviet Union share many similarities.

B) Gorbachev should negotiate for peace.

C) the Berlin Wall should be dismantled.

D) the Soviets have long desired freedom.

The Tutorverse

Passage-Based Practice

Directions: The following passages are followed by 13 questions. After reading each passage or pair of passages, select the best answer to each question based on the information implied or stated in the passage and provided in any graphics (such as charts, tables, or graphs). Try to read each passage and answer the questions following each passage in 16 minutes or less.

Passage A *(Answers & explanations on page 338).*

For a long time, too many people and poor sanitation made London an unpleasant – and dangerous – place to live. In the summer of 1854, one of the worst outbreaks of cholera in the city's
5 history occurred in the Soho neighborhood, killing over 100 people in just days. People fled the neighborhood, hoping to escape the "bad air" they thought was causing the disease to spread.

Today, we know that cholera is caused by a
10 bacterial infection, and mainly affects the small intestine. The disease strikes swiftly and soundly; profuse diarrhea and vomiting manifest within days – sometimes even hours – of exposure, resulting in extreme dehydration and, in many
15 cases, death. Though today cholera is easily cured if treated quickly, the people of 1854 London knew little about the disease and how it spread. As a result, over 600 people died of cholera before the outbreak was over.

20 At the time, many scientists believed in the miasma theory of "bad air," which stated that diseases such as cholera were caused by polluted air or air filled with the vapors of rotting organic matter – two things that rapidly industrializing
25 London had in abundance. One physician by the name of John Snow, however, did not subscribe to conventional wisdom. He reasoned that there might be another mechanism for the spread of disease, and set out to find out what it was.

30 Snow began his investigation by speaking with residents who lived on or around Broad Street, the heart of the outbreak. He asked them about their behavior, including where they worked, who they had been in contact with, and from where they
35 drew their water. Based on his investigation, Snow drew a map, carefully recording the location of each instance of cholera.

A pattern soon became clear: most instances of cholera centered around the Broad Street public
40 water pump. In fact, Snow was able to determine that almost every victim drew water from this

particular pump. Determined to uncover the culprit behind the outbreak, Snow took water samples from the pump and performed both chemical and
45 microscopic examinations on those samples. His tests were inconclusive.

Not easily dissuaded, Snow then turned to the information obtained from his interviews. He learned that none of the workers at the Broad
50 Street brewery contracted cholera, despite the fact that the brewery was just one block away from the pump in question. Snow learned that the brewery workers were given a daily beer allocation, and that none of the workers drank water from the
55 pump. A nearby factory was surrounded by sick people, but no one who worked in the factory itself contracted cholera; Snow learned the factory had its own water supply. Even distant cases of cholera could be traced back to the Broad Street pump.
60 One woman, who lived relatively far away from the Broad Street pump, succumbed to cholera. When Snow questioned her family, he learned that she sent for water from the Broad Street pump because she liked its taste.

65 Snow's data was enough to convince the local parish to shut down the pump and persuade other physicians that cholera spread through contaminated water – not through the air. Snow's method of mapping the disease was something
70 other physicians swiftly adopted. Scientists today still use Snow's methods to trace the sources of outbreaks. As a result of his work uncovering the cause of the 1854 outbreak, Snow is widely credited as the father of epidemiology, which
75 focuses on the incidence, transmission, and control of disease.

It would take London quite some time to clean up the city. Just four years later, a hot London summer combined with the pollution in the River
80 Thames resulted in conditions so bad that the residents called it The Great Stink. These conditions, along with Snow's data, inspired

The Tutorverse

engineers to build new sewers to move waste away
from the water supply, ending an era of cholera
85 outbreaks.

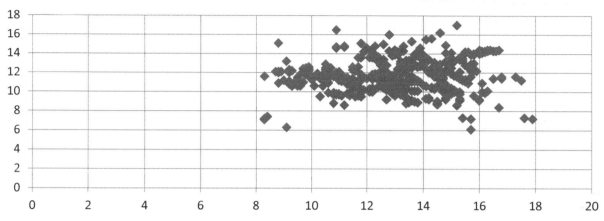

Distribution of 1854 Cholera Victims (meters)

1 Which statement best captures the events detailed in the passage?
A) An experiment is conducted to prove a theory.
B) Doctors debate scientific evidence.
C) Innovative thinking leads to lifesaving changes and discoveries.
D) A discovery is made that changes the landscape of a city.

2 Over the course of the passage, the focus shifts from
A) the description of an outbreak to the application of a scientific technique.
B) the dangers of disease to its proper prevention.
C) a city's polluted past to its modern sewage systems.
D) describing theories of disease transmission to specific examples of outbreaks.

3 The point of view of the narrator can best be described as
A) a skeptic who does not think much of medical science.
B) a biased scientist describing an important discovery.
C) an impartial reporter of events.
D) a scholar discussing a scientific controversy.

4 In the context of the passage, the author's use of the phrase "swiftly and soundly" (line 11) is primarily meant to convey the idea that
A) cholera moves from on person to another quickly.
B) cholera is a devastating disease.
C) cholera can be easy to treat.
D) cholera is a thorough disease.

5 As it is used in line 13, "exposure" most nearly means
A) an outlook or point of view.
B) gaining experience or knowledge.
C) coming into contact with something.
D) taking a risk or a chance.

6 Which statement best captures John Snow's central assumption as he began his research?

A)   Cholera is likely spread via air pollution or rotting organic matter.

B)   There may be another factor contributing to the spread of cholera.

C)   Cholera is likely spread through bacteria in polluted water.

D)   Data and mapping will persuade London residents to stop polluting.

7 In the third paragraph (lines 20-29), the description of what scientists thought caused cholera mainly serves to

A)   reveal John Snow's motivation for researching the problem.

B)   emphasize the apathy that many felt toward outbreaks of disease.

C)   introduce a key theory used in the understanding of the spread of disease.

D)   show how Snow's theories were met with resistance.

8 As it is used in line 28, "mechanism" most nearly means

A)   a system of parts.

B)   a machine.

C)   a contrivance.

D)   a process.

9 Snow was able to prove a connection between the cholera victims and the Broad Street pump by

A)   analyzing water from the pump under a microscope.

B)   drinking beer from the Broad Street brewery.

C)   discovering that cholera is caused by bacteria.

D)   learning that nearly all victims got their water from the pump.

10 The sixth paragraph (lines 47-64) serves mainly to show that

A)   Snow was equal parts stubborn and inquisitive.

B)   collecting data and information can help prevent the spread of disease.

C)   clean water and good sanitation is the key to preventing the spread of disease.

D)   nineteenth century scientists were wrong about the cause of disease.

11 Which choice provides the best evidence for the answer to the previous question?

A)   Lines 9-11 ("Today, we…intestine")

B)   Lines 20-25 ("At the time…abundance")

C)   Lines 47-48 ("Not easily…interviews")

D)   Lines 60-61 ("One woman…cholera")

12 In lines 48-55, the author most likely describes the water situation at the brewery in order to

A)   disparage Snow's methodologies.

B)   demonstrate the logic behind Snow's argument.

C)   comment on the unreliability of the people Snow interviewed.

D)   support the idea that cholera spread through the air.

13 Which statement is supported by the passage and by the information in the graph?

A)   The Broad Street pump is likely located at point (10,6).

B)   Bacteria and unsanitary conditions are the root cause of the outbreak.

C)   There was likely more than one cause for the outbreak.

D)   There is a strong correlation between the location of cholera cases and the cause of the outbreak.

Passage B *(Answers & explanations on page 338).*

Love it or hate it, pop music is, it would seem, an indelible part of our collective global culture. Sharing similarities with rock and roll, pop came into its own during the '50s and '60s and has held
5 positions at the top of sales charts ever since. Though pop was nurtured in the West, today, pop can be found around the world: K-pop in Korea; J-pop in Japan; Europop throughout Europe; Turkish pop in Turkey. The popularity of, well, the popular
10 music genre, is undeniable.

It used to be that one needed to consult the music industry sales charts to grasp the magnitude of pop music's appeal. *Thriller*, by the King of Pop Michael Jackson, is arguably the most
15 commercially successful album of all time. *Thriller* spent over two years on Billboard's charts, and occupied the number one spot for over 35 weeks. According to the Recording Industry Association of America, Epic Records, and Legacy
20 Records, *Thriller* has sold over 100 million copies worldwide, and only a third of those sales derived from the United States.

Today, we need look no further than social media and online media outlets to ascertain the
25 popularity of pop music and pop stars. As of March 2015, pop stars Katy Perry, Justin Bieber, and Taylor Swift occupied the top three slots on the social network Twitter, with 84.1 million, 76.8 million, and 72.5 million followers, respectively.
30 By comparison, then-president Barack Obama commanded only 70.9 million followers. The most viewed videos of all time on video-sharing website Youtube? As of March 2015, the top ten most viewed videos of all time all featured pop stars.
35 Psy, a Korean pop star, appears in the number one slot with 2.5 billion views; Meghan Trainor, an American pop star, comes in at number ten with 1.3 billion views; together, all ten videos account for just shy of *15 billion views*.
40 But what makes pop music so popular, anyway?

John Seabrook explores this question in great detail in his book *The Song Machine*. Pop is famous for its musical hooks – those parts of a
45 song that are so catchy that they get stuck in people's heads. As a musical concept, a hook can be applied to a melody or a rhythm, and can consist of a riff or phrase that embodies the spirit of the song. According to Seabrook, early pop
50 needed but one hook per song. Today, a song typically has multiple hooks to ensure that a listener will not, in his or her infinite boredom, immediately find a different song to play.

Because of this, a remarkable sameness
55 pervades the pop music industry. Many famous pop songs today sound curiously similar – at least, from a purely musical perspective. Pop songs are not always written by their performers. In fact, a handful of writers are responsible for the lion's
60 share of pop hits. Karl Martin Sandberg, Mikkel Eriksen, and Lukasz Gottwald, for example, are responsible for some of the most popular songs of the 21st century – songs performed by famous boybands and pop divas and superstars alike. This
65 cabal of songwriters, guided by a keen ear and enabled by technology, has created music's version of the Golden Goose – one that lays multi-platinum colored, sonic eggs. Popular songs are carefully dissected – everything from the chords to
70 structure to choruses, beats, and hooks are carefully mapped out and often replicated. Indeed, careful listening will show that many pop songs share beats so similar that they are virtually identical – only melodies, and not beats, it turns
75 out, can be protected by copyright laws.

Clearly, the masters of the pop universe have found something that people like. With hundreds of millions of dollars on the line, why fix, as the saying goes, what isn't broken? 15 billion views
80 can't be wrong, right?

Top 10 Most Followed Entities on Twitter: March 2015

- Pop Celebrity
- Other Entity
- Other Celebrity

1 Over the course of the passage, the author's focus shifts from
A) asserting a claim to defending countering arguments.
B) describing different concepts to promoting one particular concept.
C) establishing an idea to explaining the reasoning behind it.
D) telling a personal anecdote to drawing conclusions from that narrative.

2 The second paragraph serves to
A) explain a musical concept.
B) demonstrate the popularity and success of pop music.
C) describe the songwriting process in today's pop music industry.
D) explain the reason for pop music's popularity and success.

3 The third paragraph is primarily concerned with
A) comparing the popularity of different pop stars with non-musical celebrities.
B) establishing that social media is an alternate way of measuring popularity and success.
C) proving that K-pop and American pop compete with each other for popularity.
D) quantifying the monetary success of the pop music industry.

4 Data in the graph most strongly supports which of the following statements?
A) Lines 16-18 ("*Thriller* spent…weeks")
B) Lines 23-25 ("Today, we…stars")
C) Lines 38-39 ("Together, all…views")
D) Lines 77-80 ("With hundreds…right")

5 Which choice best summarizes the fifth paragraph?
A) A musical theory is explained in context.
B) An informative book is reviewed.
C) Questions about pop music's success are raised.
D) Descriptions of pop music's many elements are offered.

6 In context of the passage, a "hook" can best be described as
A) a key aspect of a song's lyrics.
B) an aspect of a song's melody.
C) any attention-grabbing musical element.
D) part of a song's rhythm.

7 According to the author, modern music listeners
A) are devoted to particular artists and genres.
B) demand artistic creativity.
C) enjoy listening to different sounds, rhythms, and melodies.
D) have access to many musical options.

8 As used in line 55, "pervades" most nearly means
A) conquers.
B) enables.
C) permeates.
D) represents.

9 According to the passage, why do so many songs sound the same?
A) Many songs are written by the same people.
B) Musical artists often look to emulate Michael Jackson's *Thriller*.
C) Pop songs must contain similar hooks.
D) Pop stars often work together in musical collaborations.

10 Which of the following choices best support the answer to the previous question?
A) Lines 13-15 ("*Thriller*, by…time")
B) Lines 50-53 ("Today, a…play")
C) Lines 58-64 ("In fact…alike")
D) Lines 79-80 ("15 billion…right")

11 In context, the "Golden Goose" mentioned in line 67 refers to
A) a moniker for "popular song."
B) a musical formula for writing songs.
C) the color representing songs with high commercial success.
D) the nickname for the cabal of songwriters.

12 According to the passage, songs are "carefully dissected" (line 69) in order to
A) protect artistic integrity.
B) ensure that new songs do not violate laws.
C) understand why not all songs are popular.
D) create new commercially successful songs.

13 With which of the following statements would the author of the passage most likely agree?
A) Songwriters must be more original.
B) Songwriters should not be permitted to write for more than one pop star.
C) Pop stars lack the artistic integrity of songwriters.
D) Pop music is a lucrative business.

The Tutorverse

Passage C *(Answers & explanations on page 339).*

Sam Anderson was making excellent time on his practice cross-country run. Tired of the usual routes, Sam decided to part ways with the rest of his team and take the long path that wound up
5 through the hills behind the high school. Just as he glanced down at his watch and smiled between breaths at his pace, he felt something grab his ankle. Before he knew what happened, he was a tangle of arms and legs, lying in a mess of leaves,
10 branches, and roots.

Sam's bewilderment gave way to a grimace as pain shot up from his ankle through his leg. An overgrown root gripped his foot like a vice. Sam looked around, trying to get his bearings. He
15 recognized the nearby house, and his stomach sank. The dilapidated building was shaded by overgrown, unkempt trees and painted the color of gloom. He was trapped behind Mr. Rush's house.

Despite being very much alive, Mr. Rush was
20 a ghost. Sam and his friends had been making up stories about Mr. Rush for years. They'd say, "He's cruel to kids!" or "He lives with forty cats, each one meaner than the next!" Sam had even created his own story: that if you got too close to
25 his house, Mr. Rush would kill you and bury you in his yard. Sam didn't really believe any of this was true, but he liked telling the stories anyway because his friends were always impressed by the creativity and goriness of them.
30 Lying on the ground, the stories about Mr. Rush quickly pushed the pain out of Sam's mind. Freeing himself from his captor, Sam wanted to run away, but the pain was so intense that he couldn't even stand. With the rest of the team
35 miles away and his phone in the locker room, Sam had no way, short of screaming, of calling for help – something he did not want to do for fear of rousing Mr. Rush.

As Sam agonized over the best course of
40 action, he saw someone emerge from Mr. Rush's house and walk toward him. Before he knew it, a tall, thin man with a gray beard stood before him, green eyes glowing below a wide-brimmed hat. Sam gasped, suddenly terrified that the stories
45 were true.

"Are you all right?" the man asked.

"I-I...t-twisted my ankle," Sam stammered.

The man knelt down beside Sam and asked, "Can you stand?"

50 Sam tried to move his leg again, but hissed as he tried to move it.

"Don't move," Mr. Rush said as he walked back toward his house.

Sam half expected Mr. Rush to return with his
55 legendary rusty shovel. Truth and fiction blurred as Sam's stomach churned. He couldn't leave – he couldn't even stand – and Mr. Rush could do whatever he wanted to Sam.

But Mr. Rush returned empty handed.
60 "There is an ambulance on its way."

"Th-thanks," said Sam uncertainly.

"I should look into having that root cut down. My son once tripped in the same spot."

Sam had only ever known Mr. Rush to be a
65 loner. "You have a son?"

"Yes. He moved from Smithfield some time ago."

"Why?" Sam knew the answer as soon as he asked the question. Though he loved Smithfield
70 and knew it to be vibrant and inhabited by friendly people, he also knew that the people of Smithfield loved to talk.

Mr. Rush glanced down at his feet, away from Sam. "Couldn't live with the shame, I suppose."
75 "Shame about what?"

Mr. Rush furrowed his brow and fixed his gaze on Sam. "You mean you haven't heard the stories?"

Sam's stomach began to churn for an entirely
80 different reason. "What stories?"

"People have been telling stories about me since my days as a high school teacher."

"You taught at the high school?"

"Indeed. I thought I was well liked by my
85 students until I failed the wrong one. That boy was so humiliated by failing my class, he began to make up stories about me. At first, I thought he was just bitter, but it soon became clear he was trying to get me fired. The stories became
90 increasingly terrible. I didn't think anyone would believe the words of an angry boy over a teacher who had been a part of the community for years. I was wrong."

"You were fired?"
95 Mr. Rush nodded. "And the stories persisted. It seems the stories with the least truth have the greatest longevity."

Sam's leg throbbed as he tried to move it. He
could hear the wail of an ambulance in the
100 distance. "I'm sorry," he said. "You seem like a
nice man."

But Mr. Rush appeared not to hear him.
"I know what they say about me."
Sam did, too. He planned to change that.

1   Which choice best summarizes the passage?
A)   A character describes why he's afraid of a
     man who lives in town and considers the
     reasons why.
B)   A group of boys terrorize a man in town
     that they fear.
C)   A young man learns that a man who lives
     in town is not what he expected.
D)   A scary man shows the boys in town why
     they should be afraid of him.

2   Over the course of the passage, the main focus of
the narrative shifts from
A)   concern a character has about another
     resident in town to a growing
     understanding and appreciation of that
     person.
B)   ambivalence a character feels toward his
     town to a growing appreciation of the
     town and the people who live there.
C)   fear a character has about another person
     to fear that the person will do something
     bad to the town.
D)   value a character attaches to telling stories
     about someone in his community to being
     forced to give up the stories.

3   The author is primarily concerned with
A)   telling a story about a man who lives in a
     small town.
B)   explaining why it is important to run with
     a partner.
C)   teaching a lesson about the power of
     speech.
D)   questioning the way society treats its older
     citizens.

4   The passage most strongly suggests that Mr.
Rush
A)   lurks around town.
B)   is rarely seen in public.
C)   terrorizes children.
D)   haunts the high school.

5   Which choice provides the best evidence for the
answer to the previous question?
A)   Line 19-20 ("Despite being…ghost")
B)   Line 23-26 ("Sam had…yard")
C)   Line 41-43 ("Before he…hat")
D)   Line 44-45 ("Sam gasped…true")

6   How does Sam's injury affect how he views Mr.
Rush?
A)   Mr. Rush's behavior confirms Sam's
     worst fears.
B)   The injury confirms for Sam that Mr.
     Rush's house is dangerous.
C)   Mr. Rush gives Sam more ammunition for
     scary stories about him.
D)   Mr. Rush's help makes Sam see him in a
     different light.

7   As used in line 33, "intense" most nearly means
A)   fragrant.
B)   vigorous.
C)   overwhelming.
D)   impassioned.

8   In the context of the passage, the author's use of
the sentence, "Sam's stomach …reason," (lines
79-80) is primarily meant to convey the idea that
A)   Sam feels nauseated.
B)   Sam feels guilty.
C)   Sam feels angry.
D)   Sam feels afraid.

9   The way the Smithfield community views Mr.
Rush is best described as
A)   loathing of a man who was once a bad
     teacher.
B)   fear of a man who no one really
     understands.
C)   ambivalence about a man who has lived in
     town for a long time.
D)   concern about a man who lives in a run-
     down house.

The Tutorverse

10 As used in line 70, "vibrant" most nearly means
A) bright.
B) vigorous.
C) lively.
D) nervous.

11 The author's main purpose in mentioning Mr. Rush's son in lines 62-74 is to
A) surprise the reader with new information about a character.
B) create sympathy for an otherwise unsympathetic character.
C) give evidence to support a character's assumption.
D) contradict something the author stated earlier in the passage.

12 In lines 96-97 ("It seems…longevity"), Mr. Rush most likely means
A) People like to spread gossip because juicy stories are entertaining.
B) Reputations take a long time to establish but are easily destroyed.
C) Hurtful stories can be very educational.
D) People are more likely to believe lies than the truth.

13 The end of the story implies that Sam is most likely to
A) continue to make up scary stories about Mr. Rush to others in the community.
B) encourage the community to repair Mr. Rush's house in order to make it more safe.
C) make up stories about someone else, to divert attention from Mr. Rush.
D) tell the people of Smithfield more positive stories about Mr. Rush.

The Tutorverse

Passage D *(Answers & explanations on page 340).*

The following passages are adapted from the 1792 letters of Thomas Jefferson and Alexander Hamilton, respectively.

Passage 1

Some have argued in support of the national debt, yet fail to acknowledge that the current debt
5 has become so large that the government cannot pay it back without borrowing more. Accumulating debt has limited the government's sources of revenues that could have helped allay costs accrued by the ordinary necessities and
10 exigencies of government. As it is, there are already murmurings against further taxation, and yet we are obliged to strain our citizens until they clamor for relief.

Furthermore, the assumption by the federal
15 government of state debts has resulted in geographic conflict. I can scarcely contemplate a more incalculable evil than the breaking of the union into two or more parts. Whenever Northern and Southern prejudices come into conflict, the
20 latter have been sacrificed and the former soothed, such that owers of debt tend to be Southern and holders of it tend to be Northern. Further conflict will be the result if nothing changes.

The irredeemable purpose of our national debt
25 was to transfer it to foreign countries so that they might invest in our future. Worse, our attempts to generate revenue, such as circulating bank bills and paper money, have corrupted a portion of the legislature. Corrupt members of Congress now aim
30 to eliminate limitations on borrowing and spending, changing the law to favor themselves. I fear that if this continues, we are doomed to grant too much power to those corrupt politicians, and will be no better off than the monarchy in England.

35 No threat to our government is greater than the corruption of the legislature. They have the power to form the most corrupt government on Earth if the means of their corruption is not prevented. The only hope is that representation changes during the
40 next election, though new representation may not be enough to undo all which the preceding legislature has done; some new members will probably share interest with the present majority. If the next legislature continues with the policies

45 of their predecessors, I cannot predict what the result will be. Our monetary system must be reformed to prevent further corruption.

Passage 2

50 A leading point likely to generate questions in the administration of government finances is the expediency of assuming state debts by the federal government. Yet the truth is such that assuming
55 state debts does away with thirteen complicated and conflicting systems of finance, and that doing so gives new strength to the federal government.

Mr. Jefferson has made clear his dislike of our present funding system, calling into question the
60 expediency of funding any debt at all. While he has not advocated directly for the undoing of what has already been done, he does censure the whole system on principle. If he continues, the end will be a subversion of the entire system.

65 The result of his trying to undermine the system has resulted in a great debate, the likes of which have taken to the halls of Congress. For his part, Mr. Jefferson has incorrectly insinuated that public money under my particular direction had
70 been unfaithfully applied, and that this application resulted in undue advantages for many speculators. Mr. Jefferson alleges that corruption is the result; others have argued that continuing to fund the national debt is a perfect Pandora's box.

75 Whatever the original merits of and present faults of the funding system, after having been so solemnly adopted and after so great a transfer of property under it, what would become of the government should it be reversed? What of our
80 national reputation? What are we to think of those politicians who would deny the legislature the power to bind the nation by contract in an affair of property? For this is precisely the case of the debt.

Mr. Jefferson is disposed to narrow federal
85 authority. He has argued that taking such power away from the states is unfriendly to liberty. I argue, however, that centralizing our debt is vital to maintaining the union.

The Tutorverse

1   What choice best summarizes Passage 1?
    A)   The national debt causes legislative corruption.
    B)   The national debt seemed like good policy, but has failed.
    C)   The national debt is dangerous for a number of reasons.
    D)   The national debt is contributing to higher taxes.

2   According to the author of Passage 1, maintaining the current monetary system could result in
    A)   conflict with foreign countries.
    B)   a more powerful federal government.
    C)   a corrupt legislature.
    D)   much needed tax relief.

3   As used in line 14, "assumption" most nearly means
    A)   accepting as true without proof.
    B)   taking on responsibility.
    C)   arrogance or presumption.
    D)   appearing to be something.

4   The most likely reason the author of Passage 1 mentions the state debts in the second paragraph is to
    A)   assign blame for the federal government's dysfunctional management of money.
    B)   outline a likely cause of future disputes between the states.
    C)   emphasize the dangers of borrowing more money from the states.
    D)   provide an example of why the current monetary system is more detrimental than beneficial.

5   The author of Passage 1 strongly suggests that the next election will
    A)   change very little.
    B)   result in some change, but that further reforms will be needed.
    C)   prevent further corruption.
    D)   lead to the election of politicians who will make the necessary reforms.

6   The central claim of Passage 2 is that the national debt
    A)   is important and integral to the maintenance of the Union.
    B)   is part of a system with immaterial flaws.
    C)   has not resulted in corrupt behavior.
    D)   is only opposed by people who do not understand it.

7   The author of Passage 2's attitude toward the allegations of corruption is best described as
    A)   haughty.
    B)   dismissive.
    C)   apprehensive.
    D)   pompous.

8   Which choice best describes the developmental pattern of Passage 2?
    A)   The author makes general statements and supports them with examples.
    B)   The author makes general statements and refutes specific arguments.
    C)   The author discusses the benefits and drawbacks of a system of finance.
    D)   The author makes arguments and offers specific evidence as support.

9   In the context of Passage 2, the author's use of the phrase "Whatever the...system" (lines 75-76) is primarily meant to convey that
    A)   merits and flaws are irrelevant; only consequences of change are important to consider.
    B)   the purpose of the system has changed, and therefore so should the system.
    C)   the original system was flawless and is still relevant.
    D)   all systems of government are inherently flawed because people are flawed.

10   On which of the following points would the authors of both passages likely agree?
    A)   Creating the national debt was a good policy.
    B)   The national debt should be eliminated.
    C)   Reform is needed to prevent corruption.
    D)   Corruption is a threat to democracy.

The Tutorverse

11 Which statement best describes the relationship between Passage 1 and Passage 2?

A) Passage 2 responds to the arguments advanced in Passage 1.

B) Passage 2 details the problems described more generally in Passage 1.

C) Passage 2 attacks the character of the author of Passage 1.

D) Passage 2 provides several possible solutions to issues described in Passage 1.

12 The author of Passage 1 would most likely respond to the discussion of reputation in lines 79-83, Passage 2, by claiming that

A) doing nothing will likely cause further damage to the country's reputation.

B) the country's reputation is an important thing to maintain.

C) corruption in the legislature is a worse consequence than a loss of reputation.

D) eliminating the debt will save the country's reputation.

13 Which choice from Passage 1 provides the best evidence for the answer to the previous question?

A) Lines 10-13 ("As it...relief")

B) Lines 14-16 ("Furthermore...conflict")

C) Lines 31-34 ("I fear...England")

D) Lines 35-36 ("No threat...legislature")

The Tutorverse

Passage E *(Answers & explanations on page 341).*

In the 19th and early 20th centuries, millions of Europeans emigrated to the United States. Many wrote "America letters" back home. This passage concerns the effect of one such letter on a young woman in Sweden.

Eleanora closed the front door and stood with her back against it. Outside, she heard the hoofbeats of Lars' horse and the slick sound of his sleigh's runners on the snow-covered ground.

5 After tonight, she had no doubt that Lars intended to ask for her hand. He had kissed her as they sat in the sleigh behind Peterson's general store, watching the stars.

She had let him kiss her, knowing that it was 10 something they should only be doing if they were betrothed. But she had no fear. Lars was reliable. She had the feeling that he intended to propose tonight, except that she had interrupted him, complaining that her feet were getting cold.

15 They weren't actually any colder than they had been for the last half hour. She just hadn't wanted to have him ask her. Not yet.

Was that foolish of her? She was eighteen now and it was high time she started to raise a family. 20 Most of her friends already had, or were planning to marry that summer.

Except Agnes. Agnes had surprised everyone by going to America. By herself. She hadn't even told Eleanora, her best friend, what she had been 25 planning.

Agnes had always been different. Her mother had died when Agnes was only three. Ever since, her father had complained about the expense of raising a girl who would never be able to do a 30 man's work on the farm.

He wouldn't miss Agnes, thought Eleanor. Then she smiled. Agnes wouldn't miss him either.

Just today, Eleanor had received a letter from Agnes. It was a surprise to see her neat 35 handwriting on the envelope. Eleanora put her hand inside her purse, touching the letter. She had carried it all day long, reading it over and over.

Agnes had a job working as a maid in a wealthy family's home. She had her own room in 40 the house and took her meals there, too. So she could save practically everything she earned.

"You wouldn't believe how many buildings there are here," Agnes had written. "And there are so many wagons and carts going from place to 45 place. Everybody moves so fast. But it's so much fun. It seems like nobody goes to bed until ten o'clock or even later! There's something happening all the time."

Agnes liked that, Eleanora knew. Something 50 happening all the time. She was always restless here in Skara, where you had to go to bed early because work started before the sun came up.

What would it be like to live there, Eleanora wondered. She had some money saved from 55 selling needlework. If only…

Eleanora noticed that Mama had left a lamp burning in the parlor. She went to turn it out, and was surprised to find Mama there, knitting socks, even though the church bell had already struck 60 eight.

Mama gave her a look, and at first Eleanora feared she might give her a scolding. It was awfully late to be out.

Instead, Mama asked, "Did you and Lars have 65 a good time?"

"Oh, yes," Eleanora answered. She didn't want to tell Mama about the kiss.

After a moment, Mama said, "He didn't say anything you'd want to tell me?"

70 Eleanora shook her head. "No, Mama. Not yet. But he will. You know Lars. He's reliable."

Mama nodded. "He's a good young man," she said. "But you shouldn't let him become too familiar unless…" She trailed off, but Eleanora 75 knew what she meant.

"By the way," Mama continued, "you didn't let me read the letter that came from Agnes."

Eleanora took off her coat and sat down by the fireplace. "Oh, I threw it away, Mama. She just 80 said some silly things. Nothing you'd be interested in."

Mama put her knitting in a bag and stood up. "I'm going to bed," she said. "You'd better not stay up much later."

85 "I won't, Mama," said Eleanora. "I just want to sit by the fire and warm up."

Mama left and Eleanora looked into the remnants of the logs that would soon burn out. She took the letter from her purse and dropped it into 90 the fire. It blazed up.

Lars was reliable. Next time she would let him ask.

1   Which of the following best captures what happens in the passage?
    A)   A young woman goes on a date.
    B)   A young woman is influenced by a letter.
    C)   A young woman deceives her mother.
    D)   A young woman reaches a decision.

2   Over the course of the passage, the main focus of the narrative shifts from
    A)   Eleanora's indecision to her decision.
    B)   Lars proposing marriage to Eleanora's deciding to accept.
    C)   Eleanora's kissing Lars to her concealing it from her mother.
    D)   Eleanora's refusing to marry Lars to her changing her mind.

3   The passage implies that Eleanora may best be thought of as
    A)   an envious friend.
    B)   a devoted daughter.
    C)   an undecided young woman.
    D)   an impatient girlfriend.

4   The narrator frequently describes Lars as "reliable" (lines 11, 71, 91). In this context, the word is most likely meant to convey the idea that Lars is
    A)   punctual.
    B)   a diligent worker.
    C)   honorable.
    D)   not easily dissuaded.

5   Based on the passage, which choice most nearly describes the difference between Eleanora and Agnes?
    A)   Eleanora has a better relationship with her father than Agnes does.
    B)   Eleanora does not have as strong a work ethic as Agnes.
    C)   Eleanora has a stronger sense of duty than Agnes does.
    D)   Eleanora is more flighty than Agnes.

6   The main purpose of lines 42-48 ("You wouldn't...time") is to show how
    A)   different Agnes' life was in America.
    B)   many people lived in Agnes' new home.
    C)   shallow life in America seemed to Eleanora.
    D)   much money Agnes was saving.

7   The passage most strongly suggests that Eleanora
    A)   is deeply in love with Lars.
    B)   thinks Agnes has made a foolish decision.
    C)   considers going to America herself.
    D)   feels sorry for Agnes.

8   Which choice provides the best evidence for the answer to the previous question?
    A)   Lines 22-25 ("Except Agnes...planning")
    B)   Lines 38-41 ("Agnes had...earned")
    C)   Lines 53-55 ("What would...only")
    D)   Lines 91-92 ("Lars was...ask")

9   The passage most strongly suggests that Eleanora's mother waited up for her because
    A)   She wanted to see the letter from Agnes.
    B)   She expected that Lars might have asked Eleanora to marry him.
    C)   She didn't like Eleanora staying out so late.
    D)   She worried that Eleanora would go to America.

10 Which choice provides the best support for the answer to the previous question?
    A)   Lines 57-60 ("She went...eight")
    B)   Lines 61-63 ("Mama gave...out")
    C)   Lines 68-69 ("After a...me")
    D)   Lines 76-77 ("By the...Agnes")

11 As used in line 74, "familiar" most likely means
    A)   close.
    B)   attached.
    C)   impertinent.
    D)   neighborly.

The Tutorverse

12 What is the most likely reason the author of the passage describes Eleanora telling her mother that she threw away Agnes' letter (lines 79-81)?

A) He wants to indicate that Eleanora doesn't trust her mother's judgment.

B) He wants to indicate that Eleanora doesn't want her mother to know she is tempted by what Agnes wrote.

C) He wants to indicate that Eleanora is secretive.

D) He wants to indicate that Eleanora desires to follow Agnes.

13 What is the main idea of the last two paragraphs of the passage?

A) Eleanora has made up her mind to marry Lars.

B) Eleanora has decided to follow Agnes to America.

C) Eleanora is angry that Agnes is living a better life.

D) Eleanora wants to have time to decide what to do.

The Tutorverse

Passage F *(Answers & explanations on page 341).*

This passage is excerpted and adapted by from a speech entitled "Space Exploration: Real Reasons and Acceptable Reasons" given by Michael D. Griffin, Administrator of the National Aeronautics and Space Administration, in 2007.

In the practical sense, space really is about spin-offs, as many have argued. But it's not about spin-offs like Teflon, Tang and Velcro as the public is so often told – and which in fact did not
5 come from the space program. And it's not about spin-offs in the form of better heart monitors or cheaper prices for liquid oxygen for hospitals. Yes, you get those things and many more; and they are real benefits. But that's not the right level on which
10 to view the matter. The real spin-offs are at a higher level. We need to look at a broader landscape.

What is the economic value to a society of upgrading the precision to which the entire
15 industrial base of that society works? Anyone who wants to…be a subcontractor or supplier or who even wants to supply nuts, bolts and screws to the space industry, must work to a higher level of precision than human beings had to do before the
20 space industry came along. And that fact absolutely resonates throughout our entire industrial base. What is the value of that? I can't calculate it, but I know it's there.

What is the scientific value of discovering the
25 origins of our universe? Or of discovering that literally 95 percent of the universe consists of dark energy or dark matter, terms for things that we as yet know nothing about?…Is it even conceivable that one day we won't learn to harness them? As
30 cavemen learned to harness fire, as people two centuries ago learned to harness electricity, we will learn to harness these new things. It was just a few years ago that we discovered them, and we would not have done so without the space program. What
35 is the value of knowledge like that? I cannot begin to guess. A thousand years from now there will be human beings who don't have to guess; they will know; and they will know we gave this to them.

Let's think for a moment about national
40 security. What is the value to the United States of being involved in enterprises that lift up human hearts everywhere when we do them? What is the value to the United States of being engaged in such projects, doing the kinds of things that other
45 people want to do with us, as partners?…I would submit that the highest possible form of national security, well above having better guns and bombs than everyone else, well above being so strong that no one wants to fight with us, is the security which
50 comes from being a nation which does the kinds of things that make others want to work with us to do them. What security could we ever ask that would be better than that, and would give more of it to us, than the space program?

55 What do you have to do? How do you have to behave, to do space projects? You have to value hard work. You have to live by excellence, or die from the lack of it. You have to understand and practice both leadership and followership; and
60 both are important. You have to build partnerships; leaders need partners and allies, as well as followers. You have to be willing to defer gratification, to spend years doing what we do, and then stand back and see if it works. We learn how
65 to leave a legacy, because we work on things that not all of us will live to see – and we know it. And we learn about accepting the challenge of the unknown, where we might fail, and to do so not without fear or apprehension, but to master it, to
70 control it and to go anyway.

These are lessons that we all need to learn, and they are lessons the space business teaches us. And I would submit that our country is a better place for those who have learned those lessons.

75 These are the values that the space program brings. This is why it must be supported. And this is why, although we don't acknowledge it, we don't admit it and most of us don't understand it. This is why if we didn't have a space program, we
80 Americans would feel less than ourselves. We can never allow that to happen.

NASA Shuttle Launches & Technological Spin-offs

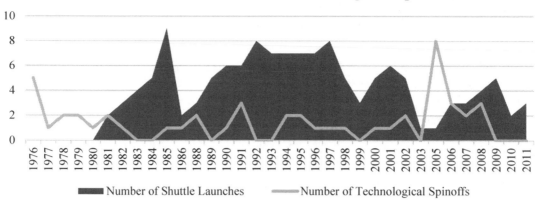

Source: NASA

1   Which of the following choices reflects the structural development of the passage?
   A)   A scientific principle is explained using a question-and-answer format.
   B)   A hypothesis is tested and the findings explained in the form of a narrative.
   C)   A particular point of view is advanced by answering a series of questions.
   D)   A personal opinion is explained using concrete facts and statistics.

2   The central idea of the first paragraph is that
   A)   most benefits of the space program are short-term in nature.
   B)   not all benefits of the space program are tangible or measurable.
   C)   the only benefits of the space program that matter are those that can be quantifiable.
   D)   the space program is responsible for a number of important commercially available inventions.

3   Which concept is supported by the passage and by the data presented in the graph?
   A)   The number of technological spin-offs exceeds launches, therefore justifying the space program.
   B)   The space program has resulted in a number of technological spin-offs.
   C)   The space program is too expensive to be justifiable in the long-term.
   D)   The value of technological spin-offs justifies the space program's existence.

4   The author suggests that the true economic value of the space program is represented by
   A)   better heart monitors.
   B)   improving the entire industrial base.
   C)   nuts, bolts, and screws.
   D)   Teflon, Tang, and Velcro.

5   Which choice best summarizes the third paragraph?
   A)   A question is answered by an analogy.
   B)   A strange scientific concept is explained.
   C)   An anecdote is used to make a comparison.
   D)   An argument is refuted using statistics.

6   As used in lines 30-32, "harness" most nearly means
   A)   abuse.
   B)   domesticate.
   C)   join.
   D)   utilize.

7   The author makes a comparison between fire, electricity, and dark energy to
   A)   determine the most powerful natural phenomena.
   B)   discuss potential military and defense applications of the space program.
   C)   suggest that the space program focus more on scientific discoveries.
   D)   underscore the vast, untapped potential of space program discoveries.

The Tutorverse

8 Based on the passage, the author would most likely support which national security policy?
A) Building more powerful bombs, guns, and other weapons.
B) Fostering stronger economic, scientific, and ideological allies.
C) Investing in space-based defense systems and technologies.
D) Supporting larger and more powerful armies, navies, and air forces.

9 Which selection best supports the answer to the previous question?
A) Lines 15-20 ("Anyone who…along")
B) Lines 32-34 ("It was…program")
C) Lines 39-40 ("Let's think…security")
D) Lines 45-52 ("I would…them")

10 Why does the author mention the qualities necessary to execute a space program?
A) It emphasizes intangible, higher-order spin-offs that may not have an obvious short-term payoff.
B) It illustrates that Americans do not value long-term payoffs.
C) To admonish Americans for a lack of courage, excellence, and leadership.
D) To encourage readers to pursue other rewarding pursuits.

11 Over the course of the passage, the author repeatedly raises questions about "value" in order to
A) counter different objections to the space program's existence.
B) support numerous concerns about the space program's effectiveness.
C) accept the various doubts about the space program's benefits.
D) emphasize the importance of quantifiable value to evaluating the space program.

12 According to the passage, why would the loss of the space program make Americans "feel less than ourselves"?
A) The space program has taken away resources from other important social programs.
B) The space program inspires Americans to improve and strive for higher-level values.
C) The space program makes Americans feel more important and powerful.
D) The space program played a historical role in elevating America's global status.

13 "The space program must be required to produce more commercially viable spin-offs in the short-term."

Regarding the above statement, the author would likely
A) agree, because politicians need to see tangible results from the space program.
B) agree, because the space program is too expensive otherwise.
C) disagree, because many benefits of the space program are intangible and long-term in nature.
D) disagree, because the space program is purely about scientific discovery.

The Tutorverse

Passage G *(Answers & explanations on page 342).*

Movies are big business. According to some estimates, as of March 2015, the top ten highest grossing films of all time – as measured by ticket sales – collectively generated nearly $17 billion.
5 Of these ten films, nine are firmly rooted in the action/adventure genre; moviegoers love, it would seem, big explosions and shiny special effects.

But gross sales are not the only measure of a movie's success. In business, a return on
10 investment (ROI) refers to the ratio of profit to the amount of money invested, and is often shown in percentage form. The higher the percentage, the better, as this indicates a proportionally larger amount of profit than capital risked in the
15 investment. Return on investment as a concept can be used to analyze any business venture – including the business of making movies.

If, instead of using gross box office sales, one considers return on investment as a metric of
20 success, the list of the top ten most successful films of all time changes dramatically. Instead of being dominated by action/adventure movies, five of the top ten movies with the highest ROIs fall squarely in the horror genre. As it turns out,
25 blockbuster action/adventure movies are very expensive to produce, while horror movies are relatively inexpensive.

But how is it that a movie with a budget of approximately $0.5 million can profit nearly $89
30 million (an ROI of nearly 18,000%)? What is it about scary movies that captivates audiences to such a degree that a movie can profit 180 times its investment?

To answer such questions, one must turn to
35 human biology.

Current research suggests that brain chemistry contributes strongly to people's love of (or aversion to) horror movies. When most people encounter a perceived threat (or are exposed to
40 thrilling circumstances), the nervous system reacts by flooding the body with hormones. This process, dubbed the fight-or-flight response, is responsible for releasing a host of chemicals – such as adrenaline – that produce a variety of reactions in
45 the body: the heart beats faster; breath quickens; muscles tense; vision narrows – all of this designed to help a person survive a stressful or dangerous situation. The science behind these reactions is complicated and highly technical, but
50 as it relates to movies, the star of the show is dopamine.

As a hormone, dopamine plays a large role in a number of different centers of the brain. Most famously, perhaps, is its role in the reward centers
55 of the brain. As with most things in the human body, the feeling of pleasure and happiness is very complicated. To say that dopamine causes pleasure would be a gross oversimplification. Instead, dopamine has a significant impact on our
60 expectations. If our expectations are exceeded or surprised, dopamine contributes to the sense of elation at the positive outcome. This is why gambling can be so addicting: the possibilities presented by unknown outcomes are such that an
65 unexpectedly good outcome (say, finding that one has been dealt a royal flush, for example) feels good.

Research suggests that horror movies trigger a similar response in the body. A particularly
70 suspenseful or thrilling scene, for example, is thought to elicit a flood of dopamine, the effect of which will depend on the viewer's expectations and the outcome of the scene. In essence, a horror movie can serve as a catalyst for the release of
75 dopamine, adrenaline, endorphins, and the host of other chemicals that heighten the senses.

It's no wonder, then, that there are die-hard fans of horror movies. Horror movies do not necessarily need the best visual or sound effects to
80 hold their own at the box office, as action/adventure movies typically do. Horror movies need only penetrate the human psyche – to tap into the unconscious of the human mind and to make viewers face their fears. And this can be
85 accomplished on a budget a fraction of the size of their action/adventure counterparts.

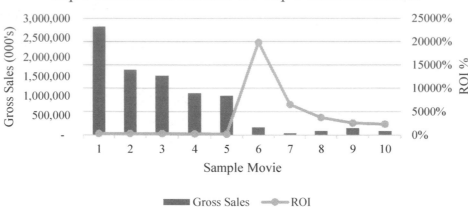

Top 5 Action/Adventure vs. Top 5 Horror Movies

1. The primary purpose of the passage is to
   A) compare horror movies with action/adventure movies.
   B) convince the reader to watch more horror movies.
   C) describe why horror movies are entertaining.
   D) explain how and why horror movies can be successful.

2. According to the passage, the movies with the highest grossing ticket sales of all time are primarily movies in the
   A) action/adventure genre.
   B) comedy genre.
   C) drama genre.
   D) horror genre.

3. The main idea of the second paragraph is that
   A) business concepts do not apply to the arts, like movie-making.
   B) higher percentages are always better than high dollar amounts.
   C) ROI is a viable measure of a movie's success.
   D) ticket sales are a viable measure of a movie's success.

4. The purpose of including the third paragraph is to
   A) explain that ROI is the preferred metric for measuring success.
   B) illustrate that some movies are successful under both criteria.
   C) illustrate that some movies are successful under one criteria can be less successful under another.
   D) reinforce the notion that ticket sales are the preferred metric for measuring success.

5. The questions posed in lines 28-33 have the effect of
   A) convincing the reader that ROI is more valuable than ticket sales.
   B) convincing the reader to invest in horror movies.
   C) explaining differences between ROI and ticket sales.
   D) introducing the main idea of the passage.

6. Relative to the overall structure of the passage, the fifth paragraph serves to
   A) bridge two seemingly different topics.
   B) establish the tone of the passage.
   C) provide answers to a questions.
   D) support the argument being advanced.

7 Which choice best describes what takes place in the sixth paragraph (lines 36-51)?
A) A biological process is described.
B) Different movie genres are compared.
C) Moviegoer characteristics are measured.
D) Two measures of success are debated.

8 As used in line 58, "gross" most nearly means
A) complete.
B) disgusting.
C) honest.
D) repugnant.

9 By mentioning gambling in lines 62-67, the author is better able to
A) compare gamblers and moviegoers in later paragraphs.
B) describe the sensation of watching action/adventure movies.
C) explain how dopamine contributes to a sense of happiness.
D) illustrate the concept of ROI as a gambler would see it.

10 According to the passage, some people like horror movies because
A) some scenes can result in a flight-or-flight response.
B) of shiny special effects and big explosions.
C) they are tired of blockbuster action/adventure movies.
D) they desire to confront their fears

11 Which selection best supports the answer to the previous question?
A) Lines 6-7 ("Moviegoers love…effects")
B) Lines 73-76 ("In essence…senses")
C) Lines 78-81 ("Horror movies…do")
D) Lines 81-84 ("Horror movies…fears")

12 Based on the passage, if approached about investing in a horror movie, the author might most likely
A) refuse, stating that action/adventure movies can be more profitable.
B) refuse, because the science behind the success of horror movies is unclear.
C) accept, because horror fans pay more per ticket than action/adventure fans.
D) accept, stating that horror movies can have a high ROI.

13 Based on the statements made in the passage, what can be inferred about the genre of the sample movies provided in the graph following the passage?
A) Only movies 6-9 are action/adventure.
B) Only movies 6-9 are horror.
C) Even numbered movies are horror.
D) Odd numbered movies are horror.

PLEASE DO NOT WRITE ON THE PAGES IN THIS BOOK. TAKE PHOTOCOPIES OF THE ONES YOU NEED.

The Tutorverse

Passage H *(Answers & explanations on page 343).*

This passage is excerpted from a speech delivered by Nelson Mandela in 1964. Mandela, a South African anti-apartheid revolutionary who opposed the government's system of racial segregation, was accused and later convicted of a number of sedition-related charges. This speech was delivered in court as part of Mandela's defense.

The lack of human dignity experienced by Africans is the direct result of the policy of white supremacy. White supremacy implies black inferiority. Legislation designed to preserve white
5 supremacy entrenches this notion. Menial tasks in South Africa are invariably performed by Africans. When anything has to be carried or cleaned the white man will look around for an African to do it for him, whether the African is
10 employed by him or not. Because of this sort of attitude, whites tend to regard Africans as a separate breed. They do not look upon them as people with families of their own; they do not realize that we have emotions – that we fall in love
15 like white people do; that we want to be with their wives and children like white people want to be with theirs; that we want to earn money, enough money to support our families properly, to feed and clothe them and send them to school. And
20 what 'house-boy' or 'garden-boy' or laborer can ever hope to do this…

The only cure is to alter the conditions under which Africans are forced to live and to meet their legitimate grievances. Africans want to be paid a
25 living wage. Africans want to perform work which they are capable of doing, and not work which the Government declares them to be capable of. We want to be allowed to live where we obtain work, and not be endorsed out of an area because we
30 were not born there. We want to be allowed and not to be obliged to live in rented houses which we can never call our own. We want to be part of the general population, and not confined to living in our ghettoes. African men want to have their wives
35 and children to live with them where they work, and not to be forced into an unnatural existence in men's hostels. Our women want to be with their men folk and not to be left permanently widowed in the reserves. We want to be allowed out after
40 eleven o'clock at night and not to be confined to our rooms like little children. We want to be allowed to travel in our own country and to seek work where we want to, where we want to and not where the Labor Bureau tells us to. We want a just
45 share in the whole of South Africa; we want security and a stake in society.

Above all, My Lord, we want equal political rights, because without them our disabilities will be permanent. I know this sounds revolutionary to
50 the whites in this country, because the majority of voters will be Africans. This makes the white man fear democracy.

But this fear cannot be allowed to stand in the way of the only solution which will guarantee
55 racial harmony and freedom for all. It is not true that the enfranchisement of all will result in racial domination. Political division, based on color, is entirely artificial and, when it disappears, so will the domination of one color group by another. The
60 ANC[5] has spent half a century fighting against racialism. When it triumphs as it certainly must, it will not change that policy.

This then is what the ANC is fighting. Our struggle is a truly national one. It is a struggle of
65 the African people, inspired by our own suffering and our own experience. It is a struggle for the right to live.

During my lifetime I have dedicated my life to this struggle of the African people. I have fought
70 against white domination, and I have fought against black domination. I have cherished the ideal of a democratic and free society in which all persons will live together in harmony and with equal opportunities. It is an ideal for which I hope
75 to live for and to see realized. But, My Lord, if it needs be, it is an ideal for which I am prepared to die.

[5] African National Congress: During Mandela's time, an organization dedicated to the protest of the government's apartheid policies enforcing racial segregation. Mandela was an active member in the organization.

1   The first two paragraphs focus on
    A)   appealing to logic and reason, and the last four on appealing to emotions.
    B)   describing a problem, and the last four on justifying a solution.
    C)   debating different solutions, and the last four on appealing to emotions.
    D)   justifying a solution, and the last four on describing a problem.

2   The primary idea of the passage is that
    A)   racial equality should be guaranteed under the law.
    B)   changes to a few government policies should be made.
    C)   black South Africans should create a separate government.
    D)   white South Africans should be more kind to their black counterparts.

3   According to Mandela, many white South Africans view black South Africans as
    A)   equals.
    B)   superior.
    C)   legitimate.
    D)   inferior.

4   Which choice best summarizes the second paragraph?
    A)   A number of demands are made based on isolated circumstances.
    B)   Examples of injustices are enumerated and used to advance a demand.
    C)   Racially motivated injustices are discussed and condemned.
    D)   The reason for injustices are explored and debated.

5   The author most likely includes examples in the second paragraph in order to
    A)   demonstrate that equality for Africans is not unreasonable.
    B)   emphasize that the white government can never again control Africans.
    C)   explain the consequences should racial equality not be attained.
    D)   illustrate why white South Africans view Africans as a separate breed.

6   According to the second paragraph, the Africans are forced to do certain work
    A)   as a matter of preference.
    B)   because of a lack of education.
    C)   because of government policies.
    D)   due to permanent disabilities.

7   Which choice from the passage supports the answer to the previous question?
    A)   Lines 10-12 ("Because of…breed")
    B)   Lines 17-19 ("That we…school")
    C)   Lines 41-44 ("We want…to")
    D)   Lines 47-49 ("Above all…permanent")

8   In context, "disabilities" (line 48) most nearly means
    A)   physical infirmities.
    B)   political concessions.
    C)   political differences.
    D)   socioeconomic disadvantages.

9   Mandela suggests that "racial harmony and freedom for all" will result in
    A)   a situation where blacks will control politics in South Africa.
    B)   disenfranchisement of white South Africans.
    C)   equality of representation in South African politics.
    D)   further fighting and violence.

10 According to Mandela, white South Africans fear democracy because there would be more black voters than white. Which statement from the passage suggests that this fear is unfounded?
    A)   Lines 3-4 ("White supremacy…inferiority")
    B)   Lines 32-34 ("We want…ghettoes")
    C)   Lines 57-59 ("Political division…another")
    D)   Lines 64-67 ("It is…live")

11 Mandela claims that the purpose of the ANC is to
    A)   establish a separate country for Africans.
    B)   overthrow the non-African government.
    C)   protest black domination.
    D)   secure equal rights for Africans.

The Tutorverse

12 In context of lines 69-71, Mandela's use of the words "white domination" and "black domination" mainly has what effect?

  A) It clarifies that Mandela has fought for one domination in the past, and has changed his mind.

  B) It emphasizes equality by showing that domination by either race is intolerable.

  C) It indicates that Mandela sees domination as a matter of racial superiority.

  D) It suggests that political equilibrium can only be achieved through domination.

13 By including the last sentence in the passage, Mandela

  A) apologizes for his actions and seeks forgiveness.

  B) dares the court to render a guilty verdict.

  C) emphasizes his dedication to freedom and equality for all.

  D) invites white leaders to martyr him.

Passage I *(Answers & explanations on page 344).*

Grandfather stood at the edge of the enclosure, his gaze intent on something in the distance. Priya stood behind her father's father, looking around the wide meadow beyond, wondering what she
5 was supposed to be looking for. As far as she could tell, this zoo enclosure was empty, save for a smattering of trees with long, wispy branches.

"Ah, there it is," said Grandfather.

At first, Priya saw nothing, but then a large,
10 gray animal lumbered out from between the trees.

Grandfather turned to Priya, a twinkle in his eye. "What do you suppose that is?"

"Grandfather! It's obviously an elephant!"

"Oh? Obviously? How do you know?"
15 "Because it's huge! It has big ears and a long trunk!"

"It is not so obvious to everyone. Did I ever tell you the tale of the blind men and the elephant?"
20 Priya laughed and shook her head, for Grandfather was full of old stories, but she couldn't recall this one.

Grandfather watched the elephant and held up his hand, a sure sign he was about to launch into
25 one of his fables. "Perhaps not all is as it seems," he said mysteriously, pointing at the elephant.

Priya humored her grandfather, asking, "What do you mean?"

He smiled. "Many years ago, the men where
30 I'm from in India were always arguing. Some said the depth of the oceans is infinite, and some said it is finite. Some said the world is round, and some said it is flat. Some said there is life after death, and some said there is not. Some said there is a
35 higher power, and some said there is not. Every man insisted that his truth was the absolute truth. But the king said that truth was relative, and that he would prove it."

Grandfather leaned on the fence around the
40 enclosure and examined the elephant.

Priya rolled her eyes, and indulged her grandfather. "How did he prove it?"

"Well, the king told his servants to gather all of the blind men in the kingdom. Once the blind
45 men were assembled, the king brought out an elephant. To the blind men, he said, 'This is an elephant.' He told the blind men to step forward and touch a different part of the elephant. He repeated, 'This is an elephant.' Each blind man
50 repeated, 'This is an elephant.' Then he asked the blind men, 'What is an elephant like?' What do you think an elephant is like, Priya?"

Priya looked at the elephant sauntering lazily across the meadow toward a tree. "Big," she said.
55 "Huge. Rough skin. Floppy ears. Long trunk."

"It seems obvious, does it not?" nodded Grandfather.

"Yes, Grandfather," Priya replied, although she was not quite sure anymore, and was curious
60 about where the story was going.

Grandfather nodded again, and continued telling the story.

"The king asked the blind men, 'Tell me – what is an elephant like?' Remember, each blind
65 man had only felt one part of the elephant. So those who had felt its ears said things like, 'An elephant is like a rough blanket.' Those who had felt the tusks said, 'An elephant is hard like a spear.' Those who had felt the trunk said, 'An
70 elephant is long like a rope.' Those who had felt the body said, 'An elephant is huge as a barn.' Those who felt the feet said, 'An elephant is tall like a pillar.' Those who felt the tail said, 'An elephant is long and bristly like a broom.'"
75 "Yes," said Priya. "An elephant is all of those things."

"Ah," said Grandfather, "but maybe not. Each of the blind men asserted that his understanding of the elephant was the truth. 'This is an elephant!'
80 they declared to the king! And the king was delighted. He said to the men of his kingdom that, in a way, we are all blind men asserting our understanding of the truth."

Now Priya understood. For behind the large,
85 lumbering elephant was a small, baby elephant. Not all elephants were huge after all.

She walked away from the enclosure and crossed the road to another. There, a pair of giraffes nibbled at the leaves on a tree. "Do you
90 have any stories about giraffes?" Priya asked.

Grandfather chuckled. "I believe I do."

1   Which choice best summarizes the text?
    A)   A man tells his granddaughter a
         humorous, yet witty, story.
    B)   A man teaches his granddaughter
         interesting facts about animals.
    C)   A story is used to teach someone about a
         philosophical concept.
    D)   A man tells his granddaughter a story
         about elephants to demonstrate how truth
         is always clear.

2   Which choice best describes the developmental
    pattern of the passage?
    A)   The telling of a story is followed by an in-
         depth analysis of the story's themes.
    B)   A story from the past is framed within a
         conversation from the present.
    C)   The merits of an amusing anecdote are
         debated.
    D)   A theory is proposed, discussed, and
         ultimately refuted.

3   The main purpose of Grandfather's story about
    the elephant is to
    A)   explain why elephants possess certain
         physiological features.
    B)   teach a lesson about perception and the
         nature of truth.
    C)   illustrate ancient Indian culture through
         storytelling.
    D)   elucidate how best to win an argument.

4   At the beginning of the passage, how does Priya
    feel about her grandfather's stories?
    A)   Grandfather's stories show he is extremely
         wise.
    B)   Grandfather's stories are interesting and
         she is curious to hear one.
    C)   Grandfather's stories are so boring that
         they border on being annoying.
    D)   Grandfather's stories are copious and
         usually silly.

5   Which choice provides the best evidence for the
    answer to the previous question?
    A)   Lines 11-12 ("Grandfather turned… eye")
    B)   Lines 20-22 ("Priya laughed…one")
    C)   Lines 23-25 ("Grandfather watched…
         fables")
    D)   Lines 58-60 ("Although she…going")

6   In line 36, "absolute" most nearly means
    A)   unrestricted.
    B)   adulterated.
    C)   qualified.
    D)   conclusive.

7   The passage most strongly suggests that the king
    asked specifically to gather blind men because he
    knows that
    A)   they have never seen an elephant and
         would be surprised.
    B)   they possess other heightened senses that
         will allow them to identify elephants.
    C)   they understand the world differently from
         people who can see.
    D)   they are learned philosophers and
         profoundly wise thinkers.

8   In context of the passage, the author repeats the
    sentence "This is an elephant," in lines 46-50, in
    order to
    A)   ensure that each blind man understood that
         he was handling an elephant.
    B)   convince the blind men that an elephant is
         made up of its parts.
    C)   illustrate that the truth is whatever the king
         says is the truth.
    D)   argue that an elephant's traits make it easy
         to identify.

9   In line 53, "sauntering" most nearly means
    A)   sneaking around.
    B)   walking at a leisurely pace.
    C)   galloping to a random location.
    D)   navigating a winding road.

10 Which best supports the argument Grandfather
    makes by telling the story?
    A)   Just as each blind man understands the
         elephant differently from others, so too do
         all men see truth differently from others.
    B)   Just as the blind men will never fully
         understand the nature of an elephant,
         neither can people ever obtain truth.
    C)   Truth is elusive, just as the nature of an
         elephant eludes the blind men.
    D)   Truth is unchanging and singular, just as
         an elephant is a large, rough-skinned
         animal.

The Tutorverse

11 Based on the passage, the blind men who believed that an elephant is "hard like a spear" had touched the elephant's
A) ears.
B) trunk.
C) nails.
D) tusks.

12 The description of how each blind man understands the elephant (lines 63-74) mainly serves to
A) underscore the fact that truth is subjective and relative to different people.
B) explain that the blind men had no idea what an elephant looked like as a whole.
C) liken the blind men's explanations with everyday objects.
D) compare what the blind men think the elephant looks like with what Priya says about elephants.

13 Which choice provides the best evidence that Priya no longer views her grandfather's stories as silly?
A) Lines 20-22 ("Priya laughed… one")
B) Lines 27-28 ("Priya humored… mean")
C) Lines 75-76 ("An elephant… things")
D) Lines 89-90 ("Do you…asked")

The Tutorverse

Passage J *(Answers & explanations on page 345).*

This passage is excerpted and adapted from an article written by Louise Herrick Wall for *Century Illustrated Monthly Magazine: Volume 72.* In this 1906 work, entitled "Heroic San Francisco," Wall describes her first-hand account of the great 1906 San Francisco earthquake, one of the most devastating natural disasters in American history.

Horror, panic, dread, terror – these are the words that have been most lavishly used by the local and Eastern press in describing the effect of the extraordinary disasters that have rushed upon

5   us here in San Francisco during the last two weeks, filling every hour since the great earthquake shock of the morning of April 18 – and the vastly more disastrous succeeding days of the fire – with a tempest of hurrying events. And yet to the

10   thousands who have been caught within the whirlpool of the most intense activity the words seem unreal, crude, and essentially false to the spirit that animates the whole mass of the people who are living with passionate energy through this

15   time. The truth is that despair is not to be seen on any face, nor the droop of it weighing upon any shoulder, nor the ring of it heard in any voice, except where extreme old age or habitual self-indulgence has already set its mark.

20   Early in the morning of April 19, twenty-four hours after the heaviest shocks, when the earth still quaked at short intervals and the walls of wrecked buildings crumbled in at a puff of wind; when the fire had swept the Mission and most of the

25   waterfront bare, and was rushing against and overwhelming the great business blocks of the main thoroughfares, at that moment attacking the heart of San Francisco itself; when Market Street was the flue through which the fire sucked its air

30   from the bay…I walked the whole length of San Francisco from the ferry to army headquarters in the Presidio and back again, and made a number of detours into the burning city, as far as the bayonets of the fire-line of guards would permit, over hot

35   debris and under festoons of half-melted, fallen wires, where the city in its first hot haste was vomited out upon these ruined streets; and yet I saw no despair upon any human face…

In the confusion people met your gaze

40   abstractedly; if questioned, they would answer, and return instantly to their interrupted tasks. All were intent on some immediate furious effort to save from the approaching fire what was left to them of family and possessions. The broken ant

45   hill, with its myriad escaping ants each carrying pupae, grub, or some burden greater than himself, is neither less nor more tragic to look upon than these eager human creatures in their determined effort to save their own. In many you saw the

50   tightening of the will that is a strong joy to the strong, and the fight for life quickened by the near rumble and jar of dynamite and fanned by the flame-beaten air laden with ash and cinder. The breeze swept scorching from the south, where the

55   fire was swallowing a fresh block of houses every ten or fifteen minutes. The whole sky in that quarter was steam and smoke, torn by wallowing bursts of flame…

From a hundred heaps of rescued treasure

60   gramophones lifted their foolish, brazen mouths. Invalids rode in baby-carriages or across the locked hands of men or on shutters, or on mattresses of woven wire. One sick woman, whose hip had been injured before the disaster, was

65   pushed from near the City Hall to the ferry on two bicycles lashed together, catamaran fashion, and steadied over the debris by her sons. She was four days on the bed they had improvised for her of a chair tied to the wheels before she reached a place

70   of safety. Babies were born on doorsteps, and mothers delivered before their time by those who were kind enough to stop and help. There is no way to exaggerate the extraordinary pain, hardship, and, above all, the killing suspense

75   suffered during the flight, but at every point it was met and matched by heroism, ingenuity, family tenderness, and disinterested devotion.

"This awful time may not be worth the suffering it has cost," cried a young soldier,

80   himself pallid with nights of work and watching, "but it is worth all the money it has cost – all, and more."

It has been wonderful and stirring to see the kindness, the magnanimity, the absolute absence

85   of greed in taking advantage of one another's misfortunes. It takes more than pain or loss to make a tragedy when the spirit of a free people

The Tutorverse

burns up strong and clear to meet its fate as it has
burned in stricken San Francisco.

**Figure 1: 1989 Earthquake Intensity (USGS)
(USGS)**

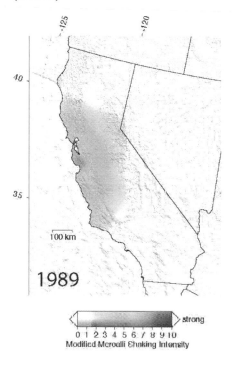

Figure 2: 1906 Earthquake Intensity

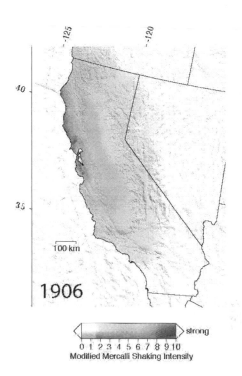

---

1 Over the course of the passage, the author's
focus

A) shifts from contradicting an argument to
telling a story.

B) shifts from explaining a theory to telling a
story.

C) does not shift, remaining focused on
relating events and observations.

D) does not shift, remaining focused on
explaining a theory.

2 On which point does the author disagree with the
East coast press?

A) The cause of the resulting fire.

B) The impact of the earthquake on the
different parts of the city.

C) The people's reaction and behavior in
response to the disaster.

D) The severity of the disaster in terms of
ground shaking intensity.

3 Which selection best supports the answer to the
previous question?

A) Lines 1-5 ("Horror, panic…weeks")

B) Lines 15-19 ("The truth…mark")

C) Lines 72-75 ("There is…flight")

D) Lines 78-82 ("This awful…more")

4 As used in line 13, "animates" most nearly
means

A) drives.

B) enraptures.

C) frightens.

D) rescues.

5 Which statement best summarizes the second
paragraph?

A) A person describes her observations of a
disaster, removed from immediate danger.

B) A person describes her observations while
walking through a disaster zone.

C) A person questions the reason for a
disaster and its impact on people.

D) A person reviles the behavior of some
people and praises that of others.

The Tutorverse

6 What caused the "walls of wrecked buildings" to crumble in the author's presence?
A) Fire.
B) Ground movement.
C) People.
D) Wind.

7 "Furious," as used in line 42, most nearly means
A) angry.
B) chaotic.
C) intense.
D) livid.

8 The author makes a comparison of the situation to a "broken ant hill" (lines 44-45) in order to
A) condemn the selfishness of certain people.
B) demean the actions of the people.
C) downplay the severity of the disaster.
D) vividly illustrate human activity.

9 The author includes the example of sick, injured, and pregnant people (lines 59-72) in order to
A) advance the argument that people faced hardship together, not giving in to fear.
B) compare the actions of normal citizens with those of soldiers.
C) contrast the behavior of people with those of ants.
D) emphasize the degree of difficulty suffered by San Francisco's people.

10 As a result of the earthquake and subsequent fire, the author suggests that people in San Francisco have
A) resorted to looting and anarchy.
B) fallen into despair and panic.
C) helped one another through the disaster.
D) remained calm and collected.

11 The author includes the sentence "There is…devotion" (lines 72-77) in order to
A) convince the reader that the media are completely incorrect in their reports of the disaster.
B) emphasize the difficulty experienced by the people of San Francisco.
C) highlight the only positive qualities displayed by San Francisco's citizenry.
D) illustrate that media outlets have missed a critical aspect of the disaster's aftermath.

12 The main idea of the second to last paragraph (lines 78-82) is that
A) soldiers were employed to help the citizens of San Francisco.
B) the earthquake brought out the best in the citizens of San Francisco.
C) the earthquake resulted in the loss of an incalculable amount of money.
D) the resulting human suffering is nothing compared to the loss of money.

13 Do Figure 1 and Figure 2 support the author's primary claim?
A) No, because the passage does not compare the 1906 earthquake with others.
B) No, because the passage suggests that the intensity was much greater than shown in the figures.
C) Yes, because earthquake intensity is a matter of intense debate.
D) Yes, because the figures corroborate the author's descriptions.

The Tutorverse

Passage K *(Answers & explanations on page 346).*

Passage 1

Thomas Hobbes, son of an English clergyman,
5 was born prematurely in 1588 – the same year that
the Spanish Armada brought an invading army to
England's shores. Hobbes later said his mother
gave birth to twins: "myself and fear."
Though the Armada was ultimately
10 unsuccessful, Hobbes' political writings were
heavily influenced by the era's fear and
uncertainty.
Hobbes posited that in their "natural" state,
where there is no organized government, humans
15 exist in "continual fear, and danger of violent
death." He wrote that "the life of man [is] solitary,
poor, nasty, brutish, and short." There is, in the
natural state, a constant conflict between people.
As a consequence, Hobbes wrote, people can
20 only live in peace together under subjection to the
absolute power of a common master. At the time
Hobbes first set down his views, this "master" was
England's king, Charles I, and the social contract
between the king and his subjects was absolute and
25 indissoluble. "The subjects to a monarch cannot
cast off monarchy," Hobbes wrote.
But Hobbes' theory would be put to the test.
King Charles and England's representative
legislature, Parliament, did not often see eye to
30 eye. In 1629, King Charles made the unpopular
decision to dissolve Parliament. Following a long
and bloody revolution, the King was convicted of
treason and sentenced to death. As Charles stood
before a crowd gathered to see him die, the king
35 gave a very Hobbesian speech: "A subject and a
sovereign are clean different things…. If I would
have given way…for to have all laws changed
according to the Power of the Sword, I needed not
to have come here and therefore…I am the martyr
40 of the people."
The sword had triumphed and a military
leader, Oliver Cromwell, became head of the new
government: the Commonwealth of England. The
people had, in the end, cast off their monarch.
45 Hobbes, who had at first sided with the
royalists, went on to refine his theory. Hobbes
wrote what many consider to be his greatest work,
Leviathan, in which he set out the powers of the
Commonwealth. A central tenant of the *Leviathan*

50 was the importance, power, and inviolability of the
state.

Passage 2

John Locke, the son of an English lawyer, was
born in 1632. The English Civil War erupted when
John was ten; his father served on the side of the
55 Parliamentary forces. While Locke studied at
Oxford University to become a doctor, the death of
Oliver Cromwell resulted in the restoration of the
English monarchy, with Charles II ascending the
throne. Locke became the personal physician of
60 Lord Shaftesbury, one of the king's political
opponents in the new Parliament.
Around this time Locke wrote his *Two
Treatises of Government,* setting forth a view of
government as a contract, of sorts, between subject
65 and ruler. By participating in a society, people
voluntarily relinquish certain rights so that the
laws of the state can ensure impartial justice and
protection for all.
Most importantly, Locke believed that the
70 powers of government should be divided to
prevent a ruler from attaining absolute power.
"Nobody can desire to have me in his absolute
power unless it be to compel me by force to that
which is against the right of my freedom – that is,
75 to make me a slave," he wrote. If such a ruler did
seize power, Locke left no doubt about the right of
the citizens to rebel: "It is lawful for me to treat
him as one who has put himself into a state of war
with me – that is, kill him if I can."
80 Such ideas were dangerous during the
restoration of the monarchy, and Locke was forced
to flee to the Netherlands. Many years later, the
popularity of the monarchy began to wane again.
Charles II's successor, James II, was removed. But
85 this time Parliament left no doubt that it held the
ultimate power. It passed laws restricting the
power of the monarchy.
Almost a century later, Locke's ideas
engendered a new revolution, albeit different from
90 one that he might have imagined. Thomas
Jefferson, Alexander Hamilton, and James
Madison cited Locke as their inspiration when
they wrote the Declaration of Independence that
separated the American colonies from England.
95 Locke had declared that among the natural rights

The Tutorverse

of people were "life, liberty, and property" – echoes of which can be found in the Declaration: "All men are created…with certain unalienable

100 rights, that among these are life, liberty, and the pursuit of happiness."

---

1 Which of the following best summarizes the political views of Thomas Hobbes, as set forth in Passage 1?

A) The sovereign receives his power through the will of the people.

B) The sovereign receives his power through force of arms.

C) The sovereign's authority cannot be challenged.

D) The sovereign's authority lasts only as long as he rules wisely.

2 Passage 1 suggests that over time, Hobbes' philosophy changed from

A) fear of the sovereign to full acceptance of the sovereign's right to rule.

B) justification of the king's right to rule to justification of the Commonwealth.

C) submission to the ruler to opposition to the Commonwealth.

D) living under no government to living under a government in which all citizens had a role.

3 In line 35, the author calls the speech given by King Charles I "Hobbesian." In what way do the king's words resemble Hobbes' philosophy?

A) Charles contends that he had surrendered his authority, he would have lived, though this would have been a violation of his right to rule.

B) Charles states that he is the sovereign, not a subject, which automatically exempts him from execution.

C) Charles shows no fear of execution, implying that he is not like the people who Hobbes said live in "continual fear."

D) Charles tries to reason with the crowd, just as Hobbes would have.

4 Why might Hobbes have written approvingly of the Commonwealth, despite the fact that he had earlier sided with the royalists?

A) He was forced to do so by the new government.

B) He realized that his earlier theory was completely flawed.

C) He understood that a ruler need not necessarily be a monarch.

D) He felt Charles I was too weak to be king.

5 Passage 2 suggests that Locke's philosophy

A) changed while he was in the Netherlands.

B) was consistent throughout his career.

C) varied depending on the prevailing ruler.

D) led him to encourage England's colonies to rebel.

6 Based on the information provided in Passage 2, it may be inferred that the author believes

A) that the political events in Locke's lifetime influenced his political views.

B) that the political events in Locke's lifetime were not as influential as events were to Hobbes.

C) that the form of government under which Locke lived was relatively unchanging.

D) that Locke's patriotic feelings strongly influenced his political views.

7 Which choices provide the best evidence for the answer to the previous question?

A) Lines 55-59 ("While Locke…throne")

B) Lines 69-71 ("Most importantly…power")

C) Lines 80-82 ("Such ideas…Netherlands")

D) Lines 88-90 ("Almost a…imagined")

8 In passage 2, why does the author say the American Revolution was different from the one that Locke might have imagined?
A) It was led by the common people.
B) It was inspired by the monarchy itself.
C) It was rooted in the theory of natural rights.
D) It led to the creation of a new country.

9 As used in line 89, "engendered" most likely means
A) feminized.
B) inspired.
C) negated.
D) endangered.

10 Which statement best describes the relationship between the two passages?
A) Passage 1 describes the advances in political thought since the work described in Passage 2.
B) Passage 2 refutes the arguments described in Passage 1.
C) The two passages describe differing views on the relationship between citizens and sovereigns.
D) The two passages describe complementary views on the relationship between citizens and sovereigns.

11 Based on the two passages, on which point would Hobbes and Locke most likely disagree?
A) Whether a monarchy can be inherited.
B) Whether a ruler should be subject to the death penalty.
C) Whether subjects have the right to rebel against the ruler.
D) Whether people would survive without a government.

12 How might Hobbes respond to Locke's view that the powers of government should be divided?
A) Hobbes might agree that the powers should be divided as long as they were absolute.
B) Hobbes might disagree because all power had to be concentrated in the hands of a single person or entity.
C) Hobbes might agree that if the subjects of the ruler demanded a division of powers it should be granted.
D) Hobbes might disagree because people would not obey a divided government.

13 According to Passage 2, how might Locke respond to the statement made in Passage 1, lines 25-26 ("The subjects...monarchy")?
A) He might respond that the Parliament was the only viable form of government.
B) He might respond that the natural rights of people included life, liberty, and property.
C) He might respond that it is just to rebel against a ruler who has deprived citizens of their rights.
D) He might respond that the restoration of the monarchy was accomplished without force.

The Tutorverse

Passage L *(Answers & explanations on page 347).*

This passage is adapted from the National Woman Suffrage Association published in 1876 addressed to all women of the United States. It was not until the 19th amendment that women in the United States were permitted the right to vote.

Let us dedicate the dawn of the Second Century to securing justice to Woman.

For this purpose, we ask you to circulate a petition to Congress asking an amendment to the
5 United States Constitution that shall prohibit the disfranchising of any citizen on account of gender. We have already sent this petition throughout the country for the signatures of those men and women who believe in the citizen's right to vote…

10 Having petitioned to both our State and National lawmakers for years, many from weariness and despair have vowed to appeal no more; for our petitions, they say, are piled up by the tens of thousands, unheeded and ignored. Yet,
15 it is possible to roll up such a mammoth petition, borne into Congress on the shoulders of stalwart men, that we can no longer be neglected or forgotten. Statesmen and politicians, alike, are conquered by majorities. We urge the women of
20 this country to make now the same united effort for their own rights, that they did for the slaves at the south, when the 13th amendment was pending. Then a petition of over 300,000 was rolled up by the leaders of the suffrage movement, and
25 presented in the Senate by the Hon. Charles Sumner. But the leading statesmen who welcomed woman's untiring efforts to secure the black man's freedom, frowned down the same demands when made for herself. Is not liberty as sweet to her as to
30 him? Are not the political disabilities based on gender as grievous as those of color? Is not a civil rights bill that shall open to woman the college doors, the trades and professions – that shall secure her personal and property rights, as
35 necessary for her protection, as for that of the colored man?

And yet the highest judicial authorities have decided that the spirit and letter of our National Constitution are not broad enough to protect
40 Woman in her political rights; and for the redress of her wrongs they remand her to the State. If this Magna Charta of Human Rights can be thus narrowed by judicial interpretations in favor of class legislation, then we must demand an
45 amendment that in clear, unmistakable language, shall declare the equality of all citizens before the law.

Women are citizens, first of the United States, and second of the State wherein they reside: hence,
50 if robbed by State authorities of any right founded in nature or secured by law, they have the same right to national protection against the State, as against the infringements of any foreign power. If the United States government can punish a woman
55 for voting in one State, why has it not the same power to protect her in the exercise of that right in every State? The Constitution declares it the duty of Congress to guarantee to every State a republican form of government, to every citizen
60 equality of rights. This is not done in States where women, thoroughly qualified, are denied admission into colleges, which their property is taxed to build and endow; where they are denied the right to practice law and are thus debarred
65 from one of the most lucrative professions; where they are denied voice in the government, and thus while suffering all the ills that grow out of the giant evils of intemperance, prostitution, war, heavy taxation and political corruption, stand
70 powerless to effect any reform. Prayers, tears, psalm-singing and expostulation are light in the balance, compared with that power at the ballot box that converts opinions into law. If Women who are laboring for peace, temperance, social
75 purity and the rights of labor, would take the speediest way to accomplish what they propose, let them demand the ballot in their own hands, that they may have a direct power in the government. Thus only can they improve the conditions of the
80 outside world and purify the home. As political equality is the door to civil, religious and social liberty, here our work must begin.

Constituting as we do one-half the people, bearing the burdens of one-half the National debt,
85 equally responsible with man for the education, religion and morals of the rising generation, let us with united voice send forth a protest against the present political status of Woman, that shall echo and re-echo through the land. In view of the
90 numbers and character of those making the demand, this should be the largest petition ever yet

rolled up in the old world or the new; – a petition
that shall settle forever the popular objection that
"Women do not want to vote."

95

Population of the United States

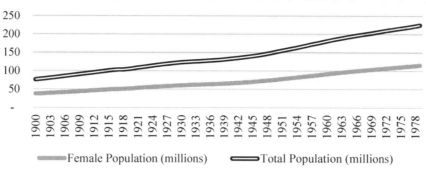

Source: U.S. Census Bureau

1 The main purpose of the passage is to
A) galvanize support for women's voting rights.
B) accuse women of inaction and complacency.
C) rebut a popular objection about women's desire to vote
D) mollify those who did not support women's voting rights.

2 All of the following choices describe the mood of the passage EXCEPT?
A) impatient
B) frustrated
C) brooding
D) determined

3 Which choice most nearly reflects the overall structure of the passage?
A) A conflict is resolved through mutual debate.
B) A problem is described and multiple solutions debated.
C) A problem is dismissed based on popular objection.
D) A problem is described and a solution advanced and justified.

4 According to the passage, the author would most likely
A) protest racial equality.
B) support racial equality.
C) leave racial equality to the courts.
D) be neutral on the issue of racial equality.

5 Based on the passage, the author most likely feels that Senator Sumner's actions are
A) justifiable.
B) hypocritical.
C) disingenuous.
D) prevaricating.

6 Which choice best supports the answer to the previous question?
A) Lines 18-19 ("Statesmen and…majorities")
B) Lines 19-22 ("We urge…pending")
C) Lines 23-26 ("Then a…Sumner")
D) Lines 26-29 ("But the…herself")

7 The author's main purpose in posing a series of questions (lines 29-36) is to
A) illustrate how racial equality differs from gender equality.
B) cast doubt on the legitimacy of racial equality.
C) ask readers to respond to the questions directly.
D) liken an attained form of equality with an unattained form.

The Tutorverse

8   After explaining how judicial authorities will not grant women equal political rights, the author
A)   suggests voting for new judges.
B)   encourages women to pray more.
C)   urges women to no longer pay taxes.
D)   moves to demand an amendment to the Constitution.

9   The author most likely uses the examples in lines 61-70 ("denied admission…reform") in order to
A)   appeal to the reader's emotions, intelligence, and sense of fairness.
B)   highlight problems that will not go away when equality is won.
C)   enumerate a specific list of demands to be made in petition.
D)   provide circumstantial evidence to support a point of view.

10   The phrase "light in the balance" (lines 71-72) most nearly means
A)   vital.
B)   trivial.
C)   dazzling.
D)   considerable.

11   Data provided in the graph provides the most direct support for which idea in the passage?
A)   Women should be able to vote because they are equally responsible for raising children.
B)   Women should be able to vote because they pay for half the national debt.
C)   Women should be able to vote because they are half the citizenry.
D)   Women should be able to vote because the petition has millions of signatures.

12   The author uses the phrase "echo and re-echo" (lines 88-89) primarily to
A)   describe the actual sound of women shouting for justice.
B)   encourage women to sign the petition.
C)   popularize the demands made in the passage.
D)   emphasize that unity of purpose will result in far-reaching political power.

13   Why does the author expect that a petition will solve the objection to women's right to vote described in the last sentence of the passage?
A)   A large petition signed by women will prove that women want to vote.
B)   A large petition will silence judges who do deny women the right to vote.
C)   The petition will result in an act of Congress, which will state that women want to vote.
D)   The petition will garner support from racial minorities.

The Tutorverse

Passage M *(Answers & explanations on page 348).*

This passage is adapted from Louisa May Alcott's 1875 novel *Eight Cousins.*

Dr. Alec's eyes twinkled, but he said very soberly, –

"Rose, are you vain?"

" I'm afraid I am," answered a very meek

5 voice from behind the veil of hair that hid the red face.

"That is a sad fault." And he sighed as if grieved at the confession.

"I know it is, and I try not to be; but people

10 praise me and I can't help liking it, for I really don't think I am repulsive."

The last word and the funny tone in which it was uttered were too much for Dr. Alec and he laughed in spite of himself, to Rose's great relief.

15 "I quite agree with you; and in order that you may be still less repulsive, I want you to grow as fine a girl as Phebe."

"Phebe!" and Rose looked so amazed that her uncle nearly went off again.

20 "Yes, Phebe; for she has what you need: health. If you dear little girls would only learn what beauty is and not pinch and starve and bleach yourselves out so, you'd save an immense deal of time, money, and, pain. A happy soul in a healthy

25 body makes the best sort of beauty for man or woman. Do you understand that, my dear?

"Yes, sir," answered Rose, much taken down this comparison with the girl from the poorhouse. It nettled her sadly, and she showed that it did by

30 saying quickly, –

"I suppose you would like to have me sweep and scrub, and wear an old brown dress, and go round with my sleeves rolled up, as Phebe does?"

"I should very much if, you could work as

35 well she does, and show as strong a pair of arms as she can. I haven't seen a prettier picture for some time than she made of herself this morning, up to the elbows in suds, singing like a blackbird while she scrubbed on the back stoop."

40 "Well I do think you are the strangest man that ever lived!" was all Rose could find to say after this display of bad taste.

"I haven't begun to show my oddities yet, so you must make up your mind to worse shocks than

45 this," he said, with such a whimsical look that she was glad the sound of a bell prevented her showing more plainly what a blow her little vanities had already received.

"You will find your gift up in auntie's parlor,

50 and there you can amuse her and yourself by rummaging to your heart's content; I've got to be cruising round all the morning getting my room to rights," said Dr. Alec as they rose from breakfast.

"Can't I help you, uncle?" asked Rose, quite

55 burning to be useful.

"No, thank you. I'm going to borrow Phebe for a while, if Aunt Plenty can spare her."

…

"Uncle will find that I can do some things that

60 Phebe can't; so now!" thought Rose, with a toss of the head as she flew to her aunt and her long desired gift.

1 Which answer choice best summarizes the passage?
- A)   A painful memory is recalled.
- B)   Two family members have a conversation.
- C)   A doctor sees and treats a patient.
- D)   Different points of view are argued.

2 Over the course of the passage, Rose's attitude toward Dr. Alec can best be described as
- A)   unchangingly dutiful.
- B)   at first dutiful, later becoming disrespectful.
- C)   at first disrespectful, later becoming dutiful.
- D)   at first dutiful, later becomes disbelieving, and finally reverting back to dutiful.

The Tutorverse

3 The passage suggests that Dr. Alec views Rose's admission of vanity
A) with wholly contemptable.
B) as entirely repulsive.
C) as at least somewhat humorous.
D) with great relish.

4 Based on the passage, with which statement would Dr. Alec most likely agree?
A) Beauty is reflected in a person's work ethic.
B) Beauty is derived from a person's material wealth.
C) Beauty is largely about a person's frame of mind and physical health.
D) Beauty is represented by gift-giving and generosity.

5 Which choice best provides evidence for the answer to the previous question?
A) Lines 15-17 ("I quite…Phebe")
B) Lines 24-26 ("A happy…woman")
C) Lines 34-36 ("I should…can")
D) Lines 49-51 ("You will…content")

6 In line 29, the use of the word "nettled" most nearly means
A) offended.
B) blistered.
C) itched.
D) disappointed.

7 The author includes Dr. Alec's statement about Phebe "singing like…stop" (lines 38-39) in order to emphasize
A) Rose's vanity and superficiality.
B) the difference between Rose and Phebe.
C) Phebe's ability to carry a tune.
D) Dr. Alec's broader philosophy about beauty.

8 Rose most likely views Phebe as
A) a superior to be emulated.
B) a peer to be respected.
C) an inferior to be ignored.
D) an equal to be acknowledged.

9 As it is used in lines 54-55, the phrase "quite burning" most closely means
A) eager.
B) enraged.
C) embarrassed.
D) languid.

10 Which choice best describes the relationship between Rose and Dr. Alec?
A) They have known each other for a long time, and are very familiar with one another's personalities.
B) They have had limited interaction and have little interest in getting to know one another.
C) There is an undercurrent of animosity between Rose and Dr. Alec.
D) Rose and Dr. Alec are not well acquainted yet, but desire to be.

11 Which choice best provides evidence for the answer to the previous question?
A) Lines 7-8 ("That is…confession")
B) Lines 12-14 ("The last…relief")
C) Lines 40-45 ("Well I…this")
D) Lines 51-53 ("I've got…breakfast")

12 The main purpose of lines 46-48 is to
A) explain the rationale behind Dr. Alec's theory of beauty.
B) establish an important shift in the direction of the passage's plot.
C) illustrate how the conversation with Dr. Alec is affecting Rose.
D) describe Dr. Alec's motivation for speaking with Rose.

13 The author uses the phrase "so now!" (line 60) in order to illustrate
A) Rose's determination to impress Dr. Alec.
B) Rose's disdain for Dr. Alec's theories.
C) Rose's incorrigible personality.
D) Rose's preoccupation with material things.

The Tutorverse

Passage N *(Answers & explanations on page 349).*

This passage is excerpted from Jane Addams' 1902 work *Democracy and Social Ethics*. Addams, a political activist and philosopher, played a large role in advancing the cause of what is now known as social work.

We are learning that a standard of social ethics is not attained by travelling a sequestered byway, but by mixing on the thronged and common road where all must turn out for one another, and at

5 least see the size of one another's burdens…There are many indications that this conception of Democracy is growing among us. We have come to have an enormous interest in human life as such, accompanied by confidence in its essential

10 soundness. We do not believe that genuine experience can lead us astray any more than scientific data can.

We realize, too, that social perspective and sanity of judgment come only from contact with

15 social experience; that such contact is the surest corrective of opinions concerning the social order, and concerning efforts, however humble, for its improvement. Indeed, it is a consciousness of the illuminating and dynamic value of this wider and

20 more thorough human experience which explains in no small degree that new curiosity regarding human life which has more of a moral basis than an intellectual one.

The newspapers, in a frank reflection of

25 popular demand, exhibit an omnivorous curiosity equally insistent upon the trivial and the important. They are perhaps the most obvious manifestations of that desire to know, that "What is this?" and "Why do you do that?" of the child. The first dawn

30 of the social consciousness takes this form, as the dawning intelligence of the child takes the form of constant question and insatiate curiosity.

Literature, too, portrays an equally absorbing though better adjusted desire to know all kinds of

35 life. The popular books are the novels, dealing with life under all possible conditions, and they are widely read not only because they are entertaining, but also because they in a measure satisfy an unformulated belief that to see farther, to know all

40 sorts of men, in an indefinite way, is a preparation for better social adjustment – for the remedying of social ills…

Partly through this wide reading of human life, we find in ourselves a new affinity for all men,

45 which probably never existed in the world before.

Evil itself does not shock us as it once did, and we count only that man merciful in whom we recognize an understanding of the criminal. We have learned as common knowledge that much of

50 the insensibility and hardness of the world is due to the lack of imagination which prevents a realization of the experiences of other people. Already there is a conviction that we are under a moral obligation in choosing our experiences,

55 since the result of those experiences must ultimately determine our understanding of life. We know instinctively that if we grow contemptuous of our fellows, and consciously limit our intercourse to certain kinds of people whom we

60 have previously decided to respect, we not only tremendously circumscribe our range of life, but limit the scope of our ethics.

We can recall among the selfish people of our acquaintance at least one common characteristic

65 — the conviction that they are different from other men and women, that they need peculiar consideration because they are more sensitive or more refined. Such people "refuse to be bound by any relation save the personally luxurious ones of

70 love and admiration, or the identity of political opinion, or religious creed." We have learned to recognize them as selfish, although we blame them not for the will which chooses to be selfish, but for a narrowness of interest which deliberately selects

75 its experience within a limited sphere, and we say that they illustrate the danger of concentrating the mind on narrow and un-progressive issues.

We know, at last, that we can only discover truth by a rational and democratic interest in life,

80 and to give truth complete social expression is the endeavor upon which we are entering. Thus the identification with the common lot which is the essential idea of Democracy becomes the source and expression of social ethics. It is as though we

85 thirsted to drink at the great wells of human experience, because we knew that a daintier or less potent draught would not carry us to the end of the journey, going forward as we must in the heat and jostle of the crowd.

1   Which of the following choices best describes the overall structure of the passage?
    A)   A general theory is contradicted by real-world examples.
    B)   A general theory is followed by a series of specific supporting points and explanations.
    C)   A general theory is presented and debated.
    D)   A hypothesis is advanced, analyzed, and retracted.

2   In line 2, the author uses the phrase "travelling a sequestered byway" mainly to describe
    A)   bearing other people's burdens.
    B)   living a sheltered life.
    C)   performing charitable works.
    D)   staying off of crowded roads.

3   Which statement best summarizes the second paragraph?
    A)   Intellectual understanding of humanity is greater than moral understanding.
    B)   Moral understanding of humanity differs from social experience.
    C)   Newspapers help expand people's range of social experiences.
    D)   Many benefits arise from the desire to gain a wide range of social experiences.

4   The main purpose of the third and fourth paragraphs is to
    A)   help publishers sell more newspapers and novels.
    B)   illustrate that one can gain social experience simply by reading.
    C)   provide examples of educational reading materials.
    D)   support the author's ideas surrounding social curiosity and learning.

5   According to Addams, reading novels is beneficial primarily because
    A)   authors are effective at convincing people to remedy social ills.
    B)   books are more developed than newspapers and other forms of writing.
    C)   books provide a way to view different people in different circumstances.
    D)   doing so is entertaining, offering a valuable distraction from daily troubles.

6   Based on the passage, the cause of "much of the insensibility and hardness of the world" (lines 49-50) is due to
    A)   a deficiency of social empathy.
    B)   deliberate selfishness.
    C)   moral obligation.
    D)   unconscious biases.

7   Addams suggests that a narrow scope of ethics can be caused by
    A)   being accepting of a wide range of opinions and creeds.
    B)   deliberately curbing breadth of social interactions.
    C)   leading luxurious lives full of love and admiration.
    D)   reading too many newspapers and novels.

8   According to the passage, selfish people care little about
    A)   people with different beliefs.
    B)   reading newspapers or novels.
    C)   the success of democracy.
    D)   those with similar sensitivities.

9   Which selection best supports the answer from the previous question?
    A)   Lines 56-62 ("We know…ethics")
    B)   Lines 68-71 ("Such people…creed")
    C)   Lines 71-77 ("We have…issues")
    D)   Lines 81-84 ("Thus the…ethics")

The Tutorverse

10 If asked to vote on a policy affecting a wide range of people, what might, according to the passage, a selfish person reason about his or her decision?

- A) It is necessary to consider the impact of the policy on a wide range of people.
- B) It is unnecessary to consider the impact of the policy on a wide range of people.
- C) The best decision will be one made after a thorough understanding of the policy's impact on all people.
- D) The worst decision will be one made that considers only personally important issues.

11 The central idea of the last paragraph is that

- A) crowded roads are full of the common people.
- B) intellectual ethics should guide social expression.
- C) social ethics must guide policy making.
- D) the truth can be found in a number of places.

12 As used in line 86, "daintier" most nearly means

- A) choosier.
- B) fancier.
- C) more accessible.
- D) more delicate.

13 Throughout the passage, the author uses the phrase "social ethics," which in context refers to

- A) a set of diverse experiences.
- B) equality of different classes of people.
- C) tangible customs and traditions.
- D) a set of rules governing a group of people.

The Tutorverse

Passage O *(Answers & explanations on page 350).*

This passage is excerpted and adapted from Nathaniel Pitt Langford's 1905 *The Discovery of Yellowstone Park*. Langford's publication documented the events of the 1870 Washburn Expedition to Yellowstone.

The place where I obtained the best and most terrible view of the canyon was a narrow projecting point situated two or three miles below the lower fall. Standing there or rather lying there
5 for greater safety, I thought how utterly impossible it would be to describe to another the sensations inspired by such a presence. As I took in this scene, I realized my own littleness, my helplessness, my dread exposure to destruction,
10 my inability to cope with or even comprehend the mighty architecture of nature…A sense of danger, lest the rock should crumble away, almost overpowered me. My knees trembled, and I experienced the terror which causes men to turn
15 pale and their countenances to blanch with fear, and I recoiled from the vision I had seen, glad to feel the solid earth beneath me and to realize the assurance of returning safety.

The scenery surrounding the canyon and falls
20 on both banks of the Yellowstone is enlivened by all the hues of abundant vegetation. The foot-hills approach the river, crowned with a vesture of evergreen pines. Meadows verdant with grasses and shrubbery stretch away to the base of the
25 distant mountains, which, rolling into ridges, rising into peaks, and breaking into chains, are defined in the deepest blue upon the horizon. To render the scene still more imposing, remarkable volcanic deposits, wonderful boiling springs, jets of heated
30 vapor, large collections of sulphur, immense rocks and petrifications abound in great profusion in this immediate vicinity. The river is filled with trout, and bear, elk, deer, mountain lions and lesser game roam the plains, forests and mountain fastnesses.
35 The two grand falls of the Yellowstone form a fitting completion to this stupendous climax of wonders. They impart life, power, light and majesty to an assemblage of elements, which without them would be the most gloomy and
40 horrible solitude in nature. Their eternal anthem, echoing from canyon, mountain, rock and woodland, thrills you with delight, and you gaze with rapture at the iris-crowned curtains of fleecy foam as they plunge into gulfs enveloped in mist
45 and spray. The stillness, which held your senses spellbound as you peered into the dismal depths of the canyon below, is now broken by the uproar of waters; the terror it inspired is superseded by admiration and astonishment, and the scene, late
50 so painful from its silence and gloom, is now animate with joy and revelry.

The upper fall, as determined by the rude means of measurement at our command, is one hundred and fifteen feet in height. The river
55 approaches it through a passage of rocks which rise one hundred feet on either side above its surface. Until within half a mile of the brink of the fall the river is peaceful and unbroken by a ripple. Suddenly, as if aware of impending danger, it
60 becomes lashed into foam, circled with eddies, and soon leaps into fearful rapids. The rocky jaws confining it gradually converge as it approaches the edge of the fall, bending its course by their projections, and apparently crowding back the
65 water, which struggles and leaps against their bases, warring with its bounds in the impatience of restraint, and madly leaping from its confines, a liquid emerald wreathed with foam, into the abyss beneath. The sentinel rocks, a hundred feet
70 asunder, could easily be spanned by a bridge directly over and in front of the fall, and fancy led me forward to no distant period when such an effort of airy architecture would be crowded with happy gazers from all portions of our country…
75 Very beautiful as is this fall, it is greatly excelled in grandeur and magnificence by the cataract half a mile below it, where the river takes another perpendicular plunge of three hundred and twenty feet into the most gloomy cavern that ever
80 received so majestic a visitant. Between the two falls, the river, though bordered by lofty precipices, expands in width and flows gently over a nearly level surface until its near approach to the verge. Here a sudden convergence in the rocks
85 compresses its channel, and with a gurgling, choking struggle, it leaps with a single bound, sheer from an even level shelf, into the tremendous chasm. The sheet could not be more perfect if wrought by art…Every object that meets the vision
90 increases its sublimity. There is a majestic harmony in the whole, which I have never seen before in nature's grandest works.

The Tutorverse

1. Throughout the passage, the narrator's attitude repeatedly shifts between
   A) anxiety and gratitude.
   B) amazement and appreciation.
   C) curiosity and terror.
   D) fear and dread.

2. The main idea of the first paragraph is that
   A) the author is in immediate danger.
   B) the author is not very articulate.
   C) Yellowstone is filled with wildlife.
   D) Yellowstone is sublime.

3. As used in line 2, the word "terrible" most nearly means
   A) awe-inspiring.
   B) nauseating.
   C) serious.
   D) unpleasant.

4. The primary purpose the author includes a detailed description in lines 11-18 is to
   A) express how the beauty of the scenery was worth the risks taken.
   B) counsel readers to avoid dangerous situations by being better prepared.
   C) help the reader imagine himself in the shoes of the author.
   D) warn readers that Yellowstone should not be visited without a guide.

5. Which statement best summarizes the third paragraph?
   A) Dangerous circumstances are described in detail.
   B) Different reasons to visit Yellowstone are enumerated.
   C) The influence of the waterfalls on the surroundings is described.
   D) The physical properties of each waterfall is separately described.

6. The "eternal anthem" in line 40 refers to
   A) the color of the waterfalls.
   B) the sound of the canyon walls.
   C) the sound of the waterfalls.
   D) the sound of the wildlife.

7. The author's use of the phrase "as if aware of impending danger" (line 59) has which effect?
   A) It compares the water to a nervous person, causing the reader to feel fearful.
   B) It contrasts the water's appearance with earlier descriptions of the water's sound.
   C) It personifies the water, causing the reader to feel a sense of wonder.
   D) It personifies the water, making the paragraph more dramatic and engaging.

8. According to the passage, the river that is "peaceful and unbroken" (line 58) becomes rough due to
   A) bears fishing for trout.
   B) excessive vegetation.
   C) rocks that churn the water.
   D) the swimming of trout.

9. Which of the following best supports the answer to the previous question?
   A) Lines 19-21 ("The scenery...vegetation")
   B) Lines 32-34 ("The river...fastnesses")
   C) Lines 61-69 ("The rocky...beneath")
   D) Lines 69-74 ("The sentinel...country")

10. By including his thoughts on the possibility of a bridge spanning the river (lines 69-74), it can reasonably be inferred that the author would support which of the following statements?
    A) Growth and development are more valuable than conservation.
    B) People should be allowed to build whatever they want wherever they want.
    C) The beautiful view must be made available to the public.
    D) Tourism revenue is more important than preserving nature.

11. The word "cataract" (line 77) most nearly means
    A) scenery.
    B) view.
    C) flood.
    D) waterfall.

The Tutorverse

12 According to the passage, the author feels that
A)   the upper fall is the more beautiful.
B)   the lower fall is the more beautiful.
C)   both falls are equally beautiful.
D)   it is impossible to judge one fall more beautiful than the other.

13 Based on the description in the last paragraph, the most appealing feature of the lower fall is
A)   the cavern into which the water falls.
B)   the loudness of the falling water.
C)   the smoothness of the falling water.
D)   the volume of water that falls.

Passage P *(Answers & explanations on page 351).*

Passage 1

In September of 2015, after years of deliberation, Nepal adopted a new constitution. Since then, leaders in India have expressed some reservations regarding certain aspects of the new document, and have requested that, in the nominal name of equality, a series of amendments be made. These revisions would have a significant impact on minority groups living along the Nepal-India border. Indian leaders worry that certain new clauses in Nepal's constitution may infringe on the rights of these minority groups, and that violence along the border may result.

Many politicians in Nepal believe that the Indian government has overstepped its bounds. Though India has a vested interest in a stable Nepal, Nepal is ultimately, like India, a sovereign state – one that has as much right as its neighbors to enact its own constitution. On the other hand, some minority groups may indeed be at risk of having their rights limited by more powerful political parties in Nepal. Some of these groups fear that the political elite have exerted unfair influence in the drafting of the new constitution. The drawing of new state lines, for example, has generated a significant amount of backlash – backlash that India fears can lead to violent conflict in the coming years.

Still, many observers point out the hypocrisy in India's protestations. India still experiences much of the discrimination against women and members of the lesbian, gay, bisexual, and transgender (LGBT) community that has been explicitly banned under Nepal's new constitution. To some, it is rich that India would point a finger at potential issues in Nepal's constitution when India itself suffers from the very shortcomings that they allege are problems with Nepal's constitution. In fact, India's actions have had the unintended effect of uniting the political parties of Nepal against India.

Passage 2

At the conclusion of a decade-long civil war, Nepal won the right to hold elections and establish a legislature, departing from a centuries-old monarchy. Enacting a constitution to govern the country has since proven to be a long and difficult process; while several legislatures have come and gone, the nation's constitution has only just been finalized. The primary reason for such a long delay in the ratification of the constitution has to do with the diversity of opinion on how best to frame the country's most important governing document.

The constitution adopted by Nepal in 2015 is revolutionary for the strides it has made toward ensuring equal rights for all its people. Among other things – such as abolishing the death penalty and providing free access to education for all citizens – the new constitution marks Nepal as the first Asian country to explicitly recognize the rights of LGBT people. The document states clearly that "no discrimination shall be made against any citizen in the application of general laws on the grounds of religion, color, caste, tribe, sex, sexual orientation, bodily condition, disability, status of health, marital status, pregnancy, financial status, origin, language or region, ideological conviction."

In theory, the new constitution is fair and progressive. However, there are concerns that the practical application of the constitution leaves many groups vulnerable. Nepal is a diverse nation, and many observers are concerned that the constitution may not protect all groups of people adequately. The legislature intended to divide the nation into seven states, but the borders of those states are a matter of significant contention because they are important in determining the balance of power in the legislature. Because the ruling party is primarily comprised of upper-class men, many other groups are concerned that, by drawing state borders a certain way, the ruling party has implicitly limited the ability of other groups to represent themselves in the legislature. Thus, despite the explicit decree in the constitution, women and minority groups may still face discrimination.

The Tutorverse

1 What statement best summarizes Passage 1?
A) The intricate details of a new constitution are discussed.
B) The effects of a new constitution are discussed.
C) A particular point of view is advanced.
D) A specific question is raised and answered.

2 The most likely reason the author of Passage 1 mentions violent conflict in lines 26-29 is to
A) present a counterargument to ideas mentioned earlier in the paragraph.
B) support the idea that the new laws are the cause of violence.
C) emphasize the dangerous results of aggressive diplomacy.
D) blame India for violence in Nepal.

3 In the context of Passage 1, the author's use of the phrase "overstepped its bounds," (line 16) is primarily meant to convey that
A) the new borders between the countries are in dispute.
B) Indian troops have crossed the border into Nepal.
C) the Indian government may have acted inappropriately.
D) Indian diplomacy is ineffective and offensive.

4 As used in line 18, "sovereign" most nearly means
A) supreme.
B) royal.
C) independent.
D) effective.

5 The author of Passage 1 most likely
A) supports India in its diplomatic actions.
B) supports Nepal's new constitution.
C) holds an ambivalent point of view on Nepal's constitution.
D) advocates for frequent foreign intervention.

6 The author of Passage 1 indicates some view India's diplomatic strategy as duplicitous because
A) Nepal's constitution is a violation of international law.
B) India's constitution is stronger than Nepal's.
C) Nepal's politicians are insincere and hypocritical.
D) India itself struggles with some of the issues they decry in Nepal.

7 The central claim of Passage 2 is that the Nepalese constitution
A) is progressive and easily implemented in practice.
B) is well-intentioned but will do little to curb discrimination.
C) has more anti-discrimination provisions than the Indian constitution.
D) does little to improve an otherwise flawed legislature.

8 According to Passage 2, why might women and minorities still face discrimination despite provisions in the new Nepalese constitution?
A) The constitution does not explicitly mention women and minorities.
B) India still experiences such discrimination, and the border with Nepal is ill-defined.
C) The ruling party in Nepal is mostly male and upper class.
D) Nepal is a diverse nation with no unifying culture.

9 Which choice best describes the developmental pattern of Passage 2?
A) The author describes a problem and offers solutions.
B) The author explains the rationale for a decision.
C) The author discusses the benefits and possible drawbacks of a policy.
D) The author makes an argument and offers specific examples as support.

The Tutorverse

10 On which of the following points would the authors of both passages likely agree?
   A) India is wrong to intervene in Nepalese affairs.
   B) Nepal has an obligation to discuss its constitution with India.
   C) Creating a constitution that satisfies everyone involved is very difficult.
   D) Democracy in the region may be in danger.

11 Which statement best describes the relationship between Passage 1 and Passage 2?
   A) Passage 1 and Passage 2 approach the same topic from different angles.
   B) Passage 1 and Passage 2 take opposing views on the same issue.
   C) Passage 2 responds to arguments advanced in Passage 1.
   D) Passage 1 responds to arguments advanced in Passage 2.

12 The author of Passage 1 would most likely respond to the possibility of discrimination raised in Passage 2 by
   A) arguing that the discrimination will lead to conflict with India.
   B) suggesting that Nepal's mistakes, if any, are its own to make.
   C) claiming that the constitution will have a number of compensating benefits.
   D) countering that Nepal may benefit from adopting India's anti-discrimination provisions.

13 Which choice provides the best evidence for the answer to the previous question?
   A) Lines 17-20 ("Though India…constitution")
   B) Lines 26-29 ("The drawing…years")
   C) Lines 30-31 ("Still, many…protestations")
   D) Lines 36-39 ("To some…constitution")

The Tutorverse

Passage Q *(Answers & explanations on page 351).*

This passage adapted from Kate Chopin's *The Awakening*, originally published in 1899. The setting is New Orleans, Louisiana, at the end of the 19th century. Edna Pontellier is a mother and wife living in a Creole society.

Edna still felt dazed when she got outside in the open air. The Doctor's carriage had returned for him and stood before the porch. She did not wish to enter the carriage, and told Doctor
5 Mandelet she would walk; she was not afraid, and would go alone. He directed his carriage to meet him at Mrs. Pontellier's, and he started to walk home with her.

Up – away up, over the narrow street between
10 the tall houses, the stars were blazing. The air was mild and caressing, but cool with the breath of spring and the night. They walked slowly, the Doctor with a heavy, measured tread and his hands behind him; Edna, in an absent-minded way, as
15 she had walked one night at Grand Isle, as if her thoughts had gone ahead of her and she was striving to overtake them.

"You shouldn't have been there, Mrs. Pontellier," he said. "That was no place for you.
20 Adèle is full of whims at such times. There were a dozen women she might have had with her, unimpressionable women. I felt that it was cruel, cruel. You shouldn't have gone."

"Oh, well!" she answered, indifferently. "I
25 don't know that it matters after all. One has to think of the children some time or other; the sooner the better."

"When is Léonce coming back?"

"Quite soon. Sometime in March."
30 "And you are going abroad?"

"Perhaps – no, I am not going. I'm not going to be forced into doing things. I don't want to go abroad. I want to be let alone. Nobody has any right – except children, perhaps – and even then, it
35 seems to me – or it did seem –" She felt that her speech was voicing the incoherency of her thoughts, and stopped abruptly.

"The trouble is," sighed the Doctor, grasping her meaning intuitively, "that youth is given up to
40 illusions. It seems to be a provision of Nature; a decoy to secure mothers for the race. And Nature takes no account of moral consequences, of arbitrary conditions which we create, and which we feel obliged to maintain at any cost."
45 "Yes," she said. "The years that are gone seem like dreams – if one might go on sleeping and dreaming – but to wake up and find – oh! well! perhaps it is better to wake up after all, even to suffer, rather than to remain a dupe to illusions all
50 one's life."

"It seems to me, my dear child," said the Doctor at parting, holding her hand, "you seem to me to be in trouble. I am not going to ask for your confidence. I will only say that if ever you feel
55 moved to give it to me, perhaps I might help you. I know I would understand, and I tell you there are not many who would – not many, my dear."

"Some way I don't feel moved to speak of things that trouble me. Don't think I am ungrateful
60 or that I don't appreciate your sympathy. There are periods of despondency and suffering which take possession of me. But I don't want anything but my own way. That is wanting a good deal, of course, when you have to trample upon the lives,
65 the hearts, the prejudices of others – but no matter – still, I shouldn't want to trample upon the little lives. Oh! I don't know what I'm saying, Doctor. Good night. Don't blame me for anything."

"Yes, I will blame you if you don't come and
70 see me soon. We will talk of things you never have dreamt of talking about before. It will do us both good. I don't want you to blame yourself, whatever comes. Good night, my child."

1. Which choice best describes what happens in the passage?
   A) A peaceful carriage ride is described.
   B) Neighborhood gossip is shared amongst friends.
   C) A woman's troubles are related to a trusted advisor.
   D) Politics are debated between rivals.

2. Over the length of the passage, the author's focus shifts from
   A) describing Edna's thoughts to demonstrating her thoughts through dialogue.
   B) describing the setting to describing Edna's thoughts.
   C) illustrating Dr. Mandelet's concern to illustrating Edna's sense of apathy.
   D) describing Edna's past to guessing at Edna's future.

3. The narrator's description in lines 14-17 ("Edna, in…them") serves to
   A) compare the gaits of Dr. Mandelet and Edna.
   B) set the scene and describe Edna's frame of mind.
   C) describe Dr. Mandelet's observations.
   D) create a tense and suspenseful mood.

4. According to the passage, the trip to visit Adèle left Edna feeling
   A) satisfied.
   B) petulant.
   C) moved.
   D) ambivalent.

5. Which choice provides the best evidence for Edna's feelings in the answer to the previous question?
   A) Lines 14-17 ("Edna, in…them")
   B) Lines 18-19 ("You shouldn't…said")
   C) Lines 24-25 ("Oh, well…all")
   D) Lines 31-32 ("Perhaps…things")

6. It can be reasonably inferred that Léonce is
   A) someone who Edna respects.
   B) someone who has controlled Edna.
   C) a close friend of Dr. Mandelet's.
   D) another medical professional.

7. The words "oh, well" and "oh! well!" in lines 24 and 47 serve to develop Edna's character by
   A) providing an example of her fickle nature.
   B) showing how she is superficial and vapid.
   C) underscoring her sadness and feeling of hopelessness.
   D) mitigating her earlier incoherency.

8. The eighth paragraph (lines 31-37) serves to
   A) describe Edna's frame of mind.
   B) explain Edna's views on children.
   C) highlight the change in Edna's speech patterns.
   D) illustrate the love Edna has for Mandelet.

9. The "meaning" that Dr. Mandelet grasps intuitively (line 39) refers to
   A) social obligations.
   B) economic responsibilities.
   C) religious obligations.
   D) hedonistic distractions.

10. The author's main purpose in describing how Mandelet holds Edna's hand (lines 51-53) is to
    A) show how Mandelet loves Edna.
    B) demonstrate the close relationship between the two.
    C) illustrate the lengths to which the doctor will go to scam her.
    D) undermine the reader's confidence in Mandelet.

11. As used in line 54, the word "confidence" most nearly means
    A) trust.
    B) poise.
    C) forgiveness.
    D) self-assurance.

12. Throughout the passage, Edna appears to think about her children as
    A) a passing curiosity.
    B) treasures to be cared for devoutly.
    C) bothersome and unworthy of her attention.
    D) at once precious yet also pernicious.

13. Which choice best supports Edna's point of view, expressed in the answer to the previous question?
    A) Line 33 ("I want…alone")
    B) Lines 45-50 ("The years…life")
    C) Lines 62-67 ("But I…lives")
    D) Lines 67-68 ("I don't…anything")

The Tutorverse

Passage R *(Answers & explanations on page 352).*

The following passage is adapted from Hiram Bingham's 1913 account of his exploration of Machu Picchu two years earlier, published in *National Geographic*. Hiram's expedition begins at the small town of Cuzco.

The road, following in large part an ancient footpath, is sometimes cut out of the side of sheer precipices, and at others is obliged to run on frail brackets propped against the side of overhanging
5 cliffs. It has been an expensive one to build and will be expensive to maintain. The lack of it prevented earlier explorers from penetrating this canyon. Its existence gave us the chance of discovering Machu Picchu.
10   On the sixth day out from Cuzco we arrived at a little plantation called Mandorpampa. We camped a few rods away from the owner's grass-thatched hut, and it was not long before he came to visit us and to inquire our business. He turned out
15 to be an Indian rather better than the average, but overfond of "fire-water." His occupation consisted in selling grass and pasturage to passing travelers and in occasionally providing them with ardent spirits. He said that on top of the magnificent
20 precipices nearby there were some ruins at a place called Machu Picchu, and that there were others still more inaccessible at Huayna Picchu, on a peak not far distant from our camp. He offered to show me the ruins, which he had once visited, if I
25 would pay him well for his services. His idea of proper payment was 50 cents for his day's labor. This did not seem unreasonable, although it was two and one-half times his usual day's wage.
    Leaving camp soon after breakfast I joined the
30 guide, and, accompanied by a soldier that had been kindly loaned me by the Peruvian government, plunged through the jungle to the river bank, and came to a shaky little bridge made of four tree trunks bound together with vines and stretching
35 across a stream only a few inches above the roaring rapids.
    On the other side we had a hard climb; first through the jungle and later up a very stiff, almost precipitous, slope. About noon we reached a little
40 grass hut, where a good-natured Indian family who had been living here for three or four years gave us welcome and set before us gourds full of cool, delicious water and a few cold boiled sweet potatoes.
45   Apart from another hut in the vicinity and a few stone-faced terraces, there seemed to be little in the way of ruins, and I began to think that my time had been wasted. However, the view was magnificent, the water was delicious; and the
50 shade of the hut most agreeable. So we rested a while and then went on to the top of the ridge. On all sides of us rose the magnificent peaks of the Urubamba Canyon, while 2,000 feet below us the rushing waters of the noisy river, making a great
55 turn, defended three sides of the ridge, on top of which we were hunting for ruins. On the west side of the ridge the three Indian families who had chosen this eagle's nest for their home had built a little path, part of which consisted of crude ladders
60 of vines and tree trunks tied to the face of the precipice.
    Presently we found ourselves in the midst of a tropical forest, beneath the shade of whose trees we could make out a maze of ancient walls, the
65 ruins of buildings made of blocks of granite, some of which were beautifully fitted together in the most refined style of Inca architecture. A few rods farther along we came to a little open space, on which were two splendid temples or palaces. The
70 superior character of the stone work, the presence of these splendid edifices, and of what appeared to be an unusually large number of finely constructed stone dwellings, led me to believe that Machu Picchu might prove to be the largest and most
75 important ruin discovered in South America since the days of the Spanish conquest.

---

1 The overall structure of the passage can best be described as
    A)   a chronological account of events.
    B)   an explanation of solutions to a problem.
    C)   alternating examples of cause and effect.
    D)   shifting perspectives on a discovery.

2 According to the narrator, previous explorers were not able to discover Machu Picchu due to a lack of
    A)   safe and traversable paths.
    B)   an amiable and knowledgeable guide.
    C)   Peruvian government support.
    D)   proper hiking and camping equipment.

The Tutorverse

3 Which choice best summarizes the second paragraph of the passage?
A) The narrator describes a dangerous situation.
B) The narrator describes a monumental discovery.
C) The narrator describes his camp and his future guide.
D) The narrator describes the surrounding flora and fauna.

4 It can be inferred, from the comment that the owner of Mandorpampa is "better than average" (line 15), that the narrator
A) admires the natives for their way of life.
B) has a low opinion of the natives he's met.
C) has had few interactions with the natives.
D) regards the natives with a great deal of respect.

5 The phrase "ardent spirits," as used in lines 18-19, most likely refers to
A) alcoholic beverages.
B) ghosts and apparitions.
C) grass and pasturage.
D) religious advice.

6 The narrator feels that payment for his guide's help is
A) akin to extortion.
B) fair and equitable.
C) tantamount to theft.
D) too expensive.

7 Which choice best supports the answer to the previous question?
A) Lines 14-16 ("He turned…firewater")
B) Lines 16-19 ("His occupation…spirits")
C) Lines 23-25 ("He offered…services")
D) Lines 27-28 ("This did…wage")

8 As used in line 39, "precipitous" most nearly means
A) doubtful.
B) rapid.
C) steep.
D) unexpected.

9 The central idea of the fifth paragraph is to show that
A) food and water from high in the mountains tasted better.
B) the mountain dwellings were highly defensible and safe.
C) the narrator doubted the success of the excursion, but still enjoyed the trip.
D) the natives were able to live high in the mountains.

10 The author's use of the phrase "eagle's nest" (line 58) serves to
A) describe the wildlife observed on his ascent.
B) emphasize the elevation and isolation of his present location.
C) illustrate the crude and shoddy construction of his hosts' home.
D) quantify the amount of time it took to climb up the mountain.

11 The word "rods" used in lines 12 and 67 refers to
A) a form of punishment.
B) a unit of measurement.
C) sticks found on the ground.
D) tent poles.

12 According to the narrator, the discovery of Machu Picchu is important because
A) of its beautiful surroundings
B) of the quality of the city's construction.
C) of the remote location of the city.
D) of the use of granite as a building material.

13 The narrator includes a detailed description of Machu Picchu's appearance in order to
A) convince the Peruvian government to fund more expeditions.
B) dramatize an otherwise uneventful expedition.
C) entice readers to visit Machu Picchu.
D) justify his belief as to the magnitude of the discovery.

The Tutorverse

Passage S *(Answers & explanations on page 353).*

Well-designed and carefully executed psychology experiments often contribute greatly to our understanding of human behavior and the inner workings of the mind. Yet many

5 psychologists often cross moral or ethical lines while pursuing their work. These restrictions, codified today in the American Psychological Association's Code of Conduct, summarize the ethical standards by which psychologists are held

10 accountable.

The first of these principles is that of beneficence and nonmaleficence – that is, psychologists should never harm the people they work with and should rather work towards helping

15 those people. In the case of a doctor-patient relationship, this principle seems straightforward. But psychologists often work with people who are not patients. A psychologist performing research, for example, often works with test subjects, or

20 people who participate in the experiment as part of the experiment itself. The principle of nonmaleficence applies equally to both patients and the subjects of psychological experiments.

These principles are, perhaps deliberately,

25 broad, leaving room for interpretation as to what precisely "harm" means. Some psychologists have found themselves mired in, at best, an ethical dilemma, while others have found themselves on ethically dubious ground. Take, for example, the

30 famous Milgram experiment, which tested the extent to which people would blindly follow authority.

There were three people involved in each replication of the experiment: the person running

35 the experiment, a volunteer subject, and an actor (who was hired to pretend to also be a volunteer subject). The experiment began by assigning each person a role. The person running the experiment would always be designated as a stern,

40 authoritative Experimenter. Meanwhile, the actor and subject would draw slips of paper to determine their roles. However, the assignments were not, in fact, random; the actor would always claim to draw the role of Learner, thus leaving the role of

45 Teacher to the subject. Once the roles had been assigned, the Learner and Teacher were separated such that the Learner would go behind a partial wall. Thus the Learner and Teacher could hear each other, but not see each other.

50 The Experimenter would then give instructions to the Teacher. The Teacher was given a list of word pairs to teach the Learner. After reading the list of word pairs to the Learner, the Teacher would begin to ask questions. Each question

55 consisted of one of the first words from a word pair on the list, followed by four possible answer choices. The Learner was to indicate his or her answer choice by pressing a button, which would indicate to the Teacher if the question was correct

60 or incorrect. If the answer was correct, the Teacher would read the next question. If the answer was incorrect, the Teacher was instructed to administer an electric shock to the learner, with the strength of that shock increasing with each incorrect

65 answer. The Experimenter would then give the Teacher a sample shock, and the entire process would begin.

There was, in fact, no actual electric shock administered to the Learner. In fact, upon being

70 separated from the subject, the actor would activate a recording that was designed to play sounds specific to each shock level. Once the shocks reached higher levels, the actor would bang on the wall and otherwise vocally express to the

75 Teacher his or her discomfort or pain. Thus, it appeared to the subject that he or she was actually administering painful shocks to another subject.

The result of the experiment was very interesting. Most subjects exhibited a number of

80 behaviors that showed their reluctance to continue the experiment; some Teachers wanted to check on the well-being of the Learner, while other Teachers would laugh nervously or display other signs of stress and mental discomfort, like

85 sweating, and shaking. Some Teachers were very insistent that the experiment be stopped; but it wasn't until a determined Teacher would ask five times that the stern and unwavering Experimenter would finally yield.

90 In the end, 65% of subjects would see the experiment through to the end, believing themselves to have – despite their reservations and mental and emotional anguish – administered the maximum intensity 450-volt shock to a complete

95 stranger.

Milgram's experiment, though enlightening with respect to the lengths at which people will go to follow instructions, was criticized by some for

The Tutorverse

the stress it placed on the test subjects. Many
100 observers argued that Milgram had violated the
ethical principle of nonmaleficence.

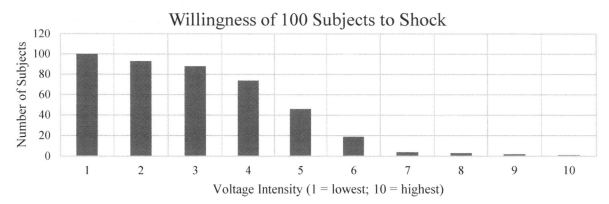

Willingness of 100 Subjects to Shock

1 Which choice best describes what happens over the course of the passage?
A) A principle is described through the perspective of a particular example.
B) A story is related chronologically.
C) An argument is advanced and supported with a specific example.
D) Consequences of a specific action are explained in detail.

2 Which statement best describes the main idea of the second paragraph?
A) A psychologist's work should never cause harm.
B) Doctors and psychologists must follow different rules.
C) Psychologists can only perform research with patients.
D) Treatment of patients and subjects are governed by different standards.

3 As used in line 29, "dubious" most nearly means
A) duplicitous.
B) explicit.
C) notorious.
D) questionable.

4 In context of the passage as a whole, the fourth, fifth, and sixth paragraphs serve what function?
A) To convince the reader that the experiment was poorly conceived.
B) To describe the experiment in context of ethical ambiguity.
C) To illustrate the findings and results of the experiment.
D) To provide instruction so as to make the experiment repeatable.

5 According to the passage, the subject of Milgram's experiment took on which role?
A) Experimenter
B) Learner
C) Observer
D) Teacher

6 By removing the Learner from the Teacher's sight, Milgram can
A) allow the Learner to rest for the experiment's duration.
B) deceive the Teacher into thinking that he/she is shocking the Learner.
C) ensure that the Teacher focuses on reading the proper questions.
D) measure the effect of sound stimulus on the Teacher.

The Tutorverse

7   The shock level would increase based on
A)   the Experimenter's whims.
B)   the Learner's tolerance levels.
C)   the Teacher's whims.
D)   the number of incorrect answers.

8   The effect of the recordings played by the actors was that
A)   Teachers believed they were shocking Learners.
B)   Teachers knew that the answer choice given by Learners was correct.
C)   Teachers knew that the answer choice given by Learners was incorrect.
D)   Teachers understood that they had performed the experiment correctly.

9   By using the phrase "finally yield" (line 89), the author implies that
A)   few Experimenters were willing to finish the experiment.
B)   few Teachers were interested in stopping the experiment early.
C)   the Experimenter would press reluctant Teachers to continue the experiment.
D)   the Teacher would generally insist on continuing the experiment.

10   According to the author, some observers believed Milgram had violated ethical standards because
A)   subjects suffered negative psychological side-effects.
B)   subjects were reluctant to continue the experiment.
C)   the actors were forced to feign injury.
D)   the experimenters were stern and unwavering.

11   Which of the following choices best supports the answer to the previous question?
A)   Lines 72-75 ("Once the...pain")
B)   Lines 79-81 ("Most subjects...experiment")
C)   Lines 81-85 ("Some Teachers...shaking")
D)   Lines 86-89 ("But it...yield")

12   Does the chart support the conclusion reached in lines 90-95?
A)   Yes, because there was always a subject who was willing to administer a maximum intensity shock.
B)   Yes, because about 65% of subjects were willing to administer a medium-intensity shock.
C)   No, because the voltage intensity in the chart does not match the maximum voltage described in the passage.
D)   No, because the chart shows that less than 20% of subjects were willing to shock at the highest intensity.

13   Which choice best describes the author's point of view on Milgram's experiment?
A)   The author agrees that the experiment was inappropriate and violated ethical standards.
B)   The author agrees with Milgram that the experiment did not violate ethical standards.
C)   The author remains impartial, simply explaining the experiment and its results.
D)   The author suggests that the American Psychological Association rule on the experiment's ethicality.

The Tutorverse

Passage T *(Answers & explanations on page 354).*

"Are you going to try out for the basketball team?"

Brian, who had been looking at a poster announcing tryouts that afternoon, turned to behold the face of Roselle Robinson, who was standing behind him.

Actually, he had been mentally composing a school song for basketball season. But this was Roselle Robinson. So he asked her, "Do you think I should?"

"You're good enough to make the team," she said sheepishly.

Even though that sounded like a compliment, Brian knew that in a high school as small as this one, almost anybody who tried out would make the team.

"There are half a dozen guys taller and faster than me," he told Roselle. "I wouldn't be a starter."

"You're just a sophomore," she said. "I bet you'll start next year. But you want to show Coach your potential this year, and don't forget: you can improve with practice."

Brian must have looked unconvinced, because Roselle added coyly, "And anyway, I'd come to see you play."

Well, if he needed an incentive, that was a fairly good one.

Brian didn't pay much attention to classes that afternoon, because he was picturing himself making a spectacular dunk while Roselle cheered him on from the stands. It didn't matter that he was a couple inches short of six-foot and had never dunked a basketball in his life. As Roselle had said, he could improve with practice.

The tryouts were fairly boring. Coach had developed a series of skill tests that assessed each player's prowess. He started by timing the players as they ran laps around the gym. Then he scrutinized how well they dribbled and passed the ball. And finally, he required that the players shoot from various places on the court.

Brian wasn't the best in these drills, but he wasn't the worst either. After a while, his mind began to wander.

Coach started sending players to sit in the bleachers. He picked all seven seniors, so it was obvious to Brian that Coach was selecting players who had made the team. Then, he chose five juniors and a freshman – a freshman who was six-foot six, so there was no mystery why he was selected.

That left three sophomores. Coach told them that he could only take two more players, and that he would make his decision by how proficient they were at shooting free throws. Free throws, Coach added, were just about the easiest thing in basketball. So the three remaining tryouts would each shoot until they missed.

The first player, Victor, who Brian recognized from English class, stepped up to the line. While he was shooting, the remaining sophomore, Harold, asked Brian if he was nervous.

"Not really," Brian replied evenly. "You?"

Harold nodded. He *did* look nervous. "I've got to make this team," he told Brian. "My mother says so."

Brian started to laugh, but then realized Harold was serious. "Why would your mother want you to make the team that badly?" he asked.

"Because she thinks I can get into college if I'm a good enough player."

From what Brian had seen, Harold would never be that good. But why tell him that?

Victor made eight free throws before missing. "You're up," Coach told Harold.

Harold stepped to the line and aimed carefully. He made the first shot.

As Brian stood watching, he thought about Harold. Brian knew that Harold's mother was holding down two jobs to support her three children on her own. But still…would Harold ever get a basketball scholarship? Maybe he'd improve with practice. Yeah, right.

Harold made four free throws, and then missed.

Brian stepped up to the line. He knew he could make more than four. The first one went through without even hitting the rim. The second was just about that easy. And the third.

He stood bouncing the ball, looking at the rim. Finally, he took the shot.

The ball bounced off the front of the rim.

It wasn't really that difficult to miss without anybody suspecting. He gave Harold a half-smile and walked off to the locker room as Harold headed toward the bleachers.

On his way to the locker room, Brian started making up the words to a song. A song about
100 Roselle. She'd be more impressed by that than by

watching him sit on the bench during basketball games.

---

1 Which of the following best summarizes the passage?
- A) A high school student tries out for the basketball team.
- B) A high school student is faced with a difficult choice and learns about himself in the process.
- C) A high school student tries to impress his girlfriend by playing basketball.
- D) A high school student tries to win a scholarship to college by playing basketball.

2 Over the course of the passage, the main focus of the narrative shifts from describing
- A) Brian's motivation behind trying out for the basketball team to his decision to let Harold take his place on the team.
- B) Brian's desire to impress Roselle to his decision to let Harold impress Coach and win a scholarship.
- C) Brian's determination to make the basketball team to his regret that he isn't good enough to pass Coach's tests.
- D) Brian's decision to impress Roselle to his decision to focus on pursuing his passion for music instead.

3 As used in line 25, "coyly" most nearly means
- A) convincingly.
- B) quietly.
- C) coquettishly.
- D) impulsively.

4 The author uses the phrase "improve with practice" three times: in lines 23, 35, and 83-84. Over the course of the passage, the connotation of the phrase changes from that of
- A) encouragement to sarcasm.
- B) hopefulness to despair.
- C) insincerity to annoyance.
- D) fantastic to realistic.

5 Based on the passage, which choice best describes Brian's primary reason for trying out for the basketball team?
- A) He daydreams about being a popular player.
- B) He thinks practice will improve his skills.
- C) He wants to impress Roselle.
- D) He is a good friend of Harold's.

6 Based on the information in the passage, it can reasonably be inferred that Brian is
- A) naïve.
- B) ambitious.
- C) ambivalent.
- D) magnanimous.

7 Which choice provides the best evidence of the answer in the previous question?
- A) Lines 13-16 ("Even though…team")
- B) Lines 43-45 ("Brian wasn't…wander")
- C) Lines 68-70 ("Brian started…asked")
- D) Lines 94-95 ("It wasn't…suspecting")

8 What is the most likely reason the author includes the sentences in lines 29-35?
- A) He wants to show that Brian is unfocused and a poor student.
- B) He wants to show that Brian's candidacy is uncontestable.
- C) He wants to contrast Brian's fantasy with reality.
- D) He wants to show that Brian is unaware of his limitations.

9 As used in line 38, "prowess" most likely means
- A) mental fortitude.
- B) team spirit.
- C) willingness to learn.
- D) athletic ability.

The Tutorverse

10 The main purpose of lines 68-70 ("Brian started…asked") is to

    A)   show that Brian is lighthearted, even during tryouts.

    B)   introduce the idea that Harold wants very much to make the team.

    C)   remind the reader that not everybody who tries out will make the team.

    D)   make the point that Brian's decision can affect Harold's mother.

11 When it comes to the basketball tryouts, we can infer from the passage that Harold

    A)   is confident he will make the team.

    B)   worries about what other students will think of him.

    C)   dislikes Brian for being a more skilled player.

    D)   feels pressured by his mother to make the team.

12 What is the most likely reason the author of this passage describes Brian's thoughts about Harold's family life in lines 80-84?

    A)   He wants to show Brian's motivation for allowing Harold to make the team.

    B)   He wants to show how Harold has struggled in life.

    C)   He wants to indicate what kind of students attend this high school.

    D)   He wants to show why Harold is not a skilled player.

13 The last two paragraphs of the passage (lines 94-102) serve primarily to

    A)   explain why Brian misses the fourth free throw on purpose.

    B)   demonstrate how Brian plans to conceal his unselfish act from Roselle.

    C)   show that Brian is not unhappy that he has given up a chance to make the basketball team.

    D)   emphasize Brian's interest in music.

The Tutorverse

Passage U *(Answers & explanations on page 355).*

On a global scale, what is a state? How does it differ from a nation? And what rights do states have that nations do not? Does a new state exist when it says it does?

5   Such questions may, on the surface, appear to have simple answers. The Montevideo Convention of 1933, for example, indicates that a state exists only if it possesses "a permanent population, a defined territory, government, and capacity to
10 enter into relations with other states." In fact, however, answers to these – and other matters related to the issue of sovereignty – are often nuanced and wreathed in semantics.

Situated approximately 110 miles across a
15 narrow straight from China, the small island of Taiwan has been making big waves in international relations for decades. To understand the nature of these issues, one must first understand the history of Taiwan and its
20 complicated relationships with its Asian neighbors.

Taiwan was originally settled by the ancestors of today's Taiwanese aborigines, an ethnic group all to its own. By the 17th century, the ethnic Han Chinese had taken control of the island, integrating
25 the island into the Qing dynasty's empire on the mainland. Following a war with Japan in the late 19th century, Taiwan was ceded by China to Japan. Taiwan would again change hands following the conclusion of the Second World War, with Japan's
30 agreement to return Taiwan to China as part of its terms of surrender.

The Chinese Civil War complicated the matter of Taiwan's return. From 1927 to 1937, forces loyal to the nationalist party of China clashed with
35 those loyal to the communist party of China. The two ideological adversaries suspended hostilities in 1937, when they united to repel a Japanese invasion as part of the Second World War. China's civil war resumed a year after the end of the
40 Second World War, in 1946. Though Japan had officially surrendered control of Taiwan, a new, more vexing question arose: which China would control Taiwan?

Military operations in the Chinese Civil War
45 effectively ceased in late 1949, whereupon the leader of the communist forces, Mao Zedong, proclaimed Beijing to be the capital of the newly founded People's Republic of China (PRC). The nationalist forces, led by Chiang Kai-shek, left
50 mainland China for Taiwan, proclaiming Taipei to be the capital of the Republic of China (ROC). Ever since (and as of the date of this publication), the PRC and ROC have operated as independent countries; the relationship between the PRC and
55 the ROC are, at best, complicated – especially when it comes to the topic of the island, the people, and the government.

Mainland China maintains that it is the only legitimate Chinese state. It argues that the ROC
60 has continued to operate as an illegitimate government ever since the 1949 founding of the PRC. It asserts, furthermore, that because the Chinese Civil War was never legally concluded with a peace treaty or armistice, that both factions
65 (the PRC and ROC) belong to the same sovereign entity, which is controlled by the PRC. The ROC in Taiwan, obviously, disagrees. It argues that it meets all requirements of statehood under the Montevideo Convention and therefore, should be
70 recognized as a fully sovereign and independent state.

The international community's view of the situation is best described as political. In 1952, United Nations General Assembly Resolution 505
75 suggested that the Chinese communists of the PRC were rebels against the ROC. In 1971, however, the United Nations General Assembly Resolution 2758 officially recognized the government of PRC as the only representative of China to the United
80 Nations. Since then, the PRC has refused diplomatic relations with any state that officially recognizes the ROC, though it does not view economic, cultural, or other such exchanges as diplomatic relations. The United States, for
85 example, is a long-time ally of the ROC, even supporting Taiwan through the sale of military arms and training. The United States acknowledges – rather than recognizes – the PRC's assertion that Taiwan is a part of China.
90 Despite the fact that the ROC and PRC share a common ancestry, and despite the fact that both the ROC and PRC conduct trade with other countries – and with one another – the political conflict between the ROC and PRC has, as of this
95 writing, yet to be resolved. Precluding the possibility of future violence, the future of ROC-PRC relations will likely be decided by the definition of seemingly innocuous words: sovereignty, recognition, support, opposition, and
100 so on.

The Tutorverse

Year	Number of Countries Recognizing ROC	Period over Period Change	Number of Countries Recognizing PRC	Period over Period Change
1969	71	N/A	48	N/A
1971	68	-4%	53	10%
1973	31	-54%	89	68%
1978	21	-32%	112	26%
1986	23	10%	134	20%
1990	28	22%	139	4%
2012	23	-18%	172	24%
2013	22	-4%	172	0%

1 Which choice best captures the shift in focus that takes place over the course of the passage?
A) The author contemplates an issue, then debates both sides using historical anecdotes.
B) The author presents both sides of an argument, then focuses on historical background information.
C) The author provides historical context, then argues in favor of one side of a debate.
D) The author provides historical context, then describes different aspects of a disagreement.

2 The primary purpose of the passage is to
A) convince the reader to side with a particular point of view.
B) describe the circumstances complicating certain international relations.
C) educate the reader about a country's complicated history.
D) paint a vivid picture of life in a period of conflict.

3 Regarding the conflict between the ROC and PRC, the author
A) at first sides with the PRC, but then sides with the ROC.
B) at first sides with the ROC, but then sides with the PRC.
C) believes the international community has settled the conflict.
D) remains neutral throughout the passage.

4 The author includes a history of Taiwan's international relations in order to
A) provide the necessary context for understanding the ROC-PRC conflict.
B) illustrate how modern disputes pale in comparison to historical disputes.
C) describe the roots of the Chinese Civil War.
D) highlight historical tensions between the ethnic Chinese and the Japanese.

5 According to the passage, the Chinese Civil war was paused in order to
A) determine the governance of the island of Taiwan.
B) establish the PRC and ROC.
C) fight the Japanese during World War II.
D) review historical documents discussing Taiwan's governance.

The Tutorverse

6   Which choice best supports the answer to the previous question?
- A)   Lines 28-31 ("Taiwan would...surrender")
- B)   Lines 33-35 ("From 1927...China")
- C)   Lines 35-38 ("The two...War")
- D)   Lines 40-42 ("Though Japan...Taiwan")

7   The ROC and PRC were established after
- A)   fighting between nationalists and communists ceased in 1949.
- B)   Japan surrendered control of Taiwan.
- C)   the 1937 suspension of hostilities.
- D)   the United States intervened in the region.

8   Which statement most effectively summarizes the seventh paragraph (lines 58-71)?
- A)   Only the PRC is justified in its position.
- B)   Only the ROC is justified in its position.
- C)   The PRC and ROC interpret sovereignty differently.
- D)   The Chinese Civil War is to blame for the present-day ROC-PRC conflict.

9   What reason does the author give to suggest that the international community's view on the ROC-PRC conflict is "political" (line 73)?
- A)   Historically, the ROC was more powerful politically than the PRC.
- B)   Resolution 505 and Resolution 2758 contradict each other.
- C)   The United States acknowledges the PRC's assertion.
- D)   Today, the PRC is more powerful politically than the ROC.

10   Does the data provided in the table support the author's statements about the international community's view on ROC-PRC relations?
- A)   No, because it ignores the years immediately following the founding of the ROC.
- B)   No, because it shows that the PRC has more supporters.
- C)   Yes, because it demonstrates that support for the ROC and PRC is essentially balanced.
- D)   Yes, because it shows declining recognition for ROC over time, and increasing recognition for PRC over time.

11   Based on the information provided in the passage, why might the PRC refuse diplomatic relations with countries that recognize the ROC?
- A)   Economic trade between the ROC and other countries is prohibited and detrimental to the PRC.
- B)   Military support between the ROC and other countries endangers the PRC.
- C)   To recognize the ROC would be to recognize the Montevideo Convention.
- D)   To recognize the ROC would contradict the PRC's policy that there is only one China, which is ruled by the PRC.

12   By emphasizing the difference between "acknowledges" and "recognizes" in describing the United States' view of the PRC's assertion (line 88), the author
- A)   condemns the United States' stance on the subject.
- B)   minces words in order to confuse the broader issue.
- C)   sides with the PRC in its assertion about the ROC.
- D)   supports the idea that semantics play a large role in international politics.

13   As used in line 98, "seemingly innocuous" most nearly means
- A)   definitely debatable.
- B)   ostensibly incontrovertible.
- C)   possibly preventable.
- D)   superficially dangerous.

Passage V *(Answers & explanations on page 356).*

The term "GMO" gets thrown around a lot, these days. Short for "genetically modified organism," GMOs have been making headlines recently for the role they play in the global food
5 chain.

In principle, the modification of genetic material in a laboratory is similar to the modification of genetic material practiced for millennia by farmers and the breeders of livestock.
10 Selective breeding, a process which takes place over generations, is a process by which people choose organisms with desirable qualities for reproduction. In the case of animals, a famous example of selective breeding is the domesticated
15 dog. Early humans carefully selected wild wolves that were more obedient and loyal than others. Those wolves were given advantages that their wild counterparts did not have – the protection of people, food, and shelter, for example – and were
20 bred with other domesticated wolves to produce yet more domesticated wolves. Over time, these wolves became the dogs we know of today.

Many of the plants that have supported the rise of civilization had much more humble origins. The
25 plant we know of today as corn – high as an elephant's eye – actually started off as a tiny, grass-like plant. Desiring sweeter, juicier apples, farmers reserved the seeds of the best apples to plant the next season. Disliking the large seeds
30 found in many fruit, such as bananas and watermelons, horticulturalists artificially promoted the dissemination of specific plants that exhibited the desired qualities – sometimes by growing cuttings of the original specimen, other times by
35 cross-pollinating plants with different qualities.

In all circumstances, people took advantage of naturally occurring mutations that resulted in desirable changes in organisms; people simply helped these mutants gain a larger foothold in the
40 world.

Modern science has accelerated the process of genetic modification and has unlocked the ability to combine genes across entirely different biological domains of life. To grasp the enormity
45 of that statement, consider that plants, animals, and fungi are all part of domain eukarya, and that it is now possible to combine eukarya genes with genes from the other two domains – bacteria and archaea.

50 A famous example of this kind of genetic modification is *Bt* corn. *Bt*, short for *Bacillus thuringiensis*, is a bacterium that produces toxins lethal to insects. *Bt* has, since 1928, been used as a pesticide to kill insects and improve the yield of
55 produce. But it was not until 1995 that the genes responsible for the insect-killing toxins were isolated and combined with the genes of corn. *Bt* corn proved so successful at staving off insects that the *Bt* genes were subsequently introduced
60 into other plants, like cotton and potatoes.

Proponents of GMOs point to the varied and impactful ways that GMOs contribute to quality of life. These supporters argue that GMOs like *Bt* organisms increase the productivity of farms,
65 reduce the amount of chemical pesticides used on farms, have no material impact on the overall environment, and can even offer higher nutritional value than unmodified organisms. According to the USDA, for the 15 years following the
70 introduction of *Bt* corn into the food supply, the amount of chemical pesticide used per acre of corn decreased by some 90%. Golden Rice (another result of the mixing of plant and bacteria genes), engineered in the early 2000s, provides four to five
75 times more Vitamin A than regular white rice.

If the practice of genetically modifying organisms has taken place for thousands of years, and if there are so many benefits to using GMOs, why do so many people today resist GMOs,
80 especially in the food supply?

Moral and ethical reservations notwithstanding, people are most often concerned with the impact of GMOs on both human and environmental health. There are concerns that,
85 despite testing and oversight by government agencies, the long-term influence of GMOs on an organism as complex as a human is, at best, unknown, and at worst, detrimental. Most testing is, after all, conducted on mice and other mammals
90 – not humans. Just as alarming are the myriad ways in which GMOs might impact the environment, again despite testing and government regulation. Such concerns follow a similar vein: the ecosystem is so complex, and people
95 understand so little about how life interacts with other life, that, though the chances are small, GMOs will invariably have negative consequences on the environment and threaten the very security

The Tutorverse

of the food supply which it was designed to
100 protect.

Figure 1
Insecticide Usage After *Bt* GMO Introduction Introduction

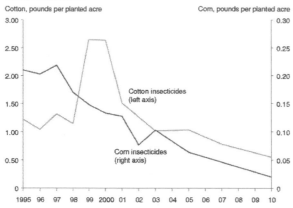

Source: USDA, Economic Research Service using data from USDA, National Agricultural Statistics Service, Agricultural Chemical Usage Reports and Quick Stats.

Figure 2
Herbicide Usage After *Bt* GMO

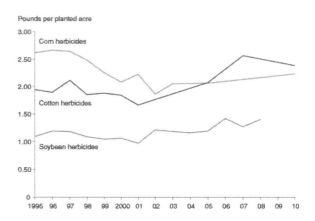

Source: USDA, Economic Research Service using data from USDA, National Agricultural Statistics Service, Agricultural Chemical Usage Reports.

---

1   The main purpose of the passage is to
    A)   convince readers that GMOs are safe.
    B)   educate readers about the issue of GMOs.
    C)   persuade readers that GMOs are unsafe.
    D)   recommend a specific policy on GMOs.

2   Which choice best summarizes what takes place in the second and third paragraphs?
    A)   A genealogical analysis of modern-day dogs is conducted.
    B)   A horticultural perspective of fruit is related.
    C)   A hypothesis is supported with findings from an experiment.
    D)   A scientific process is explained using specific examples.

3   The author's use of the phrase "high as an elephant's eye" is used to
    A)   compare today's corn crops to today's fruit crops.
    B)   decry the nutritional value of today's corn.
    C)   draw a connection between the genetic modification of animals and plants.
    D)   stress the significant differences produced in an organism by selective breeding.

4   The author includes the fourth paragraph in order to
    A)   emphasize that all genetic modification serves the same principal purpose.
    B)   highlight differences between selective breeding and today's genetic modifications.
    C)   clarify his position on genetically modified organisms.
    D)   describe procedural details pertaining to genetic modification.

5   According to the passage, what has allowed people to combine genes across domains of life?
    A)   Selective breeding.
    B)   Modern scientific processes.
    C)   Powerful agricultural interests.
    D)   Similarities between bacteria and eukarya.

6   All of the following arguments are advanced in favor of using GMOs EXCEPT
    A)   that GMOs increase the quantity of food produced.
    B)   that GMOs increase the quality of food produced.
    C)   that GMOs decrease the amount of herbicides used.
    D)   that GMOs decrease the amount of pesticides used.

The Tutorverse

7 The data in Figure 1 supports which conclusion?
A) Yields of *Bt* corn increased from 1995-2010.
B) *Bt* corn is more nutritious than non *Bt* corn.
C) Growing *Bt* corn decreased the usage of herbicides.
D) Growing *Bt* corn decreased the usage of pesticides.

8 The use of questions in the second to last paragraph (lines 76-80) shifts the focus of the passage from
A) describing an argument to explaining a scientific process.
B) describing one side of an argument to describing an opposing argument.
C) describing statistical information to relating an allegorical anecdote.
D) explaining a scientific process to describing an argument.

9 "Myriad," as used in line 90, most nearly means
A) confusing and unclear.
B) obvious and dangerous.
C) seemingly infinite.
D) temptingly convenient.

10 Based on the passage, the author suggests that an overarching objection to the use of GMOs is a(n)
A) combination of corporate greed and disregard for human health.
B) false and excessive confidence in people's ability to understand complexity.
C) lack of government oversight and scientific testing.
D) unhealthy alliance between government and powerful economic interests.

11 Which selection best supports the answer to the previous question?
A) Lines 72-75 ("Golden Rice…rice")
B) Lines 81-84 ("Moral and…health")
C) Lines 88-90 ("Most testing…humans")
D) Lines 93-100 ("Such concerns…protect")

12 Which interpretation of the data provided in Figure 2 from 1995 to 2010 would opponents of GMOs most likely cite to support their view?
A) After the introduction of *Bt*, herbicide usage increased in cotton and soybean crops.
B) After the introduction of *Bt*, herbicide usage decreased in cotton and soybean crops.
C) After the introduction of *Bt*, herbicide usage in corn crops decreased.
D) After the introduction of *Bt*, all use of herbicide decreased.

13 "There is no difference between the results of today's process of genetic modification and those of selective breeding."

According to the passage, which party would most likely agree with the above statement?
A) Opponents of GMOs, because it is a morally and ethically wrong statement.
B) Opponents of GMOs, because it suggests that today's GMOs are potentially dangerous.
C) Proponents of GMOs, because it is an undisputed, widely accepted scientific fact.
D) Proponents of GMOs, because it suggests that today's GMOs are as safe as organisms resulting from selective breeding.

The Tutorverse

Passage W *(Answers & explanations on page 357).*

Mary found sleep too difficult to capture. For
5   hours, she had been listening to the storm raging
outside her window. But it was not merely the
storm that kept her awake. That evening, the five
of them had gathered around the fireplace. Byron
had found a book of ghost stories, and he read
10 them aloud in his deep, dramatic voice.

Combined with the crashing of thunder, it
didn't take long for the stories to have the effect
Byron wanted. He grinned as he saw the others
glance uneasily into the darkness beyond the
15 fireplace. Byron enjoyed exercising power over
others, and frightening them was one way he did
that.

At last, he closed the book and looked around
at the others. "I propose a contest," he said. "Let
20 us see which of us can write the best ghost story."

That was very like him – to propose a contest
that he would obviously win. The most famous
writer in the world, suggesting a writing contest?
What chance would the others have?

25 In her heart, Mary wished she could think of a
story good enough to enter the contest. She knew it
was foolish to think that a girl still in her teens
could vie with Byron for literary achievement.
Even her paramour, Percy Shelley, was a far better
30 writer than she could ever hope to be.

But all her life she had lived in the shadow of
her famous parents, both of whom were writers.
Her mother had urged women to claim rights equal
to those enjoyed by men. Mary had been given her
35 mother's name, and felt in some way that this
obliged her to carry on her mother's crusade.
Perhaps she could do that by writing a story that
was as good as any written by a man.

Mary's mind continued to race. When she and
40 Percy were in Germany, they saw a ruined castle.
What was its name? Castle Frankenstein. She
began to imagine what kind of man might have
lived there.

He would be like Percy, she decided. Curious
45 about new things. Ready to experiment. And
daring. He must be daring.

She closed her eyes, because thinking of that
revived a painful memory. Percy's daring spirit
caused him to rush his little family from place to
50 place. He always wanted to see and experience
new things. And when Mary's baby had been sick,
Percy had not wanted to stop to let her rest. The
little girl had died.

It hadn't been his fault, Mary told herself. Not
55 really. The tiny creature had been sickly from the
start. She would have died anyway. Mary had
rubbed her thin little arms and legs for hours,
trying to bring her back to life. But nothing could
do that. Not even Percy could do that.

60 Or could he? Mary had listened as Byron and
Percy had discussed the life force. People, animals,
birds, fish, plants—all had the power of life. But
then, they died, and once that happened, they
could not live again. What was it that caused some
65 things to live?

Byron had said a man in Italy had caused a
dead frog's leg to move by touching it with
electricity. But that had not made the frog come
alive.

70 The sound of thunder, close by, startled Mary
out of her reverie. Lightning, she thought.
Lightning was a kind of electricity, people said.
But how could you use it to bring a frog back to
life?

75 And even if the frog did somehow live again,
that would not be a very scary story.

There was a book that Mary had when she was
a child. It was filled with pictures. She
remembered one in particular. It showed a man, a
80 giant really, standing over a bed in which a child
was sleeping. She had forgotten the story, but she
recalled that the picture had seemed frightening.

A flash from a lightning bolt lit up Mary's
bedroom. She opened her eyes and saw him there.
85 Saw that strange giant creature standing over her
bed. She pulled the covers over her head.

It was only her imagination, she knew. But
then she cried out, even though no one could hear:
"I have found my story!"

The Tutorverse

1   What choice best summarizes the passage?
    A)   A person wishes to be a great writer.
    B)   A person recalls a book she read.
    C)   A person finds inspiration for her story.
    D)   A person wants to meet another person's challenge.

2   Over the course of the passage, the main focus of the narrative shifts from
    A)   Mary's eagerness to excel to her sudden fright at the appearance of a vision.
    B)   Mary's hope that she could win the contest to her fear that Percy will change her life.
    C)   Mary's doubts that she could win the contest to her discovery of an idea that would help her write a winning story.
    D)   Mary's sadness about her baby's death to her eagerness to prove worthy of her mother.

3   In this passage, Mary can best be thought of as
    A)   a devoted mother.
    B)   a burdened daughter.
    C)   an ungrateful guest.
    D)   an ambitious young woman.

4   The author's use of the phrase "the others...fireplace" (lines 13-15) is likely meant to convey the idea that
    A)   Byron's guests worried about the storm.
    B)   Byron's guests found it boring to listen to so many stories.
    C)   Byron's guests were getting sleepy.
    D)   Byron's guests were made uncomfortable by the stories he read.

5   As used in line 15, "exercising" most nearly means
    A)   working out.
    B)   making use of.
    C)   limiting.
    D)   discovering.

6   Which choice most nearly expresses the effect of Mary's bearing her mother's name?
    A)   Mary felt she had to be a good mother.
    B)   Mary felt she had to show women were equal to men.
    C)   Mary felt she had to surpass Byron.
    D)   Mary felt she had to do daring things.

7   Based on the passage, Mary most likely
    A)   admired Percy's qualities.
    B)   was jealous of Percy.
    C)   would never forgive Percy.
    D)   found Percy hard to understand.

8   Which choice provides the best evidence for the answer to the previous question?
    A)   Lines 29-30 ("Even her...be")
    B)   Lines 44-46 ("He would...daring")
    C)   Lines 56-58 ("She would...life")
    D)   Lines 60-62 ("Or could...life")

9   The passage most strongly suggests that Percy
    A)   was more talented than Mary.
    B)   was a vain person.
    C)   was a self-centered person.
    D)   was a scientist and philosopher.

10 Which portion of the passage provides the best textual evidence for the answer to the previous question?
    A)   Lines 29-30 ("Even her...be")
    B)   Lines 44-46 ("He would...daring")
    C)   Lines 48-53 ("Percy's daring...died")
    D)   Lines 60-65 ("Or could...live")

11 The main purpose of lines 60-65 ("Mary had...live") is to
    A)   examine the meaning of life.
    B)   compare frogs to humans.
    C)   create sympathy for Mary's loss of a child.
    D)   introduce the idea of resurrection.

12 The author most likely mentions the discussion Byron and Percy have about the life force to
    A)   show that Mary wasn't allowed to be part of the men's discussions.
    B)   show where Mary got the idea of bringing a creature back to life.
    C)   show that the men were interested in science.
    D)   show that the men did not see how a good story could be made with the life force.

13 What is the main idea of the last three paragraphs of the passage?
    A)   A strange man has entered Mary's room.
    B)   A picture in a book has frightened Mary.
    C)   A flash of lightning inspired Mary.
    D)   Mary thinks of a man who will make her story frightening.

The Tutorverse

Passage X *(Answers & explanations on page 358).*

This passage is excerpted and adapted from a 1910 speech delivered by Theodore Roosevelt to a large audience at the University of Paris (the Sorbonne).

Today I shall speak to you on the subject of individual citizenship, the one subject of vital importance to you, my hearers, and to me and my countrymen, because you and we are great citizens
5 of great democratic republics. A democratic republic such as ours – an effort to realize its purpose of government by, of, and for the people – represents the most gigantic of all possible social experiments, the one fraught with great
10 responsibilities alike for good and evil. The success of republics like yours and like ours means the glory, and our failure of despair, of mankind; and for you and for us the question of the quality of the individual citizen is supreme…With you
15 here, and with us in my own home, in the long run, success or failure will be conditioned upon the way in which the average man, the average woman, does his or her duty, first in the ordinary, every-day affairs of life, and next in those great
20 occasional cries which call for heroic virtues. The average citizen must be a good citizen if our republics are to succeed. The stream will not permanently rise higher than the main source; and the main source of national power and national
25 greatness is found in the average citizenship of the nation. Therefore it behooves us to do our best to see that the standard of the average citizen is kept high; and the average cannot be kept high unless the standard of the leaders is very much higher.
30 It is well if a large proportion of the leaders in any republic, in any democracy, are, as a matter of course, drawn from the classes represented in this audience today; but only provided that those classes possess the gifts of sympathy with plain
35 people and of devotion to great ideals. You and those like you have received special advantages; you have all had the opportunity for mental training; many of you have had leisure; most of you have had a chance for enjoyment of life far
40 greater than comes to the majority of your fellows. To you and your kind much has been given, and from you much should be expected. Yet there are certain failings against which it is especially

incumbent that both men of trained and cultivated
45 intellect, and men of inherited wealth and position should especially guard themselves, because to these failings they are especially liable. And if yielded to, their – your – chances of useful service are at an end. Let the man of learning, the man of
50 lettered leisure, beware of that cheap temptation to pose to himself and to others as a cynic, as the man who has outgrown emotions and beliefs, the man to whom good and evil are as one. The poorest way to face life is to face it with a sneer. There are
55 many men who feel a kind of twisted pride in cynicism; there are many who confine themselves to criticism of the way others do what they themselves dare not even attempt. There is no more unhealthy being, no man less worthy of
60 respect, than he who either really holds, or feigns to hold, an attitude of sneering disbelief toward all that is great and lofty, whether in achievement or in that noble effort which, even if it fails, comes to second achievement. A cynical habit of thought
65 and speech, a readiness to criticize work which the critic himself never tries to perform, an intellectual aloofness which will not accept contact with life's realities – all these are marks not, as the possessor would fain to think, of superiority but of
70 weakness…
It is not the critic who counts; not the man who points out how the strong man stumbles or where the doer of deeds could have done them better. The credit belongs to the man who is
75 actually in the arena, whose face is marred by dust and sweat and blood; who strives valiantly; who errs, who comes short again and again, because there is no effort without error and shortcoming; but who does actually strive to do the deeds; who
80 knows great enthusiasms, the great devotions; who spends himself in a worthy cause; who at the best knows in the end the triumph of high achievement, and who at the worst, if he fails, at least fails while daring greatly, so that his place shall never be with
85 those cold and timid souls who neither know victory nor defeat.

The Tutorverse

1   Which of the following statements best captures the overall progression of the passage?
    A)   A theory is explained, a warning issued, and inspiration provided.
    B)   Actions are advocated for, warnings are heeded, and inspiration is challenged.
    C)   Ideas are shared, rebuttals acknowledged, and a revised theory developed.
    D)   Motivations are challenged, theories explained, and warnings delivered.

2   Which choice best summarizes what takes place in the first paragraph?
    A)   A man argues for a change in political doctrine.
    B)   A man shares his opinion on civic responsibility.
    C)   An audience listens to a lecture on political strategy.
    D)   An audience listens to a moral and ethical philosophy.

3   According to Roosevelt, the success of a democratic republic owes primarily to
    A)   a country's governing bodies.
    B)   actions of everyday people.
    C)   the soundness of their economy.
    D)   the strength of their legal framework.

4   In lines 22-23, water level is used as a metaphor for the relationship between
    A)   education and democracy.
    B)   leaders and ordinary citizens.
    C)   national greatness and a nation's lakes and rivers.
    D)   national greatness and the performance of civic duties.

5   According to Roosevelt, his audience has what civic responsibility?
    A)   To be heroic in daily life.
    B)   To be leaders and represent all people.
    C)   To advocate only for their interests.
    D)   To share their wealth and power.

6   The "plain people" mentioned in lines 34-35 most likely refers to the
    A)   average citizenry.
    B)   intelligent citizenry.
    C)   sympathetic citizenry.
    D)   good citizenry.

7   Roosevelt extols his audience to guard against
    A)   disbelief.
    B)   leisure.
    C)   optimism.
    D)   greed.

8   What function does Roosevelt's interjection of "your" (line 48) serve?
    A)   To clarify the person to whom he speaks.
    B)   To specify the applicability of his advice.
    C)   To widen the scope of his warning.
    D)   To emphasize the relevance of his message to the audience.

9   In context, the phrase "man of lettered leisure" as used in lines 49-50, most likely refers to
    A)   educated but lazy people.
    B)   ignorant, hardworking people.
    C)   inexperienced, jaded people.
    D)   well-educated, privileged people.

10 Based on the passage, we can infer that a cynic, when observing another's failings, would most likely comment with
    A)   encouragement and reassurance.
    B)   respect and deference.
    C)   ridicule and criticism.
    D)   suggestions and support.

11 Which excerpt from the passage provides the best evidence for the answer to the previous question?
    A)   Lines 28-29 ("And the...higher")
    B)   Lines 33-35 ("But only...ideals")
    C)   Lines 71-74 ("It is...better")
    D)   Lines 74-76 ("The credit...blood")

12 In context of the last paragraph, the use of the word "arena" in line 75
    A)   compares critics to gladiators.
    B)   captures the essence of a struggle.
    C)   is a metaphor for privilege.
    D)   is analogous in meaning to success.

13 The main idea of the last paragraph is that
    A)   enthusiasm can be extinguished in even the bravest man.
    B)   intellectual aloofness is preferable to the cold taste of defeat.
    C)   struggling is only worthwhile if the outcome is success.
    D)   there is honor and greatness positivity, and none in negativity.

Passage Y *(Answers & explanations on page 359).*

Passage 1

   Ever since the Roman author Tacitus, people have said, "Success has a thousand fathers; failure is an orphan." So it is with the film many people regard as the greatest of all time: *Citizen Kane.*

5   At the time of its release in 1941, *Citizen Kane* was not a smash hit. Even though it received nine Oscar nominations, it won only one: Best Screenplay. Writing credit had originally been given to Orson Welles, the young writer, director, 10 and star of the movie. However, Herman J. Mankiewicz, a "script doctor" known for his quality edits, protested that he was the true author. He appealed to the Screen Writers Guild, which awarded him co-credit for the script. The two men 15 shared the Oscar.

   By the end of 1942, the United States was at war, and people weren't interested in a biopic about a man whose dying word was about a lost sled. The movie rested in a studio vault for the 20 next decade.

   In the 1950s, the film began to appear on television, which, like the movie, was a black-and-white medium. Even on the small screen, people recognized its power, and the studio re-released 25 the film in art theaters. College students flocked to it. A poll taken in 1962 by the influential British magazine *Sight and Sound* rated *Citizen Kane* as the greatest movie ever made, a position it held until 2012.

30   By then, a controversy had broken out as to who should be given credit for the script. On the fiftieth anniversary of the film's release, *New Yorker* critic Pauline Kael published a 50,000-word essay in which she promulgated the idea that 35 Mankiewicz had essentially written the script by himself.

   Two months later, the critic for the *Village Voice,* Andrew Sarris, published a scathing rebuttal to Kael. He argued that much of the plot 40 of *Citizen Kane* had come from a biography written by Ferdinand Lundberg. Another critic later revealed that Mankiewicz and yet another writer had started from a 300-page script (too long for a movie of the finished length) that was written 45 by Welles.

   So who did write *Citizen Kane*? Maybe, like the ending of the movie itself, the answer is a mystery.

Passage 2

50   *Citizen Kane,* today considered one of the greatest motion pictures of all time, was almost destroyed before it could be seen by a mass audience.

   The director, Orson Welles, had caused a 55 sensation when his radio drama *War of the Worlds,* presented as a series of fictional news bulletins about invaders from another planet, caused panic among people who had tuned in late and didn't realize it was just a play.

60   RKO, a minor Hollywood studio, offered Welles a contract to make a movie for them. Welles demanded complete creative control of the project, something that was virtually never granted in Hollywood. And he was, after all, only 24 years 65 old.

   The studio finally agreed. But now Welles faced another problem: finding a project that would justify his enormous reputation. He settled on *Citizen Kane.*

70   Welles always denied that he intended to base his film on the life of powerful newspaper publisher William Randolph Hearst. Yet there were some obvious similarities between the two. The film's protagonist, Kane, owned sensationalist 75 newspapers and, like Hearst, had a lady friend whose show business career he sponsored. Both Kane and Hearst were immensely wealthy and lived on legendary estates. But those who knew Hearst personally found that, above all, Welles had 80 captured the real-life publisher's imperious personality.

   The production was shrouded in secrecy. For a time, the film was known simply as RKO 281. A columnist for the Hearst papers even praised it 85 without knowing what it was about. But when details started to leak out, Hearst waged a campaign to destroy the film. His friend, Louis B. Mayer, head of a rival studio, offered RKO more money than the film's entire budget if only RKO 90 would destroy the film.

   But RKO stuck to its guns, and released the film. Hearst's newspapers refused to advertise the

The Tutorverse

film, hurting box-office receipts. The film wasn't a
flop, but neither was it a great success. It would
95 take years for *Citizen Kane* to work its way into

the hearts and minds of audiences around the
world.

---

1 Which choice best summarizes Passage 1?
- A) Herman J. Mankiewicz has not been fully credited for writing *Citizen Kane*.
- B) Orson Welles falsely took credit for writing *Citizen Kane*.
- C) The original story for *Citizen Kane* was taken from a book.
- D) There is controversy surrounding the authorship of *Citizen Kane*.

2 In lines 1-3 the author of Passage 1 quotes Tacitus. How do the Roman writer's words relate to the content of the passage?
- A) As *Citizen Kane* became more acclaimed, the controversy over who wrote it became more heated.
- B) Tacitus was the inspiration for *Citizen Kane*.
- C) It is clear that Orson Welles is the only author of *Citizen Kane*.
- D) *Citizen Kane* has too many authors for anyone to receive full credit for writing it.

3 In line 11, the author's use of the term "script doctor" to describe Mankiewicz suggests that
- A) Mankiewicz was a published author.
- B) Mankiewicz had a light touch when he improved existing scripts.
- C) Mankiewicz was famous for writing original scripts.
- D) Mankiewicz was usually hired to modify existing scripts.

4 As used in line 34, "promulgated" most nearly means
- A) questioned.
- B) posited.
- C) prolonged.
- D) researched.

5 Over the course of Passage 2, the focus of the passage shifts from
- A) Welles' artistic differences with RKO.
- B) Welles' struggles to his ultimate triumph.
- C) Welles' insistence on creative control to his defiance of Hearst.
- D) Welles' radio career to the end of his movie career.

6 The author of Passage 2 implies
- A) that *Citizen Kane* is actually based on Hearst's life.
- B) that the similarities between Kane and Hearst are coincidental.
- C) that Welles' intention was to ridicule Hearst.
- D) that Welles actually admired Hearst.

7 Which choice provides the best evidence for the answer to the previous question?
- A) Lines 66-68 ("The studio…reputation")
- B) Lines 72-81 ("Yet there…personality")
- C) Lines 85-87 ("But when…film")
- D) Lines 91-94 ("But RKO…success")

8 In lines 70-81 ("Welles always…personality"), the author is attempting to show that
- A) Hearst was justified in trying to suppress the film.
- B) Welles was justified in denying the film was about Hearst.
- C) The many similarities make it probable that Hearst was the inspiration for the film.
- D) Welles, in his portrayal of Kane, slandered Hearst.

The Tutorverse

9 The author's use of the word "sensationalist" in line 74 implies that he thinks

A) Hearst published attention-grabbing but vacuous articles.

B) Hearst's newspapers were simultaneously thought-provoking and interesting.

C) Hearst won many sensational awards in the field of journalism.

D) Hearst newspapers only published articles about serious and important topics.

10 Which statement best describes the relationship between the two passages?

A) Passage 1 is critical of Welles, while Passage 2 views him favorably.

B) Passage 1 has to do with events that occurred after the film's release, while Passage 1 concerns events before the film's release.

C) The two passages describe opposing views of the film's authorship.

D) Passage 1 discusses authorship of the film script, while Passage 2 describes the struggle to advertise it.

11 Based on the two passages, how might Welles have responded to the charge that the true author of the film's script was Mankiewicz?

A) He might have argued that Mankiewicz was hired only as a consultant.

B) He might have argued that RKO had ultimate control over the writing of the script.

C) He might have argued that Mankiewicz did not make any substantial contributions to the script.

D) He might have argued that Hearst never suggested that Mankiewicz wrote the script.

12 How does the author's stance toward Welles in Passage 1 differ from the author's stance in Passage 2?

A) In Passage 1, the author is critical of Welles, while in Passage 2, the author portrays Welles favorably.

B) In Passage 1, the author portrays Welles favorably, while in Passage 2, the author's portrayal is neutral.

C) In Passage 1, the author is neutral toward Welles, while in Passage 2, the author portrays him favorably.

D) In Passage 1, the author portrays Welles favorably, while in Passage 2, the author is more critical.

13 What is the primary difference in the text structure of the two passages?

A) Passage 1 describes a controversy and the outcome. Passage 2 describes a controversy but not the outcome.

B) Passage 1 describes a controversy but not the outcome. Passage 2 describes a controversy and the outcome.

C) Passage 1 poses a question and gives possible answers. Passage 2 advances an argument.

D) Passage 1 advances an argument. Passage 2 poses a question and gives possible answers.

Passage Z *(Answers & explanations on page 359).*

Plastic is everywhere. Few among us think about the amount of plastic we use each day – in part because so much plastic is recyclable. However, according to the Environmental
5 Protection Agency, only about seven percent of all of the plastic waste in the U.S. was recycled in 2009. Worse yet, most plastic materials are not simply "reshaped" into their derivative products. For example, it's not possible to turn a plastic
10 bottle into another plastic bottle; plastic bottles are, instead, usually repurposed to make a lower-quality plastic product that can't be recycled again later.

Thus, a great deal of plastic actually gets
15 thrown away. Much of this waste plastic makes its way to the ocean, where it threatens the entire ecosystem. The Great Pacific Garbage Patch is a swirling vortex of debris between the coasts of California and Japan. A plastic bottle tossed into
20 the ocean by a careless beachgoer in California gets caught in oceanic currents and eventually winds up swirling around the Garbage Patch, where instead of biodegrading, it breaks up into tiny fragments. Thanks to the widespread use of
25 plastics in everything from fishing nets to water bottles, the Garbage Patch has grown to the size of a continent!

The Garbage Patch is an environmental nightmare. Some plastics can take hundreds of
30 years to fully biodegrade, while others, like those made with Polyethylene Terephthalate, will virtually never fully break down. Those plastics that do break down often leach toxic chemicals into the water. One chemical, bisphenol A (BPA),
35 which results from the decomposition of certain plastics, is poisonous to animals.

Plastic waste is, therefore, a threat not only to much of the marine life in the oceans, but also to life here on land. Animals that are lucky enough to
40 avoid choking on or becoming tangled in plastic unwittingly consume those same tiny pieces of plastic that leach chemicals like BPA into the water. Over time, these chemicals build up in the food chain, as smaller animals are consumed by
45 larger ones. The ocean's apex predators often contain toxic amounts of plastic and chemicals; many of the ocean's top predators – like tuna, for example – are on dinner menus around the world.

Plastic also threatens the ecosystem by
50 disrupting the food chain at the very beginning. Plastic waste blocks sunlight, reducing the amount of energy available to algae and other autotrophs, which form the building blocks of the entire oceanic ecosystem. The dying off of autotrophs
55 sends shockwaves through the entire ecosystem: those populations of small animals that feed on algae begin to shrink, as do the larger animals that feed on those small animals. The negative impact of plastics on the ocean's tiniest creatures have a
60 profound impact on the ocean's largest animals.

All of this should give us pause about the amount of plastic we use each day. The good news is that there is much that we can do to reduce the amount of plastic waste in the world.

65 One of the best ways to reduce our plastic waste is to reduce our use of plastic in the first place. Plastic water bottles are among the worst offenders, a source of many of the most common pollutants. Instead of reaching for a new water
70 bottle every time we're thirsty, we can invest in reusable and refillable bottles. Many conveniences that we accept without much thought – like the plastic utensils we receive when taking food to go, or the plastic sandwich bags we use to pack our
75 lunches – can be replaced by reusable versions of the same.

There are many plastic alternatives. Instead of using plastic bags to carry our groceries, we can use cloth bags. Instead of buying laundry detergent
80 packaged in plastic containers, we can choose to buy detergent packed in cardboard. Even buying fresh food can cut down on waste; many processed and frozen foods come in plastic containers that can't be reused.

85 It's important that we become more informed and self-aware of the environmental consequences of our collective actions. If nothing else, it is in our own self-interest to protect the environment from the deleterious effects of plastic waste.

1   The central claim of the passage is that
     A)   Little can be done to slow down the growth of the Great Pacific Garbage Patch.
     B)   Plastic thrown out on beaches eventually ends up in the Great Pacific Garbage Patch.
     C)   People should use less plastic because the waste is harmful to the world's ecosystem.
     D)   Buying fewer plastic products will help to decrease the amount of plastic waste.

2   Over the course of the passage, the main focus of the passage shifts from the
     A)   description of a problem to possible solutions for that problem.
     B)   an analysis of a problem to a description of that problem's trends.
     C)   study of plastic use to the impact of plastic waste on the environment.
     D)   description of an oceanic problem to the description of a global problem.

3   The author suggests that
     A)   people don't realize how much plastic they buy and throw away.
     B)   people deliberately discard plastics and refuse to recycle.
     C)   companies are to blame for putting plastic in their products.
     D)   there aren't enough alternatives to using plastic products.

4   Which choice provides the best evidence for the answer to the previous question?
     A)   Lines 1-3 ("Few among…recyclable")
     B)   Lines 4-7 ("However, according…2009")
     C)   Lines 14-15 ("Thus, a…away")
     D)   Lines 15-17 ("Much of…ecosystem")

5   Which of the following best summarizes the second paragraph (lines 14-27)?
     A)   The Great Pacific Garbage Patch is a symbolic representation of plastic waste.
     B)   Plastic waste has created the Great Pacific Garbage Patch.
     C)   Fishing nets and water bottles are responsible for the Great Pacific Garbage Patch.
     D)   The Great Pacific Garbage Patch is large but harmless.

6   In lines 28–32, the author likely explains how long some plastics take to break down in order to
     A)   explain how plastic waste interrupts the food chain.
     B)   emphasize the magnitude of a problem.
     C)   refute a previously stated counterclaim.
     D)   call for the creation of biodegradable plastics.

7   As it is used in lines 33 and 42, "leach" most nearly means
     A)   rely.
     B)   utilize.
     C)   combine.
     D)   release.

8   According to the passage, in which of the following ways does plastic waste affect the food chain in the ocean?
     A)   Some animals intentionally eat plastic.
     B)   People have less fish to eat.
     C)   Apex predators eat plastic instead of smaller animals.
     D)   Plastic waste disrupts the food chain by blocking sunlight.

The Tutorverse

9 Based on the passage, how might the author of the passage respond to the following statement:

Plastic waste has not been shown to have any negative impact on tuna fish populations.

A) The author would agree, because plastic waste only affects small fish and turtles.

B) The author would agree, because plastic affects only the ocean's largest creatures.

C) The author would disagree, because plastic disrupts the entire food chain.

D) The author would disagree, because tuna eat plastic that floats in the ocean.

10 The main rhetorical effect of lines 61-64 is to

A) describe why plastic waste is bad news.

B) transition from focusing on a problem to focusing on a solution.

C) question whether plastic is really needed in most products.

D) anticipate objections to the passage's primary argument.

11 In the seventh paragraph (lines 65-76), the author mentions plastic water bottles in order to

A) introduce a novel idea about improving recycling.

B) illustrate that it is easy to use less plastic.

C) underscore difficulties associated with giving up plastic.

D) answer a possible objection about giving up plastic.

12 In lines 77-84, the author

A) refutes numerous counterclaims to her argument.

B) makes sweeping claims about her argument.

C) strengthens her argument by providing specific examples.

D) describes an assumption central to her argument.

13 According to the passage, how does buying fresh food cut down on plastic waste?

A) Prepared foods are often stored in single-use containers.

B) Fresh food is available at places that recycle plastics.

C) Some products are packaged in cardboard, which is easier to recycle.

D) Fresh food can be carried in cloth bags.

The Tutorverse

Part Two: Writing & Language

Overview

The second part of the SAT is the Writing & Language Test, which requires that students review passages and select answer choices that represent the best revisions to those passages. These revisions encompass both basic grammatical corrections as well as improvements that enhance the passage's expression of ideas. These passages cover a number of different topics (humanities, social studies, science, and industry/commerce) and styles (persuasive, expository, and nonfiction narrative), and are on average 425 words in length.

On the Actual Test

Students will have 35 minutes to answer 44 total questions addressing 4 total passages. Each passage will span several pages, and will be displayed in the left-hand column of the page. In the right-hand column of each page will be displayed the questions. There are 11 questions per passage, 5 of which pertain to grammar, and 6 of which pertain to improving the passage's expression.

Scattered throughout the passage itself will be the numbers 1-11 appearing in white surrounded by a dark-colored box (for example, **1**). These numbers correspond to the question numbers in the right-hand column. There are also other numbers which you might find in the passage itself. Questions that are enclosed in square brackets (for example, [1]) denote sentence numbers, and are used to number the order of sentences in a paragraph. Paragraph numbers are denoted with a series of dashes that precede the paragraph (for example, "---1 ---" will appear before the first paragraph in a passage). The questions in the right-hand column will make reference to specific sentence or paragraph numbers.

It won't be possible to know in advance what combination of passage topic and style students will encounter on the test.

Types of Questions

The Writing & Language Test of the SAT draws from a bank of 28 question categories, 18 of which pertain to grammar, and 10 of which pertain to improving expression. Therefore, because there are only 11 questions per passage, not every question set accompanying a passage will include every question category. In fact, a question set may contain multiple instances of a question category. Furthermore, each category of question may be represented in a number of different ways. A summary of each of these 28 categories is provided below.

Standard English Conventions
- ✒ *Complete Sentences.* Understand what makes a complete sentence and how to correct a sentence fragment or run-on sentence to make it a complete sentence.
- ✒ *Subordination & Coordination.* Properly use punctuation and conjunctions to form grammatically complete sentences and logically correct thoughts.
- ✒ *Parallel Structure.* Correct a sentence that is internally inconsistent in terms of voice, word placement, use of preposition, and other elements that affect parallelism.
- ✒ *Modifiers.* Recognize and resolve problems affecting modifiers (i.e. dangling or misplaced modifiers).
- ✒ *Shifting Tenses, Mood, Voice.* Diagnose and correct a grammatical problem pertaining to incorrectly changing verb tense (perfect, future, past, etc.) and mood (indicative, imperative, subjunctive).
- ✒ *Pronoun Clarity.* Identify and rectify inconsistent or inappropriate changes between the person and number of pronouns as well as vague or ambiguous pronouns.
- ✒ *Possessive Determiners.* Understand the differences and correct usage of possessive determiners (i.e. "your" vs. "you're").
- ✒ *Subject-Verb Agreement.* Determine whether or not the number of verbs and subjects agree (i.e. plural forms vs. singular forms of verbs and nouns) and correct any disagreements.
- ✒ *Noun-Agreement.* Determine whether or not the number of two related nouns agree and correct any disagreements.

The Tutorverse

- *Frequently Confused Words.* Recognize and correct commonly misused words (i.e. homophones – words that sound the same when spoken but are spelled differently and have different meanings).
- *Logical Comparison.* Ensure that incorrect or illogical comparisons between nouns are corrected.
- *Conventional Expression.* Identify and correct misused idioms as well as other standards of writing convention (i.e. the proper usage and placement of prepositions).
- *End-of-Sentence Punctuation.* Properly use punctuation to signal the end of a sentence (or correct improperly used punctuation).
- *Within-Sentence Punctuation.* Properly use punctuation to separate different parts of a sentence (or correct improperly used punctuation).
- *Possessive Nouns & Pronouns.* Properly utilize and punctuate nouns and pronouns to signal possession (or correct for improperly punctuated nouns and pronouns).
- *Punctuating a Series.* Properly use punctuation to separate items in a list or series (or correct for improper punctuation used).
- *Parenthetical Expressions & Nonrestrictive Clauses.* Properly punctuate nonessential information (or correct for improperly punctuated information that is essential to the sentence).
- *Unnecessary Punctuation.* Identify and eliminate punctuation that confuses the sentence or results in a grammatically incorrect sentence.

Improving Expression

- *Proposition.* Add or revise a sentence which encompasses the author's main idea.
- *Focus.* Add, revise, or delete a sentence based on its relevance (or irrelevance) to the author's purpose.
- *Support.* Add or revise a sentence that best supports the author's main idea.
- *Quantitative Information.* Add or revise a sentence based on information from an information graphic to strengthen or otherwise improve the passage.
- *Organization.* Improve transitions between ideas, sentences, and paragraphs.
- *Logical Sequence.* Improve the logical flow of a paragraph, or of the passage itself.
- *Style/Tone.* Add or revise word choice to ensure consistency of style or to achieve a desired outcome.
- *Syntax.* Add or revise word choice to combine sentences or achieve a desired outcome.
- *Precision.* Revise word choice to best serve the contextual meaning.
- *Concision.* Revise word choice to achieve economy and minimize redundancy.

Understanding each of the above categories is essential.

How to Use This Section

The goal of this section is to help familiarize students with both the type of passages that may be encountered on the SAT as well as the type of questions that may be asked on the SAT. Recognizing that many students have not received formal grammar training, we have split this section up into 3 units:

- *Guided Practice – Standard English Conventions*
- *Guided Practice – Improving Expression*
- *Passage-Based Practice – Improving Expression*

In the *Guided Practice – Standard English Conventions* unit, we explore each of the 18 grammar-related question categories separately. English grammar is an expansive and nuanced topic about which many (large) books have been written. This workbook does not explore such intricacies; instead, this book focuses on building those skills necessary to successfully navigate the Writing & Language portion of the SAT. As such, this section is designed to help students who have minimal formal grammar training quickly learn basic grammar concepts. This section also provides valuable reinforcement for students with some existing grammar training. Students who have received extensive grammar training may wish to skip this section. Students desiring additional grammar reinforcement or who need additional help with grammar should seek guidance from a trusted and experienced educator or utilize the many grammar resources available in print and online. We have deliberately removed grammar from passage-based exercises in order to provide more focused

The Tutorverse

grammar practice and since these questions can be answered without context of passage. Students will be able to practice passage-based grammar questions in *Part Five: Practice Test*.

In completing the *Guided Practice – Standard English Conventions* unit, consider making use of the *Grammar Glossary* included in the *Answer Explanation* section of this book. This glossary will be helpful for students who are unfamiliar with many of the formal elements of grammar.

In the *Guided Practice – Improving Expression* unit, students are introduced to passage-based writing questions that are focused on Improving Expression. The primary differences between the question sets found in this unit and those found on the actual test are as follows:

- the passages in this unit are accompanied by question sets that contain all 10 of the 10 question categories related to Improving Expression; each passage on the actual exam contains 6 of the 10 possible question categories.
- the question sets in this unit do not contain any grammar questions; each passage on the actual test is accompanied by a set of 4 grammar questions.
- each question in this unit is labeled with the question category to which it belongs; the actual test does not label or classify any question.

The aforementioned differences are intended to help students to become familiar with and start to recognize the different question categories that may appear on the actual test as they pertain to Improving Expression. Take as much time as needed in this unit.

The *Passage-Based Practice – Improving Expression* unit builds on the *Guided Practice – Improving Expression* unit that precedes it. In the former, question category labels have been removed.

The best way to prepare for the actual test is for students to give themselves approximately 10 minutes to finish each passage and question set in this unit – this is approximately 1 minutes per question, including time spent reading the passage (which is based on an approximation of the time allotment per question on the actual test).

We recommend that students practice at least 2 grammar topics and 2 passage-based question sets per week in preparing for the exam (though this number should, of course, be tailored to fit a student's individual study plan).

Over the course of their studies, students should not be surprised to encounter words that are unfamiliar to them.

In fact, we encourage students to make a list of unfamiliar or difficult words, whether they appear in passages, questions, answer choices, or answer explanations. This is a natural way to build not only vocabulary, but also the ability to infer a words meaning through context (and is, in fact, a worthwhile habit to carry into everyday reading and writing). Consider writing down the definition of each word as well as a sentence using the word. Students may also want to consider writing down whether the word has a positive or negative association, and any root words that can help them to remember the word.

Lastly, a quick note on formatting: as noted above in "On the Actual Test," question numbers will be denoted with a white number surrounded by a dark-colored box (for example, **1**). In this book, questions are denoted with a grey number surrounded by a dark-colored outline (for example, 1).

Tutorverse Tips & Strategies

In addition to tips and strategies outlined in the *Test Overview* section of this workbook, consider employing the following Writing & Language Test-specific suggestions:

- *Practice grammar and focus on tricky topics.*
  Many students do not receive formal grammar training in school. Use this workbook to diagnose areas that require additional time and attention. Then, identify the most appropriate resources (online, in print, or with a tutor or trusted educator) to get even more practice.

The Tutorverse

☞ *Learn the Writing & Language Test question categories.*
The stronger a student's command of the Writing & Language Test's question categories, the more quickly he or she will be able to identify and classify questions on the actual exam. This will save the student precious time on the actual exam.

☞ *Make sure to assess Improving Expression questions in context.*
Students are allowed to make notes and otherwise mark up their test booklet (though only answers included on the answer sheet will be scored). As students read through the passage, they should think about and make note of (underline or circle) important information that is relevant to the categories of questions commonly found on the Writing & Language Test. For example, knowing that there will be 6 Improving Expression questions on each passage, students should be able to make notes in the margins when they come across information that relates to one of the 10 Improving Expression questions.

Guided Practice – Standard English Conventions

Grammar Glossary

To make the most of their grammar practice, students should feel free to consult the *Grammar Glossary* in the *Answer Explanation* section of this workbook if they come across any unknown grammar elements.

Directions: Each topic in this unit contains several questions. Each question contains a sentence, and part (or all) of each sentence is underlined. Each of the four answer choices per question represents a possible revision related to the underlined portion of the sentence. Choose the answer choice that represents the best possible action to take to improve the quality of writing in the sentence. Some questions include an answer choice of "NO CHANGE," which you should choose if it is best to leave the relevant part of the sentence unchanged.

Complete Sentences

(Answers & explanations on page 361).

A complete sentence not only has a subject and predicate, but also forms a complete thought. These questions assess the student's ability to identify complete sentences and to revise grammatical issues affecting the completeness of a sentence (i.e. a sentence fragment or a run-on sentence).

1   Whenever she gets tired and likes to take a nap.
  A) NO CHANGE
  B) She
  C) She,
  D) Whenever, she

2   Hungry as a result of his long and tiring workout.
  A) NO CHANGE
  B) As
  C) Hungry as
  D) He was hungry as

3   We decided to bring dessert to the dinner party they decided to bring snacks and drinks.
  A) NO CHANGE
  B) party, they
  C) party – they
  D) party. They

4   Dogs often like to chase cats, cats often like to chase mice.
  A) NO CHANGE
  B) cats, and cats
  C) cats: cats
  D) cats…cats

5   The restaurant was very busy and crowded with diners; we decided to eat at a different establishment.
  A) NO CHANGE
  B) diners or we
  C) diners, we
  D) diners we

6   The jungle gym was filled with children they were using all of the equipment and laughing as they played.
  A) NO CHANGE
  B) children, who
  C) children, they
  D) children and

7   The toy store ran out of the season's most popular gift the shoppers were incensed.
  A) NO CHANGE
  B) gift for the
  C) gift, the
  D) gift; the

8   Martin sneezes several times whenever there is a cat nearby.
  A) NO CHANGE
  B) times whenever, there
  C) times; whenever there
  D) times whenever. There

The Tutorverse

9 Some newspaper publications are losing readers to other types of news <u>media. These</u> companies are adopting new strategies for retaining readers.
A)   NO CHANGE
B)   media, these
C)   media these
D)   media, although these

10 Many shoppers complain about the lack of retail <u>options, yet</u> do little to support small businesses.
A)   NO CHANGE
B)   options: yet
C)   options. Yet
D)   options; yet

11 Neglecting his tenants for years at a <u>time. The</u> absentee landlord lost his right to collect rent.
A)   NO CHANGE
B)   time, the
C)   time; the
D)   time and the

12 Retirees are happiest in warmer parts of the United <u>States. Like Florida</u> and Arizona.
A)   NO CHANGE
B)   States, like Florida
C)   States. Such as Florida
D)   States. Including Florida

Subordination & Coordination

(Answers & explanations on page 362).

The logical use of conjunctions is referred to as subordination and/or coordination (depending on the types of conjunctions used, i.e. subordinating or coordinating conjunctions). These questions test the student's ability to identify and correct illogically used conjunctions.

1 <u>Before</u> his failed attempt at stealing second base, the runner decided that it wasn't worth the exertion.
A)   NO CHANGE
B)   While
C)   Because
D)   After

2 <u>During</u> juggling six bowling pins and a sword, the street performer wowed the tourists with his ability to ride a unicycle at the same time.
A)   NO CHANGE
B)   While
C)   That
D)   As soon as

3 <u>As soon as</u> the original movie had done so well at the box office, the movie studio greenlit the sequel just days after the original's release.
A)   NO CHANGE
B)   Though
C)   Because
D)   While

4 Justine was excited as ever to go to the theme park, <u>since</u> she was deathly afraid of heights and was prone to motion sickness.
A)   NO CHANGE
B)   if
C)   unless
D)   even though

5 The spoiled child knew that he could always get his way just by crying, <u>whether</u> he was well-behaved or not.
A)   NO CHANGE
B)   as soon as
C)   whenever
D)   once

6 Products with more reviews sell more frequently than products with fewer reviews, <u>but</u> retailers incentivize shoppers to leave reviews.
A)   NO CHANGE
B)   so
C)   and
D)   for

The Tutorverse

7 The restauranteur needed to choose between either the bigger building in a quiet neighborhood <u>and</u> a smaller building in a more bustling part of town.
A) NO CHANGE
B) for
C) from
D) or

8 The car had been taken to the mechanic's for repairs only yesterday, <u>yet</u> it nevertheless broke down today while I was driving to the supermarket.
A) NO CHANGE
B) so
C) for
D) or

9 Amie expected her parents to be very angry when she did poorly on the math test, <u>for</u> her parents were in fact more concerned than upset.
A) NO CHANGE
B) or
C) but
D) so

10 The thief received a lenient sentence, <u>but</u> his testimony had convinced the judge that extenuating and truly piteous circumstances had led to the crime.
A) NO CHANGE
B) from
C) nor
D) for

11 Advocates of recycling maintain that there are many benefits to the practice, not least of which are that it eases the burden on the environment <u>and</u> saves people money.
A) NO CHANGE
B) but
C) nor
D) yet

12 The author was successful <u>where</u> he knew how to tell a captivating story and treated writing like a job.
A) NO CHANGE
B) although
C) so
D) because

Modifiers

(Answers & explanations on page 363).

Modifiers are words or phrases that describe something else, and can sometimes be confusing or ambiguous when arranged in certain ways, as with misplaced, dangling, or squinting modifiers.

1 Kathleen, an avid fan of movies, has seen <u>every movie, practically made</u>.
A) NO CHANGE
B) every movie made practically
C) practically every movie made
D) practically, every movie made

2 With his tinted sunglasses on, Jack <u>could see what was hardly written</u> in large, block lettering.
A) NO CHANGE
B) could hardly see what was written
C) could see what hardly was written
D) could see what was written hardly

3 <u>The dog chased after the tennis ball with a bushy wagging tail.</u>
A) NO CHANGE
B) The dog with a bushy, wagging tail chased after the tennis ball.
C) The dog with a bushy tail chased after the wagging tennis ball.
D) The dog wagging, chased with a bushy tail, after the tennis ball.

4 The Hamiltons <u>signed the unfavorable agreement with a grudge</u>.
A) NO CHANGE
B) signed the unfavorable grudge agreement
C) signed the unfavorable agreement
D) grudgingly signed the unfavorable agreement

The Tutorverse

5 While playing the lead in *King Lear*, the audience groaned as the actor delivered yet another boring and unconvincing performance.

A) NO CHANGE

B) The audience groaned as the actor, while playing the lead in *King Lear*, delivered yet another boring and unconvincing performance.

C) The audience groaned, while playing the lead in *King Lear*, as the actor delivered yet another boring and unconvincing performance.

D) The audience groaned as the actor delivered yet another boring and unconvincing performance, while playing the lead in *King Lear*.

6 Collecting into tiny pools, Forrest watched the icicles hanging from the trees slowly melt onto the sidewalk.

A) NO CHANGE

B) Forrest watched the icicles collecting into tiny pools, hanging from the trees slowly melt onto the sidewalk.

C) Forrest watched the icicles hanging from the trees slowly melt onto the sidewalk, collecting into tiny pools.

D) Melting from the trees slowly onto the sidewalk, Forrest watched the icicles collecting into tiny pools.

7 Shining from a new coat of car polish, Jeremy wondered how many compliments his car would earn.

A) NO CHANGE

B) Jeremy, shining from a new coat of car polish, wondered how many compliments his car would earn.

C) Jeremy wondered how many compliments his car would earn, shining from a new coat of car polish.

D) Jeremy wondered how many compliments his car, shining from a new coat of car polish, would earn.

8 Casey eagerly watched the kitten nervously take its first wobbly steps, dripping with excitement and pride.

A) NO CHANGE

B) Dripping with excitement and pride, Casey eagerly watched the kitten nervously take its first wobbly steps.

C) Casey eagerly watched the kitten nervously dripping with excitement and pride take its first wobbly steps.

D) Nervously taking its first wobbly steps, the kitten watched Casey, dripping with excitement and pride.

9 Reading complex sentences quickly improves one's vocabulary.

A) NO CHANGE

B) Reading complex sentences improves one's vocabulary quickly.

C) Quickly, reading complex sentences improves one's vocabulary.

D) Reading, quickly, complex sentences improves one's vocabulary.

10 The teacher said after the math lesson that the students would be able to enjoy recess.

A) NO CHANGE

B) The teacher said that the students after the math lesson would be able to enjoy recess.

C) The teacher said that the students would be able to enjoy recess after the math lesson.

D) The teacher said that the students would be after the math lesson able to enjoy recess.

11 The business owner instructed her store employees to take the holidays off and to enjoy the time off with friends and family.

A) NO CHANGE

B) The business owner instructed at the store employees to take the holidays off and to enjoy the time off with friends and family.

C) The business owner at the store instructed employees to take the holidays off and enjoy the time with friends and family.

D) The business owner instructed employees to take the holidays off at the store and to enjoy the time off with friends and family.

12 Professors who energetically deliver their lectures are often perceived to be both more approachable and more knowledgeable.

A) NO CHANGE

B) deliver their lectures are often energetically perceived

C) deliver their lectures are often perceived energetically

D) deliver their energetically lectures are often perceived

Shifting Tenses, Mood, Voice, and Number

(Answers & explanations on page 364).

In every sentence, the verbs must agree in tense (past, present, future, etc.), mood (indicative, imperative, or subjunctive), and number (singular or plural). The voice of the sentence must also be internally consistent. These questions test the student's ability to identify and modify inappropriate changes in these elements.

1 When he realized he was going to be late for his flight, Terry is jumping out of bed and frantically searched for his passport.

A) NO CHANGE

B) has been jumping

C) jumped

D) will have been jumping

2 Because he had been receiving unusually high returns, Dominic will be continuing to invest in the stock market in the future.

A) NO CHANGE

B) had been continuing

C) will have been continuing

D) will have continued

3 It took the camp counselors over three hours to find Tony, who will hide behind the giant stack of firewood after hearing the scary campfire story.

A) NO CHANGE

B) will have hidden

C) has been hiding

D) had been hiding

4 Call the principal tomorrow morning and you tell her what happened today.

A) NO CHANGE

B) told

C) tell

D) telling

5 Decide now to avoid confusion and save time and money later on.

A) NO CHANGE

B) you avoid

C) avoiding

D) your avoiding

6 Though acting immediately can sometimes be the best course of action, so too can bide your time be most prudent.

A) NO CHANGE

B) biding

C) bide

D) biding your

The Tutorverse

7 If you <u>were</u> a trillionaire, then I would be Mickey Mouse!
A) NO CHANGE
B) was
C) are
D) is

8 It is imperative that all managers <u>are</u> present at the beginning of the quarterly conference call.
A) NO CHANGE
B) be
C) is
D) being

9 Arthur had spent the entire day playing video games; his mother felt that <u>the entire day had been wasted by him</u>.
A) NO CHANGE
B) he had wasted the entire day
C) he was wasting the entire day
D) the entire day will have been wasted by him

10 If you receive a perfect score on the exam, it <u>leads</u> to many opportunities.
A) NO CHANGE
B) will have led
C) led
D) may lead

11 To others, Jim makes a ceremony of his morning coffee routine, <u>as the beans, water, and various implements are treated like holy treasures by him.</u>
A) NO CHANGE
B) with the beans, water, and various implements being treated like holy treasures by him
C) as he treats the beans, water, and various implements like holy treasures
D) having treated the beans, water, and various implements like holy treasures

12 Though peeling grapefruit usually seemed like a chore, <u>Jim felt, on particularly stressful days, that it was actually therapeutic</u>.
A) NO CHANGE
B) it was felt by Jim to be, on particularly stressful days, therapeutic
C) it has been felt by Jim to be, on particularly stressful days, therapeutic
D) Jim having felt, on particularly stressful days, that it actually seems therapeutic

Parallel Structure

(Answers & explanations on page 365).

Parallelism is a general term referring to consistent and logical construction of a sentence. This could mean writing with a consistent tense and voice, and with appropriate conjunctions and prepositions.

1 Tomorrow, I will need to wash the car, clean the air conditioners, and <u>resealing</u> the driveway.
A) NO CHANGE
B) reseal
C) have resealed
D) reseals

2 Donovan had prepared for the big test by studying diligently and <u>exercises</u> regularly.
A) NO CHANGE
B) will be exercising
C) exercising
D) had been exercised

3 When it comes to figure skating, <u>jumps and spinning</u> can be difficult to master and dangerous to attempt.
A) NO CHANGE
B) jumping and spins
C) to jump and spinning
D) jumping and spinning

4 I know that I should take the job in Sydney and <u>relocate to Australia</u>.
A) NO CHANGE
B) be relocated to Australia
C) be relocating to Australia
D) be relocated in Australia

The Tutorverse

5 Learning is very important to your future, so it is imperative that you prioritize <u>studying</u>.
   A) NO CHANGE
   B) having studies
   C) studies
   D) to be studying

6 Bethany was nervous about leaving her home unoccupied for the next several months, <u>so a caretaker is hired by her to housesit</u>.
   A) NO CHANGE
   B) so she hired a caretaker to housesit
   C) so a caretaker was hired by her to housesit
   D) so that a caretaker will have been hired by her to housesit.

7 I was worried by the frightful thought that the bus would be stopped by the authorities, that the road would be made slippery by the rain, <u>and that the driver would fall asleep</u>.
   A) NO CHANGE
   B) and that the driver falls asleep
   C) and that the driver would be overcome by sleep
   D) and that the driver would be falling asleep

8 School will be cancelled on Wednesday, Thursday, and <u>on Friday</u>.
   A) NO CHANGE
   B) in Friday
   C) at Friday
   D) Friday

9 Pollen, ubiquitous during the late months of spring, <u>was in the air and all the kitchen countertops</u>.
   A) NO CHANGE
   B) was in the kitchen countertops and the air
   C) was in all the kitchen countertops, and on the air
   D) was in the air and on all the kitchen countertops

10 Working as a physician is not only very lucrative <u>but also is very</u> rewarding.
   A) NO CHANGE
   B) but very also
   C) but also very
   D) but is very

11 The critic wasn't sure whether or not he liked the painting; the piece was either a brilliant stroke of originality or <u>he really liked it</u>.
   A) NO CHANGE
   B) a hackneyed imitation
   C) he really didn't like it
   D) it was very popular

12 Because the weather outside is so frightful, the deacon suggested that we should stay inside, <u>have drank</u> hot chocolate, and enjoy a spirited conversation.
   A) NO CHANGE
   B) drink
   C) drunk
   D) be drinking

Pronoun Clarity

(Answers & explanations on page 366).
Pronouns must clearly refer to a specific person, place, or thing – otherwise known as an antecedent.

1 Upon winning the lottery, Larry decided that <u>he</u> would donate half of the remaining winnings to charity.
   A) NO CHANGE
   B) it
   C) they
   D) someone

2 The engineer knew that if <u>it wasn't</u> pumped out soon, the bilge water would sink the ship.
   A) NO CHANGE
   B) the pump wasn't
   C) he wasn't
   D) they weren't

The Tutorverse

3 <u>In the guidebook, he suggests</u> that the best way to see the country is to follow his itinerary.
A) NO CHANGE
B) In the guidebook, she suggests
C) They suggest, in the guidebook,
D) In the guidebook, the author suggests

4 He turned down the music for them because <u>they were</u> too loud.
A) NO CHANGE
B) the sound was
C) he was
D) it were

5 Hoping that carrying out the heist in the middle of the night might help him remain undetected, <u>the burglar</u> – to disastrous effect – forgot that jackhammering through a bank vault would be very noisy.
A) NO CHANGE
B) someone
C) him
D) she

6 Very pleased with the employee's performance over the past year, the executive gave the punctual and high-performing employee <u>her</u> bonus.
A) NO CHANGE
B) his
C) a
D) someone's

7 Both the yacht and the sailboat that crashed into it were so old that <u>it</u> would not be repaired; instead, both would simply be scrapped.
A) NO CHANGE
B) the vessel
C) one
D) they

8 The investment bankers and the corporate attorneys were waiting in the conference room when, unceremoniously, <u>both parties were</u> informed that the client would no longer move ahead with the merger and would not require any banking or legal services.
A) NO CHANGE
B) some were
C) somebody was
D) they were

9 In the United States, many people like to shop the sales immediately after their Thanksgiving Day dinners, though <u>they</u> are short and often not very good.
A) NO CHANGE
B) the sales
C) these
D) those

10 At the doctor's office, <u>he said that she</u> had a vitamin deficiency that, while not life-threatening, should be rectified as soon as possible with a course of supplements.
A) NO CHANGE
B) the doctor said that Harriet
C) he said that Harriet
D) they said that they

11 As the stranger approached the agoraphobic man (who was trying his best to avoid people), <u>he</u> said, "Excuse me, please."
A) NO CHANGE
B) anyone
C) the former
D) it

12 Justine plays both the piano and the violin, though she enjoys playing <u>it</u> more.
A) NO CHANGE
B) them
C) the violin
D) some

The Tutorverse

Possessive Determiners

(Answers & explanations on page 367).

These questions test the student's ability to distinguish between when and where to use possessive determiners (which are used like adjectives) and possessive pronouns (which are used like nouns).

1   The best part of the movie was, in <u>mine</u> opinion, the scene where the villain delivers a long-winded monologue.
    A)   NO CHANGE
    B)   my
    C)   me
    D)   I

2   Though national political issues tend to generate more media coverage, local political issues are arguably more impactful to <u>you're</u> daily life.
    A)   NO CHANGE
    B)   your'
    C)   yours
    D)   your

3   Nicolaus Copernicus was a great thinker who made many important discoveries; <u>his</u> brilliant ideas and revolutionary theories continue to influence science today.
    A)   NO CHANGE
    B)   him
    C)   he
    D)   his'

4   Marie Curie, famed physicist and chemist, was the first woman to win a Nobel Prize, which was awarded to her for <u>hers</u> work associated with radiation.
    A)   NO CHANGE
    B)   she's
    C)   her
    D)   her's

5   Jury duty affords ordinary citizens the opportunity to observe and participate in the rule of law; <u>its</u> importance to a free and democratic society cannot be understated.
    A)   NO CHANGE
    B)   it'
    C)   it's
    D)   its'

6   The widespread of use of plastic bottles, which can take hundreds of years to biodegrade, is an environmental hazard in <u>it's</u> own right.
    A)   NO CHANGE
    B)   its
    C)   it
    D)   its'

7   Some philosophers contend that <u>our</u> greatest concerns in life should be about making decisions that maximize utility.
    A)   NO CHANGE
    B)   ours
    C)   we
    D)   us

8   We decided that our contribution to the group project would be the presentation and that <u>they're</u> contribution would be the paper.
    A)   NO CHANGE
    B)   theirs
    C)   their
    D)   their's

9   The principal decided that there would be no reprieve from detention until someone from <u>there</u> group confessed to the prank.
    A)   NO CHANGE
    B)   they're
    C)   theirs
    D)   their

10 The celebrity chefs who judged the baking contest found it difficult to decide <u>who's</u> cookies, Norma's or Claudia's, were better.
    A)   NO CHANGE
    B)   whose
    C)   whom's
    D)   whomever's

The Tutorverse

11 When playing a game with many people, it can be confusing to remember <u>whose</u> turn it is.
A) NO CHANGE
B) who's
C) whom's
D) whomevers

12 Watching his creation take life for the first time, the doctor exclaimed, "<u>Its</u> alive!"
A) NO CHANGE
B) Its'
C) It's'
D) It's

Possessive Nouns & Pronouns

(Answers & explanations on page 368).

Like questions in the Possessive Determiners category, questions in this category require the student to correctly use nouns, pronouns, and punctuation to show possession.

1 Local geography plays a large role in determining the <u>Miami and New York City's</u> climates, which are very different from one another.
A) NO CHANGE
B) Miami's and New York City's
C) Miamis and New York City's
D) Miami's and New York Cities'

2 <u>Simon and Judith's</u> home, which they purchased together in 2005, has tripled in value during the interceding years.
A) NO CHANGE
B) Simon's and Judith's
C) Simons and Judiths
D) Simon and Judiths'

3 Because they must contend with tired and disgruntled flyers, the <u>flight attendants</u> least favorite routes to fly are red-eye flights.
A) NO CHANGE
B) flight attendant's
C) flight attendant
D) flight attendants'

4 The <u>chairmans'</u> objections to the sale was moral in nature; he did not want to sell the environmentally sustainable company to a less environmentally conscientious company.
A) NO CHANGE
B) chairmans
C) chairman's
D) chairman

5 <u>Camillas preference</u> for pink was apparent, as everything she owned was one shade of pink or another.
A) NO CHANGE
B) Camilla's preference
C) Camillas' preference
D) Camilla's preference's

6 Dexter's uncanny ability to quickly understand concepts others found difficult earned him the moniker "boy genius," which would stay with him for much of <u>its</u> life.
A) NO CHANGE
B) his'
C) his
D) their

7 The publisher believed that the book, with <u>it's</u> fresh take on age-old issues, would lead to wildfire sales, and paid the author accordingly.
A) NO CHANGE
B) its
C) its'
D) their

8 Monica was eventually able to prove to her roommate, Joshua, that <u>her's</u> was the right way to do dishes.
A) NO CHANGE
B) hers'
C) she's
D) hers

The Tutorverse

9   "Hey!" shouted Jerry, "That slice of apple pie isn't <u>your's</u>! I saved it after Thanksgiving dinner and froze it, so it's mine!"
A)   NO CHANGE
B)   your'
C)   yours'
D)   yours

10   Zachary, always responsible and self-reliant, felt that it was his responsibility to have stopped the toilet leak, not <u>theirs</u>.
A)   NO CHANGE
B)   their's
C)   theirs'
D)   there's

11   <u>Our's</u> was the most popular chili at the contest, prevailing over even those of world-famous chefs.
A)   NO CHANGE
B)   Ours
C)   Ours'
D)   Our

12   It was all of the <u>crew members'</u> opinion that the captain was unfit for duty.
A)   NO CHANGE
B)   crew member's
C)   crew members's
D)   crew members

Subject-Verb Agreement

(Answers & explanations on page 368).

These questions test the student's ability to correctly choose the appropriate verb number to correspond with the subject number (i.e. singular vs. plural).

1   The camp for girls <u>are situated</u> by a lake some five hours away from the closest town.
A)   NO CHANGE
B)   is situated
C)   were situated
D)   exist

2   In addition to political success, many senators <u>are</u> also successful in business.
A)   NO CHANGE
B)   was
C)   is
D)   becomes

3   Everybody in Kaisha's class <u>were</u> afraid of snakes, so the science teacher changed the class project to be about the lifecycle of frogs, instead.
A)   NO CHANGE
B)   are
C)   was
D)   have been

4   For many conspiracy theorists, it is widely accepted that all of the gold said to be held in Fort Knox <u>are</u> nothing more than a hoax.
A)   NO CHANGE
B)   is
C)   possesses
D)   utilizes

5   Every member of the local labor union <u>were instructed</u> to participate in the strike.
A)   NO CHANGE
B)   are instructed
C)   have been instructed
D)   was instructed

6   A general rule of thumb when cooking for guests is that a pound of meat can feed two people; so, for a party of twenty people, ten pounds of meat <u>are</u> sufficient.
A)   NO CHANGE
B)   is
C)   were
D)   have been

The Tutorverse

7 Mathematics, a subject that many people deem irrelevant to their daily lives, <u>are</u> fundamental to many of the technological luxuries we take for granted.
A) NO CHANGE
B) were
C) have been
D) is

8 The CEO decided that the financial and operational functions of the company <u>are</u> so interrelated that a combined department should be created.
A) NO CHANGE
B) is
C) has been
D) was

9 My long-time mentor and close friend <u>request</u> that he be invited to all future meetings.
A) NO CHANGE
B) requests
C) ask
D) demand

10 The teacher, counselor, or principal <u>are proctoring</u> the standardized test.
A) NO CHANGE
B) is proctoring
C) have been proctoring
D) were proctoring

11 Even though it was bedtime, neither Bill's three daughters nor Bill's son <u>is</u> ready for bed.
A) NO CHANGE
B) were
C) are
D) am

12 Dorothy's forgetfulness became a real liability when she forgot where she kept her passport and <u>were</u> late for an important flight.
A) NO CHANGE
B) have been
C) were being
D) was

Noun-Agreement
(Answers & explanations on page 369).
As subjects and verbs must agree in number, so too must logically related nouns also agree in number.

1 Bellagio <u>is a municipalities</u> in the Italian province of Como that is famous for its beautiful lake.
A) NO CHANGE
B) are municipalities
C) is a municipality
D) are municipality

2 Jupiter and Saturn are, respectively, the fifth and sixth <u>planet</u> from the Sun yet differ in orbital periods by nearly 17.6 Julian years.
A) NO CHANGE
B) celestial body
C) satellite
D) planets

3 The billionaire's gala <u>were the events</u> of the season, attracting politicians, socialites, celebrities, and others in the upper crust.
A) NO CHANGE
B) was the event
C) was the events
D) were the event

4 The car show attracted thousands of people and displayed hundreds of cars <u>in model</u> ranging from the antique to the futuristic.
A) NO CHANGE
B) of type
C) in models
D) as example

The Tutorverse

5 Because money is inextricably tied to success in modern American politics, politicians and their campaign managers often find it necessary to hold numerous fundraisers, which <u>are events</u> such as dinners and auctions designed to generate monetary contributions.
A) NO CHANGE
B) are event
C) is events
D) is an event

6 When the football team's equipment disappeared overnight, many suspected the rival team of having a hand in making <u>the gears</u> disappear.
A) NO CHANGE
B) the gear
C) the equipments
D) them

7 Upon finding an oasis in the desert, the travelers experienced indescribable <u>happiness</u>.
A) NO CHANGE
B) happinesses
C) contentments
D) blisses

8 <u>Unease's</u> spread through the crowd as they worried about the welfare of the injured player.
A) NO CHANGE
B) Uneases
C) Uneasiness'
D) Unease

9 After nearly a decade, the city's orchestra – the country's most respected <u>musical ensembles</u>, in fact – opened its doors to new members.
A) NO CHANGE
B) musical ensemble
C) musical groups
D) groups of musician

10 The student government could not agree amongst <u>themself</u> about how best to decorate the spring formal.
A) NO CHANGE
B) themselves'
C) them
D) themselves

11 Over time, the faculty have developed <u>procedure</u> for dealing with tardy or absent students.
A) NO CHANGE
B) a procedures
C) procedures
D) procedure's

12 The candles were put in the <u>holder</u> and tastefully situated throughout the apartment.
A) NO CHANGE
B) holders
C) votive
D) candlestick

Logical Comparison
(Answers & explanations on page 370).
Where noun-agreement requires that related nouns agree in number, questions in the logical comparison category test the student's ability to ensure that logical comparisons (between nouns) are being made.

1 Temperatures in Antarctica can be much, much colder than <u>Africa</u>.
A) NO CHANGE
B) all of Africa
C) those in Africa
D) some of Africa

2 The weight of a Bengal tiger is greater than <u>common house cats</u>.
A) NO CHANGE
B) all common house cats
C) a common house cat
D) that of a common house cat

The Tutorverse

3 The price of some handbags can be higher than <u>the price of other accessories,</u> though all handbags essentially serve the same purpose.
A) NO CHANGE
B) the price of some other things
C) most other accessories
D) the price of other handbags

4 Like <u>yesterday,</u> the front page of today's newspaper was plastered with details of the politician's scandal.
A) NO CHANGE
B) yesterday's cover
C) the day before
D) the previous day

5 The amount of potassium found in a kiwifruit is comparable to <u>that found in a banana.</u>
A) NO CHANGE
B) a banana
C) bananas
D) those bananas

6 After a year, the chef concluded that Marcus' ability to make delicious sauces was better than <u>anyone else.</u>
A) NO CHANGE
B) anyone else's skill
C) anyone he had ever seen
D) anyone else's sauce

7 The opportunities afforded to graduates of elite universities can be very different from <u>some non-graduates.</u>
A) NO CHANGE
B) other people
C) those afforded to non-graduates
D) those afforded to other degrees

8 Hummingbirds must drink many times their bodyweight in order to sustain their high metabolism, consuming more calories per ounce than <u>many other animals do.</u>
A) NO CHANGE
B) the consumption of other animals
C) calories of other animals
D) ounces of other animals

9 The amount of lead in crystal glassware is much higher than <u>normal, everyday glassware.</u>
A) NO CHANGE
B) normal, everyday glasswares
C) any normal, everyday glassware
D) what is found in normal, everyday glassware

10 Many believe that bagels made in New York City are superior <u>to Los Angeles</u> due to differences in the water used in the boiling process.
A) NO CHANGE
B) to those made in Los Angeles
C) from Los Angeles'
D) to Los Angeles'

11 For the most part, sports cars have a greater capacity for acceleration and a higher maximum top speed than <u>do minivans.</u>
A) NO CHANGE
B) other sports cars
C) all cars
D) machines

12 New Yorkers are often divided on whether the West Side is <u>better than living on the East Side.</u>
A) NO CHANGE
B) better than life on the East Side
C) better than the East Side
D) better than living life on the East Side

The Tutorverse

Frequently Confused Words

(Answers & explanations on page 371).

These questions test the student's ability to distinguish among frequently misused words.

1 Regular exercise and a balanced diet are important to <u>you're</u> health and wellbeing.
A) NO CHANGE
B) your
C) yore
D) you've

2 By signing a contract, the parties to the contract each <u>except</u> the terms and conditions.
A) NO CHANGE
B) accept
C) excerpt
D) exert

3 Not sure how her friends had convinced her to see the scary movie, Jamie could not <u>bare</u> to watch without covering her eyes with her fingers.
A) NO CHANGE
B) bore
C) beer
D) bear

4 Unable to speak the local language, Jonas decided that the strange noises were in fact meant as a <u>complement</u>.
A) NO CHANGE
B) compilation
C) compliment
D) complication

5 <u>Whether</u> or not the students pass the test is incumbent solely on how much they study.
A) NO CHANGE
B) Weather
C) Wether
D) Wither

6 In order to reach the evil genius' secret lair, one must travel <u>threw</u> a dark and treacherous tunnel.
A) NO CHANGE
B) thorough
C) through
D) throughout

7 As soon as he realized that he had forgotten his keys, he remembered that he had forgotten his <u>wallet, to</u>.
A) NO CHANGE
B) wallet two
C) wallet, two
D) wallet, too

8 <u>In they're</u> excitement to go to the beach, they barely remembered to pick up sunscreen from the store.
A) NO CHANGE
B) In their
C) In there
D) In those

9 In my school, it is the vice principal's responsibility to <u>mete</u> out any necessary disciplinary actions in accordance with the school's policies.
A) NO CHANGE
B) meet
C) meter
D) meat

10 Jennifer, who did not enjoy more mainstream attractions, declined to see the crowded and touristy <u>sight</u>.
A) NO CHANGE
B) sighs
C) sights
D) cites

11 In order to test the team's <u>meddle</u>, the coach always ran an exhausting practice during the first week of the season.
A) NO CHANGE
B) mettle
C) metal
D) medal

12 Movie trailers are designed to <u>peak</u> the interest of potential moviegoers.
A) NO CHANGE
B) pick
C) pique
D) peek

The Tutorverse

Conventional Expression

(Answers & explanations on page 371).

These questions test the student's ability to choose the most appropriate common expressions. This may involve identifying mondegreens and choosing correct idioms.

1   Learning to ride a bike can be an abject lesson in the value of perseverance; despite falling off the first few times, most people are eventually able to ride without assistance.
A)   NO CHANGE
B)   an object lesson
C)   an expensive lesson
D)   an unreal lesson

2   The customer stared incredulously at the instructions that read, "Please fax a copy to our office." He could not believe that, in this day in age, he needed to fax anything.
A)   NO CHANGE
B)   day on age
C)   day or age
D)   day and age

3   For some people, an expensive bottle of wine and a good-tasting bottle of wine are one and the same.
A)   NO CHANGE
B)   one in the same
C)   one of the same
D)   one or the same

4   The feud between the Hatfields and the McCoys, two families each with a deep-seeded hatred for the other, is a well-known story.
A)   NO CHANGE
B)   depleted
C)   deep-seated
D)   deep seeded

5   With such a huge lead over the visiting team, the elated fans of the home team knew, for all intensive purposes, that the game was over.
A)   NO CHANGE
B)   for every intent and purpose
C)   for each intensive purpose
D)   for all intents and purposes

6   I've seen bad movies before, but the latest animated film based on Shakespeare's *Macbeth* really takes the cake!
A)   NO CHANGE
B)   tastes the cake
C)   bakes the cake
D)   sells the cake

7   Problems with the roof and foundation becoming apparent only after we purchased the house, the town government, to insult and to injure, advised us that the entire second floor did not have the proper permits and would need to be torn down.
A)   NO CHANGE
B)   add insult to injury
C)   insult and injure
D)   insure and inspect

8   Despite thousands of hours of planning, research, and development, the new show failed to impress test audiences. The writers and producers of the show had no choice but to go back to the drawing board.
A)   NO CHANGE
B)   back to the drawing room
C)   back into the drawing room
D)   back on the drawing board

9   Though Avery only admitted that she felt within the weather, her mother knew, given her fever and lack of appetite, that she was actually very sick.
A)   NO CHANGE
B)   on top of the weather
C)   throughout the weather
D)   under the weather

10   Having spent the last several weeks compiling and cataloging evidence, the attorney said to the defendant, "There's nothing more we can do. The ball is in court."
A)   NO CHANGE
B)   in the court
C)   in their court
D)   on their court

The Tutorverse

11 It was unlike Valentine to <u>beat through the bush</u>; Jill knew him to be much more candid and open with his opinions, sometimes being so forthright that his honesty offended those unaccustomed to his personality.
A) NO CHANGE
B) beat around the bush
C) beat into the bush
D) beat the bush

12 Swarup, having waited all day to tell his father about his college acceptance, was just about to share the good news when his mother nonchalantly <u>heard it straight from the horse's mouth</u>.
A) NO CHANGE
B) let sleeping dogs lie
C) pulled the wool over his eyes
D) let the cat out of the bag

End-of-Sentence Punctuation

(Answers & explanations on page 372).

The questions in this category focus on the appropriate use of punctuation to conclude a sentence.

1 Do you know what will be covered on tomorrow's <u>test!</u>
A) NO CHANGE
B) test?
C) test.
D) test…

2 Someday, I would very much like to travel <u>to Africa?</u>
A) NO CHANGE
B) to Africa –
C) to Africa,
D) to Africa.

3 The tennis match was the most exciting game I had <u>ever seen!</u>
A) NO CHANGE
B) ever seen?
C) ever seen;
D) ever seen:

4 The students were all very excited for the <u>field trip.</u>
A) NO CHANGE
B) field trip…
C) field trip?
D) field trip –

5 After turning left onto Grand Street, walk three more blocks and then turn right onto <u>Main Street:</u>
A) NO CHANGE
B) Main Street,
C) Main Street.
D) Main Street?

6 Miranda asked, "Where are the boots that match <u>this belt</u>"?
A) NO CHANGE
B) this belt?".
C) this belt?"
D) this belt?

7 Did Ashley really say, "It's none of <u>your business?"</u>
A) NO CHANGE
B) your business"?
C) your business."?
D) your business"

8 I can't believe Bill just yelled, "We're not going to take <u>it anymore!"</u>
A) NO CHANGE
B) it anymore!"!
C) it anymore"!
D) it anymore!".

9 Once she reached the top of the mountain, the hiker shouted, "I'm on top of <u>the world…"</u>
A) NO CHANGE
B) the world!"
C) the world".
D) world?"

10 When I tripped and fell, the first thing my mother said to me was, "You should really be <u>more careful".</u>
A) NO CHANGE
B) more careful."
C) more careful…"
D) more careful"…

The Tutorverse

11 "You can't do this to me!" Walt shouted at Jessie. "Don't you know <u>who I am?"</u>
    A) NO CHANGE
    B) who I am."
    C) who I am"!
    D) who I am"?

12 In reply to the waiter's question, Sharon said, "I'm allergic to <u>shellfish." "Is</u> the bread freshly baked?"
    A) NO CHANGE
    B) shellfish"; "Is
    C) shellfish: is
    D) shellfish. Is

Within-Sentence Punctuation

(Answers & explanations on page 373).

The questions in this category focus on the appropriate use of punctuation within sentences.

1 Jordan always said he only needed two things to be ha<u>ppy, friends</u> and family.
    A) NO CHANGE
    B) happy: friends
    C) happy; friends
    D) happy…friends

2 Sarah was eager to return home to see her childhood <u>friends – if</u> she could get a ride!
    A) NO CHANGE
    B) friends: if
    C) friends; if
    D) friends. If

3 The influential restaurant critic was famously <u>ill-tempered, therefore,</u> the restaurant staff worked diligently to make him happy.
    A) NO CHANGE
    B) ill-tempered – as such
    C) ill-tempered; therefore
    D) ill-tempered: as such

4 Because she had recently moved to a new <u>city Beverly</u> was sometimes lonely.
    A) NO CHANGE
    B) city, Beverly
    C) city; Beverly
    D) city: Beverly

5 California is suffering from a major <u>drought; umbrellas</u> are a common sight in the rainy city of London.
    A) NO CHANGE
    B) drought, umbrellas
    C) drought – umbrellas
    D) drought. Umbrellas

6 Forgetting to set her alarm <u>clock; the</u> star athlete was late for her big game and caused her team to lose the important match.
    A) NO CHANGE
    B) clock, the
    C) clock – the
    D) clock: the

7 Percy had stayed up too late watching <u>television, thus;</u> he was late for his first meeting of the day.
    A) NO CHANGE
    B) television – thus,
    C) television. Thus;
    D) television; thus,

8 The firefighters were <u>perplexed when the brick building on the corner</u> spontaneously caught fire.
    A) NO CHANGE
    B) perplexed, when the brick building on the corner
    C) perplexed when the brick building, on the corner
    D) perplexed when the brick building on the corner,

9 The <u>sleek stealthy</u> cat pounced on the unsuspecting mouse.
    A) NO CHANGE
    B) sleek…stealthy
    C) sleek, stealthy
    D) sleek; stealthy

The Tutorverse

10 "Watch out for that tree!", shouted the narrator.
A) NO CHANGE
B) tree!," shouted
C) tree!" shouted
D) tree,"! shouted

11 Galileo Galilei was a famous scientist born in the sixteenth century.
A) NO CHANGE
B) sixteenth-century.
C) sixteenth centuries.
D) sixteenth-centuries.

12 It is important to observe proper technique when brushing one's teeth; brushing with too much force, for example, can injure the gums and wear enamel.
A) NO CHANGE
B) teeth, brushing
C) teeth – brushing
D) teeth: brushing

Punctuating a Series

(Answers & explanations on page 374).

These questions test the student's ability to identify and modify punctuation (such as commas, colons, and semicolons) used to designate and separate items in a list or series.

1 Today is a beautiful day because the sun is shining, the birds are singing, and the breeze is blowing gently.
A) NO CHANGE
B) shining the
C) shining – the
D) shining: the

2 Many health experts advise people to limit their consumption of fast foods because of high levels of fat salt and cholesterol.
A) NO CHANGE
B) fat, salt,
C) fat salt,
D) fat; salt,

3 The teacher asked his students to bring three items on the field trip, sunscreen, money for lunch, and a pen.
A) NO CHANGE
B) trip; sunscreen
C) trip: sunscreen
D) trip. Sunscreen

4 During my career, I have worked in three different places: Phoenix, Arizona, New York City, and San Francisco.
A) NO CHANGE
B) Arizona; New York City; and
C) Arizona; New York City: and
D) Arizona, New York City;

5 The three coworkers – Cheryl, Blake and Daniel – often argued about the right way to perform their shared responsibilities.
A) NO CHANGE
B) coworkers, Cheryl, Blake, and Daniel,
C) coworkers; Cheryl, and Blake, and Daniel
D) coworkers, Cheryl; Blake; and Daniel;

6 The Kingfisher a yacht and a sailboat participated in a dangerous three-way race around the globe.
A) NO CHANGE
B) Kingfisher, a yacht, and a sailboat
C) Kingfisher; a yacht; and a sailboat
D) Kingfisher, a yacht and a sailboat,

7 Cooking is one of my favorite pastimes: it relaxes, rejuvenates, and refreshes my mind; it affords me an opportunity to work with my hands; and it provides me with something delicious to eat.
A) NO CHANGE
B) pastimes, it relaxes, rejuvenates
C) pastimes; it relaxes; rejuvenates
D) pastimes: it relaxes; rejuvenates

The Tutorverse

8 For many, gardening <u>is a</u> great way to relieve stress, enjoy the outdoors, and get some exercise.
A) NO CHANGE
B) is: a
C) is; a
D) is – a

9 Holidays offer many people a great opportunity to enjoy time with friends and <u>family and donate</u> time, money, or goods to charitable organizations; and otherwise relax by the fireplace with a good book.
A) NO CHANGE
B) family donate
C) family; donate
D) family: donate

10 When determining the path of a projectile, it is important to consider several <u>factors; velocity</u>, or the speed that the projectile travels; acceleration, or the rate at which the velocity changes; and the effect of gravity on both the velocity and acceleration.
A) NO CHANGE
B) factors: velocity
C) factors, velocity
D) factors. Velocity

11 The term "succulents" can refer to a number of different <u>plants; such as the</u> baby jade, giant agave, and pincushion cactus.
A) NO CHANGE
B) plants. Such as the
C) plants, such as the
D) plants: such as the

12 Before you leave for vacation, <u>remember, close the windows – set the alarm – and lock the door</u>.
A) NO CHANGE
B) remember: to close the windows, set the alarm, and lock the door
C) remember to close the windows, set the alarm, and lock the door
D) remember; close the windows; set the alarm; and lock the door

Parenthetical Expressions & Nonrestrictive Clauses

(Answers & explanations on page 375).

Nonrestrictive clauses and parenthetical expressions refer to those elements of a sentence that are unessential to the sentence's core meaning. The questions in this category require the student to identify and properly punctuate such elements.

1 Though Marcus hated getting <u>wet, almost</u> as much as a cat hates getting wet, he decided that participating in the charity water balloon toss was worth the risk.
A) NO CHANGE
B) wet – almost
C) wet (almost
D) wet, (almost

2 Good oral hygiene is a matter of routine – that is, doing something repeatedly until it becomes second <u>nature – and</u> technique.
A) NO CHANGE
B) nature, and
C) nature) and
D) nature, – and

The Tutorverse

3 Though Adam dislikes eating eggs, he loves pasta with _carbonara (a traditional_ Italian sauce made with egg and cheese).
A) NO CHANGE
B) _carbonara,_ (which is a traditional
C) _carbonara,_ which, is a traditional
D) _carbonara,_ a traditional

4 Miniature golf which is also known as "mini golf" is a game that is popular with children and adults alike.
A) NO CHANGE
B) golf, which is also known as "mini golf," is
C) golf which is also known as "mini golf," is
D) golf, which is also known as "mini golf" is

5 The nearby residents questioned why the boat (that was docked at the end of the pier) remained there through the winter when other boats usually left for warmer waters.
A) NO CHANGE
B) boat, that was docked at the end of the pier, remained
C) boat that was docked at the end of the pier, remained
D) boat that was docked at the end of the pier remained

6 The questions – that confuse patients the most are those that are phrased in medical jargon that only trained professionals understand.
A) NO CHANGE
B) questions, which
C) questions that
D) questions – which

7 There was no question that in the days and weeks to come, residents of the town devastated by the hurricane would face many difficult challenges.
A) NO CHANGE
B) question, that, in
C) question that, in
D) question that (in

8 Under the mistaken impression – probably caused by his unfamiliarity with the local culture – Frank realized that the food on display was not, in fact, free.
A) NO CHANGE
B) impression – probably,
C) impression, which was
D) impression, that was

9 Judge Jamie who was famous for throwing the book at repeat offenders, surprised the media with her surprisingly and uncharacteristically lenient sentence.
A) NO CHANGE
B) Jamie, who
C) Jamie – who
D) Jamie (who

10 The politicians, who refused to pledge allegiance to the new government's manifesto were immediately put under surveillance for possibly harboring treasonous sympathies.
A) NO CHANGE
B) politicians (who
C) politicians, (who
D) politicians who

11 Unable to decide which color to paint the walls (turquoise was so calming, but ocher so warming), the client instructed the interior decorator to flip a coin.
A) NO CHANGE
B) walls, turquoise was so calming, but ocher so warming, the
C) walls, turquoise was so calming, but ocher so warming – the
D) walls (turquoise was so calming, but ocher so warming) the

12 The family was amazed and ecstatic that the antique steamer trunk, which crossed the Atlantic on the Mayflower, sat unscathed in the ashes of the fire.
A) NO CHANGE
B) trunk which
C) trunk. Which
D) trunk; which

The Tutorverse

Unnecessary Punctuation

(Answers & explanations on page 376).

Punctuation must only be used where required; the questions in this category test the student's ability to identify and remove extraneous punctuation.

1 Cheetahs are one of nature's most effective <u>hunters possessing</u> both stealth and speed.
   A)   NO CHANGE
   B)   hunters possessing,
   C)   hunters, and
   D)   hunters, possessing

2 Over the roar of the crowd, Cindy yelled, "Doesn't this <u>music rock, Brenda?</u>"
   A)   NO CHANGE
   B)   music rock Brenda
   C)   music, rock, Brenda
   D)   music, rock Brenda

3 Eventually undergoing a <u>vibrant rejuvenation, the</u> city's piers, once used by merchants and titans of commerce, suffered from widespread neglect for over a decade.
   A)   NO CHANGE
   B)   vibrant rejuvenation the
   C)   vibrant, rejuvenation, the
   D)   vibrant, rejuvenation the

4 When the <u>cold rainy season</u> sets in, many of the city's residents believe that they suffer from Seasonal Affective Disorder, or a type of depression that is related to changes in general weather patterns.
   A)   NO CHANGE
   B)   cold, rainy season
   C)   cold, rainy, season
   D)   cold and rainy, season

5 Multinational <u>corporations often very large and bureaucratic,</u> use their size and influence to their advantage by lobbying politicians and otherwise influencing public policy.
   A)   NO CHANGE
   B)   corporations often very large and bureaucratic
   C)   corporations, often very large and bureaucratic,
   D)   corporations, often very large and bureaucratic

6 In the past, physicians would often send their patients to convalesce in an <u>out-of-the-way town</u> surrounded by bucolic countryside.
   A)   NO CHANGE
   B)   out of the way town
   C)   out of the way, town
   D)   out, of the way, town

7 Until scientists downgraded Pluto from a planet to a dwarf <u>planet there</u> were nine planets in our solar system.
   A)   NO CHANGE
   B)   planet, there
   C)   planet. There
   D)   planet; there

8 Investment in scientific and medical advancement is something that <u>experts on all sides</u> of the <u>political spectrum</u> tend to deem important.
   A)   NO CHANGE
   B)   experts, on all sides, of the political spectrum,
   C)   experts, on all sides of the political spectrum
   D)   experts on all sides of the political spectrum,

9 Some <u>research, suggests that the rise of 24-hour-a-day news stations</u> contributes to feelings of nervousness and anxiety among the elderly.
   A)   NO CHANGE
   B)   research suggests that, the rise, of 24-hour-a-day news stations,
   C)   research, suggests that the rise of 24-hour-a-day news stations,
   D)   research suggests that the rise of 24-hour-a-day news stations

10 Though, on the surface, there appear to be many differences between Eastern and Western <u>philosophy, closer</u> examination of these schools of thought reveals the fact that many core principles are, in fact, very similar.

A) NO CHANGE
B) philosophy closer
C) philosophy; closer
D) philosophy. Closer

11 From the shores of <u>Aruba it's possible, on a clear, sunny day</u> to see all the way to the South American continent.

A) NO CHANGE
B) Aruba it's possible on a clear sunny day
C) Aruba, it's possible, on a clear, sunny day,
D) Aruba, it's possible, on a clear sunny day,

12 The cookie jar was placed high on a <u>hard to reach</u> shelf.

A) NO CHANGE
B) hard-to-reach
C) hard, to reach,
D) hard to reach,

Guided Practice – Improving Expression

Directions: Each of the following passages is accompanied by several questions. These questions will ask you to consider how to revise the passage in order to improve the expression of ideas. A passage may be accompanied by one or more graphics (such as charts, tables, or graphs) that you must consider when assessing revisions. Some questions will address underlined portions of a passage. Others will ask you to assess a specific place in a passage, or assess the passage as a whole.

Read each passage and choose the answer to each question that most effectively improves the passage's quality of writing. Some questions include an answer choice of "NO CHANGE," which you should choose if it is best to leave the relevant part of the passage unchanged.

The Gambler's Fallacy *(Answers & explanations on page 377).*

--- 1 ---

If you flip a standard, perfectly balanced American coin, what are the chances that it will land heads-side up?

--- 2 ---

You would be right to predict that there would be a 50% chance that the coin will land heads-side up. In this case, the statistical laws governing the probability of a coin landing heads-side up aligns closely with intuition and our everyday experiences.

--- 3 ---

Now, **1** <u>maybe</u> consider the following scenario. Imagine that you have just seen a coin being flipped ten times in a row, and each time the coin has landed heads-side up. **2** <u>You are told that the coin is perfectly fair and balanced. You are then asked to predict the outcome of an eleventh coin flip.</u> What would you do? In this scenario, is a tails-side up result any more or less likely than a heads-side up result?

1 *[Style/Tone]*
The writer wants to convey an informal tone, consistent with the rest of the passage. Which choice best accomplishes this goal?
A) NO CHANGE
B) let's
C) you must
D) I invite you to

2 *[Syntax]*
Which choice most effectively combines the underlined sentences?
A) You are told that the coin is perfectly fair and balanced and are asked to predict the outcome of an eleventh coin flip.
B) You are told that the coin is perfectly fair and balance and you are asked by someone to predict the outcome of an eleventh coin flip.
C) You are told that the coin is perfectly fair and balanced whose outcome can be predicted.
D) You are told that the coin is perfectly fair and balanced and must predict the outcome of an eleventh coin flip?

The Tutorverse

--- 4 ---

Like many cognitive biases, The Fallacy is observable in real-world behavior. **3** A famous example of The Fallacy influencing people's behavior took place in 1913, at a casino in Monte Carlo. The game? Roulette. The result? The loss of millions of francs.

--- 5 ---

In psychology, the term *cognitive bias* refers to any type of reasoning that deviates from rational judgment. In the scenario described above, the most rational **4** judgement would be to follow the statistical law that each flip of a coin is independent of other flips. To deviate from this law – in this case, by assigning greater probability of one outcome over another based on previous outcomes – is an example of a cognitive bias called The Gambler's Fallacy. In the scenario imagined above, to believe that "I have seen an unusually high number of heads-side up outcomes, so surely the next outcome of a coin flip will be tails-side up" is to succumb to The Gambler's Fallacy. The Fallacy is a powerful example of what happens when **5** intuition and everyday experiences are prioritized over statistical law and rational thought.

3 *[Support]*

At this point, the writer is considering whether or not to add the following information:

In fact, many controlled experiments and studies confirm that The Fallacy is real.

Should the addition be made here?

A) Yes, because the sentence supports the primary purpose of the paragraph.

B) Yes, because the information is relevant to information described later in the passage.

C) No, because the information is irrelevant to the scenario imagined earlier in the passage.

D) No, because the sentence does not support the primary purpose of the paragraph.

4 *[Precision]*

A) NO CHANGE

B) decision

C) conviction

D) certitude

5 *[Proposition]*

Which choice most clearly ends the paragraph with a restatement of the writer's primary claim?

A) NO CHANGE

B) people unfairly prioritize rational thought over everyday experiences.

C) psychologists classify cognitive disorders based on everyday experiences.

D) statistical law trumps powerful, intuitive experiences.

--- 6 ---

In European roulette, a slotted wheel with 37 small pockets is spun in one direction, and a ball is spun in the other direction on a track along the circumference of the wheel, just above the pockets. Each slot is **6** <u>non-sequentially numbered</u>, and each number is alternatingly colored red or black **7** <u>(with the exception of the number zero, which is colored green)</u>. Among other ways to win, gamblers can choose to bet on whether the ball will come to rest in a red, black, or green slot. **8**

6 *[Concision]*
A) NO CHANGE
B) purposefully and randomly numbered
C) numbered in a way that can be confusing even for professional gamblers
D) numbered such that no consecutive numbers are next to each other

7 *[Focus]*
The writer is considering removing the underlined part of the sentence. Should the underlined part remain, or be removed?
A) Remain, because it helps illustrate the appearance of a roulette wheel.
B) Remain, because it is important to the reader's understanding of different roulette outcomes.
C) Removed, because it confuses the reader and complicates the passage.
D) Removed, because the information is irrelevant to the various outcomes of a game of roulette.

8 *[Organization]*
Which choice most effectively sets up the information that follows?
A) In American roulette, there are 38 small pockets due to the inclusion of a double-zero slot, which also adds another green pocket to the wheel.
B) Another way to win at roulette is to bet on which number the ball will land on – a bet that has a low probability, but a high payout.
C) Some gamblers like to bet on red, while others prefer black; regardless of the color preference, these players have a similar chance to win.
D) On August 18, 1913, the ball landed on black-colored slots 26 times in a row, a highly improbable – but not impossible – occurrence.

The Tutorverse

--- 7 ---

By the time the ball came to rest on a black slot for the fifteenth time in a row – **9** an already unbelievably rare run – The Gambler's Fallacy had already begun to influence the gamblers' behavior. Players began to increase their bets significantly, assuming that the next ball *had* to land on a red slot. For the next eleven spins of the wheel, these bettors lost their ever-growing wagers. By the end of the run, the casino had made millions of francs.

Probability of a Ball Landing on Black (European Roulette)	
Number of Consecutive Spins	Probability
1	0.48649
2	0.23667
3	0.11514
4	0.05601
5	0.02725
6	0.01326
7	0.00645
8	0.00314
9	0.00153
10	0.00074
11	0.00036
12	0.00018
13	0.00009
14	0.00004
15	0.00002

Question 10 asks about the passage in its entirety.

9 *[Quantitative Information]*
At this point, the author is considering revising the underlined portion with specific information from the table that supports the central idea of the sentence. Which choice most effectively replaces the underlined portion?
A) NO CHANGE
B) an outcome with nearly a 1 in 2 chance of happening
C) an outcome with only a 2 in 100,000 chance of happening
D) an outcome with a seven in a billion chance of happening

Consider the passage as a whole when answering question 10.

10 *[Logical Sequence]*
In order to make the passage most logical, paragraph 4 should
A) remain where it is now.
B) be moved after paragraph 5.
C) be moved after paragraph 1.
D) be moved before paragraph 7.

Stranger in a Brave New Land *(Answers & explanations on page 377).*

The term "science-fiction" was coined in the **1** 1920s and it was thought up by writer and editor Hugo Gernsback, who was influenced by writers Edgar Allan Poe, H.G. Wells, and Jules Verne, among others. Since its inception, science-fiction literature has been characterized by prophetic, speculative, and sometimes dystopian themes. Though often set in far-away lands and alien environments, the themes discussed in science-fiction literature are always, in some way, relevant to contemporary society. **2** Science-fiction authors continue to explore the unknown by challenging preconceived ideas and subjecting norms to extenuating circumstances. **3** Science-fiction literature is an important genre that should continue to be studied today.

1 *[Concision]*
A) NO CHANGE
B) 1920s. Hugo Gernsback, writer and editor,
C) 1920s. Writer and editor
D) 1920s by writer and editor

2 *[Support]*
The writer wants to add a sentence in this spot. Which sentence is the best choice?
A) During and immediately after the Cold War period, for example, themes involving space travel and nuclear proliferation were a reaction to the perils of space travel and Cold War anxiety.
B) Science-fiction writers often create plots and stories that are firmly rooted in and limited to modern society's current body of knowledge.
C) Writers were looking at important issues of the time, and this was seen in their works.
D) Science-fiction writers usually lived in the past, often focused on learning from history.

3 *[Proposition]*
Which statement most effectively replaces the underlined sentence as a closing statement for the paragraph?
A) Science fiction literature has always been relevant to the contemporary world, despite – or because of – its technologically-saturated and futuristic settings.
B) Even though it has not been as popular as other genres, it is still an important genre to study.
C) With themes that are irrelevant to society, science-fiction literature is always an important genre to study.
D) Science-fiction literature needs to be studied as many other forms of literature are derivative of this genre.

The Tutorverse

Science fiction literature has looked beyond the confines of terrestrial knowledge while simultaneously presenting critiques of contemporary society. Robert Heinlein, one of the "Big Three" science-fiction writers (along with Isaac Asimov and Arthur C. Clarke), considered the effects that space travel would have on **4** humans. Science-fiction writer Robert Heinlein's works simultaneously delved into conformist themes in human society. His 1961 novel *Stranger in a Strange Land*, considered one of the most popular works of science-fiction, deals with religion, institutions, and the idea of cultural relativism.

Authors in this genre have also focused on technological innovation. Arthur C. Clarke, a leader of British science-fiction, is most widely known for the novel *2001: A Space Odyssey*. In this novel, Clarke touched on a wide range of themes, notably the perils of technology and its influence on humanity. Clarke, like other notable science-fiction writers, explored the possibilities of technological progress. **5**

Novel	Novel Publish Year	Technology Predicted	Technology Creation Year
From Earth To The Moon	1865	Moon Landing	1969
Looking Backward	1888	Debit Card	1977
The Land Ironclads	1903	Tanks	1916
Brave New World	1931	Anti-depressants	1950

4 *[Syntax]*
At the underlined part, which answer choice most effectively combines the two sentences?
A) humans; this famous writer
B) humans, and
C) humans; notably his works might
D) humans: he also wrote works that

5 *[Quantitative Information]*
The author would like to add one of the following sentences at this point. Using the information graphic provided, which sentence is most appropriate?
A) Science-fiction writers are the primary source of ideas for new inventions and innovations.
B) Only the most scientifically trained science-fiction writers are able to successfully predict future technologies.
C) Though creative, writers of science-fiction literature are rarely successful in their imaginings of future technologies.
D) In fact, the Big Three are known for predicting technological advances, sometimes decades before their realization.

The Tutorverse

Science-fiction literature also confronts issues of chaos and turmoil, often brought about by human society's reactions to cataclysmic events. **6** <u>Isaac Asimov, a professor of biochemistry, focused on themes of human society and the human condition.</u> His short story "Nightfall" (1941), widely regarded as one of the most important works in the genre, is a story of a planet named Lagath that is bathed in constant illumination by six suns. Lagath is soon threatened by the coming of darkness, a result of an eclipse of one of its suns. **7** <u>Asimov uses this setting to address some pressing social and cultural issues.</u>

[1] In *Brave New World* (1932), British author Aldous Huxley **8** <u>construed</u> a world in which scientific advancement resulted in fundamental changes in society. [2] Over eight decades later, Huxley's novel, which contemplates ideas of autonomy, identity, and population control, is still read widely in schools and universities. [3] **9** <u>Today,</u> we see the influence of science-fiction literature in the media, and even in the classroom. [4] The ideas of Huxley and "the Big Three" are still relevant today, with similar themes even being explored in popular films, such as *The Matrix* and *Gravity.* **10**

6 *[Style/Tone]*
A) NO CHANGE
B) Isaac Asimov focused on themes of human society and the human condition, and he was a professor of biochemistry.
C) A professor of biochemistry, Isaac Asimov focused on themes of human society and the human condition.
D) Isaac Asimov was a professor of biochemistry. He focused on themes of human society and the human condition.

7 *[Focus]*
The author is considering the following revisions. Which answer choice illustrates the best possible revision?
A) Asimov uses this story to warn about the dangers of human behavior.
B) In this story, Asimov sees the perils of human nature.
C) This story is a good example of the themes that science-fiction literature addresses.
D) Asimov uses this setting to speculate on the behaviors of human society when faced with an apocalyptic event.

8 *[Precision]*
A) NO CHANGE
B) supposed
C) imagined
D) conveyed

9 *[Organization]*
Which choice provides the most logical introduction to the sentence?
A) NO CHANGE
B) Eventually
C) Someday
D) Nevertheless

10 *[Logical Sequence]*
In order to make this paragraph most logical, sentence 3 should
A) remain where it is now.
B) be moved before sentence 1.
C) be moved after sentence 1.
D) be moved after sentence 4.

The Tutorverse

Can You Hear Me? *(Answers & explanations on page 378).*

As congestion and traffic jams in major cities gum up aging and overcrowded roadways, and businesses grow and scale internationally, telecommuting is becoming an increasingly attractive option for employers and employees alike.

[1] Telecommuting, sometimes called remote work or telework, is a work arrangement in which the employee does not necessarily work from a centralized or main office. [2] Better technology has allowed many employees to work away from a main office, as long as they have access to the internet. [3] There are two schools of thought on the practice: it either decreases or increases productivity. [4] However, more evidence supports the idea that working remotely can increase productivity and decrease stress, leading to a happier and more satisfied workforce. [5] Some say working from home leads to employees goofing off and being less productive. **1**

Removing or minimizing commutes is a key part of **2** creating less stress for employees who have long commutes that are stressful. **3** Most commuters experience the same type of stress. One such stressor is related to the monetary cost associated with commuting, which can be high whether one drives or takes mass transit. Annually, the average telecommuter spends nearly $7,000 less on transportation than do their commuter counterparts. Another such stressor is related to physical health. Sitting for extended periods of time, and the stress of maneuvering through heavy traffic, can cause commuters to gain weight, develop back problems, have higher blood pressure, and be at higher risk for heart attack. Psychologically, workers who commute more than 45 minutes each day are also **4** generally less happy.

1 *[Logical Sequence]*
To make this paragraph most logical, sentence 4 should be placed
A)   where it is now.
B)   before sentence 2.
C)   before sentence 3.
D)   after sentence 5.

2 *[Concision]*
A)   NO CHANGE
B)   reducing stress for people who would otherwise have to travel a long distance.
C)   making the lives of employees easier and less prone to stress.
D)   reducing employee stress levels.

3 *[Organization]*
Which choice is most effective to introduce the ideas that follow?
A)   NO CHANGE
B)   Stressors associated with commuting are numerous and varied.
C)   For many office workers, stress is just a part of the job.
D)   Commutes are not as big a stressor as working with a difficult boss.

4 *[Style/Tone]*
A)   NO CHANGE
B)   abjectly miserable and sad.
C)   in need of a good pick-me-up.
D)   working way too hard.

Many studies show that telecommuting has a number of other benefits. Some studies have shown that employees who telecommute are more efficient in and satisfied with both their jobs and personal lives. These employees generally waste less time surfing the Internet or chatting with other **5** <u>employees. They</u> also have more leisure time, as they spend less time on mundane chores and the actual act of commuting.

Companies who allow their workers to telecommute can save money on the work place itself. Many companies have discovered that they are able to decrease the size of their office and reduce **6** <u>overhead costs</u>, such as those associated with furniture, electricity, heating, and cooling. Some proponents of telecommuting suggest that, with reduced operating costs, companies can create new jobs, as well. **7**

5 *[Syntax]*
Which choice most effectively combines the sentences at the underlined portion?
A) NO CHANGE
B) employees, but
C) employees, nevertheless they
D) employees; or they

6 *[Precision]*
A) NO CHANGE
B) overage costs
C) excessive costs
D) superfluous costs

7 *[Focus]*
At this point, the writer is considering adding the following sentence.

Telecommuting can have an environmental impact by causing fewer cars to be on the road.

Should the writer make this addition here?
A) Yes, because it supports the central idea of the paragraph, that telecommuting is good for both employers and employees.
B) Yes, because it provides an additional detail about why telecommuting helps companies.
C) No, because it contradicts the claim that telecommuting is good for employers.
D) No, because it introduces irrelevant details that blurs the focus of the central idea of the paragraph.

The Tutorverse

Telecommuting, however, is not without its drawbacks. Many telecommuters report working during their vacations due to pressure from deadlines or their employees. In fact, many telecommuters feel they need to work harder than they would in the office, due to a lack of visibility. **8** Studies also show that employees who work in environments in which they talk to their coworkers face-to-face tend to be more innovative. As such, telecommuters may not benefit from the creative and innovative synergies associated with working in an office.

Still, the benefits of telecommuting outweigh the drawbacks, and more and more companies and employees seem to recognize this fact. **9** Many employees are interested in telecommuting. **10** Telecommuting is great for everyone.

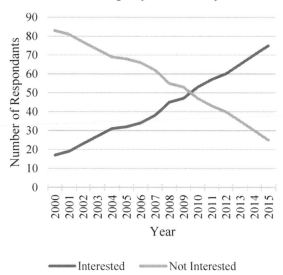

Interest in Telecommuting: 100-Employee Survey

8 *[Support]*
At this point, the writer is considering adding the following sentence.

Traditional offices promote inefficiency among employees, so working remotely is actually an important way to promote productivity.

Should the writer make this addition here?
- A) Yes, because it promotes the central idea of the paragraph, that telecommuting is good for employees.
- B) Yes, because it refutes a claim in the previous sentence that telecommuters are lazy.
- C) No, because it does not support the central idea of the paragraph.
- D) No, because it supports the notion that telecommuting has many benefits.

9 *[Quantitative Information]*
Which proposed revision offers an accurate interpretation of the data in the chart?
- A) NO CHANGE
- B) Over time, more and more people are interested in telecommuting.
- C) Over time, telecommuting has lost some of its appeal.
- D) Virtually all employees are interested in telecommuting.

10 *[Proposition]*
Which choice most clearly ends the passage with a statement of the writer's primary claim?
- A) NO CHANGE
- B) Telecommuting is not for everyone, but some employers offer it to some of their employees.
- C) Telecommuting can benefit employers and employees alike, creating a happier, more productive workforce while simultaneously creating cost savings.
- D) Telecommuting is the best way for employers to save money.

Table For 118, Please *(Answers & explanations on page 378).*

The average person possesses at best a passing understanding of the periodic table of elements; at worst, the table is nothing more than a confusing jumble of letters and numbers. For scientists, however, the periodic table of elements is a living, breathing guide that helps bring order and understanding to the chemical and atomic worlds.

The periodic table of elements, which systematically organizes elements by their atomic number, electron configurations, and chemical properties, **1** takes on many forms and can be represented in many different ways. Indeed, since its 1789 inception, the table has grown from a mere 33 elements to a whopping 118 elements (as of 2015). Antoine de Lavoisier is widely credited with publishing the first list of elements in his *Traité Élémentaire de Chimie* (Elementary Treatise of Chemistry), which included such elements as oxygen, nitrogen, and hydrogen. Curious minds would go on to build upon Lavoisier's work, each adding to his or her predecessor's accomplishments. **2** Alexandre de Chancourtois, in his 1862 publication, identified additional elements and organized them into a spiraling chart that expanded outward according to atomic weight. **3** The then-known 62 elements were classified by John Newlands into eight groups, based on their physical properties, in 1864. It was not until 1869 that Dmitri Mendeleev published a periodic **4** table of elements. This table is similar in organization to the table used today.

1 *[Concision]*
A) NO CHANGE
B) has evolved over time. ✓
C) can be represented in many different and unique ways.
D) has many formats, styles, and types.

2 *[Support]*
At this point, the author wants to add another sentence. Which of the following is most appropriate?
A) Josiah Gibbs, in his 1876 publication, established the concept of free energy.
B) John Dalton, in his 1808 publication, describes atomic theory and the law of multiple proportions.
C) William Proust, in his 1827 publications, classified biomolecules into carbohydrates, lipids, and proteins.
D) Johann Döbereiner, in his 1829 publication, identified more elements and classified them into a table of triads.

3 *[Style/Tone]*
Which of the following choices best maintains the sentence structure previously established in the paragraph?
A) NO CHANGE
B) In 1864, John Newlands classified the then-known 62 elements into eight groups, based on their physical properties.
C) John Newlands, in his 1864 table, classified the then-known 62 elements into eight groups, based on their physical properties.
D) The then-known 62 elements were classified, in 1864, by John Newlands, into eight groups, based on their physical properties.

4 *[Syntax]*
Which choice most effectively combines the sentences at the underlined part?
A) table of elements, similar in organization
B) table of elements which is similar in organization
C) table of elements; similar in organization
D) table of elements similar in organization

The Tutorverse

[1] In his publication, *The Dependence Between the Properties of the Atomic Weights of the Elements,* Mendeleev posited that elements with similar chemical properties have similar or regularly increasing atomic weights; that the more widely diffused elements have similar atomic weights; that there existed many unknown elements, among many other theories. [2] Mendeleev's theories have stood the test of time – they have remained true and have been confirmed by repeatable experiments and new discoveries. **5** [3] Indeed, as the list of known elements grew over the years (as Mendeleev had predicted), the periodic table remained **6** fundamentally unchanged. [4] Mendeleev's table of elements, organized into rows and columns, reflected certain rules and theories that governed the chemical world. **7**

5 *[Quantitative Information]*
At this point, the author is considering adding the following graphic. Should the author include this graphic?

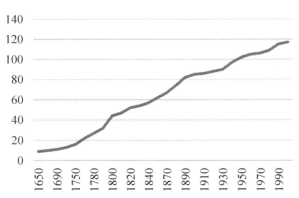

Cumulative Number of Known Elements

A)   Include, because the data on the graph supports the idea that the Mendeleev's theories have stood the test of time.

B)   Include, because the information from the graph illustrates how elements have increasing atomic weights.

C)   Exclude, because the information from the graph shows that the number of known elements has been increasing.

D)   Exclude, because the data on the graph does not support the idea that Mendeleev's theories have stood the test of time.

6 *[Precision]*
A)   NO CHANGE
B)   officially
C)   superficially
D)   surprisingly

7 *[Logical Sequence]*
In order to make this paragraph most logical, sentence 4 should
A)   remain where it is now.
B)   be moved before sentence 1.
C)   be moved before sentence 2.
D)   be moved before sentence 3.

8 Mendeleev's table paved the way for future chemists and physicists, providing a framework for analyzing chemical interactions and behavior. **9** <u>In the near future</u>, illustrious thinkers such as Henry Moseley and Glenn Seaborg were able to use an ever-growing table of elements in their research and experiments. In many ways, even now, in the 21st century – after the 2015 discovery of the 118th element – the periodic table still resembles Mendeleev's original creation. **10** As history has shown, it is likely that the periodic table as we know it will continue to grow and change with each new chemical discovery.

8 *[Proposition]*
Which of the following sentences could most effectively be used as a topic sentence of the paragraph?

A) Mendeleev's table is as useful to scientists today as it was to scientists when he created it.

B) Mendeleev's table was useful during his time, but is no longer relevant in modern science.

C) Mendeleev's contributions to science extend beyond the creation of a lasting periodic table.

D) In order to continue to make discoveries, scientists must study how Mendeleev created his table.

9 *[Organization]*
Which choice provides the most logical transition to the sentence?

A) NO CHANGE

B) Regrettably

C) Subsequently

D) Previously

10 *[Focus]*
At this point, the author is considering including the following sentence:

In fact, Mendeleev's periodic table is so popular that it hangs on the walls of almost every classroom.

Should the author include the sentence?

A) Yes, because it shows how Mendeleev's creation has had a lasting impact, even in modern society.

B) Yes, because it answers a question asked earlier in the passage, resolving a claim made by the author.

C) No, because the sentence is not concerned with describing one of Mendeleev's contributions.

D) No, because the sentence does not relate to how Mendeleev's periodic table has continued to evolve.

Passage-Based Practice – Improving Expression

Directions: Each of the following passages is accompanied by several questions. These questions will ask you to consider how to revise the passage in order to improve the expression of ideas. A passage may be accompanied by one or more graphics (such as charts, tables, or graphs) that you must consider when assessing revisions. Some questions will address underlined portions of a passage. Others will ask you to assess a specific place in a passage, or assess the passage as a whole.

Read each passage and choose the answer to each question that most effectively improves the passage's quality of writing. Some questions include an answer choice of "NO CHANGE," which you should choose if it is best to leave the relevant part of the passage unchanged. Spend no more than 10 minutes per passage & question set.

Junior! *(Answers & explanations on page 379).*

Indiana Jones: fedora-wearing, whip-wielding, satchel-bearing professor, archaeologist, explorer, and treasure-hunter.

Though many have daydreamed about finding long-lost treasures and outsmarting **1** rafts of ill-tempered thugs, few have come close to living out the fictional life of Jones.

Yet few is more than none, and Hiram Bingham III is one of those **2** precious few.

Like Jones, Bingham was a dedicated academic; Bingham received a bachelor's degree from Yale, a master's degree from the University of California, **3** and some additional degrees from Harvard. Bingham was as prolific a teacher as he was a learner, holding teaching positions at Harvard, Princeton, and Yale.

Bingham's interest in South and Latin America is evidenced by the numerous positions he held over the course of his life: lecturer, South American History and Geography (1907-1910); curator, Collections on South American History (1908-1930); **4** professor of Latin American History from 1915 to 1924. Yet Bingham was most famous not for rousing lectures, but for his 1911 expedition to South America that would result in one of the greatest archaeological rediscoveries of the century: the ruins of Machu Picchu.

1
A) NO CHANGE
B) cadres
C) blocs
D) societies ✓

2
A) NO CHANGE
B) exquisite ✓
C) valuable
D) beloved

3
A) NO CHANGE
B) another master's degree from Harvard, and a doctorate from Harvard
C) and another master's degree – as well as a doctorate – from Harvard ✓
D) and, also from Harvard, another master's degree, as well as a doctorate

4 Which of the following maintains the stylistic pattern established earlier in the sentence?
A) NO CHANGE
B) Latin American History professor (1915-1924).
C) professor, from 1915 to 1924, of Latin American History.
D) professor, Latin American History (1915-1924). ✓

[1] Bingham's first trip to the Peruvian town of Cuzco, in 1909, left him yearning to see more of what the Incas had built. [2] During that time, he visited the ruins of Choqquequirau, which was widely believed to be the last capital of the Inca civilization. [3] However, based on his studies, Bingham believed differently: that the last capital of the Incas still remained to be found. [4] Though not a trained archaeologist, Bingham was determined to prove his theory, and organized the 1911 expedition to do so, securing financial support from Yale, the National Geographic Society **5** and taking a sabbatical until further notice. **6**

From Cuzco, Bingham and the rest of the expedition began their exploration, traveling first to Urubamba, then to Ollantaytambo, and on the sixth day after their arrival in Cuzco, to a small plantation called Mandorpampa. **7** According to Bingham's 1913 account of the expedition, published in *National Geographic*, the owner of the Mandorpampa, Melchor Arteaga, made a living selling "grass and pasturage to passing travelers."

5 Which choice best results in a sentence that most closely supports the point developed in the paragraph?
A)   NO CHANGE
B)   and logistical support from both the United States and Peruvian governments.
C)   and suggesting that colleagues from Harvard lead the expedition instead.
D)   and excusing himself from further research responsibilities.

6 The writer wants to add the following sentence somewhere in this paragraph.

With his expedition in tow, Bingham returned to Cuzco in June of 1911.

The most logical placement for this sentence is immediately
A)   after sentence 1.
B)   after sentence 2.
C)   after sentence 3.
D)   after sentence 4.

7 The writers is considering removing the underlined sentence. Should the sentence remain, or be removed?
A)   Remain, because it establishes Melchor's identity.
B)   Remain, because it illustrates the relationship between Melchor and Bingham.
C)   Removed, because it is irrelevant to the comparison between Bingham and Jones.
D)   Removed, because the information blurs the focus of the passage.

The Tutorverse

Upon meeting Melchor, Bingham inquired as to the location of any nearby ruins. **8** <u>Through his interpreter, Bingham learned that there were indeed ruins very close by. He learned that Melchor would be happy to lead the way there.</u>

   9 <u>The rest is, as they say, history.</u>

   Melchor did indeed lead Bingham to the ruins of Machu Picchu. Bingham would go on to orchestrate several more expeditions to excavate, catalogue, and preserve the now-famous ruins. And though Bingham didn't find a long-lost biblical relic or recover any sacred stones from a murderous cult, as Jones did in his famous adventures, **10** <u>Bingham and Jones have more in common than most people realize.</u>

8 Which choice most effectively combines the underlined sentences?

- A) Through his interpreter, Bingham learned that there were indeed ruins very close by – and that Melchor would be happy to lead the way there.
- B) Bingham learned that there were indeed ruins very close by, and that the owner of Mandorpampa would lead him there, with his interpreter.
- C) Bingham's interpreter, who translated what Melchor said, indicated that Melchor would be happy to lead the way to the ruins that were very close by.
- D) Bingham learned, when Melchor replied, through Bingham's translator, that there were ruins nearby, and that he would lead him there.

9 Which choice creates the most effective transition between paragraphs?

- A) NO CHANGE
- B) That's, as they say, all she wrote.
- C) And that's, as they say, the real deal.
- D) And that was, as they say, the final straw.

10 Which choice most effectively results in the best conclusion to the paragraph and passage?

- A) NO CHANGE
- B) many people nevertheless believe Jones was based on Bingham's life.
- C) the descendants of the Incas are grateful to Bingham for recovering their history.
- D) he took credit for a discovery that really wasn't his to take.

Living Shorelines *(Answers & explanations on page 380).*

Many scientists agree that the earth's climate is changing, **1** and that this change has a significant impact on the environment. These scientists warn that a warming global climate is resulting in everything from rising sea levels to more powerful and destructive storms. One of the primary drivers of this climate change is the accumulation of greenhouse gases, such as carbon dioxide, in the atmosphere.

[1] One way to fight climate change is to manage levels of carbon dioxide in the atmosphere. [2] People must actively manage climate change. [3] The National Oceanic and Atmospheric Administration (NOAA) suggests that some coastal ecosystems dubbed "living shorelines" may be one such solution to the problem of excessive atmospheric carbon dioxide. [4] These shorelines are **2** made with natural materials such as plants, sand and rocks. **3**

All plants use carbon dioxide to grow, sequestering atmospheric carbon dioxide in their biomass (such as leaves and roots). The carbon stored in coastal ecosystems **4** is known as coastal blue carbon. A salt marsh is one common type of coastal **5** ecosystem. It can store two to three times as much carbon as an equally sized tropical forest. In North Carolina, for example, the living shorelines developed by scientists at NOAA can store enough carbon to offset 64 metric tons of carbon dioxide each year – the pollution equivalent to burning 7,500 gallons of gasoline. If the entire North Carolina shoreline were developed this way, its 850 miles of coast could combat the pollution equivalent of using more than 100,000 gallons of gasoline.

1 Which choice provides the most appropriate introduction to the passage?
A) NO CHANGE
B) but disagree as to the impact on the environment.
C) but are uncertain as to the environmental impact.
D) and that the impact on global climate remains debatable.

2
A) NO CHANGE
B) protected and stabilized
C) propped up
D) moved or created

3 To make this paragraph most logical, sentence 2 should be placed
A) where it is now.
B) before sentence 1.
C) after sentence 3.
D) after sentence 4.

4
A) NO CHANGE
B) can also be referred to by some as
C) is also, often, called
D) is referred to by people who work there as

5 Which choice most effectively combines the sentences at the underlined portion?
A) ecosystem, but it can
B) ecosystem: it can
C) ecosystem that can
D) ecosystem; however, it can

The sequestration of carbon dioxide is not only limited to salt marshes. NOAA has studied coastal blue carbon in mangrove and seagrass beds, **6** which are also pretty great at carbon storage. In fact, **7** some ecosystems are better at storing carbon than others.

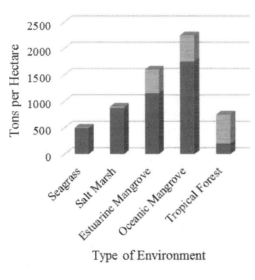

Biomass Profile:
Living Coastlines

Tons per Hectare / Type of Environment

▪ Sequestered Carbon   ▪ Other Biomass

Adapted from the National Oceanic and Atmospheric Administration, 2015.

6
A) NO CHANGE
B) which are pretty nifty ecosystems.
C) which are also lush, gorgeous ecosystems that store critical carbon.
D) which also have a strong capacity to store carbon.

7 Using the data from the graphic provided, which of the following choices would be the best revision to the underlined portion of the sentence?
A) NO CHANGE
B) when measured as a percentage of total biomass, seagrass is among the most efficient carbon sequestration ecosystem.
C) estuarine mangroves can, in terms of total carbon captured per hectare, sequester more carbon than any other ecosystem.
D) salt marshes are the least effective ecosystem when it comes to sequestering carbon.

The Tutorverse

Because coastal environments are so effective and efficient at removing carbon dioxide from the atmosphere, it is crucial to prevent damage to existing coastlines and to bolster at-risk coastlines. When these habitats are destroyed, whether by natural or man-made forces, their ability to capture carbon dioxide is lost. Worse yet, the destruction of coastal habitats releases carbon back into the atmosphere. **8** Living shorelines are gaining attention as natural and effective alternatives to traditional shoreline stabilization techniques, such as the building of sea walls. By reducing erosion and buttressing coastal environments from storms, **9** living shorelines can benefit the ecosystem in terms of food production and water quality improvements.

Reducing and offsetting levels of atmospheric carbon dioxide is an important part of managing climate change. **10** Scientists and volunteer groups can do more to fight against climate change.

8 At this point, the writer is considering adding the following sentence.

The leading cause of destruction to these habitats is development for housing, ports, and other commercial facilities.

Should the writer make this addition here?
A) Yes, because it supports the central idea of the paragraph, that coastal habitats are threatened by man-made forces.
B) Yes, because it provides additional details about the coastal habitats the writer wants to protect.
C) No, because it contradicts the claim that creating sea walls is the only step needed to fight climate change.
D) No, because it introduces irrelevant details that do not support the central idea of the paragraph.

9

A) NO CHANGE
B) conservationists can build a natural wall to prevent erosion.
C) people can prevent the loss of an important habitat that stores carbon.
D) people will have healthier drinking water and cleaner air.

10 Which choice most clearly ends the passage with a statement of the writer's primary claim?
A) NO CHANGE
B) Although climate change is irreversible, there are still things people can do to prevent against the harmful effects of rising temperatures.
C) People should work to build strong living shorelines to keep shores intact and reduce the damaging effects of carbon dioxide.
D) People must do whatever they can to fight the dangerous effects of climate change on our shorelines.

Rosebud *(Answers & explanations on page 380).*

[1] "Rosebud" – the word alone is enough to set movie critics and aficionados atwitter. [2] The word is the first spoken in *Citizen Kane*, which debuted in 1941 and was co-written, directed, and produced by Orson Welles. [3] Critics consistently rank *Citizen Kane* as one of the best movies ever produced. [4] Regular moviegoers appear to share in critics' **1** passion or appreciation; in a recent poll, *Citizen Kane* was ranked as the 67th best movie of all time. **2**

3 But what is it about *Citizen Kane* that so impresses critics? While there are many aspects of the movie that impress critics, it boils down to one thing: innovation. In terms of movie making, *Citizen Kane* **4** was revolutionary, groundbreaking, and progressive, pushing the boundaries of the art form by utilizing novel and creative techniques.

Citizen Kane **5** did not follow a simple chronological order. The movie begins with its protagonist uttering his dying word. From there, the movie flashes back to Kane's childhood, and tells the story of his life from the perspectives of his forgetful associates. The viewer is often uncertain as to whether or not the flashbacks – which often overlap and run into one another – appear in chronological order. **6** Ultimately, what the viewer knows about Kane is unclear, as the narrators are unreliable.

1   Which should the writer add to describe how regular moviegoers feel about *Citizen Kane?*
- A) passion, reserve, or appreciation
- B) passion, furor, or appreciation
- C) passion, conception, or appreciation
- D) passion, admiration, or appreciation

2   To make this paragraph most logical, sentence 4 should be placed
- A) where it is now.
- B) before sentence 1.
- C) before sentence 2.
- D) after sentence 2.

3   Which choice would be the most appropriate introduction to the paragraph?
- A) *Citizen Kane*, though revolutionary in 1941, is today valued academically rather than artistically.
- B) There are few aspects of *Citizen Kane* that have stood the test of time.
- C) *Citizen Kane* is a celebrated landmark in filmmaking.
- D) Critics are impressed by *Citizen Kane*.

4
- A) NO CHANGE
- B) caused a dramatic and exciting change
- C) was revolutionary
- D) promoted dangerous new ideas

5   Which of the following best connects the sentence with the preceding paragraph?
- A) was one of the first movies made that
- B) respected movie-making tradition and
- C) was conservative and canonical and
- D) was predictably formulaic and

6   The writer is considering deleting the underlined sentence. Should the sentence be kept or deleted?
- A) Kept, because it effectively summarizes the paragraph's main idea.
- B) Kept, because it provides a transition to the next paragraph.
- C) Deleted, because it does not support the main idea of the paragraph.
- D) Deleted, because it contradicts what was stated earlier in the paragraph.

The Tutorverse

Another innovation often cited by critics is the frequent use of deep focus. This special camera technique allows everything in a scene – the foreground, background, and middle-ground – to be captured and in simultaneous focus, which approximates images viewed by the human eye. The extensive use of deep focus was, at the time, a departure from tradition. Earlier movies typically focused the camera on the center of interest, allowing **7** ancillary images to recede out of focus. Because all images are in focus, a great deal of thought had to be put into how best to direct **8** the viewer's attention. As a result, the movement of people and objects within each scene became very important.

Just as *Citizen Kane* explored new ways to tell a story within each scene, so too did it find new ways to transition between scenes. One such transition is a called a wipe. The visual effect of a wipe is such that one image disappears from the screen while another comes into view; this can sometimes result in abrupt changes between scenes. *Citizen Kane* introduced what became known as the invisible wipe, which disguises itself as part of **9** the scene; the result is a smooth and often subliminal change between scenes.

These techniques are just a few of many cinematic innovations that keep critics raving about *Citizen Kane*. **10** And whether one is a movie critic or a regular moviegoer, one has *Citizen Kane* to thank for many elements of moviemaking often taken for granted.

7
A) NO CHANGE
B) peripheral
C) substantive
D) essential

8 The author is considering revising the underlined portion. Which revision is most appropriate?
A) NO CHANGE
B) the viewer's attention, therefore
C) the viewer's attention – resulting in
D) the viewer's attention, and, as a result,

9 The author is consider revising the passage. Which is the best choice?
A) NO CHANGE
B) the scene; with the final result being
C) the scene, and the ultimate result is
D) a scene. The result is

10 At this point, the author wants to include the following graphic and the following statement:

Top Grossing Films of 1941

Rank	Title	Studio
1	Sergeant York	Warner Bros.
2	Honky Tonk	MGM
3	Louisiana Purchase	Paramount
4	A Yank in the RAF	20th Century Fox
5	How Green Was My Valley	20th Century Fox
30	Citizen Kane	RKO

Adapted from Box Office Digest, 1942.

Due to its cinematic innovations, *Citizen Kane* was highly regarded and performed well in the 1941 box offices.

Should this be included?
A) Yes, because Orson Welles was a creative artist, as illustrated by the chart.
B) Yes, because the data from the chart and the statement made support the main idea of the passage.
C) No, because there is no correlation made in the chart between box office success and innovation.
D) No, because the studio was relatively unknown, as indicated by the chart.

Keys to the Kingdom *(Answers & explanations on page 381).*

Smartphones and the software applications created for them have changed the way people live, work, and play. Need to quickly transfer money to a friend? There's an app for that. Need to catch a ride to work? There's an app for that, too. **1** Is there a software program to forecast the weather? Absolutely.

[1] But smartphones and apps have done more than just make life easier or more entertaining. [2] Entire industries have **2** sprung up around potential business opportunities that smartphones and apps unlock. [3] Thanks to the popularity of smartphones and apps, software engineers are some of the most in-demand professionals out there. [4] On top of this monetary compensation are the perks – catered lunches and dinners, high-end coffees and teas, and a host of other fringe benefits that sound, at times, more suited for a country club than a workplace: **3** free copies, office supplies, and overtime. [5] Even more valuable, at times, is the propensity for business owners to part with valuable equity stakes in order to attract the right engineering talent. **4**

1 Which choice best matches the stylistic choices made earlier in the paragraph?

A) NO CHANGE

B) There is also an app to find out the weather forecast.

C) There's also an app to find out what the weather is.

D) Need to know tomorrow's weather? There's an app for that, as well.

2

A) NO CHANGE

B) generated

C) sprung up and surfaced around

D) surfaced near the vicinity of

3 Which choice provides the most relevant detail?

A) NO CHANGE

B) salaries, bonuses, and health insurance.

C) daycare, sleeping pods, and massages.

D) parking, salaries, and bonuses.

4 Where is the most logical place in this paragraph to include the following sentence?

Software engineers today can expect salaries that rocket far into the six-figures – with bonuses to match.

The best placement for the above sentence is immediately before

A) sentence 1.

B) sentence 2.

C) sentence 3.

D) sentence 4.

The Tutorverse

5 <u>Many people wonder how they can become engineers themselves.</u> The answer lies in the economics of an app or other web-based service. With just a few knowledgeable engineers, it's possible for a company to quickly build and offer their idea to the public. Many apps and web-based services are highly scalable – once an app or program is built, it can service a million people almost as easily as it could service a hundred. The potential for business is **6** <u>huge: a</u> popular app can quickly generate millions of dollars.

Of course, competition in the world of apps is huge – hundreds, if not thousands, of apps vie for the increasingly **7** <u>fathoming</u> and oftentimes fickle eye of the consumer. This competition is beginning to manifest also in the labor market, where engineers face increasing competition for the most coveted jobs. Because the compensation is so high and the perks are so good, **8** <u>some</u> students are becoming interested in pursuing a career in software engineering.

Composition of Majors: 2005

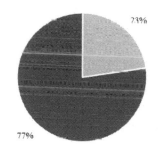

23%

77%

▪ Software Engineering ▪ All Other Majors

Composition of Majors: 2015

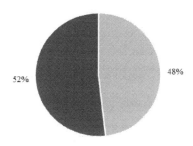

52%   48%

▪ Software Engineering ▪ All Other Majors

5 Which choice provides the most appropriate introduction to the paragraph?
A) NO CHANGE
B) But just why do software engineers command such a high premium?
C) When did software engineering become such a popular profession?
D) What types of people are most suited to work in software engineering?

6 Which of the following choices most effectively combines the underlined sentences?
A) NO CHANGE
B) huge and a
C) huge; a
D) huge, a

7
A) NO CHANGE
B) discerning
C) uninterested
D) imaginative

8 The author wants the information in the underlined portion to correspond with the information provided in the two charts. Which choice represents the best choice of words?
A) NO CHANGE
B) fewer and fewer
C) a proportionally larger number of
D) an inappropriate amount of

Perhaps the day will come when there are simply too many software engineers, and not enough engineering jobs to go around. **9** It's not inconceivable then, that software engineers might even go the way of the once-indispensable telephone operator!

If there exists a concern that the software engineer field will become fully saturated, such a concern must certainly be a long, long way off. Most things we take for granted are powered by computers and commanded by software programs; often times, we don't even realize that computers are involved. This does not, however, necessarily mean that the demand for apps will always exist. **10**

9 The writer is, at this point, considering deleting the underlined sentence. Should the sentence be deleted or kept?

A) Deleted, because the example provided in the sentence does not support the preceding conjecture.

B) Deleted, because the passage is primarily about software engineers, not telephone operators.

C) Kept, because the passage is primarily concerned with comparing one profession with another.

D) Kept, because the sentence offers an example of a profession whose popularity ebbed and flowed.

10 The author would like to include a conclusion that conveys how the popularity of professions changes over time. Which sentence best accomplishes this goal?

A) Still, some fields will exist in perpetuity, regardless of fads and trends, perks and benefits.

B) It wasn't that long ago that the word "app" referred to an appetizer, not a software program.

C) Nevertheless, we will find it difficult to get by without our apps and, by extension, our engineers.

D) Engineers used to build bridges; today, they build apps; tomorrow, they will build other things.

Determination: The Stuff of Stars *(Answers & explanations on page 382).*

Edwin Hubble was born in 1889 in Marshfield, Missouri. Hubble showed great academic **1** determination despite putting forth little effort. He received a scholarship to and attended the University of Chicago, working there as a lab assistant under Nobel Prize-winning physicist Robert Millikan. Eventually, Hubble graduated from the University of Chicago with a degree in Mathematics and Astronomy, and earned a Rhodes scholarship to Oxford.

While at Oxford, Hubble pursued law rather than his passion, which was astronomy. This decision was due to a promise Hubble made to his dying father, who never accepted his love of astronomy. **2** Though Hubble completed his legal studies and even practiced law for a year, he could not, despite the promise he had made to his father, resist the allure of astronomy. Hubble returned to the University of Chicago and received a doctorate in the field. Shortly thereafter, he began working at California's Mount Wilson Observatory. There, **3** Hubble helped the work of and complete the new construction of its Hooker Telescope.

The Hooker Telescope was the largest and most powerful telescope of its time. Having access to such a piece of equipment gave Hubble and his colleagues unprecedented opportunities to explore the far reaches of space. **4** Hubble's discoveries would go on to turn astronomy on its head.

[1] It was 1923, when Hubble focused the Hooker Telescope on the Andromeda Nebula and found that it contained stars that were like the ones in our own galaxy. [2] Hubble examined images of the same area taken previously by other astronomers and realized that he was looking at special types of stars that were useful in measuring distances. [3] After performing his analysis, Hubble concluded that he was in fact looking at an entirely separate galaxy – one containing millions of stars. [4] However, Hubble's evidence was ironclad, and within a few years most astronomers were convinced that our Milky Way galaxy was but one of many in a far greater universe. [5] This conclusion clashed with the conventional wisdom that our galaxy was the only one in the universe. **5**

1
A) NO CHANGE
B) energy
C) prowess
D) indications

2 Which choice provides the most logical introduction to this sentence?
A) NO CHANGE
B) Whenever
C) As soon as
D) Before

3
A) NO CHANGE
B) Hubble helped complete the pending construction of the Hooker Telescope.
C) the Hooker Telescope was completed due to Hubble.
D) Hubble helped complete the Hooker Telescope.

4 The writer is considering deleting the underlined sentence. Should the sentence be kept or deleted?
A) Kept, because it underscores the importance of Hubble's contributions to astronomy.
B) Kept, because it explains the literal impact Hubble had on astronomy.
C) Deleted, because these discoveries are not relevant to the Hooker Telescope.
D) Deleted, because The Hubble Telescope was not his own creation.

5 To make this paragraph most logical, sentence 5 should be placed
A) where it is now.
B) before sentence 3.
C) after sentence 1.
D) before sentence 4.

Hubble would go on to make some of the most **6** significant discoveries **7** in modern astronomy. One such discovery came in 1929. By examining galaxies' distance from Earth, Hubble discovered that all galaxies seemed to be receding away from the Milky Way with velocities that increased in proportion to their distance from us. This observation became known as Hubble's Law, and overturned the conventional view of a static universe. **8** Hubble's Law demonstrated that the universe itself was expanding – an important corollary to the prevailing Big Bang Theory.

Sample Galaxies: Distance vs. Speed

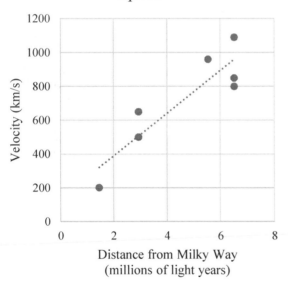

Adapted from the National Aeronautics and Space Administration, 2015.

Science is, perhaps, fortunate that Hubble followed his passion and went against his father's wishes. Without Hubble's **9** intellect and his steadfast dedication for his life's passion, our understanding of the universe would likely be very different. **10**

6

A) NO CHANGE
B) enormous
C) weighty
D) gargantuan

7 Which choice most effectively combines the sentences at the underlined portion?

A) in modern astronomy, one such discovery came in 1929.
B) in modern astronomy, including one in 1929.
C) in modern astronomy; one of the major discoveries came in 1929.
D) in modern astronomy and one such discovery came in 1929.

8 The writer is considering removing the included graph. Should the author do so?

A) Yes, because the data provided was from the outdated Hooker Telescope.
B) Yes, because subsequent data has disproven the data provided in the graph.
C) No, because the graph proves that the universe is static.
D) No, because the graph provides an example of Hubble's Law.

9 The writer wants to add a third trait to describe Hubble. Which choice is best?

A) intellect, apathy, and his steadfast dedication
B) intellect and loyalty, as well as his steadfast dedication
C) intellect and curiosity, as well as his steadfast dedication
D) intellect, patience, and steadfast dedication

10 Which choice would most appropriately serve as the concluding sentence of the passage?

A) Edwin Hubble's discovery led to the Big Bang Theory.
B) Success is one part passion and two parts perseverance.
C) If one follows one's passions and pursues one's dreams, success will always follow.
D) Edwin Hubble was instrumental in a number of groundbreaking astronomical discoveries.

New York's Beanstalks *(Answers & explanations on page 382).*

The Chrysler Building is so well liked that its significance in the history of architecture is often overlooked.

[1] The building's architect, William Van Alen, studied at the Pratt Institute in New York City and worked for several prominent architects in New York City before he won a scholarship to study at the École des Beaux-Arts in Paris. [2] When he returned to New York, Van Alen partnered with H. Craig Severance and they began to design large commercial buildings together. [3] Personal differences led to the end of the partnership in 1924. [4] Van Alen's time in France strongly affected his design aesthetic and he became interested in modernism and other new types of architecture. **1**

2 Developers at the time wanted to challenge conventional wisdom about what could be built, which created a race to build the world's tallest building. **3** Van Alen and Severance were caught up in the fray, as architects of the Chrysler Building and the Bank of Manhattan Trust Building at 40 Wall Street, respectively. Construction on both buildings occurred nearly simultaneously. Both architects tweaked their designs and took advantage of new technological advances – such as elevators and innovations in steel construction – with the hopes of being the architect associated with the taller building.

1 In order to make this paragraph the most logical, sentence 4 should
A) remain where it is now.
B) be moved before sentence 1.
C) be moved after sentence 1.
D) be moved after sentence 2.

2 Which choice would be the most effective topic sentence of the paragraph?
A) Van Alen and Severance helped advance the race to build the world's tallest building.
B) Van Alen and Severance kept tweaking their designs to try to beat each other in designing the tallest building.
C) Technology had made building taller structures possible.
D) The plan for the Bank of Manhattan Trust Building should have led to a taller structure than the Chrysler Building.

3 Which choice most logically introduces the sentence?
A) NO CHANGE
B) Van Alen and Severance were related
C) Van Alen and Severance were apathetic
D) Van Alen and Severance were disabused

Construction on the Chrysler Building began in September of 1928. **4** The Chrysler Building remains the world's tallest brick **5** building. Most of the weight of the building is supported by steel. Building a structure taller than any that previously existed was something of a puzzle for the building's designers, who had to account for factors like wind resistance and how to ensure the safety of the workers laying the bricks. Chrysler also wanted an efficient air-conditioning system in his building, which **6** brought into existence new innovations in climate control technology.

4 At this point in the passage, the writer is considering adding the following sentence.

Approximately 3,826,000 bricks were laid by hand around a steel structure.

Should the writer make this addition here?
A)   Yes, because it adds an interesting detail that supports the main idea.
B)   Yes, because it reinforces the main point about the Chrysler Building's architectural significance.
C)   No, because it introduces details that aren't important to understanding the main idea of the paragraph.
D)   No, because it blurs the paragraph's focus by introducing a new point that goes unexplained.

5 Which choice most effectively combines the sentences at the underlined portion?
A)   building, and most of the weight
B)   building, though most of the weight
C)   building, most of the weight
D)   building, mostly weighing

6

A)   NO CHANGE
B)   usefully brought about
C)   led to
D)   created a need for

But in the end, the building at 40 Wall Street **7** <u>was a monstrosity</u>. Upon completion, Severance and his partners crowned themselves builders of the world's tallest building. But Van Alen had a trick up his sleeve. Workers had been secretly constructing a 125-foot spire inside the building. **8** <u>When it was added, the Chrysler building stood at 1,046, the first man-made structure taller than 1,000 feet and the new tallest building in the world.</u>

Van Alen's triumph was short-lived. The Empire State Building took the world's tallest building crown less than a year **9** <u>later</u>. Still, the Chrysler Building is **10** <u>a gorgeous, sparkling jewel of the New York skyline.</u>

Timeline of Tall Buildings		
<u>Name of Building</u>	<u>Year Built</u>	<u>Height (ft)</u>
World Building	1890	309
Manhattan Life Building	1894	348
Park Row Building	1899	391
Singer Building	1908	612
Metropolitan Life Tower	1909	700
Woolworth Building	1913	792
Bank of Manhattan Building	1930	927
Chrysler Building	1930	1046
Empire State Building	1931	1250
One World Trade Center	1972	1368
Sears Tower	1974	1451

7
A) NO CHANGE
B) was much taller.
C) was very ugly.
D) was more expensive.

8 The writer is considering deleting the underlined sentence. Should the writer do this?
A) Yes, because the sentence contains details that do not support the main idea of the paragraph.
B) Yes, because it does not provide a transition to the next paragraph.
C) No, because the details support the main idea that the Chrysler Building is important to architectural history.
D) No, because it continues the explanation of how Van Alen used tricks to beat Severance to make the tallest building.

9 Which choice best completes the sentence based on the data in the table?
A) later by over 200 feet, remaining the tallest for some 40 years.
B) later by over 100 feet, briefly the tallest building in the world.
C) later by over 200 feet, quickly replaced by other taller buildings overseas.
D) later by over 200 feet, before being replaced by the Sears Tower.

10
A) NO CHANGE
B) one of the coolest buildings ever built.
C) a favorite of architects around the world, inspiring them to build ever taller.
D) a reminder of how, along with 40 Wall Street, the Empire State Building, and the World Trade Center, buildings challenged conventional notions.

The Tutorverse

Masters of the Universe *(Answers & explanations on page 383).*

The financial crisis of 2007-2008 is widely regarded as the worst financial crisis since the Great Depression of the 1930s. From July 2008 to July 2009, the crisis cost the United States **1** an incalculable amount of its Gross Domestic Product (GDP). The superficial cause of the crisis was the bursting of the housing bubble and the economic instability that resulted. **2** At its core, however, was a system riddled with perverse incentives that encouraged reckless risk taking.

[1] As the value of homes and the mortgages on those homes rapidly lost value, the entire financial infrastructure of the United States was shaken to its foundation. [2] Many financial institutions had invested in and traded assets (such as properties and mortgages) that they knew to be virtually worthless. [3] Yet these institutions continued to artificially prop up the value of such assets until they could do so no more. [4] Some financial institutions folded entirely, having been dragged into bankruptcy by the very actions that had for years sent profits soaring. **3**

1 At this point, the author would like to include specific information that supports the main idea of the paragraph. Which choice best completes the sentence with relevant and accurate information based on the graph?

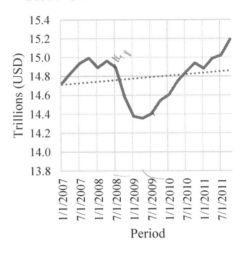

Real GDP: United States

A) NO CHANGE
B) precisely one trillion dollars
C) approximately half a trillion dollars
D) approximately half a billion dollars

2 Which of the following choices most effectively concludes the paragraph with a statement of the passage's primary aim?
A) NO CHANGE
B) In spite of this
C) Nevertheless, along the fringes
D) Notwithstanding the housing crisis

3 The most logical place in this paragraph to include the following sentence is after which sentence?

Yet other institutions, due to their critical importance to the economy at large, were rescued from bankruptcy by the American taxpayer.

A) Sentence 1
B) Sentence 2
C) Sentence 3
D) Sentence 4

The Tutorverse

4 According to many academics, industry insiders, and regulators, human behavior was ultimately to blame. After all, any business – including those financial institutions involved in the crisis of 2007-2008 – is made up of people. In a business, groups of people make decisions together. How could – or, why would – groups of otherwise rational, intelligent people **5** unwittingly risk not only their own businesses, but also the health and welfare of the broader society?

The people who were implicit in causing the financial crisis were highly incentivized to pursue risky (and, by their nature, potentially profitable) investments. **6** Asset managers, for example, are often compensated based on the value of their portfolio of assets. Similarly, asset traders are often paid a commission on trades executed. Coupled with the incentive to pursue personal fortune was the ability to externalize the negative consequences of their risk-taking behavior. The asset managers and traders, for example, were not risking their own **7** money. The asset managers and traders were risking the money of their company and their company's shareholders, instead.

4 Which choice provides the best transition between the current and preceding paragraphs?
A) But how did so many companies allow this to happen in the first place?
B) What were some of the consequences of the bankruptcies?
C) Would it ever be possible to quantify the magnitude of the crisis?
D) Why was it necessary for taxpayers to rescue these companies?

5 If the author desires to convey an accusatory tone about the actions of business decision makers, which of the following best accomplishes this goal?
A) NO CHANGE
B) deliberately jeopardize
C) reluctantly gamble
D) mistakenly imperil

6 At this point, the writer is contemplating deleting the underlined sentence. Should the author make this deletion?
A) Yes, because the paragraph is not primarily concerned with asset manager compensation.
B) Yes, because the information presented does not advance the paragraph's central focus.
C) No, because the information presented provides context for arguments described later.
D) No, because the paragraph is concerned with describing compensation structures.

7 Which choice most effectively combines the two sentences at the underlined section?
A) NO CHANGE
B) money, but were risking
C) money; the asset managers and traders were risking
D) money. Those risked

8 Together, the strong incentive to take risks and the ability to **9** <u>abdicate</u> responsibility for taking those risks proved to be a one-two punch to both the financial sector and the economy at large.

What, then, can be done to prevent another devastating economic collapse? Rather than enacting reactive laws (that can – and have, historically – been circumvented through loopholes), the government should enact laws that address the problems of **10** <u>a person's motivation</u> and responsibility.

8 The author would, at this point, like to add another supporting example of why responsible parties were able to avoid risk. Which of the following choices best accomplishes this goal?

A) They knew that they were taking risks, but knew also that the amount of money they could make was worth the risk.

B) Commissions were high; asset managers and traders were willing to sacrifice the broader economy for personal gain.

C) Shareholders are, famously, shortsighted, and care little if the actions of today prove detrimental tomorrow – so long as profit can be made.

D) Furthermore, the government had previously – as it did in this crisis as well – allowed responsible parties to walk free, focusing instead on staunching economic losses.

9

A) NO CHANGE
B) relinquish
C) bear
D) shirk

10 CONCISION

A) goals
B) incentive
C) experiences
D) circumstance

Money Matters *(Answers & explanations on page 384).*

For many Americans, an understanding of economic policy consists of a superficial understanding of phrases such as "deficit spending," "GDP," and "tax cuts." However, economic policy impacts many levels and aspects of **1** society. Economic policies affect such sectors as the healthcare, manufacturing, education, banking, and insurance sectors. Therefore, it is **2** perfunctory that the public become informed about different types of economic policies.

In the United States today, economic policy is generally influenced by two theories: demand-side (Keynesian) economics and supply-side economics. "Keynesian" refers to economist John Maynard Keynes, a former economic advisor to President Franklin D. Roosevelt. Central to Keynesian thought is the belief that economic activity is driven by the demand for goods and services; therefore, Keynesians structure the tax code with a focus on increasing the buying power of the multitudinous middle and lower classes, while promoting tax hikes to those few in the upper tax brackets. Keynesian economists also believe that the government should intervene in a depressed economy in order to **3** right the ship.

On the contrary, "supply-siders" believe that stimulating supply and limiting government intervention is the key to reviving a sluggish economy. Influential in the development of the supply-side philosophy was economist Milton **4** Friedman. Friedman developed his economic philosophy "monetarism," a precursor to supply-side economics, as a direct criticism of Keynesian economic principles. The focus of Friedman's philosophy is the control of the supply of **5** money, which allows the economy to fix itself. Further, supply-siders believe that controlling the supply of money directly influences **6** inflation.

1
A) NO CHANGE
B) society; such sectors as
C) society, such as
D) society. This includes

2
A) NO CHANGE
B) imperative
C) informative
D) dubious

3 Which choice would be most effective in replacing the underlined phrase with a clear, focused idea?
A) continue to print money and strengthen the money supply.
B) restructure the tax code to restore an effective debt to GDP ratio.
C) make the free market more functional.
D) restore buying power, which is an important component of an economic recovery.

4 Which answer choice most effectively combines the two sentences at the underlined part?
A) Friedman; he was an economist that
B) Friedman; Friedman
C) Friedman: he was the man who
D) Friedman, who

5
A) NO CHANGE
B) money. Many individuals feel that this lets the economy fix itself.
C) money; this, supply-siders feel, will allow the economy to fix itself.
D) money. This allows the economy to correct mistakes.

6 At this point, the writer wants to add one of the following choices. Which choice is best?
A) inflation, which cannot be controlled by the government.
B) inflation, which only affects supply-side economists.
C) inflation, which influences the prices of and demand for goods and services.
D) inflation, which affects the ability of businesses to buy goods and services.

The Tutorverse

[1] When the economy is in recession, the government should, under Keynesian economic theory, spend heavily – even deep into debt – in order to move the economy toward recovery. [2] The two philosophies differ in the methods used to stimulate a sluggish economy. [3] In general, Keynesian economics relies on government spending to boost a nation's economic growth. [4] Keynesians believe that by doing so, government spending can improve, or even replace, economic growth in the absence of consumer spending or private investment. **7**

8 <u>Supply-side</u> economists believe that an economy can be most effectively stimulated by increasing the net wealth possessed by those with the most disposable income: the wealthy and the "job creators." Historically, supply-siders believe that instead of spending excess capital on purchases (demand), the wealthy will invest in things that increase "supply": new businesses, factories, innovation, etc. **9**

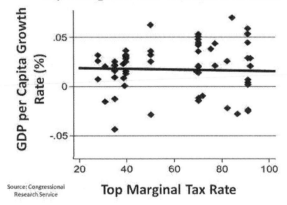

GDP Per Capita Growth Rate and the Top Marginal Tax Rates, 1945-2010

Source: Congressional Research Service

© *Congressional Research Service, 2012.*

In order to make informed decisions, individuals must develop an understanding of economic theory. Otherwise, the public can be easily misled by phrases often heard in political discourse, such as "getting America back to work" and "restoring the middle-class." **10** <u>It is important to know about the economics of these phrases.</u>

7 In order to make this paragraph most logical, sentence 1 should
A) remain where it is now.
B) be moved after sentence 2.
C) be moved after sentence 3.
D) be moved after sentence 4.

8 Which choice best connects the sentence with the previous paragraph?
A) Conversely, supply-side
B) Similarly, supply-side
C) Analogously, supply-side
D) Ultimately, supply-side

9 At this point, the author is considering including the graph provided. Should the author include the graph?
A) Include, because it supports the statements made by the supply-siders.
B) Include, because it lends authority to the author's primary argument.
C) Exclude, because the graph is confusing and difficult to interpret.
D) Exclude, because the data in the graph does not support the statements made by the supply-siders.

10 The author is considering the following revisions. Which answer choice illustrates the best possible revision?
A) Individuals need to know what these phrases mean on a personal level in order to be knowledgeable voters.
B) If an individual is unclear about what these phrases mean, then he or she should be prevented from voting.
C) Without clear knowledge of these phrases and the economic proposals put forth by those seeking office, individuals might be unable to distinguish between rhetoric and effective policies.
D) If society does not seek a clear understanding of these phrases, then elections will continue to be controlled by those who have the most wealth.

Cellular Breakthroughs *(Answers & explanations on page 384).*

Stem cells are characterized by two important **1** features. The two features are as follows: first, they are unspecialized cells capable of replicating themselves through cellular division; second, under certain conditions, they can transform from unspecialized cells into specialized cells. These distinct characteristics have encouraged scientists to study stem cells for their potential medical benefits; the resulting research has provided scientists with a wide range of medical applications. **2** They are also great at repairing damaged tissue in some organs. Due to the regenerative and reparative potential of stem cells, research in this field **3** is a vital course of study in our understanding of biology and the future of medicine.

[1] In 1981, scientists discovered ways to derive embryonic stem cells from early mouse embryos; this was a significant achievement at the time. [2] **4** Scientists work primarily with two kinds of stem cells: embryonic stem cells and non-embryonic ("adult") stem cells. [3] This led to a breakthrough in 1998, when the study of mouse stem cells led scientists to discover a technique that can be used to derive stem cells from human embryos – this allowed scientists to grow human stem cells in the laboratory. [4] In 2006, scientists made another advance by identifying conditions that allow some specialized adult cells to be "reprogrammed" genetically to adopt a stem cell-like state. **5**

6 Stem cells are important. In some adult tissues, such as those found in the brain, cells do not regenerate when lost through injury, disease, or normal wear and tear.

1 Which answer choice most effectively combines the two sentences at the underlined part?
A) NO CHANGE
B) features: first,
C) features, and the first is that
D) features; first is

2
A) NO CHANGE
B) For example, specialized stem cells are able to replace worn out or damaged tissues in certain organs.
C) They are great for a variety of reasons, but notably for repairing damaged tissue in organs.
D) One reason being their importance in repairing damaged organs.

3
A) NO CHANGE
B) is important to our understanding, learning, and knowledge of
C) is a vital course of study to learn about
D) is vital to our understanding of

4
A) NO CHANGE
B) There are countless types of stem cells
C) One stem cell has been proven to work
D) Research suggests a plethora of options

5 In order to make this part of the paragraph most logical, sentence 2 should
A) remain where it is now.
B) be moved before sentence 1.
C) be moved after sentence 3.
D) be moved after sentence 4.

6 What statement most effectively replaces the underlined sentence as a topic sentence for the paragraph?
A) Stem cells are important and need to continue to be studied.
B) Stem cell research has resulted in many medical breakthroughs.
C) Stem cells can help an individual in many ways.
D) Stem cells continue to be important in the study of biology.

The Tutorverse

The induced pluripotent stem cell (iPSC), discovered as a result of a 2006 study on the specific conditions needed to "reprogram" specialized adult cells, makes it possible to regenerate previously irreplaceable cells, like those found in the brain. **7** In addition to the discovery of iPSCs, advances are also being made in other medical fields. Laboratory studies are being conducted to test the efficacy of stem cells in screening new drugs for potency and safety, as well as to learn more about the causes of birth defects. And, given their **8** complex nature, stem cells may also result in new treatments for diseases such as diabetes. **9**

Stem cell research continues to advance both our understanding of cellular replication and our ability to treat medical conditions. **10** It is a topic of debate today. In fact, scientists believe that stem cells may be able to help with organ transplants by minimizing or mitigating an organ transplant recipient's risk of organ rejection. Stem cell research is one of the most interesting areas of biological study today, with seemingly limitless potential.

Stem Cell Publications by Type

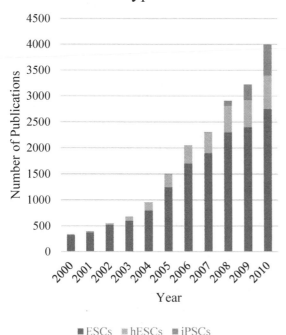

Adapted from eurostemcell.org, 2013.

7 The writer wants to add a sentence in this spot. Which sentence is the best choice?

A) This type of cell has not been found to aid in tissue regeneration.

B) This type of stem cell is difficult to work with in the laboratory, therefore limiting the practicability of stem cell research.

C) iPSCs have important qualities, but their effectiveness in human organ regeneration is still not clear.

D) iPSCs are important because they represent a single source of cells that can replicate other cell types in the body.

8

A) NO CHANGE

B) malleable

C) impressive

D) unstable

9 The author is considering adding the graphic at the end of the passage and the statement below:

In fact, the increasing number of papers published on the topic of stem cell research underscores the importance of the field.

Based on the graphic, should the author make this addition?

A) No. It does not connect to the increasing use of iPSCs.

B) No. It does not relate to medical applications and the treatment of diseases.

C) Yes. It illustrates a strong correlation between the number of publications and the importance of stem cell research.

D) Yes. It helps the reader see the growing difficulties in categorizing stem cell research.

10 The author is considering the following revisions. Which answer choice illustrates the best possible revision?

A) NO CHANGE.

B) However, the costs of funding stem cell research continue to increase.

C) There are many moral and ethical issues surrounding stem cell research.

D) Scientists are only beginning to scratch the surface of possible stem cell applications.

Data-mancy *(Answers & explanations on page 385).*

--- 1 ---

Data scientists gather, analyze, and interpret data in order to help businesses make **1** more informed decisions than without data science. By its very nature, data science is focused both on the past and on the future. Practitioners consult the records of past events – be it the number of people who like to shop for shoes on Wednesday mornings or the frequency that a person visits his or her favorite coffee shop – in order to identify patterns that might be useful in determining future events – in this case, estimating how many people will shop for shoes next Wednesday morning, or when a person will next visit his or her favorite coffee shop.

--- 2 ---

The desire to know what the future holds comes as naturally to people as does breathing. Since the beginning of recorded history, people have sought to **2** contemplate the future. From the oracles of ancient Greece to the palm readers of modern day China, cultures past and present have held in high esteem those who claim to be able to predict things that have **3** yet to be. To the list of fortune tellers, soothsayers, clairvoyants, and prophets we can add another: data scientist.

--- 3 ---

Though there are various methods by which a fortune can be told, many follow very particular sets of rules and utilize equally particular tools **4**: tarot cards in cartomancy; bones, stones, or even dice in cleromancy; precious stones in lithomancy. For the data scientist, however, the future is revealed through statistics.

--- 4 ---

5 Data scientists today develop tools to help them predict the future. Supported by increasingly advanced hardware, different software are being created that help data scientists distill even the largest amounts of information to the

1
A) NO CHANGE
B) better and improved decisions with better results.
C) informed decisions with data science.
D) more informed decisions.

2
A) NO CHANGE
B) divine
C) appreciate
D) dream about

3 Which choice most effectively combines the sentences at the underlined portion?
A) NO CHANGE
B) yet to be and to the list
C) yet to be; to the list
D) yet to be, to the list

4 The author is contemplating deleting the underlined portion of the sentence. Should the author make this deletion?
A) Yes, because the underlined portion is irrelevant to the paragraph.
B) Yes, because the underlined portion confuses the main idea of the passage.
C) No, because the underlined portion provides a useful comparison to the rest of the paragraph.
D) No, because the underlined portion supports the main idea of the passage.

5 The author wants to ensure that the first sentence of the paragraph summarizes the paragraph's main idea. Which of the following choices best accomplishes this goal?
A) NO CHANGE
B) Information is power, and data scientists are powerful.
C) Every craftsman has his tool, and data scientists use technology.
D) Data scientists rely too heavily on computers and not enough on intuition.

most salient of learnings. New software, such as machine learning programs, data visualization models, and artificial intelligence, are helping data scientists to recognize patterns and trends never before seen. Decision makers in government and business alike have already begun to recognize data science's ability to help them make more informed decisions. As technology continues to advance at a breakneck pace, so too will data science's importance to our everyday lives. **6**

--- 5 ---

7 <u>Because of this</u>, data science shares many of the same faults as its less math-oriented predecessors. The imperfect nature of data sets can often cause an analysis to result in false-positives and false-negatives. And even if there were a perfect set of data, the biases and errors in interpretation that are part and parcel with being human can never be fully removed.

--- 6 ---

Ultimately, for all the technology and reliance on mathematics, data science **8** <u>may just be a newer, shinier attempt at</u> solving **9** <u>a magnanimous</u> problem: knowing what tomorrow will bring.

Refer to the entire passage when answering Question 10.

6 At this point, the author desires to include an example that will emphasize the idea conveyed in the preceding sentence. Does the following sentence accomplish this goal?

In fact, with the advent and widespread use of software that tracks and reports on a person's physical activity, we are already beginning to see data science make an appearance at the personal level.

A) Yes, because personal fitness tracking software was developed very quickly.
B) Yes, because personal fitness tracking software is an example of an everyday application.
C) No, because personal fitness tracking software cannot replace a doctor's advice.
D) No, because personal fitness tracking software is unrelated to data science.

7 Which choice presents the most logical introduction to the sentence?
A) NO CHANGE
B) Likewise,
C) However,
D) Conceivably,

8 The author wishes to continue to temper the optimism of earlier paragraphs. Which choice best accomplishes this goal?
A) NO CHANGE
B) is the final word in
C) has definitely upped the ante when it comes to
D) fails to present a reliable method for

9
A) NO CHANGE
B) a juvenile
C) an unimaginable
D) an insurmountable

Consider the passage as a whole when answering question 10.

10 In order to make the passage most logical, paragraph 1 should
A) remain where it is now.
B) be moved after paragraph 2.
C) be moved after paragraph 4.
D) be moved before paragraph 6.

The Tutorverse

Soul Crisis *(Answers & explanations on page 386).*

On July 15th, 1979, President Jimmy Carter **1** addressed the nation. He made the address from the Oval Office. In this address, titled the "Crisis of Confidence" speech, President Carter discussed many important themes. **2** Somewhat among his concerns was the issue of energy and an American reliance on foreign oil. However, there was another issue that hit even closer to home. Carter was the first post-World War II president to address an internal threat to American democracy: an obsession with consumption and a detachment from society.

3 There were no other presidents who were able to convey this idea since the end of World War II. President Carter began his speech with an appeal to ethos, reading from letters sent to him by concerned Americans. Some of these letters included comments, such as the following: "Don't talk to us about politics or the mechanics of government, but about an understanding of our common good." Carter **4** lamented the fact that it would not be legislation that would ameliorate these concerns, nor would it be solved by those in elected positions. Instead, Carter saw a "crisis of confidence" looming on the American horizon.

[1] **5** This crisis, deemed a "fundamental threat to American democracy," did not threaten the political and civil liberties of the American people, nor was it militaristic in nature. [2] Instead, Carter said this crisis struck at the "heart and soul and spirit of our national will." [3] It was an existential crisis that clouded the meaning of an individual's life and hastened the loss of unity in America. [4] Ultimately, Carter felt that this crisis threatened to erode the social and the political fabric of America. [5] The foundation of this crisis rested in America's shift from being a nation that prided itself on family, faith, hard work, and community to one that worshipped self-indulgence and consumption. [6] Our identities were being shaped by what we could consume and not by what we do or our quality of character. **6**

1   At the underlined portion, which choice most effectively combines the sentences?
A)   addressed the nation; he made the address from the Oval Office.
B)   addressed the nation, from the Oval Office.
C)   addressed the nation from the Oval Office.
D)   addressed, from the Oval Office, the nation.

2

A)   NO CHANGE
B)   Coincidentally,
C)   Paramount
D)   However,

3   Which choice establishes the most effective topic sentence?
A)   NO CHANGE
B)   Carter drew inspiration for his speech both from everyday examples and from personal observation.
C)   Carter's public speech mirrored his private lack of motivation and drive.
D)   Prior to World War II, many presidents had expressed concerns similar to Carter's

4

A)   NO CHANGE
B)   knew
C)   praised the fact
D)   championed the fact

5   Which of the following most effectively connects the sentence with the previous paragraph?
A)   NO CHANGE
B)   The problem
C)   The change
D)   The revolution

6   In order to make this paragraph most logical, sentence 4 should
A)   remain where it is now.
B)   be moved before sentence 1.
C)   be moved after sentence 2.
D)   be moved after sentence 6.

The Tutorverse

Carter's speech was met with mixed reactions. At the time, some publications hailed it as a diagnosis of a wayward nation, while others pejoratively dubbed it the "Malaise Speech," hinting at the undertones of exasperation. **7** Still, the themes that Carter covered – consumption, identity, and unity – **8** which still resonate today are all themes that America continues to deal with. Looking back, it seems almost as if Carter had a crystal ball with which he glimpsed the future –a future where **9** Americans can enjoy peace and prosperity.

Average Household Debt as a Percentage of Disposable Personal income

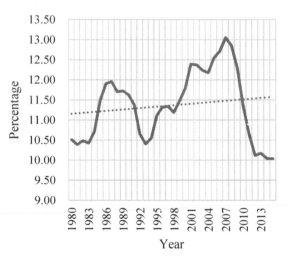

Adapted from The Federal Reserve Board, 2016.

10 Many pundits enjoy analyzing Carter's speech. Whether or not President Carter's speech was considered a success at the time of its broadcast might be a moot point today. In comparing the concerns expressed in the "Malaise Speech" to current issues, we may find that there are more bridges than gaps.

7 At this point, the writer wants to add one of the following sentences. Which sentence is the best choice?

A) Nevertheless, some viewed the speech as especially prescient, while others viewed it as depressingly pessimistic.

B) Today, however, the speech is largely seen as a failure and an example of a political mistake.

C) But, when asked about the speech today, Carter does not regret it.

D) However, many individuals who offered an analysis at the time of the speech were soon discredited.

8

A) NO CHANGE

B) are all themes that America continues to deal with and still resonate today

C) which, still resonating today, are all themes that America continues to deal with

D) are all themes that America continues to deal with

9 Which of the following is the best revision based on information from the graph?

A) NO CHANGE

B) everyone in America has enough.

C) Americans spend money they don't have.

D) saving – not spending – is the norm.

10 The author is contemplating removing the underlined sentence. Should the author make this change?

A) Yes, because the enjoyment of pundits is irrelevant to the main idea of the passage.

B) Yes, because pundits represent public opinion and are highly respected.

C) No, because the sentence effectively summarizes the main idea of the passage.

D) No, because the sentence connects to earlier statements made about the "Malaise Speech."

Hammer, Meet Feather (*Answers & explanations on page 386*).

1 Over the millennia, people have attempted to explain natural phenomena in countless – and often creative – ways. Fire and lightning are just a couple of examples of these phenomena that have given birth to some of the world's most famous myths and legends. Yet, as a result of scientific inquiry and the development of the scientific method, our understanding of such things as **2** fire and lightning have advanced significantly beyond the stories and speculation of antiquity.

Repeatable and observable experiments have facilitated the advancement of the scientific body of knowledge. In the case of what we now know of as gravity, experiments have been **3** middling in developing our current understanding of the phenomena.

One particularly famous experiment was said to have been conducted by Galileo Galilei. Prior to this experiment, the general consensus amongst thinkers, scientists, and philosophers was that heavier objects – objects with more mass – fall faster than lighter objects, or objects with less mass. Indeed, even today, observation of normal, **4** everyday occurrences that are commonplace seems to support this theory **5**; after all, a dropped hammer will hit the ground faster than a feather dropped from the same place.

1 Which choice most effectively introduces the paragraph?
A) There are many imaginative explanations of natural phenomena, some of which have become famous stories.
B) The only explanation of natural phenomena is those that are advanced by scientific inquiry.
C) Science has enriched our understanding of phenomena that was once mysterious and incomprehensible.
D) The scientific method has resulted in stories and speculations that are more elaborate than those of antiquity.

2 At this point, the author wants to revise the sentence. Which of the following is most appropriate?
A) NO CHANGE
B) fire, lightning, and earthquakes
C) fire, lightning, and tornados
D) fire, lightning, and tidal waves

3
A) NO CHANGE
B) inconsequential
C) incontrovertible
D) invaluable

4
A) NO CHANGE
B) everyday occurrences
C) daily events
D) mundane, and routine occurrences

5 The writer is considering deleting the underlined part of the sentence. Should this sentence be removed or kept?
A) Kept, because the example helps clarify how a theory is supported by observation.
B) Kept, because hammers and feathers are relevant to the understanding of gravity.
C) Removed, because hammers and feathers are irrelevant to the understanding of gravity.
D) Removed, because the example does not support the claim made in the rest of the sentence.

The Tutorverse

Today, we know that the reason the feather will fall more slowly than the hammer is because of friction caused by **6** air resistance, since the feather has a relatively large surface area, molecules in the air play a large part in slowing down the feather's descent. Similarly, because the hammer has a smaller surface area than the feather, the effect of molecules in the air on the hammer's descent is less than the effect of molecules in the air on the feather's descent.

[1] According to Vincenzo Viviani, one of Galileo's students, Galileo climbed to the top of the Leaning Tower of Pisa with two heavy balls. [2] Though Galileo's experiment didn't explain the theory of air resistance, it did prove that mass had nothing to do with the speed of an object's free fall. [3] These balls, though of similar shape and density, had different masses; that is, they had different weights. [4] When Galileo dropped these two balls from the Tower, he found that they hit the ground at the same time. [5] According to Viviani's account, this experiment led Galileo to conclude – rightly – **7** that all objects fall with the same rate of acceleration, regardless of their mass. **8**

9 While the historical veracity of this account is questionable, the experiment serves as a way to visualize and understand the concept of constant acceleration applied to objects in free fall. Along with experiments conducted by many other thinkers, Galileo's theories have **10** been established and have advanced our collective understanding of gravity and the motion of objects in free fall.

Free Fall Time (seconds)

Object	Weight (grams)	Atmosphere (air present)	Vacuum (no air present)
Falcon Feather	30	2.28	0.38
Aluminum Hammer	1320	0.45	0.38

Note: All objects assumed to be dropped from the same height. Values included in this chart are hypothetical.

6 Which of the following most effectively combines the sentences at the underlined part?
A) air resistance: since
B) air resistance. Since
C) air resistance – since
D) air resistance…since

7 Which choice most accurately and effectively represents information from the table?
A) NO CHANGE
B) that heavier objects fall with a faster rate of acceleration
C) that lighter objects fall with a faster rate of acceleration
D) that all objects fall with a different rate of acceleration, depending on their weight

8 In order to make this paragraph most logical, sentence 2 should
A) remain where it is now.
B) be moved before sentence 1.
C) be moved after sentence 3.
D) be moved after sentence 5.

9 Which of the following maintains the sentence pattern established by the rest of the paragraph?
A) NO CHANGE
B) The experiment serves as a way to visualize and understand the concept of constant acceleration applied to objects in free fall despite the questionable veracity of this account.
C) The experiment, despite the questionable veracity of this account, serves as a way to visualize and understand the concept of constant acceleration applied to objects in free fall.
D) The experiment serves as a way to visualize and understand the concept of constant acceleration applied to objects in free fall, while the historical veracity of this account is questionable.

10 The author wants to include a conclusion that highlights the importance of Galileo's theories. Which choices best accomplishes this goal?
A) NO CHANGE
B) been proven
C) at times been useful
D) helped to shape modern science

Mile by Mile *(Answers & explanations on page 387).*

--- 1 ---

Without sleep, the human body begins to fall apart. Sleep is critical to everything that we do. It affects how well we process information, learn new things, socialize, and respond to physical stimuli. There is much science still does not understand about sleep, but what we do know is that sleep is a necessary aspect of cognition. The brain forms new neural pathways while sleeping, refreshing our ability to perform both mental and physical duties, **1** such as read a book or fly an airplane.

--- 2 ---

2 Sleep is the most important thing and must be prioritized each day. What happens in everyday life when a person gets less sleep than necessary? Even losing an hour or two of sleep per night will have negative consequences. One of the more dangerous consequences of lack of sleep can be found on America's roads and highways. According to the National Heart, Lung, and Blood Institute, drowsiness is implicated in roughly 100,000 car accidents a year. About 1.5% of these accidents prove fatal. Getting sufficient sleep is important for all drivers, but should be absolutely mandatory for drivers of large tractor-trailers. **3**

--- 3 ---

The issue of fatigued truckers is so important that it has made headlines. A 2014 New York Times article describes how a truck driver drove his tractor-trailer for nearly 11 hours before plowing into cars stopped on the highway, killing ten people. That same article described another incident, where a tractor-trailer slammed into a van, critically injuring one passenger and killing another. In both instances, though there were other contributing factors, lack of sleep was **4** inculcated as the primary reason for the accidents. In all likelihood, both of these accidents – and many of the 100,000 accidents likely caused by drowsiness – were preventable.

1 Which choice results in a sentence that best supports the point developed in the paragraph, and passage as a whole?
A) NO CHANGE
B) for example watch a movie or ride a bicycle.
C) for instance write a book or paint a room.
D) like answer questions on a test or drive a car safely.

2 Which choice is most effective at setting up the information that follows in the rest of the paragraph?
A) NO CHANGE
B) Sleep plays an important role in many aspects of cognition.
C) But we don't always get as much sleep as we need.
D) The consequences of getting too much sleep are as worrisome as getting too little sleep.

3 The author is considering including the following sentence at this point.

Drives of large tractor-trailers should be required to attend accident prevention classes.

Should this sentence be included?
A) Yes, because the sentence supports the earlier claims made about accidents.
B) Yes, because the sentence supports the earlier claims made about sleep.
C) No, because the sentence digresses from the primary purpose of the paragraph.
D) No, because the sentence contradicts the importance of sleep.

4
A) NO CHANGE
B) indicted
C) implicated
D) indoctrinated

The Tutorverse

--- 4 ---

Have you ever spent a restless night chasing sleep only to have it elude you until morning? Have you ever then tried, the next day, to drive a **5** <u>long distance? If so,</u> then you know exactly just how important sleep can be.

--- 5 ---

The government has finally begun to take the necessary steps to help curtail the number of fatigue-related incidents. Effective 2012, the Federal Motor Carrier Safety Administration (FMCSA) ruled that **6** <u>the upper limit of the number of hours</u> a trucker can legally work each week be reduced from 82 hours to 70 hours, and that a driver cannot drive for longer than 11 hours a day; by comparison, a common standard workweek is 40 hours long, typically split over five eight-hour days. Such a ruling appears to be supported by the facts **7**. Still, the rule is, **8** <u>understandably,</u> unpopular with the trucking industry. Truckers are often paid by the mile, and businesses thrive or wither by the timeliness of their deliveries.

Percentage of crashes due to fatigue as a function of hours driven

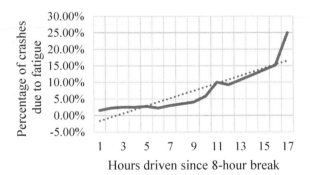

--- 6 ---

Ultimately, so long as we as a society put the value of human life above that of money and profits, we **9** <u>should weigh the costs and benefits of the FMCSA's ruling.</u>

Consider the previous passage as a whole when answering question 10.

5 Which choice represents the most effective combination of the underlined portion?
A) NO CHANGE
B) long distance,
C) long distance?
D) long distance; if so,

6
A) NO CHANGE
B) the maximum number of hours
C) the most number of hours that can be worked by
D) the threshold of hours that cannot be exceeded by

7 Which of the following best completes the sentence with relevant and accurate data from the graph?
A) NO CHANGE
B) as a large percentage of accidents due to fatigue happen after 11 hours of driving.
C) as proportionally few accidents due to fatigue happen after 11 hours of driving.
D) as a disproportionate number of all accidents happen after 11 hours of driving.

8 In context, which choice best maintains a neutral and unbiased tone?
A) NO CHANGE
B) pejoratively
C) unbelievably
D) absurdly

9 Which choice most clearly ends the paragraph with the author's primary claim?
A) NO CHANGE
B) must better understand the role of sleep in human biology.
C) should interview truckers regarding the FMCSA's ruling.
D) must acknowledge the logic of and adhere to the FMCSA's ruling.

Consider the passage as a whole when answering question 10.

10 To improve the logical flow of the passage, paragraph 4 should
A) remain where it is now.
B) be moved before paragraph 1.
C) be moved after paragraph 5.
D) be moved after paragraph 6.

There Can Be Only One *(Answers & explanations on page 387).*

The study of philosophy covers a wide range of topics. Epistemology, for example, is the study of truth and knowledge, spawning such schools of thought as skepticism, rationalism, and empiricism. Metaphysics, on the other hand, is concerned with the study of existence and the relationship between the **1** mind and the body; and the study of aesthetics is centered on understanding beauty, judgment, and perception.

Yet perhaps the most practical of all philosophical branches of study is that of political philosophy. This branch of philosophical study seeks to flesh out the intricacies of interpersonal relationships; that is, what rules should govern the myriad ways people interact with one another, and why? As Aristotle suggested – and later, modern psychology proved – human beings are social animals. People live in communities of various sizes; for many, family and friends represent the most **2** complex of communities. Rules governing the interaction amongst friends and family seem, at least on the surface, to be governed by love, respect, and a reciprocating sense of empathy. **3** Bigger communities are more difficult to govern because of differing backgrounds, opinions, and hopes. And how is it possible, outside of social or familial circles (and indeed, sometimes even within them), to collectively decide on rules governing everything from common courtesy to the orderly transfer of wealth and property to the administration of justice **4** and to the waging of war?

1 In context, which choice best combines the underlined portion?
A)   NO CHANGE
B)   mind and the body. The study
C)   mind and the body as well as the study
D)   mind, body, and study

2
A)   NO CHANGE
B)   enjoyable
C)   important
D)   atomic

3 The writer wants to engage the reader to think critically about the difficulty of governing large groups of people. Which revision best accomplishes this goal?
A)   NO CHANGE
B)   Do you think that bigger communities are easier or more difficult to govern?
C)   But what happens when the community grows larger, and encompasses people with different backgrounds, points of views, desires, and values?
D)   As a result of differing value systems and perspectives on how a society should function, larger communities are more difficult to govern.

4 The author is deciding whether or not to delete the underlined portion of the sentence. Should the author keep or delete this portion?
A)   Keep, because it provides a powerful example of how political philosophy can influence an important policy.
B)   Keep, because it is used figuratively to illustrate how philosophical disputes can lead to conflict.
C)   Delete, because it fails to support the primary purpose of the paragraph, which is to explain the importance of political philosophy.
D)   Delete, because results in a conclusion that is contradictory to the statements made earlier in the paragraph.

The Tutorverse

What political philosophy offers is a framework through which people view both the individual and the collective. Since ancient times, political philosophers have **5** <u>grappled with questions having real-world implications</u>: What is the justification for any political authority? What obligations do individuals have to their government, and do governments have to their constituents? What is the best system for organizing individuals into larger and larger communities?

[1] It was Karl Marx and his Marxism that questioned why so much belonged to so few **6**, after all, that inspired the idea of communism – a political philosophy so potent that it ushered in a new world order and brought about the Cold War.

5   Which choice most appropriately transitions between the previous sentences and introduces the information that follows?

A)   NO CHANGE

B)   confused theoretical questions with real-world application

C)   misinterpreted political philosophies from the past to disastrous effect

D)   questioned the real-world implications of political philosophy

6   At this point, the author would like to add the following graphic. Should the author do so?

Distribution of Global Wealth by Population

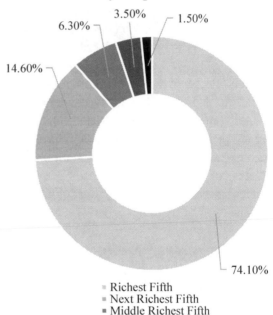

Adapted from the United Nations Development Programme, 2005.

A)   Yes, because the philosophers often think in terms of numbers and graphics.

B)   Yes, because the data in the chart supports the claims made in the sentence.

C)   No, because the data in the chart does not support the claims made in the sentence.

D)   No, because the data in the chart suggests that other philosophies may be more practical.

[2] **7** <u>So many thousands of people have in the past made an effort</u> to answer these questions and implement their corollaries – sometimes to a revolutionary end. [3] Such answers inform on governments' rules and laws under which all citizens – regardless of their own individual ideologies – must adhere. [4] How will taxes be spent, and what amount must each person contribute; who must serve in the military, and under what circumstances; **8** <u>who can befriend whom</u> – implicit behind the rules that govern these and countless other matters is the *why*, which is something decided by a government's political philosophy. [5] It is the *why* that has sparked fierce debate and even ignited war. **9**

10 <u>What other branch of philosophy has made such an impact?</u>

7
A) NO CHANGE
B) People with different backgrounds and insights have tried repeatedly
C) Countless people have in vain sought
D) Many have attempted

8 Which choice gives another supporting example that is most similar to the examples already in the sentence?
A) NO CHANGE
B) how many people in each community is optimal
C) who goes to jail, and for what reasons
D) who may be allowed to immigrate, and for what purpose

9 To improve the cohesion and flow of this paragraph, the author is considering changing the location of sentence 1. Sentence 1 should
A) remain where it is now.
B) be moved after sentence 3.
C) be moved after sentence 4.
D) be moved after sentence 5.

10 The writer would like to include a concluding sentence that highlights the importance of political philosophy. Which choice best accomplishes this goal?
A) NO CHANGE
B) Only a few other branches of philosophy can make such a claim.
C) Clearly, political philosophy is superior to other branches of philosophy.
D) People must consider the reasons behind their actions.

The Tutorverse

Part Three: Math

Overview

The third and fourth parts of the SAT are the Math Tests, one of which does not allow the use of calculators, the other of which does allow the use of calculators. Some questions are multiple choice, while others are student-produced responses. These tests assess the student's ability to solve both standard and context-based math questions as they relate to the following units:

- 🐢 Algebra: linear equations; systems of equations; graphing linear equations
- 🐢 Data Analysis: ratios; proportions; percentages; probabilities; working with quantitative data
- 🐢 Advanced Math: creating algebraic expressions; solving and graphing quadratic and nonlinear equations
- 🐢 Additional Math Topics: area/volume; trigonometry; right triangles; unit circle; various theorems.

On the Actual Test

On the third part of the SAT (Math – No Calculators), students will have 25 minutes to answer 20 questions. 15 of these 20 questions will be multiple choice, and the remaining 5 questions will be student-produced responses. Of the 20 questions, 9 will relate to Advanced Math, 8 to Algebra, and 3 to Additional Math Topics.

On the fourth part of the SAT (Math – Calculators), students will have 55 minutes to answer 38 question. 30 of these 38 questions will be multiple choice, and the remaining 8 questions will be student-produced responses. Of the 38 questions, 17 will relate to Data Analysis, 11 to Algebra, 7 to Advanced Math, and 3 to Additional Math Topics.

It won't be possible to know in advance which math topic will be covered by multiple choice or student-produced responses.

How to Use This Section

Each of the 4 math units are further divided by topic. Many of these topics are related, but

- 🐢 Unit: Algebra
    - 🐢 Solving Linear Equations & Inequalities
    - 🐢 Solving Systems of Equations
    - 🐢 Linear Equations, Inequalities, & Systems in Word Problems
    - 🐢 Linear Equations, Inequalities, & Systems on the Coordinate Grid
    - 🐢 Absolute Value
- 🐢 Unit: Data Analysis
    - 🐢 Ratios & Proportions
    - 🐢 Linear & Exponential Growth
    - 🐢 Interpreting Graphs & Tables
    - 🐢 Additional Data Analysis & Statistics
- 🐢 Unit: Advanced Math
    - 🐢 Working with Polynomials
    - 🐢 Working with Polynomial Factors in Expressions & Equations
    - 🐢 Quadratic Functions & Equations
    - 🐢 Exponents & Radicals
    - 🐢 Systems of Equations
    - 🐢 Function Notation
    - 🐢 Graphs of Functions
    - 🐢 More Word Problems

The Tutorverse

- Unit: Additional Math Topics
  - Geometry
  - Equations of Circles
  - Trigonometry
  - Radians
  - Imaginary & Complex Numbers

There is a *Guided Practice* section for each of the above-listed math topics. These sections are designed to help build students' fluency in each topic by progressing from the more basic to the more advanced. The workbook will clearly indicate which questions should or should not be attempted with the use of a calculator. Students should take as much time as they need working through each topic's *Guided Practice* section.

There is a *Mixed Practice* section for each of the above-listed units. These sections contain a sampling of questions from each topic comprising the given unit. The workbook will clearly indicate which questions should or should not be attempted with the use of a calculator. We recommend that students give themselves approximately 1 minute and 15 seconds per question in each unit's *Mixed Practice* section. This emulates the average amount of time allotted per math question on the actual exam.

We recommend that students practice at least 2 *Guided Practice* topics per week in preparing for the exam (though this number should, of course, be tailored to fit a student's individual study plan).

Tutorverse Tips & Strategies

In addition to tips and strategies outlined in the *Test Overview* section of this workbook, consider employing the following Math-specific suggestions:

- *Don't assume you have to use a calculator, even on the calculator section.*
  Sometimes, students spend too much time plugging away at their calculators and not enough time thinking about the question itself. Oftentimes, questions do not require a calculator to solve. Instead, think about the question itself and how it might be possible to use any multiple choice answer choices to help solve the question.
- *Commit important formulas, theorems, and identities to memory.*
  The exam provides a list of basic formulas, relationships, and rules at the beginning of the math section, but it's best not to spend time flipping back and forth trying to apply a formula to a particular question. Instead, students should attempt to memorize as many important rules and theorems as possible – especially ones that may help save time on the actual exam.
- *Work out your answers on paper if you need to.*
  Many students attempt to solve math questions mentally. We strongly recommend students layout their work on paper. This helps not only ensure that calculations are performed correctly, but also facilitates a final review (if time allows) of answer choices on the actual exam.

The Tutorverse

Reference Equations & Formulas

At the beginning of each math section (sections 3 and 4 of the actual exam) will be a sheet of reference formulas and equations. Some of these formulas and equations are reproduced below, which you may find on the test. These formulas and equations will be helpful to know for some, but not all problems on the test. As we mentioned previously, it is prudent to commit as many of these formulas to memory as possible.

A circle has 360 degrees of arc.
A circle has 2π radians of arc.
The sum of the measures of all angles in a triangle is 180.

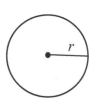

$A = \pi r^2$

$C = 2\pi r$

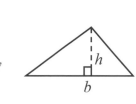

$A = lw$

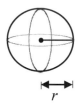

$A = \dfrac{1}{2}bh$

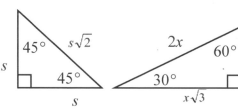

Special Right Triangles

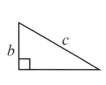

$c^2 = a^2 + b^2$

$V = \pi r^2 h$

$V = \dfrac{4}{3}\pi r^3$

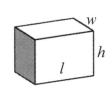

$V = lwh$

$V = \dfrac{1}{3}\pi r^2 h$

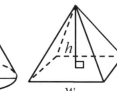

$V = \dfrac{1}{3}lwh$

The Tutorverse

Algebra

Guided Practice – Solving Linear Equations & Inequalities

(Answers & explanations begin on page 389).

Multiple Choice – No Calculator

1 If $\dfrac{x-1}{2} = k$ and $k = 4$, what is the value of x?
- A) 2
- B) 3
- C) 8
- D) 9

2 If $2x + 4 = 20$, what is the value of $4x + 5$?
- A) 8
- B) 13
- C) 32
- D) 37

3 If $\dfrac{5}{6}x - \dfrac{1}{6}x = \dfrac{2}{3} + \dfrac{1}{2} + \dfrac{5}{6}$, what is the value of x?
- A) 2
- B) 3
- C) 5
- D) 6

4 If $\dfrac{x+3}{4} = g$ and $g = 5$, what is the value of x?
- A) 20
- B) 18
- C) 17
- D) 6

5 $8(x - 1) = x(a + 3) - 8$
In the equation shown above, a is a constant. For what value of a does the equation have infinitely many solutions?
- A) 0
- B) 1
- C) 4
- D) 5

Student Produced Response – No Calculator

1 $-3(2x - 2.5) = -5(3x - 1.5)$
What is the solution to the equation above?

2 If $5c - 12 \geq 8$, what is the least possible value of c?

3 If $3x + 7 = 22$, what is the value of $6x - 8$?

4 If $\dfrac{5}{8}x - \dfrac{3}{8}x = \dfrac{3}{4} + \dfrac{1}{2}$, what is the value of x?

5 $2(\dfrac{1}{2} - p) = \dfrac{3}{4} + 8p$
What is the solution to the equation above?

6 $-3(4x - 2.8) = -5(4x - 2.8)$
What is the solution to the equation above?

Multiple Choice – Calculator

1 If $2b - 4 > 6$, which of the following best describes all possible values of b?
- A) any value less than $\dfrac{1}{2}$
- B) any value greater than 1
- C) any value less than $\dfrac{3}{2}$
- D) any value greater than 5

2 If $12 + 3x$ is 10 more than 17, what is the value of $4x$?
- A) 3
- B) 5
- C) 20
- D) 40

The Tutorverse

3 If $\dfrac{1}{2}g = \dfrac{3}{5}$, what is the value of g?

A) $\dfrac{6}{5}$

B) $\dfrac{4}{3}$

C) $\dfrac{3}{5}$

D) $\dfrac{5}{6}$

4 If $\dfrac{1}{4}a > -\dfrac{5}{8}$, which of the following best describes the possible range of values of a?

A) $a > -\dfrac{5}{2}$

B) $a > -\dfrac{5}{32}$

C) $a < -\dfrac{5}{32}$

D) $a < -\dfrac{5}{2}$

5 If $6 + 9x$ is 20 more than 4, what is the value of $5x$?

A) 2
B) 10
C) 18
D) 22

6 If $7x + 3 = 38$, what is the value of $4.5x$?

A) 5
B) 17.5
C) 22.5
D) 28

7 If $\dfrac{x+2}{x+1} = 5$, what is the value of x?

A) -3

B) $-\dfrac{3}{4}$

C) $\dfrac{3}{4}$

D) 3

8 $x + 2x + 3 = 3(-5x + 4) - 6$
What is the value of x?

A) $-\dfrac{1}{6}$

B) $\dfrac{1}{6}$

C) 1

D) 6

9 Which of the following numbers is NOT a solution of the inequality $2x + 3 \geq 3x - 2$?

A) -6
B) -4
C) 4
D) 6

10 $2 + 8x - 3 = (a + 1)x - 1$
In the equation above, a is a constant. For what value of a does the equation have infinitely many solutions?

A) 2
B) 5
C) 7
D) 12

11 If $2a - 3 \geq 1$, what is the least possible value of $2a + 3$?

A) 2
B) 3
C) 7
D) 9

12 Let x and y be numbers such that $-y < x < y$. Which of the following must be true?

    I. $x > 0$

    II. $x > y$

    III. $|x| < y$

A) I only
B) II only
C) III only
D) I and III only

13 If $4 > -2x - 5$, which inequality represents the possible range of values of $-10x - 25$?

A) $-10x - 25 > -0.5$
B) $-10x - 25 < -0.5$
C) $-10x - 25 < 20$
D) $-10x - 25 > 20$

The Tutorverse

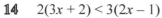

14 $2(3x + 2) < 3(2x - 1)$
Which of the following best describes the solutions to the above inequality?
A) All real numbers
B) $x < -\dfrac{7}{6}$
C) $x > \dfrac{7}{12}$.
D) No solution

15 $-x + 5 + 12x > -8 + 11x + 2$
In the equation shown above, x is a constant. For what value of x does the inequality have infinite solutions?
A) All real numbers
B) $x > -\dfrac{1}{2}$
C) $x > 5$
D) No solution

16 The sum of three numbers is 670. One of the numbers, x, is 50% more than the sum of the other two numbers. What is the value of x?
A) 335
B) 402
C) 432
D) 455

17 If x is the average (arithmetic mean) of m and 8, y is the average of $2m$ and 12, and z is the average of $3m$ and 16, what is the average of x, y, and z in terms of m?
A) $m + 6$
B) $m + 12$
C) $2m + 9$
D) $3m + 18$

The Tutorverse

Guided Practice – Solving Systems of Equations

(Answers & explanations begin on page 390).

Multiple Choice – No Calculator

1
$$3x + 2y = 2$$
$$2y - x = -6$$
What is the solution (x,y) to the system of equations above?
A) $(2,-2)$
B) $(2, 2)$
C) $(2,-4)$
D) $(2, 4)$

2
$$\frac{x}{y} = 4$$
$$3(y+1) = x$$
If (x,y) is the solution to the system of equations above, what is the value of y?
A) 1
B) 3
C) 9
D) 12

3
$$x + y = 3$$
$$3x + 2y = 12$$
Which of the following ordered pairs (x,y) satisfies the system of equations above?
A) $(-2,-2)$
B) $(3, -3)$
C) $(6, -3)$
D) $(3, 6)$

4
$$2x + 3y = -6$$
$$3x - 2y = 17$$
If (x,y) is a solution to the system of equations above, what is the value of $x - y$?
A) 11
B) 9
C) 7
D) 5

5
$$3x - y = y + 8$$
$$x + 2y = 8$$
Based on the system of equations above, what is the value of the product of xy?
A) 2
B) 6
C) 8
D) 16

Multiple Choice – Calculator

1
$$x = 2y$$
$$y = 2x$$
How many solutions does the system of equations have?
A) 0
B) 1
C) 2
D) infinitely many

2
$$3x + 2y = -2$$
$$6x + ay = -6$$
In the system of equations above, for which value of a does the system have no solutions?
A) 2
B) 3
C) 4
D) 6

The Tutorverse

3

$$2x + b = y$$
$$2y + b = x$$

In the equations above, b is a constant. How many solutions does this system have?

A) 0
B) 1
C) 2
D) infinitely many

4

$$2x + b = 3x - 5$$
$$2y + c = 3y - 5$$

In the equations above, b and c are constants.

If b is equal to c plus $\frac{1}{2}$, which of the following is true?

A) x is y plus $\frac{1}{6}$.

B) x is y plus $\frac{1}{2}$.

C) x is y plus 1.

D) x is y minus $\frac{1}{2}$.

5

$$-3x = 6y + 12$$
$$2(2y + 3) = 3x - 2$$

What is the solution (x,y) to the system of equations above?

A) $(0,-2)$
B) $(-2,0)$
C) $(0, 2)$
D) $(2,-2)$

6

$$3x + 5y = -2$$
$$6x - ay = -4$$

In the system of equations above, a is a constant. For what value of a does the equation have infinite solutions?

A) -10
B) -5
C) 5
D) 10

7

$$-10x = -5y + 15$$
$$4y + 3 = 12x - 5$$

How many solutions does the system of equations have?

A) 0
B) 1
C) 2
D) infinitely many

8

$$-2x = 6y + 8$$
$$3(ay + 5) = 4x - 3$$

For which value of a does the system have no solutions?

A) -4
B) -3
C) $-\frac{1}{3}$
D) 4

Student Produced Response – Calculator

1

$$ax + by = 10$$
$$3x + 4y = 20$$

In the system of equations above, a and b are constants. If the system has infinitely many solutions, what is the value of $\frac{a}{b}$?

2

$$y \le -15x + 54$$
$$y \le 3x$$

On the xy-plane, if a point with coordinates (a,b) lies in the solution set of the system of inequalities above, what is the maximum possible value of b?

3

$$3x + 2y = -4$$
$$2(x - 4) = 3y$$

How many solutions does the above system of equations have?

Guided Practice – Linear Equations, Inequalities, & Systems in Word Problems

(Answers & explanations begin on page 392).

Multiple Choice – No Calculator

1 Jack and Amy work at an electronics store, and one of their duties is to email customers when the items they've ordered are ready to be picked up in the store. One afternoon, Jack sent m email messages each hour for 3 hours. Amy sent a email messages each hour over 4 hours. Which of the following represents the total number of emails sent by Jack and Amy that afternoon?
A) $7ma$
B) $12ma$
C) $3m + 4a$
D) $4m + 3a$

2 $w = 4.5a + 2$
A veterinarian uses the model above to estimate the weight, w, of a kitten, in ounces, in terms of the kitten's age, a, in weeks, between when the kitten is 8 and 16 weeks old. Based on the model, what is the estimated increase, in ounces, in the kitten's weight each week?
A) 38
B) 36
C) 6.5
D) 4.5

3 A restaurant has 15 tables that can sit a total of 86 people. Some tables seat 4 people and others seat 6 people. How many tables sit 6 people?
A) 2
B) 7
C) 8
D) 13

4 $a = 1.0 + 0.2x$
$s = 0.4 + 0.4x$
In the equations above, a and s represent the price per pound, in dollars, of aluminum and steel, respectively, at a scrap yard, plus an additional surcharge, x weeks after delivery to the yard. What was the price per pound of aluminum when it was the same as the price per pound of steel?
A) $1.20
B) $1.60
C) $2.00
D) $5.00

5 While training for a swim meet, Toby created a training schedule in which the distance he swims each week is increased by a constant amount. If Toby's training schedule requires that he swim 400 meters in week 4 and 1,000 meters in week 16, which of the following best describes how the distance Toby swims every week changes between week 4 and week 16 of his swimming schedule?
A) Toby increases his swim distance by 5 meters every week.
B) Toby increases his swim distance by 100 meters every week.
C) Toby increases his swim distance by 100 meters every 2 weeks.
D) Toby increases his swim distance by 50 meters every 2 weeks.

6 A charity organization is recruiting volunteers for a fundraiser. Each volunteer can sign up to set up tables before the event or hand out flyers during the event. A volunteer can set up 6 tables per hour or hand out 20 flyers per hour. There are 180 tables and 300 flyers. If the volunteers each work a 3-hour shift, how many volunteers does the organization need?
A) 5
B) 10
C) 15
D) 20

7 $d = 145 + 0.1x$
$p = 75 + 0.2x$
In the equations above, d and p represent the price, in dollars, of down coats and pea coats, respectively, x days after Labor Day last year. What was the price of a down coat when it was equal to the price of a pea coat?
A) $145
B) $152
C) $205
D) $215

The Tutorverse

8 Jane bought 4 paperback and 2 hardcover books at a used book store and spent a total of $36. Her friend, Sarah, bought 3 paperbacks and 5 hardcover books and spent a total of $69. What would be the total cost, in dollars, of 1 paperback and 1 hardcover?

A) 2
B) 5
C) 9
D) 15

9 Dara works in a clothing store and earns a percent of the price of each item sold as a commission, in addition to her regular hourly salary. Her manager calculates her weekly paycheck by using the expression $14h + 0.10p$, where h is equal to the number of hours she works and p is equal to the total price of the items sold. Which of the following is the best interpretation of 0.10 in the expression?

A) Dara earns $0.10 for every item sold.
B) Dara's commission goes up $0.10 for each item she sells.
C) Dara's commission is equal to 10% of the total price of the items she sells.
D) Dara works 10 hours every week.

10 The twelfth grade class is holding a bake sale for student activities. Cookies cost $2 each and brownies cost $3 each. The class is hoping to earn at least $500. Students have provided a total of 400 cookies and brownies. Solving which of the following systems of equations yields the number of cookies c and brownies b the twelfth grade class needs to sell to make its goal?

A) $b + c < 400$
$3c + 2b \geq 500$

B) $b + c < 400$
$3c + 2b \leq 500$

C) $b + c \leq 400$
$2c + 3b \geq 500$

D) $b + c < 400$
$\dfrac{c}{2} + \dfrac{b}{3} \geq 500$

11 $b = 6.5 + 0.5x$
$f = 4.5 + 0.7x$

A collector created a formula to represent roughly how much trading cards appreciate in value. In the equations above, b and f represent the price, in dollars, of baseball and football cards, respectively, x years after the cards were released. After how many years are baseball and football cards equal in value?

A) 5
B) 10
C) 50
D) 100

12 At a sporting goods store, baseballs cost $3 each and tennis balls cost $2 each. A physical education teacher has a $150 budget and wants to buy at least 50 baseballs and tennis balls in total. Solving which system of inequalities will help him determine how many baseballs, b, and tennis balls, t, to buy?

A) $b + t \leq 50$
$3b + 2t \geq 150$

B) $b + t \geq 50$
$3b + 2t \leq 150$

C) $b + t \geq 50$
$3b + 2t \geq 150$

D) $b + t \leq 50$
$3b + 2t \leq 150$

13 A bakery sells muffins in boxes of 4 and cupcakes in boxes of 6. At the end of the day, the baker does an inventory and sees that they have sold 30 boxes and a total of 140 cupcakes and muffins. How many boxes of muffins did the bakery sell?

A) 10
B) 15
C) 20
D) 25

The Tutorverse

14 Gina sells custom-made tee-shirts at a craft fair. She sold twice as many shirts on Saturday as she did Friday. If she sold 26 shirts on Friday and x is equal to the number of shirts she sold Saturday, which of the following equations is true?

A) $26x = 2$

B) $2x = 26$

C) $\dfrac{x}{2} = 26$

D) $x + 26 = 2$

Student Produced Response – No Calculator

1 $a = 10 + 0.1m$

$b = 5.5 + 0.25m$

In the equations above, a and b represent different Wi-Fi plan options at a hotel, with a given base price, in dollars, and an additional surcharge per minute. After how many minutes will both plans have the same price?

2 A butcher shop sells chicken for $3 per pound and pork for $4 per pound. If the shop sold a total of 15 pounds of meat one day and made $50, how many pounds of chicken did it sell?

3 The temperature of the ocean decreases at a constant rate as the depth increases. In one part of the ocean, the temperature at the surface is 22°C and the temperature at 500 meters below the surface is 14°C. For every additional 100 meters, the temperature decreases by k°C, where k is a constant. What is the value of k?

4 $t = 2.6 - 0.5x$

$l = 1.8 - 0.3x$

In the equations above, t and l represent the price per square foot of tile and linoleum flooring, respectively, at a home improvement store, x weeks after delivery to the store. What was the price per square foot of tile, in dollars, when it was the same as the price per square foot of linoleum?

5 Tamara owns a gym and wants to start offering yoga classes. Each yoga class is 1.5 hours long. Instructors are paid $40 per hour, but Tamara doesn't want to spend more than $1,000 on instructors. What is the maximum number of yoga classes Tamara can offer per week?

Multiple Choice – Calculator

1 A magazine has both print and online subscriptions available. A print subscription costs $12.50 per month and an online subscription costs $9.99 per month. Which of the following expressions represents the amount, in dollars, the magazine receives for subscriptions if there are x print subscriptions and y online subscriptions?

A) $12.50x + 9.99y$

B) $12.50x - 9.99y$

C) $9.99x + 12.5y$

D) $9.99x - 12.5y$

2 A premium cable channel has a monthly subscription fee of $9.98. Viewing programming on the channel is included in the membership fee, but there is an additional $2.50 fee to watch on-demand programming. For one month, Sam's bill was $17.48. How many on-demand programs did Sam watch that month?

A) 1

B) 2

C) 3

D) 4

The Tutorverse

3 Last week, Joanna worked 12 more hours than Rafael. If they worked a combined total of 64 hours, how many hours did Joanna work?
A) 52
B) 38
C) 26
D) 12

4 Admission at a theme park is $12.50 for adults and $6.75 for students. A twelfth grade class went to the theme park. There were 209 adults and students on the trip in all, and the total admission fee was $2,118. Solving which of the following systems of equations yields the number of adults, x, and the number of students, y, who went to the theme park?

A)
$$x + y = 2,118$$
$$12.5x + 6.75y = 209$$

B)
$$x + y = 209$$
$$6.75x + 12.5y = 2,118$$

C)
$$x + y = 209$$
$$12.5x + 6.75y = 2,118$$

D)
$$x + y = 209$$
$$12.5x + 6.75y = 2,118 \times 2$$

5 A small library has a maximum capacity of 15,000 books. When the shelves are full, librarians remove old books to make space for the new ones. On January 1st, the library had 13,500 books. Each month, they receive an additional 95 books. If y represents the time, in months, after January, which of the following inequalities describes the set of months where the library is at or above capacity?
A) $15,000 - 95 \leq y$
B) $15,000 \leq 95y$
C) $15,000 - 13,500 \geq 95y$
D) $13,500 + 95y \geq 15,000$

6 A TV network sells ads in 30-second and 60-second time slots. A 30-minute TV program has 6 minutes of ads. The network airs programming for 18 hours a day. The network sold a total of 325 slots one day and filled every available ad minute. Solving which of the following systems of equations yields the number of 30-second ads, x, and the number of 60 second ads, y, that aired in one 18-hour period?

A)
$$x + y = 325$$
$$0.5x + y = 216$$

B)
$$x + y = 325$$
$$0.5x + y = 1,080$$

C)
$$x + y = 216$$
$$0.5x + y = 325$$

D)
$$x + y = 325$$
$$0.5x + 6 = 108$$

7 A cereal factory ships boxes of cereal that are 8 ounces or 14 ounces. Let x be the number of 8-ounce boxes and y be the number of 14-ounce boxes. The cereal ships in cases that can carry at most 12 boxes and the total weight cannot exceed 96 ounces. Which of the following systems of inequalities represents this relationship?

A)
$$8x + 14y \leq 96$$
$$x + y \leq 12$$

B)
$$\frac{x}{8} + \frac{y}{14} \leq 96$$
$$x + y \leq 12$$

C)
$$8x + 14y \leq 12$$
$$x + y \leq 96$$

D)
$$x + y \leq 96$$
$$8x + 14 \leq 96$$

8 At a sandwich shop, a foot-long sandwich, f, costs \$2.50 more than a six-inch sandwich, s. One family orders 2 foot-long sandwiches and 4 six-inch sandwiches for a total of \$37.70. Which system of equations could you use to find the cost of a foot-long sandwich?

A) $f = 2.5s$
$2f + 4s = 37.7$

B) $f = s + 2.5$
$2f + 4s = 37.7$

C) $f = s + 2.5$
$2f - 4s = 37.7$

D) $f = 2.5s$
$4f - 2s = 37.7$

9 A plane has a maximum fuel capacity of 5,300 gallons. The airline requires that the pilot fly no more than 400 minutes before refueling. A one-way flight to a certain destination requires 2,000 gallons of fuel and 190 minutes of flight time. How many round trips can the pilot make before having to refuel?

A) 1
B) 2
C) 3
D) 4

10 Certain shipping crates can hold either 50 pounds or 80 pounds each. Let x be the number of 50-pound crates and y be the number of 80-pound crates. A truck can hold either 30 boxes or a weight of 2,000 pounds. Which of the following systems of inequalities represents this relationship?

A) $x + y \leq 2,000$
$50x + 80y \leq 2,000$

B) $\dfrac{x}{50} + \dfrac{y}{80} \leq 2,000$
$x + y \leq 30$

C) $50x + 80y \leq 30$
$x + y \leq 2,000$

D) $50x + 80y \leq 2,000$
$x + y \leq 30$

11 At a pottery store, each cup costs \$6.50 less than each plate. If Maggie spends a total of \$55.50 for 5 cups and 3 plates, what is the price of each cup?

A) \$3.50
B) \$4.50
C) \$6.50
D) \$11.00

12 $d = \dfrac{1}{2}p + 65$
$s = 200 - p$

In the equations above, d is equal to the quantity of a product displayed for sale at a store at p, the price in dollars and s is equal to the quantity of the product that the store sold. At what price will the quantity of the product displayed be equal to the quantity of the product sold?

A) \$90
B) \$100
C) \$115
D) \$135

13 In a trivia game, each player starts with k points and loses 5 points each time a question is answered incorrectly. If a player gains no additional points but answers 30 questions incorrectly has a score of 50 points, what is the value if k?

A) 0
B) 100
C) 200
D) 300

The Tutorverse

14 Every morning, Sharon bikes at a constant speed of 9 miles per hour and then walks at 3 miles per hour to get to her job. Her goal is to travel the 6 miles to work in less than 1 hour. If Sharon bikes b miles and walks w miles, which of the following systems represents Sharon's goal?

A) $\dfrac{b}{9}+\dfrac{w}{3}<1$
$b+w=6$

B) $\dfrac{b}{9}+\dfrac{w}{3}\geq 1$
$b+w<6$

C) $9b+3w\geq 6$
$b+w=1$

D) $9b+3w<1$
$b+w\geq 6$

15 It takes Michaela 90 minutes and 3 sheets of paper to complete a writing assignment. It takes her 20 minutes and 1 sheet of paper to complete a math assignment. Michaela is required to spend more than 300 minutes to complete assignments and she can use as many as 20 sheets of paper. If w represents the number of writing assignments and m is the number of math assignments, which system of inequalities represents Michaela's homework?

A) $90w+20m\leq 300$
$3w+m\geq 20$

B) $90w+20m>300$
$3w+m\leq 20$

C) $\dfrac{90}{w}+\dfrac{20}{m}>300$
$3w+m<20$

D) $90w+20m>20$
$3w+m\leq 300$

16 $s=5.5h+\dfrac{t}{6}$

$t=0.15d$

The first equation above shows the earnings of a server at a certain restaurant for a night's work, where s is equal to the total earnings, in dollars, h is equal to the number of hours worked, and t is equal to the total amount of tips all servers earned, in dollars. Tips are, on average, 15% of the total dinner sales in dollars, d. If the restaurant made \$785 in dinner sales one night, how much did one server make during an 8 hour shift, rounded to the nearest cent?

A) \$19.73
B) \$44.00
C) \$47.72
D) \$63.63

17 A school is building a rectangular playground. Due to space constraints, the length, x, of the playground must be at least 20 feet longer than the width, y, and the perimeter will not be greater than 2,000 feet. Solving which of the following systems of inequalities yields the length and width of the playground?

A) $x-y\geq 20$
$2x+2y\leq 2,000$

B) $x-y\leq 20$
$2x+2y\geq 2,000$

C) $x-y\geq 20$
$2x+2y\geq 2,000$

D) $x-y\leq 20$
$2x+2y\leq 2,000$

18 A movie theater sells tickets for adults and children. One customer buys 4 adult tickets and 8 child tickets; the cost is \$116.00. Another customer buys 6 adult tickets and 2 child tickets and spends \$89.00. How much does an adult ticket cost?

A) \$8.50
B) \$10.00
C) \$12.00
D) \$14.50

The Tutorverse

19 Concert tickets cost $12 for students and $15 for adults. If Jason spends at least $90 but no more than $105 on x student tickets and 2 adult tickets, which is a possible value of x?

A) 3
B) 5
C) 7
D) 8

20 A comic book store sells new superhero comics for $3.50 each and new graphic novels for $12.50 each. If one day, the store sold 40 more superhero comics than graphic novels and made $700 in total sales, how many superhero comics did the store sell?

A) 35
B) 40
C) 75
D) 100

21 A copy shop charges $1.00 per visit to use its copy machine and an additional fee of $0.10 per page. Which of the following represents the total charge, t, in dollars, to use this copy machine to make n copies in one visit?

A) $t = 1.10n$
B) $t = 1.00 + 10n$
C) $t = 1.00 + 0.10n$
D) $t = 1.10 + n$

22 Jake is driving cross country. Gas costs $2.19 per gallon at the gas station chain that he prefers. On average, he can drive 23 miles per gallon of gas. He plans to drive 400 miles each day. Which of the following expressions represents the total cost, in dollars, of the gas needed for traveling x days?

A) $2.19x \div (400 \div 23)$
B) $2.19(x \cdot 400 \cdot 23)$
C) $2.19[(400 \div 23)x]$
D) $2.19(400 \div 23) \div x$

23 Courtney is measuring the height of geologic features from sea level, which has an altitude of 0 feet. The lowest elevation Courtney measures has an altitude of x feet. One feature is 4 times x plus 10 feet high, which Courtney calculates as being 6 feet above sea level. What is the height of another feature that is 2 times x plus 5 feet?

A) −4
B) −1
C) 3
D) 4

24 Mr. Lopez is redoing the front walkway at his house and deciding where to buy materials and rent tools for the project. The table below shows the materials' cost and daily rental costs for three different stores.

Store	Cost of Materials M ($)	Rental cost of wheelbarrow W ($ per day)	Paver saw ($ per day)
A	500	25	70
B	450	20	80
C	550	15	85

The total cost, y, for buying materials and renting the tools in terms of the number of days, x, is given by $y = M + (W + K)x$. For what number of days, x, will the total cost of buying the materials and renting the tools from Store B be less than or equal to the total cost of buying the materials and renting the tools from Store A?

A) $x \leq 5$
B) $x \geq 5$
C) $x \leq 10$
D) $x \geq 10$

25 A machine packs 18 boxes of cereal into a carton. It fills c cartons in 1 hour. Which equation shows how many cartons the machine fills in 5 minutes?

A) $\dfrac{18c \cdot 5}{60}$

B) $5c \cdot 60$

C) $\dfrac{5c}{60}$

D) $\dfrac{5c \cdot 60}{18}$

26 John brings a water cooler holding n fluid ounces of water to distribute to all of the athletes on the football team. If he gives each player 8 fluid ounces of water, he will have 76 fluid ounces of water left over. In order to give each player 10 fluid ounces of water, he will need an additional 30 ounces. How many players are there?

A) 10

B) 41

C) 53

D) 106

Student Produced Response – Calculator

1 A geologist in Texas has calculated that the average erosion rate for the Gulf Coast is 2.4 feet per year. According to the geologist's estimate, how long will it take, in years, for the Texas Gulf Coast to erode by 36 feet?

2 A florist sells a bouquet of roses for $25 and a bouquet of daisies for $15. If one day, the florist sold 30 more bouquets of roses than daisies and made a total of $1,350, how many bouquets of roses did the store sell?

3 A landscaping company placed two orders with a nursery. The first order was for 13 bushes and 4 trees and totaled $485. The second order was for 6 bushes and 2 trees and totaled $230. The bills do not list a per-item price. What would be the total cost of 1 bush and 1 tree?

4 Geoff and Damon took turns driving their car across the country. The trip took a total of 55 hours. Geoff drove 15 hours more than Damon did. If Geoff's average speed was 55 miles per hour, what was the total distance he drove?

5 Pete bought a pair of pants and a backpack at a department store. The sum of the prices before sales tax was $78.00. There was no sales tax on the pants and a 6% sales tax on the backpack. The total Pete paid, including the sales tax, was $80.40. what was the price, in dollars, of the pants?

The Tutorverse

Guided Practice – Linear Equations, Inequalities, & Systems on the Coordinate Grid

(Answers & explanations begin on page 396).

Multiple Choice – No Calculator

1   Jane opened a savings account with $500. Each month, she deposits $150. Which graph represents v, the value of the savings account, as a function of t, the number of months since the account was opened?

A)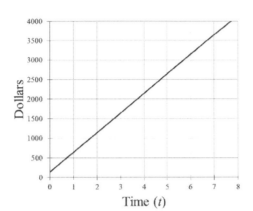

C)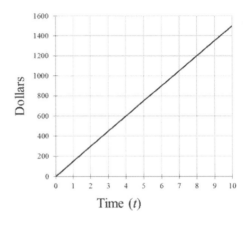

B)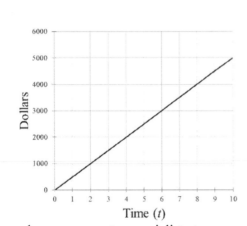

D)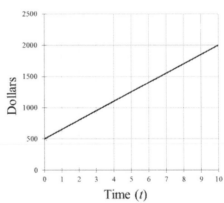

2   Jake works as a computer specialist at an electronics store. Each week, he receives a certain number of computers that need to be repaired. The number of computers he has left to fix at the end of each day can be estimate with the equation $C = 95 - 12d$, where C is the number of computers left and d is the number of days he has worked that week. What is the meaning of the value 95 in the equation?

   A)   Jake repairs computers at a rate of 95 per day.

   B)   Jake repairs computers at a rate of 95 per hour.

   C)   Jake starts each week with 95 computers to fix.

   D)   Jake will complete the repairs within 95 days.

3    $2x + 5y = -2$

     $3y - x = 12$

What is the solution (x,y) to the system of equations above?

   A)   (6,2)

   B)   (2,6)

   C)   (–6,2)

   D)   (6,–2)

4   Which of the following equations represents a line that is parallel to the line with equation $y = 4x + 3$?

   A) $-4x + y = 12$

   B) $4x + 2y = 8$

   C) $2x + y = 6$

   D) $-2x + 2y = 3$

The Tutorverse

5

$$y = ax + 1$$
$$ax - y = 6$$

In the system of equations above, a is a constant. The system has x-intercepts at $(1,0)$ and $(-6,0)$, respectively. If the system has no solutions, what is the value of a?

A) -6
B) -1
C) 0
D) 1

6 A line on the xy-plane passes through the origin and has a slope of $\dfrac{1}{5}$. Which of the following points lies on the line?

A) $(1,5)$
B) $(5,1)$
C) $(0,5)$
D) $(5,5)$

Student Produced Response – No Calculator

1 A hotel charges guests for the use of its Wi-Fi. To calculate the cost for each guest, the hotel uses the function $c = ah + 10$, where the cost c is a function of a, the hourly rate (in dollars per hour), and h, the number of hours, plus a $10 flat fee. A guest pays $26 for 8 hours of Wi-Fi use. What was the hourly rate, in dollars per hour?

Multiple Choice – Calculator

1 If the relationship between the total cost, y, of renting ski equipment from Store A and the number of days, x, for which the equipment is rented is graphed on the xy-plane, what does the slope of the line represent?

A)   The total cost of the rental.
B)   The number of items rented.
C)   The daily rental fee.
D)   The total cost of each item rented.

7 A sports equipment store rents out pairs of roller skates. They calculate the cost of the rental using the function $c = 7h + b$, where h is the number of hours a pair of roller skates can be rented for, b is a flat charge that varies based on the type of roller skate model, and c is the total cost of the rental. If Sue paid $26 to rent a pair of roller skates for 3 hours, what was the surcharge for the pair?

A) 2
B) 3
C) 5
D) 7

8 Which of the following equations represents a line that is perpendicular to the line with equation $y = -6x + 1$?

A) $-6x + y = 3$
B) $12x + 2y = 4$
C) $x + 6y = 3$
D) $x - 6y = 18$

2 The graph of a line on the xy-plane has slope 3 and contains the point $(1,9)$. The graph of a second line passes through the points $(2,3)$ and $(4,1)$. If the two lines intersect at the point (a,b), what is the value of $a + b$?

2

$$y = ax - 4$$
$$bx - y = 4$$

In the system of equations above, a and b are both constants, and the system has infinite solutions. If the value of b is 4, what is the value of a?

A) -4
B) 4
C) 6
D) 8

3

$$y = 2x - 3$$
$$x - y = 3$$

A system of two equations is shown above. How many solutions does the system have?
A) Zero
B) One
C) Two
D) Infinite

4

$$y = 3x - 2$$
$$3x - y = 5$$

A system of two equations is shown above. How many solutions does the system have?
A) Zero
B) One
C) Two
D) Infinite

5

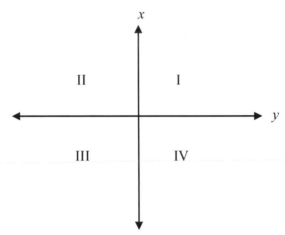

If the system of inequalities $y \geq -3x + 1$ and $y > -\frac{1}{3}x + 1$ is graphed on the xy-plane above, which quadrant contains no solutions to the system?
A) Quadrant II
B) Quadrant III
C) Quadrant IV
D) There are solutions in all four quadrants.

6 Line l on the xy-plane contains points from each of Quadrants I, II, and III, but no points from Quadrant IV. Which of the following must be true?
A) The slope of the line l is undefined.
B) The slope of the line l is zero.
C) The slope of the line l is positive.
D) The slope of the like l is negative.

7 Joanne drew a map to show Maple Street and Elm Street in a coordinate plane. She graphed Maple Street using the equation $y = 2x - 4$ and Elm Street using the equation $y = -3x + 6$. At what point on the xy-plane will the two streets meet?
A) $(0, -2)$
B) $(-2, 0)$
C) $(0, 2)$
D) $(2, 0)$

8

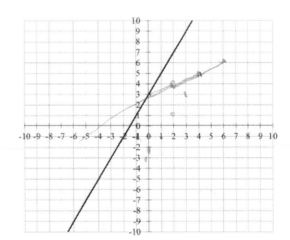

The graph above shows a line on the xy-plane. Which of these is the equation of a perpendicular line?
A) $2x - y = 3$
B) $y = -2x + 3$
C) $2y + x = 6$
D) $-2y + x = 4$

The next two questions refer to the below information:

Water Evaporation by Day

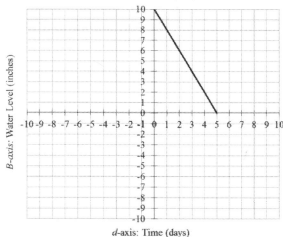

d-axis: Time (days)

The graph above displays the amount of water left in a bucket, B, after the water has been left to evaporate in the sun for d days.

9 What does the B-intercept represent in the graph?
   A) The amount of water in the bucket on the first day.
   B) The total amount of water that evaporated.
   C) The total number of days it took for all the water to evaporate.
   D) The amount of water that evaporated on the first day.

10 Which of the following represents the relationship between d and B?
   A) $B = 2d$
   B) $B = 2d + 10$
   C) $B = -2d + 10$
   D) $B = -2d$

Student Produced Response – Calculator

1
$$y = -bx + 5$$
$$bx - y = 3$$

In the system of equations above, b is a constant. On a coordinate grid, the graphs of the equations intersect at point (1,1). What is the value of b?

The next two questions refer to the below information:

A bakery tracked how many loaves of bread they baked per hour over h hours and recorded the data in the following graph:

Loaves of Bread Baked Over Time

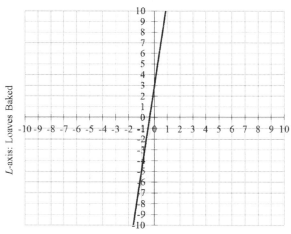

h-axis: Time (hours)

11 What does the L-intercept represent in the graph?
   A) The total number of loaves baked.
   B) The total number of hours when bread is baked.
   C) The increase in the number of loaves baked per hour.
   D) The number of loaves the bakery had when they started tracking.

12 Which of the following represents the relationship between h and L?
   A) $L = 8h$
   B) $L = 8h + 3$
   C) $L = \frac{3}{8}h + 3$
   D) $L = -8h + 3$

2 Johnson's Paint Company estimates the price of painting a house in dollars, using the expression $30 + 12nh$, in which there is a flat fee of $30, an hourly rate of $12, n is equal to the number of painters, and h is equal to the number of hours. Clark's Paint Company estimates a similar job using the expression $42 + 10nh$. Dawn wants to hire one of the companies to paint her house using 3 painters. How many hours will it take for the jobs to be the same price from both companies?

The Tutorverse

Guided Practice – Absolute Value

(Answers & explanations begin on page 398).

Multiple Choice – No Calculator

1 If $|x-4|+3=7$, which of the following is a possible value of x?
A)   0
B)   3
C)   4
D)   7

2 Which of the following expressions is equal to 0 for some value of x?
A) $|x-2|-2$
B) $|2-x|+2$
C) $|x+2|+2$
D) $|x-2|+2$

3 Solve $|5x+4|+10=2$.
A)   –8
B)   4/5
C)   2
D)   There is no solution.

4 If $|2-4x|>10$, which of the following is a possible value of x?
A)   –4
B)   –1
C)   2
D)   3

5 The requirements to join a dance group state that dancers must be within 4 inches of 70 inches tall. Which of the following inequalities can be used to assess which dancers are the correct heights?
A) $|h-4|\le 70$
B) $|h-4|\ge 70$
C) $|h-70|\le 4$
D) $|h-70|\ge 4$

6 If $f(x)=|5-4x|$, then $f(2)=$
A) $f(-2)$
B) $f(-1)$
C) $f(4)$
D) $f(\frac{1}{2})$

7 If a is a negative number and b is a positive number, what is the absolute value of a plus the absolute value of b?
A) $-a+b$
B) $-(a+b)$
C) $-a-b$
D) $a+b$

Student Produced Response – No Calculator

1 $|x-3|-7=-5$

What is the least value of x that satisfies the equation above?

2 $|8-k|=5$

$|k-2|=11$

What is the value of k that satisfies both equations?

3 A band releases a new single. Weekly sales s (in thousands) increase steadily for a while and then decrease as given by the function $s=-2|t-20|+40$ where t is the time in weeks. What was the maximum number of singles sold in week number one?

The Tutorverse

Multiple Choice – Calculator

1 For what value of n is $|n-2|+2$ equal to 0?
A) 0
B) 2
C) 4
D) There is no such value of n.

2 Which of the lettered points in the figure below has coordinates (x,y) such that $|x|-|y|=3$?

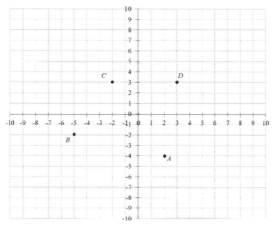

A) A
B) B
C) C
D) D

3 A carpenter is buying a metal rod for a project. The ideal diameter is 2.5 inches with an allowable error of at most 0.05 inches. He measures all of the rods available at the store. Which size, in inches, should he buy?
A) 2.4418
B) 2.4671
C) 2.5512
D) 2.6518

4 Let x and y be numbers such that $-y < x < y$. Which of the following must be true?
   I. $x > 0$
   II. $y > 0$
   III. $|x| < y$
A) I only
B) III only
C) II and III only
D) I, II, and III

5 The ideal diameter of a gear for a certain type of clock is 12.25 mm. An actual diameter can vary by as much as 0.06 mm. Which of the following shows the range of possible diameters for the clock gear?
A) $|x-12.25| \le 0.06$
B) $|x+12.25| \le 0.06$
C) $|0.06+x| \le 12.25$
D) $|x-0.06| \ge 12.25$

6 Simplify $-|3^2-10|+|-(3)^2-2|$
A) 9
B) 10
C) 11
D) 12

7 The temperature on Mars roughly satisfies the inequality $|t-75| \le 145$ where t is the temperature in Fahrenheit. Which of the following shows the range of temperatures on Mars?
A) $-220 < t < 220$
B) $-70 \le t \le 145$
C) $70 \le t \le 220$
D) $-220 \le t \le 70$

8 The average temperature in Minneapolis last week was 34°F. The temperature fluctuated between 7 degrees cooler or warmer. Which equation represents the high and low temperature, t, in Minneapolis last week?
A) $|t+7| = 34$
B) $|t+34| = 7$
C) $|t-7| = 34$
D) $|34-t| = 7$

9 If $|26x| = 13$, the possible values for x are
A) only $\frac{1}{2}$ and $-\frac{1}{2}$.
B) all real numbers for which $-\frac{1}{2} \le x \le \frac{1}{2}$.
C) all real numbers except $\frac{1}{2}$ and $-\frac{1}{2}$.
D) all real numbers for which $-2 \le x \le 2$.

The Tutorverse

10 At a factory, a machine fills bags with coffee beans. After the bags are filled, another machine weighs them. If the bag's weight differs from 16 ounces by more than 0.5 ounces, the bag is rejected. Which equation could be used to find the heaviest and lightest acceptable weights?

A) $|x - 0.5| = 16$

B) $|x - 16| = 0.5$

C) $|x + 0.5| = 16$

D) $|x + 16| = 0.5$

11 Dominique is baking pastries. The oven is set to 180°C but vacillates 5°C during baking. Which of the following represents all the temperatures that the oven reaches during baking?

A) $|x - 5| \leq 180$

B) $|x - 180| \geq 5$

C) $|x - 180| \leq 5$

D) $|x - 5| \geq 180$

12 It usually takes Jane between 30 and 40 minutes to drive to visit her friend's house. The house is 25 miles away. Which of the following shows the range of speed, in miles per hour, that Jane likely travels to get to her friend's house?

A) $|x - 30| \leq 10$

B) $|x - 43.75| \leq 6.25$

C) $|x - 50| \leq 12.5$

D) $|x + 37.5| \leq 12.5$

13 If $x < 0$, $|-x| =$

A) $-x$

B) x

C) 0

D) $-|x|$

Student Produced Response – Calculator

1 The average score on Mr. Rodriguez's chemistry final was a 72. Mr. Rodriguez calculated that the rest of the scores varied by ±15% of the average, which can be represented by the inequality $|x - 72| \leq 10.8$. What score did the lowest-scoring student receive on the test, rounded to the nearest whole number?

2 A café owner hangs art on the walls that is also for sale. She sets the price for each painting at $110.00, but she has given instructions to her employees that the price can vary by as much as 15%. Employees use the inequality $|x - 110| \leq 16.5$ to calculate the possible prices. What is the lowest possible price an employee could offer for a painting, in dollars?

3 Tom earned $100 last week. He has budgeted $30 to spend at the movies, and he wants to keep his spending within $5 of his budget. A ticket costs $7.50. A medium popcorn costs $3.75. A soft drink costs $2.25. His spending at the movies can be represented by the inequality $|s - 30| \leq 5$, where s equals Tom's total spending. If he buys a medium popcorn and soft drink just for himself, and also buys movie tickets for himself and his friends, what is the maximum number of friends he can bring with him while staying within his preferred budget?

The Tutorverse

Mixed Practice – Algebra

(Answers & explanations begin on page 399).

Multiple Choice – No Calculator

1 If $3x = 27$, what is the value of $6x + 5$?
A) 9
B) 30
C) 54
D) 59

2 For a certain brand of snack bars, the peanut butter bars have 40 more calories than the dried fruit bars. If 3 peanut butter bars and 4 dried fruit bars have a total of 750 calories, how many calories does 1 peanut butter bar have?
A) 84
B) 90
C) 130
D) 360

3 Julio needs to score at least an 80 on his next math test in order to maintain his A average, which is an average of 90 or higher. His next test has a maximum point score of 100. Which of the following inequalities describes all the possible scores that Julio can get on his test and maintain his A average?
A) $|x - 80| \le 100$
B) $|x - 100| \le 80$
C) $|x - 90| \le 10$
D) $|x - 10| \le 90$

4

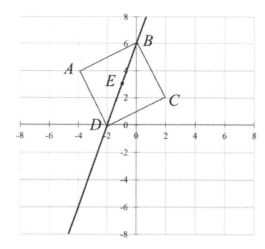

On the *xy*-plane above, *ABCD* is a square and point *E* is the center of the square. The coordinates of points *B* and *E* are $(0,6)$ and $(-1,3)$ respectively. Which of the following is an equation of the line that passes through points *A* and *C*?
A) $y = 3x + 6$
B) $y = -3x - 6$
C) $y = \frac{1}{3}x + 2\frac{2}{3}$
D) $y = -\frac{1}{3}x + 2\frac{2}{3}$

5
$$3x + b = 4x - 7$$
$$3y + c = 4y - 7$$
In the equations above, *b* and *c* are constants. If *b* is *c* plus $\frac{1}{2}$, which of the following is true?
A) *x* is *y* plus $\frac{1}{4}$.
B) *x* is *y* plus $\frac{1}{2}$.
C) *x* is *y* plus 2.
D) *x* is *y* plus 4.

The Tutorverse

Student Produced Response – No Calculator

1
$$ax - y = -3$$
$$y = bx - 5$$
In the system of equations above, a and b are constants and $a \neq b$. The system has one solution at $(1,-1)$. What is the value of b?

2   If $3a - 5 \geq 1$, what is the least possible value of $3a + 5$?

Multiple Choice – Calculator

1   When 3 times the number x is added to 9, the result is 3. What number results when 2 times x is added to 15?
A) -2
B)   5
C)   11
D)   14

2   Lisa and Stacey ate dinner out together. The price of Lisa's dinner was x dollars, and the price of Stacey's dinner was $3.00 more than the price of Lisa's dinner. If Lisa and Stacey split the cost of the meal evenly and each paid a 18% tip, which of the following expressions represents the amount, in dollars, each of them paid? (Assume there is no sales tax.)
A) $0.18x + 0.2$
B) $1.5x + 0.06$
C) $1.18x + 0.27$
D) $1.36x + 1.5$

3   Which of the following numbers is NOT a solution of the inequality $3b - 3 \geq 5b + 5$?
A) -6
B) -5
C) -4
D) -3

4   Sean wants to download songs and podcasts to his smart phone. Every song requires 3.5 megabytes of data, and every podcast requires 20 megabytes of data. Sean wants to download 25 songs and podcasts, but he only has 300 megabytes available on his phone. What is a possible number of podcasts Sean can download?
A)   12
B)   15
C)   17
D)   20

5
$$|m - 4| = 5$$
$$|k + 5| = 10$$
In the equations above $m < 0$ and $k < 0$. What is the value of $m - k$?
A) -16
B) -5
C)   4
D)   14

Student Produced Response – Calculator

1
$$a = 26 + 0.3x$$
$$b = 18 + 0.5x$$
In the equations above, a and b represent the price per square foot of Alex's and Berenice's houses, respectively, x months after they each purchased them. What was the price per square foot of Alex's house, in dollars, when it was the same as the price per square foot of Berenice's house?

The Tutorverse

Data Analysis
Guided Practice – Ratios & Proportions
(Answers & explanations begin on page 401).

Multiple Choice – Calculator

1 If $y = kx$, where k is a constant, and $y = 42$ when $x = 7$, what is y when $x = 9$?
A) 49
B) 54
C) 63
D) 72

2 A bakery sells cupcakes for $2.75 each, or a dozen for $21. How much cheaper is the unit price of the cupcakes sold by the dozen than one sold individually?
A) $0.75
B) $1.00
C) $1.75
D) $4.89

3 Comparing the growth of two dogs, Dora notices that Rover has gained 30% more weight than Spot. When Dora first observed both dogs, they both weighed 20 kg and Rover now weighs 46 kg. How much does Spot weigh now?
A) 35.4 kg
B) 40.0 kg
C) 53.8 kg
D) 59.8 kg

4 A rectangle is 20 meters long and 20 meters wide. If the length is increased by 10% and the width is decreased by 10%, what is the new area?
A) 320
B) 396
C) 400
D) 484

5 A rectangle is 50 feet long and 40 feet wide. The length is decreased by 20% and the width is increased by 20%. What is the percent decrease in the area, rounded to the nearest percent?
A) 0%
B) 1%
C) 4%
D) 10%

6 A bike messenger is paid $5 per delivery and can on average deliver one package every 15 minutes. If she worked five hours on Thursday and four hours on Friday, how much money did she earn in those two days if her rate of delivery was equal to the average?
A) $36
B) $300
C) $180
D) $144

The next two questions refer to the following information.
In a sales position, the salesperson's earnings are in direct proportion to the number of items sold. If the salesperson sells 40 items, he earns $1,500.

7 How much will the salesperson earn if he sells 180 items?
A) $5,200
B) $5,850
C) $6,275
D) $6,750

8 The salesperson uses 67% of his earnings for living expenses. The remainder is placed in a savings account. How much will the salesperson place in the savings account after selling 40 items?
A) $495
B) $1,005
C) $1,320
D) $2,680

9 On Wednesday of Spirit Week, a survey was done of the juniors wearing the school colors. Out of 650 students, 48% were wearing the school colors. How many juniors were *not* wearing the school colors that day?
A) 312
B) 338
C) 360
D) 384

The Tutorverse

10 The spacecraft New Horizons took 9.5 years to travel from Earth to Pluto, a distance of 4.67×10^9 miles. What was the approximate average speed for the trip in miles per hour?

A) 3.23×10^7
B) 1.35×10^6
C) 5.61×10^4
D) 2.24×10^4

11 The atomic weight of the element mercury, in atomic mass units (amu), is approximately 200 amu. The atomic weight of cerium is approximately 30% less than that of mercury. Which of the following best approximates the atomic weight, in amu, of cerium?

A) 60 amu
B) 140 amu
C) 194 amu
D) 158 amu

12 A high school senior reviewed 25% more pages in her science textbook on Thursday than on Wednesday. If the total number of pages she reviewed on Thursday was 40, how many pages did she review on Wednesday?

A) 15
B) 32
C) 50
D) 65

13 A smartphone that regularly costs $600 is on sale for 40% off. A customer used a coupon for an additional discount on the marked sale price at checkout. If the final price of the smartphone is $252, what additional discount was applied to the sale price?

A) 5%
B) 18%
C) 30%
D) 43%

14 The density of an object is equal to the mass of the object divided by the volume of the object. Aluminum has a density of 2.7 grams per cubic centimeter. What is the mass, in grams, of a sample of aluminum with a volume of 8 cubic centimeters?

A) 0.3375
B) 2.96
C) 10.7
D) 21.6

15 A quality assurance analyst chooses 7 of every 200 widgets manufactured to inspect for quality of the manufacturing process. To ensure the same percentage of widgets checked, how many widgets should the analyst inspect from 35,000 produced?

A) 775
B) 1,225
C) 1,550
D) 1,725

16 1 furlong = 660 feet
1 mile = 5,280 feet
A wheat farmer drives his tractor 3 miles in one morning. How many furlongs did he drive?

A) 27
B) 24
C) 18
D) 15

17 1 acre = 43,560 square feet
1 square yard = 9 square feet
A real estate developer bought 3.5 acres of land. For development purposes, he divides the land into square yards on a topographical map. How many square yards did he buy?

A) 1,372,140
B) 112,011
C) 16,940
D) 1,383

The Tutorverse

18   14 pounds = 1 stone
1 pound = 16 ounces
A British doctor calculates the average weight of an adult male as 11.9 stone. What is the average weight of an adult male, in ounces?
A)   2,665.6
B)   2,332.4
C)   41.9
D)   13.6

19   When Ms. Martinez negotiated her annual salary 10 years ago, it was agreed that she would receive a raise every year of 5% of her starting salary. Her annual salary this year is $72,000. What was her first year's salary?
A) $22,000
B) $43,100
C) $44,200
D) $48,000

20   1 ounce = 28.35 grams
1 pound = 16 ounces
A jeweler is buying gold at 20% below the current market value of $40 per gram. Approximately how much will he pay for a gold necklace that weighs 0.1 pounds?
A) $54.4
B) $363
C) $1,451
D) $1,814

21   Last year, a driving instructor taught 300 students, 240 of which passed their driving test on the first try. This year, the instructor taught 240 students, 144 of which passed their driving test on the first try. Which of the following best approximates the percentage of all of the instructor's students in the past two years who passed their driving test on the first try?
A)   60%
B)   70%
C)   71%
D)   80%

22   A certain family kept track of their annual spending last year. The following table shows their results.

Expenses	Percentage of Total Income
Rent	26
Food	10
Car Expenses	14
Clothing	3
Insurance	9
Entertainment	4
Taxes	34

If the family spent $1,920 on clothing last year, approximately how much was spent on rent, in thousands of dollars?
A)   6
B)   17
C)   58
D)   64

23   Light can travel approximately 300 million meters in one second. What is that speed, in kilometers per minute?
A) 5×10^3
B) 1.8×10^7
C) 5×10^9
D) 1.8×10^{13}

24   A car is moving at a speed of 30 miles per hour. Which expression has a value equal to the car's speed, in feet per minute? (*Note: There are 5,280 feet in 1 mile.*)
A) $\dfrac{30 \times 5,280}{60}$
B) $\dfrac{60 \times 5,280}{30}$
C) $\dfrac{30 \times 60}{5,280}$
D) $\dfrac{60}{30 \times 5,280}$

The Tutorverse

25 In a certain high school, the ratio of boys to the entire student population is $\frac{3}{7}$. If there are 1,200 girls in the school, how many boys are there?
A) 300
B) 400
C) 900
D) 1,100

26 The average car contains approximately 330 pounds of aluminum and 2,400 pounds of steel. If a car manufacturer uses 200 tons of aluminum in one day, approximately how many pounds of steel does it use?
A) 57,000
B) 850,000
C) 3,000,000
D) 1,000,000,000

27 A car factory manufactures 10 cars every 12 minutes. Assuming the factory never closes, how many cars can it make in 12 hours?
A) 10
B) 100
C) 600
D) 7,200

28 An architect is designing a gallery space for an artist using the Golden Ratio. He wants the ratio of the length to the height of the feature wall to equal 1.618. If the wall is 13 feet high, approximately how long will the wall be?
A) 8
B) 11
C) 15
D) 21

29 Madden filled her car's gas tank to the top and then drove her car at a constant spend along a highway for one hour, using 16% of the gas in the tank. If her gas tank is depleted at a constant rate, approximately how many more hours will she be able to drive?
A) 5.25
B) 6.25
C) 15
D) 16

30 Between 1970 and 2006, carbon monoxide emissions in the United States fell from 197 million tons to 89 million tons, while sulfur dioxide emissions fell from 31 million tons to 15 million tons. Which had the greater percent decrease?
A) carbon monoxide emissions, because its 54.8% decrease is greater than a 51.6% decrease
B) carbon monoxide emissions, because its 48.4% decrease is greater than a 45.2% decrease
C) sulfur dioxide emissions, because its 54.8% decrease is greater than a 51.6% decrease
D) sulfur dioxide emissions, because its 48.4% decrease is greater than a 45.2% decrease

31 In 2011, the total world strawberry production in tons was 4,594,539, of which 1,312,960 tons were produced in the United States. What percent of the world's strawberries in 2011 were produced in places outside the United States?
A) 3.5
B) 28.6
C) 49.9
D) 71.4

The Tutorverse

Student Produced Response – Calculator

1   A woman is jogging at a rate of 2 meters per second. What is the woman's speed, rounded to the nearest integer, in feet per minute? (*Note: There are 0.305 meters in one foot.*)

2   Joni Construction is planning to pave over a park to build a parking lot. On the blueprint, the park takes up 120 in². The scale on the map shows that 1 in = 10 meters. They are planning on using one ton of concrete to build every 200 m² of the parking lot floor. Approximately how many tons of concrete will be needed to cover the entire park?

3   Susan took 8 math tests over the course of one semester. Her average score on the first 3 tests was 84. Her average score on her last 5 tests was 92. What was the overall average of all 8 tests?

4   The highest grossing film released in 2015 earned $935.8 million in ticket sales, which was 8.4% of the total amount earned in ticket sales by all films released that year. What was the total amount of money earned by all films, in billions of dollars, rounded to the nearest tenth of a billion?

Guided Practice – Linear & Exponential Growth

(Answers & explanations begin on page 404).

Multiple Choice – Calculator

1   Which of the following functions would describe the total amount, *A*, a bank customer would receive, in dollars, on a deposit of $10,000 at an annual percentage rate of 15% compounded annually for *t* years?

A) $A = 10,000(1.015)^t$

B) $A = 10,000(11.5^t)$

C) $A = 10,000(1 + 0.15)^t$

D) $A = 10,000(0.15)^t$

2   Which of the following statements is *not* an example of exponential growth?
A)   Every year, the amount of interest earned at a fixed rate during that year is added to the principle.
B)   Every year, the amount of amount of money which earns interest increases by the amount of interest earned the previous year.
C)   Every year, the principle increases based on the amount of interest accrued from the previous year.
D)   Every year, the amount of money added to the account is constant.

3   Which one of the following sequences would be considered an example of exponential growth?

A) $\dfrac{1}{2}, \dfrac{3}{2}, \dfrac{5}{2}, \dfrac{7}{2}, \dfrac{9}{2}$

B) $\dfrac{2}{3}, \dfrac{4}{9}, \dfrac{8}{27}, \dfrac{16}{81}, \dfrac{32}{243}$

C) $\dfrac{3}{2}, \dfrac{9}{4}, \dfrac{27}{8}, \dfrac{81}{16}, \dfrac{243}{32}$

D) $4, 8, 12, 16, 20$

4   The population of lizards in a park is observed over the course of eighteen weeks, as shown in the table below.

Lizard Population

Week of Observation	Number of Lizards Observed
Initial Population	250
Week 3	220
Week 6	190
Week 9	160
Week 12	130
Week 15	100
Week 18	70

Which of the following best describes the relationship between time and the observable population of lizards during the eighteen weeks?
A)   Increasing linear
B)   Decreasing linear
C)   Exponential growth
D)   Exponential decay

5   The rule of 72 is a method of approximation based on the compound interest formula to determine how long an amount will take to double, given a fixed annual rate of interest. By dividing 72 by the annual rate of return, investors can roughly estimate the number of years it will take for the initial amount to double. Approximately how many years will it take for an initial amount of $240 to accrue enough interest to become $480 at a fixed annual interest rate of 6%?
A)   6
B)   8.33
C)   12
D)   72

The Tutorverse

6 The chart below displays the number of bacteria observed in a sample.

Expected Number of Bacteria

Time of Observation	Number of Bacteria
2:00 PM	100,000
2:30 PM	150,000
3:00 PM	225,000
3:30 PM	

The bacteria's method of reproduction leads to exponential growth. What is the expected number of bacteria at 4:00PM?

A) 300,000
B) 337,500
C) 375,000
D) 506,250

The next two questions refer to the information below:

The formula below is used for estimating the growth of a certain colony of bacteria based on the number of bacteria initially in the sample:

$$N_{NOW+20} = N_{NOW} + 0.7N_{NOW}\left(1 - \frac{N_{NOW}}{K}\right)$$

7 If $N_{NOW} = 10,000$ and $K = 50,000$, what is N_{NOW+20}, the number of bacteria twenty minutes from now?

A) 13,500
B) 15,600
C) 18,400
D) 19,700

8 What will be the value of K if the desired number of bacteria at the end of 20 minutes (N_{NOW+20}) is 14,200 and the initial number is 10,000?

A) 25,000
B) 30,000
C) 35,000
D) 40

9 An investor earned 100% annually on her investment in a strong performing business and reinvested her earnings into that business. Which of the following choices describes the growth of the amount she originally invested?

A) the amount will double every year
B) the amount will be 100 times larger each year
C) the amount will be unchanged each year
D) the amount will be $100 greater each year

10 Which of the following equations below describes the amount of interest that would be lost as a result of the interest rate on an annually compounded account decreasing from 9% to 7%?

A) $A = P(1 - 0.2)^t$

B) $A = P\left(\left(1 + \dfrac{9}{100}\right)^t - \left(1 + \dfrac{7}{100}\right)^t\right)$

C) $A = P(1.2)^t$

D) $A = P(0.8)^t$

11 In a wildlife refuge, the number of prairie dogs is observed over a four year period. The initial population, observed the first year as 16,000, and each succeeding year is recorded in the table below.

Prairie Dog Observation

Year of Observation	Number of Prairie Dogs Observed
1	16,000
2	20,000
3	25,000
4	31,250

What is the percent increase added to the population each year?

A) 50%
B) 37.5%
C) 33%
D) 25%

12   Two banks offer the same interest rate on deposits. One bank compounds annually and the other compounds semiannually. Which formula below would be used to calculate the difference, A_D, between the total value of an account compounded semiannually versus annual compounding on an initial amount of P dollars at rate r percent for t years?

A) $A_D = P\left(\left(1 + \dfrac{2}{r}\right)^{\frac{t}{2}}\right) - (1 + r)^t$

B) $A_D = P \cdot r^t - P \cdot r \cdot t$

C) $A_D = P\left(\left(1 + \dfrac{2r}{2}\right)^{2t} - (1 + r)^t\right)$

D) $A_D = P\left(\left(1 + \dfrac{r}{2}\right)^{2t} - (1 + r)^t\right)$

Student Produced Response – Calculator

1 $\dfrac{25}{9}, \dfrac{125}{27}, \dfrac{625}{81}, \dfrac{3{,}125}{243}$

In the above sequence of exponentially increasing numbers, what is the common ratio that is being raised to increasing integer powers?

2   The chart below displays the observed number of perch in an underwater wildlife preserve over the course of three years.

Perch Population Over Time

First Observation	4,290
1 year after first observation	4,590
2 years after first observation	4,912
3 years after first observation	5,255

What is the annual percentage growth of the number of perch in the underwater preserve during the three recorded years, to the nearest whole percent? (*Ignore the percent symbol when entering your answer.*)

3   During the first year of life, a certain species of panda increases its weight by 40% every six months. By what percent will the panda have increased its weight after 1 year?

13   One bank in town has a promotion to attract new savings accounts. The bank offers three different levels of compounding interest, depending on how much is deposited. All three levels set the savings rate of interest to the same percent as the number of times per year the account is compounded. The highest rate is compounded monthly. If an annual compounding would result in the rate of 1% and a semiannual compounding would set the savings rate equal to 2%, which general formula below would describe the amounts in each of three accounts if n is the number of times the interest is compounded per year?

A) $A = 2^{nt} P \;\; A = 2^{nt} P$

B) $A = 1.2^{nt} P$

C) $A = P(1 + n)^{2nt}$

D) $A = P(1.01)^{nt}$

4   Exponential growth has been observed in a certain species of rabbit at a wildlife preserve as summarized in the chart below.

Wildlife Preserve Rabbit Population

Year of Observation	Number of Prairie Dogs Observed
1	1,600
2	2,000
3	2,500
4	

At the rate deduced from the chart, what would be the expected number of rabbits in the fourth year?

5   Mark was looking at the chart shown below of the annually reported amounts for an account into which he had invested $40,000.

Account Balance Over Time

Year	Amount
0 (Initial Amount)	$ 40,000
1	$ 43,200
2	$ 46,656

What is the annual percentage rate of growth, based on annual compounding?

6   A scientist discovers a new element. When he exposes 48 grams of the element to oxygen, a chemical reaction happens and the amount of the element remaining decreases by 0.6g per second. When he exposes 48 grams of the element to hydrogen, a chemical reaction happens and the amount of the element remaining decreases by half of itself every 12 seconds. How many more grams are left of the oxygen-exposed element than the hydrogen-exposed element after one minute?

7   Two competing astrophysicists have each created a computer model that can discover new stars in the universe beyond the Milky Way. The first astrophysicist's model found 10 new stars on the first day and, every day after, finds twice as many new stars as the previous day. The second astrophysicist's model found 200 new stars on the first day and, every day after, finds 125 more new stars than the previous day. How many more stars does the first astrophysicist find than the second astrophysicist on Day 10?

Guided Practice – Interpreting Graphs & Tables

(Answers & explanations begin on page 406).

Multiple Choice – Calculator

1   Michelle does aerobic exercise for one hour every day. The graph below shows her target heart rate at different times during her workout.

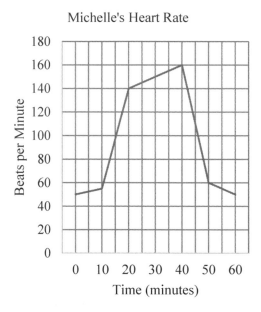

On which interval is the target heart rate strictly increasing then strictly decreasing?
A)   Between 0 and 20 minutes
B)   Between 10 and 30 minutes
C)   Between 30 and 50 minutes
D)   Between 40 and 60 minutes

2   Which of the following graphs best shows a strong negative association between *x* and *y*?
A)

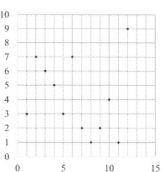

B)

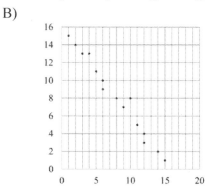

C)

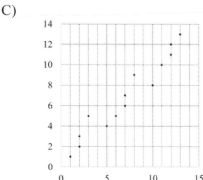

D)

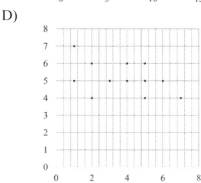

3 Jennifer is planning a school assignment. The table below shows information about the assignment.

Category	Measurement
# of hours Jennifer plans to spend on assignment per day	2
# of hours for research	3
# of pages in the assignment	15
# of words per page	500
# of words Jennifer writes per minute	70
# of words in the assignment	7,500

If Jennifer completes the assignment at the rate given in the table, which of the following is the closest to the number of days Jennifer will need to complete the assignment?

A) 2
B) 3
C) 5
D) 6

4

Highway Toll Traffic

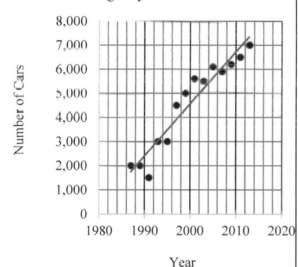

Year

According to the line of best fit in the scatterplot above, which of the following best approximates the year in which the number of cars that passed through the toll was estimated to be 6,500?

A) 2005
B) 2007
C) 2010
D) 2013

5

The graph above shows Joe's distance from his house during a 3-hour bike ride. He stopped for 30 minutes to take photos in a park. Based on the graph, which of the following is closest to the time he finished taking photos and continued his bike ride?

A) 1:20
B) 2:00
C) 2:50
D) 3:10

6 The table below represents ticket sales for 35 productions put on at the Chestertown Theater, categorized by genre and intended audience.

Chestertown Theater Productions

	Comedy	Drama	Musical	Total
Child	4	2	6	12
Any	5	3	2	10
Adult	3	5	5	13
Total	12	10	13	35

What fraction of the movies is dramas intended for adults?

A) $\dfrac{1}{7}$

B) $\dfrac{2}{7}$

C) $\dfrac{1}{3}$

D) $\dfrac{5}{13}$

The Tutorverse

The next two questions refer to the below information:

The scatter plot below shows the recorded high temperatures in September for a town in Minnesota.

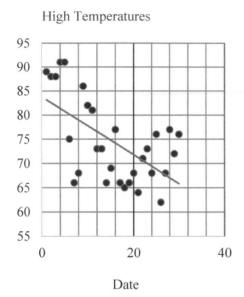

High Temperatures

Date

7   Based on the line of best fit to the data shown, which of the following values is closest to the average daily decrease in temperature?
A)   1°F
B)   3°F
C)   5°F
D)   20°F

8   Based on the graph, which of the following show the general trend in temperatures?
A)   The temperature generally increased throughout the month.
B)   The temperature generally decreased throughout the month.
C)   The temperature increased until September 15 and then generally decreased.
D)   The temperature generally remained steady throughout the month.

9   The scatter plot below shows how the interval between eruptions and the length of each eruption has changed over time.

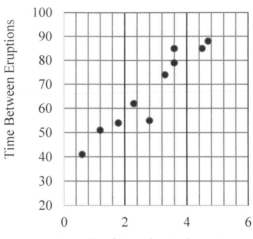

Geyser Eruptions

Length of Eruption (minutes)

If a line of best fit were drawn, which would best approximate the length of the eruption after an 80-minute interval?
A)   2 minutes
B)   3 minutes
C)   4 minutes
D)   5 minutes

10   A survey was conducted of people who voted in a recent Senate election in one district. The table below displays a summary of the survey results.

Age	Candidate A	Candidate B	Total
18–29	255	383	638
30–44	656	684	1,340
45–64	1,801	1,200	3,001
65 or over	604	737	1,341

According to the table, for which age group did the greatest percentage of people within that age group vote for Candidate B?
A)   18–29
B)   30–44
C)   45–64
D)   65 or over

The next two questions refer to the below information:

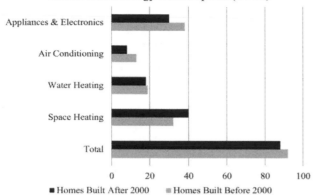

United States Energy Consumption (BTUs)

■ Homes Built After 2000   ▓ Homes Built Before 2000

The bar graph above shows energy consumption in millions of British thermal units (Btu) in the United States, by type of heating or cooling, for homes built before 2000 and homes built after 2000.

11 In a scatterplot of this data, where energy consumption in homes built before 2000 is plotted along the x-axis and energy consumption in homes built after 2000 is plotted along the y-axis for each of the given energy uses, how many data points would be above the line $y = x$?

A) 1
B) 2
C) 4
D) 5

12 A researcher noticed that the number of household appliances in the average house built since 2000 has gone up by 15%. Which of the following conclusions is most valid?

A) A decrease in the amount of energy consumed by an appliance leads to a decrease in the number of appliances installed in a house.
B) An increase in the amount of energy consumed by an appliance leads to an increase in the number of appliances installed in a house.
C) A decrease in the amount of energy consumed by an appliance leads to an increase in the number of appliances installed in a house.
D) Both energy consumption and the number of appliances per house has increased since 2000.

13 If the number of bacteria in a petri dish doubles each hour, which of the following graphs could model the number of bacteria?

A)

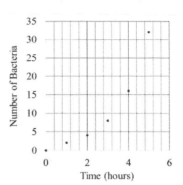

B)

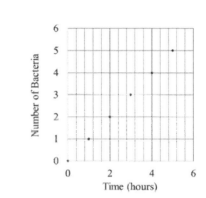

C)

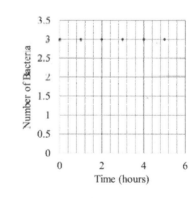

D)

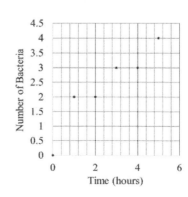

The Tutorverse

The next two questions refer to the below information:

E-Book Sales by Price

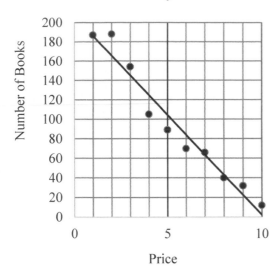

A bookstore sells e-books through its website and tracks the number of sales of books at different price points. The equation for the line of best fit is $y = 196 - 18x$.

14 How many of the different price points sold more than was expected based on the line of best fit?
A) 2
B) 3
C) 5
D) 6

15 What is the best interpretation of the meaning of the *x*-intercept (not pictured) of the line of best fit?
A) The store would be giving away books for free.
B) There would be at least 10 books sold.
C) There would be 196 books sold.
D) Virtually no books would be sold at a price point of more than $10.

The next two questions refer to the below information:

A vacation home rental company tracked the average nightly price of 21 homes. The scatterplot below shows the number of bathrooms in each home and the price of the home per bathroom, along with the line of best fit and the equation for the line. The equation of the line of best fit is $y = 90 - 9x$.

Nightly Price of Home Rental

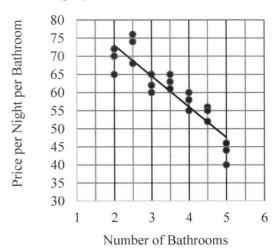

16 According to the line of best fit, approximately how much would it cost to rent a home with three-and-a-half bathrooms for one night? (Round your answer to the nearest dollar.)
A) $55
B) $60
C) $65
D) $205

17 What is the best interpretation of the meaning of the slope of the line of best fit?
A) For each additional full bathroom, the rental price of the home decreases by $9.
B) For each additional full bathroom, the average price per bathroom decreases by $9.
C) For each additional full bathroom, the rental price of the home decreases by $90.
D) For each additional full bathroom, the average price per bathroom decreases by $4.50.

The Tutorverse

18 Tanisha opened a bank account that earns 1.5% interest compounded annually. Her initial deposit was $200. If Tanisha does not deposit any additional money, which of the following functions gives the total amount A, in dollars, that will be in Tanisha's account after t years?

A) $A = 200(1.015t)$

B) $A = 200(1.15t)$

C) $A = 200(1.015)^t$

D) $A = 200(1.15^t)$

19

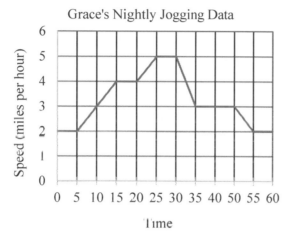

Grace's Nightly Jogging Data

Each evening, Grace jogs for 60 minutes. The graph above shows Grace's speed during a particular night's jog. Which segment of the graph represents the times when Maria's speed is the greatest?

A)   The segment from (5,2) to (15,4).

B)   The segment from (25,5) to (30,5).

C)   The segment from (35,3) to (50,3).

D)   The segment from (55,2) to (60,2).

The next two questions refer to the below information:

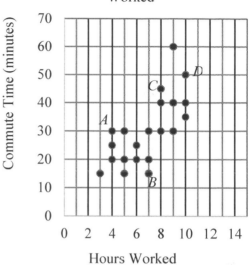

Employee Commutes vs. Hours Worked

The human resources department at a large company created the above scatterplot to examine the relationship between the length of time employees typically work in the office and the time they take to commute to the office.

20 How many hours does the person who lives farthest from the office typically work?

A)   8

B)   9

C)   10

D)   Cannot be answered from the given information

21 The labeled points represent different employees. Which labeled employee spends the most time commuting per hour worked?

A) A (4,30)

B) B (6,25)

C) C (8,45)

D) D (10,50)

The Tutorverse

Student Produced Response – Calculator

1   The graph below shows the annual smart phone sales at an electronics store. According to the graph, the number of smart phone sales in 2012 is what fraction of those sold in 2015?

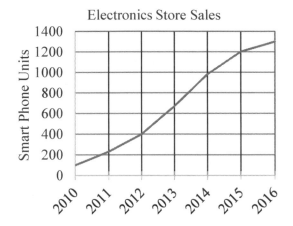

Electronics Store Sales

The next two questions refer to the below information:

A clothes store tracked sales of t-shirts for six months in the graph below.

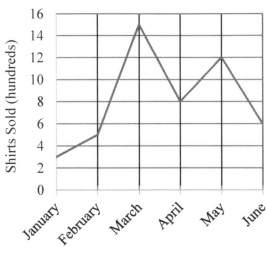

Clothing Store Sales

Month

2   According to the graph, the number of shirts sold in January is what fraction of those sold in April?

3   According to the graph, how many more shirts were sold in the month with the most sales than the month with the least sales?

The Tutorverse

Guided Practice – Additional Data Analysis & Statistics

(Answers & explanations begin on page 408).

Multiple Choice – Calculator

1   The number of households who have switched to using renewable energy in their homes instead of fossil fuels in 5 countries is shown in the chart below.

Renewable Energy in Five Countries

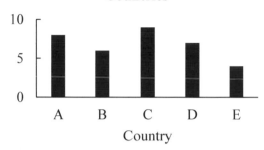

If the total number of households using renewable energy is 34,000, what is an appropriate label for the vertical axis of the graph?

A)   Number of households (in tens)
B)   Number of households (in hundreds)
C)   Number of households (in thousands)
D)   Number of households (in tens of thousands)

2   The table below shows the distribution of age and gender for 100 people who visited an amusement park.

Gender	Under 18	18 or Older	Total
Male	15	40	55
Female	10	35	45
Total	25	75	100

If one out of every 100 amusement park visitors is chosen to win a free ticket, what is the probability that the winner will be either a male or a female over age 18?

A) $\dfrac{75}{100}$

B) $\dfrac{40}{100}$

C) $\dfrac{35}{100}$

D) $\dfrac{25}{100}$

3   The years that constitute certain milestones in the population of the world are shown in the table below.

Year	Population (millions)
1650	508
1750	790
1800	980
1850	1,260
1900	1,650
1950	2,557
2000	6,088
2050*	9,408

*Estimated. Source: U.S. Census Bureau

Which of the following best describes the relationship between time and the estimated world population during these years?

A)   Increasing linear
B)   Decreasing linear
C)   Exponential growth
D)   Exponential decay

4

Number of Eggs per Carton	Price
1	$ 1.00
6	$ 3.50
12	$ 4.99
18	$ 5.89

Based on the table above, which of the following is the least amount of money needed to purchase exactly 100 eggs?

A) $36.95
B) $43.92
C) $60.00
D) $100.00

The Tutorverse

5 A researcher polled 100 subway commuters during the morning rush hour to find out which kind of pass they used to pay for their ride. The result of this poll is shown in the chart below.

Subway Pass Usage

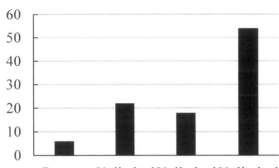

The sum of the commuters who used Pay Per Ride passes and Unlimited Day Passes is approximately what percent of all commuters polled?

A) 22%
B) 28%
C) 46%
D) 54%

6 A quality control researcher at an electronics company is testing the life of the company's batteries in certain smart phones. The researcher selects 100 batteries at random from the daily output of the batteries and finds that the average life of the batteries has a 95% confidence interval of 8-12 hours with normal phone use. Which of the following conclusions is the most reasonable based on the confidence interval?

A) It is plausible that the true average life of batteries produced by the company that day is between 8 and 12 hours.
B) It is plausible that the true average life of all batteries ever produced by the company is between 8 and 12 hours.
C) 95% of all the batteries produced by the company have a life between 8 and 12 hours.
D) 95% of all the batteries ever produced by the company have a life between 8 and 12 hours.

7 A sports team is deciding whether to implement new security measures to prevent tickets to games from being resold illegally. Capacity at the stadium is 20,000 people, and the security team estimates that there are 45 people per game who purchased tickets illegally. The security manager estimated the results of a new security measures as shown in the table below.

	Illegal Tickets Detected	Tickets Allowed	Total
Illegal Tickets	38	7	45
Legal Tickets	12	19,943	19,955
Total	50	19,950	20,000

According to the manager's estimates, if illegal tickets are detected, what is the probability that the customer did *not* attempt to use an illegal ticket?

A) 0.19%
B) 0.25%
C) 24%
D) 76%

8 A certain calculus professor offers all of the students in his course an additional study session before each exam. The students who attended the additional study session did better on the exam than students who didn't attend. Which of the following is an appropriate conclusion?

A) Attending the additional study session will cause an improvement for any student who takes any math class.
B) Attending the additional study session will cause an improvement for any student who takes a calculus class.
C) Attending the additional study session was the cause of the improvement for the students at this university who took this professor's calculus class.
D) No conclusion about cause and effect can be made regarding students at this university who attended the additional study session and their performance on the exam.

The Tutorverse

9

Science Class Enrollment by Gender

Class	Male	Female	Total
Biology	45	52	97
Chemistry	39	50	89
Physics	36	38	74
Total	120	140	260

A group of high school students responded to a survey that asked which science course they were currently enrolled in, the results of which were recorded in the table above. Which of the following categories accounts for 15% of all survey respondents?

A)   Females taking biology
B)   Females taking chemistry
C)   Males taking chemistry
D)   Males taking biology

10

Heights of Athletes

59	60	60	61	62	63
63	64	65	65	66	67
67	67	68	69	70	78

The table above lists the heights, to the nearest inch, of a random sample of female athletes competing at a track meet. The outlier measurement of 78 inches is an error. Of the mean, median, and range of the listed values, which will change the most if the 78-inch measurement is removed from the data?

A)   Mean
B)   Median
C)   Range
D)   The mean, median, and range will all change by the same amount.

Questions 11 and 12 refer to the following information.

Proposed Annual County Budget (millions USD)

Department	2014	2015	2016
General	3.14	3.55	3.05
Health	6.48	7.54	8.56
Public Protection	7.32	7.45	7.63
Public Assistance	6.85	6.54	6.56
Recreation & Culture	0.65	0.7	0.85
Other	1.15	1.25	1.36
Total	25.59	27.03	28.01

The table above lists the annual budget, in millions of dollars, for a county in California.

11   Which of the following best approximates the average rate of change in the annual budget for Public Protection in this county from 2014 to 2016?
A) $130,000 per year
B) $155,000 per year
C) $180,000 per year
D) $1,550,000 per year

12   Of the following, which department's ratio of its 2014 to its 2016 budget is closest to the Recreation & Culture department's ratio of its 2014 to its 2016 budget?
A)   Health
B)   Public Protection
C)   Public Assistance
D)   Other

13

Home Sale Prices

The scatterplot above shows home sale prices and square footage for several homes in a certain town. The line of best fit is also shown, and has equation $y = .8529x + 71$. Which of the following best explains how the number 71 in the equation relates to the scatterplot?

A)   The smallest house in the town costs $71 per square foot.

B)   The cheapest house in the town costs $71,000.

C)   Land costs about $71,000 per square foot.

D)   Even tiny houses are likely to cost at least $71,000.

14   A researcher conducted a survey to determine whether people in a certain city preferred shopping at big chains or at independently-owned stores. The researcher surveyed 23 people who were shopping downtown on a Saturday, three of whom refused to respond. Which of the following factors makes it least likely that a reliable conclusion can be drawn about the shopping preferences of all of the people in the city?

A)   Sample size.

B)   Population size.

C)   The number of people who refused to respond.

D)   Where the survey was conducted.

15   Eight students each took a shift in the park to count the number of birds spotted in a 1-hour period. Each student was in the park for exactly 1 hour and no shifts overlapped. Their data is shown in the table below.

Student	Number of Birds
A	32
B	27
C	54
D	43
E	35
F	48
G	32
H	29

What is the mean number of birds spotted each hour?

A)   27

B)   32

C)   33.5

D)   37.5

Questions 16 and 17 refer to the following information.

Because the gravitational pull is different on different planets, weight varies depending on the strength of the gravitational pull. The table shows the approximate weight of a 150-pound person on different planets.

Planet	Weight (pounds)
Mars	56.5
Mercury	56.7
Uranus	133.3
Venus	136.0
Saturn	159.6
Neptune	168.7
Jupiter	354.6

16   Based on this data, what is the weight of a 175-pound person on Saturn?

A)   164.5 pounds

B)   184.6 pounds

C)   186.2 pounds

D)   413.7 pounds

The Tutorverse

17 An object on Earth weighs 100 pounds. On which planet would the same object have an approximate weight of 236 pounds?
A) Venus
B) Jupiter
C) Uranus
D) Neptune

18 In order to determine if a change to a car engine gave the car better gas mileage, a research study was conducted. From all the cars produced by a factory in a given week, 50 were randomly selected. Half of them were tested with the new engines, and the other half kept the old engines. The resulting data showed that cars with the new engines had significantly better gas mileage as compared to the old engines. Based on the design and result of the study, which of the following is an appropriate conclusion?
A) The new engines cause substantial improvements in gas mileage.
B) The new engines will improve the gas mileage of any cars they are used in.
C) The new engines improve gas mileage better than other manufacturing changes.
D) The new engines are likely to improve gas mileage for the car model this factory produces.

19

Gender	Yes	No
Male		
Female		
Total	110	45

The incomplete table above summarizes, by gender, the number of students who play at least one sport for a tenth-grade class at a high school. There are twice as many female students who play sports than female students who don't and 3 times as many male students who play a sport as those who don't. Which of the following is closest to the probability that a student who plays a sport selected at random is female?
A) 0.23
B) 0.41
C) 0.45
D) 0.55

20 A researcher asked office workers in two different cities about how many cups of coffee they typically drink each day and recorded the results in the chart below.

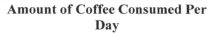

Amount of Coffee Consumed Per Day

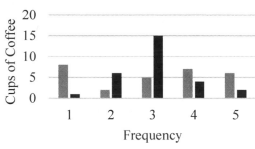

■ City A ■ City B

Which of the following is true about the data shown?
A) The standard deviation of cups of coffee consumed per day in City A is larger than that of City B.
B) The standard deviation of cups of coffee consumed per day in City B is larger than that of City A.
C) The standard deviation of cups of coffee consumed per day City A is the same as that of City B.
D) The standard deviation of cups of coffee consumed per day in these cities cannot be determined with the data provided.

21 A football team scores an average of 11 points per game over 4 games. If the team scored 7, 18, and 6 points at 3 games, respectively, how many points did they score in the 4th game?
A) 11
B) 13
C) 15
D) 17

22

Students Enrolled by Geographic Region

Class	Northeast	Midwest	South	West
Freshman	2,345	1,018	1,164	1,465
Sophomore	1,987	1,672	1,011	1,234
Junior	2,015	1,212	1,332	1,115
Senior	1,874	1,341	1,216	1,102
Total	8,221	5,243	4,723	4,916

The table above shows the number of students enrolled in a large northeastern university, in four geographic regions and class groups. Based on the table, if a student is chosen at random, which of the following is closest to the probability that the student was a junior from the Midwest?

A)   0.05
B)   0.14
C)   0.21
D)   0.25

23

Day	Minutes
1	3.0
2	2.9
3	2.7
4	2.6
5	2.4
6	2.3
7	2.1
8	2.0

Each day for eight days, Wendy ran a lap around the track. The table above shows the time, in minutes, it took Wendy to run each lap. If the track is 0.25 miles around, which of these is the best approximation Wendy's average speed, in miles per hour?

A)   20
B)   10
C)   6
D)   2.8

24   Amar bowled 3 games. During the first two games, he scored 116 and 148 points, respectively. How many points must he have scored in the third round to have an average score of 134?

A)   132
B)   134
C)   138
D)   166

25

Cookbook Recipes

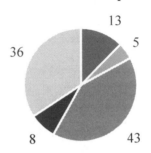

- Appetizers
- Soups
- Entrees
- Snacks
- Desserts

The table above shows the distribution of recipes in a cookbook. Of the mean, median, and range of the values listed, which will change the most if a chapter with 25 side dish recipes is also included in the book?

A)   Mean
B)   Median
C)   Range
D)   They will all change by the same amount.

26   For a class test, the mean score was 71, the median score was 74, and the standard deviation of the scores was 6. The teacher decided to add 5 points to each score due to a grading error. Which of the following statements must be true for the new scores?

     I.   The new mean score is 76.
     II.   The new median score is 79.
     III. The new standard deviation of the scores is 11.

A)   I only
B)   II only
C)   I and II only
D)   I, II, and III

The Tutorverse

27

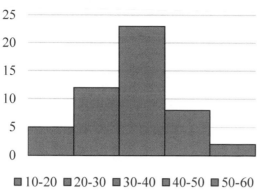

Hours Workd by Clothing Store Employees Last Week

■ 10-20 ■ 20-30 ■ 30-40 ■ 40-50 ■ 50-60

The histogram above shows the number of hours worked last week by 50 employees of a clothing store. In the histogram, the first bar represents all workers who worked at least 10 hours but less than 20 hours; the second represents all workers who worked at least 20 hours but less than 30 hours; and so on. Which of the following could be the median and mean number of hours worked for the 50 employees?

A)   Median: 25, Mean: 24
B)   Median: 34, Mean: 26
C)   Median: 35, Mean: 36
D)   Median: 42, Mean: 40

28 At a gym with 121 members, 54 members are enrolled in a martial arts class and 23 are enrolled in a yoga class. Of the members taking kickboxing or yoga, 12 are taking both classes. How many members are not taking either course?

A)   32
B)   44
C)   56
D)   68

Student Produced Response – Calculator

1 The average temperature in Chicago for 6 days is 66°F. If, on the 7th day, the temperature is 52°F, what is the average temperature, in degrees Fahrenheit, for all 7 days?

2

Manatee Length (ft.)
9.5
8.8
8.3
9.2
x

In a study, manatees in one part of Florida were measured and tagged. If the range of data is 2 feet, what is the least possible value of x?

3

Player	Number of Home Runs
Albert Pujols	560
Alex Rodriguez	687
Babe Ruth	714
Barry Bonds	762
Hank Aaron	755
Ken Griffey, Jr.	630
Mark McGwire	583
Mickey Mantle	536
Reggie Jackson	563
Sammy Sosa	609
Willy Mays	660

The table above lists the number of home runs hit over the careers of 11 prominent baseball players at a certain point in time. According to the table, what is the mean number of career home runs of these players? (Round your answer to the nearest whole number.)

4 A product sold through an online store receives customer satisfaction ratings between 0 and 10, inclusive. In the first 5 ratings the store received, the average (arithmetic mean) of the ratings was 7. What is the least value the store can receive for the 6th rating and still be able to have an average of at least 8 for the first 10 ratings

5 The average score for 18 students on an exam is 82. Two more students take the test, averaging a score of 76 between them. What is the total class average (rounded to the nearest tenth) if these two students are added to the 18?

6

T-Shirt Sales

	18-34	35-49	50+	Total
Before	82	23	12	117
During	22	18	10	50
After	108	44	23	175
Total	212	85	45	342

The table above shows the distribution of t-shirt sales at a theater before, during, and after a concert, arranged by age of concert-goer. If one t-shirt customer will be randomly selected to win tickets to the band's next show, what is the probability that the winner will be someone aged 35-49 who purchased a t-shirt after the concert? (Write your answer as a decimal rounded to the nearest hundredth.)

7 The 20 students taking calculus this school year scored an average of 80 points on their midterm exam. If the average score of 19 of the students was 79, what was the score of the 20th students?

Mixed Practice – Data Analysis

(Answers & explanations begin on page 410).

Multiple Choice – Calculator

1   The graph shows the number of points scored by each member of a basketball team during the past season. There is one bar missing.

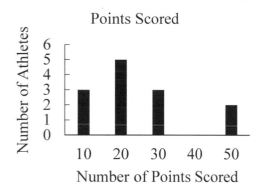

If the median of the data is 20, which of the following could be the number of athletes that scored 40 points?

A)   2
B)   3
C)   4
D)   5

2   Ignoring air friction, an apple falls from a tree with an acceleration of 9.8 m/s² (9.8 meters per second, per second). The speed with which the apple falls (the number of meters traveled per second) can best be described as which of the following?
A)   constant
B)   constantly increasing
C)   constantly decreasing
D)   indeterminable

3   Two members on a rowing team, Tom and Everett, are comparing the time it takes them to row 2,000 meters. Tom is faster than Everett, but Everett argues that he has improved his time over the past six months more than Tom. The table below shows the number of minutes each took to row 2,000 meters six months ago and at a recent practice.

	Six months ago	Current
Tom's 2000-meter time	9:00	8:00
Everett 2000-meter time	12:00	10:00

Over the past six months, by what percentage did each runner improve his time?
A)   Tom improved his time by 11.1%; Everett improved his time by 20%.
B)   Tom improved his time by 12.5%; Everett improved his time by 20%.
C)   Tom improved his time by 11.1%; Everett improved his time by 16.7%.
D)   Tom improved his time by 12.5%; Everett improved his time by 16.7%.

4   The Thompsons are shopping for a new house. They have narrowed their choices down to their four favorites and have recorded the size of each house and the price, as shown below.

House	Size (sq. ft.)	Price (thousands)
Harrison Street	900	$350
Wingspread Road	1,100	$400
Howell Boulevard	1,400	$450
Bennett Avenue	1,500	$500

Based on the information in the table, which house has the lowest cost per square foot?
A)   Harrison Street
B)   Wingspread Road
C)   Howell Boulevard
D)   Bennett Avenue

5 The graph below shows the 10 fastest times sprinters ran the 100 meter dash, graphed against the age of each sprinter.

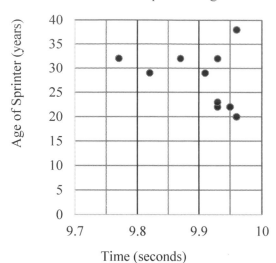

100 Meter Dash: Speed vs. Age

How long did it take the oldest sprinter, in seconds, to finish the 100 meter dash?
A) 9.77
B) 9.87
C) 9.91
D) 9.96

6 The histogram shows the perimeters of all the parks in a certain town.

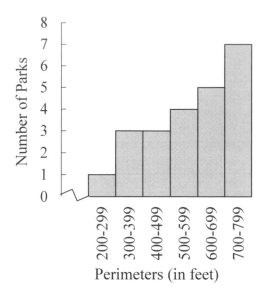

Which of the following could be the median perimeter?
A) 429
B) 513
C) 602
D) 789

Student Produced Response – Calculator

1 An entomologist is studying a species of fruit fly in a controlled environment and currently has 500 of these fruit flies. The population of this species that the botanist expects to grow next month, $N_{\text{next month}}$, can be estimated from the number of fruit flies this month, $N_{\text{this month}}$, according to the following equation:

$N_{\text{next month}} =$

$N_{\text{this month}} + 0.2\,(N_{\text{this month}})\left(1 - \dfrac{1}{K} \cdot N_{\text{this month}}\right)$

If K is a constant representing the maximum number of fruit flies the environment can support, what is the value of K if the number of fruit flies the following month ($N_{\text{next month}}$) is 580?

2 Jason is planning to drive across the country.

Number of hours Jason plans to drive per day	6
Average speed (miles per hour)	40
Miles per gallon of gas	36
Fuel tank capacity (in gallons)	18
Total Number of Miles	2,522

According to the chart above, if Jason starts the trip with a full tank of gas, how many times will he have to refill the tank?

3 A penguin habitat is 60% female. If there are 300 male penguins, how many female penguins are there?

The Tutorverse

Advanced Math
Guided Practice – Working with Polynomials
(Answers & explanations begin on page 411).

Multiple Choice – No Calculator

1 $7x^2 - 4x + 8$

$3x^2 - x + 7$

Which of the following is the sum of the two polynomials shown above?

A) $10x^2 - 3x + 15$

B) $10x^2 - 5x + 15$

C) $10x^4 + 4x^2 + 15$

D) $10x^4 - 5x^2 + 15$

2 $(4x + 3)(5x - 10)$

Which of the following is equivalent to the expression above?

A) $9x - 7$

B) $20x^2 - 30$

C) $20x^2 - 25x \quad 30$

D) $20x^2 - 55x \quad 30$

3 $5(3x + 1)(2x + 1)$

Which of the following is equivalent to the expression above?

A) $60x$

B) $25x^2 + 10$

C) $30x^2 + 5$

D) $30x^2 + 25x + 5$

4 $\dfrac{1}{2}(2x + 4)(x + 1)$

Which of the following is equivalent to the expression above?

A) $x^2 + 2$

B) $x^2 + 3x + 2$

C) $x^2 + 6x + 4$

D) $\dfrac{1}{2}x^2 + \dfrac{3}{2}x + 1$

5 $7x(2x + 1) + 3(2x + 1)$

Which of the following is equivalent to the expression shown above?

     I. $(7x + 3)(2x + 1)$

     II. $14x^2 + 13x + 3$

A)   Only I

B)   Only II

C)   I and II

D)   Neither I nor II

6 If $\dfrac{20}{ab} = 10$ what is the value of $\dfrac{32}{a^2 b^2}$?

A)   2

B)   4

C)   8

D)   16

7 If $\dfrac{x}{y} = 3$ what is the value of $\dfrac{6y}{x}$?

A)   3

B)   2

C)   1

D)   0

8 If $x > 3$, which of the following is equivalent to $\dfrac{\dfrac{1}{x+4} + 1}{\dfrac{2}{x-2}}$?

A) $\dfrac{x-3}{2x+8}$

B) $\dfrac{x-3}{x+4}$

C) $\dfrac{2x+10}{x^2+x-12}$

D) $\dfrac{x^2+2x-10}{2x+8}$

The Tutorverse

9 If $0 < x < 7$, which of the following is equivalent to $\dfrac{\dfrac{x+5}{x+4}}{\dfrac{x-7}{2x+8}}$?

A) $\dfrac{2x+10}{x-7}$

B) $\dfrac{x+5}{2x-14}$

C) $\dfrac{2x^2+40}{x^2-28}$

D) $\dfrac{x^2-2x-35}{2x^2+16x+32}$

10 $4a^4 + 20a^2b^2 + 25b^4$

Which of the following is equivalent to the expression shown above?

A) $(4a+25b)^4$

B) $(2a+5b)^4$

C) $(4a^2+25b^2)^2$

D) $(2a^2+5b^2)^2$

11 $\dfrac{a+3}{x} + \dfrac{b-5}{2x}$

Which of the following is equivalent to the expression above?

A) $\dfrac{a+b-2}{x}$

B) $\dfrac{a+b-2}{2x}$

C) $\dfrac{2a+b+1}{2x}$

D) $\dfrac{a+2b-7}{2x}$

12 The expression $(3x-6)^3$ is equivalent to which of the following?

A) $9x^3 - 216$

B) $9x^3 - 36x^2 + 36$

C) $27x^3 - 162x^2 + 324x - 216$

D) $27x^3 + 162x^2 - 324x + 216$

13 The expression $\dfrac{6x-1}{x+4}$ is equivalent to which of the following?

A) $\dfrac{6-1}{4}$

B) $6 - \dfrac{1}{4}$

C) $6 - \dfrac{1}{x+4}$

D) $6 - \dfrac{25}{x+4}$

14 If $x > 0$, which of the following is equivalent to $\dfrac{3}{x+2} - \dfrac{2}{x^2+4x+4}$?

A) $\dfrac{3x+4}{x^2+4x+4}$

B) $\dfrac{1}{x^2+4x+4}$

C) $\dfrac{-1}{x^2+3x+2}$

D) $\dfrac{3x^2+10x+10}{x^2+6x^2+12x+8}$

15 If $\dfrac{y+1}{x} = \dfrac{6}{7}$, which of the following must also be true?

A) $\dfrac{y}{x} = -\dfrac{1}{7}$

B) $\dfrac{y}{x} = \dfrac{6x-7}{7x}$

C) $\dfrac{y}{x} = \dfrac{5}{7}$

D) $\dfrac{y}{x} = \dfrac{5}{7x}$

16 $f(x) = (x-5)^2 - 1$

Which of the following is an equivalent form of the function f above in which the roots of f appear as constants or coefficients?

A) $f(x) = (x-6)^2$

B) $f(x) = x^2 - 10x + 24$

C) $f(x) = (x-5)(x-1)$

D) $f(x) = (4-x)(6-x)$

The Tutorverse

Student Produced Response – No Calculator

1. $4x(2x+3)+5(4x+1)=ax^2+bx+c$

   In the equation above, a, b, and c are constants. If the equation is true for all values of x, what is the value of b?

2. $x^4-18x^2+81=0$

   For what real, positive value of x is the equation above true?

3. $x^3-7x^2+3x-21=0$

   For what real value of x is the equation above true?

4. $6x^4(x^4-2)=-6$

   If $x>0$, what is one possible solution to the equation above?

Multiple Choice – Calculator

1. The expression $64w^6-v^6$ is equivalent to which of the following?

   A) $(8w^3-v^3)^2$

   B) $(4w^2-v^2)^3$

   C) $(4w^3-v^3)^3$

   D) $(8w^3-v^3)(8w^3+v^3)$

2. $f(x)=(x+3)(x-7)$

   Which of the following is an equivalent form of the function f above in which the minimum value of f appears as a constant or coefficient?

   A) $f(x)=x^2-21$

   B) $f(x)=(x-2)^2-25$

   C) $f(x)=(x+3)^2-7$

   D) $f(x)=x^2-4x-21$

3. $f(x)=x^2$

   $g(x)=x^2-6x+19$

   What is the difference in the minimum values of the functions $f(x)$ and $g(x)$ above?

   A) 3

   B) 6

   C) 10

   D) 19

Student Produced Response – Calculator

1. $(7x^2+2x-4)-5(x^2-3x+2)$

   If the expression above is rewritten in the form ax^2+bx+c, where a, b, and c are constants, what is the value of b?

2. $3xy-15x+y^2-c$

   In the polynomial above, c is a constant. If the polynomial is divisible by $y-5$, what is the value of c?

3. $x^3=2x(24-x)$

   If a, b, and c represent the solutions of the equation above and $a<b<c$, what is the value of c?

The Tutorverse

Guided Practice – Working with Polynomial Factors in Expressions & Equations

(Answers & explanations begin on page 413).

Multiple Choice – No Calculator

1 If $\dfrac{t+3}{t-3} = 6$, what is the value of t?

   A)   3

   B) $\dfrac{6}{5}$

   C) $\dfrac{15}{7}$

   D) $\dfrac{21}{5}$

2 The function f is defined by a polynomial. Some values of x and $f(x)$ are shown in the table below.

x	$f(x)$
0	2
1	0
2	2
3	10

Which of the following must be a factor of $f(x)$?

   A) $x+1$
   B) $x-1$
   C) $x+2$
   D) $x-2$

3 The function f is defined by a polynomial. Some values of x and $f(x)$ are shown in the table above.

x	$f(x)$
-3	0
0	-1
1	0
2	6

Which of the following must be a factor of $f(x)$?

   A) $x-3$
   B) $x-2$
   C) $x+1$
   D) $x+3$

4 The function f is defined by a polynomial. Some values of x and $f(x)$ are shown in the table above.

x	$f(x)$
0	1
2	3
4	7
6	0

Which of the following must be a factor of $f(x)$?

   A) $x-6$
   B) $x-4$
   C) $x-2$
   D) $x-1$

5 What is the remainder when $4x^2 - 2x + 9$ is divided by $(x-1)$?

   A)   0
   B)   11
   C)   13
   D)   15

6 What is the remainder when $9x^2 + 5x - 2$ is divided by $(x+3)$?

   A)   0
   B)   4
   C)   34
   D)   64

7 For a polynomial $p(x)$, the following information is given: $p(-3) = 0$ and $p(2) = 4$. Which of the following must be true about $p(x)$?

   A) $x-3$ is a factor of $p(x)$
   B) $x-6$ is a factor of $p(x)$
   C)   The remainder when $p(x)$ is divided by $x-2$ is 4.
   D)   The remainder when $p(x)$ is divided by $x-4$ is 2.

8 If $\dfrac{2}{x} = \dfrac{10}{x+24}$, what is the value of $\dfrac{x}{2}$?

A) $\dfrac{1}{3}$

B) 3

C) 5

D) 6

9 If $\dfrac{x}{x+6} = \dfrac{1}{4}$, what is the value of $\dfrac{1}{x+6}$?

A) $\dfrac{1}{2}$

B) $\dfrac{1}{4}$

C) $\dfrac{1}{6}$

D) $\dfrac{1}{8}$

Student Produced Response – No Calculator

1 When $8x^2 - 20x + 40$ is divided by $4x - 6$ the result is $2x - 2 + \dfrac{R}{4x-6}$ where R is a constant. What is the value of R?

2 $\dfrac{1}{t+2} = \dfrac{-2}{t+10} + \dfrac{1}{4}$

If t is a solution to the equation above and $t > 0$, what is the value of t?

Multiple Choice – Calculator

1 If $\dfrac{t-3}{t-5} = 7$, what is the value of t?

A) $\dfrac{8}{3}$

B) $\dfrac{16}{3}$

C) $\dfrac{21}{5}$

D) $\dfrac{3}{35}$

2 If $\dfrac{3t}{t+6} = \dfrac{1}{10}$, what is the value of t?

A) $-\dfrac{60}{7}$

B) $\dfrac{1}{20}$

C) $\dfrac{6}{29}$

D) 5

3 What is the remainder when $x^2 - 7x + 12$ is divided by $x - 3$?

A) 0

B) 3

C) 4

D) −4

4 For a polynomial $p(x)$, the value of $p(4)$ is -1. Which of the following must be true about $p(x)$?

A) $x - 5$ is a factor.

B) $x - 1$ is a factor.

C) $x + 1$ is a factor.

D) The remainder when $p(x)$ is divided by $x - 4$ is -1.

5 $\dfrac{x+2}{x+11} = \dfrac{2y}{5y}$

The equation above is true for all values of $y \neq 0$. What must be the value of $x + 11$?

A) 5

B) 10

C) 15

D) 20

6 $\dfrac{30x^2 - 26x - 19}{ax - 6} = 6x + 2 - \dfrac{7}{ax - 6}$

The equation above is true for all values of $x \neq \dfrac{1}{6}$. What is the value of a?

A) 5

B) −5

C) 24

D) −24

The Tutorverse

7 $\dfrac{8x^2 - 22x - 9}{2x + b} = 4x + 3 + \dfrac{12}{2x + b}$

The equation above is true for all values of

$x \neq \dfrac{b}{2}$, where b is a constant. What is the

value of b?

A) -11
B) -7
C) -3
D) 1

Student Produced Response – Calculator

1 $\dfrac{2}{t-1} + \dfrac{1}{6} = \dfrac{5}{t+2}$

If t is a solution to the equation above and $t < 12$, what is the value of t?

2 When $7x^2 - 38x + 88$ is divided by $7x + 4$

the result is $x - 6 + \dfrac{R}{7x + 4}$, where R is a

constant. What is the value of R?

3 $\dfrac{10x^2 - 34x - 6}{5x + 8} = 2x - 10 + \dfrac{R}{5x + 8}$

What is the value of the constant R in the equation above?

The Tutorverse

Guided Practice – Quadratic Functions & Equations

(Answers & explanations begin on page 415).

Multiple Choice – No Calculator

1 Which of the following does NOT have the same solutions as the other three equations?
   A) $x^2 + x - 20 = 0$
   B) $x^2 - x - 20 = 0$
   C) $(x-4)(x+5) = 0$
   D) $(x-4)(2x+10) = 0$

2 What are the solutions to $x^2 + 2x - 35 = 0$?
   A) $-7, 5$
   B) $-5, 7$
   C) $-5, -7$
   D) $-2, 35$

3 What are the solutions to $2x^2 + 3x + 1 = 0$?
   A) $1, 2$
   B) $1, \dfrac{1}{2}$
   C) $-1, -2$
   D) $-1, -\dfrac{1}{2}$

4 What are the solutions to $x^2 + 5x + 2 = 0$?
   A) $\dfrac{5 \pm \sqrt{17}}{2}$
   B) $\dfrac{-5 \pm \sqrt{17}}{2}$
   C) $\dfrac{5 \pm \sqrt{33}}{2}$
   D) $\dfrac{-5 \pm \sqrt{33}}{2}$

5 What are the solutions to $x^2 + 1 = -4x$?
   A) $2 \pm \sqrt{3}$
   B) $-2 \pm \sqrt{3}$
   C) $\dfrac{1 \pm \sqrt{17}}{2}$
   D) $\dfrac{-1 \pm \sqrt{17}}{2}$

6 $x^2 - 8x + 16 = 0$
   How many real solutions does the equation above have?
   A)   0
   B)   1
   C)   2
   D)   4

7 What are the solutions to $3x(x+2) = 1$?
   A) $\dfrac{-1 \pm \sqrt{2}}{3}$
   B) $\dfrac{-3 \pm \sqrt{17}}{2}$
   C) $-1 \pm \dfrac{\sqrt{6}}{3}$
   D) $-1 \pm \dfrac{2\sqrt{3}}{3}$

8 If $(ax + 4)(bx + 5) = 6x^2 + cx + 20$ for all values of x, and $a + b = 5$, what are two possible values for c?
   A)   2 and 3
   B)   8 and 15
   C)   10 and 12
   D)   22 and 23

9 $(x + a)(x + b) = x^2 + cx - 7$
   In the equation above, a, b and c are integers and the equation is true for all values of x. What are two possible values for c?
   A)   −1 and 7
   B)   −1 and −7
   C)   −6 and 6
   D)   −8 and 8

10 If $(x + a)(x + b) = (x + 3)^2 + 11$ for all values of x, what is the value of ab?
   A)   11
   B)   14
   C)   20
   D)   33

The Tutorverse

11   The function $f(x) = x^2 - 10x + 25$ passes through the points $(a,0)$ and $(0,b)$. What is the value of $a + b$?
A) -10
B) 10
C) 20
D) 30

12   The function $f(x) = 25x^2 - 9$ passes through the points $(-k,0)$ and $(k,0)$. What is the value of k?
A) $\dfrac{3}{5}$
B) $\dfrac{5}{3}$
C) $\dfrac{9}{25}$
D) $\dfrac{25}{9}$

13 $(3x + 2)(ax + b) = cx^2 + d$
In the equation above, a, b, c and d are non-zero integers and the equation is true for all values of x. Which of the following MUST be negative?
A) a
B) b
C) $a+b$
D) ab

14   The functions $f(x) = -x^2 + 8x - 7$ and $g(x) = x^2 - 8x + 17$ are graphed on the xy-plane. The graphs of f and g intersect at the points (a,k) and (b,k). What is the value of k?
A)   2
B)   5
C)   6
D)   7

Student Produced Response – No Calculator

1   What is the product of the solutions of $(x+4)^2 = 1$?

15   The functions $f(x) = 16 - x^2$ and $g(x) = x^2$ are graphed on the xy-plane. The graphs of f and g intersect at the points $(-a,b)$ and (a,b). What is the value of a?
A)   4
B)   8
C) $2\sqrt{2}$
D) $2\sqrt{3}$

16 $g(x) = \dfrac{1}{x^2 - 4x + 8}$
For how many values of x is the function $g(x)$ above undefined?
A)   0
B)   1
C)   2
D)   There are infinitely many values.

17   A swimming pool is 3 meters deep. Its length is 4 meters longer than twice its width. If the pool can hold 60 cubic meters of water, which of the following equations can be used to find the width, x, of the pool?
A) $x^2 + 2x + 10 = 0$
B) $x^2 + 4x + 20 = 0$
C) $x^2 + 2x - 10 = 0$
D) $x^2 + 12x - 60 = 0$

2 $f(x) = \dfrac{1}{x^2 - 5x - 14}$
For what positive value of x is the function $f(x)$ above undefined?

The Tutorverse

Multiple Choice – Calculator

1 Which of the following has NO real solution?

    I. $x^2 + 7x - 3 = 0$

    II. $4x^2 + 4x + 1 = 0$

    III. $x^2 + 2x + 5 = 0$

A) I only
B) II only
C) III only
D) I and II

2 What is the sum of all values of r that satisfy $3r^2 + 21r + 36 = 0$?

A)   −7
B)   7
C)   −21
D)   12

3 Three functions, f, g, and h are given below. Which of these functions is/are undefined when $x = 2$?

$$f(x) = \frac{1}{(x-2)^2 + (x-4)^2}$$

$$g(x) = \frac{3x}{x^2 - 6x + 8}$$

$$h(x) = \frac{x-2}{x^2 + 10x + 16}$$

A) f only
B) g only
C) h only
D) g and h

4 A hiker walks at a speed of $\dfrac{x}{2}$ miles per hour for $x + 2$ hours. At that time, he reaches a mountain, where he hikes for 3 additional hours at half of his original speed. If the hiker walked a total of 15 miles, which equation can be used to find the value of x?

A) $x^2 + 5x - 30 = 0$
B) $x^2 + 5x - 15 = 0$
C) $2x^2 + 7x - 56 = 0$
D) $2x^2 + 7x - 60 = 0$

5 A woman left her home and drove north for $3x$ hours at a speed of $\dfrac{2x}{3}$ miles per hour. Then she realized she had forgotten something at home. She began driving south at her original speed. After driving south for 30 minutes, she was 50 miles from her home. Which equation could be used to find the value of x?

A) $x^2 - 15x - 25 = 0$
B) $x^2 - 45x - 25 = 0$
C) $6x^2 - x - 150 = 0$
D) $6x^2 + x - 150 = 0$

Student Produced Response – Calculator

1 If $x > 0$ and $3x^2 + 14x - 5 = 0$, what is the value of x?

2 What is the sum of the solutions of $2x^2 + 35 = 17x$?

3 $$h(x) = \frac{1}{(x-7)^2 + 2(x-7) + 1}$$

For what value of x is the function $h(x)$ above undefined?

The Tutorverse

Guided Practice – Exponents & Radicals

(Answers & explanations begin on page 418).

Multiple Choice – No Calculator

1 Which of the following is equivalent to $a^{\frac{4}{5}}$, for all values of a?

A) $\sqrt{a^{\frac{2}{5}}}$

B) $\sqrt{a^{5}}$

C) $\sqrt[5]{a^{\frac{1}{4}}}$

D) $\sqrt[5]{a^{4}}$

2 If $2x - y = 18$, what is the value of $\dfrac{4^{x}}{2^{y}}$?

A) 2^{2}

B) 2^{18}

C) 4^{2}

D) The value cannot be determined from the information given.

3 $\sqrt{3k^{2}+9} - x = 0$
If $k > 0$ and $x = 6$ in the equation above, what is the value of k?

A) 1

B) 2

C) 3

D) 6

4 A news website with is gaining subscribers at the rate of 3% per year. The company had 4 million subscribers at the start of 2014. Assume the company continues to gain new subscribers at the same rate and that it does not lose subscribers. Which of the following functions, s, models the number of subscribers (in millions) the website gains t years after the start of 2014?

A) $s(t) = 4(1.03)^{t}$

B) $s(t) = 4(0.97)^{t}$

C) $s(t) = 4(0.03)^{t}$

D) $s(t) = 4(1.03)t$

5 If $\dfrac{x^{a}}{x^{b}} = x$, $x > 1$, what is the value of $b - a$?

A) -1

B) 3

C) 5

D) 7

6 If $10^{ab} = 1,000$, where a and b are positive integers, which of the following is a possible value of a?

A) 2

B) 3

C) 6

D) 10

7 A radioactive substance decays 3% each day. If the initial amount of the substance was 400 grams, which of the following functions f models the remaining amount of the substance, in grams, t days later?

A) $f(t) = 400(0.03)^{t}$

B) $f(t) = 0.03(400)^{t}$

C) $f(t) = 400(0.97)^{t}$

D) $f(t) = 0.97(400)^{t}$

8 $x - 6 = \sqrt{x - 6}$
What is the solution set for the above equation?

A) $\{6\}$

B) $\{7\}$

C) $\{-6,7\}$

D) $\{6,7\}$

9 If m and k are positive integers and $m^{2}k^{-1} = 10m$, what is m^{-1} in terms of k?

A) $\dfrac{k}{10}$

B) $\dfrac{\sqrt{k}}{10}$

C) $\dfrac{1}{10k}$

D) $\dfrac{10}{k}$

The Tutorverse

Student Produced Response – No Calculator

1 If $5x^2 = 4y = 20$, what is the value of x^2y?

2 If $\dfrac{x^{a^2}}{x^{b^2}} = x^{36}$, $x > 1$, and $a + b = 4$, what is the value of $a - b$?

3 If $a = 3\sqrt{3}$ and $2a = \sqrt{3x}$, what is the value of x?

Multiple Choice – Calculator

1 $P(t) = 2,000 \times 2^{\frac{t}{2}}$
Scientists study cultures of organisms in a lab. The population P of the organisms in the culture t days after the culture began is modeled by the function above. By how many organisms does the population increase from $t = 2$ to $t = 4$?
A)   2,000
B)   4,000
C)   8,000
D)   16,000

2 If a, b, and c are different positive integers and $2^a \times 2^b \times 2^c = 64$, then $2^a + 2^b + 2^c =$
A)   12
B)   14
C)   17
D)   32

3 $\sqrt{x+16} = x - 4$
For all values of x greater than 4, the equation above is equivalent to which of the following?
A) $x = x^2$
B) $x = x^2 + 16$
C) $x = x^2 - 8x$
D) $x = x^2 - 8x + 16$

4 Greg purchased a car for $20,000. The value of the car decreases 20% every year. The value, in dollars, of the car n years from the date of purchase is given by the function V, where $V(n) = 20,000(0.8)^n$. How many years from the date of purchase will the value of the car be $10,240?
A)   1
B)   2
C)   3
D)   4

5 If k is a positive integer, what is the least value of k for which $\sqrt{\dfrac{5k}{4}}$ is an integer?
A)   4
B)   5
C)   20
D)   80

6 $A - \sqrt{s(s-a)(s-b)(s-c)}$
To determine the area of a triangle using the lengths of each side of the triangle, use Heron's Formula (above). The length of each side of the triangle is represented by a, b, and c. s is equal to $\dfrac{1}{2}$ of the triangle's perimeter.
What is the area of a triangle with side lengths of 6, 10, 12 units?
A) $4\sqrt{14}$
B) $8\sqrt{14}$
C) $64\sqrt{28}$
D) $421\sqrt{8}$

7 $\sqrt{4x^2 + 1} = 2x + 1$

Which values of x make the above equation true?

A) $x = 0$
B) $x > 0$
C) $x < 0$
D) The value cannot be determined with the information given.

8 The administration at a large university implemented a new policy to make the university more exclusive, which resulted in a decrease in student population of 10 percent every 4 years. If the population at the university when this policy was adopted was 25,000 students, which of the following expressions represents an estimate of the student population t years from the time of adoption?

A) $25,000(0.1)^{4t}$

B) $25,000(0.9)^{4t}$

C) $25,000(0.1)^{\frac{t}{4}}$

D) $25,000(0.9)^{\frac{t}{4}}$

9 The population of bees in a major city is in decline. If the city had an estimated 500,000 bees and they are dying off at the rate of 5% per year, approximately how many bees will there be in the city in ten years?

A) 30,000
B) 100,000
C) 300,000
D) 450,000

Student Produced Response – Calculator

Questions 1 and 2 refer to the following information.

The price of one share of stock in a certain company is worth $270 today. A stock analyst believes the stock will lose 24% of its value each week for the next three weeks. The analyst uses the equation
$V = 270(r)^t$ to model the value V, of the stock after t weeks.

1 How many weeks will it take for the value of the stock to decrease by $114?

2 If this trend continues, how many weeks will it take for $V \le \$50$?

3 $\sqrt{x^2 - t^2} = 2t - x$

If x and t are positive numbers that satisfy the equation above, what is the value of $\frac{x}{t}$?

The Tutorverse

Guided Practice – Systems of Equations

(Answers & explanations begin on page 419).

Multiple Choice – No Calculator

1 $y = 2x - 3$

$y = x^2 + 6x$

Which of the following ordered pairs represents a solution (x,y) to the system of equations above?

A) $(1,-1)$
B) $(1,3)$
C) $(-1,-3)$
D) $(-1,-5)$

2 $y = x^2 + ax + b$

$x = -3$

In the system of equations above, a and b are constants. For which of the following values of a and b does the system of equations have exactly two real solutions?

A) $a = 5, b = 6$
B) $a = 6, b = 9$
C) $a = -1, b = -6$
D) None of these

3 $x^2 + y^2 = r^2$

$y = |rx|$

In the system of equations above, r is a constant and $r \neq 0$. The solution(s) of this system can be found in

A) Quadrant I only
B) Quadrants I and II
C) Quadrants III and IV
D) Cannot be determined without knowing the value of r.

4 Which of the following is a system of equations with exactly two solutions (x_1, y_1) and (x_2, y_2) where $y_1 = y_2$?

A) $x + y = 5$ and $x + 2y = 5$
B) $x + y = 5$ and $2x + y = 5$
C) $x^2 + y^2 = 9$ and $y = 0$
D) $x^2 + y^2 = 9$ and $x = 0$

5 $y = 2x - 10$

$x = y^2 - 2y$

How many ordered pairs (x,y) satisfy the system of equations shown above?

A) 0
B) 1
C) 2
D) There are infinitely many ordered pairs.

6 $y = x^2 + 4$

$y = ax^2 + b$

In the system of equations above, a and b are constants. For which of the following values of a and b does the system of equations have no real solution?

A) $a = \dfrac{1}{2}, b = 2$
B) $a = 2, b = 2$
C) $a = \dfrac{1}{2}, b = 6$
D) $a = -1, b = 4$

7 $y = x^3 + 15x$

$y = cx^2$

In the system of equations above, c is a constant. For which of the following values of c does the system of equations have exactly three real solutions?

A) -5
B) 3
C) 8
D) None of these

The Tutorverse

8 $3x + 4y = 0$

$y = \dfrac{9}{4}x^2 - 6x + 3$

If (x,y) is a solution of the system of equations above, what could be the value of y?

A) $-\dfrac{3}{4}$

B) $\dfrac{3}{4}$

C) $-\dfrac{4}{3}$

D) $\dfrac{4}{3}$

Student Produced Response – No Calculator

1 $y = x^2 - x - 35$

$x = y$

If (x,y) is a solution of the system of equations above and $x > 0$, what is the value of x?

2 $y + 4 = |x - 2|$

$x + 2y = 200$

If (x,y) is a solution of the system of equations above and $x < 0$, what is the value of y?

Multiple Choice – Calculator

1   Which of the following does NOT represent the same system of equations as the other three choices?

A) $y = x^2 + 2x + 1$

$y = -2x + 6$

B)   A system of equations with a unique solution at $(4,1)$

C)

Function I		Function II	
x	y	x	y
−1	0	−1	8
0	1	0	6
1	4	1	4

D)

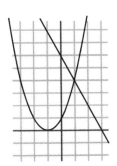

2 $y = (x - 3)(x - 7)$

$4x + y = 13$

Which of the following ordered pairs represents a solution (x,y) to the system of equations above?

A) $(3,0)$
B) $(2,4)$
C) $(2,5)$
D) $(3,7)$

The Tutorverse

3 $y = (x-2)(x+12)$

$y = (x+5)^2 - 49$

How many ordered pairs (x,y) satisfy the system of equations shown above?

A)   0
B)   1
C)   2
D)   There are infinitely many ordered pairs.

4 $y = 5x^2 + x + 8$

$y = 3x^2 + 4$

How many ordered pairs (x,y) satisfy the system of equations shown above?

A)   0
B)   1
C)   2
D)   There are infinitely many ordered pairs.

Student Produced Response – Calculator

1 $x = -4$
$y - x^3 + 300$
If (x,y) is a solution of the system of equations above, what is the value of y?

5 $4x + y = 0$

$y = mx^2 + n$

In the system of equations above, m and n are constants. For which of the following values of m and n does the system of equations have exactly one real solution?

A) $m = 2, n = 8$
B) $m = 2, n = 2$
C) $m = -2, n = 2$
D) $m = -1, n = 4$

2 $y = 5(x^2 - 4x + 4)$

$y = x^2 - 1$

If (x,y) is a solution of the system of equations above, what could be the value of x?

Guided Practice – Function Notation

(Answers & explanations begin on page 421).

Multiple Choice – No Calculator

1 If $f(x) = 5g(x)$ and $g(x) = 2x + 1$, what is $f(4)$?
- A) 9
- B) 20
- C) 41
- D) 45

2 A function f satisfies $f(7) = 6$ and $f(6) = 2$. A function g satisfies $g(6) = 7$ and $g(2) = 0$. What is the value of $f(g(6))$?
- A) 0
- B) 2
- C) 6
- D) 7

3 What is the value of $f(f(10))$ in the table below?

x	1	10	100	1,000	10,000
$f(x)$	1,000	10,000	10	100	1

- A) 1
- B) 100
- C) 1000
- D) 10,000

4 If $g(x) = 2x + 7$ and $f(g(x)) = \sqrt{2x + 3}$, which of the following describes $f(x)$?
- A) $\sqrt{x + 4}$
- B) $\sqrt{x - 4}$
- C) $\sqrt{2x + 4}$
- D) $\sqrt{2x - 4}$

5 $g(x) = ax^2 - 2ax + 6$

For the function g defined above, a is a constant. What is the value of $g(2)$?
- A) 0
- B) 4
- C) 6
- D) Cannot be determined from the information given.

6 A function f satisfies $f(a) = b$ and $f(b) = c$. A function g satisfies $g(a) = c$ and $g(b) = a$. What is the value of $g(f(a))$?
- A) a
- B) b
- C) c
- D) bc

7 If $f(x) = x^2 - 9$ and $g(x) = x + 5$, what is $f(g(x))$ equal to?
- A) $x^3 + 5x^2 - 9x - 45$
- B) $x^3 - 45$
- C) $x^2 + 10x + 16$
- D) $x^2 + x - 4$

8 The table below shows some values of the linear function f. Which of the following defines f?

n	1	2	3	4
$f(n)$	1	3	5	7

- A) $f(n) = n + 2$
- B) $f(n) = 2n - 1$
- C) $f(n) = 3n - 2$
- D) $f(n) = 4n - 5$

9 The table below shows some values of the linear function f. Which of the following defines f?

n	1	2	3	4
$f(n)$	1	4	7	10

- A) $f(n) = n + 4$
- B) $f(n) = 2n - 1$
- C) $f(n) = 3n - 2$
- D) $f(n) = 4n - 6$

10 If $f(x) = 2x + 4$, which of the following is equal to $4x + 8$?
- A) $f(2)$
- B) $f(2x)$
- C) $f(2x + 2)$
- D) $f(2x + 4)$

The Tutorverse

11 If $f(x) = x^2 + 2$ and $g(x) = 5x$, which of the following is equal to $f(g(x)) - g(f(x))$?

A) 0

B) $x^2 - 5x + 2$

C) $5x^3 + 10x$

D) $20x^2 - 8$

12 If $y(x) = \sqrt{x^2 - 6}$ which of the following is equivalent to $y(y(x))$?

A) $\sqrt{x^2 - 6}$

B) $\sqrt{x^2 - 6} - 6$

C) $\sqrt{x^2 - 12}$

D) $\sqrt{(x^2 - 6)^2 - 6}$

Student Produced Response – No Calculator

1 If $g(x) = 3x + 4$ and $f(x) = g(x) + 10$, what is $f(3)$?

Multiple Choice – Calculator

1 $g(x) = cx^2 - 6$

For the function g defined above, c is a constant and $g(2) = 6$. What is the value of $g(-2)$?

A) 6

B) 3

C) -6

D) -18

2 $f(x) = ax - 4$

For the function f defined above, a is a constant and $f(2) = 16$. What is the value of $f(3)$?

A) 26

B) 24

C) 10

D) -1

13 The function $f(x)$ is graphed on the xy-plane. The graph $y = g(x)$ is equivalent to the graph $y = f(x)$ reflected over the y-axis. Which of the following correctly relates $f(x)$ and $g(x)$?

A) $f(x) = g(x)$

B) $f(x) = g(-x)$

C) $f(x) = -g(x)$

D) $f(x) = -g(-x)$

14 The function $p(x)$ is graphed on the xy-plane. The graph $y = q(x)$ is equivalent to the graph $y = p(x)$ translated 4 units up and then reflected over the x-axis. The graph $y = r(x)$ is equivalent to the graph $y = p(x)$ reflected over the x-axis and then translated 4 units up. Which of the following correctly relates $q(x)$ and $r(x)$?

A) $q(x) = r(x)$

B) $q(x) = -r(x - 4)$

C) $q(x) = -r(x) - 4$

D) $q(x) = r(x) - 8$

2 $f(x) = x^2 - 13x + 40$

For the function f above, $f(0) = f(a)$ where a is a constant and $a > 0$. What is the value of a?

3 If $f(x) = x^2 - 3$ and $g(x) = 4x - 4$, which of the following is true for all values of x?

A) $f(x) = -f(x)$

B) $f(x) = f(-x)$

C) $g(x) = -g(x)$

D) $g(x) = g(-x)$

4 If $f(x) = 3x - 4$ and $g(x) = 2x + 2$, what is the value of $f(g(3))$?

A) 40

B) 20

C) 12

D) 8

5　The graph of $y = f(x)$ is shown below. If $g(x) = 2f(-x)$, which of the following is the graph of $y = g(x)$?

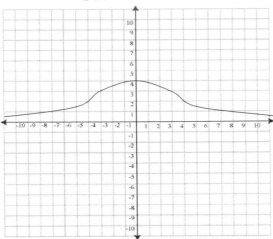

A)

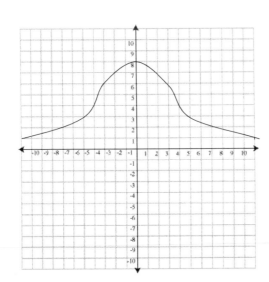

C)

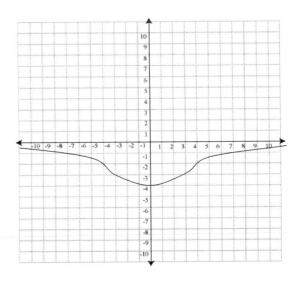

B)

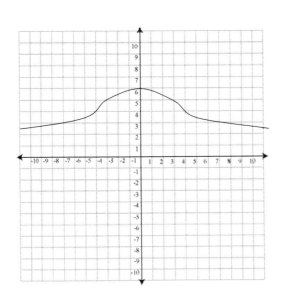

D)

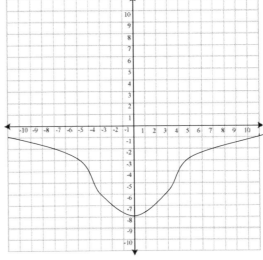

The Tutorverse

6 If $f(x) = 4x + 6$, what is $f(-5x)$ equal to?

A) $-x + 6$

B) $-20x + 6$

C) $-20x - 30$

D) $-20x^2 - 30x$

Student Produced Response – Calculator

1 If $f(x) = 2x - 4$ and $g(x) = 3f(x)$, what is $g(20)$?

2 If $h(x) = f(x) + g(x)$ and $g(x) = 3x + 7$ and $f(x) = 2x + 5$, what is $h(2)$?

3 The graph of $y = f(x + 6)$ is shown below.

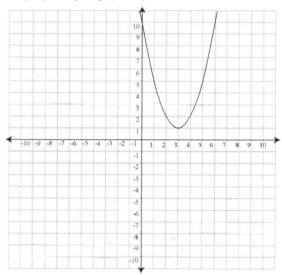

For which value of x, rounded to the nearest whole number, must $f(x) = 1$?

Guided Practice – Graphs of Functions
(Answers & explanations begin on page 423).

Multiple Choice – No Calculator

1 The graph of which of the following functions on the *xy*-plane has *x*-intercepts at –3 and 2?

A) $f(x) = (x+3)(x-2)$

B) $g(x) = (x-3)(x+2)$

C) $h(x) = (x-3)^2 + 2$

D) $k(x) = (x+2)^2 - 3$

2 Which of the following equations has a graph on the *xy*-plane for which *y* is always greater than or equal to 0?

A) $y = |x| - 1$

B) $y = x^2 - 1$

C) $y = (x-1)^2$

D) $y = x^3 - 1$

3 On the *xy*-plane, the parabola with the equation $y = (x-5)^2$ intersects the line with equation $y = 4$ at two points, *A* and *B*. What is the length of $\overline{AB}$?

A)   4

B)   6

C)   8

D)   10

4 If $f(x) = \sqrt{2x-8}$, the domain of the function is equal to

A)   all real numbers.

B)   all real numbers greater than or equal to 8.

C)   all real numbers greater than or equal to 4.

D)   all real numbers greater than or equal to 2.

5 What is the range of the function $f(x) = x^2 + 2x + 2$?

A)   All real numbers.

B)   {–1, 1}

C) $y \geq 1$

D)   The range is undefined.

6

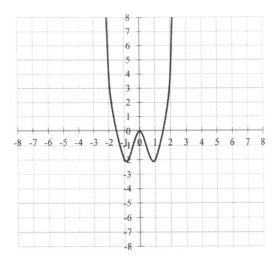

The function $f(x) = x^4 - 3x^2$ is graphed on the *xy*-plane as shown above. If *k* is a constant such that the equation $f(x) = k$ has 4 solutions, which of the following could be a value of *k*?

A)   3

B)   1

C)   0

D)   –1

7 $y = a(x-2)(x+6)$

In the quadratic equation above, *a* is a nonzero constant. The graph of the equation on the *xy*-plane is a parabola with vertex (*c*,*d*). Which of the following is equal to *d*?

A)   –4*a*

B)   –8*a*

C)   –12a

D)   –16a

8

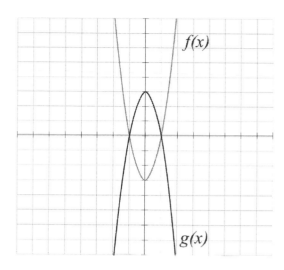

The functions *f* and *g* are defined by $f(x) = 3x^2 - 3$ and $g(x) = -3x^2 + 3$, and graphed on the *xy*-plane above. The graphs of *f* and *g* intersect at the points $(k,0)$ and $(-k,0)$. Which of the following could be the value of *x*?

A) $\dfrac{1}{2}$

B)   0

C)   1

D)   2

9

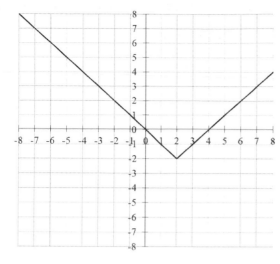

The graph above shows *f(x)*. Which equation is equal to *f(x)*?

A) $f(x) = |x|$

B) $f(x) = |x - 2|$

C) $f(x) = |x - 2| - 2$

D) $f(x) = (x - 2) - 2$

Student Produced Response – No Calculator

1   On the *xy*-plane (1,5) lies on the graph of the function $f(x) = bx + 2$. What is the value of *b*?

2   On the *xy*-plane, the parabola with the equation $y = (x - 4)^2$ intersects the line with equation $y = 25$ at 2 points, *A* and *B*. What is the length of $\overline{AB}$?

Student Produced Response – Calculator

1   On the *xy*-plane, (3,2) lies on the graph of the function $f(x) = 2x^2 - bx + 2$. What is the value of *b*?

2   The function *f* is defined by $f(x) = x^3 + 3x^2 + kx - 6$, where *k* is a constant. On the *xy*-plane, the graph of *f* intersects the *x*-axis at a single point, namely (1,0). What is the value of *k*?

3   $y = a(x + 1)(x - 3)$

In the quadratic equation above, *a* is a nonzero constant. The graph of the equation on the *xy*-plane is a parabola with vertex (1,–8). What is the value of *a*?

3   Suppose the graph of *f(x)* = x^2 is translated 2 units left and 1 unit up. If the resulting graph represents *g(x)*, what is the value of *g(3)*?

The Tutorverse

Multiple Choice – Calculator

1 $y = x^2 - 7x + 12$

The equation above represents a parabola on the xy-plane. Which of the following equivalent forms of the equation displays the x-intercepts of the parabola as constants or coefficients?

A) $y - 12 = x^2 - 7x$

B) $y - 1 = (x - 3)^2$

C) $y = x(x - 7) + 12$

D) $y = (x - 3)(x - 4)$

2

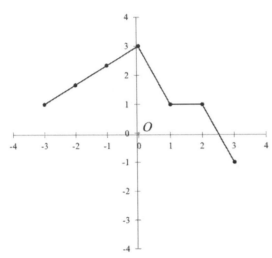

The complete graph of the function f is shown on the xy-plane above. Which of the following are equal to 1?

    I. $f(-3)$
    II. $f(1)$
    III. $f(2)$

A)   I only

B)   II only

C)   II and III only

D)   I, II, and III

3 $y = x^2 - 8x + 12$

The equation above represents a parabola on the xy-plane. Which of the following equivalent forms of the equation displays the xy-coordinates of the vertex of the parabola as constants or coefficients?

A) $y - 12 = x^2 - 8x$

B) $y = (x - 10)(x + 2)$

C) $y = (x - 2)(x - 6)$

D) $y = (x - 4)^2 - 4$

4   If $f(-x) = f(x)$ for all real numbers x and if $(1,4)$ is a point on the graph of f, which of the following points must also be on the graph of f?

A) $(-4,-1)$

B) $(-1,-4)$

C) $(-1,4)$

D) $(1,-4)$

5   The function f is defined by $f(x) = 2x^3 + x^2 + kx + 4$, where k is a constant. On the xy-plane, the graph of f intersects the x-axis at a single point, namely $(-1,0)$. What is the value of k?

A) -6

B)   1

C)   3

D)   4

6 $y = x^2 + 6x + 9$

The equation above represents a parabola on the xy-plane. Which of the following equivalent forms of the equation correctly displays the x-intercepts of the parabola as constants or coefficients?

A) $y - 9 = x^2 + 6x$

B) $y - 1 = (x + 2)(x + 4)$

C) $y = x(x + 6) + 9$

D) $y = (x + 3)^2$

7   For a rational function $\dfrac{x^2 + 4x + 2}{x + 2}$, there is a vertical asymptote at $x = a$. What is the value of a?

A) -2

B)   0

C)   2

D)   4

8   What is the smallest value that belongs to the range of the function $f(x) = 2|x - 4| + 2$?

A) -2

B)   0

C)   2

D)   4

The Tutorverse

9

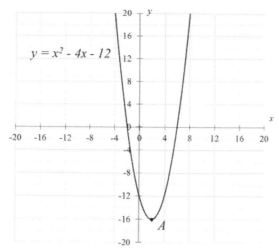

Which of the following is an equivalent form of the equation of the graph shown on the *xy*-plane above, from which the coordinates of vertex *A* can be identified as constants in the equation?

A) $y = (x-2)(x+6)$

B) $y = (x+2)(x-6)$

C) $y = (x-4)^2$

D) $y = (x-2)^2 - 16$

10 On the *xy*-plane, the graph of function *f* has *x*-intercepts at −2, −1, and 2. Which of the following could define *f*?

A) $f(x) = (x-2)^2(x-1)$

B) $f(x) = (x-2)(x-1)(x+2)$

C) $f(x) = (x+2)(x+1)(x-2)$

D) $f(x) = (x+2)^2(x+1)$

11 Suppose the graph of $f(x) = -x^2$ is translated 3 units left and 1 unit up. If the resulting graph represents $g(x)$, what is the value of $g(-2)$?

A) −1

B) 0

C) 1

D) 2

12

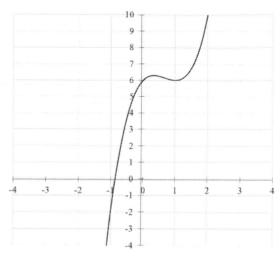

If $f(x) = 2x^3 - 4x^2 + 2x + 6$, which of the following statements are true?

   I.   The function *f* is increasing for $x \geq 1$.

   II. The equation $f(x) = 0$ has two real solutions.

   III. $f(x) \geq 6$ for all $x \geq 0$.

A) I only

B) II only

C) I and II

D) I and III

13 What is the range of the function defined by $f(x) = \dfrac{1}{x} - 2$?

A) All real numbers.

B) All real numbers except −2.

C) All real numbers except 0.

D) All real numbers except 2.

14 Which of the following values of *x* is in the domain of the function $f(x) = \dfrac{x-2}{x^2 + 3x - 10}$?

A) −5

B) 0

C) 2

D) The domain includes all real numbers.

15

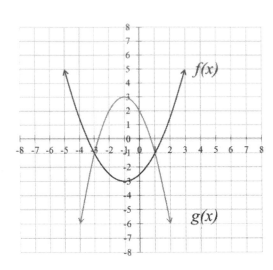

Graphs of the functions *f* and *g* are shown on the *xy*-plane above. For which of the following values of *x* does $f(x) + g(x) = 0$?

A)   –3
B)   –1
C)   1
D)   3

16   If *k* is a positive constant and $k \neq 1$, which graph could be the graph of $y + x = k(x - y)$ on the *xy*-plane?

A)

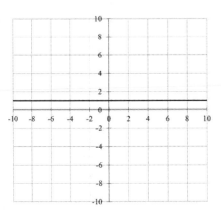

C)

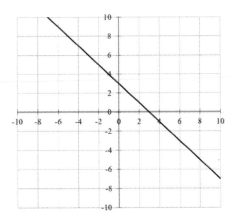

B)

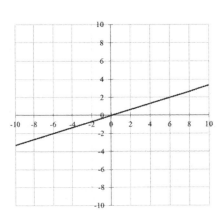

D)

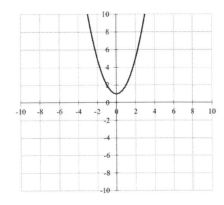

The Tutorverse

Guided Practice – More Word Problems
(Answers & explanations begin on page 425).

Multiple Choice – No Calculator

1   The bill, b, for a particular cell phone plan is calculated using the formula $b = 0.45m + 40$ where m is the number of extra minutes that the person has used above their monthly contract. Which of the following expresses the number of extra minutes in terms of the bill?

A) $m = \dfrac{b + 40}{0.45}$

B) $m = \dfrac{b - 40}{0.45}$

C) $m = \dfrac{40 - b}{0.45}$

D) $m = \dfrac{0.45}{b + 40}$

2   At a particular fitness center, customers get their first two yoga classes for free, and after that the classes cost $12 each. The cost, c, of taking y yoga classes can be modeled by the equation $c = 12y - 24$ for all $y \geq 2$. Which of the following expresses the number of yoga classes in terms of the cost?

A) $y = \dfrac{c}{12} + 2$

B) $y = \dfrac{c}{12} + 24$

C) $y = \dfrac{c}{12} - 2$

D) $y = \dfrac{c}{12} - 24$

3   $w = -0.5y^2 + ay + b$

The equation above gives the hourly wage, w, of an employee who has worked at the company for y years. Which of the following gives a in terms of w, y, and b?

A) $a = w + b - 0.5y$

B) $a = \dfrac{w - b + 0.5}{y}$

C) $a = \dfrac{w - b}{y} + 0.5y$

D) $a = \dfrac{w + b}{y} - 0.5y$

The next two questions refer to the below information:

$$C(t) = 100 - t$$
$$L(t) = 2t + 33$$

Two customers at a restaurant order coffee and lemonade. As the beverages sit on the table, their temperatures change. The function $C(t)$ gives the temperature of the coffee t minutes after it is served. The function $L(t)$ gives the temperature of the lemonade t minutes after it is served.

4   How will the temperature of the lemonade change over a period of 10 minutes?
A)   The temperature will increase by 2 degrees.
B)   The temperature will decrease by 10 degrees.
C)   The temperature will increase by 20 degrees.
D)   The temperature will increase by 53 degrees.

5   If the temperature of the lemonade increases by 10 degrees, the temperature of the coffee will
A)   increase by 10 degrees.
B)   decrease by 5 degrees.
C)   decrease by 10 degrees.
D)   decrease by 20 degrees.

The Tutorverse

The next two questions refer to the below information:

$$R = \frac{\sqrt{P}}{2}$$

A company uses the formula above to calculate an employee's rating, R, based on the number of projects, P, that he or she completes.

6   Which of the following expresses the number of projects an employee completed in terms of their rating?
A) $P = 2R$
B) $P = 4R$
C) $P = 2R^2$
D) $P = 4R^2$

7   Anna completed 9 times as many projects as Brenda. Brenda's rating will be what fraction of Anna's rating?

A) $\dfrac{1}{3}$

B) $\dfrac{1}{9}$

C) $\dfrac{2}{3}$

D) $\dfrac{2}{9}$

8   An animal's height, h, in inches, when it is m months old is modeled by the function $h(m) = \dfrac{1}{6}m + 20$. How does the animal's height change over the course of one year?
A)   Its height increases by 2 inches.
B)   Its height increases by 12 inches.
C)   Its height increases by 20 inches.
D)   Its height increases by 22 inches.

The next two questions refer to the below information:

$$h = \frac{w}{5r^2}$$

The formula above is used to calculate the number of hours, h, that it takes for a circular field of radius r to absorb w gallons of water.

9   Which of the following expresses the square of the radius in terms of the number of hours and gallons of water?

A) $r^2 = \dfrac{5h}{w}$

B) $r^2 = \dfrac{w}{5h}$

C) $r^2 = \dfrac{h}{5w}$

D) $r^2 = \dfrac{hw}{5}$

10   The same amount of water is poured onto Field A and Field B, but on Field B, it takes 4 times as long for the water to be absorbed. The radius of Field B is what fraction of the radius of Field A?

A) $\dfrac{1}{2}$

B) $\dfrac{1}{4}$

C) $\dfrac{1}{8}$

D) $\dfrac{1}{16}$

11   A factory builds hollow plastic cubes. The mass, m, of each cube can be calculated using the formula $m = 6ds^2$ where d is the density of the plastic and s is the length of each side of the cube. If the density of the plastic is doubled and the length of each side is halved, how does the mass change?
A)   The mass is doubled.
B)   The mass is unchanged.
C)   The mass is halved.
D)   The mass is quartered (divided by 4).

The Tutorverse

12 $h = -3t^2 - 3t + 60$

The equation above expresses the height, h, of a rock in feet above the bottom of a lake t seconds after it is thrown into the lake. How many seconds will pass from when the rock is thrown until it hits the bottom of the lake?

A) 4
B) 5
C) 9
D) 10

Student Produced Response – No Calculator

1 The formula $PV = nRT$ is known as the ideal gas law, and is useful to predict the behavior of a gas under ideal conditions. In this equation, P represents the pressure of the gas, V represents the volume, n represents the amount of gas, R is the universal gas constant, and T is the temperature. In a particular lab experiment, the volume of a gas is doubled, the temperature is multiplied by 1.5, and the amount of gas is multiplied by 20. Under ideal conditions, the pressure of this gas will be multiplied by what number?

Multiple Choice – Calculator

1 A truck is carrying boxes of bricks. The total weight of the truck's cargo is calculated by the expression $n(bK + w)$ where n is the number of boxes, b is the number of bricks per box, K is a constant, and w is the weight of an empty box. If the brick company decides to start making their bricks with a heavier material, which of the quantities in the expression would change?

A) n
B) b
C) K
D) w

13 $c = dpk$

The formula above gives the total cost, c, of gasoline when a car drives a distance of d miles and pays a price of p dollars per gallon of gasoline. The quantity k in this formula could represent which of the following?

A) The amount of gasoline required for the trip.
B) The amount of gasoline required per mile.
C) The number of miles driven per gallon of gasoline.
D) The number of times the car stops to refill the gasoline.

2 $m = 12t^2l$

If a metal rod has length l and thickness t, then its mass, m, is calculated using the formula above. Two rods have the same mass, but one has thickness t and the other has thickness $\frac{3}{2}t$. What is the ratio of the length of the thicker rod to the length of the thinner rod? (Grid your answer in fraction form.)

2 $h = -16t^2 + 65t$

The equation above expresses the height, h, in feet, of a ball t seconds after it is launched from the ground with an upward velocity of 65 feet per second. After approximately how many seconds will the ball hit the ground?

A) 3.5
B) 4.0
C) 4.5
D) 5.0

The Tutorverse

3 A sprinter finds that his time, t, in seconds, for the 100-meter dash depends on the hours of sleep, s, that he gets the night before the race. This relationship is modeled by the function $t(s) = s^2 - 16s + 75$. Which of the following equivalent forms of $t(s)$ shows, as constants or coefficients, the minimum possible time that he can run the race and the amount of sleep that results in that minimum time?

A) $t(s) = (s-8)^2 + 11$

B) $t(s) = s(s-1) - 15(s-5)$

C) $t(s) = s(s-10) - 3(2s-25)$

D) $t(s) = s(s-16) + 75$

4 $$\frac{\pi d}{4} = \sqrt{\frac{w}{p}}$$

The equation above shows the relationship between the diameter, d, of a cylindrical column of liquid, its weight, w, and the average pressure, p, exerted by the liquid. Which of the following correctly expresses w in terms of d and p?

A) $w = \dfrac{\pi d \sqrt{p}}{4}$

B) $w = \dfrac{\pi d^2 p}{4}$

C) $w = \dfrac{\pi d^2}{16 p}$

D) $w = \dfrac{\pi^2 d^2 p}{16}$

5 $$P = \frac{r}{r+b}$$

The probability, P, of picking a red marble out of a bag containing r red marbles and b blue marbles is calculated using the formula above. Let D represent the probability of picking a red marble if r is doubled but b remains the same. Which of the following equations expresses D in terms of P?

A) $D = P$

B) $D = 2P$

C) $D = \dfrac{2P}{P+1}$

D) $D = \dfrac{2P}{2P+1}$

6 A vehicle manufacturer estimates that if a particular vehicle is driven at a velocity of v miles per hour, then its gas mileage, m, in miles per gallon is $m(v) = -\dfrac{1}{10}v^2 + 4v$. Which of the following equivalent forms of $m(v)$ shows, as constants or coefficients, the maximum possible gas mileage and the velocity that results in that maximum gas mileage?

A) $m(v) = 4v - \dfrac{1}{10}v^2$

B) $m(v) = -\dfrac{1}{10}(v^2 - 40v)$

C) $m(v) = 4v\left(1 - \dfrac{1}{40}v\right)$

D) $m(v) = -\dfrac{1}{10}(v-20)^2 + 40$

7 The number of cells, c in a test tube after t minutes is modeled by the equation $c = ke^{rt}$. If r in the equation is replaced with $2r$, how will the value of c change?

A) The value of c will be doubled.

B) The value of c will be squared.

C) The value of c will be multiplied by e.

D) The value of c will be multiplied by e^{rt}.

Student Produced Response – Calculator

The next two questions refer to the below information:

At the beginning of the week a certain pond had 270 cubic meters of water. Evaporation caused the amount of water in the pond to decrease by 12% each day. The equation $V = 270(r)^t$ models the volume, V, of the pond after t days.

1 What is the value of r?

2 To the nearest cubic meter, what is the volume of the pond after 3 days?

3 $$B = \frac{m}{h^2}$$

The body mass index (B) of a person who has mass m and height h is calculated using the formula above. If two people have the same mass, but one has height h and the other has height $0.9h$, what is the ratio (to the nearest hundredth) of the taller person's body mass index to the shorter person's body mass index?

Mixed Practice – Advanced Math
(Answers & explanations begin on page 428).

Multiple Choice – No Calculator

1 $9\sqrt{x^3} + 3 = x - 6$

For all values of x greater than 0, the equation above is equivalent to which of the following?

A) $x^3 = \dfrac{x-9}{9}$

B) $x^3 = x^2 - 18x$

C) $x^3 = \dfrac{x^2 - 18x + 81}{81}$

D) $x = \sqrt{\dfrac{x^2 - 18x + 81}{81}}$

2 $c = kx^2 + 20x + b$

The equation above gives the cost of tiling a bathroom that is x feet long and x feet wide. Which of the following gives k in terms of x, b, and c?

A) $k = \dfrac{c - b - 20}{x^2}$

B) $k = \dfrac{c + b + 20x}{x^2}$

C) $k = \dfrac{c - b}{x^2} - 20$

D) $k = \dfrac{c - b}{x^2} - \dfrac{20}{x}$

3 $y = 3x^2 - 8x + 36$

$y = 2x^2 + 2x + 11$

If (x,y) is a solution of the system of equations above, what is the value of $x + y$?

A)   10
B)   25
C)   47
D)   76

4   A science student determines that the amount of energy, E, required to carry a water balloon a distance d can be represented by the equation $E = kdr^3$ where r is the radius of the water balloon and k is a constant. If the distance and radius are both doubled, the energy will be multiplied by

A)   2
B)   4
C)   8
D)   16

5   A function f satisfies $f(1) = 0$ and $f(0) = -1$.

A function g satisfies $g(-1) = 2$ and $g(0) = 1$.

What is the value of $g(f(0))$?

A) -1
B)   0
C)   1
D)   2

6   Which of the following equations has exactly one real solution?

    I. $x^2 - 6x + 9 = 0$

    II. $x^3 + 5x = 0$

    III. $x^2 - 4 = 0$

A)   I only
B)   I and II
C)   II and III
D)   III only

7 $y = x^2 + 4x + 4$

The equation above represents a parabola on the xy-plane. Which of the following equivalent forms of the equation displays the x-intercepts of the parabola as constants or coefficients?

A) $y - 5 = x^2 + 4x$

B) $y = (x + 2)^2$

C) $y = x(x + 2) + 4$

D) $y = (x + 4)^2$

The Tutorverse

Multiple Choice – Calculator

1 $\dfrac{t}{t-2}+\dfrac{1}{t-4}=\dfrac{2}{t^2-6t+8}$

If t is a solution to the equation above, what is the value of t?

A) 6
B) 4
C) 2
D) −1

2 If $\dfrac{4}{x-1}=\dfrac{7}{x+8}$, what is the value of x?

A) $\dfrac{3}{25}$

B) $\dfrac{25}{3}$

C) 13

D) $\dfrac{1}{7}$

3 If $f(x)=2x-7$, what is $f(x+4)$ equal to?

A) $2x+1$
B) $2x-3$
C) $8x-7$
D) $2x^2+x-28$

4 A teacher bought 30 books. Out of those 30 books, there were x books that cost 10 dollars each. The rest of the books cost $\dfrac{x}{2}$ dollars each. If the total cost of the 30 books was $200, which equation could be used to find the value of x?

A) $x^2-50x+400=0$
B) $x^2+20x-400=0$
C) $2x^2+3x-40=0$
D) $3x^2+2x-40=0$

5 $y-6=-(x+2)^2$
$2x+y=3$

How many ordered pairs (x,y) satisfy the system of equations shown above?

A) 0
B) 1
C) 2
D) There are infinitely many ordered pairs.

6 Which of the following is NOT divisible by $x-8$?

A) $x^4(x-8)+17(x-8)$
B) $(x-8)(x+2)+6$
C) x^3-13x^2+40x
D) x^2y-64y

Student Produced Response – Calculator

1 Joe's savings account has a balance of $1,325. The account earns 2% interest compounded annually. If Joe has left the money in the account for 5 years with no additional deposits or withdrawals, how much money did he initially deposit into the account?

2 Suppose the graph of $f(x)=x^3$ is translated 3 units left and 2 unit up. If the resulting graph represents $g(x)$, what is the value of $g(2)$?

The Tutorverse

Additional Math Topics

Guided Practice – Geometry

(Answers & explanations begin on page 429)

Multiple Choice – No Calculator

1 In the figure below, line segments *AB* and *DE* are parallel. A surveyor needs to find the distance *BC* across a swamp.

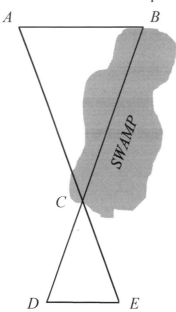

Note: Figure not drawn to scale.

The length of *DE* is 4 meters, *AB* is 12 meters, *DC* is 5 meters, and *EC* is 6 meters. What is the length of *BC*?

A)   12 meters
B)   15 meters
C)   18 meters
D)   21 meters

2 An oil storage container is a right circular cylinder that has a diameter of 20 meters and height of 8 meters. What is the volume of the oil storage container in cubic meters?

A) 640π
B) 800π
C) $1,280\pi$
D) $3,200\pi$

3

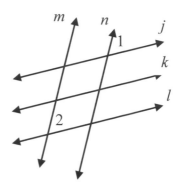

Note: Figure not drawn to scale.

In the figure above, lines *j*, *k*, and *l* are parallel to each other and lines *m* and *n* are parallel to each other. If the measure of ∠1 is 65°, what is the measure of ∠2?

A)   25°
B)   65°
C)   115°
D)   135°

4 In the figure below, lines *m* and *n* are parallel, and line *n* intersects segment *BC* at point *D*.

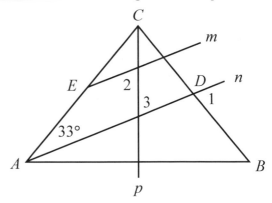

Note: Figure not drawn to scale.

If angle *CAD* = 33° and ∠1 = 78°, what is the measure of angle *ACB*?

A)   69°
B)   73°
C)   75°
D)   78°

The Tutorverse

5 In the figure below, ∠DCA = 105° and ∠BAC = 35°.

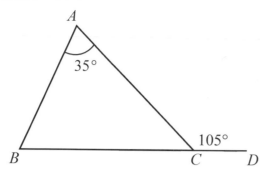

Note: Figure not drawn to scale.

What is the measure of ∠ABC?

A) 60°
B) 65°
C) 70°
D) 75°

6

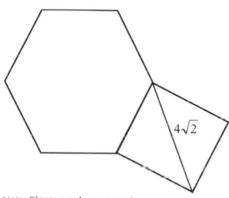

Note: Figure not drawn to scale.

In the picture above, a regular hexagon is attached to a square with diagonal distance of $4\sqrt{2}$. One side of the square is equal to one side of the hexagon. Find the area of the hexagon.

A) $96\sqrt{3}$
B) $48\sqrt{3}$
C) $24\sqrt{3}$
D) $18\sqrt{3}$

Questions 7 and 8 refer to the following image.

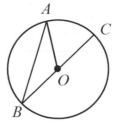

Note: Figure not drawn to scale.

7 In the figure above, if the central angle AOC = 60°, find the measure of angle ABC.

A) 15°
B) 20°
C) 30°
D) 60°

8 In the figure above, if central angle AOC = 56°, what is the angle OAB?

A) 14°
B) 28°
C) 56°
D) 62°

9 In the figure below, point O is the center of the circle, line segments LM and KM are tangent to the circle at points L and K, respectively, and the segments intersect at point M.

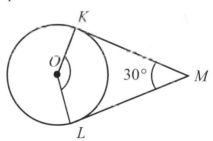

Note: Figure not drawn to scale.

If the circumference of the circle is 720, what is the length of major arc LK?

A) 300
B) 480
C) 600
D) 660

The Tutorverse

10 In the figure below, lines s, t, and u intersect at a point.

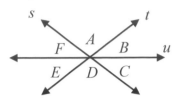

If the measures of angles $A + B = C + D$, which of the following must be true?

    I. $B + C + D = A + F + B$
    II. $E = C$
    III. $A = D$

A)   III only
B)   I and III only
C)   II and III only
D)   I, II, and III

11

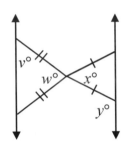

Note: Figure not drawn to scale.

In the figure above, the two vertical lines are parallel, angle $v = 40°$ and angle $w = 2x°$. What is angle $y°$?

A)   110°
B)   115°
C)   125°
D)   140°

12 In the figure below, triangle ABC is inscribed in a semicircle with a diameter of 20. Angle BAC subtends arc BC, which is 60°.

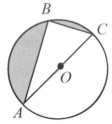

Note: Figure not drawn to scale.

What is the area of the shaded region?

A) $50\pi - 10\sqrt{2}$
B) $50\pi - 50\sqrt{3}$
C) $100\pi - 10\sqrt{2}$
D) $100\pi - 50\sqrt{3}$

13 In the figure below, a right circular cylinder and a right circular cone are drawn, but not to scale.

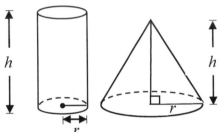

Which of the following conditions will always result in the cone and cylinder having equal volumes?

I. The cone has a base radius one third the radius of the cylinder and the height of the cone is nine times the height of the cylinder.

II. The cylinder has a base radius twice the radius of the cone and the cone's height is twelve times the cylinder's height.

III. The cone and cylinder have the same base radius and the height of the cylinder is one third the height of the cone.

A)   I and II only
B)   I and III only
C)   II and III only
D)   I, II, and III

The Tutorverse

Student Produced Response – No Calculator

1

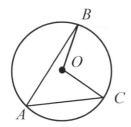

Note: Figure not drawn to scale.

In the figure above, angle *BAC* is 43° and subtends arc *BC*. What is the measure, in degrees, of central angle *BOC*?

2 In the figure below, the height of the triangle *ABC* is the length of the segment *BD*.

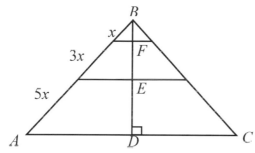

Note. Figure not drawn to scale.

If *BD* = 90 and segment *AB* is split into parts with proportions as shown, find the length of *DE*.

Multiple Choice – Calculator

1 As shown on the figure below, a cabin is designed so that the roof rests on the ground. The intersections of the roof lines and first floor, second floor, and attic are in the proportions shown. The entire structure is 32 feet tall.

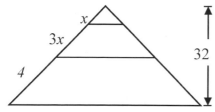

Note: Figure not drawn to scale.

What is the height of the first floor?
A) 28 feet
B) 24 feet
C) 20 feet
D) 16 feet

3 In the figure below, isosceles triangle *ABC* is inscribed in a semicircle.

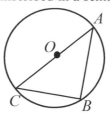

Note: Figure not drawn to scale.

If the circumference of the circle is 8π, what is the area of the triangle *ABC* in square units?

2 A bush and a tree cast shadows 2 meters and 15 meters long, respectively. The height of the bush is measured at 0.7 meters. What is the height of the tree?
A) 1.75 meters
B) 5.25 meters
C) 10.5 meters
D) 17.3 meters

The Tutorverse

3 In the figure below, the minor arc length $AB = 1.58$ cm and angle $x = 8°$.

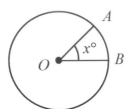

Note: Figure not drawn to scale.

Which of the following is the closest to the radius of the circle?

A)   3.06 cm
B)   6.10 cm
C)   9.13 cm
D)   11.32 cm

4

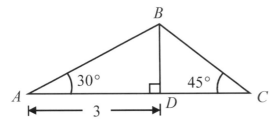

Note: Figure not drawn to scale.

Find the length of side BC in the figure above.

A) $\sqrt{2}$
B) $3\sqrt{2}$
C) $\sqrt{6}$
D) $3\sqrt{6}$

5 The figure below shows a circle with radius 12. A central angle $x°$ subtends an arc length between 23 and 24.

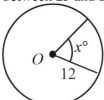

Note: Figure not drawn to scale.

Find the range of integer answers for x.

A) $105 \le x \le 109$
B) $110 \le x \le 114$
C) $115 \le x \le 119$
D) $120 \le x \le 124$

6 Captain Tom is sailing his ship from a port to an island. The direct route is 57 miles. When a storm comes, he decides to take a detour by heading 25 miles north until he is directly east of the island, then sailing west directly towards the island, as shown below.

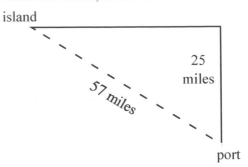

Note: Figure not drawn to scale.

To the nearest mile, how many miles west does Captain Tom have to sail to reach the island?

A)   13
B)   32
C)   51
D)   62

7 In the figure below, a right circular cone has a slant height of 12 cm and the altitude makes a 30° angle with the slant height.

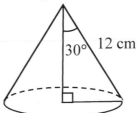

Note: Figure not drawn to scale.

Which of the following is closest to the volume of the cone, in cubic centimeters?

A)   65.3
B)   130.6
C)   195.9
D)   391.8

8 Two geometric solids, a pyramid with square base and a rectangular solid, have equal volumes. Which of the following pairs have equal volume?

A) A pyramid with base sides 6 and height 4; a rectangular solid with dimensions $9 \times 3 \times 2$

B) A pyramid with base sides 3 and height 4; a rectangular solid with dimensions $3 \times 3 \times 2$

C) A pyramid with base sides 9 and height 3; a rectangular solid with dimensions $3 \times 3 \times 9$

D) A pyramid with base sides 6 and height 8; a rectangular solid with dimensions $3 \times 4 \times 6$

9

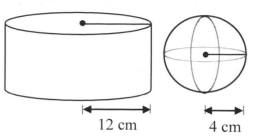

12 cm   4 cm

Note: Figure not drawn to scale.

A sphere with a radius of 4 centimeters is filled with liquid and then poured into an empty right circular cylinder with a radius of 12 centimeters. Which of the following is closest to the height of the liquid in the cylinder?

A) 0.593 cm
B) 21.3 cm
C) 67.0 cm
D) 85.3 cm

Student Produced Response – Calculator

1 In the figure below, the measure of $\angle ABC$ is $20°$ and the measure of $\angle BAC$ is $80°$.

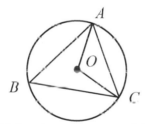

If the circumference of the circle is 720, what is the arc length of AB?

2 A spherical volleyball, when fully inflated, holds 288π cubic inches of air. What is the diameter of the volleyball, in inches?

Guided Practice – Equations of Circles
(Answers & explanations begin on page 432)

Multiple Choice – Calculator

1 $(x-6)^2 + (y+8)^2 = 16$
A circle on the *xy*-plane has the equation shown above. Which of the following correctly describes the location of the center of the circle and the length of its radius?
A)   Center: (6,–8)
     Radius: 4
B)   Center: (6,–8)
     Radius: 8
C)   Center: (–6,8)
     Radius: 4
D)   Center: (–6,8)
     Radius: 8

2 A circle on the *xy*-plane has its center at (5,–4) and radius 8. Which of the following is an equation of the circle?
A) $(x+5)^2 + (y-4)^2 = 16$
B) $(x-5)^2 + (y+4)^2 = 16$
C) $(x+5)^2 + (y-4)^2 = 64$
D) $(x-5)^2 + (y+4)^2 = 64$

3 A circle on the *xy*-plane has its center at (–3.6,–13.4) and radius $\sqrt{8}$. Which of the following is an equation of the circle?
A) $(x+3.6)^2 + (y+13.4)^2 = 2$
B) $(x-3.6)^2 + (y-13.4)^2 = 2$
C) $(x+3.6)^2 + (y+13.4)^2 = 8$
D) $(x-3.6)^2 + (y-13.4)^2 = 8$

4 A circle on the *xy*-plane has its center at $(\frac{1}{6}, \frac{5}{7})$ and radius $\frac{2}{3}$. Which of the following is an equation of the circle?
A) $(x+\frac{1}{6})^2 + (y+\frac{5}{7})^2 = \frac{4}{9}$
B) $(x-\frac{1}{6})^2 + (y-\frac{5}{7})^2 = \frac{4}{9}$
C) $(x+\frac{1}{6})^2 + (y+\frac{5}{7})^2 = \frac{4}{6}$
D) $(x-\frac{1}{6})^2 + (y-\frac{5}{7})^2 = \frac{4}{6}$

5 A circle with center *M* is graphed on the *xy*-plane.

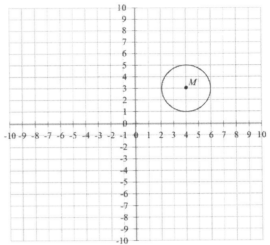

Which of the following is an equation of the circle?
A) $(x+4)^2 + (y+3)^2 = 2$
B) $(x-4)^2 + (y-3)^2 = 2$
C) $(x+4)^2 + (y+3)^2 = 4$
D) $(x-4)^2 + (y-3)^2 = 4$

6 A circle on the *xy*-plane has its center at (–8,11). If the point (4,11) lies on the circle, which of the following is an equation of the circle?
A) $(x+8)^2 + (y-11)^2 = 12$
B) $(x-8)^2 + (y+11)^2 = 12$
C) $(x+8)^2 + (y-11)^2 = 144$
D) $(x-8)^2 + (y+11)^2 = 144$

7 $x^2 + (y+3)^2 = 16$
The graph of the equation above on the *xy*-plane is a circle. If the center of the circle is translated 1 unit up and the radius is increased by 1, which of the following is an equation of the resulting circle?
A) $(x-1)^2 + (y+3)^2 = 17$
B) $(x-1)^2 + (y+3)^2 = 25$
C) $x^2 + (y+2)^2 = 25$
D) $x^2 + (y+4)^2 = 17$

8 $x^2 + y^2 = 25$

The graph of the equation above on the *xy*-plane is a circle. If the center of the circle is translated 2 units up and the radius is decreased by 1, which of the following is an equation of the resulting circle?

A) $x^2 + (y+2)^2 = 16$

B) $x^2 + (y+2)^2 = 36$

C) $x^2 + (y-2)^2 = 16$

D) $x^2 + (y-2)^2 = 36$

9   Which of the following is an equation of a circle on the *xy*-plane with center (2,5) and a radius with endpoint (2,2)?

A) $(x-2)^2 + (y-5)^2 = 9$

B) $(x+2)^2 + (y+5)^2 = 16$

C) $(x+2)^2 + (y-2)^2 = 9$

D) $(x-2)^2 + (y-5)^2 = 16$

10   A circle in the *xy*-plane has a diameter with endpoints at (−4,−2) and (8,−2). Which of the following is an equation of the circle?

A) $(x-2)^2 + (y+2)^2 = 36$

B) $(x+2)^2 + (y-2)^2 = 36$

C) $(x-2)^2 + (y+2)^2 = 64$

D) $(x+2)^2 + (y-2)^2 = 64$

11 $(x-4)^2 + (y-5)^2 = 36$

Which of the following circle graphs is best represented by the equation shown above?

A)

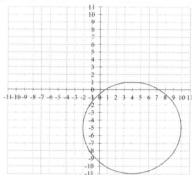

B)

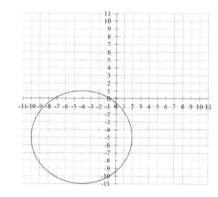

C)

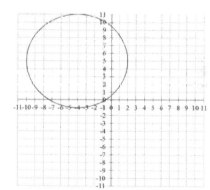

D)

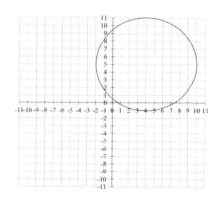

The Tutorverse

12 A circle with center C is graphed on the xy-plane.

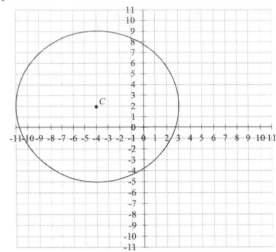

Which of the following is an equation of the circle?

A) $(x+4)^2 + (y-2)^2 = 14$

B) $(x-4)^2 + (y+2)^2 = 14$

C) $(x+4)^2 + (y-2)^2 = 49$

D) $(x-4)^2 + (y+2)^2 = 49$

13 $x^2 + (y-7)^2 = 9$

The graph of the equation above on the xy-plane is a circle. If the center of the circle is translated 2 units to the left and the radius is increased by 7, which of the following is an equation of the resulting circle?

A) $(x-2)^2 + (y-7)^2 = 16$

B) $(x+2)^2 + (y-7)^2 = 16$

C) $(x-2)^2 + (y-7)^2 = 100$

D) $(x+2)^2 + (y-7)^2 = 100$

14 Which of the following could be an equation of a circle in the xy-plane with a diameter having one endpoint at $(6,-6)$ and a length of 14?

A) $(x+1)^2 + (y+6)^2 = 49$

B) $(x+6)^2 + (y-1)^2 = 49$

C) $(x-1)^2 + (y+6)^2 = 196$

D) $(x-6)^2 + (y-1)^2 = 196$

15 $(x-3)^2 + (y+2)^2 = 25$

The graph of the equation above in the xy-plane is the resulting circle after another circle was translated 3 units to the right and the radius was increased by 3. Which of the following is an equation of the original circle before the transformation?

A) $x^2 + (y+2)^2 = 4$

B) $x^2 + (y+2)^2 = 64$

C) $(x-6)^2 + (y+2)^2 = 4$

D) $(x-6)^2 + (y+2)^2 = 64$

Student Produced Response – Calculator

1 A circle on the xy-plane has center $(4,4)$ and a radius with endpoint $(0,7)$. What is the radius of the circle?

2 $x^2 + 4x + y^2 - 12y = 41$

The graph of the equation above on the xy-plane is a circle. What is the diameter of the circle?

3 $x^2 - 6x + y^2 - 16y = 27$

The graph of the equation above on the xy-plane is a circle. What is the diameter of the circle?

Guided Practice – Trigonometry

(Answers & explanations begin on page 434)

Multiple Choice – No Calculator

1

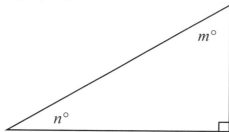

Note: Figure not drawn to scale.

In the right triangle above, cos(*n*) = 0.8.
What is sin(*m*)?

A) 0.2
B) 0.4
C) 0.6
D) 0.8

2

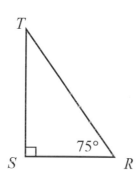

Note: Figure not drawn to scale.

Which expression is equivalent to sin(75°)?

A) cos(*T*)
B) cos(*R*)
C) sin(*T*)
D) sin(*S*)

3 Two acute angles, *A* and *B*, have measures
a° and *b*° respectively and sin(*a*°) = cos(*b*°).
If *a* = *k* + 6 and *b* = 3*k* + 4, what is the value
of *k*?

A) 1
B) 7
C) 20
D) 45

4

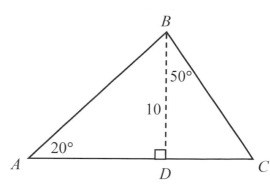

Note: Figure not drawn to scale.

Which of the following is equal to the length
of *AD*?

A) 10tan(70°)
B) 10tan(50°)
C) 10tan(20°)
D) 10sin(20°)

5

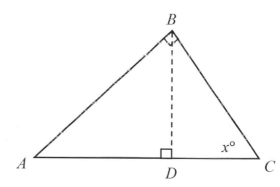

Note: Figure not drawn to scale.

In the figure above, *ABC* and *BDC* are both
right triangles. Which of the following
expressions must be equal to the length of
the segment *BD*?

A) tan(*x*°)*AD*

B) $\dfrac{1}{\tan(x°)}AD$

C) sin(*x*°)*DC*

D) $\dfrac{1}{\tan(x°)}DC$

Student Produced Response – No Calculator

1

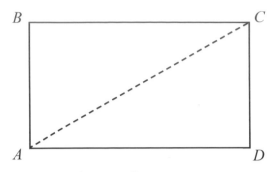

Note: Figure not drawn to scale.

In the rectangle *ABCD* above, the length of *AB* is 6 and the length of BC is $6\sqrt{3}$. What is the measure, in degrees, of ∠*CAD*?

Multiple Choice – Calculator

1

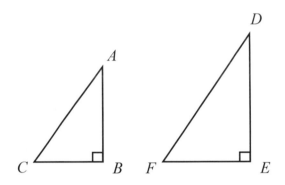

Note: Figure not drawn to scale.

In the figure above, right triangle *ABC* is similar to right triangle *DEF*. Vertices *A*, *B*, and *C* correspond to vertices *D*, *E*, and *F* respectively. If sin(*A*) = 0.45, what is the value of sin(*D*)?

A)   0.89
B)   0.55
C)   0.45
D)   0.20

2

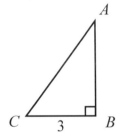

Note: Figure not drawn to scale.

It is given that
$\sin(65°) \approx 0.9063, \cos(65°) \approx 0.4226$, and
$\tan(65°) \approx 2.1445$. The length of *CB* is 3 and the measure of ∠*BCA* is 65°. Which of the following is closest to the length of *AC*?

A)   1.26
B)   3.29
C)   6.42
D)   7.14

The Tutorverse

3

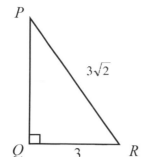

Note: *Figure not drawn to scale.*

What is the measure in degrees of $\angle PRQ$ in the figure shown?

A) 60
B) 50
C) 45
D) 30

Student Produced Response – Calculator

1

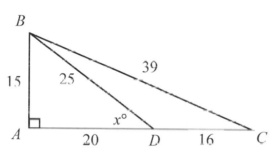

Note: *Figure not drawn to scale.*

In the figure above, what is $\cos(x°)$ as a fraction in simplest form?

2 Right triangle *ABC* has sides 5 m., 12 m., and 13 m. If the side opposite to angle *A* is 12 m., then what is cos *A*?

4

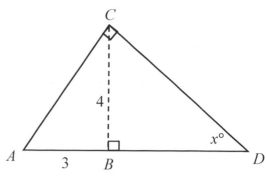

Note: *Figure not drawn to scale.*

In the figure above, right triangle *ABC* is similar to right triangle *CBD*. The lengths of segments *AB* and *BC* are 3 and 4 respectively. Which of the following inequalities is true about the value of $\sin(x°)$?

A) $0 \le \sin(x°) < 0.5$

B) $0.5 \le \sin(x°) < 0.7$

C) $0.7 \le \sin(x°) < 1$

D) $1 \le \sin(x°)$

3

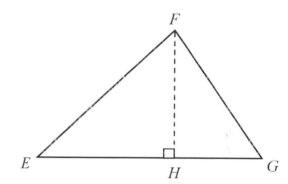

Note: *Figure not drawn to scale.*

The measure of angle *FEH* is 30°, the measure of angle *FGH* is 45° and the height *FH* of the triangle is 14 inches. Given that $\sqrt{2} \approx 1.41$ and $\sqrt{3} \approx 1.73$, what is the length of *EG* to the nearest inch?

4 In triangle *XYZ*, the measure of $\angle Y$ is 90°, the measure of $\angle X$ is $x°$, *YZ* = 12 and *XZ* = 13. What is the value of $\tan(x°)$?

Guided Practice – Radians

(Answers & explanations begin on page 435)

Multiple Choice – No Calculator

1

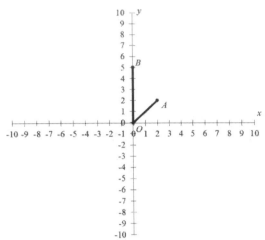

In the figure above, the coordinates of point A are (2,2). What is the measure, in radians, of angle AOB?

A) $\dfrac{\pi}{8}$

B) $\dfrac{\pi}{4}$

C) $\dfrac{\pi}{3}$

D) $\dfrac{\pi}{2}$

2 $\sin(C) = \cos(C)$

The equation above is true for some $\angle C$. What is the measure of $\angle C$ in radians?

A) $\dfrac{\pi}{4}$

B) $\dfrac{\pi}{3}$

C) $\dfrac{\pi}{2}$

D) π

3 Which of the following is true for any acute angle x?

A) $\sin(x) = \cos(\pi - x)$

B) $\sin(x) = \cos(x - \pi)$

C) $\sin(x) = \cos\left(\dfrac{\pi}{2} - x\right)$

D) $\sin(x) = \cos\left(x - \dfrac{\pi}{2}\right)$

4

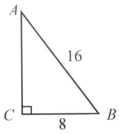

Note: Figure not drawn to scale.

What is the measure in radians of $\angle A$ in the figure above?

A) $\dfrac{\pi}{6}$

B) $\dfrac{\pi}{4}$

C) $\dfrac{\pi}{3}$

D) $\dfrac{\pi}{2}$

5

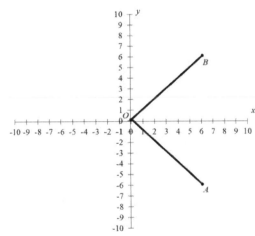

In the figure, the coordinates of point A are (6,–6) and the coordinates of point B are (6,6). What is the measure in radians of $\angle AOB$?

A) $\dfrac{\pi}{4}$

B) $\dfrac{\pi}{3}$

C) $\dfrac{\pi}{2}$

D) $\dfrac{2\pi}{3}$

The Tutorverse

6 In a unit circle centered on the origin, the point A has coordinates $(1,0)$ and point B lies on the terminal side of angle AOB, where O is the origin. The measure of angle AOB is $210°$. What is the measure of angle AOB in radians?

A) $\dfrac{\pi}{3}$

B) $\dfrac{2\pi}{3}$

C) $\dfrac{5\pi}{6}$

D) $\dfrac{7\pi}{6}$

Student Produced Response – No Calculator

1

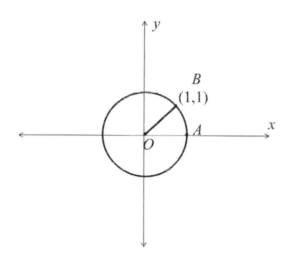

On the xy-plane above, O is the center of the circle, and the measure of $\angle AOB$ is $\dfrac{\pi}{a}$ radians. What is the value of a?

2 In a circle with center O, central angle AOB has a measure of $\dfrac{7\pi}{8}$ radians. The area of the sector formed by central angle AOB is what fraction of the area of the circle?

The Tutorverse

Multiple Choice – Calculator

1

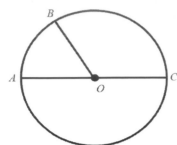

The measure of $\angle BOA$ in the figure above is $\dfrac{\pi}{6}$. What is the measure of $\angle COB$?

A) $\dfrac{\pi}{3}$

B) $\dfrac{5\pi}{6}$

C) $\dfrac{7\pi}{6}$

D) $\dfrac{11\pi}{6}$

2

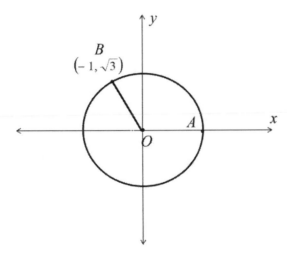

On the xy-plane above, O is the center of the circle. What is the measure in radians of $\angle AOB$?

A) $\dfrac{\pi}{3}$

B) $\dfrac{2\pi}{3}$

C) $\dfrac{3\pi}{4}$

D) $\dfrac{5\pi}{6}$

3

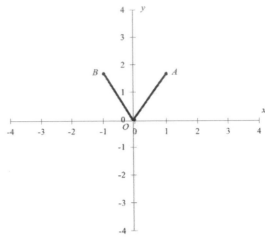

In the figure above, the coordinates of point A are $\left(1, \sqrt{3}\right)$ and the coordinates of point B are $\left(-1, \sqrt{3}\right)$. What is the measure in radians of $\angle AOB$?

A) $\dfrac{\pi}{6}$

B) $\dfrac{\pi}{4}$

C) $\dfrac{\pi}{3}$

D) $\dfrac{2\pi}{3}$

4

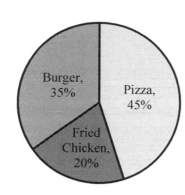

Students were asked which fast food they preferred and the results are shown in the pie chart above. What is the measure in radians of the central angle of the sector representing pizza?

A) $\dfrac{2\pi}{45}$

B) $\dfrac{9\pi}{40}$

C) $\dfrac{9\pi}{20}$

D) $\dfrac{9\pi}{10}$

Student Produced Response – Calculator

1 In a circle with center O, central angle AOB has a measure of $\dfrac{3\pi}{5}$ radians. The length of the arc intercepted by angle AOB is what fraction of the circumference of the circle?

5 Angles A and B are supplementary. The measure of angle A is twice the measure of angle B. What is the measure of angle B in radians?

A) $\dfrac{\pi}{3}$

B) $\dfrac{\pi}{2}$

C) $\dfrac{2\pi}{3}$

D) π

Guided Practice – Imaginary & Complex Numbers

(Answers & explanations begin on page 437)

Multiple Choice – No Calculator

1   Which of the following is equal to $i^2 + i^2$?
(Note: $i = \sqrt{-1}$)
A) i^4
B) $2i^4$
C) 0
D) -2

2   Which of the following is equal to
$(3 + 4i) + (7 + 6i)$? (Note: $i = \sqrt{-1}$)
A) $7 + 13i$
B) $10 + 10i$
C) $10 - 10i$
D) $10 - 10i^2$

3   Which of the following is equal to
$(4 + 2i) - (7 - 2i)$? (Note: $i = \sqrt{-1}$)
A) -3
B) $-3i$
C) $-3 + 4i$
D) $-3 - 4i$

4   Which of the following is equal to
$-6i(3 - 2i)$? (Note: $i = \sqrt{-1}$)
A) $12 - 18i$
B) $-12 - 18i$
C) $-18 + 12i$
D) -30

5   Which of the following is equal to
$12i(4 + 3i)$? (Note: $i = \sqrt{-1}$)
A) $36 - 48i$
B) $-36 + 48i$
C) $-36 - 48i$
D) 84

6   Which of the following is equal to $\dfrac{12 + 8i}{2}$?

(Note: $i = \sqrt{-1}$)
A) 10
B) $10i$
C) $6 + 4i$
D) $6 + 8i$

7   Which of the following is equal to
$5i^4 - 5i^2 - 5$? (Note: $i = \sqrt{-1}$)
A) -5
B) 0
C) 1
D) 5

8   Which of the following is equal to
$(-5i^2) - (-3 - 7i^2)$? (Note: $i = \sqrt{-1}$)
A) 1
B) $-3 - 12i^2$
C) $3 - 12i^2$
D) $3 + 2i^2$

9   Which of the following is equal to
$5i^3(4 - 2i^2)$? (Note: $i = \sqrt{-1}$)
A) $10i$
B) $20 - 10i$
C) $30i$
D) $-30i$

10   Which of the following is equal to
$8i(7 - 3i)$? (Note: $i = \sqrt{-1}$)
A) $-24 + 56i$
B) $24 + 56i$
C) $56 + 24i$
D) $32 + 56i$

11   Which of the following is equal to
$(4 - i)^2$? (Note: $i = \sqrt{-1}$)
A) $15 - 8i$
B) $15 + 8i$
C) $17 - 8i$
D) $17 + 8i$

12   Which of the following is equal to
$(5 - 5i)(4 + 4i)$? (Note: $i = \sqrt{-1}$)
A) 40
B) $40 - 40i$
C) $20 - 20i$
D) $20 - 40i - 20i^2$

The Tutorverse

13 Which of the following is equal to i^{32}?
(Note: $i = \sqrt{-1}$)
A) i
B) $-i$
C) 1
D) -1

14 Which of the following is equal to i^{47}?
(Note: $i = \sqrt{-1}$)
A) i
B) $-i$
C) 1
D) -1

15 Which of the following is equal to
$(4 + 2i)(3 - 7i)$? (Note: $i = \sqrt{-1}$)
A) $12 - 14i^2$
B) -2
C) $-2 - 22i$
D) $26 - 22i$

16 Which of the following is equal to
$(8 - 3i)(8 + 3i)$? (Note: $i = \sqrt{-1}$)
A) 55
B) $64 - 6i$
C) $64 - 9i$
D) 73

17 Which of the following is equal to
$(i + 1)(i - 1)$? (Note: $i = \sqrt{-1}$)
A) 0
B) $-2 + i$
C) $-2 - i$
D) -2

18 Which of the following is equal to $\dfrac{7}{2i}$?
(Note: $i = \sqrt{-1}$)
A) $\dfrac{7}{4}$
B) $\dfrac{-7}{4}$
C) $\dfrac{7i}{2}$
D) $\dfrac{-7i}{2}$

19 Which of the following is equal to $\dfrac{9i}{1 + 8i}$?
(Note: $i = \sqrt{-1}$)
A) $\dfrac{9 + 72i}{9}$
B) $\dfrac{72 + 9i}{65}$
C) $\dfrac{9 - 72i}{9}$
D) $\dfrac{72 - 9i}{65}$

20 Which of the following is equal to $\dfrac{9 - 4i}{-5i}$?
(Note: $i = \sqrt{-1}$)
A) $\dfrac{9i + 4}{5}$
B) $\dfrac{13}{5}$
C) $\dfrac{9i - 4}{5}$
D) $\dfrac{-9i + 4}{5}$

21 Which of the following is equal to
$i + i^2 + i^3 + i^4$? (Note: $i = \sqrt{-1}$)
A) 0
B) $2 + 2i$
C) $2 - 2i$
D) i^{10}

22 Which of the following is equal to $\dfrac{4}{2 + 3i}$?
(Note: $i = \sqrt{-1}$)
A) $\dfrac{8 + 12i}{5}$
B) $\dfrac{8 - 12i}{13}$
C) $\dfrac{8 + 12i}{13}$
D) $\dfrac{-4}{5}$

23 $\dfrac{8-3i}{2+i}$

If the expression above is rewritten in the form $a + bi$, where a and b are real numbers, what is the value of a? (Note: $i = \sqrt{-1}$)

A) $\dfrac{13}{5}$

B) $\dfrac{19}{5}$

C) $\dfrac{13}{3}$

D) $\dfrac{14}{3}$

24 Which of the following is equal to

$\dfrac{5}{5+i} + \dfrac{i}{5-i}$? (Note: $i = \sqrt{-1}$)

A) $\dfrac{12}{13}$

B) $\dfrac{1}{4}$

C) $5 + i$

D) $1 - 5i$

Student Produced Response – No Calculator

1 What is the value of the following expression: $(5 + 6i) + (4 - 6i)$? (Note: $i = \sqrt{-1}$)

2 What is the value of the following expression: $i^4 - 6i^2 + 9$? (Note: $i = \sqrt{-1}$)

3 What is the value of the following expression: $(4 + 5i)(4 - 5i)$? (Note: $i = \sqrt{-1}$)

4 What is the value of the following expression:

$\dfrac{i^3}{-5i}$? (Note: $i = \sqrt{-1}$)

5 What is the value of the following expression: $(-2 - 8i)(-2 + 8i)$? (Note: $i = \sqrt{-1}$)

6 What is the value of the following expression:

$\dfrac{i^7}{-i}$? (Note: $i = \sqrt{-1}$)

7 What is the value of the following expression:

$\dfrac{2-i}{2+i} + \dfrac{2+i}{2-i}$? (Note: $i = \sqrt{-1}$)

The Tutorverse

Mixed Practice – Additional Math Topics

(Answers & explanations begin on page 439)

Multiple Choice – No Calculator

1

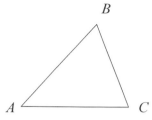

Note: Figure not drawn to scale.

In the figure above, A and C are acute angles and $\sin(A) = \cos(C)$. What is the measure, in degrees, of angle B?

A) 120
B) 90
C) 60
D) 45

2 Which of the following is equal to $(12 + 2i)^2$?

(Note: $i = \sqrt{-1}$)

A) 140
B) $148 + 48i$
C) $144 + 48i$
D) $140 + 48i$

3 Which of the following is an equation of a circle on the xy-plane with center $(2,4)$ and a radius with endpoint $(8,-4)$?

A) $(x+2)^2 + (y+4)^2 = 36$

B) $(x-2)^2 + (y-4)^2 = 64$

C) $(x-2)^2 + (y-4)^2 = 100$

D) $(x-2)^2 + (y-4)^2 = 196$

4

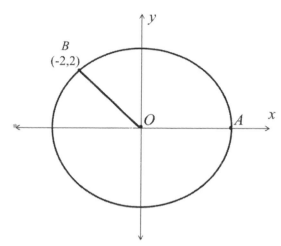

On the xy-plane above, O is the center of the circle. What is the measure in radians of angle AOB?

A) $\dfrac{\pi}{4}$

B) $\dfrac{\pi}{3}$

C) $\dfrac{3\pi}{2}$

D) $\dfrac{3\pi}{4}$

5 $\dfrac{10 + 40i}{-3 + 5i}$

If the expression above is rewritten in the form $a + bi$, where a and b are real numbers, what is the value of b? (Note: $i = \sqrt{-1}$)

A) -170
B) -5
C) 5
D) 170

The Tutorverse

6 $(x-4)^2 + (y-2)^2 = 49$

Which of the following circle graphs is best represented by the equation shown above?

A)

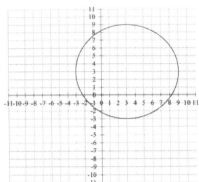

B)

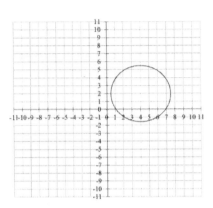

C)

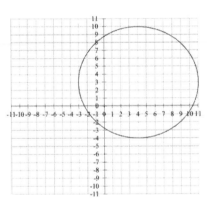

D)

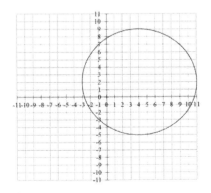

7

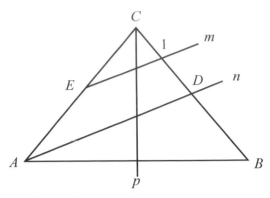

Note: Figure not drawn to scale.

In the above figure, lines *m* and *n* are parallel, and line *n* intersects segment *BC* at point *D*. If angle 1 = 98° and angle *DAB* = 12°, what is angle *DBA*?

A)   55°
B)   70°
C)   86°
D)   90°

Multiple Choice – Calculator

1   In the figure below, a rocket engine is constructed from a right circular cylinder with a right circular cone attached to the top.

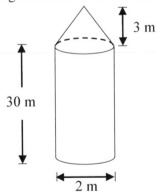

Note: Figure not drawn to scale.

Both the cone and cylinder have diameters of 2 meters, the height of the cylinder is 30 meters, and the height of the cone is 3 meters. Find the volume of the rocket engine in cubic meters.

A)   30π
B)   31π
C)   33π
D)   62π

The Tutorverse

Part Four: Essay

Overview

The Essay portion of the SAT is optional. Students will only need to take the Essay if they sign up (and pay) for it when registering for the test.

The Essay prompt is always the same: read a persuasive passage, and write an essay explaining how the author crafts and supports the argument in the passage. The persuasive passage will vary from test to test, but will generally be around 700 words long (about a page in length).

Students have 50 minutes to read the passage and write the essay.

Tutorverse Tips & Strategies

Read & Take Notes

The first step is to read the passage carefully and dissect the argument. One of the best ways to do this is to underline and label each element in an argument, making notes in the margins if necessary. Pay attention to and label or write down the following elements of an argument:

- **Claims** – statements of a point of view, (e.g. an opinion, as opposed to a fact)
- **Assumptions** – things taken for granted and assumed to be true (e.g. the ideas that must be true in order for the argument to make sense, but that aren't always supported by facts)
- **Support** – evidence that is offered up to justify a claim (e.g. facts like statistics, quotes, related ideas, etc.)
- **Conclusions** – the claim of the passage that logically results from the assumptions, claims, and support

Many students find the acronym "CASC" helpful to remember the elements of an argument.

Once the elements of the argument – the CASC – have been identified, take a step back and look at the overall structure of the passage. Ask how the author uses the CASC elements – What order are they in? Does the author focus on some elements but not others? Can the elements be further broken down and categorized? Is there something missing that would make the argument more clear?

Outline & Write

Once you've finished reading and taking notes on the elements of the argument, it is important to spend time outlining the essay itself. Remember, the prompt asks that students analyze the elements of the argument and explain *how* the argument is constructed – *how* the passage is persuasive. The prompt *does not* ask the student to form an opinion on the passage's topic, or ask whether the student agrees with the arguments in the passage.

Be sure to determine the thesis – main point – of the essay, which should succinctly explain how the author crafts the argument in the passage. The rest of the essay should expand upon this thesis using specific evidence from the passage. Cite lines and parts of the passage to support the interpretation offered by the thesis; explain how the author uses figurative language or adjectives to influence the reader's opinion; describe the flow of the argument.

The essay itself should *only* be written on the lined pages of the answer booklet.

Proofread

Be sure to reserve time to proofread the essay. Check for proper grammar, punctuation, capitalization, etc.

The Tutorverse

Practice Passages

The best way to prepare for the Essay section of the SAT is to practice reading, planning, writing, and proofreading an essay under a time limit. This section contains nine persuasive passages covering a wide range of topics. The prompt for each passage is the same: write an essay describing how the author crafts the argument in the passage and how the author uses each element of an argument to persuade the reader. Set a timer for 50 minutes and write your essay on a separate piece of lined paper.

With practice, students should develop an individualized strategy to approximate on the actual exam, splitting the 50 minutes given into smaller allotments to complete each step of the writing process (i.e. 10 minutes to read and take notes, 10 minutes to outline, 25 minutes to write, 5 minutes to proofread).

There is no answer key for this section of the workbook. Instead, ask a trusted educator to review your essay. Be sure to discuss each metric scored on this part of the test: Reading, Analysis, Writing (see the How to Use this Book: Scoring & Reporting section of this workbook for more information). Also discuss with your tutor, teacher, mentor, or family member how much time you spent on each step of the writing process.

Practice Passage 1

1. Clinical trials for new medical treatments are a crucial part of determining whether new and experimental treatments can effectively treat infectious disease. In the United States, clinical trials are closely regulated and monitored by the Food and Drug Administration (FDA), and scientists are required to follow very specific procedures. One such procedure relates to the use of a control group. Because a number of factors can affect the results of a clinical trial, such as small differences in the testing environment, control groups are created to help prevent any biases from affecting results and conclusion. In medical studies, researchers will often place patients in separate groups: one that receives the new, experimental treatment, and one that receives a placebo (usually a substance that is believed to have minimal impact on a person's health, like a sugar pill) or the standard course of treatment. The latter is generally referred to as the control group. Data from each group is then reviewed to determine whether or not the new treatment is safe and effective. This process alone can take years.

2. Because ensuring the safety and efficacy of a new treatment is a key aspect of the clinical trial process, is it ever acceptable to forego the use of a control group? What happens when the disease being treated has a high mortality rate and spreads quickly? These were questions scientists faced during the 2014 Ebola outbreak in West Africa.

3. The Ebola virus is as debilitating as it is contagious; on average, symptoms manifest between eight to ten days after exposure, and many cases prove fatal within only days of first contracting the disease. Some survivors also suffer from chronic health problems for the rest of their lives. Because there is no known cure for the disease, scientists worked hard during the outbreak to find a treatment. But because of the deadly nature of the virus, the use of a standard clinical trial process presented an ethical dilemma. Creating a control group would have left a group of patients without the new treatment, requiring doctors to instead providing patients with the often ineffective standard treatments for Ebola: fluids, pain medication, and antibiotics. Yet, doctors didn't know if the new drugs would substantially increase the odds the patient would survive, or if there would be problematic side effects. The doctors were stuck between a rock and a hard place.

4. Administering treatment without following clinical trial protocols posed an ethical problem for doctors working in West Africa. Doctors from the National Institute of Allergy and Infections Diseases (NIAID) argued that foregoing control groups was an appropriate course of action only if it met all of the following criteria: that the drug had no side effects, was known to successfully treat the disease, and that there was little variability in results. At the time, it was simply not possible to know whether or not such a strict criteria

The Tutorverse

could be met.

5. Yet the NIAID doctors were not on the ground with actual patients, viewing the situation from a safe distance instead. Doctors at the outbreak sites argued that, in cases like this, delaying treatment to patients in order to conduct clinical trials to ascertain the answers to questions posed by the NIAID could actually cost lives. Since the existing standard of care was so ineffective, it seemed logical to try the experimental treatments, which at least had the hope of saving lives that would most likely be lost anyway. Many of these treatments seemed promising because they'd been derived from patients who had actually survived Ebola.

6. Ultimately, the World Health Organization allowed doctors to administer new drugs without using a control group. The crisis had reached the level that delaying potentially effective treatments was ultimately more costly than conducting proper trials. Doctors in West Africa created a framework for their trials that enabled them to make quick decisions about the efficacy of the drugs they were using, especially in comparison with the normal standard of care. In the end, many of the treatments used did in fact prove effective at treating the disease: countless lives were spared.

7. Oftentimes, difficult ethical questions – such as those raised during the Ebola outbreak concerning the use of experimental drugs – can often be answered by asking a simple question: Do the pros outweigh the cons? Under most circumstances, standard clinical trials for new medical treatments are the best way to ensure the efficacy and safety of new drugs. However, in times of crisis, a better approach may be to follow the precedent set in West Africa.

Practice Passage 2

1. School budgets across the America are getting slashed, and music programs are often among the first to go. Cutting music programs might save money now, but doing so is a long-term disservice to students. Music programs do much more than simply teach children to play instruments; studies have shown that music education has wide-reaching academic and social benefits for students.

2. Music begins to enrich students as early as age two, and should therefore be a part of early childhood education. According to the Children's Music Workshop, an advocacy group that offers music classes to students in the Los Angeles area, learning music at a young age better prepares students for formal learning once they begin grade school. Music class requires students to listen, repeat sounds, and move. Studying music can also help students learn and memorize information; young learners are more likely to remember something if they learn it in song, and music can help older students with memorization as well.

3. Early musical training can also facilitate language development. Learning music helps students better make sound-to-meaning associations, which they can then apply to learning to read. Music also has a positive effect on the left side of the brain, especially the area where people process language. Studying music has been shown to help students remember verbal information, which can help them succeed academically.

4. This verbal component of music education has a number of benefits for students. Not only do students involved in music read and process language better than their peers, but they also develop better skills and techniques for interacting with other people. Dr. Kyle Pruett, a clinical professor of child psychiatry at Yale School of Medicine, argues further that this language development is important for the way students socialize. "Language competence is at the root of social competence," he says. "Musical experience strengthens the capacity to be verbally competent."

5. Music doesn't just help with verbal skills. Students who take music classes may also perform better in math. According to the National Association for Music Education (NAFME), learning music helps students with pattern recognition, spatial relationships, creative thinking, and other skills required to succeed at math.

The Tutorverse

Reading music also requires counting skills and the ability to understand fractions and patterns, skills that young students learn in music class and can apply to their other academic subjects.

6. Music education has also been shown to raise intelligence quotient (IQ) scores. A study conducted by E. Glenn Schellenberg at the University of Toronto at Mississauga found that students who took piano and voice lessons tested, on average, three IQ points higher than their peers who did not have music lessons. Another study conducted by Ellen Winner and Gottfried Schlaug of Boston College and Harvard Medical School, respectively, found that students who took music class for fifteen months could better distinguish between different kinds of sounds and were better at fine motor tasks than students who did not take music classes.

7. Perhaps the most remarkable part of music education is that it has been shown to raise test scores. According to NAFME, students who have taken music classes earn higher SAT scores than students who have not; on average, the former score 63 points higher on the verbal section and 44 points higher in math than the latter. According to a study by Christopher Johnson, a professor of music education and music therapy at the University of Kansas, elementary school students with access to quality music programs scored about 22 percent higher in English and 20 percent higher in math scores on standardized tests than their peers at schools with neglected programs. Johnson has put forth the likely explanation that the concentration and focus required to learn music can be applied to standardized testing, which helps raise scores.

8. There are a number of other benefits to learning music: music can be relaxing and help students relieve stress; students who study an instrument tend to have better discipline when it comes to studying and academics; playing in an ensemble promotes teamwork. With all of these benefits – and many more that have yet to be quantified and studied – having a solid music program is an essential part of any education. Rather than eliminating music programs from schools, we should better fund them for the benefit of our students.

Practice Passage 3

1. Many Americans would likely agree that talking freely about a political candidate should be protected by the Constitution. But what about contributing money to political candidates? In theory, anyone should have the right to show support for a political candidate however he or she deems appropriate; in practice, the same laws that protect an individual's rights to contribute to a campaign also allow corporations and special interest groups to donate immense sums of money toward political campaigns. Though the latter are fewer in number, the wealth and power of these few are so great that they are often able to sway the outcome of entire elections. Rather than representing the interests of the many, elections are often bought and paid for by the rich and powerful; therefore, in order to keep elections fair and preserve the essence of democracy, limits should be placed on campaign spending.

2. There is much evidence that heavy spending on political advertisements can sway the outcome of an election. In 2004, a group called the Swift Boat Veterans for Truth (SBVT) launched an expensive advertising campaign against presidential candidate John Kerry, calling into question his military record. Some experts believe that the aggressive SBVT campaign cost Kerry the election. In modern American politics, advertising plays a large role in shaping public opinion. And it takes money – a lot of money – to advertise.

3. Though it remains illegal for non-individuals to donate money directly to candidates, organizations and groups of people can contribute money to candidates in slightly less direct ways. The landmark court case *Citizens United vs. Federal Election Commission* ("Citizens United") paved the way for corporations, unions, and other coordinated, like-minded groups to donate significant amounts of money toward the indirect support of candidates. Citizens United allowed these groups to buy advertisements, sponsor events,

The Tutorverse

and fund other political activities that can heavily influence any given election. One of the results of the ruling has been the creation of the political action committee (PAC), organizations that are directly affiliated with political candidates in all but name. Wealthy donors can contribute money to a PAC, which then spends that money on any candidate whose interests are aligned with their own.

4. However, there's some debate over how much influence these PACs actually have. Many of the republican candidates campaigning in the 2016 presidential election, such as Jeb Bush, were supported by very well-funded PACs. Despite the support of large sums of money and the advertisements purchased, Bush's campaign was ultimately ineffective: Bush dropped out of the race early in the primary season. Conversely, Bernie Sanders ran a campaign largely based on donations from individuals. Sanders was able to run a close primary race against party favorite Hillary Clinton despite this type of funding, garnering widespread attention for his revolutionary ideas.

5. Even if, in terms of electoral success, there is no correlation between "having" a PAC and "not having" one, there's no question that a powerful advertising campaign has the power to sway public opinion and undermine the democratic process. Democracy needs a free exchange of ideas in order to thrive. In the twenty-first century, this exchange most often happens in the media, where special interests can buy TV advertisements or launch social media campaigns to express their opinions. Since the cost of advertising is significant, it's hard for some politicians that don't have as much money to compete with those who are better-funded. Although some politicians have had success with soliciting small donations, when a few wealthy individuals can donate enough money to dominate the discussion, they jeopardize the free exchange of ideas. Despite the poisonous influence money has on the democratic process, the Citizens United ruling guaranteed such unrestricted freedom to spend under the First Amendment.

6. But the right to free speech guaranteed under the First Amendment is not unlimited. Court precedent has shown that speech presenting a "clear and present danger" is not necessarily protected under the First Amendment. If one accepts the premise that unrestricted campaign spending causes a clear danger to democracy, then one must also accept that such spending should not remain unlimited and cannot be afforded absolute protection under the First Amendment. Limitations on the kind of spending favored by PACs, for example, would level the playing field, better allowing the voices of the poor and middle class to be heard alongside the voices of the wealthy. In a democracy, no one interest is more important than another. In order to ensure that the democratic process is not undermined, it is the role of the government to ensure that all ideas are given an equal opportunity to be heard.

Practice Passage 4

1. In the 1950s, a man with a factory job could expect a good salary, a nice benefits package, and a healthy pension when he retired. If the man with the steady job in the '50s was a union member, his union fought to make sure he received fair pay and good benefits. But are unions still relevant in our modern economy?

2. Throughout the nineteenth century, many activists fought for labor reform. It wasn't until the formation of the American Federation of Labor (AFL) in 1886, however, that labor interests became organized. The founders of the AFL believed that workers should stand together with other workers in similar trades and that they should collectively advance concrete, job-related goals. AFL leadership believed that a means to these ends was to carry out strikes and peaceful protests. By employing these tactics, many workers were able to negotiate more favorable agreements. In addition to improving the economic circumstances of their members, the national organization also fought to improve working conditions.

3. By the turn of the century, the AFL and other organizations had made strides toward improving work conditions for men in certain trades, but it had not done much to improve working conditions for everyone.

Immigrants and women, for example, continued to work in crowded factories under dangerous conditions.

4. On one afternoon in March, 1911, Frances Perkins was having tea with friends when the group heard a commotion outside. The nearby Triangle Shirtwaist Factory – a modern-day sweatshop where several hundred women, many of them young immigrants, worked six days a week for little pay – was on fire. Perkins ran outside to see what was happening. The horror of the fire – one of the deadliest workplace disasters at the time in America – resonated deeply with Perkins. Inspired to crusade for better working conditions, she became an outspoken advocate for workers, and was eventually selected to be Secretary of Labor under President Franklin Roosevelt – the first woman appointed to the president's cabinet. Perkins was an instrumental part of shaping Roosevelt's New Deal, a set of policies intended to help Americans recover from the Great Depression. By the end of World War II, 12 million workers were union members, and unions had become a key part of the industrial economy.

5. Although it took tragedies like the Triangle Shirtwaist Factory fire to engender significant change, a number of measures to improve worker safety were soon implemented after sustained public outcry about unsafe work conditions. Witnesses to the fire saw women jump out of the burning building to their deaths and, like Frances Perkins, were inspired to fight for change. They believed that employers had an obligation to make conditions safe for their employees. In New York State, thirty new labor laws were enacted, including new requirements for sprinkler systems, regular fire drills, and updated equipment for skyscrapers. At the national level, pressure from unions and increased awareness about workplace safety eventually resulted in the passage of the Occupational Safety and Health Act of 1970 (OSHA). Administered through the Department of Labor, OSHA continues to ensure safe working conditions for private-sector workers.

6. With many safety concerns having since been addressed, and with a shift in the economy away from more dangerous manufacturing and industrial jobs toward relatively safer commercial and service oriented jobs, the power of unions has begun to wane. Still, though union membership has continued to decline in the decades since World War II, unions continue to fight for workers. This is largely because there continues to exist between many employers and employees a rift. In a 2003 bid to save money, a large, well-known grocery store company attempted to shift the cost of healthcare on to its 70,000 employees. As a result, the employees went on strike for four months, ultimately costing the company an estimated $2 billion. If workplace safety was the rallying cry that powered unions of the 20th century, then healthcare might be the rallying cry that powers the unions of the 21st century. Ultimately, the employees' union helped to resolve the issue.

7. So long as employer and employee interests are not fully aligned, unions will always have a role to play. So far, unions have helped to ensure that employees across a number of industries have a safe place to work, can access to the healthcare they need, and receive fair compensation. Who knows what tomorrow's unions will champion.

Practice Passage 5

1. Coral reefs are like cities: large, complex communities with a great deal of structure and diversity. Can you imagine what the United States would be like if New York City or Los Angeles suddenly disappeared? The loss of coral reefs would have a similar impact on the ocean.

2. Thousands of marine species call coral reefs their home. Unfortunately, the rise in ocean temperatures, increased water acidity, and influx of invasive species are killing coral reefs around the world. This results in a significant threat to marine life in the regions where such life relies on coral reefs for places to live, hide, eat, and mate. Existing preservation and conservation efforts aren't enough: we must also create artificial reefs.

The Tutorverse

3. Off the coast of southern California sits the Eureka Oil Rig. It's a forty-year-old oil platform that was once used to harvest oil from the marine oil fields off the coast of Los Angeles. Today, this oil platform and others like it have become significant marine ecosystems unto themselves; they are home to thriving communities of fish and other sea life. In fact, according to Milton Love, a professor of marine biology at the University of California Santa Barbara, "They are more productive than coral reefs." Dr. Love has pointed out that because of where these oil platforms are located, they have become perfect habitats for marine life. The discovery of new ocean life and an increase in the population of a few species of fish have inspired some conservation groups to advocate for the conversion of more decommissioned oil platforms into artificial reefs. This, they argue, would be preferable to destroying the platforms.

4. This stance is not necessarily popular with some environmentalists. Because there have been several environmentally devastating oil spills around the California platforms – including a particularly destructive one in 2015 – some activists oppose the idea of leaving the platforms standing. Linda Krop, an environmental lawyer with the Environmental Defense Center, has argued that leaving the platforms is akin to rewarding oil companies, because the companies would not have to pay to remove them. However, scientists like Dr. Love continue to point out that the platforms have come to serve as man-made homes for large populations of marine life. For many, the benefits to the marine species living around the oil platforms outweigh the risks of leaving the platforms.

5. There are other, less controversial ways to create artificial reefs. Over on the East Coast, near the Delaware shoreline, scientists are turning old subway cars into artificial reefs. The Red Bird Reef – named for the old, red New York City subway cars nicknamed Redbirds – is booming. These old subway cars were dropped into the ocean with the intent of creating homes for a number of Atlantic Ocean species, including muscles, sponges, and bass. Jeff Tinsman, from the Delaware Department of Natural Resources and Environmental Control, calls these artificial reefs "luxury condominiums for fish." The results were successful beyond expectations; in fact, the reefs became overcrowded with small fish, and larger fish like tuna and mackerel began to swim around the reefs looking for lunch. Subway cars, it turns out, are just the right size to welcome fish to make homes and are durable enough to stay put even in strong ocean currents. Even as Delaware seeks to expand their reef by getting new cars, other states have started to compete for New York City's decommissioned subway cars to build artificial reefs of their own.

6. Inspiration for these sunken subway car reefs came from an accidental discovery: that underwater shipwrecks often become home to a great many marine species. Shipwrecks make such good artificial reefs that now, decommissioned ships are sometimes intentionally sunk. One place some of these ships are laid to rest is the Florida Keys National Marine Sanctuary. The sunken ships in this nature preserve have provided a habitat for countless fish and other marine species.

7. These artificial reefs are not just a boon for marine life; they are also good for local economies. Artificial reefs attract divers, fisherman, and snorkelers. Disposing of industrial remnants – such as oil platforms and subway cars – has an unexpected environmental benefit for a vast number of marine species. Although we should also continue to preserve existing, natural coral reefs, creating artificial reefs is a good way to ensure many ocean species continue to thrive.

Practice Passage 6

1. "In my fifth-grade class I was only able to read books about white boys and their dogs," says eleven-year-old Marley Dias of New Jersey. "I understood that my teacher could connect with those characters, so he asked us to read those books. But I didn't relate to them, so I didn't learn lessons from those stories." Marley's experience is sadly not unique. As the United States population becomes increasingly diverse, many readers are having a hard time seeing themselves in the characters central to the books they read.

The Tutorverse

2. This is due in part to what many view as the homogeneity of the publishing industry itself. According to some industry insiders, because there are so many applicants for jobs in the publishing industry, and because publishing is based largely in cities where the cost of living is very high, the people who tend to break into publishing are young, affluent, and white – people who have the ability to work for years in entry-level, low-salary positions before growing into managerial positions. The result is an industry where many in positions of power think and view the world in similar ways. Most publishing employees love books and want to make sure they put out the best books they can, but because the people sitting in editorial board meetings have similar backgrounds, interests, and experiences, many don't think to look for books beyond their repertoire. The result of this is that many of the books published, particularly those for younger readers, feature white characters.

3. Everyone benefits from greater diversity in publishing. A wider range of books increases opportunities for readers to learn new things or find themselves reflected in characters they might not otherwise imagine. More of an effort should be made to foster diversity in the publishing industry, both within publishing houses and in the books they produce.

4. Thankfully, the paradigm has begun to shift. Small presses have started publishing a greater variety of books, particularly those that feature people of color or members of the lesbian, gay, bisexual, and transgender (LGBT) community. Even mainstream publishers are starting to broaden their new book lists. Unfortunately, these books are often relegated to their own section of the bookstore, which decreases the chance that a casual browser will pick one up. A major publisher, Harlequin, for example, publishes romance novels with African American protagonists; but the books are often shelved far from other romance novels. LGBT fiction is frequently shelved in the nonfiction section of bookstores – a counterintuitive practice that confuses shoppers. Worse yet, such books are often absent from schools and libraries.

5. Marley Dias didn't just understand this problem – she set out to fix it. To address this problem, she started a book drive. Using the hashtag #1000blackgirlbooks, she set out to collect 1,000 books featuring black girl protagonists for her school library and for a library in Jamaica, her mother's homeland. The hashtag went viral on social media; in short order, Mary had exceeded her 1,000-book goal. Large corporations donated books and money, and Marley even appeared on popular television shows.

6. The movement to increase the availability of diverse books has spread to adult books, too. Controversy arose after an annual publishing convention came under fire in 2014 for having a panel of authors consisting entirely of white men and women. "It was 30 authors that were all white and the only diversity was the Grumpy Cat," says Ellen Oh, author and co-founder of We Need Diverse Books. "And I think at that point the anger and the disappointment of a lot of people just kind of overflowed and we decided to really talk about why this was so important." Out of this lack of diversity grew the #WeNeedDiverseBooks hashtag. The response surpassed the movement's expectations. "These were clear reflections…that diversity was not just important to a small section of authors who had been talking about it for years; that it was actually important to the world," says Oh. As a result, the convention organizers prioritized putting together a panel on diverse books at the next event.

7. The publishing industry has made some progress toward diversifying the books produced, but there is still work to be done. Social media campaigns, book drives, integrating bookshelves, and other methods of bringing attention to the problem can highlight the kinds of books that have previously been marginalized. Hopefully, more readers will soon be able to see more books featuring characters that reflect their experiences.

The Tutorverse

Practice Passage 7

1. Marketers use a number of different techniques to persuade consumers to buy products. Some of these methods can be deceptive, preying on consumers' emotions or otherwise manipulating them into buying a product. Many consumers are generally aware of common forms of manipulation: bright colors, emotional appeals, and positive association, for example. But some practices are much more insidious. In order to make more informed purchasing decisions, it's a good idea to be aware of what some marketers are doing to grab our attention.

2. One way that for-profit companies make their products seem more appealing is by associating non-profit causes with their products. One prominent example are pink products offered in support of breast cancer awareness. So many products now come in pink versions or with pink labels that the many have taken to calling the process of using breast cancer awareness to sell products "pinkwashing." Although proceeds from the sales of products like pink toilet paper to pink keychains do go to charitable organizations, marketers want consumers to think that a much larger contribution to the charity is being made than actually is. First, a good deal of the money goes toward awareness-raising organizations, not organizations that research cancer prevention. Second, only a small fraction of each sale – sometimes as little as a penny per dollar spent! – is donated to cancer research related organizations; many companies also put a cap on how much of their profits they are willing to donate. Worst of all, some beauty products sold with pink labels may themselves actually contain substances that are known to or suspected of causing cancer themselves!

3. Advertisers also capitalize on panic and paranoia, preying on consumers' fear of disease to sell products to them. Antibacterial products, for example, sell very well. During an outbreak of disease (or even during a time of year when more people tend to be sick), advertisers will tout their antibacterial products, such as hand gels, kitchen and bathroom cleaners, and soaps, as part of a health and hygiene routine that can help prevent the spread of disease. The marketing, however, is less than truthful; in reality, not all illnesses are created equal. Contracting the flu, which is caused by a virus, for example, isn't preventable by using antibacterial products. Many strains of the flu pass through the air, so using these products won't do much to prevent the spread of the disease. Some companies have started making antiviral tissues aimed at preventing the common cold – never mind the fact that there are so many hundreds of strains of viruses that cause the common cold that there's no way a single tissue could prevent the spread of them all.

4. Perhaps no marketing practices are as insidious as those employed online. Even the most casual user of the internet may have noticed that advertisements on many websites display information about products or companies recently viewed online. This is because advertisers are constantly gathering data using software that can track everything from a person's browsing habits to credit card purchases to brand preferences. Companies can target these advertisements to such a high degree of specificity that consumers will generally only see advertisements for personally interesting products. This form of targeted marketing is so effective and devious that it can subliminally influence a purchasing decision before the consumer is even aware of a product. Many popular social media sites play a role in this process by feeding advertisers data they've collected from their users. For example, if a group of women in one social media group all have school-aged children, marketers can display advertisements for products that might appeal to parents of school-aged children. Though consumers can avoid some of this by using ad-blocking software and by changing social media privacy settings, they should be aware of free products and services. The old adage applies now more than ever: "If you aren't paying for the product, you are the product."

5. Because some practices used by advertisers are deceptive at best and dangerous at worst, it's good to be aware of how these marketing tricks work. When looking at an advertisement or new product, carefully read the fine print. Savvy consumers can make better buying choices and avoid paying for goods and services they don't need or that don't actually work as advertised.

The Tutorverse

Practice Passage 8

1. As students in the United States continue to fall behind the rest of the world, and as an increasing number of our students struggle with standardized testing, we should rethink our approach to education in this country.

2. One way we can reform education in the United States is to follow the models set forth in Scandinavian countries. According to the Organization for Economic Cooperation and Development (OECD), Denmark and Finland have some of the best education systems in the world; based on math and science scores, Finland ranks sixth in the world compared to the twenty-eighth-ranked United States. Though these countries generally have higher tax rates than in the United States, they put these revenues toward education, hiring strong teachers, and investing in facilities.

3. In Denmark, schools are regulated and funded by the state. All students must attend primary and lower secondary schools and pass an exam to graduate. In addition to primary and secondary school, the Danish government also funds higher education for those who want to further their studies. Students also spend more time in the classroom than in the United States. As a result, students are well equipped to transition between grades and, ultimately, into the workforce. Despite having more generous unemployment insurance plans than in the United States, unemployment rates in the former are generally lower than in the latter. Collectively, the Danish want to ensure that all citizens contribute to and are supported by the nation's economy; in addition to funding primary, secondary, and tertiary education, the government also funds vocational programs to help train people for a specific trade or industry. Denmark, then, appears to validate a study conducted by the OECD, which shows that the unemployment rate is lower among those who are better educated.

4. Finland also has a strong education program for its young citizens. Part of this strength is derived from the quality of Finland's teachers. The Finnish have set an extremely high bar for teachers, who must, prior to entering a classroom, complete more rigorous education and training than they do in the United States. Finnish teachers typically receive higher salaries and have more freedom to shape their curriculum than most public school teachers in the United States. Finland also tends to shy away from placing too great an emphasis on standardized testing, allowing teachers to tailor education for both gifted and struggling students. The result is that Finnish students routinely perform among the best in the world, with a smaller disparity between the highest and lowest performing students and higher graduation rates than in the United States. The focus on improving schools is part of a nationwide welfare program that has helped Finland keep poverty and unemployment rates significantly lower than in the United States.

5. It's worth noting that these Scandinavian countries are smaller and more homogenous than the United States, which possesses great ethnic and socioeconomic diversity. The demography of the United States is such that schools must cater to a much wider population with different needs and philosophies on education policy. Achieving Scandinavian-like education equality in the United States will be no trivial task. But just because reformation is difficult does not mean it should not be attempted. The Finnish government spends less per capita on students than the United States government does, but invests its money in smarter ways with tangible benefits for students. Perhaps the best way to achieve higher scores on standardized tests is not to restrict teachers to a set curriculum, but to empower them – who know their students best – to foster true understanding of a topic through deep learning. Perhaps the government could do more to support tertiary education and improve the general population's access to college and university-level educations.

6. Such changes will not come easily, and any victories will have been hard won. Politics will, invariable, come between what we know we should do and what we will end up doing. But we must strive toward a better future for our students, as their future is the future of our country.

The Tutorverse

Practice Passage 9

1. Did you know that when people cast their votes to elect the President of the United States, they are actually electing someone whose name they probably don't even know? In the United States, when voters choose a candidate, they are actually choosing an elector, or a member of the Electoral College who in turn votes for the president. This kind of indirect participation often accurately represents popular sentiment, but not always. Take, for example, the presidential election of 2000, when Al Gore won a greater number of popular votes – that is, the number of votes made by the general public – but still lost the presidency to George W. Bush (who won more electoral votes). Or, take the 1876 defeat of Samuel J. Tilden by Rutherford B. Hayes, where the former lost the presidency by one electoral vote despite winning the popular vote. That a system so antithetical to democracy and direct participation has persisted for so long is surprising, and is one of the reasons it should be abolished.

2. At the Constitutional Convention, the Founding Fathers fiercely debated a number of major issues, one of which was how to elect the president. In the country's infancy, most voters were locally-focused in their thinking, and the Founders reasoned that voters would be more likely to vote for candidates from their own states; thus, they reasoned, politicians from the most populous states would have undue influence over the rest of the country. They therefore conceived of the Electoral College – a system in which states are assigned electors who then choose the president on behalf of the general public.

3. The Electoral College may have seemed like a practical solution at the time, but the system quickly became outdated as the country grew and changed. One issue with this system is the aforementioned: the possibility of a candidate winning the popular vote but not the electoral vote – a scenario which seems to contradict the very premise of democracy. A separate issue has to do with the process of campaigning. Most candidates focus their efforts only on states where electoral votes are contested – known as "swing states" – and not on states they are certain they will win or lose. This means that today, the bulk of campaigning is often conducted in only a handful of states. Candidates pander to the voters in those states, making campaign promises that are often only important in those states or regions. Yet another issue has to do with the number of electors awarded to each state, which is equal to that state's number of senators and representatives. Seats in the House of Representatives can be redistributed, shifting the balance of power in the Electoral College. After the 2010 census redistributed seats in the House, a general voter in Wyoming actually has over three times the influence on the Electoral College than a general voter in California even though California is much more populous than Wyoming.

4. Most states have a winner-take-all system in place; if a candidate wins the majority of votes in that election, all of that state's electors will then vote for the given candidate. The result is that third-party candidates – that is, a candidate not subscribing to either the Democrat or Republican Party – have virtually no chance of winning electoral votes. The Founders didn't anticipate the rising power of political parties, nor their influence on the Electoral College. As a result, debate is often limited to two outspoken points of view and real progress stalemated in a quagmire of partisan politics. All of this leads to apathy among the general public – the death knell of democracy.

5. Direct democracy puts the power back in the hands of the people and cuts out the middlemen, so to speak. An engaged and involved electorate is the backbone of democracy. Putting political power back into the hands of the people would go a long way toward encouraging participation, increasing voter turnout, and ensuring that those elected to power truly represent the people. Abolishing the Electoral College would be a crucial step forward in rehabilitating America's democracy.

The Tutorverse

Part Five: Practice Test

Overview

This practice test is designed to assess your understanding of key skills and concepts covered in this workbook. It is important to take the final practice test after spending time studying and practicing.

Though this practice test assesses your mastery of certain skills and concepts that you may see on the actual exam, there are several differences between this practice test and the actual exam:

- ✏ This practice test does not include an experimental section. As of the date of this publication, the College Board has reported that students that opt out of the optional Essay will be given a 20-minute experimental section on Math, Reading, or Writing at the beginning of the exam.
- ✏ The format of the Writing & Language questions differs slightly. Question numbers on the actual Writing & Language Test will be denoted with a white number surrounded by a dark-colored box (for example, **1**). In this book, questions are denoted with a white number surrounded by a dark-colored outline (for example, **1**).

Format

The format of this practice test is similar to that of the actual test:

Practice Test Section	Questions	Time Limit
Reading Test	52	65 minutes
Writing & Language Test	44	35 minutes
Math – No Calculator	20	25 minutes
Math – Calculator	38	55 minutes
Essay (Optional)	1	50 minutes
Total (Including Essay)	**155**	**230 minutes**

Answering

Use the answer sheets provided on the next several pages to record your answers. You may wish to tear out these pages for convenience.

The Tutorverse

Answer Sheet

Section 1: Reading Test

	A B C D		A B C D		A B C D		A B C D		A B C D
1.	○ ○ ○ ○	12.	○ ○ ○ ○	23.	○ ○ ○ ○	34.	○ ○ ○ ○	45.	○ ○ ○ ○
2.	○ ○ ○ ○	13.	○ ○ ○ ○	24.	○ ○ ○ ○	35.	○ ○ ○ ○	46.	○ ○ ○ ○
3.	○ ○ ○ ○	14.	○ ○ ○ ○	25.	○ ○ ○ ○	36.	○ ○ ○ ○	47.	○ ○ ○ ○
4.	○ ○ ○ ○	15.	○ ○ ○ ○	26.	○ ○ ○ ○	37.	○ ○ ○ ○	48.	○ ○ ○ ○
5.	○ ○ ○ ○	16.	○ ○ ○ ○	27.	○ ○ ○ ○	38.	○ ○ ○ ○	49.	○ ○ ○ ○
6.	○ ○ ○ ○	17.	○ ○ ○ ○	28.	○ ○ ○ ○	39.	○ ○ ○ ○	50.	○ ○ ○ ○
7.	○ ○ ○ ○	18.	○ ○ ○ ○	29.	○ ○ ○ ○	40.	○ ○ ○ ○	51.	○ ○ ○ ○
8.	○ ○ ○ ○	19.	○ ○ ○ ○	30.	○ ○ ○ ○	41.	○ ○ ○ ○	52.	○ ○ ○ ○
9.	○ ○ ○ ○	20.	○ ○ ○ ○	31.	○ ○ ○ ○	42.	○ ○ ○ ○		
10.	○ ○ ○ ○	21.	○ ○ ○ ○	32.	○ ○ ○ ○	43.	○ ○ ○ ○		
11.	○ ○ ○ ○	22.	○ ○ ○ ○	33.	○ ○ ○ ○	44.	○ ○ ○ ○		

Section 2: Writing & Language Test

	A B C D		A B C D		A B C D		A B C D		A B C D
1.	○ ○ ○ ○	10.	○ ○ ○ ○	19.	○ ○ ○ ○	28.	○ ○ ○ ○	37.	○ ○ ○ ○
2.	○ ○ ○ ○	11.	○ ○ ○ ○	20.	○ ○ ○ ○	29.	○ ○ ○ ○	38.	○ ○ ○ ○
3.	○ ○ ○ ○	12.	○ ○ ○ ○	21.	○ ○ ○ ○	30.	○ ○ ○ ○	39.	○ ○ ○ ○
4.	○ ○ ○ ○	13.	○ ○ ○ ○	22.	○ ○ ○ ○	31.	○ ○ ○ ○	40.	○ ○ ○ ○
5.	○ ○ ○ ○	14.	○ ○ ○ ○	23.	○ ○ ○ ○	32.	○ ○ ○ ○	41.	○ ○ ○ ○
6.	○ ○ ○ ○	15.	○ ○ ○ ○	24.	○ ○ ○ ○	33.	○ ○ ○ ○	42.	○ ○ ○ ○
7.	○ ○ ○ ○	16.	○ ○ ○ ○	25.	○ ○ ○ ○	34.	○ ○ ○ ○	43.	○ ○ ○ ○
8.	○ ○ ○ ○	17.	○ ○ ○ ○	26.	○ ○ ○ ○	35.	○ ○ ○ ○	44.	○ ○ ○ ○
9.	○ ○ ○ ○	18.	○ ○ ○ ○	27.	○ ○ ○ ○	36.	○ ○ ○ ○		

The Tutorverse

Section 3: Math – No Calculator

	A B C D		A B C D		A B C D		A B C D		A B C D
1.	○ ○ ○ ○	4.	○ ○ ○ ○	7.	○ ○ ○ ○	10.	○ ○ ○ ○	13.	○ ○ ○ ○
	A B C D		A B C D		A B C D		A B C D		A B C D
2.	○ ○ ○ ○	5.	○ ○ ○ ○	8.	○ ○ ○ ○	11.	○ ○ ○ ○	14.	○ ○ ○ ○
	A B C D		A B C D		A B C D		A B C D		A B C D
3.	○ ○ ○ ○	6.	○ ○ ○ ○	9.	○ ○ ○ ○	12.	○ ○ ○ ○	15.	○ ○ ○ ○

16	17	18	19	20
/ ○ ○ ○ ○	/ ○ ○ ○ ○	/ ○ ○ ○ ○	/ ○ ○ ○ ○	/ ○ ○ ○ ○
. ○ ○ ○ ○	. ○ ○ ○ ○	. ○ ○ ○ ○	. ○ ○ ○ ○	. ○ ○ ○ ○
0 ○ ○ ○ ○	0 ○ ○ ○ ○	0 ○ ○ ○ ○	0 ○ ○ ○ ○	0 ○ ○ ○ ○
1 ○ ○ ○ ○	1 ○ ○ ○ ○	1 ○ ○ ○ ○	1 ○ ○ ○ ○	1 ○ ○ ○ ○
2 ○ ○ ○ ○	2 ○ ○ ○ ○	2 ○ ○ ○ ○	2 ○ ○ ○ ○	2 ○ ○ ○ ○
3 ○ ○ ○ ○	3 ○ ○ ○ ○	3 ○ ○ ○ ○	3 ○ ○ ○ ○	3 ○ ○ ○ ○
4 ○ ○ ○ ○	4 ○ ○ ○ ○	4 ○ ○ ○ ○	4 ○ ○ ○ ○	4 ○ ○ ○ ○
5 ○ ○ ○ ○	5 ○ ○ ○ ○	5 ○ ○ ○ ○	5 ○ ○ ○ ○	5 ○ ○ ○ ○
6 ○ ○ ○ ○	6 ○ ○ ○ ○	6 ○ ○ ○ ○	6 ○ ○ ○ ○	6 ○ ○ ○ ○
7 ○ ○ ○ ○	7 ○ ○ ○ ○	7 ○ ○ ○ ○	7 ○ ○ ○ ○	7 ○ ○ ○ ○
8 ○ ○ ○ ○	8 ○ ○ ○ ○	8 ○ ○ ○ ○	8 ○ ○ ○ ○	8 ○ ○ ○ ○
9 ○ ○ ○ ○	9 ○ ○ ○ ○	9 ○ ○ ○ ○	9 ○ ○ ○ ○	9 ○ ○ ○ ○

Section 4: Math - Calculator

	A B C D		A B C D		A B C D		A B C D		A B C D
1.	○ ○ ○ ○	7.	○ ○ ○ ○	13.	○ ○ ○ ○	19.	○ ○ ○ ○	25.	○ ○ ○ ○
	A B C D		A B C D		A B C D		A B C D		A B C D
2.	○ ○ ○ ○	8.	○ ○ ○ ○	14.	○ ○ ○ ○	20.	○ ○ ○ ○	26.	○ ○ ○ ○
	A B C D		A B C D		A B C D		A B C D		A B C D
3.	○ ○ ○ ○	9.	○ ○ ○ ○	15.	○ ○ ○ ○	21.	○ ○ ○ ○	27.	○ ○ ○ ○
	A B C D		A B C D		A B C D		A B C D		A B C D
4.	○ ○ ○ ○	10.	○ ○ ○ ○	16.	○ ○ ○ ○	22.	○ ○ ○ ○	28.	○ ○ ○ ○
	A B C D		A B C D		A B C D		A B C D		A B C D
5.	○ ○ ○ ○	11.	○ ○ ○ ○	17.	○ ○ ○ ○	23.	○ ○ ○ ○	29.	○ ○ ○ ○
	A B C D		A B C D		A B C D		A B C D		A B C D
6.	○ ○ ○ ○	12.	○ ○ ○ ○	18.	○ ○ ○ ○	24.	○ ○ ○ ○	30.	○ ○ ○ ○

(Continued on next page)

The Tutorverse

31

	/	.	0	1	2	3	4	5	6	7	8	9

32

	/	.	0	1	2	3	4	5	6	7	8	9

33

	/	.	0	1	2	3	4	5	6	7	8	9

34

	/	.	0	1	2	3	4	5	6	7	8	9

35

	/	.	0	1	2	3	4	5	6	7	8	9

36

	/	.	0	1	2	3	4	5	6	7	8	9

37

	/	.	0	1	2	3	4	5	6	7	8	9

38

	/	.	0	1	2	3	4	5	6	7	8	9

Section 5: Essay Planning Section

Section 5: Essay Response Section

Scoring

To score the practice test, use the following instructions (refer to the *Scoring & Reporting* section of this workbook for more information on scoring, terminology, and interpretation).

Step 1: Using the answer key at the end of this workbook, determine which questions were answered correctly.

Step 2: Add together the total number of questions answered correctly in each of the four sections. Enter those totals in the table below in the "# Correct Answers" column.

Step 3: For both the Reading Test and Writing & Language Test, consult the table on the next page to determine the Test Score based on the number of questions answered correctly. Enter the two Test Scores in the "Test Score" column below.

For example, if the # of Correct Answers on the Reading Test is 40, then the Reading Test Score would be 33; if the # Correct Answers on the Writing & Language Test is 31, then the Writing & Language Test Score would be 30.

Practice Test Section	# Correct Answers	Test Score
Reading Test	_____	_____
Writing & Language Test	_____	_____
Math Test – No Calculator	_____	N/A
Math Test – Calculator	_____	N/A

Step 4: Add together the Reading Test Score and the Writing & Language Test Score and multiply that number by 10 to receive your Reading & Writing Section Score. Input that number in the "Section Score" column below.

Continuing the example from Step 3: a Reading Test score and Writing & Language Test score of 33 and 30, respectively, would result in a total of 63. $63 \times 10 = 630$, the Reading & Writing Section Score.

Step 5: Add together the total number of correct answers from both Math Tests (No Calculator + Calculator). Consult the table on the next page to determine the Math Section Score based on the total number of correct answers. Record the resulting Math Section Score in the "Section Score" column below.

For example, if the total number of correct answers on both Math Tests is 35, then the Math Section Score is 600.

Step 6: Add together both the Reading & Writing Section Score and the Math Section Score. The sum is the total score (out of a 400-1600 range).

Practice Test Section	Section Score
Reading & Writing Section	_____
Math Section	_____
Total Score	_____

Note that this practice test does not provide a breakdown of subscores or cross-test scores.

The Tutorverse

# Correct Answers	Math Section Score	Reading Test Score	Writing Test Score
0	200	10	10
1	200	10	10
2	210	10	10
3	230	11	11
4	250	12	12
5	270	13	13
6	290	14	14
7	300	15	14
8	320	15	15
9	330	16	16
10	340	17	17
11	360	18	17
12	370	18	18
13	380	19	19
14	390	19	19
15	410	20	20
16	420	21	21
17	430	21	22
18	440	22	22
19	450	22	23
20	460	23	24
21	470	23	24
22	480	24	25
23	490	24	26
24	500	25	26
25	510	25	27
26	520	26	27
27	530	26	28
28	540	27	28
29	550	28	29

# Correct Answers	Math Section Score	Reading Test Score	Writing Test Score
30	560	28	30
31	570	29	30
32	580	29	31
33	580	29	32
34	590	30	32
35	600	30	33
36	610	31	33
37	620	31	34
38	630	32	35
39	630	32	35
40	640	33	36
41	650	33	37
42	660	34	38
43	670	34	39
44	680	35	40
45	680	36	
46	690	36	
47	700	37	
48	700	38	
49	710	38	
50	720	39	
51	730	40	
52	740	40	
53	580		
54	760		
55	770		
56	780		
57	790		
58	800		

The Tutorverse

Reading Test

Directions:

The following passages are followed by 10-11 questions. After reading each passage or pair of passages, select the best answer to each question based on the information implied or stated in the passage and provided in any graphics (such as charts, tables, or graphs).

52 Questions Total; 65 Minute Time Limit
Use Section 1 of the answer sheet to answer questions in this section.

Questions 1-10 are based on the below passage.

The following passage is adapted and excerpted from Solomon Northup's 1853 memoir *Twelve Years a Slave*. Northup, a free-born man, was kidnapped and sold into slavery. His memoir details his kidnapping and escape.

It was a moment of life or death. The sharp, bright blade of the hatchet glittered in the sun…If I stood still, my doom was certain; if I fled, ten chances to one the hatchet, flying from his hand
5 with a too-deadly and unerring aim, would strike me in the back. There was but one course to take. Springing towards him with all my power, and meeting him full half-way, before he could bring down the blow, with one hand I caught his uplifted
10 arm, with the other seized him by the throat. We stood looking each other in the eyes. In his I could see murder. I felt as if I had a serpent by the neck, watching the slightest relaxation of my grip, to coil itself round my body, crushing and stinging it to
15 death…

The good genius, which thus far through life has saved me from the hands of violence, at that moment suggested a lucky thought. With a vigorous and sudden kick, that brought him on one
20 knee, with a groan, I released my hold upon his throat, snatched the hatchet, and cast it beyond reach.

Frantic with rage, maddened beyond control, he seized a white oak stick, five feet long, perhaps,
25 and as large in circumference as his hand could grasp, which was lying on the ground. Again he rushed towards me, and again I met him, seized him about the waist, and being the stronger of the two, bore him to the earth. While in that position I
30 obtained possession of the stick, and rising, cast it from me, also.

He likewise arose and ran for the broad-axe, on the work-bench. Fortunately, there was a heavy plank lying upon its broad blade, in such a manner
35 that he could not extricate it, before I had sprung upon his back. Pressing him down closely and heavily on the plank, so that the axe was held more firmly to its place, I endeavored, but in vain, to

break his grasp upon the handle. In that position
40 we remained some minutes.

There have been hours in my unhappy life, many of them, when the contemplation of death as the end of earthly sorrow—of the grave as a resting place for the tired and worn out body—has
45 been pleasant to dwell upon. But such contemplations vanish in the hour of peril. No man, in his full strength, can stand undismayed, in the presence of the "king of terrors." Life is dear to every living thing; the worm that crawls upon the
50 ground will struggle for it. At that moment it was dear to me, enslaved and treated as I was.

Not able to unloose his hand, once more I seized him by the throat, and this time, with a vice-like gripe that soon relaxed his hold. He became
55 pliant and unstrung. His face, that had been white with passion, was now black from suffocation. Those small serpent eyes that spat such venom, were now full of horror—two great white orbs starting from their sockets!
60 There was "a lurking devil" in my heart that prompted me to kill the human blood-hound on the spot—to retain the grip on his accursed throat till the breath of life was gone! I dared not murder him, and I dared not let him live. If I killed him,
65 my life must pay the forfeit—if he lived, my life only would satisfy his vengeance. A voice within whispered me to fly. To be a wanderer among the swamps, a fugitive and a vagabond on the face of the earth, was preferable to the life that I was
70 leading…

I was desolate, but thankful. Thankful that my life was spared,—desolate and discouraged with the prospect before me. What would become of me? Who would befriend me? Whither should I
75 fly?

CONTINUE ➡

The Tutorverse

1

Which of the following choices best describes the passage's course of development?

A)   An unbiased accounting of events is recounted.

B)   Opinions are supported by facts and evidence.

C)   Events, sprinkled with internal dialogue, are related.

D)   A particular point of view is advanced through external dialogue.

2

Which statement best captures what happens in the passage?

A)   A man fights for no reason other than to fight.

B)   A man fights to redeem himself.

C)   A man struggles with what the future holds.

D)   A man fights for his freedom and against inner demons.

3

In the first paragraph, the narrator believes that he cannot run from the fight because

A)   his assailant is proficient with a hatchet.

B)   standing still was a better option.

C)   he is physically stronger than his assailant.

D)   he would win in hand-to-hand combat.

4

As used in line 6, "course" most nearly means

A)   class.

B)   option.

C)   sequence.

D)   schedule.

5

In context, the narrator uses the phrase "No man...king of terrors" (line 46-48) to convey the idea that

A)   though death is terrifying, one must fight against it.

B)   life can sometimes be as terrifying as death.

C)   the struggles of life are painful, though worthwhile.

D)   the grave is a peaceful resting place.

6

The idea most central to paragraph five is that

A)   all life will fight to live.

B)   life is sometimes a struggle.

C)   in life, peace is hard to come by.

D)   one's viewpoints rarely change.

7

Which choice best describes the narrator's assailant's frame of mind in the sixth paragraph?

A)   Hateful, filled with venomous thoughts.

B)   Unstable, bordering on insane.

C)   Euphoric, gladdened to have won.

D)   Fearful, scared for his life.

8

In context, the phrase "a lurking devil" (line 60) most likely refers to

A)   the assailant's primal instincts.

B)   the narrator's higher moral conscience.

C)   the narrator's baser instincts.

D)   the narrator's predicament.

9

According to the passage, the narrator ultimately ran from the fight because

A)   he had no other choice.

B)   he had lost the fight with the assailant.

C)   he had a religious epiphany.

D)   he desired the life of a fugitive.

10

The narrator feels "desolate and discouraged" by his prospects because

A)   he has injured another man.

B)   a small voice is questioning his actions.

C)   he lost a part of himself during the fight.

D)   he is unsure how best to proceed as a runaway.

CONTINUE ➡

Questions 11-20 are based on the below passage.

It hasn't always been easy to be a scientist. Today, scientists are, at the very least, tolerated by society; more often than not, they are in fact venerated. But it has not always been easy to be a
5 scientist, especially if one's convictions led one to conclusions unpopular in one's day.

Take, for example, the work of Gregor Mendel, hailed as the father of genetics. By studying the characteristics of pea plants – their
10 height, shape, color, and other physical traits – Mendel realized that, if plants with certain features were bred together, the next generation of pea plant would display those qualities. Over time, he realized that there was something at work that
15 controlled the outcome of plant combinations – something that always made the offspring of yellow and green pea plants yellow, for example. Though he did not know precisely what those forces were – forces which we know of today as
20 genes – he knew that some forces were recessive and others dominant. Though today we use these terms without giving them much thought, it was not until many years after his discovery – and, unfortunately, after his death – that the
25 significance of Mendel's work was fully appreciated. In fact, his findings were initially rejected by his peers.

Mere rejection, however unfortunate, pales in comparison to persecution at the hands of the
30 Inquisition. In 1615, Galileo Galilei's theories on heliocentrism – the idea that the bodies in the solar system revolved around the sun, not the earth – had been submitted to the Roman Inquisition by Father Niccolo Lorini. Lorini believed that Galileo
35 was reinterpreting the Bible, an activity that was prohibited by the Roman Catholic Church's

ecumenical Council of Trent. This was, unfortunately for Galileo, not his first run in with the Church, having just years prior answered to the
40 Grand Duchess of Florence. Over the course of 1615 and 1616, Galileo was forced to cease his work on heliocentrism.

Galileo obeyed – at least superficially. He focused on writing a book, which he submitted
45 formally to the Inquisition and Pope for approval. Permission for Galileo to publish the book was granted, and the book *Dialogue Concerning the Two Chief World Systems* was published in 1632. Despite the permission obtained from the Church,
50 Galileo was summoned before inquisitor Vincenzo Maculani and charged with heresy. He was formally condemned for his beliefs in 1633 and his book banned and included in the infamous *Index of Forbidden Books.*

55 Galileo danced a fine line between standing by his ideas and incurring the wrath of the most powerful force in the West. Ultimately, Galileo was sentenced to house arrest, avoiding a far more horrible fate than many of his contemporaries.
60 While under arrest at his villa near Florence, Galileo completed *Two New Sciences* – his seminal work.

Galileo did not live to see his work truly appreciated; he died in 1642 in his villa. Yet good
65 things, it is said, come to those who wait. In Galileo's case, it took over 200 years – until 1835 – for the Church to remove his 1632 book from the *Index of Forbidden Books*. It was not until 1992 – almost 160 years after his 1632 book was officially
70 unbanned – that the Church finally agreed with Galileo's theories and admitted that Galileo had been wrongfully condemned.

CONTINUE ➡

The Tutorverse

11

Which statement best captures the overall structure of the passage?
A) A question is answered with specific information.
B) A theory is debated and rejected.
C) An idea is supported by specific examples.
D) Different concepts are generally discussed.

12

As used in line 4, "venerated" most nearly means
A) endured.
B) released.
C) respected.
D) suffered.

13

Which choice best summarizes the second paragraph?
A) A general account of a scientific concept is advanced.
B) A person's accomplishments and legacy are detailed.
C) A question about history is discussed in detail.
D) An argument is made supporting a particular action.

14

With which statement would the author most likely agree?
A) Galileo had a more difficult time as a scientist than Mendel.
B) Mendel and Galileo had equally difficult times being scientists.
C) Mendel had a more difficult time as a scientist than Galileo.
D) Neither Mendel nor Galileo had a difficult time being scientists.

15

Which selection best supports the answer choice to the previous question?
A) Lines 4-6 ("But it...day")
B) Lines 26-27 ("In fact...peers")
C) Lines 28-30 ("Mere rejection...Inquisition")
D) Lines 63-40 ("Galileo did...appreciated")

16

According to the passage, Galileo ran afoul of the Inquisition in 1615 due to
A) decree by the Council of Trent.
B) his reinterpretation of the Bible.
C) the actions of Father Lorini.
D) the Grand Duchess of Florence.

17

The phrase "danced a fine line" (line 55) is used to
A) explain the rationale for Galileo's subsequent sentencing.
B) describe the Church's disapproval of Galileo's ideas.
C) rationalize Maculani's charge of heresy leveled against Galileo.
D) suggest that it was difficult for Galileo to choose between two different obligations.

18

According to the passage, as a result of the Inquisition, Galileo's punishment was
A) determined by the Pope.
B) house arrest.
C) similar to his contemporaries.
D) similar to Mendel's.

19

By including the last paragraph, the author is able to
A) condemn the Church's decision to ban Galileo's book.
B) downplay the impact of the Church's 1632 actions.
C) liken Galileo's absolution with that of Mendel's.
D) praise the Church for finally reversing its easier decision.

20

The author's attitude toward scientists can best be described as
A) apathetic.
B) disrespectful.
C) impatient.
D) sympathetic.

CONTINUE ➡

Questions 21-31 are based on the following pair of passages and graphic.

Passage 1

Few people actually enjoy having to memorize information. Humans have, for thousands of years, relied on technology – writing, photographs, and
5 now computers – to store information and augment our memories.

Yet there are times when we must memorize information. It would not do, for example, to consult a phone book each time we needed to
10 reach emergency services; instead, we memorize the numbers 9-1-1.

The same is true in education. Memorization is important because it enables us to tackle more difficult problems. If we do not memorize the
15 meanings of words, then reading and understanding a sentence would be a tedious task, involving the frequent consultation of a dictionary. Similarly, if we do not memorize facts and formulas, as we require our students to do in math
20 and science subjects, our ability to solve problems becomes that much more difficult.

Memorizing key information is a necessary and inescapable aspect of learning. Computations would be laborious indeed without memorizing the
25 multiplication table. How can students learn more advanced material without first demonstrating a command of more basic information? The simple fact remains that there is, in education, a certain pedagogy that must be followed – an order to
30 which things are learned. Just as the number one precedes the number two, and the letter A precedes the letter B, so too must the learning of addition and subtraction come before the learning of multiplication.
35 In the end, memorized information is a tool to be used in the pursuit of higher learning. We should not confuse intelligence with the ability to memorize information. Just because someone knows that the earth revolves around the sun does
40 not mean that he knows why.

Passage 2

"The M word" – the bane of many students' academic careers.

45 So often in school, students are told that they must memorize information – that this information is critical to their education, and that by memorizing information and then reproducing it on a test or exam, they will earn a good grade.
50 But why do students so resist memorization? As it turns out, memorization for the sake of memorization is boring because it lacks context. What's the cosecant of $\pi/2$? Ask an average high schooler, and he or she will hopefully tell you that
55 the cosecant of $\pi/2$ equals one. But go one step further and ask the reason why. Most students will fumble for an explanation and simply explain that they don't know – that they were told to memorize the formula and substitute the values into problems
60 on their homework or on their tests.

One can have a similar conversation with students across grade levels, from kindergarten all the way up through post-secondary school – a fact that should be alarming to parents, employers, and
65 politicians alike. The problem of rote memorization – that is, memorization without context – is most prevalent in the maths and sciences; this is intuitive, given the nature of these disciplines. But what is less intuitive is why rote
70 memorization is, itself, a problem.

Rote memorization encourages students to learn tidbits of information, the command of which can be easily assessed by standardized tests. We record the results of these tests, aggregate them,
75 and look at them as an assessment of our students' collective intelligence. But do standardized tests really measure intelligence? Some standardized tests certainly do: they are designed to measure a student's ability to reason critically and apply
80 learnings to new problems and unknown situations. But many more are not, requiring students to learn facts and formulas that demonstrate only a superficial command of the subject matter.
85 Rather than emphasizing the importance of rote memorization, we should instead be teaching our students in such a way as to support true conceptual

CONTINUE ➡

The Tutorverse

Percentage of Time Spent Memorizing vs. Learning Conceptually

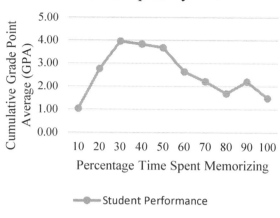

90 understanding. This process develops critical thinking skills that, though more difficult to quantify, are arguably more important than the ability to remember certain formulas. The human brain is not designed like a computer; the latter 95 more effectively stores and retrieves information, where the former demonstrates a greater potential to reason and process complex information.

Let's leave the memorizing to computers and instead teach our students to become better 100 problem solvers – to be better able to draw on their collective knowledge and experiences in order to tackle new and vexing problems of all kinds.

21

Which choice best summarizes the first two paragraphs in Passage 1?

A) Despite tools and technology, memorizing information is necessary.

B) Memorization is useful only in certain situations.

C) People do not enjoy memorizing information.

D) Technology replaces the need for people to memorize information.

22

The author of Passage 1 gives which of the following as reasons why memorization is important?

A) An overreliance on technology will result in a decline in the capacity to learn.

B) Memorizing basic information enables mastery of more complicated learning.

C) Memorizing is the key to scoring well on standardized tests.

D) Technology will sometimes fail, requiring people to memorize instead.

23

The selection which best supports the answer to the previous question can be found in

A) Lines 7-8 ("Yet there…information")

B) Lines 12-14 ("Memorization is…problems")

C) Lines 22-23 ("Memorizing key…learning")

D) Lines 36-40 ("We should…why")

24

The last sentence in Passage 1 (lines 38-40) demonstrates the author's belief that

A) intelligence is signified by one's ability to memorize information.

B) memorization is the key to learning.

C) memorization often saves time.

D) there is a difference between memorizing information and deeper understanding.

CONTINUE ➡

25

The central argument advanced in Passage 2 is that
A) many high school students require additional math reinforcement.
B) memorization and conceptual learning are equally important.
C) standardized tests never accurately assess students' intelligence.
D) there should be more of a focus on conceptual learning than on memorization.

26

The author refers to memorization as "the M word" in order to
A) demonstrate how teachers refer to memorization.
B) emphasize his disdain for the practice.
C) encourage the use of mnemonic devices to improve memorization.
D) explain why students dislike memorization.

27

The author includes the example of the cosecant (lines 53-60) in order to
A) demonstrate that memorization does not necessarily lead to understanding.
B) demonstrate why standardized testing needs to be reformed.
C) explain how mathematics requires certain concepts be memorized.
D) lament the state of high school education.

28

"Tidbit," used in line 72, most nearly refers to
A) complex patterns.
B) confusing data.
C) meaningful concepts.
D) out of context knowledge.

29

How might the author of Passage 1 respond to the cosecant example mentioned by the author of Passage 2 in lines 53-60?
A) Memorizing the cosecant of $\pi/2$ can help students to unlock deeper understanding.
B) Memorizing the cosecant of $\pi/2$ demonstrates true understanding.
C) Memorizing the cosecant of $\pi/2$ is inefficient.
D) Memorizing the cosecant of $\pi/2$ is pointless because of calculators and computers.

30

On which of the following statements would the author of Passage 1 and the author of Passage 2 most likely agree?
A) Intelligence is the ability to memorize information and process it quickly.
B) Intelligence is the ability to understand and interpret information.
C) Memorization and understanding are analogous.
D) Memorization plays a key role in learning.

31

Which passage could the information in the graph support?
A) Passage 1, because the more time spent memorizing, the higher the GPA.
B) Passage 2, because the more time spent memorizing, the lower the GPA.
C) Both passages, because data in the graph can support either passage.
D) Neither passage, because the information is irrelevant to the central claim of both passages.

CONTINUE ➡

The Tutorverse

Questions 32-41 are based on the below passage.

The following passage is adapted and excerpted from President Franklin D. Roosevelt's first Fireside Chat delivered over the radio in 1933, during one of the worst years of the Great Depression.

I want to talk for a few minutes with the people of the United States about banking – with the comparatively few who understand the mechanics of banking but more particularly with
5 the overwhelming majority who use banks for the making of deposits and the drawing of checks. I want to tell you what has been done in the last few days, why it was done, and what the next steps are going to be. I recognize that the many
10 proclamations from state capitols and from Washington, the legislation, the Treasury regulations, etc., couched for the most part in banking and legal terms should be explained for the benefit of the average citizen. I owe this in
15 particular because of the fortitude and good temper with which everybody has accepted the inconvenience and hardships of the banking holiday. I know that when you understand what we in Washington have been about I shall continue to
20 have your cooperation as fully as I have had your sympathy and help during the past week.

First of all let me state the simple fact that when you deposit money in a bank the bank does not put the money into a safe deposit vault. It
25 invests your money in many different forms of credit-bonds, commercial paper, mortgages and many other kinds of loans. In other words, the bank puts your money to work to keep the wheels of industry and of agriculture turning around. A
30 comparatively small part of the money you put into the bank is kept in currency – an amount which in normal times is wholly sufficient to cover the cash needs of the average citizen. In other words the total amount of all the currency in the
35 country is only a small fraction of the total deposits in all of the banks.

What, then, happened during the last few days of February and the first few days of March? Because of undermined confidence on the part of
40 the public, there was a general rush by a large portion of our population to turn bank deposits into currency or gold – a rush so great that the soundest banks could not get enough currency to meet the demand. The reason for this was that on the spur
45 of the moment it was, of course, impossible to sell perfectly sound assets of a bank and convert them into cash except at panic prices far below their real value.

By the afternoon of March 3rd scarcely a bank
50 in the country was open to do business. Proclamations temporarily closing them in whole or in part had been issued by the governors in almost all the states.

It was then that I issued the proclamation
55 providing for the nation-wide bank holiday, and this was the first step in the government's reconstruction of our financial and economic fabric.

The second step was the legislation promptly
60 and patriotically passed by the Congress confirming my proclamation and broadening my powers so that it became possible in view of the requirement of time to extend the holiday and lift the ban of that holiday gradually. This law also
65 gave authority to develop a program of rehabilitation of our banking facilities. I want to tell our citizens in every part of the Nation that the national Congress – Republicans and Democrats alike – showed by this action a devotion to public
70 welfare and a realization of the emergency and the necessity for speed that is difficult to match in our history.

The third stage has been the series of regulations permitting the banks to continue their
75 functions to take care of the distribution of food and household necessities and the payment of payrolls.

CONTINUE ➡

32

The primary concern of the passage is to
A) debate the merit of actions taken to solve a difficult crisis.
B) demonstrate that additional actions must be taken to prevent a crisis.
C) explain the actions taken to address a complicated issue.
D) recommend future actions that must be taken to correct a problem.

33

How does Roosevelt's focus change over the course of the passage?
A) Roosevelt alternates between providing context and explaining actions taken.
B) Roosevelt first provides context, then describes a problem and the actions taken to address that problem.
C) Roosevelt focuses solely on describing actions taken to address a problem.
D) Roosevelt remains focused on providing context and background information for the problem discussed.

34

"Temper," (line 15), most nearly means
A) disposition.
B) fury.
C) patience.
D) strength.

35

Roosevelt includes the second paragraph in order to
A) describe the actions taken to address a problem.
B) explain the precise reason why a problem took place.
C) provide people with information needed to understand a problem.
D) thank people for their patience and understanding.

36

It can be inferred from the passage that the general public's level of trust in the banking system was
A) high.
B) indeterminable.
C) low.
D) neutral.

37

According to the passage, why were banks unable to give people back their deposits when requested?
A) The banks had squandered the deposits and could not pay so many people back.
B) The banks were using deposits to distribute food and payrolls.
C) The deposits were invested, and the investments could not be converted back to enough money.
D) The government had seized the bank's money to protect people's money.

38

The selection that best supports the answer choice from the previous question is from
A) Lines 44-48 ("The reason...value")
B) Lines 51-53 ("Proclamations temporarily...states")
C) Lines 54-58 ("It was...fabric")
D) Lines 73-77 ("The third...payrolls")

39

The author's repeated use of the word "holiday" (lines 18, 55, 63, 64) serves to
A) criticize Congress' lack of timely action.
B) mock the seriousness of the banking crisis.
C) summarize Roosevelt's advice to the public.
D) emphasize the temporary nature of bank closures.

40

According to the passage, Congress
A) did not take sufficient action to help curb the impact of the crisis.
B) refused to cooperate with Roosevelt in addressing the crisis.
C) was a step behind Roosevelt in addressing the crisis.
D) worked closely with Roosevelt to address the crisis.

41

Based on the passage, the "program of rehabilitation" (lines 65-66) was enabled by
A) Congressional legislation.
B) presidential decree.
C) popular vote.
D) a national referendum.

CONTINUE

The Tutorverse

Questions 42-52 are based on the passage and graphic below.

In the 1997 film *Good Will Hunting*, Matt Damon plays an autodidactic math genius by the name of Will Hunting. In the movie, Hunting, who works as a janitor at the Massachusetts Institute of Technology, stumbles upon a highly challenging math problem posted for the school's graduate students to solve. Hunting solves the problem easily, shocking the students and faculty alike.

In real life, such seemingly miraculous events rarely happen – but they do happen.

Take, for example, the problem of the twin primes conjecture. Prime numbers, recall, are those numbers that are divisible by exactly two numbers – one and themselves. There are, of course, an infinite number of prime numbers, but what about twin primes? A twin prime is made up of a pair of prime numbers whose difference (known as a prime gap) is exactly two: for example, 41 and 43, and 101 and 103. The twin prime conjecture asks how many twin primes there are. The answer is difficult to divine because twin primes become more rare the larger the prime numbers become. Since at least 1849, mathematicians have surmised that there are an infinite number of twin primes. But such a supposition is nothing more than a conjecture; without a pure mathematical proof or rule that can be tested, the question remains unanswered.

At its core, the twin prime conjecture deals with the question of prime gaps; in particular, whether or not, for any given gap (three, a million, or two – as in the case of twin primes) between two prime numbers, there are an infinite number of prime pairs separated by that gap.

Enter Yitang Zhang.

Zhang, who earned his doctorate in mathematics from Perdue University in 1991, had found it difficult to work in academia for many years. To make ends meet, Zhang worked as an accountant and, most famously, even worked in a fast food sandwich shop. All the while, Zhang pursued his interest in number theory, a rather esoteric branch of mathematics devoted to the study of numbers and integers – including, of course, prime numbers. Zhang closely followed developments in the field, reading published scholarly works on the subject. One such scholarly work was a paper authored in 2005 by Donald Goldston, János Pintz, and Cem Yıldırım (dubbed the GPY), which came harrowingly close to definitively proving the twin prime conjecture.

After reading the paper, Zhang began working on the problem by himself. For three years, Zhang puzzled over the twin prime conjecture, to no avail; he was unable to use the methodology described in the GPY paper to prove the conjecture. Zhang decided to take a break from his work and visit a friend. It was outside in his friend's yard that an idea suddenly hit him.

By modifying the methodology described in the GPY paper, Zhang developed a theory that would shake the theoretical mathematics community to its core and result in a major milestone in the quest to understand the question of prime gaps. Zhang's theory effectively proved that there must be a specific prime gap that occurs an infinite number of times. This could be true for many prime gaps, but at least one of the prime gaps with an infinite number of pairs must be under 70 million. Such a claim had never been proven before, and was a bold statement from a previously unknown and rather obscure personality.

Zhang submitted his work, after months of drafting, to a prestigious journal of mathematics: *Annals of Mathematics.* Immediately spotting the authenticity and lucidity of Zhang's work, the reviewers at the journal published the work, resulting in great fanfare. Less than a month after he submitted his work, Zhang was invited to speak about his discovery at Harvard University. What became clear to the tightly knit community of mathematicians was that Zhang had, through force of will and a tireless diligence, discovered a theorem to go down in history – and that he had done so without anyone's help.

Though Zhang's theory did not directly prove or disprove the twin prime conjecture, it did pave the way for greater understanding of prime gaps in general, and has provided a more targeted framework for proving the twin prime conjecture. As of this writing, Zhang's theory has enabled mathematicians to refresh their work on finding a prime gap that will result in an infinite number of prime pairs. The upper limit, no longer 70 million, is now thought to be 246 – tantalizingly close to 2.

CONTINUE ➡

The Tutorverse

For All Prime Numbers Less Than 100

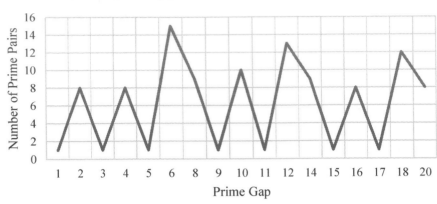

42

The author includes the example of the film *Good Will Hunting* to
A) contrast Zhang's work with Hunting's.
B) explain how fiction differs from reality.
C) explain how reality is stranger than fiction.
D) mirror Zhang's astounding work.

43

Which choice best summarizes what takes place in the third and fourth paragraphs?
A) A concept is explained and a question raised.
B) An anecdote is used to illustrate a concept.
C) Different concepts are compared and contrasted.
D) Possible answers to a question are discussed.

44

As used in line 21, "divine" most nearly means
A) absolve.
B) ascertain.
C) comprehend.
D) estimate.

45

From paragraphs 1-4 to paragraphs 5-10, how does the focus of the passage change?
A) From providing general context to arguing a point based on that context.
B) From providing general context to explaining specific information based on that context.
C) From providing general context to forming a recommendation based on that context.
D) From providing general context to telling a story based on that context.

46

The author uses the phrase "most famously...shop" (lines 40-41) to
A) contrast Zhang's ordinary life with his prodigious feat.
B) explain the inspiration behind Zhang's discovery.
C) highlight Zhang's inability to find academic work.
D) illustrate how Zhang earned his doctorate.

47

For Zhang, the GPY paper
A) failed to help him with his discovery.
B) later disproved his discovery.
C) provided the foundation for his discovery.
D) was a reminder of his failure to solve the twin prime conjecture.

CONTINUE ➡

The Tutorverse

48

According to the passage, the catalyst for Zhang's discovery was
A)   a conversation with a friend.
B)   a vacation.
C)   an undisclosed publication.
D)   the GPY paper.

49

Which selection provides the best evidence for the answer to the previous question?
A)   Lines 45-47 ("Zhang closely...subject")
B)   Lines 47-51 ("One such...conjecture")
C)   Lines 58-59 ("It was...him")
D)   Lines 60-64 ("By modifying...gaps")

50

Zhang was invited to speak at Harvard
A)   a year after earning his doctorate from Perdue University.
B)   after his theory was tested by the broader math community
C)   soon after his work was published.
D)   while he was still drafting his theory.

51

Based on the passage, the mathematics community most likely views Zhang with
A)   contempt.
B)   esteem.
C)   irreverence.
D)   trepidation.

52

Does the graph at the end of the passage support Zhang's discovery?
A)   Yes, because it proves that the twin prime conjecture is unknowable.
B)   Yes, because the graph quantifies the number of prime pairs per prime gap.
C)   No, because the question of infinite prime pairs has already been solved.
D)   No, because the graph does not identify a prime gap with infinite prime pairs.

STOP. Do not go on
until instructed to do so.

The Tutorverse

Writing & Language Test

Directions

Each of the following passages is accompanied by several questions. Some questions will ask you to consider how to revise the passage in order to improve the expression of ideas. Other questions will ask you to consider how the passage might be revised to rectify errors in sentence construction, grammar usage, and punctuation. A passage may be accompanied by one or more graphics (such as charts, tables, or graphs) that you must consider when assessing revisions.

Some questions will address underlined portions of a passage. Other questions will ask you to assess a specific place in a passage, or assess the passage as a whole.

Read each passage and choose the answer to each question that most effectively improves the passage's quality of writing or best adheres to standard writing conventions. Some questions include an answer choice of "NO CHANGE," which you should choose if it is best to leave the relevant part of the passage unchanged.

44 Questions Total; 35 Minute Time Limit
Use Section 2 of the answer sheet to answer questions in this section.

Questions 1-11 are based on the below passage and graphic.

Better to be Lucky than Good

When you think of a scientist, what qualities come to mind? Intelligence certainly comes to mind, as many scientists have demonstrated a prodigious capacity to learn new things and think critically. **1** As the life story of many scientists tells us, curiosity is also a plausible trait. But what about luck? It's not often that we liken **2** scientists too gamblers, but many of the most famous discoveries in science have been attributable to luck!

1

Which choice best matches the stylistic pattern established in the previous sentence?
A) NO CHANGE
B) Being curious might be a trait, too, as the lives of many scientists shows us.
C) Curiosity is also a plausible trait, as the life story of many scientists tells us.
D) Curiosity, as the life story of many scientists tells us, is also a plausible trait.

2

A) NO CHANGE
B) scientists to
C) scientists two
D) scientists, too,

CONTINUE ➡

The Tutorverse

Take the discovery of radioactivity as an example. Co-winner of the 1903 Nobel Prize in Physics, Antoine Henri Becquerel is widely credited with the discovery of radioactivity. But like many scientists before him, Becquerel did not set out with the deliberate intention of discovering radioactivity; **3** before long, radioactivity was a hitherto unknown concept at the time. Becquerel's discovery was the result of serendipity. **4**

Becquerel's early **5** incursions into science dealt primarily with light and the phenomenon of phosphorescence. Today, we know that phosphorescence occurs when a substance absorbs energy and releases it as an emission of light. A glow-in-the-dark toy, for example, soaks up light during the day and lights up at night. In Becquerel's day, however, phosphorescence was still very much a mystery. In order to better understand it, Becquerel conceived of an experiment.

[1] When Becquerel repeated the process, this time inserting a patterned metal sheet between the paper and the phosphorescent substance, he **6** finds that only an image of the pattern made an impression on the film. [2] Becquerel's original theory suggested that X-rays, which pass through most substances, might play a role in phosphorescence. [3] To test this, Becquerel covered photographic film (which is very sensitive to light) with black paper. [4] He then placed a phosphorescent substance on top of the paper (in this case, a uranium salt substance), and then left the whole thing out in the sun. [5] Becquerel developed the film and saw that there was an image of the substance on the film. [6] The result, Becquerel concluded, was that phosphorescent substances emitted rays that could pierce through paper and make an impression on film. **7**

As he continued his experiment, however, Becquerel came across a few very cloudy **8** days. These did not provide enough sunlight to activate the uranium salt's phosphorescence.

3
A)   NO CHANGE
B)   a blessing in disguise
C)   a flash in the pan
D)   after all

4
At this point, the author is considering adding the following sentence:

Becquerel's discovery was so important that they named the measurement of radiation – the Becquerel – after him.

Should this addition be made?
A)   No, because the sentence introduces a concept unrelated to the paragraph.
B)   No, because the sentence does not describe Becquerel's scientific process.
C)   Yes, because the sentence supports the paragraph's main idea.
D)   Yes, because the sentence highlights the importance of Becquerel's discovery.

5
A)   NO CHANGE
B)   excursions
C)   expeditions
D)   forays

6
A)   NO CHANGE
B)   found
C)   had been finding
D)   will find

7
To improve the logical flow of the paragraph, sentence 1 should be moved
A)   after sentence 2.
B)   before sentence 4.
C)   before sentence 5.
D)   before sentence 6.

8
Which choice most effectively combines the underlined portion?
A)   NO CHANGE
B)   days that
C)   days which
D)   days; these

CONTINUE ➡

The Tutorverse

He expected, upon developing the film from these days, that he would find only a weak image of the substance on the film.

To Becquerel's surprise, the image of the substance **9** clearly appeared much more than expected.

Becquerel reasoned that the phenomenon causing the image to appear **10** operated independently of light, so he conducted one more experiment. Becquerel prepared his usual equipment, only this time, in a darkroom. He put the film and uranium salt substance inside a cardboard box, and then put the box in a dark drawer. Becquerel then developed the plates. He saw that despite the darkness, the image was in fact imprinted on the film. **11** Becquerel concluded that the source of energy activating the photographic film was the uranium salt itself and not phosphorescent light.

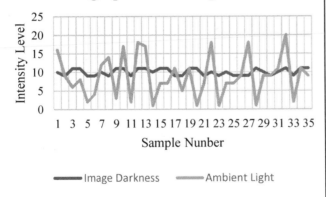

Influence of Ambient Light on Image Darkness: Uranium Salt & Photographic Film Experiment

9

A) NO CHANGE
B) appeared much more than clearly expected.
C) appeared much more clearly than expected.
D) appeared much more than expected, clearly.

10

The author desires that the information in the passage align as closely as possible with the data in the graph. Which choice best accomplishes this?
A) operated dependently on the intensity of ambient light
B) operated independently of the intensity of ambient light
C) was inversely correlated with the intensity of ambient light
D) was positively correlated with the intensity of ambient light

11

A) NO CHANGE
B) Becquerel, concluded that the source
C) Becquerel concluded that, the source
D) Becquerel concluded, that the source

CONTINUE ➡

Questions 12-22 are based on the below passage.

A Registered Increase

For many, choosing a career path can be a confusing **12** proposition, although there are so many things to think about when considering different job opportunities, after all. Oftentimes, these considerations can be mutually exclusive. For example, a job that pays well can often be stressful or require long hours or advanced degrees of study. A job that is too easy for **13** them might not be satisfying or stimulating enough, even if it pays well.

In recent years, however, many have chosen to pursue life as a registered nurse (RN). RNs perform duties as diverse as the environments in which they serve. In general, RNs coordinate and provide care and education to patients and their families. In addition to caring for the body, some RNs also provide emotional support to their **14** customers. Though RNs typically work in doctors' offices or even in the private homes of their patients, one might encounter an RN where one least expects **15** to – in hospitals, for example.

According to the United States Department of Labor's Bureau of Labor Statistics (BLS), the occupation enjoys one of the most positive outlooks in the entire economy. The BLS expects the occupation to grow 16 percent from 2014 to 2024 – an astonishingly high rate of growth **16** exceeding other occupations! As **17** the worlds population continues to grow and people continue to live longer, demand for healthcare professionals such as RNs **18** is also expected to grow and more people will need RNs. Because more and more people will continue to require both preventative care and management for chronic conditions, such as diabetes and obesity, the demand for RNs is expected to rise. As a result, average compensation for RNs is among the highest across all occupations (according to the BLS: $66,640 in May of 2014).

12
A) NO CHANGE
B) proposition. There
C) proposition. Although, there
D) proposition, whereas

13
A) NO CHANGE
B) a person
C) people
D) him

14
A) NO CHANGE
B) custodians
C) friends
D) wards

15
The author is considering revising the underlined portion to strengthen the point developed in this sentence. Which choice best accomplishes this goal?
A) NO CHANGE
B) to – at insurance companies, for example.
C) to – in nursing facilities, for example.
D) to – in health clinics, for example.

16
A) NO CHANGE
B) exceeding the rates of other occupations
C) that exceeds other occupations
D) exceeding those other occupations

17
A) NO CHANGE
B) the world population's
C) the world's population
D) the worlds' population

18
A) NO CHANGE
B) going to increase along with the number of people who need RNs
C) is also expected to grow
D) will grow like the number of people who need RNs

CONTINUE ➡

The Tutorverse

As with any job, RNs experience their fair share of challenges. Many RNs work long shifts – sometimes as long as 13 hours in a row – a practice that jeopardizes the safety of nurse and patient alike. In addition, due to the nature of their work, RNs are often exposed to pathogens at rates much higher than average. However, employers and RN advocacy groups are working together to address these and other issues. Despite such issues, RNs appear to be very satisfied with their **19** career choice; in one study conducted by a healthcare staffing firm, 90% of nurses surveyed indicated that they were very satisfied with their career choice.

20 Though requirements vary from country to country, prospective RNs in the United States have two options: obtain at least an associate's degree in **21** nursing. Or receive a diploma from an approved nursing program. After these educational requirements are met, registered nurses must also receive licensure by passing the National Council Licensure Examination-Registered Nurses. **22**

19

Which choice most effectively combines the underlined portion?
A)   NO CHANGE
B)   career choice, however, in one study
C)   career choice, in one study
D)   career choice, and in one study

20

Which choice most effectively introduces the information that follows?
A)   How does one become a registered nurse?
B)   When should one become a registered nurse?
C)   Who should consider becoming a registered nurse?
D)   Why does one become a registered nurse?

21

A)   NO CHANGE
B)   nursing; or receive
C)   nursing, or receive
D)   nursing – or receive

22

Which choice most effectively concludes the passage with a restatement of the author's main idea?
A)   Becoming an RN is probably not worth the difficult licensing requirements.
B)   Being an RN is not for everyone, especially people who do not want to work long hours.
C)   There will not be sufficient demand for RNs to justify the licensing process.
D)   Though the road to becoming an RN is long and arduous, the rewards and benefits can be great.

CONTINUE ➡

The Tutorverse

Questions 23-33 are based on the below passage.

What Do You Mean?

Most people takes for granted the fact that we can communicate clearly with one another. Yet it's nothing short of amazing that we're able to make ourselves understood to one another – to convey complicated thoughts and ideas to other people. **23** Its thanks to languages that we have become the dominant species on our planet.

But what exactly is language, and how does it work? How was language created, and how did it change over time? Why is it still a challenge to communicate with those who speak different languages? **24** Why is it that the word "dog" refers to a furry, four-legged creature that barks and bites? These questions and more **25** is the focus of linguists, or those who study language.

You might ask yourself: "How can there be a whole field of study devoted to language? There's nothing more to it than reading, writing, speaking, and listening, **26** right?" In reality, languages are as **27** complex and subtly different as the way we use them. Thus, an entire field of study centers around learning about languages: linguistics. Though the field of linguistics is actually quite **28** inexact, it can be thought of in two parts: the first has to do with the structure of a language, **29** and how language is used is the second.

23
- A) NO CHANGE
- B) It'
- C) Its'
- D) It's

24

The author is considering deleting the underlined sentence. Should this deletion be made?
- A) Yes, because the sentence blurs the focus of the paragraph.
- B) Yes, because the sentence contradicts previous statements made.
- C) No, because the sentence advances the idea of the paragraph.
- D) No, because the sentence supports an opposing point of view.

25
- A) NO CHANGE
- B) am
- C) are
- D) be

26
- A) NO CHANGE
- B) right"?
- C) right?"?
- D) right?".

27
- A) NO CHANGE
- B) complex and nuanced
- C) complex and different in many ways
- D) difficult to comprehend and different

28
- A) NO CHANGE
- B) broad
- C) duplicative
- D) narrow

29
- A) NO CHANGE
- B) and language usage is the second.
- C) and the second has to do with usage of a language.
- D) and the second pertains to language usage.

CONTINUE ➡

The Tutorverse

There are many parts to a language. The most basic component of languages are words. Morphology refers to the study of words themselves – how they are used in sentences, how they've developed over time, how some words are related to others, and so on. If words are the building blocks of a language, then sentences are the structures. **30** <u>Syntax refers to the study of sentences themselves – what rules to follow when constructing a sentence, which types of words come before others, and so forth.</u> Then, of course, are the way words are spoken – the way they sound, and what they mean. Phonology, semantics, and pragmatics refer to the study of sounds in languages – how the words themselves sound when spoken, and what they mean depending on order and context. **31**

32 <u>Unlike the study</u> of the structure of a language, the study of language usage focuses more on how people utilize languages. In historical linguistics, for example, linguists are focused on the overall changes to a language over time. They are focused on understanding how and why languages change over time. Psycholinguistics, on the other hand, is primarily concerned with studying the psychological and neurological **33** <u>factors which allows</u> people to develop linguistic skills. Psycholinguists study everything from how people learn a language to how they is able to draw on a language to convey their ideas.

30

Which choice best mirrors the stylistic patterns established in the rest of the paragraph?
A)   NO CHANGE
B)   What rules to follow when constructing a sentence, which types of words come before others, and so forth refers to syntax, the study of sentences themselves.
C)   What rules to follow when constructing a sentence, which types of words come before others, and so forth refers to the study of sentences themselves – syntax.
D)   Syntax – the study of sentences themselves – refers to the rules to follow when constructing a sentence, which types of words come before others, and so forth.

31

Which sentence best concludes the paragraph?
A)   Instead, the study of language is divided into several disciplines.
B)   Nevertheless, the study of language is divided into several disciplines.
C)   Therefore, the study of language is relatively straight forward.
D)   Thus, the study of language is divided into several disciplines.

32

Which choice best connects this paragraph with the paragraph immediately preceding it?
A)   NO CHANGE
B)   Similar to the study
C)   Despite the study
D)   In spite of the study

33

A)   NO CHANGE
B)   factors that allow
C)   factors, which allow
D)   factors, which allows

CONTINUE ➡

The Tutorverse

Questions 34-44 are based on the below passage.

It's Good to be King?

--- 1 ---

The rule of law stands in contrast to systems of **34** government, that grant ruling power, to those with the most physical, economic, or political power. Unlike in the latter, in the former, all persons are bound by the same rules and laws that govern the society. In the former, the poorest pauper and the wealthiest scion, for example, must all adhere to codified laws and ordinances. Even the **35** administrator of the government – the prime ministers, presidents, and statesmen – are bound by the rule of law. **36**

--- 2 ---

The rule of law is a fairly new concept. For centuries, many societies were organized as stratocracies, plutocracies, or monarchies, all of which conferred ruling authority on the powerful. In a stratocracy, such as the ancient Greek city-state of Sparta, society is governed by warriors. **37** Sparta, though a strong military power in its day, eventually faced isolation and decline. In a plutocracy, such as the Italian republics of Venice and Florence during the Middle Ages, ruling power is derived from economic wealth. For nearly two thousand years, the emperors of China ruled with absolute authority in the form of a monarchy, with power derived from the divine. In many such societies, the ruling class often lived by an entirely different set of laws than those governing the ruled.

34
- A) NO CHANGE
- B) government, which, grant ruling power to
- C) government, which grant ruling power, to
- D) government that grant ruling power to

35
- A) NO CHANGE
- B) administrators
- C) administrator's
- D) administrators'

36

At this point, the author is considering adding the following sentence:

In the latter society, however, the rules are not necessarily applied equally to all people.

Should this sentence be added?
- A) Yes, because the sentence clarifies the difference between different forms of government.
- B) Yes, because the sentence supports the notion that economic power is greater than rule of law.
- C) No, because the sentence does not support the primary claim of the paragraph.
- D) No, because the sentence does not logically follow from the preceding sentence.

37

The author is considering deleting the underlined sentence. Should the sentence be deleted?
- A) Yes, because the details are superfluous to the central focus of the paragraph.
- B) Yes, because the history of Sparta mirrors the history of other ancient societies.
- C) No, because the decline of Sparta is a metaphor for the rule of law.
- D) No, because the details are relevant to the central focus of the paragraph.

CONTINUE ➡

--- 3 ---

Today, many societies are governed by legal principles rather than the **38** changing whims and feelings of a given ruling regime. **39** Often referred to as the rule of law. These legal principles help settle conflicts, resolve disputes, and otherwise ensure the orderly conduct of business and interpersonal interactions.

--- 4 ---

Yet even in antiquity, the seeds of the modern rule of law were being sown. The ancient Greek philosopher Aristotle was a fervent, **40** proficient advocate of the rule of law, stating that "it is more proper that law should govern than any one of the citizens" and that "if it is advantageous to place the supreme power in some particular persons, they should be appointed to be only guardians, and the servants of the laws." Similar rumblings also surfaced in ancient China, in the **41** form of the legalist school of thought. Han Fei, a political philosopher of the second century BC, wrote in his seminal work that "the intelligent ruler…makes the law measure merits and makes no arbitrary judgment himself." Despite the cogency of Aristotle and Han Fei's arguments, few societies actually practiced the theories espoused by these legalists.

--- 5 ---

Some thousand years later, King John of England signed the Magna Carta, a document that would help **42** launch the rule of law. The Magna Carta would go on to limit the power of the monarchy, establish the rules and laws governing the people of England, and serve as a framework for other societies governed by the rule of law – including the Constitution of the United States. The **43** concept that once existed in practical obscurity, would go on to dominate global governance.

Refer to the entire passage when answering Question 44.

38
- A) NO CHANGE
- B) caprices
- C) unpredictable thoughts
- D) suggestable notions and ideas

39
- A) NO CHANGE
- B) These are often referred to as the rule of law
- C) Often referred to as the rule of law; these
- D) Often referred to as the rule of law, these

40
- A) NO CHANGE
- B) pliant
- C) outspoken
- D) authoritarian

41
- A) NO CHANGE
- B) forms of the legalist schools of thoughts.
- C) forms of the legalist school of thought.
- D) form of the legalist school of thoughts.

42
Which choice best utilizes stylistic elements encountered in the fourth paragraph?
- A) NO CHANGE
- B) mold the rule of law
- C) develop the rule of law
- D) the rule of law to take root

43
- A) NO CHANGE
- B) concept, that once existed in practical obscurity would
- C) concept that, once existed in practical obscurity would
- D) concept that once existed in practical obscurity would

44
In order to improve the cohesion and logical flow of the passage, paragraph 3 should
- A) remain where it is now
- B) be moved before paragraph 1.
- C) be moved before paragraph 2.
- D) be moved before paragraph 5

STOP. Do not go on until instructed to do so.

STOP

The Tutorverse

Math – No Calculator

Directions for questions 1-15
Solve each question by choosing the best answer from the choices provided. Fill in the appropriate circle on the answer sheet. Writing in the test booklet is allowed.

Directions for questions 16-20
Answer each question by solving the problem and entering the answer in the provided grid on the answer sheet. Though it is recommended that you write the answer in the boxes at the top of each column, you will receive credit only if the circles are appropriately filled in. Do not mark more than one circle in any column. No question has a negative answer. Some questions may have multiple answers, in which case you need only provide one answer. Mixed numbers such as $2\frac{1}{2}$ must be gridded either as 2.5 or 5/2; do not grid the answer as 21/2. Decimal answers may be rounded or truncated. Answers may be entered starting in any column. Writing in the test booklet is allowed.

Notes
1. You **may not** use a calculator.
2. The variables and expressions used are real numbers unless otherwise indicated.
3. All figures shown in this test are drawn to scale unless otherwise indicated.
4. Figures lie in a plane unless otherwise indicated.
5. The domain of a given function f is the set of all real numbers x for which $f(x)$ is a real number, unless otherwise indicated.

Reference
A circle has 360 degrees of arc.
A circle has 2π radians of arc.
The sum of the measures of all angles in a triangle is 180.

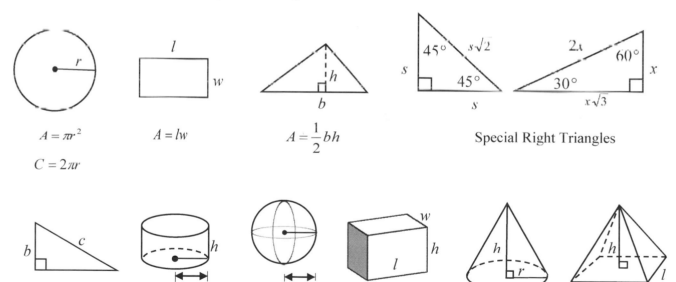

$$A = \pi r^2$$
$$C = 2\pi r$$

$$A = lw$$

$$A = \frac{1}{2}bh$$

Special Right Triangles

$$c^2 = a^2 + b^2$$

$$V = \pi r^2 h$$

$$V = \frac{4}{3}\pi r^3$$

$$V = lwh$$

$$V = \frac{1}{3}\pi r^2 h$$

$$V = \frac{1}{3}lwh$$

The Tutorverse

1

If $\frac{2}{3}w = \frac{5}{4}$, what is the value of w?

A) $\frac{8}{15}$

B) $\frac{7}{12}$

C) $\frac{5}{6}$

D) $\frac{15}{8}$

2

$$y = a(x+2)(x-4)$$

In the quadratic equation above, a is a nonzero constant. The graph of the equation on the xy-plane is a parabola with vertex (c,d). Which of the following is equal to d?

A) $-9a$
B) $-6a$
C) $-3a$
D) $-2a$

3

The relationship between a reading C on the Celsius temperature scale and a reading F on the Fahrenheit temperature scale is

$C = \frac{5}{9}(F-32)$, and the relationship between

a reading on the Celsius temperature scale and a reading K on the Kelvin temperature scale is $K = C + 273$. Which of the following expresses the relationship between readings on the Kelvin and Fahrenheit temperature scales?

A) $K = \frac{5}{9}(F-231)$

B) $K = \frac{5}{9}(F-32)+273$

C) $K = \frac{5}{9}(F-32)-273$

D) $K = \frac{5}{9}(F+32)+273$

4

The population of a small town from 2000 to 2010 can be modeled by the equation $y = 12x + 13,580$, where x represents the number of years since 2000, and y represents the total population. Which of the following best describes the meaning of the number 0.12 in the equation?

A) The total population in the year 2000.
B) The estimated increase in the population each year.
C) The estimated difference between the population in 2010 and 2000.
D) The total population in the year 2010.

5

$$y = 5x + b$$

The above equation represents a line on the xy-plane with y-intercept b. The line passes through the point $(-1,-2)$. What is the value of b?

A) -7
B) 3
C) 7
D) 9

6

Let $g(x) = x^2 - 3$.

If $f(g(x)) = \sqrt{x^2 - 6}$, which of the following describes $f(x)$?

A) $f(x) = \sqrt{x-3}$

B) $f(x) = \sqrt{x^2 - 1}$

C) $f(x) = \sqrt{x^2 - 3}$

D) $f(x) = \sqrt{x^4 - 6x^2 + 15}$

7

$$(6x^2 + 2x - 3) - (10x^2 - 2x + 5)$$

Which of the following is equivalent to the expression above?

A) $-4x^2 + 2$
B) $-4x^2 - 8$
C) $-4x^2 + 4x - 8$
D) $-4x^2 + 4x + 2$

CONTINUE

The Tutorverse

8

What is the sum of all values of m that satisfy $25m^2 - 4 = 0$?

A)   0

B) $\dfrac{2}{5}$

C) $\dfrac{4}{5}$

D) $\dfrac{4}{25}$

9

The population of a certain city increases by 6% each year. If the city's current population is 5 million, which function models the population, P, measured in millions, as a function of the number of years, t, into the future?

A) $P(t) = 5(1.06)^t$

B) $P(t) = 5(0.94)^t$

C) $P(t) - 1.06(5)^t$

D) $P(t) = 0.94(5)^t$

10

For a polynomial $p(x)$, the value of $p(-2)$ is 6. Which of the following must be true about $p(x)$?

A)   The remainder when $p(x)$ is divided by $x + 2$ is 6.

B)   The remainder when $p(x)$ is divided by $x - 2$ is 6.

C)   The remainder when $p(x)$ is divided by $x + 6$ is -2.

D)   The remainder when $p(x)$ is divided by $x - 6$ is -2.

11

$$R = \dfrac{T}{T + L}$$

An airline uses the formula above to calculate their on-time arrival rate, R, based on the number on-time arrivals, T, and the number of late arrivals, L. Which of the following expresses the number of on-time arrivals in terms of the other variables?

A) $T = \dfrac{L}{R - 1}$

B) $T = \dfrac{L}{1 - R}$

C) $T = \dfrac{RL}{R - 1}$

D) $T = \dfrac{RL}{1 - R}$

12

$$f(x) = |3x - 15|$$

For the function defined above, what is a possible value of a for which $f(a) < a$?

A)   -6

B)   -4

C)   0

D)   6

13

If $f(x) = x^2 + 1$ and $g(x) = 3x$, what is $f(g(x))$ equal to?

A) $3x^2 + 1$

B) $9x^2 + 1$

C) $3x^2 + 3$

D) $9x^2 + 3$

CONTINUE ➡

The Tutorverse

14

If $\dfrac{a+b}{a-b} = \dfrac{9}{7}$, which of the following must also be true?

A) $\dfrac{a}{b} = 8$

B) $\dfrac{a}{b} = -8$

C) $\dfrac{a+2b}{a-b} = \dfrac{10}{7}$

D) $b - a = -7$

15

$$\dfrac{-16+4i}{5+3i}$$

If the expression above is rewritten in the form $a + bi$, where a and b are real numbers, what is the value of a? (Note: $i = \sqrt{-1}$)

A) −68

B) −2

C) 2

D) 68

Student Produced Responses

16

$$ax + by = 12$$
$$2x + 5y = 72$$

In the system of equations above, a and b are constants. If the system has infinitely many solutions, what is the value of ab?

17

Steve has a budget of $1,000 for a home improvement project. He buys cans of paint for $50 each and bundles of lumber for $100 each. If he buys at least one can of paint and one bundle of lumber, what is the greatest number of cans of paint he can buy?

18

$$x^3 - 4x^2 + 9x - 36 = 0$$

For what real value of x is the equation above true?

19

In a right triangle, one angle measures $x°$, where $\cos(x°) = \dfrac{3}{5}$. What is $\sin(90° - x°)$?

20

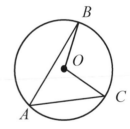

Note: Figure not drawn to scale.

In the figure above, central angle BOC is 114° and subtends arc BC. What is the measure, in degrees, of angle BAC?

STOP. Do not go on until instructed to do so.

STOP

The Tutorverse

Math – Calculator

Directions for questions 1-30

Solve each question by choosing the best answer from the choices provided. Fill in the appropriate circle on the answer sheet. Writing in the test booklet is allowed.

Directions for questions 31-38

Answer each question by solving the problem and entering the answer in the provided grid on the answer sheet. Though it is recommended that you write the answer in the boxes at the top of each column, you will receive credit only if the circles are appropriately filled in. Do not mark more than one circle in any column. No question has a negative answer. Some questions may have multiple answers, in which case you need only provide one answer. Mixed numbers such as $2\frac{1}{2}$ must be gridded either as 2.5 or 5/2; do not grid the answer as 21/2. Decimal answers may be rounded or truncated. Answers may be entered starting in any column. Writing in the test booklet is allowed.

Notes

1. You **may** use a calculator.
2. The variables and expressions used are real numbers unless otherwise indicated.
3. All figures shown in this test are drawn to scale unless otherwise indicated.
4. Figures lie in a plane unless otherwise indicated.
5. The domain of a given function f is the set of all real numbers x for which $f(x)$ is a real number, unless otherwise indicated.

Reference

A circle has 360 degrees of arc.

A circle has 2π radians of arc.

The sum of the measures of all angles in a triangle is 180.

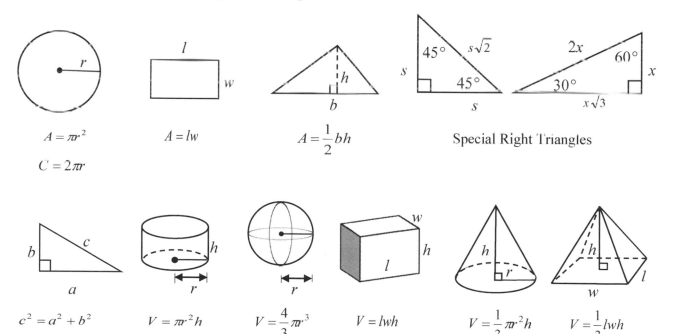

$A = \pi r^2$ $A = lw$ $A = \frac{1}{2}bh$ Special Right Triangles

$C = 2\pi r$

$c^2 = a^2 + b^2$ $V = \pi r^2 h$ $V = \frac{4}{3}\pi r^3$ $V = lwh$ $V = \frac{1}{3}\pi r^2 h$ $V = \frac{1}{3}lwh$

The Tutorverse

1

If $12 < 6 + 9mx$, which inequality represents the possible range of values of $2 + 3mx$?

A) $2 + 3mx < 4$

B) $2 + 3mx > 4$

C) $2 + 3mx < 8$

D) $2 + 3mx > 8$

2

The function f is defined by $f(x) = x^3 + 2x^2 + kx + 2$, where k is a constant. On the xy-plane, the graph of f intersects the x-axis at the point $(-2,0)$ and the y-axis at $(0,2)$. What is the value of k?

A) -1

B) 0

C) 1

D) 2

3

1,000 cubic centimeters of water is to be poured into right circular conical cups with a radius of 3 centimeters and a height of 6 centimeters, as depicted below.

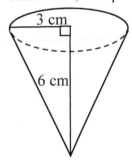

Note: Figure not drawn to scale.

What is the greatest number of cups that can be completely filled?

A) 5

B) 17

C) 18

D) 26

4

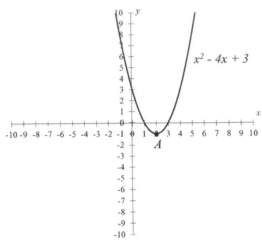

Which of the following is an equivalent form of the equation of the graph shown on the xy-plane above, from which the coordinates of the vertex A can be identified as constants in the equation?

A) $y = (x-1)(x-3)$

B) $y = (x+1)(x+3)$

C) $y = x(x-2)^2 - 3$

D) $y = (x-2)^2 - 1$

5

In a triangle ABC, the measure of angle A is $\dfrac{\pi}{4}$ and the measure of angle B is $\dfrac{\pi}{3}$. What is the measure of angle C?

A) $\dfrac{5\pi}{12}$

B) $\dfrac{7\pi}{12}$

C) $\dfrac{11\pi}{12}$

D) $\dfrac{17\pi}{12}$

CONTINUE ➡

The Tutorverse

6

Mike and Dylan own a total of 128 comic books. If Dylan owns 14 more comic books than Mike, how many comic books does Dylan own?

A) 14
B) 57
C) 71
D) 89

7

In a random sample of certain species of peas, 12 out of every 700 peas have a genetic characteristic that turns them red. What would be the expected number of peas with this characteristic in a random sample of 210,000?

A) 360
B) 3,600
C) 840
D) 8,400

8

$$x - 2y + 4$$

$$y = x^2 + \frac{1}{2}x - 2$$

If (x,y) is a solution of the system of equations above, what is the value of y?

A) -2
B) 0
C) $\dfrac{1}{2}$
D) 2

9

The force a spring exerts on an object can be represented by $F = kx$ where k is the spring constant, which measures how strong the spring is and x is the distance the spring is stretched or compressed away from its rest position. The force applied to a spring in the suspension of a certain car is 2,450 N. What is the approximate spring constant when the spring is compressed 1.5 feet, in N/ft.?

A) 1,225.5
B) 1,633.3
C) 3,675.0
D) 4,900.0

10

The retail price for a book was $30. It was marked down 20% on Black Friday. The next day, it was marked back up 30%. By what percentage did the price of the book increase from the original price to the final price?

A) 0%
B) 4%
C) 6%
D) 10%

11

The cost for vendors of using the Wi-Fi at a convention center is $0.15 per minute. Which of the following equations represents the total cost c, in dollars, for h hours of Wi-Fi use?

A) $c = 0.15(60h)$
B) $c = 0.15h + 60$
C) $c = \dfrac{60h}{0.15}$
D) $c = \dfrac{0.15h}{60}$

CONTINUE ➡

The Tutorverse

12

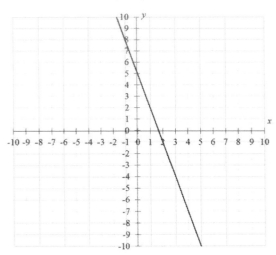

The graph above shows a line on the *xy*-plane. Which of these is the equation of a parallel line?

A) $3x + y = 4$

B) $-3x + y = 4$

C) $x - 3y = 5$

D) $3y = x + 5$

13

A certain lake contains 420,000 cubic meters of water. A government environmental agency finds a toxic level of waste in the lake and decides to drain the entire lake. The water is pumped out at a rate of 240 cubic meters per minute. How much water, in cubic meters, remains in the lake after 2 hours?

A)   60,000

B)   369,600

C)   391,200

D)   419,520

14

The average number of students per classroom at Western High School from 2000 to 2010 can be modeled by the equation $y = 0.45x + 22.5$ where *x* represents the number of years since 2000 and *y* represents the average number of students per classroom. The average number of students at Eastern High School can be similarly modeled using the function $y = 0.55x + 22.1$.

In what year did the two schools have the same average number of students per classroom?

A)   2002

B)   2004

C)   2005

D)   2008

15

When 5 times the number *x* is added to 7, the result is −13. What number results when 3 times *x* is added to 25?

A)   −13

B)   −3

C)   13

D)   37

CONTINUE ➡

The Tutorverse

Questions 16 & 17 refer to the following information:

A fruit company is concerned because some bananas become rotten while being transported to the store. The company uses the formula $S = B(0.95)^t$ to predict how many bananas will be fresh enough to sell by the time they reach the store. B represents the number of bananas that are transported and t represents the number of days that it takes for them to be transported to the store.

16

If it takes one week for the bananas to reach the store, what percentage of them are no longer fresh enough to sell when they arrive at the store?
A)   5%
B)   7%
C)   30%
D)   35%

17

Last year it took d days to transport the bananas. This year it takes $2d$ days to transport the same number of bananas. How does the value of S change from last year to this year?
A)   It is multiplied by 0.95
B)   It is multiplied by 0.95^d
C)   It is multiplied by 0.95^2
D)   It is multiplied by 0.95^{2d}

18

A circle on the xy-plane has its center at $(7,1)$. If the point $(10,5)$ lies on the circle, which of the following is an equation of the circle?
A) $x^2 + y^2 - 14x - 2y = -25$
B) $x^2 + y^2 - 14x + 2y = -25$
C) $x^2 + y^2 + 14x - 2y = -25$
D) $x^2 + y^2 + 14x + 2y = -25$

19

If $f(x) = 14x - 7$ and $g(x) = 10x - 5$, which of the following is NOT divisible by $2x - 1$?
A) $f(x)$
B) $f(g(x))$
C) $f(x)g(x)$
D) $f(x) + g(x)$

20

The table below summarizes the results of 150 students in the Biology 101 class at a university.

Biology 101 Exam Results

	Passed	Did Not Pass
Attended Review Session	82	18
Did Not Attend Review Session	33	17

If one of the students who passed is chosen at random for an interview, what is the probability that the person chosen did *not* attend the review session?

A) $\dfrac{17}{72}$

B) $\dfrac{33}{50}$

C) $\dfrac{33}{82}$

D) $\dfrac{33}{115}$

CONTINUE ➡

The Tutorverse

Questions 21 & 22 refer to the following information.

A sociologist chose 200 students at random from each of two schools and asked how many pets he or she has. The results are shown in the table below.

Students' Pets Survey

Number of Pets	Pembroke School	Elkwood School
0	60	80
1	50	40
2	40	30
3	25	25
4	25	25

There are a total of 1,800 students at Pembroke school and 2,000 students at Elkwood School.

21

What is the median number of pets for all the students surveyed?

A)   0
B)   1
C)   2
D)   3

22

Based on the survey data, which of the following most accurately compares the expected total number of students with 4 pets at the two schools.

A)   The total number of students with 4 pets is expected to be equal at the two schools.

B)   The total number of students with 4 pets at Elkwood School is expected to be 25 more than at Pembroke School.

C)   The total number of students with 4 pets at Pembroke school is expected to be 25 more than at Elkwood School.

D)   The total number of students with 4 pets at Elkwood School is expected to be 200 more than at Lincoln School.

23

The expression $(2x+5)^3$ is equivalent to which of the following?

A) $8x^3 + 125$

B) $4x^3 + 20x^2 + 25$

C) $8x^3 + 20x^2 + 50x + 125$

D) $8x^3 + 60x^2 + 150x + 125$

24

A cable company has been losing approximately 25% of its subscribers each year for the past several years, as shown in the chart below:

Year	Average annual subscribership (in thousands)
2010	318.9
2011	240.5
2012	179.4
2013	134.6
2014	100.9
2015	75.7
2016	56.8
2017 (estimated)	42.6

Which of the following best describes the relationship between time and the cable company's average annual subscribership during these years?

A)   Increasing linear
B)   Decreasing linear
C)   Exponential growth
D)   Exponential decay

CONTINUE ➡

The Tutorverse

25

$g = 60 + 0.3x$

$q = 62.25 + 0.15x$

In the equations above, g and q represent the price per square foot in dollars, of granite and quartz, respectively, at a home improvement store, plus an additional surcharge for x weeks after delivery to the store. What was the price per square foot of granite when it was the same as the price per square foot of quartz?

A) $60.00
B) $62.25
C) $64.50
D) $65.15

26

The table below gives the initial weight of a certain radioactive substance observed in a lab and allowed to decay.

Time (Days)	Weight of Sample (ounces)
0	5.22
5	4.07
10	2.92
15	1.77
20	0.62

Which of the following functions models the weight of the substance after t days?

A) $f(t) = 5.22 - 1.15t$

B) $f(t) = 5.22 - 0.23t$

C) $f(t) = 5.22 - 0.23^t$

D) $f(t) = 5.22 - 0.23^{5t}$

27

Which of the following situations describes exponential growth?

A)   An employee gets a job that pays $1000 per day.

B)   An employee's pay increases from $800 per week to $825 per week.

C)   An employee has a job that pays $1 the first day, $2 the second day, $4 the third day, and doubles the amount per day each day.

D)   The number of employees in a certain company starts at 100 and increases by 50 each year.

28

Mel placed one thermometer in direct sunlight and one in the shade and recorded the temperatures on both over a 12-hour period in the graph below.

Recorded Temperatures

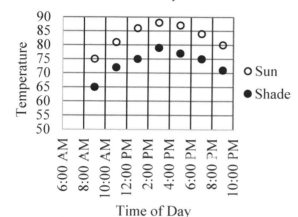

Time of Day

Which of the following statements correctly compares the average rates at which the temperatures of the two samples change?

A)   In every 2-hour interval, the magnitude of the rate of change of temperature recorded by the thermometer in the sun is greater than that of the thermometer in the shade.

B)   In every 2-hour interval, the magnitude of the rate of change of temperature recorded by the thermometer in the shade is greater than that of the thermometer in the sun.

C)   In the intervals from 9:00 to 11:00 and 11:00 to 13:00, the rates of change of temperature recorded by the thermometer in the shade are of greater magnitude, whereas in the intervals between 15:00 and 17:00 and 17:00 and 19:00, the rates of change of the temperature recorded by the thermometer in the sun are of greater magnitude.

D)   The rates of change of temperature recorded by the thermometer in the sun are roughly the same as the rates of change of temperature recorded by the thermometer in the shade.

CONTINUE ➡

Questions 29 & 30 refer to the following information.

A home improvement e-store sells 27 different kinds of hammers. The store tracked the number of hammers that were returned over the course of one year as a function of each hammer's average customer rating on a scale of 0–7. The scatterplot below shows the customer rating and the number of each type of hammer that was returned, along with the line of best fit. The equation for the line of best fit is $y = 75 - 10x$.

Hammer Return Information

29

According to the line of best fit, how many hammers would the e-store expect to be returned if its customer rating was 4.5?

A) 45
B) 39
C) 30
D) 25

30

For how many of the 27 hammers tracked was the number of hammers returned greater than the number predicted by the line of best fit?

A) 2
B) 10
C) 12
D) 27

Student Produced Responses

31

If $y = kx$, where k is a constant, and $y = 128$ when $x = 16$, what is the value of y when x is increased by 25%?

32

Aaron calculates, using a certain font and line spacing, that each page of a typed document contains at least 240 words and at most 260 words. What is the least number of pages needed for a 12,000-word document?

33

$$B = \frac{m}{h^2}$$

The body mass index B of a person who has mass m and height h is calculated using the formula above. If two people have the same mass, but one has height h and the other has height $\frac{3}{4}h$, what is the ratio of the taller person's body mass index to the shorter person's body mass index? *(Grid your answer as a fraction.)*

CONTINUE ➡

The Tutorverse

34

Sadie kept track of how far she ran each day and recorded her data in a table.

Day	Distance on Street (miles)	Distance in Park (miles)	Total
Monday		3	
Tuesday	2		
Total			10

On Monday, $\frac{3}{4}$ of the distance Sadie ran was in the park. What distance, in miles, did she run in the park on Tuesday?

35

John usually gets to work by driving 29 miles down Greenwich Street, which goes from his house to his office in a straight line. One week, Greenwich Street is closed due to construction, so John gets to work by driving 13 miles west on 57th Street, and then turning onto Harrison Street and driving north to his office. Approximately how many more miles does John have to drive by taking the detour? (*Round your answer to the nearest tenth of a mile.*)

36

There are 3 feet in one yard. A man is walking at a speed of 90 yards per minute. What is the man's speed, in feet per second?

37

From 1980 to 2015, the student body at University A grew approximately 3% per year. By contrast, during the same period, the student body at University B grew by approximately 300 students per year. If both universities had exactly 10,000 students in 1980, what was the difference between the student bodies of University A and University B in 2015?

38

$$y^2 = \sqrt{x}$$

If $y = 6$, what is the value of x?

STOP. Do not go on until instructed to do so.

The Tutorverse

Essay

Directions

In this essay, you must:

- show that you have carefully read the passage
- present a clear and logical analysis
- use language precisely

The essay must be written on the lines provided on the answer sheet, in the Essay Response Section. You may use the space provided in the Essay Planning Section of the answer sheet to formulate your thoughts.

Write on every line, do not leave too much space on either end of each line, and write in a reasonable size. The people reading and evaluating the essay are not familiar with your handwriting, so print or write legibly.

You have 50 minutes to read the passage and write an essay in response to the prompt provided.

Do not write your essay anywhere else but on the Essay Response Section; only what you write on the Essay Response Section of the answer sheet will be evaluated.

An essay on any other topic will not be evaluated.

As you read the passage below, consider how the author

- uses evidence, such as facts, figures, examples, and other information, to support claims made.
- logic to develop ideas and relate connect claims with evidence.
- utilizes stylistic elements, such as diction or emotion, to add persuasiveness to the argument.

---

1. Crop diversity is important to the security and stability of our food supply. We should not allow the convenience and affordability of "monoculture" – the cultivating of a single crop only – to blind us to the costly and dangerous consequences of relying too greatly upon any one single plant for food. In fact, there are many historical disasters that have shown us that monoculture is not only risky, but also potentially disastrous. One of the most well-known disasters resulting from monoculture was the Irish Potato Famine of the mid-nineteenth century.

2. During the seventeenth and eighteenth centuries, Irish Catholics were prevented from owning land, voting, holding office, obtaining an education, gaining any kind of professional employment, and living near large towns or cities. These stringent laws, enacted by the ruling British powers, helped mire the Irish in poverty for several generations. The Irish had no power over their circumstances; they were forced to work for British absentee landlords, paying rents by working the fields and subsisting on what little crop they had time to cultivate on their own. By the mid-nineteenth century, a census conducted by the British government found that poverty was rampant in Ireland: one-third of all Irish worked parcels of land so small that they could not support their families after paying rent to their landlords. At the time, two-thirds of the eight million Irish were dependent on agriculture for survival, even though they were not given enough land to do so. Given the paucity of land, the only crop that could be grown in sufficient quantities was the Irish Lumper potato.

3. For the Irish, the Lumper potato was not only a food staple, but also a key cog in the economic fabric of Irish society. The Lumper potato was used as feed for livestock, which were raised not only for

The Tutorverse

consumption, but for export, as well. Thus, Lumper potatoes served as the fodder that fueled the whole of Ireland. Without the potato, 19th century Ireland would have been a very, very different place – as millions of Irish would inevitably witness.

4. In the years leading up to the Great Famine, there were already signs that the crop was beginning to fail. Frost and pre-existing diseases, such as dry rot and curl, began to chip away at Ireland's very foundation. A few months after its arrival in Europe, the blight quickly spread to Ireland. By 1845, one-third to one-half of all potato crops had succumbed to the disease. A year later, in 1846, the disease had destroyed three-quarters of the crop. For the next several years, potato crop yields shrank to a mere fraction of what they had been. Famine and starvation set in, resulting in the deaths of hundreds of thousands of people and the complete collapse of the Irish economy and society. To escape the harsh reality of life without the Lumper potato, many hundreds of thousands more left the country.

5. American society today has not been forced into monoculture for social and political reasons, as the Irish were. Instead, Americans willingly accept monoculture as a matter of economic convenience and preference. In order to facilitate the mass production of food, we have come to accept the risk inherent in the cultivation of a single plant crop. This is because the mass production of our crops allows for lower prices and greater abundance. In general, Americans appear willing to trade taste, variety, and food security for lower prices.

6. In 1844, Irish newspapers reported on troubling diseases that, for two years, had attacked potato crops in America. Then in 1845, the Gardeners' Chronicle and Horticultural Gazette reported on a strange new potato blight. Though the British government found the reports troubling, they ultimately disregarded them, choosing to believe instead that the reports were exaggerated and written by alarmists.

7. Today, Americans face a similar issue. America's overreliance on its wheat crop – which, like the Lumper potato feeds man and beast alike – is a cornerstone of both the domestic and global food chain. And yet the mass cultivation of this crop is threatened by a disease called stem rust. Should America's wheat crop succumb to this disease, as the Lumper potato did to the blight, we can expect economic and social hardships akin to those experienced by Ireland in the 19th century.

8. Will we let history repeat itself? Or will we be proactive in combating this, as well as all future threats, caused by the myopic practice of monoculture?

Write an essay that explains how the author builds an argument to persuade the audience that America should avoid the practice of monoculture. In this essay, analyze the author's use of one or more of the features described at the beginning of this section (or features of your own choosing) to reinforce the logic and power of his argument. Make certain that this analysis focuses on the most relevant aspects of the passage.

Answer Keys & Explanations

Explanations: Part One – Reading
Guided Practice
Passage AA

1   *Summarizing.* D. Jurgis deals with the aftermath of his assault, which sees him arrested, charged with assault, and jailed; this leads to encounters with the law, other criminals, homeless people, and more importantly, his own thoughts. To view the passage as merely about a man's night in jail or dealing with regret misses the connection between the events and the impact of those events on the man. The narrator alludes to an injury, though this was merely a thought that Jurgis had, and did not take place.

2   *Text Structure.* B. The narrator proceeds to first describe Jurgis' arrest and jailing, then describes Jurgis' thoughts. There is no opinion or argument in these paragraphs, as the passage focuses primarily on the events surrounding Jurgis' arrest as well as the latter's thoughts and feelings.

3   *Close Reading.* A. The passage begins with Jurgis' arrest, descriptions of the policemen's blue uniforms, and the policemen who charge him with assault. Jurgis is then led to a cell.

4   *Arguments.* A. The narrator describes an injustice – the mistreatment of prisoners by the police – in the hopes that the reader will rally behind those being mistreated (in this case, Jurgis). The author's description of a miscarriage of justice is not intended to harden the reader against Jurgis or generate an understanding why the police act in such a way – in fact, the trivial nature of Jurgis' mistake is intended to cast an unfavorable light on the police.

5   *Main Ideas.* C. The paragraph describes Jurgis' cell, and tees up the setting for the rest of the passage. Jurgis' motivations are not revealed yet, and no comparison is made with another place. While Jurgis did put his face in his hands, a sign of how he is feeling, the real demonstration of his thoughts takes place in the third paragraph.

6   *Word Choice.* D. A wild beast that that has glutted itself is one that has eaten more than its fill. The narrator indicates that Jurgis was "in a dull stupor of satisfaction" and proceeds to describe how "his senses cleared" and he began to feel regretful. The simile itself compares Jurgis to such an animal, describing how Jurgis is filled with a deep sense of happiness and gratification at his actions. Jurgis is not described as being confused, only as feeling happy, and then having that happiness devolve into despair. There is nobody else jailed with Jurgis as of the third paragraph.

7   *Close Reading.* D. Jurgis' regret is fueled by the realization that Ona will lose her lodging and be unable to feed herself and her child. Jurgis would not feel the same regret if he did not care deeply about Ona, as he was, at first, very pleased with his actions.

8   *Relationships.* D. The reader knows that Jurgis was arrested for assault and battery, and can infer that the victim of his wrath was someone powerful (referred to as "the boss") who was hurting Ona. Jurgis had apparently attempted to help Ona by saving her from "the horrors that she had borne" and the "memory that would haunt her all her days." The narrator indicates that Jurgis was very respectful of policemen, especially when being jailed. Jurgis is confined with homeless people; the passage does not suggest that he himself is homeless. There is no indication that Jurgis was a thief.

9   *Point of View.* A. The narrator's tone is such that Jurgis does not truly belong in jail with a "drunken wife-beater" and "yelling maniac," feeling morally vindicated that he had done the right thing "the ends…throat" (lines 33-34). Jurgis panics at the consequences of his actions, and would likely not believe his punishment is reasonable given the hurt that had befallen Ona. Equally unlikely is the notion that he would be uncaring about his punishment – he cares very much as implied by the desperation in his thoughts: "what was to happen to him God only knew." The narrator mentions that Jurgis did not drink his coffee.

10   *Close Reading.* B. The smell of fertilizer keeps the other men in the wagon apart from Jurgis. From lines 57-61, the narrator describes how men whose breath smelled badly insult Jurgis for the smell that emanates from him. Thus Jurgis, not the wagon, police, or other men, smells of fertilizer,.

11   *Textual Evidence.* C. The description of how the breath of the homeless was fetid, yet the homeless "call down the torments of hell" upon Jurgis juxtaposes the stench of one against the other. This leads the reader to believe that earlier references to fertilizer smells are due to Jurgis.

12   *Words/Phrases in Context.* A. The word "fetid" describes something that smells extremely unpleasant. The reader knows this from context also because the men in the jail with Jurgis, who have bad breath, insult Jurgis for the way he smells. From this it can also be inferred that Jurgis smells like fertilizer.

13   *Purpose.* B. Jurgis' pacing and the description of how a "fiend" tears out "the strings of his heart" conveys a deep sadness – an anguish over the thoughts that he has grappled with all night. Jurgis regrets his actions and worries

The Tutorverse

about both his fate and Ona's. The reader can infer that Jurgis likely regrets his actions, but this regret may come short of true repentance, being driven primarily by his and Ona's fates. The passage does not suggest that Jurgis is only seeing part of the larger set of circumstances, as myopia would suggest. Any hate Jurgis has appears to have dissolved into worry and regret.

Passage BB

1   *Summarizing.* B. This is the best summary of the whole passage, which explains how scientists like Leclerc and Lamarck began to question the traditional biblical worldview and created their own ideas based on fossil evidence.

2   *Point of View.* C. The author of Passage 1 does not take sides on the matter discussed; she merely describes Leclerc's and Lamarck's theories and how those theories changed. The author does not use language characteristic of a persuasive passage (which an impassioned advocate or opinionated scientists might use), or write in a highly technical manner.

3   *Text Structure.* B. The fact that fossils of elephants were found in parts of the world where elephants did not live supported the conclusion that the elephants had migrated. This, and the example about how the skeletal structures of the animals were similar yet different show that Leclerc's ideas likely had some merit, even if they were not ultimately completely accurate.

4   *Purpose.* A. The example of giraffe's necks growing to reach higher leaves shows how Lamarck's ideas related to what he observed in nature. The author does not contrast Lamarck's ideas with Leclerc's, instead citing their similarities. The author does not take a stance on Lamarck's theory as ridiculous or fantastic.

5   *Close Reading.* C. The passage describes Leclerc's and Lamarck's ideas about the earth's history but implies the theories were not entirely accurate. In the last paragraph, the author mentions Darwin and states that Darwin studied Lamarck's work, which provided a stepping stone between the biblical view of the earth and the theory of evolution Darwin would later develop.

6   *Main Ideas.* D. The passage deals primarily with the idea that Darwin's travels helped him to formulate an idea, which later became a theory. That Darwin sailed and studied birds are just one aspect of the passage.

7   *Word Choice.* B. Each species has characteristics that are uniquely suited to the environment it lives in. For example, the beak shape of each finch is tailored toward the type of food it eats. While finches may have different coloring, the phrase is more general, introducing the idea that special traits help certain birds survive.

8   *Words/Phrases in Context.* D. The advantages Darwin described were physical traits that helped the finches, and other species, survive as their environment changed. The passage is primarily concerned with describing physical traits, as opposed to the random nature of good or bad opportunities.

9   *Relationships.* C. Darwin's views differed from earlier scientists' because Darwin thought adaptation came about over several generations, with species that had advantageous traits breeding with each other and passing those on to their offspring. This differs from the idea of spontaneous creation or a "nervous fluid." These species of finch were likely descended from one common ancestor.

10   *Main Ideas.* B. Both passages indicate that several scientists made discoveries and developed explanations for the history of life on earth, and several generations of scientists took previous conclusions and developed them further. Lamarck drew from Leclerc's work, and Darwin drew from Lamarck's and from the geology texts he read on the *Beagle*, for example.

11   *Multiple Texts.* B. Although Darwin uncovered evidence that did dispute a few of Lamarck's conclusions, Darwin more built on the work of the earlier scientists than directly refuted it. Collectively, these scientists were some of the first to come up with a non-biblical explanation for the history of life on earth, and both passages show a progression of ideas rather than one set of ideas contrasting with another.

12   *Arguments.* C. Lamarck and Darwin both share the view that traits can be passed on from one generation to another. However, they differ in that Lamarck credits a "nervous fluid" as a catalyst for changing traits, while Darwin's view was that these changes were merely the result of small differences across a population of animal – changes that compounded over time and across generations. Neither scientist viewed life as static or that it changes spontaneously.

13   *Textual Evidence.* D. Both scientists discuss the passing of traits on from one generation to the next. The other answer choices draw from other parts of the passage that do not support Lamarck's theories, or that support an incorrect answer choice from the previous question.

The Tutorverse

Passage CC

1   *Summarizing*. A. The passage is primarily concerned with describing the economic benefits of investing in infrastructure. The author mentions that American infrastructure must be improved – an idea that directly contradicts the notion that infrastructure is irrelevant. Though implicit in the author's argument, safety is not the primary concern of the passage.

2   *Main Ideas*. D. The passage describes several ways in which infrastructure development can stimulate the economy. The other answer choices either state facts contrary to evidence presented in the passage, or else focus in on only certain benefits to infrastructure development.

3   *Purpose*. D. The fact that these two groups came together in this setting and urged Congress to pass an adequate funding bill shows the need to fix the nation's grade D infrastructure. The two men were not proposing methods of funding, nor were they there with a blueprint for a bill.

4   *Quantitative Information*. C. The graph shows that as a percentage of the country's productivity, infrastructure spending has declined. This supports the statement made in lines 8-11. The graph does not illustrate why such spending would be politically contentious, or why investing in infrastructure is important to the future. The graph shows only infrastructure spending, and doesn't compare that spending with actual economic performance.

5   *Close Reading*. A. The paragraph is primarily concerned with discussing the impact of infrastructure development on jobs creation, and the benefits associated with those jobs. Transportation and luxury time are the focus of the third paragraph. The paragraph uses infrastructure development at the community level as an example, but does not make comparisons to infrastructure at the national level.

6   *Word Choice*. A. The author assumes that the reader is familiar with the idea that people such as engineers, construction workers, and people who harvest raw materials would be employed on infrastructure development projects. The use of the word "even" indicates that what follows might be surprising to some readers: that accountants, who typically don't work with their hands and work in office buildings, would also benefit from infrastructure job creation.

7   *Words/Phrases in Context*. C. A catalyst is something that causes something else to happen. In this case, the author uses the example of a new power plant to show how it can result in additional investment and growth within a community. In chemistry, a catalyst can be a chemical compound or substance, but in this case "compound" and "substance" don't accurately describe "power plant"; similarly, "incentive" mistakes the relationships between the cause and the effect – the incentive to creating a power plant are the additional businesses and services (and electricity) that will come as a result.

8   *Arguments*. B. The paragraph makes clear connections between money saved on vehicle maintenance and a family's ability to save money for other needs. This helps to strengthen the author's argument and explains how a concept as seemingly abstract as infrastructure development can have tangible results for everyday people.

9   *Textual Evidence*. B. It clearly illustrates the multiplier effect that can arise from new and improved infrastructure, notably a port, bridge, or a network of roads. The benefits for a city go beyond aiding business efficiency and productivity and job creation, and are pervasive throughout a community.

10   *Relationships*. B. Central to the author's argument are the manifold benefits that arise from investing in infrastructure. The building of a port is analogous to the building of a power plant. Though investment may lead to increased tax revenue, consumer spending, or property values, the author does little to draw a connection between these concepts.

11   *Text Structure*. C. Without specific examples and research, the author's argument would not be as strong. The examples help to show the reader real-world connections to the ideas presented. The author does not proposing infrastructure projects, nor is he concerned with explaining the government's point of view, per se. Vehicle operating cost savings and job creation are separate ideas supporting his central argument, not two ideas that are directly related.

12   *Purpose*. A. The author's arguments mirror closely Eisenhower's rationale for signing the Federal-Aid Highway Act. If one is to believe that the Act was successful in accomplishing what Eisenhower said, then one should also believe in the arguments set forth by the author.

13   *Point of View*. B. In his final address, Eisenhower connects a strong, efficient highway system with the needs of the population, economic expansion, and national security. According to the passage, Eisenhower took action by signing the Federal-Aid Highway Act of 1956, recognizing that there are many reasons for investing in infrastructure. While a president contends with many issues, clearly this action reflected the importance and high priority assigned to infrastructure.

The Tutorverse

Passage DD

1   *Text Structure*. C. Reagan's speech begins by describing the problem of communism vis-à-vis the division of Berlin. He goes on to explain why freedom has been proven by history to be better than totalitarianism, and ultimately calls on his Soviet counterpart to free his people.

2   *Summarizing*. C. Reagan's speech uses Berlin – a city split in half politically – as an example to compare the fruits of democracy and communism. The use of famous quotes enables Reagan to better make his point; they are not the primary or overarching focus of the passage. The passage culminates in a political challenge, but not before ideologies are compared and contrasted.

3   *Word Choice*. B. A scar is the result of an injury, in this case, an injury done to Berlin itself and to "freedom for all mankind." This metaphor helps to make Reagan's point more clear – that there was damage done to a city and a people, and that a reminder of it – the Berlin Wall – is symbolic of that damage. Reagan is hopeful that the wall will be dismantled (evidenced by his appeal to Gorbachev), which would represent a symbolic fading of the scar.

4   *Arguments*. A. Reagan says that "prosperity can…economic freedom" (lines 35-36). Freedom of speech is also discussed, but in context of truth and journalistic freedom. The prosperity in West Berlin happened in spite of its split from the East, not because of it.

5   *Close Reading*. B. Reagan implies that it is because of freedoms enshrined in the government that West Berlin was able to rebuild. von Weizsacker was mentioned earlier in the speech, but not in context of rebuilding. While support from the United States and unity against communism were most likely factors, Reagan's speech focuses primarily on government policies.

6   *Textual Evidence*. C. Reagan mentions that the rebuilding was done "in freedom," and precedes the paragraph in question with the notion that "other leaders…doubled" (lines 32-40). The other choices do not support the notion that freedoms guaranteed by government policies drove reconstruction.

7   *Purpose*. D. In using their native language, Reagan demonstrates respect for the Berliners' accomplishments. The joke itself applauds the positive qualities that have helped them rebuild – their courage and sense of humor, for example. Reagan adds a comment about the *schnauze,* which is a self-deprecating nod to the Berliner's macho attitude. Though Reagan remarks that the Soviets' did not count on such qualities, the joke is intended primarily to praise Berliners, not point out Soviet mistakes. If anything, such a statement would inflame, rather than defuse, tensions with the Soviet Union.

8   *Purpose*. B. By comparing a famous speech delivered by the leader of the Soviet Union to events that actually transpired, Reagan demonstrates how history has disproven the theory of communism. That such a confident prediction proved untrue speaks for itself; Reagan has no need to attack Khrushchev's personality or leadership ability. The use of the quote does not underscore Berlin's earlier suffering.

9   *Point of View*. D. Khrushchev, leader of the Soviet Union's Communist Party, would likely not have agreed that West Berlin was successful due to democracy, or freedom. While he may have wanted to claim that communism had a hand in West Berlin's success, such a claim would be unlikely, given the lack of influence communism had there. The reader can infer that Khrushchev would instead be dismissive of West Berlin's accomplishments.

10   *Relationships*. C. Reagan describes the failings of communism in order to show that an absence of freedom has negative consequences, much to the contrary of what Khrushchev predicted. Reagan was not congratulating West Berlin at the expense of East Berliners, nor was he congratulating communism on its achievements. That Reagan wished to inflame tensions is not supported by the passage.

11   *Textual Evidence*. B. Reagan follows his comments on the failings of communism with the conclusion that freedom has been proven by history, in practice, to lead to progress and prosperity. The other answer choices support incorrect answer choices in the previous question.

12   *Words/Phrases in Context*. B. From context the reader can tell that Reagan is questioning the authenticity of freedom surfacing in the Soviet Union. The sentence "or are…it" is a supposition: that the Soviets are not making real changes, but are doing things superficially. The only choice that makes sense is "misleading" – actions designed to "raise false hopes." "Perfunctory" instead suggests that the gestures were performed quickly, without effort; "vacuous" suggests that the gestures lack careful thought.

13   *Main Ideas*. C. The last paragraph famously challenges Gorbachev to approve the dismantling of the Berlin Wall and begin to open his regime to freedoms and liberties. The topics of freedom and peace are discussed, but not in context of being long-desired or something to be negotiated for.

The Tutorverse

Passage-Based Practice

Passage A

1   *Summarizing*. C. In the passage, Dr. Snow pursues his own theories and research. His thinking helped debunk the miasma theory and led to new practices and theories (such as epidemiology) that would save lives.

2   *Text Structure*. A. The passage begins by explaining conditions in London that led to the cholera outbreak and then explains how John Snow utilized a novel technique for mapping disease that both stopped the outbreak and is still used to track outbreaks today.

3   *Point of View*. C. The narrator of this article seems impartial, relating the events of the cholera outbreak and Snow's discovery without much bias. Snow himself was skeptical of conventional science of the era, but the narrator takes a more broad approach, including information about what people now know about cholera and how it spreads.

4   *Word Choice*. B. The author uses an alliterative device to convey the idea that cholera strikes quickly and is deadly if untreated. "Swiftly" describes the speed with which symptoms manifest, not how quickly the disease can spread. "Soundly" describes the dangerous symptoms that can lead in many cases to death.

5   *Words/Phrases in Context*. C. In this instance, exposure refers to someone coming into contact with cholera. Though exposure can refer to the taking of a risk, gaining of experience, or a point of view, these meanings are inappropriate in context of a disease.

6   *Close Reading*. B. Snow did not know the source of the outbreak, nor did he believe the conventional wisdom (i.e. miasma) adequately described the outbreak. His investigations were the result of this questioning of an assumption.

7   *Purpose*. A. The passage indicates that Snow was skeptical of the miasma theory of disease, which stated that bad air carried disease. Thus, he set about researching cholera victims to better understand how the outbreak spread.

8   *Words/Phrases in Context*. D. The text refers to the mechanism for disease transmission, or the natural process of disease traveling between people. In this case, the text is referring to Snow's skepticism that polluted air was the way (or process) that the disease was spreading.

9   *Relationships*. D. Snow did look at water under the microscope, but the analysis proved fruitless. Rather, learning from the victims, even those who did not live near the pump, got their water from the Broad Street helped convince Snow and local officials that the pump was the source of the outbreak.

10   *Main Ideas*. B. John Snow was able to discover the cause of the cholera outbreak through research and mapping, and his methods are still used today to study disease outbreaks. Thus, Snow's approach of looking for patterns to find the cause of disease is the main concept the author is trying to convey in the paragraph.

11   *Textual Evidence*. C. This shows that Snow's collection of data and creation of a visual model helped him identify the exact source of the outbreak, which meant local officials were able to shut down the water pump and stop the further spread of disease.

12   *Arguments*. B. The paragraph is primarily concerned with providing examples of Snow's investigative work. These examples demonstrate the logic behind Snow's assertions, and strengthen the idea that Snow's discoveries were pivotal in helping save lives.

13   *Quantitative Information*. D. Neither the graphic nor the passage indicate that the location of the cases of cholera led Snow or others to conclude that cause of cholera was bacteria. Instead, both the graphic and the passage suggest that Snow used the location of cholera cases to arrive at the conclusion that the cause of the outbreak had something to do with the water pump.

Passage B

1   *Text Structure*. C. The author first defines pop music and establishes its popularity and success in the first three paragraphs, then transitions to explaining why pop is so popular and successful. The author does not advance different arguments, or defend a particular point of view from countering points of view. The author does not use a personal anecdote.

2   *Purpose*. B. The author uses an example of a popular and successful song to demonstrate that pop as a genre is popular and success. The only musical concept described in the passage is a hook, which is described in paragraph five. The details of songwriting in the pop industry and the general explanation for the success of pop music is discussed in the latter half of the passage.

3   *Main Ideas*. B. The paragraph provides quantitative information supporting the notion that social media can demonstrate the success and popularity of pop music. The paragraph cites the number of Twitter follows and Youtube views of different pop stars and their songs. The paragraph does not provide information about money generated, or emphasize the competition between K-pop and American pop.

The Tutorverse

4   *Quantitative Information.* B. The graph displays information about entities followed on Twitter, not about Billboard's charts, or Youtube. The graph does not describe the lucrative nature of pop – merely it's popularity. It supports the notion that social media is a way to measure pop's popularity.

5   *Summarizing.* A. The paragraph discusses the concept of a musical hook, providing an explanation for what a hook is as well as its relevance to pop music. The author cites the source of this information. The paragraph does not raise questions about pop music's success, nor does it describe elements of pop music (beyond the hook).

6   *Close Reading.* C. The passage describes a hook as "those parts…heads" (lines 44-46). It then goes on to describe examples of a hook, and how they can be part of a melody, rhythm, or lyrics. The other answer choices are too specific, and would exclude other examples of hooks.

7   *Close Reading.* D. The author writes that listeners can "immediately find a different song" to listen to if they are uninterested in a song (lines 50-53). The author does not imply that listeners demand creativity; instead, the author suggests the opposite, as he cites information about how people do not appear to mind listening to songs that sound similar (lines 76-79).

8   *Words/Phrases in Context.* C. The paragraph goes on to explain how many pop songs sound very similar. Thus, the reader can infer from this sentence that the sameness of sound has permeated (spread throughout) the industry.

9   *Arguments.* A. The author suggests that many pop songs are not written by performers, but are instead written by a handful of songwriters. There is no argument advanced that *Thriller* is the template that pop songwriters follow, or that there is some requirement that pop songs contain similar hooks. The passage does not mention collaborations between performers.

10   *Textual Evidence.* C. This selection states that many popular songs used by different artists are written by the same people. This supports the previous question's answer. The other choices support incorrect answers to the previous question, or are unrelated to the issue of songs sounding the same.

11   *Word Choice.* B. The subsequent sentences describe how popular songs are analyzed and their most popular elements replicated. This results in the creation of more songs that sound similar and are similarly popular. The author implies in the last paragraph that this ability to create popular song after popular song is very lucrative. The formula – the knowledge of which elements of a song to use – is the key to creating popular and commercially successful songs.

12   *Relationships.* D. The ultimate aim of analyzing songs is to be able to produce new songs that are as successful – if not more so – than their predecessors. The passage alludes to this in the last paragraph, suggesting that "hundreds of million dollars" are on the line, and that songwriters have "found something that people like." Understanding why some songs are successful and others not is part of this process, but does not capture the ultimate goal of dissecting songs. The passage suggests that songs sound virtually identical in spite of copyright laws; thus the dissection of a song's key features does not pertain to ensuring that copyright laws are followed. Artistic integrity is not mentioned as an issue in the passage.

13   *Point of View.* D. The author maintains a neutral tone throughout the passage, raising questions and attempting to address them. Author does not advocate for any particular course of action, seeking instead to simply explain what he believes to be the facts. The author does not discuss obligations of songwriters or pop stars, or compare the integrity of songwriters and stars. Choice D represents the only statement which maintains a neutral tone, stating only facts.

Passage C

1   *Summarizing.* C. In the story, Sam and his friends are afraid of Mr. Rush. But when Sam gets injured, he learns that Mr. Rush is actually a nice man who is largely misunderstood by the community.

2   *Text Structure.* A is the best answer. At the beginning of the story, Sam has concern and fear about Mr. Rush, but over the course of the story, he learns what Mr. Rush is really like and changes his opinion. By the end of the story, Sam has vowed to change the way he behaves around Mr. Rush.

3   *Main Ideas.* C. At the surface, the story is about a man living in a small town. Running with a partner would have helped Sam when he injured his foot. However, the substance of the passage is about how words are powerful and how they can change someone's life – in this case, Mr. Rush.

4   *Close Reading.* B. The second paragraph says Mr. Rush is a ghost, which implies that he is invisible and rarely seen. The children in town avoid his house because they find him scary, but the reality is that they don't know much about him. The children in town are afraid of him, but most of the stories about him are made up, so he doesn't terrorize or haunt them.

5   *Textual Evidence.* A. The description of Mr. Rush as a ghost implies that, like a ghost, he is invisible or rarely seen. The evidence in the passage supports the idea that most of the reasons children have for being afraid are made up.

6   *Relationships*. D. Sam's experience after he falls shows him that he misjudged and probably did Mr. Rush wrong by spreading stories about him. The injury allows Sam to see Mr. Rush in a different light and change his opinion.

7   *Words/Phrases in Context*. C. "Intense" (not to be confused with "incense") refers to Sam's pain, which was so extreme that it prevented him from walking. Pain is not customarily described as invigorating or passionate – to do so would be to imply an incorrect connotation.

8   *Word Choice*. B. In the story, Sam is nervous at first because he's worried something bad will happen to him at Mr. Rush's house, but once he realized that Mr. Rush is a nice man and not as scary as he thought, Sam begins to feel guilty for the role he played in maligning Mr. Rush.

9   *Point of View*. B. The town of Smithfield generally seems to view Mr. Rush as a strange old man, and the children spread stories about him in order to scare each other. Therefore, the community's opinion of Mr. Rush is that he is uncertain and to be feared.

10   *Words/Phrases in Context*. C. Sam is using the word "vibrant" to describe the town of Smithfield, and he means that the town is lively and friendly, not that it is literally bright or colorful.

11   *Purpose*. B. The information is a little surprising, given what the reader knows about Mr. Rush to this point, but the fact that Mr. Rush has a son helps create sympathy from both Sam and the reader.

12   *Arguments*. A. In the context of the story, Mr. Rush is bemoaning the fact that the story a disgruntled student told about him has spawned a lot of other stories about him, and that people are more likely to believe the old, bad stories than the actual truth. This has had the effect of damaging his reputation.

13   *Close Reading*. D. At the end of the story, Sam vows to change what people say about Mr. Rush. Given his experience in the story and the fact that he tells Mr. Rush he seems like a nice man, it is likely that Sam will tell nice or positive stories about Mr. Rush instead of scary stories. He would not likely tell stories about someone else, given the lesson he learned from his experience.

Passage D

1   *Summarizing*. C. The passage lists a number of negative effects of the national debt, including taxation, corruption, and geographic conflict.

2   *Relationships*. C. The author of the first passage states that corruption of the legislature is the greatest threat to government, and that the current monetary system is contributing to it by allowing legislators to manipulate the law for personal gain.

3   *Words/Phrases in Context*. B. "Assumption" can have a number of meanings, but this line specifically refers to the national government assuming state government debt, which means that the national government is taking on the responsibility for paying off debts incurred by the states.

4   *Purpose*. B. The author argues one result of the federal government assuming the state debts is conflict between the state, which, in addition to the cycle of debt and the threat of corruption in the legislature, is another disastrous consequence of the current monetary system.

5   *Close Reading*. B. Though the author says that his hope is that representation changes during the next election, meaning some of the corrupt politicians will leave office, he also acknowledges that the election may not change much because the system itself is troubled. Thus, further reform is needed.

6   *Main Ideas*. A. The author argues in the first and last paragraphs that the act of the national government assuming the debts of the states has strengthened the union and is a vital part of maintaining it; before the assumption of state debts, there were thirteen different systems of finance in the country. The author argues that the simplified system is more efficient, and dismisses charges of corruption.

7   *Point of View*. B. The author of the second passage does little to address the allegations of corruption leveled against him. The use of the phrase "incorrectly insinuate" suggests that he believes the charges to be baseless, and by not addressing them directly, dismisses them entirely. The author is neither nervous nor does he think overly highly of himself.

8   *Text Structure*. B. The author makes a few general statements about the debt while also refuting specific arguments made by his opponents (for example, the importance of assuming state debts). He doesn't offer much specific evidence, but does make arguments and uses some logical explanation for why his views are valid.

9   *Word Choice*. A. The author uses this phrase to set up his next argument. He does not believe that it matters if the system is flawed or perfect; because eliminating or changing the system would have more disastrous consequences than leaving the original system in place, he argues that no changes to the system need be made.

10   *Main Ideas*. D. The authors disagree on whether the national debt is a good policy and whether it needs to be reformed or eliminated. However, it is implied that both view corruption in the government as a threat, they merely disagree on whether the national debt is a cause.

The Tutorverse

11 *Multiple Texts.* A. Passage 1 advocates eliminating the national debt because it causes corruption and conflict. Passage 2 advocates maintaining the national debt and specifically indicts the argument in Passage 1, arguing that the claims about corruption are untrue and that the national debt is key to a stable union. Passage 2 stops short of personally attacking the author of Passage 1, does not provide a solution to each of the issues pointed out in Passage 1, and is as general and sweeping as Passage 1.

12 *Arguments.* C. The author of Passage 1 argues that corruption in the legislature is the worst thing that can happen to a democracy, so he would likely argue that it is more important to eliminate the debt to stop the corruption than it is to maintain the country's reputation abroad. Furthermore, the author of Passage 1 uses the word "irredeemable" to describe the practice of owing debt to foreign countries.

13 *Textual Evidence.* D. The author says that there is no greater threat to democracy than corruption in the legislature. It can therefore be inferred that he would argue that this threat is greater than a loss of reputation.

Passage E

1 *Summarizing.* D. Choices A, B, and C are all specific elements that can be found at certain places in the passage, but only choice D summarizes what happens over the course of the entire passage.

2 *Text Structure.* A. The first parts of choices B and D do not occur in the passage. Choice C fails to capture the fact that Eleanora changes her mind.

3 *Point of View.* C. Eleanora appears to admire Agnes for her courage and for knowing what she wants; the passage does not suggest that she is jealous of Agnes. Similarly, the events of the passage show that Eleanora was in no rush to marry Lars. Eleanora deceives her mother about Agnes' letter. The passage is about Eleanora's indecision.

4 *Word Choice.* C. Eleanora knows Lars will do the right thing – the thing that is expected of him (that is, formally propose marriage before becoming more involved with Eleanora). In this passage, that has nothing to do with punctuality, work habits, or persistence.

5 *Relationships.* C. Eleanora is tempted by Agnes' letter but decides to accept Lars' proposal. The passage says nothing about Eleanora's bond with her father, nor her work ethic. Choice D is contradicted by Eleanora's decision.

6 *Purpose.* A. Choices B and D are details that add color to Agnes' description of her new life. Eleanora does not make a judgment as to whether or not the new life is good or bad – merely that it is a life that Agnes always seemed to want. Eleanora goes on to allude that she entertained the notion of going to America herself.

7 *Close Reading.* C. If Eleanora was so deeply in love with Lars, she would likely have let him propose to her (even though in the end she chooses to marry him). Instead, Eleanora toys with the idea of going to America, as reflected in lines 53-55. Eleanora admires Agnes, and thinks her brave for going to America alone and not getting married.

8 *Textual Evidence.* C. Eleanora wonders what it would be like to live in America, and considers that she has saved money she would use to pay for her passage. It can be inferred that Eleanora had difficulty choosing between going to America and marrying Lars.

9 *Close Reading.* B. Elenora's mother initially questions her about Lars. When that does not elicit the answer she is seeking, Mama follows up with a second question about what Lars might have said. There is no mention of Eleanora's traveling to America, nor of Mama's explicit disapproval of staying out too late. Agnes' letter is an afterthought that Mama does not pursue.

10 *Textual Evidence.* C. This is Mama's follow-up question, showing that she is anxious to learn if Lars "said something." In other words, did he propose? Choices A and B deal with Eleanor's fears that her mother would not approve of her staying out late. Choice D is not her mother's primary concern.

11 *Words/Phrases in Context.* B. Eleanora deliberately avoids telling her mother exactly what transpired with Lars. This section of the passage implies that Mama knows that Eleanora and Lars have feelings for each other. Mama advises Eleanora that she should not allow Lars to get physically and emotionally close unless there are plans for marriage.

12 *Arguments.* B. Eleanora desires to hide her temptation to travel to America from her mother. By lying about the contents of the letter from Agnes, Eleanora avoids a difficult conversation about America, especially since it appears that her mother supports the relationship with Lars.

13 *Main Ideas.* A. Burning the letter is a sign that Eleanora is rejecting the possibility of a new life in America, but not that Eleanora is angry with Agnes. The last line indicates Eleanora is ready to marry Lars.

Passage F

1 *Text Structure.* C. The author is concerned with explaining how the space program benefits society. He does so by answering commonly asked questions about why the space program benefits society, addressing the economy, national security, scientific value, etc.

2 *Main Ideas.* B. The author writes that, though there are immediate benefits of the space program (heart monitors, liquid oxygen, etc.), these short-term gains are not the true purpose of the space program. Instead, the author

The Tutorverse

encourages the reader to view benefits in the long-term "at a higher level" – "at a broader landscape." These longer term gains and spin-offs, he implies, are not easily named or determined (or, in the case of the answer choice, measurable).

3   *Quantitative Information.* B. The graph shows the number of shuttle launches plotted against the number of technological spin-offs. The graph does not show dollar value or otherwise of either the program or the spin-offs; it serves only to show that there exist spin-offs. The graph does not show that there are more spin-offs than launches (it shows the opposite of that).

4   *Close Reading.* B. The author writes, in the second paragraph, that the economic value is not known precisely, but that it extends to more than just specific parts of the economy involved in the space program. Nuts, bolts, and screws are all important, but the impact to the economy of improving quality and raising standards across all aspects of the industrial base is important. The author suggests that heart monitors are an example of a specific benefit, but that the true – broader – economic benefit is harder to define and affects the entire industrial base.

5   *Summarizing.* A. The author poses a question regarding the scientific value of the space program, and then answers it by using an analogy. This analogy implies that the value is long-term and so broad as to be unknowable at this time, as it has only been "a few years" since major scientific findings were discovered. The actual scientific concept of dark matter or energy is not explained, nor are statistics or anecdotes used to make the point.

6   *Words/Phrases in Context.* D. "Harness" as a verb means to control and make use of something, or else to literally put equipment on something. In context, the reader can infer that the author intends to use "harness" to mean "utilize," since he discusses things like electricity and fire – things that were once wild but that have since been controlled and used by people. "Domesticate" has a similar meaning, but is usually used to refer to animals.

7   *Arguments.* D. The author indicates that the understanding and utilizing natural phenomena is a long-term process with unknowably far-reaching implications. He cites fire and electricity - two powerful and fundamental phenomena – as examples of forces that have been tamed and put to use. The author does not use these phenomena to discuss military applications or suggest that the space program spend more energy on scientific pursuits.

8   *Point of View.* B. The author indicates that the ideal form of national security is a policy that is "well above having better guns and bombs" and "being so strong that no one wants to fight" one where nations desire to work with other nations. In other words, the ideal form of national security is to align with other nations on non-military interests, such as scientific or economic pursuits. This directly contradicts the other answer choice options.

9   *Textual Evidence.* D. The only appropriate answer choice discusses how there are non-military ways to ensure national security. The other answer choices are unrelated to this or other answer choices in the previous question.

10   *Purpose.* A. Lines 55-70 discuss the intangible qualities that are needed to run a space program. Chief among these are the delay of gratification (a focus on the long-term rather than the long-term) and the raising of standards of leadership, perseverance, and courage. It's placement in the passage, after outlining economic, scientific, and security related spin-offs, summarizes an even broader and farther reaching spin-off: the impact on people and on a society. The author does not use the paragraph to admonish Americans, or encourage them to abandon the space program for other pursuits; the author uses this paragraph to suggest the opposite be done.

11   *Word Choice.* A. Each question raised represents a common objection to the space program (i.e. it does not produce enough direct, tangible results). The effectiveness of the program is not called into question. The author does not accept doubts about the program, instead mounting a carefully composed response. Throughout the passage, the author minimizes the importance of quantifying spinoffs, instead suggesting that some value is not easily measured.

12   *Relationships.* B. The author repeatedly suggests, over the course of the passage, that the space program elevates a society – economically, scientifically, and geopolitically. The program requires discipline and determination – the ability to sacrifice for the future. These are the higher-order values discussed. The author does not discuss the historical role of the space program in terms of global status, or that it makes Americans feel "important."

13   *Point of View.* C. The author's point of view is that the space program is inherently about higher-level, longer-term values and benefits – short-term gains are secondary, though welcome. However, a requirement to focus on short-term gains would do a disservice to the program and sacrifice long-term gains.

Passage G

1   *Main Ideas.* D. The passage in general describes how there are different definitions of "success" when it comes to movies, and that horror movies are successful because of ingrained biological processes.

2   *Close Reading.* A. The first paragraph indicates that nine of the ten highest grossing movies of all time based on ticket sales are action/adventure movies (lines 4-6).

3   *Main Ideas.* C. The second paragraph introduces the idea of ROI and profit as a measure of movie success. The paragraph does not exempt movies from this measurement simply because movies are a form of art. Ticket sales

The Tutorverse

were discussed in the first paragraph. The author makes no claims about percentages other than the fact that higher ROI is better. One could have very high percentages that equate to very small amounts, for example.

4   *Purpose*. C. The third paragraph discusses how a list of "most successful" movies can look different if one considers ROI as opposed to ticket sales. The author does not take a stance on which is preferable, remaining unbiased in this regard.

5   *Word Choice*. D. The main idea of the passage does not concern the amount of money movies make, rather how biology factors into the success of horror movies. By posing questions here asking such questions, the author transitions from providing context – the definition of ROI, the amount of money made, etc. – into how biology relates to horror movies.

6   *Text Structure*. A. At first, the passage appears to be concerned with discussing the business of movies. However, the questions raised in the fifth paragraph suggest that the discussion is deeper than just the amount of money movies make. The sixth paragraph makes this clear, but suggesting that the answers to questions raised in the fifth might be answered in the later parts of the passage.

7   *Summarizing*. A. The sixth paragraph is the first paragraph to delve into biology, and discusses the flight-or-flight response and its impact on the body and mind.

8   *Words/Phrases in Context*. A. In this paragraph, the author describes how simply equating dopamine with pleasure is an oversimplification. The author does not make a judgement about the degree of this oversimplification (as calling it disgusting or repugnant would imply). By calling it a "gross" oversimplification, the reader can infer that this is a complete shortchanging of the complexity of the impact of dopamine. It is not an honest oversimplification.

9   *Arguments*. C. The paragraph is focused primarily on explaining how dopamine impacts the mind and body. The author uses the example of gambling to explain how emotions are affected by dopamine and expectations. This concept is referenced in the following paragraph, when the effect of dopamine on those who watch horror movies is described. The author does not include the example in order to compare gamblers with moviegoers, nor does the author mention ROI from a gambler's point of view.

10   *Relationships*. A. The passage indicates that "research suggests...body." This response, having been discussed at length in the preceding paragraphs, is essentially the "fight-or-flight response" mentioned in line 42 – the releasing of chemicals like dopamine, adrenaline, etc. The passage does not indicate the watchers of horror movies have an opinion on special effects, explosions, or action/adventure movies, nor does it suggest that the reason for watching horror movies is to confront one's fears.

11   *Textual Evidence*. B. The passage states that horror movies can act as a trigger for the release of hormones noted as part of the fight-or-flight response. The other selections support incorrect answer choices from the previous question.

12   *Point of View*. D. While the author does not advance a particular opinion on investing in different types of movies, the passage compares and contrasts two different views on defining the success of movies. The author would likely contradict his passage if he suggested that action/adventure movies are more profitable than horror movies. The passage does not discuss the price per ticket paid. While the author admits the science behind being scared is complicated, he does not suggest that the science is unclear.

13   *Quantitative Information*. B. The passage states that horror movies bring in less in terms of ticket sales, but are far more profitable than action movies. If there are five horror and five action/adventure movies displayed, the pattern that most fits this description is that movies 1-5 are action/adventure (showing high ticket sales but low profitability) and that movies 6-9 are horror (showing low ticket sales but high profitability).

Passage H

1   *Text Structure*. B. Mandela first describes the problem of apartheid with vivid imagery and an appeal to emotions. He cites various injustices and inequalities in order to support his accounting of the political situation. Mandela then goes on to explain what must be done – that Africans must be seen as equal under the law – and supports this theory by refuting anticipated rebuttals and using logic to justify the stability and validity of the idea. Mandela does not spend time debating specific policies, instead focusing on the overarching changes that equality will bring.

2   *Main Ideas*. A. Mandela's primary aim is to illustrate why racial equality is necessary and achievable. Rather than focus on specific policies, Mandela advocates for "a just share...society" (lines 44-46). He does not advocate for secession, nor that white South Africans simply be nicer.

3   *Point of View*. D. Mandela suggests that "whites tend to regard Africans as a separate breed" and goes on to show examples that imply that the white South Africans look down on the black South Africans.

4   *Summarizing*. B. Racially motivated injustices are sandwiched between two demands: that Africans' "legitimate grievances" be met and that Africans should have "a just share in the whole of South Africa." Though this passage discusses the reason for the widespread injustices (the government's racially exclusive policies) and condemns them, the demands are a critical aspect of the paragraph.

The Tutorverse

5   *Arguments*. A. The injustices described are already happening, and are not contingent on failing to achieve political and social equality. Mandela uses these examples to advance his argument, as the injustices should enrage all people, regardless of ethnicity or skin color. The injustices exist because the politically powerful white South Africans view blacks as a separate breed (according to Mandela), not as a reason why this view exists.

6   *Relationships*. C. The paragraph indicates that the government's labor bureau controls the jobs that the Africans can have. Like other injustices, this control extends from the government's policies. Mandela indicates that the Africans want to work in jobs that they are most suited for. The passage does not indicate that a lack of education is the cause for work assignments. The disabilities described are not physical in nature, that would prevent someone from working; rather they refer to political disadvantage.

7   *Textual Evidence*. C. Mandela states that Africans must work in jobs based solely on the labor bureau's pleasure, not based on ability or preference. The other answer choices support incorrect answer choices from the previous question, or misinterpret the cited lines.

8   *Words/Phrases in Context*. D. As used in context, Mandela refers to all of the inequalities and injustices due to formal government segregation as disabilities – that is, the disadvantages in society and in economy arising from political segregation, as well. Mandela does not use "disabilities" in the sense of physical incapacity, or in the sense that the lack of political power arises as an allowance or mere philosophical difference.

9   *Arguments*. C. Mandela writes that "It is…domination" (lines 55-57). Mandela claims that in an equal society, no one race will dominate the other – there will be fair representation. Mandela does not hint at further violence or fighting.

10   *Textual Evidence*. C. In the fourth paragraph, Mandela anticipates and counters a widespread fear. He argues that the "enfranchisement of all" will not result in racial domination, going on to say that the ANC has fought against racialism, suggesting that it will not carry out "reverse-racialism" if the cause of equality is won.

11   *Close Reading*. D. The passage does not suggest that the ANC is looking to secede from the rest of the country, nor does the ANC seek to overthrow the government. Mandela indicates that though overthrow is a fear, it is something the ANC does not support as it has "spent half a century fighting against racialism." The ANC instead supports equality, as emphasized in the second paragraph.

12   *Word Choice*. B. Rather than simply saying that racial domination of political power is bad, repeating the colors at odds – blacks and whites – emphasizes that neither side should be able to dominate the other. Equality is the only path forward. The other answer choices are contradictory to information presented in the passage.

13   *Purpose*. C. That Mandela indicates that he is willing to die for his cause is not intended to request a guilty verdict or death penalty; instead, Mandela's final thoughts in this passage are designed to show that no matter what the government does to him, he will not recant his beliefs. Mandela does not actively seek martyrdom, but is willing to accept it if necessary.

Passage I

1   *Summarizing*. C. In the story, a man and his granddaughter visit a zoo whereupon the grandfather relates a parable about elephants that enlightens his granddaughter as to the nature of truth. Priya's attitude toward the story changes over the course of the passage, as does her understanding of truth.

2   *Text Structure*. B. The author of the passage relates the story through Grandfather's conversation with Priya while at the zoo. While Priya may have found some parts amusing, the passage suggests that she was curious and intrigued near the end of Grandfather's story. Though the purpose of the story was to teach a lesson, that lesson was not analyzed or refuted in Priya's conversation with Grandfather.

3   *Main Ideas*. B. Different physiological features are described in Grandfather's story, but these features are used to illustrate a broader point – that truth is in the eye of the beholder (i.e. that truth is subjective). While the story may or may not be representative of ancient Indian culture, it certainly refrains from describing methods for winning an argument.

4   *Point of View*. D. Priya thinks he is "full of old stories," implying he tells a lot of stories. Priya also rolls her eyes, implying that she thinks the story is silly. Priya doesn't understand the wisdom of the story until the end of the passage, nor does she become curious until later on in the story. The passage does not suggest that the stories are boring or annoying.

5   *Textual Evidence*. B. Priya's laughter and her description of grandfather as being full of old stories indicates that Grandfather tells a lot of stories and Priya finds most of them silly or humorous.

6   *Words/Phrases in Context*. D. An absolute truth is a truth without qualification, adulterations, or restrictions – it is a conclusive truth. In this case, Grandfather means that the men assumed the truth as they understood it was the only truth possible. In context, "unrestricted" does not have quite the same meaning as "conclusive."

The Tutorverse

7   *Close Reading.* C. The king wanted to show that not everyone perceives the world in the same way, so truth is not absolute. The king anticipated that blind men would illustrate his point; the passage does not indicate that the blind men used heightened sense, or that they were particularly wise.

8   *Word Choice.* A. In the story, the king repeats "This is an elephant" to make sure all of the men gathered understand that he is showing them an elephant. The king does so because he knows that they will, later on in the story, illustrate his point: that each blind man saw the truth as something different.

9   *Words/Phrases in Context.* B. The elephant is meandering through its zoo enclosure, which in context means it is walking at a slow or leisurely pace.

10   *Arguments.* A. Grandfather shows Priya, through the parable of the blind men and the elephant, that truth is a matter of perspective. Grandfather's story does not illustrate that truth is singular, elusive, or unobtainable.

11   *Textual Evidence.* D. In lines 63-74, the passage describes how each of the blind men came to their conclusions. The passage indicates that those blind men who had touched the tusks believed the elephant to be hard like a spear.

12   *Relationships.* A. The point of the contrasting how each blind man described the elephant is to show that none of them were wrong, but their understanding of the elephant was different from each other. This further serves to contrast the idea that the blind men couldn't see the elephant but each felt he knew the truth of what the elephant looked like. This supports Grandfather's claim that truth is relative and not absolute.

13   *Textual Evidence.* D. Choices A and B show that Priya does not take her grandfather seriously, as she laughs and humors him. The excerpt in choice C takes place at a point in the passage when she doesn't quite understand the story yet, and is still working through understanding the point of Grandfather's story. But in choice D, Priya not only recognizes the moral of the story, but is interested in learning more.

Passage J

1   *Text Structure.* C. The author recounts personal observation, though this is framed within the context of disproving widely held beliefs about the "horror, panic, dread, terror" plaguing San Francisco after the disaster. The author's focus essentially remains unchanged, focusing on describing events rather than explaining a theory or making an argument.

2   *Point of View.* C. The author's primary contention with East coast newspapers is with their "describing the effect of the extraordinary disaster" on the population. The author does not discuss the cause of the fire, and does not contend the impact of the quake on the city. Instead, the author's contention is that people have not reacted as poorly as the press would have them suggest.

3   *Textual Evidence.* B. The selection points to the author's suggestion that the press' view of how people have reacted and their behavior is not quite complete or accurate. The author here suggests the opposite – that people have in fact well and that there is no "despair" on any face.

4   *Words/Phrases in Context.* A. The passage discusses how a "mass of people" are dealing with the disaster with "passionate energy." The sentence is specifically concerned with what "spirit" is causing those people to live with such energy – what drive, or motivation, causes the energy.

5   *Summarizing.* B. The author's descriptions are vivid and personal, describing her own point of view of the disaster. These observations help to set the scene for the rest of the passage and ultimately serve to establish why the perseverance of the people is so impressive and great. The author does not here revile people's behavior.

6   *Relationships.* D. The author attributes the crumbling walls to "the puff of wind" (line 23).

7   *Words/Phrases in Context.* C. "Furious" generally refers to a state of anger, but can also refer to an intense state. In this case, while it may seem logical that people suffering from an earthquake may be angry, it is more reasonable to suggest that "furious" is used to refer to the intensity of people's efforts to save their possessions and loved ones.

8   *Word Choice.* D. By using a metaphor likely recognized by many readers, the author elegantly illustrates the frantic and urgent comings and goings of people after the disaster. The author does not propose to demean, condemn or downplay – merely to explain as best she can what she saw.

9   *Arguments.* A. The author includes these examples of people helping other people to show that there is no selfishness – no giving in to "panic" and "dread" mentioned by newspapers. Instead, people have risen to the occasion to help others, even in the face of "horrors" and "terror." The author does not compare normal citizens with soldiers, or here compare people with ants (as done in the preceding paragraph). The difficulty of suffering has already been established, and though this also serves that purpose, the fact that people are persevering is central.

10   *Close Reading.* C. The author writes that the though there was "no way to exaggerate the extraordinary pain [and] hardship," the people have displayed "heroism, ingenuity…devotion" (lines 72-77). The author does not mention anywhere looting/anarchy. The author also does not mention the fact that the people have remained "calm and collected," instead pointing to the "furious effort" (line 42) put into saving life and possessions.

The Tutorverse

11   *Purpose.* D. The author begins the passage by stating that the press (newspaper media) report on the "horror, panic, dread, terror" of the earthquake. However, by line 77, the author has demonstrated that the city has not completely fallen to those negative qualities. The author does acknowledge that there are "horrors" and "terrors" (the burning of the city described in the second paragraph), as do the newspapers. However, the author also points out that the people have responded very well, in light of the circumstances, and not as the newspapers would have everyone believe.

12   *Main Ideas.* B. In context of the broader passage, the author is attempting to show that the suffering in San Francisco has actually brought out the best in people – their "kindness, the magnanimity" etc. The quote from the soldier is used to emphasize this point – that despite much suffering, which alone is horrible, people have prevailed and helped one another through and not resorted to violence, looting, or descended into chaos. The soldier dismisses the monetary cost.

13   *Quantitative Information.* A. The author does not provide a comparison of the 1906 earthquake with other earthquakes, nor does she quantify the intensity of the 1906 quake. The passage is not concerned with debating the intensity of earthquakes, and no data is cited in the passage. The passage focuses primarily on describing the human impact of the quake.

Passage K

1   *Summarizing.* C. Hobbes wrote, "The subjects…cannot cast off monarchy," without adding "as long as he rules wisely." A monarch's power is indissoluble. He does not describe the process whereby the sovereign receives his power.

2   *Text Structure.* B. Hobbes' early writings emphasized that the king's rule was absolute and indissoluble. After the revolution established a Commonwealth, Hobbes justified the absolute rule of the new head of government.

3   *Word Choice.* A. The speech fits in with Hobbes' early belief that a subject-sovereign relationship is the only acceptable form of government. Charles contends that if he had given in to Parliament, he would betray the subjects he has an obligation to lead. He is not really arguing that he should not be executed, nor is he claiming that his lack of fear is due to his position as king. It is not implied that he is seeking to avoid execution by reasoning with the crowd.

4   *Purpose.* C. When Hobbes originally developed his philosophy, the king was the sovereign and held the "absolute power." After the Commonwealth was established, Hobbes saw that power had shifted and adjusted his philosophy accordingly. The later theory is partially consistent with the earlier theory, in that people must submit to some ruling power. There is no evidence in the passage to support choices A or D.

5   *Close Reading.* B. The author of the passage does not imply any significant changes in Locke's philosophy, not mentioning anything about what Locke experienced while in the Netherlands. There is no mention that Locke's views varied based on the ruler. Locke himself did not encourage colonists to rebel, even though the latter were inspired by his philosophy.

6   *Close Reading.* A. Locke's early years saw radical changes in government, leading to his view that the form of government need not be permanent. His father, a Parliamentarian, may have influenced his theory that people ought fight for their "natural rights." The author of Passage 2 does not mention Hobbes directly, nor does it suggest that Locke was particularly patriotic.

7   *Textual Evidence.* A. Lines 55-59 show the rapid changes in Locke's youth, and imply that he learned to view governmental change as normal. Lines 69-71 describe the initial premise of Locke's ideas. Lines 80-82 do not relate to Locke's views. Lines 88-90 do not deal with events in Locke's lifetime.

8   *Point of View.* D. Locke envisioned and experienced revolutions that changed the ruler or the form of government, not the separation of one part of the country from another. The passage previously states that Locke believed the people have a right to rebel if their natural rights were being infringed upon.

9   *Words/Phrases in Context.* B. From the context, the reader can tell that Locke's ideas were a strong influence on Thomas Jefferson and others who wrote the American Declaration of Independence, the formal starting point of the American Revolution.

10   *Relationships.* C. Hobbes' views in Passage 1 differ sharply from Locke's views in Passage 2. The views described in Passage 1 were developed before the ones in Passage 2, not after. Though the views in each passage are different, they do not specifically refer to each other.

11   *Main Ideas.* C. Neither passage discusses whether or not a monarchy should be inherited, or whether or not people would survive without any government. Instead, both passages discuss the relationship between people and a government. Though Hobbes would likely have argued that a ruler not be subject to the death penalty, the reader doesn't have enough information about how Locke would treat the situation to know whether or not he would disagree. The reader does know that Hobbes believed the power of the sovereign or state to be absolute, while Locke did not (arguing that people had the right to rebel).

12   *Arguments*. B. Hobbes felt that for a government to be effective it should have total power. He would not likely have agreed to a division of power under any circumstances.

13   *Arguments*. C. Hobbes' early theory was that the only way for a society to function was under the rule of a monarch. Locke, however, disagreed, and said that it would be appropriate to overthrow a ruler if that ruler violated the people's rights (lines 75-79). Locke may have witnessed the restoration of a monarchy, may have supported Parliament, and did say that people had natural rights, but it is illogical to assume that Locke would respond to an argument in favor of monarchy with such statements.

Passage L

1   *Main Ideas*. A. The passage appeals to reason and emotion in order to incite the reader to rally behind supporting women's voting rights. The allusion to the fact that women could do more serves to underscore the broader point that women must rally to their own cause. Similarly, the objection raised at the very end of the passage is used as an example of what must be proven wrong, not that it has been proven wrong by the passage itself.

2   *Summarizing*. C. The passage conveys a sense of impatience and frustration, yet balances such negative feelings with determination. The setbacks described in the passage, such as lack of political and judicial support, and lack of unity and action on the part of women themselves, are not described in such a way as to be brooding (or self-piteous). Instead, they are used to illustrate the absurdity of such setbacks and create a sense of frustration and impatience. There is an undertone of hope and determination regarding the future of women's rights.

3   *Text Structure*. D. The passage describes the problem of women's political equality. This problem and the efforts made to remedy it are the subject of the first several paragraphs. The remaining paragraphs of the text relate to the solution, discussing the actions that must be taken and providing the reason why they are appropriate. The passage does not describe a debate between parties.

4   *Point of View*. B. The passage urges "women...pending" (lines 19-22). This suggests that the moral or philosophical rationale for women's rights aligns with the rights of race-based rights – that "the Constitution...rights" (lines 57-60). The author appears to have a low opinion of the courts, as indicated in fourth paragraph, and would not likely leave an important issue such as racial equality to the judiciary.

5   *Close Reading*. B. The passage describes how Sumner supported abolishing slavery, and welcomed the help of women to do so. It also describes how, when approached by women to secure rights for women, he would not help. From this the reader can imply that the author feels betrayed, and that Sumner's were unacceptable. Sumner's actions were not insincere or tentative; they were, to the author, deliberate. His refusal to help can be seen as a hypocrisy; supporting one cause of equality but not another.

6   *Textual Evidence*. D. Choices A is unrelated to the matter of Senator Sumner. Choice B showcases women's support of racial equality. Choice C describes how Sumner was happy to receive the help of women. Only choice D describes how Sumner refused to support women's political rights, even after fighting to secure the rights of slaves.

7   *Purpose*. D. The questions follow a brief discussion on the 13th amendment and racial equality attained. The author compares the plight of women in the present to the plight of the slaves years ago. The questions are designed in such a way as to lead the reader to the conclusion that there is no essential difference between the two forms of equality. The author would not be casting doubt on racial equality, having previously implied support for it.

8   *Relationships*. D. The author does not suggest voting for judges (judges are appointed), but rather wants women to form a petition demanding equal treatment under the Constitution. The author cites paying taxes as a reason for fair treatment, but does not imply that taxes go unpaid. Prayer is, according to the author, less effective than the right to vote – therefore an incentive to win the vote.

9   *Arguments*. A. The examples imply that women will have a voice in reforming such problems if the petition is successful. The examples are used as a technique to convince the reader of the emotional and logical reasonableness of the arguments advanced in the passage. The petition seeks to win women the right to vote, not to explicitly end the problems highlighted. The issues raised are pandemic to the nation, according to the author, and are not isolated to particular places.

10   *Words/Phrases in Context*. B. In context, the author describes how women need political power in order to "convert opinions into law." The author downplays the significance of means traditionally available to women – "praying, tears, psalm-singing" – suggesting that they are virtually useless next to the right to vote.

11   *Quantitative Information*. C. The graph illustrate the total and female populations in the United States over time. The graph shows, indirectly, that women account for almost exactly half of the population. The graph does not show national debt, responsibility for raising children, or petition signatures.

The Tutorverse

12　*Word Choice.* D. "Echo and re-echo" does not refer to the actual sound of women shouting. Instead it symbolizes the reverberation through society of the ideas set forth in the passage and embodied in the petition. No doubt women would be encouraged to sign the petition, and no doubt that the rationales in the passage will be popularized. Only "with united voice" would women be able to garner power enough that will change the political landscape of the whole country.

13　*Arguments.* A. The author anticipates the objection that "women do not want to vote" and knows that a large petition will prove otherwise. The author argues that the objection ignores women's voice, and the only way to voice women's opinions is through a petition.

Passage M

1　*Summarizing.* B. Rose addresses Dr. Alec as "uncle" throughout the passage, so we know that the two are related. The passage is primarily comprised of dialogue – a conversation between Dr. Alec and Rose. The passage does suggest that the dialogue is particularly painful. Instead, there are allusions to the fact that there is a lightheartedness about the conversation – Dr. Alec's laughter, for example. The passage does not implicitly or explicitly state that Rose is Dr. Alec's patient. And while it would appear that Dr. Alec and Rose have different points of view on certain matters, there is no evidence to suggest a debate or argument.

2　*Text Structure.* D. Over the course of the passage, Rose reacts in different ways toward Dr. Alec. At first, when asked about her vanity, Rose answers "meekly." When told that she should emulate Phebe, she becomes shocked and disbelieving, going on to suggest that Dr. Alec is in fact quite strange. However, by the end of the passage, Rose seeks to gain Dr. Alec's approval, hoping to prove her ability to outperform Phebe.

3　*Point of View.* C. The passage indicates that Dr. Alec "laughed in spite of himself" (line 14) and "sighed as if grieved" when Rose admitted to being vain. The tone of the confession and subsequent exchange is lighthearted, though the topic is serious. Dr. Alec uses Rose's own word ("repulsive") not in a serious way, but in an endearing way that allows him to impart some advice and discuss the subject of beauty.

4　*Arguments.* C. Dr. Alec, in lines 20-26, encourages Rose to emulate Phebe precisely because Phebe is from "the poorhouse" (and, we can infer, has little material wealth) yet still is vivacious both in spirit and in body. The passage does not suggest that Dr. Alec believes beauty to be a matter of material wealth, nor does it suggest that beauty is owed to superficial things like gift-giving. Instead, Dr. Alec states that "a happy soul in a healthy body" is all that is required for beauty.

5　*Textual Evidence.* B. Dr. Alec explicitly mentions physical health and a positive disposition as being the most important qualities of beauty. Choice A refers simply to Dr. Alec's comparison of Rose to Phebes. While hard work does play a role in Dr. Alec's definition of beauty (at least as it relates to physical health), it is not a "requirement," per se. Choice D refers to Dr. Alec's gift giving, but not in context of beauty.

6　*Words/Phrases in Context.* A. Earlier in the paragraph, we are told that Rose was "much taken down" by the comparison between her and Phebe. In the following paragraphs, we can tell that Rose addresses Dr. Alec with some irritation and sarcasm in her tone. Rose is irritated and annoyed by the fact that Dr. Alec not only compared her to Phebe, but also praised Phebe.

7　*Purpose.* D. At this point in the passage, the author has established not only Dr. Alec's theory about beauty, but also how Rose reacts to this theory. By providing an example of Phebe singing while working, Dr. Alec emphasizes to Rose specifically how Phebe emulates the qualities of a healthy body and a "happy soul."

8　*Close Reading.* C. We can infer based on the way Rose talks about Phebe that the former does not respect the latter. In line 18, Rose reacts in a shocked way that causes Dr. Alec to almost break out in laughter. We know from line 27 that Rose felt "taken down" when compared with Phebe, which is from the poorhouse. We also know that Rose challenges Dr. Alec's advice to emulate Phebe by listing in a condescending way the different attributes she associates with Phebe: doing manual labor, wearing old, ugly clothes, etc.

9　*Words/Phrases in Context.* A. After being somewhat rebuffed by her uncle (who had advised her to be more like Phebe), Rose is apparently eager to help her uncle to prove that she can display the qualities that her uncle praised in Phebe. This is echoed in the final paragraph of the passage, though she does not, according to the passage, have the opportunity to prove these qualities to her uncle quite yet.

10　*Relationships.* D. The conversation between Rose and Dr. Alec revolves around the notion of vanity and beauty. Dr. Alec asks Rose if she feels that she is vain – the first of many hints that he does not know her very well. There is concrete evidence to support this notion as described in the following question and answer explanation.

11　*Textual Evidence.* C. It becomes clear in lines 40-48 that Rose and Dr. Alec do not know each other very well, as Rose is clearly off-put by the things that Dr. Alec was saying. Dr. Alec goes on to say that he hasn't "begun to show [his] oddities yet," which implies that he and Rose are still getting to know each other.

The Tutorverse

12 *Main Ideas.* C. Rose's reaction to her conversation with Dr. Alec is made apparent throughout the passage. Here, in lines 46-48, Rose reacts not only to the culmination of her conversation with Dr. Alec about vanity, beauty, and Phebe, but also to Dr. Alec's reaction to their conversation. Rose takes much of her conversation with Dr. Alec seriously, as we find out that she was saved (by a bell) from displaying yet more of how shaken she is by her conversation. She was glad that she would not give away more about how much the conversation has influenced her thinking.

13 *Word Choice.* A. Though Rose is on her way to receive her gift, the phrase "so now!" does not underscore her vanity. Instead, in context, we know that Rose is trying to earn Dr. Alec's respect and favor, and that she wants to prove her ability to not just be like Phebe in some ways, but to be "more than" Phebe. This shows determination to impress Dr. Alec, not a disdain for his theories nor a personality that cannot be improved upon.

Passage N

1 *Text Structure.* B. Addams here presents her view of social ethics: that social experience and empathy is necessary to the advancement of a democratic society. She first sets out what the theory is, why it is important, and proceeds to support her theory. She explains how to develop social empathy, why a lack of empathy is detrimental, and how social empathy can help society. There is little debate or consideration given to opposing views; Addams has not changed her mind by the end of the passage.

2 *Word Choice.* B. Addams uses a metaphor of travelling on different roads to illustrate different ways to being part of a society. She compares traveling on a "sequestered byway" – on a road that is secluded from other roads – to travelling on a busy and commonly traversed way. In context of a society and the passage, traveling on a secluded road would be akin to living a life apart from other in society, not caring about the welfare of others. Addams does not intend this phrase to be actual travelling advice.

3 *Summarizing.* D. In this paragraph, Addams refines her theory further, explaining the benefits of social contact: that it can correct opinions regarding "social order" and how best to improve society; that it leads to a moral understanding of humanity, rather than an academic understanding. Addams does not in this paragraph describe whether moral or intellectual understanding is greater, or that social experience and contact will lead to intellectual understanding; the two are different, to Addams. The role of newspapers are discussed in the third paragraph.

4 *Purpose.* D. In the second paragraph, Addams describes how the desire to understand a "wider and more thorough human experience" is naturally occurring. This results in at least two examples of services that cater to this desire: newspapers and novels. Though Addams would certainly suggest that reading is a good place to start, she would likely suggest that this comes short actual, first-person experiences. There is no evidence to suggest that Addams wrote the passage to help sell books or papers.

5 *Arguments.* C. Addams writes that novels deal with "life under all possible conditions" and they are read because they are entertaining, but also because they help develop a wider perspective on society and how or why to fix social problems. Addams is mum on the effectiveness of authors, and stops short of saying that books are "better" than newspapers. Though entertainment is certainly a factor, Addams does not mention that distraction is the same thing – or that it would be particularly beneficial.

6 *Relationships.* A. Addams writes that it is "lack of imagination which prevents a realization of the experiences of other people." This translates to a lack of social understanding and empathy. Moral obligations are mentioned, but not in context of difficulties in the world.

7 *Relationships.* B. Addams writes that if people "consciously limit" their interactions, they will limit the richness of their lives and the scope of their ethics (lines 56-62). Such limitations preclude the accepting of a wide range of different people, though doing so does not preclude a rich or life full of love.

8 *Close Reading.* A. In lines 68-71, Addams indicates that selfish people "refuse to be bound by any relation save" those that they already identify with, stating also that this leads to a narrow view on the world. In this excerpt, "save" means "except for" and "relation" refers to a connection or relationship. Thus, selfish people do not care about people with different creeds or opinions – or, more simply, beliefs.

9 *Textual Evidence.* B. As explained above, selfish people do not care about ideas "save" those to which they already subscribe. The other answer choices do not pertain to the topic of who selfish people (do not) care about.

10 *Point of View.* B. Addams submits that the selfish person considers only his or her subscribed to beliefs, and has a narrow worldview. Therefore, it is unlikely that the person would consider other people in his or her decision making.

11 *Main Ideas.* C. The last paragraph of the passage summarizes Addams' primary idea: that social ethics is necessary in guiding government and policy making. The only way to advance democracy is to understand the lives of its constituents, and then to act upon that understanding. The passage and paragraph do not discuss the role of

The Tutorverse

intellectual ethics or suggest that "the truth" can be found in different places. The metaphor of the crowd is used to illustrate the point, and is not to be taken literally.

12   *Words/Phrases in Context.* D. In this metaphor, Addams compares human experience to a well that provides sustenance for the human journey. Anything less than the sustenance provided by the well of human experience – anything "less potent" or "daintier" – will not suffice. The passage implies that drinking from the well of experience is not as easy as simply keeping a narrow mind.

13   *Word Choice.* D. Social ethics refers to the way in which people treat one another, sometimes embodied in laws and sometimes not. Social ethics can influence a democracy's policies because the government itself represents the people's ethics. Social ethics are shaped by experiences, but is not itself an experience. The equality of different classes of people may derive from tolerant social ethics, but does not itself embody social ethics. Similarly, customs and traditions spring from social ethics, but are not themselves social ethics.

Passage O

1   *Text Structure.* B. The author's reaction toward the scenery is complicated. There are times when the author is filled with a sense of wonder, and times when he forgets everything but the beautify before him. At times, the author alludes to actually being anxious or nervous, but his concerns do not devolve into fear, dread, or actual terror. Instead, the tone of the passage is overwhelmingly positive.

2   *Main Ideas.* D. The author's primary purpose in this paragraph is to establish that the scene he views is overwhelmingly beautiful, despite a "sense of danger." This "sense" cannot be interpreted as actually being in danger. The author is not actually inarticulate – he merely uses the notion of being unable to describe "to another the sensations inspired" by his view as a way to emphasize the beauty.

3   *Words/Phrases in Context.* A. The paragraph describes the author's reaction to the scenery. Phrases such as "my helplessness" and "inability to cope with or even comprehend the mighty architecture of nature" suggest that "terrible" most nearly means "awe-inspiring." "Terrible" has multiple meanings, two of which are "unpleasant" and "serious" – but in this case, "awe-inspiring" fits best.

4   *Purpose.* C. The author communicates a deep, visceral sensation of vertigo – an unsettling feeling hardwired into people. By describing this basic feeling – the overpowering fear and how color drains from the face – the author helps the reader to better understand his own sensations and experiences.

5   *Summarizing.* C. This paragraph is concerned primarily with describing the two waterfalls and how they fit into the scenery. The author describes how "without them would be the most gloomy and horrible solitude in nature." He also mentions how "the stillness…broken by the uproar of waters." This paragraph does not discuss dangerous circumstances, nor does it call on the reader to visit Yellowstone explicitly. The falls are described in more detail in later paragraphs.

6   *Word Choice.* C. The paragraph introduces the two waterfalls both in appearance and in sound. The author likens the sound of the waterfalls (that happen to echo through the canyon walls, not emanate from the canyon walls) to an anthem – a song that helps to imbue "life, power, light and majesty" to the surrounding area.

7   *Word Choice.* D. By using action verbs such as "aware" that are normally associated with conscious beings (like people), the author helps to create a sense of drama in his writing. Without the literary device, the sentence would be less engaging, instead being a mere retelling of facts. Earlier examples of this literary device evoke a sense of wonder, but this example focuses on action and drama.

8   *Relationships.* C. The paragraph describes how the water, once peaceful, turns into rapids because of the rocks that are near the fall's edge. The passage does not mention bears or trout except in passing in earlier paragraphs. There is also no mention of excessive vegetation.

9   *Textual Evidence.* C. The "rocky jaws" are described as converging as the river narrows toward the falls, which appear to crowd the water, which "struggles and leaps" and wars with "the impatience of restraint." This best supports the idea that the river narrows and passes over rocks which cause it to no longer be smooth an placid, instead rough and turbulent.

10   *Point of View.* C. The author does not suggest that people should pay to view the waterfalls, or that money should be made from the natural beauty. He simply comments that any development would be "crowded with happy gazers." There is not enough information in the passage to support the notion that the author prioritizes tourism revenue or unrestricted development over nature.

11   *Words/Phrases in Context.* D. In context, "cataract" refers to a large waterfall. While substituting in "scenery" or "view" into the sentence might make sense, the earlier part of the sentence makes it clear that the author is comparing two waterfalls. Earlier in the passage the author alludes to "two grand falls," as well. A waterfall is not quite the same thing as a flood.

The Tutorverse

12   *Close Reading.* B. The author indicates that the upper fall is "excelled in grandeur and magnificence" by the lower fall (line 76).

13   *Arguments.* C. The author writes that "the sheet…art," referring to the sheet of water that is "sheer." The author describes the "gurgling, choking" sound of the water passing through the channel, but not the roar of the falls itself. Similarly, the cavern and volume of water are not the primary focus.

Passage P

1   *Summarizing.* B. The passage discusses in general the impact of Nepal's constitution on relations with India as well as within its own country. The author does not discuss specific details, nor does he advocate for a particular point of view or answer a particular question.

2   *Purpose.* A. The author of Passage 1 states that Nepal is "a sovereign state" and uses the phrase "on the other hand" to acknowledges an argument from the opposing point of view. The author in the second and third paragraphs presents both sides of an argument and does not take sides.

3   *Word Choice.* C. The author argues that India may be right to express concerns regarding the potential for violence along the India/Nepal border. However, the author goes on to suggest that India has acted inappropriately when it comes to requesting constitutional amendments. Actual border disputes between Nepal and India are not mentioned in the passage; only internal border disputes are mentioned.

4   *Words/Phrases in Context.* C. The word "sovereign" has many meanings. In context, the word is used to indicate that Nepal acts independently and without foreign influence.

5   *Point of View.* C. Throughout the passage, the author of Passage 1 presents multiple sides to the issue of Nepal's constitution. He uses language such as "many politicians believe," "on the other hand," "some of these groups," and "to some" to draw a line between the views expressed in the passage and his own views – whatever they may be. We do not know what the author's particular point of view is on the Nepalese constitution.

6   *Close Reading.* D. In the third paragraph, the author indicates that many observers believe India's protestations to be "hypocrisy" because "India itself…constitution (lines 36-39).

7   *Main Ideas.* B. The author of the piece points out that the document itself is fair and progressive, but it may not be fairly put into practice because of the political parties who dominate the Nepalese legislature. The author suggests that the implementation of the constitution will be difficult to carry out as fairly as intended.

8   *Relationships.* C. Despite provisions in the new constitution that explicitly state that all people of Nepal shall have equal rights regardless of gender, race, and a number of other criteria, the current ruling power in the legislature is primarily male and upper class. Therefore, an unintentional result of the new government in Nepal could be discrimination against women and minorities.

9   *Text Structure.* C. The author discusses the benefits of the new constitution in Nepal as well as explains a possible drawback. The author does not offer specific examples of the drawback, and only speaks to the problems in general.

10   *Main Ideas.* C. Both passages discuss problems associated with Nepal's constitution. In Passage 1, the author writes about Nepal's relations with India, as well as the possibility of internal violence and discrimination towards some of Nepal's own citizens. In Passage 2, the author also discusses discrimination and inequality. Thus, it is reasonable to infer that both authors would agree that creating a "perfect" constitution is at best very difficult (if not impossible).

11   *Multiple Texts.* A. Neither passage responds to specific arguments advanced in the other passage. In fact, both passages discuss the same topic – Nepal's constitution and the difficulties associated with the reality of the country – from a different perspective. Passage 1 presents different issues and different sides to each of those issues. Passage 2 focuses primarily discrimination and remains silent on the possibility of violence and impact of India's involvement.

12   *Arguments.* B. The author of Passage 1 is primarily concerned with describing the tension between India and Nepal. However, the author does make a statement supporting Nepal's sovereignty. The author of Passage 1 does little to delve into the constitution's other virtues, and implicitly disapproves of India's own experiences with discrimination.

13   *Textual Evidence.* A. The author of Passage 1 focuses primarily on India's reaction to Nepal's constitution. The sentence describing Nepal's sovereignty (or its independence) best supports the answer from the previous question which states that Nepal is responsible for the decisions it makes on its own. The other choices support incorrect answer choices from the previous question.

Passage Q

1   *Summarizing.* C. Most generally, the passage describes how Edna discusses her inner feelings of turmoil and dissatisfaction with Dr. Mandelet. While the passage hints at events occurring at Adèle's, the reader doesn't know whether gossip or politics were described. Edna decided to walk instead of ride in the carriage, talking to Mandelet on the way.

The Tutorverse

2   *Text Structure.* A. The passage begins with the third-person narration of Edna's thoughts in the first paragraph, which continues into the second paragraph. From there the entire passage is dialogue-based, showing both Dr. Mandelet's and Edna's thoughts through dialogue.

3   *Purpose.* B. This is the reader's first hint that something is weighing heavily on Edna's mind – and that this something is not new to her. While this sentence sets the scene and establishes a mood, it does not create tension.

4   *Relationships.* D. Dr. Mandelet suggests that the visit was "cruel" and that Edna should not have gone. Thus, the reader can infer that Edna would probably not be feeling "satisfied." Edna goes on to say how she doesn't think that "it matters after all," suggesting that she is ambivalent, or indifferent, to the events. The passage does not suggest that she became aggressive or particularly moved by her visit.

5   *Textual Evidence.* C. Edna's ambivalence is echoed both in how she answers (indifferently) and what she says ("I don't…all"). The other choices might suggest that Edna was feeling preoccupied, angry, or defiant.

6   *Close Reading.* B. When Dr. Mandelet changes the subject, asking about Léonce, the reader can infer that he has hit a sore subject. Edna proceeds to say that she doesn't "want to go abroad" and won't "be forced into doing things." The reader can infer that this has to do with travelling with Léonce abroad, the trigger for Edna's statement. There is no evidence to suggest that Léonce is a medical professional, or that Léonce and Mandelet have a relationship at all (the reader only know that the latter merely knows of the former).

7   *Word Choice.* C. The phrase "oh well" is typically used to convey a sense of resignation, which mirror Edna's statements in line 61 about "despondency and suffering." Edna cannot even be bother to articulate her feelings to Dr. Mandelet.

8   *Main Ideas.* A. Edna can barely complete a coherent thought, in fact leaving her sentence unfinished. This highlights her inner turmoil. Edna's speech pattern is an example of a manifestation of what is going on in her mind. She mentions children, but only in passing – as an example of the conflict in her mind.

9   *Argument.* A. In the preceding paragraph, Edna describes how she doesn't want "to be forced into doing things." This matter is made more complicated by her children. The reader can infer then that Edna desires to do something not generally approved of by society, and that she feels trapped for it. The doctor appears to agree, stating that many obligations are fabricated by people and society.

10   *Purpose.* B. In this paragraph, the doctor seeks to convince Edna to speak to him freely about the thoughts concerning her. By holding her hand, the doctor demonstrates that she can trust him. There is no indication that the doctor is in love with Edna, or has disingenuous motives.

11   *Words/Phrases in Context.* A. The reader can infer that Mandelet is a doctor of the mind – a counselor, or therapist – who listens to Edna's troubles. Based on Edna's inability to articulate her thoughts, the reader can infer that something is troubling her that is not easily put into words. Dr. Mandelet invites her to trust him so that she might be more comfortable sharing with him her thoughts, but does so without demanding it; rather, he supports the notion that she can trust him by saying that he might be able to understand her.

12   *Point of View.* D. Edna struggles with the role her children play in her life. She mentions her children as an exception to being forced to do things she doesn't want to do (lines 31-32) and discusses how she doesn't want to "trample upon the little lives" (lines 66-67). Edna views her children as a complicating factor in her life, at once something she cares deeply for, but that traps her and wears away at her. Evidently, Edna cannot stop thinking about her children (lines 57-27), yet does not think that they are wholly "good" or wholly "bad."

13   *Textual Evidence.* C. Edna's view of her children is complicated – she at once loves them and cares about them, but also feels trapped by her duty to them. This rift is expressed when she describes how she wishes to live her life, but can't bear the thought of trampling on "the little lives" – her children.

Passage R

1   *Text Structure.* A. Hiram describes his expedition chronologically, from beginning to end. This passage details his experiences immediately preceding his discovery of Machu Picchu, over the course of several days. Hiram then goes on to describe the day of discovery itself, beginning with "after breakfast," preceding to "about noon" and then later, "presently" in the ruins of Machu Picchu.

2   *Relationships.* A. Hiram describes how the road his group took ran along "sheer precipices" supported only by new, frail brackets. He cites "the lack of" roads as a reason why earlier explorers were not able to take his present path. While his guide, government support, and equipment helped, these are not alluded to in Hiram's description.

3   *Summarizing.* C. Hiram describes his meeting of his future guide to Machu Picchu, the proprietor of the small plantation Mandorpampa. He describes his surroundings only briefly, spending more time on the environment in preceding and following paragraphs. The discovery itself is not described until later in the passage, as are hazardous and difficult circumstances.

The Tutorverse

4   *Point of View.* B. By comparing the owner of Mandorpampa to other natives, the reader can infer that Hiram has met and dealt with many natives in the past. The comment certainly does not indicate that Hiram views the natives with respect or admiration; instead, one can infer the opposite.

5   *Words/Phrases in Context.* A. The guide is described as someone fond of "firewater" – a colloquial term for alcohol. He does sell "grass and pasturage to passing travelers," but also provides them with spirits. There is no indication that this means he provides them with ghosts or religious advice.

6   *Close Reading.* B. Though Hiram mentions that the guide's payment is many times his usual wages, he ultimately believes this payment to "not seem unreasonable." Hiram's afterthought – that 50 cents was many times his wage – is not intended to suggest extortion or theft.

7   *Textual Evidence.* D. As indicated in explanation 6, Hiram's comments suggest that the fee was reasonable. The other answer choices do not relate to Hiram's opinion on the amount of the fee.

8   *Words/Phrases in Context.* C. "Precipitous" can sometimes mean rapid or unexpected, but in context, Hiram uses the word to describe the walls of the canyon – the grade of the slope.

9   *Main Ideas.* C. Hiram mentions how he thought his "time had been wasted" but that he nonetheless took the time to enjoy his situation, taking note of his surroundings. The other answer choices are ancillary details that support this main idea.

10   *Word Choice.* B. Eagle's nests are usually built high in the air in locations that are difficult to reach. By comparing his present location to an eagle's nest, Hiram uses a metaphor to emphasize both how remote and how high up he is. While Hiram does comment on the rudimentary nature of the home, the metaphor is primarily intended to convey a sense of height and remoteness. Hiram does not mention any observed wildlife, and describes the passing of the day to measure time.

11   *Words/Phrases in Context.* B. It can be inferred from the passage that "rods" are a unit of measurement describing distance. In context, both usages refer to how far one thing is from another – "a few rods away from the owner's grass-thatched hut" and "a few rods farther along." There is no context to support the notion that rods were used to punish, or as tent poles, or that they were random sticks.

12   *Arguments.* B. In the last paragraph, Hiram mentions that the "superior character of the stone work" and presence of "unusually large number of finely constructed stone dwellings" leads him to the conclusion that Machu Picchu is an important discovery. That the surroundings are beautiful and granite was used are secondary facts that may support the importance. The primary claim to fame, Hiram believes, is the architecture and preservation of the site.

13   *Purpose.* D. Hiram's claim, in the last paragraph, is that Machu Picchu is important because of the pristine and high quality nature of construction. The details he adds supports this claim. There is no evidence to suggest that Hiram is appealing for more funding, or that he particularly wants readers to visit his discovery. The descriptions certainly add drama and excitement to Hiram's story, but were not added solely for that purpose.

Passage S

1   *Summarizing.* A. The principle described is that of nonmaleficence. Concerns relating to nonmaleficence are described using the Milgram experiment as an example. Though the explanation of the experiment follows a quasi-chronological order, the broader passage focuses on using the context to illustrate a situation where nonmaleficence is somewhat unclear. The author does not take sides or argue for a particular point of view.

2   *Main Ideas.* A. The paragraph discusses the principle of nonmaleficence and describes that this standard must apply to all people that a psychologist works with. The passage states that psychologists often work with patients and subjects, but that they must be held to the same standard of nonmaleficence.

3   *Words/Phrases in Context.* D. In the passage, the author explores the idea of experiments that are ethically questionable, such as the Milgram experiment, because they do not adhere strictly to the notion of nonmaleficence and fall into a grey area. In this sentence, the author describes how some psychologists are "mired" in "ethical dilemmas" while others are on "ethically dubious ground," suggesting that there are practices which are not easy to label as "ethical" or "not ethical." The ethical concerns are not explicit or clear, nor are they treacherous or infamous.

4   *Text Structure.* B. The author first introduces the idea of ethics and nonmaleficence in the first several paragraphs. The next several paragraphs frame the idea of nonmaleficence in context of a specific example – the Milgram experiment. The last several paragraphs discuss the outcome and reactions to the experiment. While the passage is written with enough detail that the experiment could in theory be repeated (ethical considerations notwithstanding), the purpose and function of the fourth-sixth paragraphs is not to give instructions.

The Tutorverse

5   *Close Reading.* D. The passage indicates in lines 46-49 that the actor would always be the Learner, and the subject would be the Teacher – the one who would ask questions and administer shocks. The purpose of the experiment was to see the lengths to which the subject would follow the Experimenter's instructions.

6   *Purpose.* B. In the experiment, the Learner was not actually shocked. However, the Teacher needed to believe that he/she was shocking the Learner. One way to accomplish this was to put the Learner out of view of the Teacher and play recordings of shocks being administered. The passage does not suggest that the Learner needed to rest or that the Teachers had a difficult time focusing on asking questions.

7   *Relationships.* D. According to lines 64-65, the strength of the shock would increase "with each incorrect answer" provided by the Learner. The Experimenter and Teacher's feelings did not influence the intensity of the shocks, and the shocks progressed regardless of the Learner's lack of tolerance.

8   *Relationships.* A. The Learners (hired actors) played prerecorded sound clips that were designed to imitate the sound of a person receiving different types of shocks. In this way, the Teachers were exposed to the supposed effect of their action (which was to administer shocks in the event of incorrect answers). The Teachers already knew that the answer choice was incorrect, because no shock would be administered in the event of a correct answer.

9   *Word Choice.* C. The paragraph discusses how many Teachers were reluctant to continue the experiment, but that they would not be permitted to stop until an Experimenter gave permission. Because the Experimenter withheld permission until a Teacher asked five times, one can infer that the Experimenter somehow convinced Teachers to continue the experiment.

10   *Arguments.* A. Earlier in the passage, the author writes that the principle of nonmaleficence states that practitioners should do no harm. Yet in Milgram's experiment, some subjects clearly suffered "signs of stress and mental discomfort" – something that could be considered a negative side-effect. Thus, for some, the experiment violated ethical standards. The mere fact that actors were hired to pretend, or that some subjects did not want to continue is not enough to suggest that the experiment violated ethical standards.

11   *Textual Evidence.* C. The passage states that the subjects exhibited nervous laughter and other signs of stress. The other selections support incorrect answer choices from the previous question, or else present other, ancillary information.

12   *Quantitative Information.* D. The passage suggests that 65% of subjects went on to administer the full, maximum-intensity shock. In the chart, the maximum-intensity shock is represented by 10, though in the passage the maximum-intensity shock is 450 volts. The difference in the unit of measurement is not a concern – what is a concern is comparing the percentage of subjects who would administer a maximum intensity shock. The chart shows that a far smaller percentage of subjects than mentioned in the passage were willing to administer the max shock.

13   *Point of View.* C. Throughout the passage, the author adopts an impartial tone, simply raising questions about the ethical concerns of psychologists and using a famous experiment as an example. The author does not draw a conclusion on the ethics of Milgram's experiment, simply stating that some viewed the experiment as a violation of ethical standards.

Passage T

1   *Summarizing.* B. A, C, and D are all specific elements that can be found at certain places in the passage, but only choice B summarizes what happens over the course of the entire passage. The passage is nominally about basketball tryouts, and Brian does want to impress Roselle, but only choice B captures the climax of the passage: Brian's decision to miss the final free throw.

2   *Text Structure.* A. The passage begins by describing Brian and his relationship with Roselle, which is the reason why Brian ultimately decides to try out for the team. From there, the passage goes on to describe the tryouts, culminating in Brian's decision to deliberately miss his final free throw.

3   *Words/Phrases in Context.* C. From context, the reader can infer that Brian wishes to impress Roselle and believes initially that the best way to do this is by trying out for the basketball team. The reader can also infer that Roselle has feelings for Brian, suggesting that she would like to see Brian play. When Brian appears unconvinced, Roselle attempts to charm and encourage him to try out for the team.

4   *Word Choice.* A. In line 23 Roselle uses the phrase to encourage Brian to try out. But in lines 83-84, it's meant to be sarcastic because even by practicing, Brian believes it is unlikely that Harold will ever be good enough to get a scholarship. The phrase is not used as a signal of despair in line 83-84. Roselle is sincere when she says it in line 23, and in lines 35, Brian doesn't regard it as being unrealistic.

5   *Relationships.* C. Though Brian daydreams about dunking the ball, he does so in context of impressing Roselle. He feels practice is actually boring and has no particular desire to improve his skills. The passage is not clear as to whether or not Brian is friends with Harold – only that the former sympathizes with the latter.

The Tutorverse

6   *Close Reading.* D. Brian gives up a place on the team because he believes Harold wants the position more. This is a generous act. If Brian were ambitious, he would likely not have deliberately missed his final free throw. If he were naïve, he might have believed he could be a starter. If he were ambivalent, he might not have known what to do and not demonstrated so much thoughtfulness in his actions.

7   *Textual Evidence.* D. The reason Brian deliberately misses the free throw is to allow Harold to make the team. The other choices do not, by themselves, indicate that Brian is generous, even though they lead to his decision.

8   *Purpose.* C. Brian's fantasy is only a daydream, and when Brian faces the choice of remaining on the team or letting Harold have his place, he is realistic enough to know his own limitations. He is influenced by Roselle, but only to achieve an unrealistic goal, which he readily abandons.

9   *Words/Phrases in Context.* D. The tests – running, passing, etc. – are designed to display each player's abilities as they relate to basketball. There is no indication that these tests are assessing the players' emotional or mental facilities.

10   *Purpose.* B. Brian may at first think Harold is joking, but sees that the latter is really serious about making the team. Up to this point, Brian seems committed to making the team. Coach has already made it clear that not everybody will make the team. Harold's mother is not mentioned until later.

11   *Point of View.* D. There is no evidence that Harold is more skilled than Brian, or that he worries about his popularity amongst his peers. The author describes Harold as nervous and worried about his tryout prospects, which is the opposite of confident.

12   *Arguments.* A. Brian's sympathy for Harold's dream that he can get a basketball scholarship is prompted by Harold's challenging home life. This fact is relevant to the passage only because of its effect on Brian's actions. Harold's home situation is not necessarily typical of other students in the school, nor is it implied to be a factor that affects his basketball skills.

13   *Main Ideas.* C. Brian's motivations are explained prior to his missing the shot. The passage does not imply that Roselle will find out about his missed shot – or that she was even in attendance. Brian's interest in music is mentioned primarily to show that he is comfortable with his decision and with who he is and how he will impress Roselle.

Passage U

1   *Text Structure.* D. Before addressing the international relations question posed by Taiwan, the author first provides historical context. She then goes on to explain how historical circumstances translated into a modern disagreement. She then describes the disagreement from different perspectives.

2   *Main Ideas.* B. The author goes to great lengths to explain the political conflict between PRC and ROC, using history as context to help the reader understand the disagreement. She is careful not to take sides, and does not conclude which side of the conflict is to be supported. While history plays a role in the structure of the passage, history itself is not the central purpose of the passage.

3   *Point of View.* D. The author remains neutral and unbiased regarding the validity of claims made by the PRC and ROC, presenting both sides equally. The matter, in her opinion has not yet been settled, by the international community or otherwise.

4   *Purpose.* A. The historical context is necessary in order to fully understand the ROC-PRC conflict. It provides the reader with the understanding that the island of Taiwan has changed hands numerous times and that, given the confusion during the Japanese surrender at the end of World War II, ownership over the island was unclear. The passage does not compare modern disputes with historical ones. The roots of the Chinese Civil War are not discussed, except as being the result of differences between nationalists and communists. Though the Chinese and Japanese have historically warred, this is only of passing relevance to the issue at hand.

5   *Close Reading.* C. The passage indicates that the Chinese Civil War was "suspended" when the nationalists and communists joined forces to "repel a Japanese invasion." The PRC and ROC were not established until after World War II. The governance of Taiwan was not settled during the brief pause.

6   *Textual Evidence.* C. The passage clearly states that the two adversaries suspended hostilities in order to fight the Japanese, who had invaded China during World War II. The other references allude to different aspects of the conflict, including the surrender of Japan (which complicated the governance of Taiwan).

7   *Relationships.* A. The author indicates in lines 44-45 that military operations ceased in late 1949 and the PRC and ROC were formed. The 1937 suspension of hostilities was only a reprieve. After the Japanese surrendered fighting between communists and nationalists in China resumed. The passage does not imply that the United States intervention in Asia resulted in the founding of the ROC and PRC.

The Tutorverse

8   *Summarizing*. C. The seventh paragraph outlines both the ROC and PRC's justifications for their position. The author does not comment on which party is more or less justified than the other. The Chinese Civil War, though referenced, is not blamed for the conflict. Instead, the paragraph focuses on the different interpretations of sovereignty.

9   *Arguments*. B. The author cites the conflicting determinations of the two United Nations General Assembly Resolutions. This implies that as political winds shift, so too does the international community's point of view on the ROC-PRC conflict.

10   *Quantitative Information*. D. The chart illustrates with numbers the idea that the international community's views have changed over time. In the passage, the author cites UN Resolution 505 and 2758 as examples. The table appears to corroborate this idea. The chart does not show "support" – it shows the number of countries that "recognize" the ROC and PRC. As illustrated in the United States' point of view, for example, such differences in semantics matters.

11   *Arguments*. D. The PRC maintains a policy that it governs the only China in existence – that the ROC is an illegitimate rogue government. It will not engage diplomatically with countries that recognize the ROC as a legitimate state, as doing so would violate its own policy. According to the passage, the PRC in fact allows other countries to trade with and otherwise engage with the ROC.

12   *Word Choice*. D. The difference between "acknowledges" and "recognizes" may seem miniscule or trivial – but that is precisely the point the author is trying to make: that the differences are a matter of semantics. The author does not side with the PRC or condemn the United States. Drawing attention to what seems to be a minor difference between words is not simply mincing words – it is proving the author's point.

13   *Words/Phrases in Context*. B. One of the author's main points is that words that seem simple to understand and incontrovertible, such as "sovereignty," are actually more complicated to define. Thus, the use of "seemingly innocuous" means that the words appear ("seemingly") to be easy to understand and incontrovertible ("innocuous"). The word "ostensibly" suggests a meaning similar to "seemingly," as does "incontrovertible" to "innocuous." The words are not "definitely debatable," as the idea revolves around the notion that the words appear incontrovertible, but actually aren't. "Innocuous" in this case should not be confused with "inoculate" (to prevent).

Passage V

1   *Main Ideas*. B. The passage describes scientific concepts in order to help the reader understand both sides of the GMO debate. The author then provides both sides of the argument. The author does not arrive at a conclusion about the validity of one side or the other, or make any recommendations. The author simply provides information, facts, and figures.

2   *Summarizing*. D. The author describes the process of selective breeding and the effect it has on organisms, offering examples (wolves and dogs; grasses and corn) to help communicate the idea. To narrow the scope of the paragraph to a discussion of dogs or fruit is to miss the broader purpose of the paragraphs. The author does not cite evidence from an experiment.

3   *Word Choice*. D. Today's corn plants are very tall – a fact that the author emphasizes using the frequently used expression "high as…eye." This contrasts the fact that the plant was originally a small plant and serves to show that an organism can undergo drastic changes as a result of selective breeding. The author does not complain about corn's nutritional value. Fruit crops are offered as another example of changes that have been made to plant species. The author does not mention elephants as an example of an organism that has been genetically modified.

4   *Purpose*. A. The paragraph states that the purpose of selective breeding and today's genetic modification are to create an organism with desirable qualities – the overall principal purpose of conducting any genetic modifications, whether through selective breeding or with today's processes.

5   *Relationships*. B. The author writes that "modern science…life" (lines 41-44). Selective breeding would not have resulted in genetic combinations between eukarya and bacteria, as it requires the breeding of the same species within a domain. The passage does not mention agricultural interests.

6   *Close Reading*. C. The seventh paragraph does not describe a decrease in herbicides used. It does describe how the nutritional value of GMOs is sometimes higher than non-GMOs, and does mention that yields increased while pesticide use decreased.

7   *Quantitative Information*. D. The data in Figure 1 shows that there is a sharp and sustained decrease in the use of insecticides – another name for pesticides – after *Bt* corn (a GMO) is introduced. The chart does not show the amount of corn produced, its nutritional value, or amount of herbicides used.

8   *Text Structure*. B. The author raises logical questions following the preceding paragraphs in order to introduce an opposing viewpoint. The third to last paragraph and last paragraph describe different sides of the GMO debate, and do not describe scientific processes or anecdotes.

The Tutorverse

9   *Words/Phrases in Context.* C. "Myriad" is an adjective that describes something that is countless, or very great in number. Thus, "seemingly infinite" best matches this definition. While the "ways in which GMOs might impact the environment" may be convenient, dangerous, or unclear – all possible arguments advanced by opponents of GMOs, the rest of the paragraph discusses how these ways may not yet be known since the environment is so complex.

10   *Arguments.* B. The author does not mention any alliance between the government and powerful economic interests, nor does it suggest that greed as a reason to reject GMOs. Instead, the author suggests that despite testing and government regulation (not because of a lack of those things), many opponents believe that the impact on GMOs is too complicated to properly understand.

11   *Textual Evidence.* D. The author suggests that people do not know enough about complex biological systems to be able to guarantee that modern GMOs will not have a negative impact. This supports the previous question, which suggests that complexity and a false sense of confidence will lead to negative and unforeseeable consequences. The other selections support incorrect answer choices from the previous paragraph, or else provides a selection which supports a proponent's view of GMOs.

12   *Quantitative Information.* A. The figure shows that the increase in herbicides used in cotton and soybean plantings has increased while those used in corn plantings decreased initially, but then gradually increased. An opponent of GMOs would likely not highlight the fact that herbicide usage initially decreased.

13   *Point of View.* D. Based on the passage, selective breeding is viewed as resulting in many widely known and "safe" organisms, like dogs and apples. Because the statement indicates that there is "no difference" in the processes, the statement implies that the results of those processes should be equally safe. There is no evidence in the passage to suggest that the statement is widely accepted or that it is ethically wrong. The passage does not imply that today's GMOs would be dangerous based on the statement.

Passage W

1   *Summarizing.* C. The other choices are all elements to be found in the passage. However, the most complete choice encompasses all of these elements.

2   *Text Structure.* C. At first, Mary has doubts about winning – even regarding the idea as impossible – but the passage ends with her discovery of an idea that gives her hope she can win. All the other choices have elements that are present in the passage, but are not the primary focus of the passage.

3   *Point of View.* D. The passage shows how Mary desires to meet Byron's challenge to write a ghost story. While Mary's role as a mother and daughter are discussed briefly, she is primarily concerned with coming up with a story.

4   *Word Choice.* D. The stories were intended to frighten, and the darkness beyond the fireplace only adds to the guests' fears. The other answers are not so clearly related to the passage and are incongruent with Byron's motivations as indicated in the passage.

5   *Words/Phrases in Context.* B. Byron wants to use his power by frightening the others. To exercise in this context does not mean to work out, or exercise, the body. Byron already knows he has power over the others, so he would not be discovering it here, nor would he limit it by trying to frighten them.

6   *Relationships.* B. Mary feels she must carry on her mother's crusade, and the passage states that the crusade is for equal rights for women. Mary feels that being a writer is one way she might carry on the crusade.

7   *Close Reading.* A. Mary's thoughts about him are all positive. She even excuses him from possibly contributing to the death of their child.

8   *Textual Evidence.* B. When Mary imagines the man in the castle to be like Percy, she attributes to him several positive qualities. Mary recognizes that Percy is a skilled writer, but does so without jealousy.

9   *Close Reading.* C. Mary regards Percy as more talented, but that does not mean that he was; nor is it certain whether or not he was a scientist or philosopher, based on the information in this passage. However, the reader knows that his desire to see new things led to his neglect of his infant daughter, which is certainly an indication of self-centeredness.

10   *Textual Evidence.* C. This part of the passage describes Percy's putting his own interests above the welfare – even the life – of his daughter. His discussions with Byron don't display his personality.

11   *Purpose.* D. Byron and Percy do not discuss the meaning of life, but the source of it, and if a creature can be resurrected from death. Mary's attempt to revive her baby is part of this general idea. In context, the lines help advance the passage by making clear Mary's pattern of thoughts.

12   *Arguments.* B. In the course of the passage, listening to this discussion planted the idea in Mary's head that creatures could be brought back to life. This began with the death of her baby, and continues with her vision of a strange giant of a man who will be the main character in her story.

The Tutorverse

13 *Main Ideas*. D. Although the other choices did happen, each of them only contributed to the flash of inspiration that is the climax of the passage. It is clear that she wants to think of some element that will make her story truly frightening. That is the man she sees in her imagination.

Passage X

1   *Text Structure*. A. Roosevelt's speech takes the following arc: he first explains the importance of civic duty and the role his audience can play in it; then he issues a warning to his audience about potential pitfalls and traps to be vigilant for while playing their role in society; finally, he seeks to inspire his audience to fulfill their role and to avoid the aforementioned pitfalls. Roosevelt's speech does not take the form of point-counterpoint, nor are his points challenged.

2   *Summarizing*. B. Roosevelt, in the first paragraph, discusses "the subject of individual citizenship" and its importance to the success of democracy. He also discusses how best to raise the quality of those individual citizens. This amounts to a discussion on civic responsibility – what leaders must do to help raise up the civic quality of individual citizens. There is no formal political doctrine, political strategy, or moral and ethical philosophy being discussed; the primary subject of discussion is a citizen's duties.

3   *Close Reading*. B. Roosevelt states that "in the…virtues" (lines 15-20). This suggests that it is the individual citizen's actions, not the structure of government or the economy or legal framework that has the greatest influence on the success of a democracy.

4   *Word Choice*. D. Roosevelt here likens a stream and its source (a spring, for example) to national greatness and its source – average citizens and their ability to perform "his or her duty." He does not make comparisons to education.

5   *Relationships*. B. It can be inferred that Roosevelt feels that in his audience are people who represent leaders – those wealthy, well educated, or powerful people. Thus, as leaders, they are held to a higher standard than average citizens, and have a duty to those citizens to empathize and fight with them. He does not imply that wealth and power must be shared, or that leadership must be unyielding.

6   *Word Choice*. A. In the first and second paragraphs, Roosevelt discusses different citizens: the average citizen and the leaders of those citizens. Roosevelt addresses, in his audience, the leaders "It is…today" (lines 31-34). He extols his audience to "sympathize with" the plain people – the average citizens. Thus, the plain people are not necessarily sympathetic, good, or intelligent – just average.

7   *Arguments*. A. Roosevelt warns his audience of the "cheap temptation…cynic" (lines 50-51). Cynics and cynicism, he goes on to say, are those that have an "attitude of sneering disbelief." Roosevelt does not warn against leisure, greed, or optimism (in fact, the opposite); he warns his well-educated, privileged audience against a lack of sympathy and "sneering disbelief."

8   *Purpose*. D. Roosevelt chooses to use the word "your" in order to speak more directly to his audience – to let them know that his message is meant for them. This does not serve to indicate the Roosevelt speaks to a single person, or that his advice is only applicable under certain circumstances. Instead, he likens the crowd to the privileged leaders he previously described, earlier in the paragraph.

9   *Words/Phrases in Context*. D. The reader can infer from earlier in the paragraph that Roosevelt is addressing those who "have received special advantages" who have had "opportunity for mental training." Thus, Roosevelt is addressing educated people. A man of leisure refers to someone who has the means – typically monetary assets – to be free from obligations and material wants. Such people can be hardworking or lazy, but are usually freed from responsibilities and wants by their wealth or privilege.

10 *Point of View*. C. According to Roosevelt, a cynic is one to "criticize work" and "points out how the strong man stumbles or where the doer of deeds could have done them better." In light of a failure, the cynic would likely not encourage, respect, or support.

11 *Textual Evidence*. C. Of cynics/critics, Roosevelt states that a cynic is one to "criticize work" and "points out how the strong man stumbles or where the doer of deeds could have done them better." The other answer choices do not address the actions of a cynic, and instead describe other aspects of the speech (such as the lofty standards to which leaders must be held, as in choice A).

12 *Word Choice*. B. An arena is where people compete. Roosevelt uses this as a metaphor not for privilege, but for struggle – the struggle and competition that spurs men to try, fail, and try again. It is the people who struggle for greatness – who are in the arena – that Roosevelt says "counts." Success may or may not be the result of a struggle – nor may wealth and privilege.

13 *Main Ideas*. D. In the last paragraph, Roosevelt describes how it is the struggle for greatness, lofty ideas, and worthy causes that is the true measure of greatness. He suggests that those that sit on the sidelines and criticize the efforts of those who fail lack mettle, comparing them to "cold and timid souls who neither know victory nor defeat."

The Tutorverse

Passage Y

1   *Summarizing*. D. Mankiewicz received co-author credit at the Oscar ceremony, and indications are that Welles certainly contributed to the script. There is no indication that Welles' claim was false. Though choice C may be correct, it does not capture the controversy around the movie's authorship.

2   *Main Ideas*. A. Because the movie became acclaimed years after its release, the question of authorship became more important. Tacitus writes that "success has a thousand fathers," implying that people always desire to latch onto something that is successful. Because *Citizen Kane* was successful, the author suggests that people tried to take credit for that success. The passage does not address the movie's inspiration or make claims about the true author.

3   *Word Choice*. D. "Script doctor" is a term that implies the writer improves scripts, rather than writes new ones. The author mentions that Mankiewicz was "known for his quality edits." It does not imply the writer was a published author or used a light touch in his work.

4   *Words/Phrases in Context*. B. Kael set forth a controversial idea in her essay. In context, "promulgated" most nearly means "posited," which means "suggests" or "believes." Kael did not question her idea – she questioned the authorship of the film, leading her to this idea. She most likely performed research, but she used the research in setting forth her idea.

5   *Text Structure*. B. The author juxtaposes the early lack of success and conflict with a powerful person against the later success of Welles' film. The author mentions that Welles' saw early success as a result of his radio program, and does not imply that he struggled with acceptance as a result of that success. Welles' demand for creative control is mentioned only in passing. There is nothing in the passage suggesting that Welles' movie career ended with *Citizen Kane*.

6   *Close Reading*. A. The author points out that though Welles denies basing his film on Hearst's life, there are many strong similarities (lines 70-81) between Hearst and the film's protagonist. Given the feedback from Hearst, one can infer that certainly Hearst did not feel the similarities to be coincidental. Nothing in the passage suggest that Welles wanted to ridicule Hearst or that the filmmaker admired the publisher.

7   *Textual Evidence*. B. The selection in choice B recounts some of the main similarities between Kane and Hearst. The other answer choices do not exemplify the fact that there are striking similarities between the fiction and real-world personalities.

8   *Purpose*. C. The similarities listed are so numerous that they suggest the film is based on Hearst's life; Kane's personal and professional life seems to strongly mirror that of Hearst's. This does not justify Hearst's actions, nor Welles' denials. The passage does not discuss the legality of Welles' work; slander is not mentioned in the passage – the reader knows only that Hearst objected to the film.

9   *Word Choice*. A. A sensationalist newspaper refers to one that publishes things that are entertaining or attention grabbing – things that cause a sensation. Sensations typically are not caused by serious, thought-provoking, or important topics (which may be boring to many readers). The author does not mention journalistic awards.

10   *Relationships*. B. The events of Passage 1 occurred after the film's release, and Passage 2 primarily discusses events beforehand. Neither passage is critical of Welles, instead offering multiple points of view. Passage 2 is not concerned with authorship. Passage 2 is not primarily concerned with advertising the film, but rather with releasing it, though it mentions that advertising was a challenge because of Hearst's dislike of the film.

11   *Arguments*. C. The passage does not suggest that Welles viewed Mankiewicz as a consultant, or that RKO had control over the writing of the script (a fact that runs contrary to the notion that Welles had creative control over the project). There is no indication that Hearst suggested Mankiewicz wrote the script. Instead, Welles would most likely have suggested that Mankiewicz's notoriety as a script doctor means that the latter did not deserve full writing credit.

12   *Point of View*. C. In Passage 1, the author does not take sides in the controversy about the film's authorship, instead presenting facts clearly and without bias. In Passage 2, the author appears to view Welles more favorably, implying that he was within his artistic rights to make the film despite how its inspiration angered a powerful man. The author in the end suggests that despite the controversy, *Citizen Kane* rightfully found its way to fame.

13   *Text Structure*. B. Both passages describe controversies, but Passage 1 does not take a stand on its outcome, saying that the true author of the film might never be known. In Passage 2, the author suggests that despite the controversy surrounding the film's release, the film ultimately became very successful. Neither passage advances an argument per se – the authors of both passages remain relatively unbiased. For example, the author of Passage 2 does not argue whether or not Welles or Hearst acted appropriately, or whether or not the film should have been released.

Passage Z

1   *Main Ideas*. C. The passage's main claim is that people should use less plastic because plastic waste contributes to problems like the Great Pacific Garbage Patch and the interruption of food chains. The passage goes on to discuss

The Tutorverse

how plastic waste can also effect land animals, like people, who rely on food from the ocean. The other answer choices address specific parts of the passage but fail to address the broader claim.

2 *Text Structure.* A. The first part of the passage discusses the problem of plastic waste and its negative impact on the environment. The passage then shifts to the possible solutions that can help curb the problem of plastic waste. The passage focuses on more than just the problem of plastic waste.

3 *Close Reading.* A. At the beginning of the passage, the author writes that "many of...recyclable." This suggests that people are not willfully and maliciously creating plastic waste, as choice B would suggest, but that instead they are simply lulled into a false sense of plastic's safety. The author does not suggest that companies are to blame for putting plastics in products, instead arguing that consumers should become more educated and make more informed decisions. The author offers several examples of plastic alternatives.

4 *Textual Evidence.* A. According to the author, many people use plastic products because they assume the ability of plastics to be recycled is environmentally friendly. The author implies that because we do not think about the amount of plastic used, we don't realize the impact of our decisions on the environment. The author does not suggest that this is willful or deliberate. The other answer choices do not support the answer to the previous question.

5 *Summarizing.* B. The paragraph discusses how plastic waste ends up in the Great Pacific Garbage Patch by traveling through currents and describe the scale of the problem. Though the Garbage Patch certainly does embody the problem of plastic waste, it is not simply a symbol, but an actual problem. The paragraph mentions fishing nets and water bottles, but is not the focus of the passage. The author does not describe the Patch as harmless, and instead says the opposite in following paragraphs.

6 *Arguments.* B. The author uses this paragraph to build her overall argument by emphasizing the problem of plastic waste. This paragraph is a logical component of the author's argument: first, the author describes the Garbage Patch, then describes how plastic waste is detrimental (including the fact that it lasts a long time) and goes on to propose several solutions. The author does not address any counterclaims in this passage, and is focused primarily on advocating for using less plastics – not creating biodegradable plastics.

7 *Words/Phrases in Context.* D. The word "leach" is a verb that is often confused with "leech." The latter refers to something that relies on something else, such as the parasite animal that feeds on blood. Here, the word means "release," as the passage discusses how plastic waste can give off chemicals like BPA into the water.

8 *Relationships.* D. In lines 49-60, the author describes how the food chain itself is disrupted by plastic waste. Plastic waste reduces energy available to autotrophs, which are the building block of the oceanic food chain. The author does not suggest that apex predators eat plastic; instead, the large predators eat small animals, which are the ones that consume plastic waste "unwittingly." The author doesn't claim that people have less fish to eat; instead, she suggests that the fish supply is being poisoned by plastic chemicals.

9 *Point of View.* C. The statement represents a possible counterclaim to the author's argument – specifically to the part of her argument that addresses the buildup of plastic chemicals in apex predators. The author would disagree with the claim, citing the fact that plastic chemicals build up in apex predators like tuna. The author would argue that this contributes to the disruption of the food chain.

10 *Word Choice.* B. The author spends the first several paragraphs describing the problem of plastic waste, and the last several paragraphs discussion potential solutions. This paragraph helps to transition between the two ideas, acknowledging the negative impacts on the environment as well as introducing the idea that there is something that can be done. The author does not raise objections to the idea that plastic waste is bad for the environment, or in this paragraph question the use of plastic in products.

11 *Arguments.* B. The author's example of water bottles helps to advance the argument that there are simple and easy ways to use less plastic. The author does not describe how using less plastic would be difficult, or raise an objection to giving up plastic. The author does not describe improving recycling, instead advocating that people invest in reusable water bottles.

12 *Close Reading.* C. The author's focus in the last three paragraphs of the passage is to argue that there are many actions that can be taken to reduce plastic waste. Lines 77-84 describe many concrete examples of how plastics can be replaced by other things, while the preceding paragraph describes how plastics can be reused or declined entirely. The author does not refute a counterclaim, or make general claims in this paragraph. The assumption that plastic waste is bad (and therefore should be curbed) is not described in this paragraph, but in the first several paragraphs of the passage.

13 *Relationships.* A. The passage explains that a lot of frozen and prepared foods are packaged in plastic containers that can't be reused, meaning that most probably get thrown away instead of recycled, and thus contribute to the plastic waste problem. The author does not draw a correlation between recycling centers and fresh food, nor are cardboard or cloth bags cited as a way in which fresh foods can help reduce plastic waste.

The Tutorverse

Explanations: Part Two – Writing & Language

Grammar Glossary

The explanations in this section make frequent reference to elements of grammar. To maximize the efficacy of the answer explanations, we have included the following Grammar Glossary.

- 🐟 Sentence – a sentence must have a predicate (most generally, a verb) and a subject (of that predicate/verb). It may also have other words that help to form a complete thought.
  - 🐟 Subject – usually a noun or pronoun; the person, place, or thing that the sentence is actually about
  - 🐟 Predicate – what the subject of the sentence is doing
- 🐟 Clause – a group of words that has a predicate and subject
  - 🐟 Independent clause – a clause that can also stand alone as a sentence (a clause that also contains a complete thought)
  - 🐟 Dependent (subordinated) clause – a clause that cannot stand alone as a sentence (a clause that does not contain a complete thought)
- 🐟 Phrase – a group of words that does not contain the sentence's verb or subject
  - 🐟 Prepositional phrase – a group of words beginning with a preposition but ends with a noun (acts like an adjective, or adverb)
  - 🐟 Participial phrase – phrase beginning with a participle (a verb that ending in –ing, which acts like an adjective or adverb)
- 🐟 Fragment – a group of words that lacks any one or more of the three elements that form a sentence; sometimes a dependent clause written as if it was an independent clause.
- 🐟 Run-on – two independent clauses joined together without appropriate or sufficient punctuation and/or conjunctions
  - 🐟 Fused sentence – a run-on sentence resulting from the lack of any punctuation
  - 🐟 Spliced comma – a run-on sentence resulting from the inappropriate use of a comma to join two independent clauses
- 🐟 Compound sentence – two independent clauses joined together with appropriate or sufficient punctuation and/or conjunctions
  - 🐟 Conjunction – a word that joins two clauses together; frequently preceded by punctuation
    - 🐟 Coordinating conjunction – connects two clauses of equal importance (i.e. two independent clauses); *and, but, or, so, for, nor, yet*
    - 🐟 Subordinating conjunction – connects a dependent clause to an independent clause; *after, before, if, since, while, etc.*
    - 🐟 Correlative conjunction – pairs of words that signal a relationship between two elements in a clause (i.e. either/or, both/and, neither/nor)
- 🐟 Verb Tense – at its most basic, the different forms of a verb that indicate when an action takes place (i.e. in the past, present, or future; whether something continues to happen)
- 🐟 Verb Mood – indicate the author's attitude in terms of what the intention is: to show a statement of fact (indicative), issue a command (imperative), or propose a statement contrary to fact (subjunctive)
- 🐟 Number (verb, noun) – indicates whether a verb or noun is singular or plural
- 🐟 Preposition – a word that links a noun to another word, often describes the position of that noun (i.e. in, etc.)
- 🐟 Voice – refers to the way a sentence is written where the subject performs the action indicated by the verb (active) or where the verb acts upon the subject (passive)

Guided Practice – Standard English Conventions

Complete Sentences

1 B. As written, the sentence is a fragment, lacking a complete thought. What happens when "she" gets tired and likes to take naps? "Whenever" is a subordinating conjunction and cannot stand alone at the beginning of this sentence. Removing it, in this case, is the best option. Otherwise, we could rewrite the sentence as "She likes to take naps whenever she gets tired." The two sentences, though having different meanings, are both grammatically correct.

2 D. As written, it is unclear what the phrase "hungry as a result of" applies to. We know that the cause of the hunger was "his long and tiring workout," but is the same person who worked-out also hungry? Choice D clarifies this for us and turns a fragment into a grammatically correct sentence with a complete thought.

3 D. The sentence as written is a run-on sentence. More specifically, it is a fused sentence – a grammatically incorrect sentence where two independent clauses are joined together without the proper punctuation. Though a semicolon would be acceptable, it is not a provided option. A period most effectively separates two independent ideas.

The Tutorverse

4 B. As written, this sentence is also a run-on sentence. The sentence suffers from a spliced comma, or a comma that is used to incorrectly join two independent clauses. Colons typically signify that a list of items follows. Ellipses are used to show that some thought has been omitted. Neither the colon nor the ellipses is used correctly in this case. The coordinating conjunction "and" is preceded by a comma and serves to join the two independent clauses.

5 A. Choice B results in an illogical idea. Choice C results in a comma splice, and choice D results in a fused sentence. The semicolon signals a pause between sentences greater than a comma but less than a period, but only works with logically related sentences.

6 B. The sentence is another example of a fused sentence. Choice B corrects the sentence by clarifying that the people using the equipment were the children. Choice C results in a comma splice and choice D results in a fused sentence that is grammatically incorrect, implying that the jungle gym was using the equipment and laughing while playing.

7 D. A semicolon correctly joins two related independent clauses. Choice B results in an illogical idea and choice C results in a comma splice. As written, the sentence is fused. Alternatively, we could introduce a subordinating conjunction such as "when" to the beginning of the sentence and a comma after "gift" – thus the independent clause would read "The shoppers were incensed" and the dependent clause "when the toy store ran out of the season's most popular gift" would tell the reader more about the situation.

8 A. The subordinating conjunction "whenever" helps to connect the independent clause "Martin sneezes several times" with the dependent clause "whenever there is a cat nearby." Other options leave the dependent clause standing alone, creating a fragment.

9 A. The two sentences are properly punctuated with a period separating two independent clauses. Inserting a comma or omitting any punctuation would result in a comma splice or fused sentence, respectively. Adding a subordinating conjunction is inappropriate, as the resulting sentence would be illogical.

10 A. Using a period or semicolon would result in a sentence fragment with a subordinated clause ("yet…businesses") standing alone. A colon is inappropriate as no list of items follows it. The comma used in this sentence is actually optional, since the sentence is an example of a simple compound sentence. In longer, more complicated compound sentences, commas necessarily precede coordinating conjunctions.

11 B. By introducing a period or semicolon, the sentence is inappropriately split into two halves, with a participle phrase being treated as a complete sentence ("Neglecting his tenants for years at a time"). Using the word "and" to replace the comma results in a fused sentence.

12 B. As written, the first sentence is a proper sentence. However, the second sentence is not, as it does not contain a complete thought. To integrate the information – examples of warmer parts of the United States, a comma is needed. Changing prepositions – from "like" to "such as" or "including" – does not correct the sentence, as what results continues to be an incomplete sentence.

Subordination & Coordination

1 D. In this sentence, the subordinated clause explains why the runner decided stealing a base was not worthwhile. Though this reason is because of the failed attempt to steal second base, "because" would require the word "of" to properly explain this thought. "While" is typically used to show that something is contradictory to another, or that something happened at the same time as something else. It would not make sense that the runner would decide to stop stealing second base without trying, as "before" would suggest.

2 B. "While" tells the reader that something occurred at the same time as something else. "During" is typically used to describe a noun, such as a juggling act. "That" and "as soon as" result in sentences that are missing some critical parts of speech, such as additional nouns and verbs to describe the action.

3 C. "Because" is used to indicate that something happened as a result of something else. In this case, the result of good performance at the box office was approval for a sequel. "Though" and "while" generally indicate that something to the contrary happened as a result of something else; it would not make much sense that a sequel *not* be approved as a result of good box office performance of the original movie. As written, the sentence is somewhat contradictory – was the sequel greenlit after the original's release, or as soon as the original did well at the box office?

4 D. "Since" functions much as "because" does, signaling that something happened as a result of something else. "If" and "unless" introduce a conditional of some kind; in this case, if Justine was afraid of heights and prone to motion sickness, she probably would not be excited to go to the theme park. "Even though" functions like "while" in that it shows that something happened in spite of something else.

5 A. "Whether" functions like a qualifier, telling us that something is contingent on something else. The sentence is illogical when the other answer choices are used because they do not describe the circumstances under which the child gets his way.

The Tutorverse

6   B. Coordination simply refers to the proper and logical use of coordinating conjunctions, which include the following words: or, nor, but, yet, so, for, and. Coordinating conjunctions typically connect two independent clauses, which is to say that they connect two clauses that could stand as independent sentences, but are in some way related. In this sentence, the fact that reviews are good for business means that the retailers will want to incentivize reviews. In this case, because one thing logically results in another, the word "so" is the most appropriate conjunction.

7   D. In this sentence, the restauranteur must choose amongst different options. The word "or" signals that only one of something can happen (and is frequently used with the word "either" as a correlative conjunction), where "and" signals that both of the things being referenced can happen. "For" suggests that the clause following it was the reason for the clause that preceded it, which is not the case in this sentence.

8   A. "Yet" is often used to show that two things are contradictory. In this case, it makes sense that one would not expect a car that had only recently been taken in for repairs to break down so soon after the maintenance had been performed. It does not make sense to use "so" or "for" since doing so would suggest that one would expect a recently repaired car to break down the next day or that the car was taken in for repairs yesterday when it broke down today. "Or" suggests that only one of things happened, when both, in fact, happened.

9   C. "But" is often used to show how one thing should have happened when it in fact did not. In this sentence, Amie's parents had a very different reaction than Amie expected. Amie's expectation wasn't shaped by her parents' actual reaction, as "for" would suggest; neither were her parents' reaction shaped by Amie's expectations, as "so" would suggest. As both events happened, "or" is inappropriate to use in this sentence.

10   D. The thief received a lenient sentence because of his testimony, not in spite of it. "For" makes a strong connection between the leniency and the testimony, showing that the testimony is what caused the thief to receive a lenient sentence. The contrary, as suggested by "but," is illogical. The other answer choices result in an illogical and incorrect sentence.

11   A. Both of the benefits mentioned are reasons why advocates maintain that recycling is a good practice. There is nothing in the sentence to suggest that the environmental benefit would preclude monetary savings (as "but" would do) or that saving money is bad (as "yet" would do). "Nor" is typically used with "neither" as a way to show that no possible event can take place, which is clearly not the intention of the sentence.

12   D. Is the best choice. The subordinating conjunction "because" is used to show that what follows (the subordinated clause, in this case) describes more about what precedes it (the independent clause, in this case). The independent clause states that the author was successful, and the subordinated clause describes reasons why, or how, this was accomplished. It does not make sense that the author was be successful in spite of his ability to tell a captivating story, as "although" would suggest. "So" suggests that the information in the subordinated clause took place because of the information in the independent clause, which in this case is illogical.

Modifiers

1   C. Modifiers are words or phrases that describe (or modify) other parts of a sentence. Modifiers tell us more information and paint a more detailed picture about a sentence's primary nouns and verbs. Modifiers can be adjectives, adverbs, adjective or adverb clauses, and verb or prepositional phrases. In general, modifiers should be placed as closely as possible to the thing that it modifies. Confusion can arise when the modifiers are placed "far away" from the things they modify. In this case, the meaning of the sentence changes significantly depending on where the modifier "practically" (an adverb) is placed. As written and as suggested in choice B, the sentence means that Kathleen has seen every movie which was made practically. Choice D suggests that Kathleen was practical in her watching of every movie ever made. Only choice C makes sense in context of the fact that she is a fan of movies; as used in this choice, "practically" tell us more about how many movies Kathleen has seen, and means "nearly all" in context of the sentence. In this case, the modifier "practically" is misplaced, resulting in a misplaced modifier and a logically confusing sentence.

2   B. In this case, "hardly" (an adverb) describes "see" and should be placed before the verb "see." As it is written, the modifier "hardly" is misplaced. The other choices do not reflect the fact that Jack could not see what was written because of his sunglasses. In these cases, it sounds like Jack could see well with his sunglasses on, except for the fact that the writing on the street sign is not written clearly or well.

3   B. The modifier in this sentence ("with a bushy wagging tail") is an adjective clause, or a clause that acts like an adjective. In this case, the adjective clause modifies the noun "dog," though it is misplaced and results in a confusing and grammatically incorrect sentence. As written, it is unclear whether or not the dog is chasing after a tennis ball that possesses a bushy, wagging tail. Choice B places the modifier most closely with the noun that it modifies, resulting in a grammatically correct and unambiguous sentence.

4   D. The modifier in this sentence ("with a grudge") is an adverb clause, or a clause that acts like an adverb. In this case, the adverb clause modifies the verb "signed," though it is misplaced and results in a confusing sentence. As

The Tutorverse

written, it is unclear whether or not the agreement has a grudge, or whether the Hamiltons signed a grudging agreement. By changing the phrase "with a grudge" to "grudgingly," the sentence is clear that the Hamiltons did not wish to sign the unfavorable agreement, but did so anyway. While choice C is grammatically correct, the resulting sentence does not carry the same meaning as the original, which clearly intended to convey the unwilling nature of the signing.

5   B. The modifier "while playing the lead in *King Lear*" is a dangling modifier – a modifier that modifies nothing in the sentence as written. Without it, the sentence is grammatically correct, yet with it, the sentence is confusing and ambiguous: was the audience groaning as the actor played the lead in *King Lear*, or was the audience – for some reason – playing the lead in *King Lear* and groaning simultaneously? Only choice B correctly places the modifier close to the modified thing (the actor) and clarifies the sentence.

6   C. "Collecting into tiny pools" is a dangling modifier. As with question 5, without this modifier, the sentence is grammatically correct, though with it, the sentence is confusing: is Forrest collecting into tiny pools, or are the icicles that hang from trees (or the melted icicles)? Only choice C correctly and unambiguously places the modifier close to the modified thing (the melted icicles).

7   D. "Shining from a new coat of car polish" is, as written, a dangling modifier. By moving it close to the modified thing (the car) and offsetting it with commas (into what is known as a parenthetical expression), the sentence becomes more clear. Otherwise, it may seem that Jeremy himself was shining from a new coat of car polish.

8   B. It doesn't make sense that the kitten, which is nervously taking its first steps, would be dripping with excitement and pride. Thus, it makes the most sense that the modifier "dripping with excitement and pride" would modify how Casey watched the kitten. The other choices remain ambiguous.

9   B. The word "quickly" is, as written, a squinting modifier; that is, a modifier that can reasonably modify multiple things in the sentence. In this case, the sentence could mean that reading complex sentences at a rapid pace can improve one's vocabulary. Or, the sentence could mean that reading complex sentences can improve, at a rapid pace, one's vocabulary. Choice B is the only selection that properly clarifies this sentence.

10   C. As with question 9, the modifier can apply to a number of different things. The modifier here is "after the math lesson" and could apply to when the teacher told the class, when the recess will happen, or more confusingly, to students. Choice C is the only choice that clarifies the modifier appropriately.

11   A. The modifier "at the store" is ambiguous in choices B-D.

12   A. The modifier "energetically" is an adverb, which can describe more about an action (verb). In the sentence, there are two verbs: "deliver" and "perceived." The modifier should be placed closest to that which it modifies. In this case, it does not make logical sense that the "energetically" modify "perceived." Doing so results in an illogical or confusing sentence. Instead, the adverb should modify "deliver."

Shifting Tenses, Mood, Voice, and Number

1   C. Verbs must agree in tense, and tenses relate to time. The three main verb tenses relate to the past (something that happened in the past), present (something that is happening now), and future (something that will happen in the future). Each of these three tenses are further divided into the simple, progressive, perfect, and perfect progressive tenses, which each indicate when something has been (or is being or will be) done. In this sentence, the verb "realized" is written in the past simple tense. Therefore, the verb "jump" should also be written in the past simple tense as "jumped." The other forms of the verb "jump" are written in various forms of the present or future tense.

2   A. The subordinated clause "because…returns" describes why "Dominic…future," the independent clause. In the former, the clause's main verb "had been receiving" is written in the past perfect progressive form, which tells how Dominic had continuously received high returns before his decision to continue investing in the future. In the latter, the clause's main verb "will be continuing" is written in the future progressive form, telling how Dominic has not yet invested, but will do so at some point in the future. The sentence is illogical if "continue" is written in the past perfect progressive ("had been continuing"), the future perfect form ("will have continued"), or the future perfect progressive ("will have been continuing").

3   D. The sentence suggests that the counselors had already found Tony, which means that Tony must have already hidden after hearing the scary story and subsequently been found by the counselors. Since this is the case, neither the future simple tense "will hide" nor the future perfect tense "will have hidden" make sense; neither does the present perfect progressive form "has been hiding." Only the past perfect progressive form "had been hiding" makes sense, as the hiding has already taken place and describes how Tony had hidden for some extended period of time.

4   C. In addition to tenses, verbs can also be classified by mood. There are three moods: the indicative, the imperative, and the subjunctive. The vast majority of verbs are used in the indicative mood, which states a fact or indicates a state of being. The imperative mood is used to indicate a request or a command. The subjunctive mood is used to express a wish or state something contrary to fact. In this sentence, the verb "call" is written in the imperative mood, telling someone to make a phone call. Choice C expresses the verb "tell" in the imperative mood. The other choices are written in the indicative mood, including "you tell."

5   A. In this sentence, a command is being issued; thus, the imperative mood is called for. "Avoid" is already written in the imperative mood (like "decide"), where "avoiding" is written in the indicative mood (as in "Avoiding trouble is beneficial."). "You avoid" is also written in the indicative mood (as in "You avoid a lot of responsibility."); "your avoiding" is used incorrectly in this sentence, and is also written in the indicative mood (as in "Your avoiding of the matter is harmful.")

6   D. "Bide your (time)" is written in the imperative mood, instructing someone to wait. This mood conflicts with the mood of "acting," which is written in the indicative mood. "Biding your" matches the verb tense and mood with "acting." Note that the other choices omit some variant of "you," resulting in a grammatically incorrect sentence.

7   A. The subjunctive mood (only used with the verbs "be" and "were") are used to show something contrary to a fact or to express a wish or request. Since the author is not likely to be a fictional character in reality, the person the author addresses is not likely a trillionaire. The indicative verbs "was," "is," and "are" are not appropriate to use. The phrase "would be" is often a clue that the verb in question should be in the subjunctive mood.

8   B. Though choice A may seem intuitive, the sentence expresses a (rather firm) request of managers that currently is not the case (i.e. the mangers are not all present at the call). "Are," "is," and "being" are all indicative moods, and are inappropriate for this type of sentence. In this case, the verb "be" is an example of the present subjunctive, where in question 7 "were" was an example of the past subjunctive.

9   B. In the first independent clause, "spent" is the past simple tense of "spend." The first clause is also written in the active voice, where Arthur, the subject of the sentence, is doing the action described by the rest of the sentence (i.e., wasting the day). In the second clause, after the semicolon, the subject of the sentence is "the day," upon which some action was performed (i.e. Arthur's wasting, described in the passive voice). To correct for the change in voice, the second clause should show that Arthur had wasted the day, as it does in the first clause. The progressive form of "waste" ("was wasting") is inappropriate, as the action being referred to has already ceased. Choice D is incorrect is it is also written in the passive voice. More practice on active and passive voice can be found in the Parallel Structure section.

10   D. The sentence describes a hypothetical situation which requires that the conditional mood be used. The word "may" properly reflects the possibility that a perfect score can lead to many opportunities. It would not be appropriate to use any forms of the past tense of the verb "lead."

11   C. Along with choice B, the subordinated clause ("as ...him") is written in the passive voice where the independent clause ("Jim...routine") is written in the active voice. To correct this, choice C uses the present simple tense of "treat" (which is congruent with the present simple tense of "make") to show that the action is being performed on the beans, water, and implements by Jim.

12   A. The sentence as written maintains the active voice; in addition, verb tenses agree (i.e. "felt" is written in the past simple tense, as is "seemed"). The other answer choices either convert part of the sentence into the passive voice, or inappropriately shift between various verb tenses.

Parallel Structure

1   B. One of the rules for writing with parallel construction is to ensure that verb tenses agree within the sentence, as was introduced in the previous section. In this sentence, the verbs "wash" and "clean" are written in the future simple tense; so too should the verb "reseal" be in future simple tense.

2   C. The independent clause "Donovan...test" contains a verb written in the past perfect tense ("had prepared") indicating that the preparation was something that had taken place already. The subordinated clause "by...regularly" explains more about the preparation. The sentence indicates that Donovan prepared by "studying" (progressive). Thus, the verb "exercise" should also be written in the progressive form ("exercising") as opposed to A (present simple), B (future progressive), or D (past perfect progressive).

3   D. "Skating" is a gerund, or a word that begins with a verb and ends in –ing that acts like a noun. Writing with parallel construction means using the same form of nouns. Here, to complement "skating," the best choice is "jumping" and "spinning." Other forms of "jump" and "spin" may appear to be grammatically correct, but fail at establishing parallel construction in the sentence.

4   A. The voice of a sentence also affects whether or not a sentence is written with parallel structure. In this case, the sentence is written in the active voice, where the subject is actively *doing* what the verb tells us. Among other issues, the other choices change the second part of the sentence to be written in the passive voice, where the verb is *being done to* the subject.

5   A. "Learning" and "studying" are both gerunds that reflect the appropriate parallelism in the sentence. The other choices do not reflect this construction and result in an awkward or incorrect sentence.

The Tutorverse

6 B. The first part of the sentence is written in the active voice, so the second part of the sentence should also be written in the active voice. Only choice B is written in the active voice.

7 C. The sentence is largely written in the passive voice – "I" was "worried by"; "bus" would be "stopped by"; "road" would be "made slippery by." As written, and as in choices B and D, the action of the driver falling asleep is written in the active voice. Only choice C correctly expresses the passive voice.

8 D. While there is nothing grammatically wrong with the sentence as written per-se, parallelism applies to the use of prepositions such as "on" in a sentence. Within a sentence, care must be taken that the proper prepositions precede a noun or phrase. Here, the preposition "on" applies appropriately to each day of the week; thus, there is no need to use another "on" before "Friday."

9 D. The appropriate preposition to use with "countertop" is "on" (one does not generally find anything besides the countertop "in a countertop"). Therefore, D is the only appropriate choice, as "air" and "countertops" require different propositions. It is also generally appropriate to organize items in a list by degree of importance or specificity; in this case, the items progress from more general to more specific.

10 C. Writing with parallel construction can also mean ensuring that the placement of conjunctions is consistent throughout the sentence. In this sentence, the correlative conjunctions "not only" is placed after the verb "is"; the correlative conjunction "but also" is placed before the verb "is." To correct the parallelism in the sentence, the conjunction "but also" should follow "is." However, repeating "is" is unnecessary, as the verb "is" serves the entire predicate ("not...rewarding").

11 B. Parallel construction requires that the clauses being correlated by conjunctions such as "either" and "or" are logical. In this case, the piece is either something creative and original or it was not. Popularity is irrelevant in this sentence. We do not know for sure whether or not the critic does in fact like the painting. Thus, only B is logical, as the piece was either original or an imitation.

12 B. The sentence is largely written in the simple present tense – "is," "stay," and "enjoy." Therefore, "drink" should also be written in the simple present tense, as it is in choice B. "Drank" and "drunk" are the simple past and past participle forms of "drink," and "be drinking" is the progressive form of the simple present.

Pronoun Clarity

1 A. A pronoun (a word that replaces a noun) must have a clear antecedent, otherwise the sentence can become confusing or ambiguous. In this case, "he" refers to Larry, the person who had just won the lottery. By adding another pronoun, such as "it," "they," or "someone," the sentence becomes ambiguous at best and confusing at worst. For example, what is the "it" that would donate to charity? Who are the "they" or who is the mysterious "someone"?

2 A. An antecedent need not always precede the pronoun. In this sentence, the pronoun "it" refers to bilge water, which needs to be pumped out of the bottom of a ship. "He" and "they" are not appropriate pronouns to refer to bilge water. The bilge water must be pumped out, not the pump itself.

3 D. Unlike in the first two questions, this sentence is vague in that we do not know who is doing the suggesting. The use of "he," "she," and "they" do not correct the problem of clarifying who is doing the suggesting. This sentence, as written, is an example of a sentence where there is no clear antecedent (the person suggesting could be the author, a character, an interviewee, etc.). Only by clearly suggesting that it is "the author" who is doing the indicating does the sentence become more clear.

4 B. It is unclear whether "they" refers to a group of people or to the source of the loudness. By clarifying "the sound was," we are no longer confused by whether or not the volume was turned down because the group of people was too loud or if the surroundings were too loud. The other answer choices are nonsensical or grammatically incorrect.

5 A. Using the pronouns as suggested in choices B and C would result in a vague sentence – one where we do not know who forgot that jackhammering would be noisy. "The burglar" is used appropriately to inform the reader that it was the thief who made the mistake. "She" conflicts with what we already know: that the subject of the sentence is already referred to as "him."

6 C. As written, "her" could refer to either the executive or the employee; so too could "his" refer to both the employee and the executive, since we do not know either's gender. Using "a" helps to clarify the ownership of the bonus. This question is an example of a pronoun with more than one possible antecedent.

7 D. "It" could refer to either the yacht or the sailboat, as could "the vessel," resulting in confusion as to which boat, if any, is being discussed. From the second independent clause after the semicolon, we know that both boats will not be repaired and would be scrapped instead. Therefore, "they" appropriately refers to both the yacht and the sailboat and makes logical sense in context of this sentence.

The Tutorverse

8   A. By using "they," "somebody," or "some," the sentence is confusing as to who the informed persons are. The original phrasing, referring to both parties – that is, both the investment bankers and corporate attorneys – is most clear, having clear antecedents. "They were" could refer to one group of people or both – it is unclear and therefore not the best choice.

9   B. In this sentence, the word "they" could refer to the people who do the shopping, the actual after-dinner sales, or even the dinners themselves – another example of a pronoun with more than one possible antecedent. "These" and "those" do not clarify the sentence any more than "they." Only by repeating "the sales" in the dependent clause after the second comma in the sentence does the sentence become clear. Alternatively, "the former."

10   B. It is unclear, as originally written, who "he" and "she" refer to. Choice B lets us know that the doctor told Harriet that the latter had a vitamin deficiency. The other choices, "he" and "they" are still unclear about who is speaking to whom (or who "they" are).

11   C. The pronoun "he" is unclear: is the sentence referring to the stranger, or to the agoraphobic man? In order to clarify, the best choice is "the former," as "anyone" and "it" are as vague or inappropriate. Pronouns must have a clear antecedent to which they refer. In this case, "former" refers to "stranger," letting the reader know who spoke the sentence.

12   C. The pronoun "it" could refer to "piano" or "violin" and, as written, it is unclear which instrument it refers to. Only "the violin" clarifies the meaning of the sentence.

Possessive Determiners

1   B. Possessive determiners are used like adjectives; they accompany nouns and apply to nouns just like adjectives do. Possessive pronouns are used like nouns; they take the place of nouns. "My" is a possessive determiner and "mine" is a possessive pronoun (variations of the nouns "I" and "me"). In this sentence, "mine" is used incorrectly. The word "my" applies to "opinion."

2   D. "You're" is a contraction, abbreviating "you are," and is inappropriate in this sentence. "Your" is the possessive determiner and "yours" is the possessive pronoun. The word "your" lets the reader know that the writer is referring to the daily life of "you."

3   A. "His" is both a possessive determiner and a possessive pronoun (where "him" and "he" are simply pronouns). By using "his," we know that we are referring to Copernicus' brilliant ideas and revolutionary theories. There is no such word as "his'."

4   C. "Hers" is a possessive pronoun, and "her" is a possessive determiner. In this sentence, the possessive determiner is needed to show that the work belongs to Marie Curie. There is no such word as "her's," and "she's" is a contraction of "she is."

5   A. "Its" is a possessive determiner, which here shows that the importance refers to jury duty. "It's" is a contraction of "it is" and is incorrect to use in this sentence. There is no such word as "it'" or "its'."

6   B. In this case, the contraction "it's" is inappropriate. If used, the reader would be confused as to what the "right" referred to.

7   A. "Our" is a possessive determiner where "ours" is a possessive pronoun. In this case, "our" lets us know who has concerns.

8   C. The possessive determiner "their" lets the reader know whose contribution would be the paper. In this case, it is some group of people. "They're" is a contraction of "they are" and is inappropriate and illogical to use. "Theirs" is a regular pronoun that does not show possession. "Their's" is not a word.

9   D. The possessive determiner must be used to let the reader know whose group must confess. "There" is an adverb that describes where someone or something is, was, or will be.

10   B. "Who's" is a contraction of "who is" and is not appropriate to use here (it does not make sense that someone would be a cookie). The possessive determiner "whose" is the only grammatically correct choice here. Note that "whom's" and "whomever's" are not words.

11   A. "Whose" is used appropriately here and should not be changed, as it describes who the turn belongs to. The contraction "who's" is inappropriate here.

12   D. "It's" is a contraction of "it is" and is appropriate in this sentence as it would read "It is alive!" "Its" is the possessive form used to show that something belongs to "it" and is inappropriate in this case.

Possessive Nouns & Pronouns

1   B. As written, the sentence suggests that Miami and New York City jointly possess the same climate. However, we know from the sentence that the climate in each city is different. Adding an " 's" to the end of each noun signifies that there are two separate climates being discussed. In the case of proper and regular nouns, an apostrophe is needed to signify possession.

2   A. Unlike in question 1 of this section, two nouns jointly possess the same object. In this case, we know that Simon and Judith purchased their home together. The punctuation as written reflects this joint ownership, which follows the last of the nouns that possess.

3   D. From the sentence, we know that the subject of the sentence is plural ("they" is used to refer to flight attendants). Because we know that the subject is plural, the proper punctuation to use to signify the possessive of a plural noun is an apostrophe at the end of the word. Adding an " 's" would signify that only one flight attendant shares the opinion expressed in the sentence.

4   C. There is only one chairman in this case (as indicated by the "he" used after the semicolon), so we know the noun is singular. To signify possession, an " 's" is added to the end of the singular noun. As written, the sentence suggests that there are several chairman.

5   B. The sentence suggests that there is only one Camilla (as indicated by "she"). We know that an apostrophe is needed to indicate that we are talking about her preference. To do so, an apostrophe between the "a" and the "s" of "Camillas" is needed. No apostrophe is needed in preference, as there is nothing that is possessed by "preference" (unlike "preference" itself, which is possessed by Camilla).

6   C. The pronoun "it" is used to refer to an object or thing and generally not to a person. The possessive form of "it" is "its." In this case, the sentence is referring to Dexter's life and the appropriate possessive pronoun to use is "his." Remember, possessive pronouns replace the noun that it refers to, where possessive determiners accompany the nouns they refer to. "His" is special in that it is both a possessive pronoun and possessive determiner. Both "its" and "his" are exceptions to the general rule that possession is indicated with an apostrophe.

7   B. "It's" is a contraction that means "it is"; in this sentence, the possessive form "its" is needed to refer to the book's fresh take on old issues.

8   D. The possessive pronoun "hers" is used to refer to Monica's way of doing dishes. There is no apostrophe needed to indicate possession (it is not a word).

9   D. The possessive pronoun "yours" does not require an apostrophe to show possession.

10   A. The possessive pronoun "theirs" does not require an apostrophe to show possession.

11   B. The possessive pronoun "ours" does not require an apostrophe to show possession.

12   A. We know from the word "all" that the sentence references more than one person's opinion, and that the opinion is attributable to these people. The plural of "crew member" is "crew members"; to indicate possession, add an apostrophe after "crewmembers" (but not another "s"). Note that choice D represents only the plural of "crew member" and does not show possession. Choice B indicates only that there is a single crew member.

Subject-Verb Agreement

1   B. Singular subjects must be matched with singular verbs, as plural verbs must be used with plural subjects. The matching of singular verbs with singular subjects and plural verbs with plural subjects is the act of ensuring subject-verb agreement, or ensuring that the verb and subject numbers agree. Identifying the subject is critical. The girls, the lake, the time, and the town are all nouns, but only the camp is the subject. The prepositional phrase "for girls" describes "camp" while the entire phrase "some five hours away from the closest town" describes the general location. The subject, therefore, is "camp." The verb "are" is plural, and the subject "camp" is singular. Therefore, the only correct choice is B, using the verb "is."

2   A. The noun "senators" is already plural, which already agrees with the plural verb "are." Other choices are singular verbs and do not agree with the plural subject, which in this case is "senators."

3   C. Certain indefinite pronouns such as "everybody" may seem like they should be plural (since it does talk about more than one person), but they are actually singular. Therefore, only the singular verb "was" is appropriate here (think of "everybody" as a single unit).

4   B. In some cases, indefinite pronouns that sound like they should be accompanied with a plural verb (such as "all" in this case) should actually be accompanied by singular verbs. In these cases, it is important to look at the object of the prepositional phrase (that we ignored when determining the subject in Question 1 of this section) to determine the number of the verb.

5   D. Whenever the word "every" appears in front of a word or group of words, the verb associated with those words should be singular. "Was" is the only singular answer choice.

6   B. When describing an amount of something as a single group or unit, a singular verb should accompany the subject. In this sentence, "ten pounds of meat" is treated like a unit, so the singular verb "is" is the best choice.

The Tutorverse

7   D. In this sentence, the subject is "mathematics," which is a singular noun that ends in "s." Though "mathematics" appears to be a plural noun that should be accompanied by a plural verb, it should actually be accompanied by the singular verb "is." There are many such nouns that appear plural but are actually singular (a clue about this is found in the clause, where "a subject" refers to "mathematics").

8   A. Compound subjects (in this case, financial functions and operational functions) that are joined by the word "and" take a plural verb (in this case, "are").

9   B. Some compound subjects that are joined by the word "and" are actually treated as singular if they are thought of as a single unit. In this case, the friend is also the long-time mentor, and should be accompanied by a singular verb such as "requests."

10   B. Singular subjects that are joined by "or" or "nor" (in this case, "teacher," "counselor," and "principal") are accompanied by a singular verb (no matter how strange it might sound to say the resulting sentence aloud). In this case, "is" is the only singular verb. Similarly, plural subjects joined by "or" or "nor" should be accompanied by plural verbs.

11   A. When a singular subject and a plural subject ("Bill's son" and "Bill's three daughters," respectively) are joined by "or" or "nor," the number of the verb follows the number of the subject closest to it. In this case, "Bill's son" is closest to the verb of being, "is/are/was/were," etc. Thus we should choose the singular verb of being: "is."

12   D. The verb "was" must be congruent and match in number with the subject ("Dorothy"), which is singular in number (there is only one Dorothy). Therefore, the only singular verb of "be" is the past tense verb "was"; "have" and "were" are both plural (i.e. "they were" or "they have").

Noun-Agreement

1   C. Two related nouns (for example, a subject and a modifying word or phrase containing a noun) must have the same number. Problems arise when a noun and its modifier disagree in number; for example, if the noun is singular but the modifier is plural. In this case, the proper noun "Bellagio" is a singular noun (the name of a single place). The noun "Bellagio" is modified by the phrase "is a municipality," which describes more about "Bellagio." Because "Bellagio" is singular, it is appropriate to use the singular noun "municipality" with the appropriate singular verb "is."

2   D. In this sentence, there are two nouns: Jupiter and Saturn. Taken together, "Jupiter and Saturn" is a plural noun (which is followed by the plural verb "are"). The word "planet" modifies both Jupiter and Saturn, and should also be pluralized as "planets."

3   B. The noun "gala" is modified by the phrase "the events of the season." By ignoring the prepositional phrase "of the season," we know that the main modifier of "gala" is "events." However, "gala" – a count noun (that is, a noun that can be counted) – is singular, so "events" should be as well; therefore, only the singular noun "event" (accompanied by the singular verb "was") is appropriate.

4   C. The plural count noun "cars" is described by the noun "model" which should also be plural. "Models" is the only plural noun offered as a choice.

5   A. Because this sentence is complex, start by stripping away details, or parts of the sentence that are not necessary to the core meaning of the sentence. The part of a sentence that starts with "because" and ends in some punctuation (in this case, a comma) is a dependent clause and generally not essential to the core meaning of the sentence. In this case, the entire clause "Because…politics" is unnecessary to the core meaning of the sentence. Similarly, the clause "which…contributions" is unnecessary to the core meaning of the sentence – it only serves to tell the reader more about fundraisers. Because the sentence's purpose is to explain that politicians and their managers hold fundraisers (as indicated in the independent clause "politicians…fundraisers"), we know that the two nouns that must match in number are "fundraisers" (also a count noun) and "events." Because the former is plural, so too should the latter be plural.

6   B. Some nouns, such as "equipment," are called noncount (or mass) nouns. Unlike count nouns (i.e. "a hundred cars"), noncount nouns cannot be numbered. These nouns are always singular, so the nouns that are used to modify them should also be singular. In this case, "gear" is the most clear singular noun offered in the answer choices. "Them" results in an indefinite pronoun, which makes the sentence vague.

7   A. As with "equipment," "happiness" is a noncount noun and is always treated as a singular noun. Therefore, even though the happiness belongs to more than one traveler, it is written in the singular.

8   D. Another noncount noun, "unease" is always treated as a singular noun. The possessive forms of the word are inappropriate to use, as the sentence is not describing the worry felt by unease; rather, the sentence is describing the unease and worry of the crowd.

The Tutorverse

9 B. "Orchestra" is a collective noun. Collective nouns are able to take a singular or plural form depending on the use. In this case, "orchestra" is referring to a single group of musicians (as suggested by "the city's orchestra," not "orchestras." Therefore, the singular noun "musical ensemble" is the best choice.

10 D. The collective noun "government" can be treated either as a singular or plural noun depending on context. Here, the government is being treated as an entity comprised of many people who cannot agree with each other. Therefore, "themselves" is the best choice. Note that a singular form "itself" would also be grammatically correct, though the choice is not offered here. There is no such word as "themself."

11 C. In this case, the collective noun "faculty" can either be paired with "has" or "have." However, the noun "procedure" must be written in the appropriate number in context of the sentence. "A procedure" would signal a single procedure, where "procedures" would signal many. Either works in this sentence grammatically, though only one is given as an answer choice.

12 B. We know from the sentence that there is more than one candle in the apartment ("candles" and "were" are both plural. The word "holder" is related to the word "candles" and should also be plural, otherwise it would be illogical that one candleholder could be spread throughout an apartment. While votives and candlesticks can also hold candles, they are all singular.

Logical Comparison

1 C. When a sentence compares two things, it is important to clearly and precisely identify the two things being compared. An easy way to do this is to remove prepositional phrases or other descriptive phrases. In this sentence, the things being compared are temperatures, not places themselves, as the prepositional phrase "in Antarctica" might suggest. Though it would be proper to compare "temperatures in Antarctica" with "temperatures in Africa," an equally acceptable way to compare the two temperatures would be to use the word "those" to refer to "temperatures." Without the word "those," the sentence compares temperatures with Africa itself, or something vague having to do with Africa (in the case of "all" and "some").

2 D. In this sentence two different weights are being compared – that of a tiger and that of a common house cat. Of the given choices, only "that of a common house cat" properly indicates that two different weights are being compared. Using any other choice would incorrectly compare the weight of a tiger and house cats themselves (as opposed to the weight of a common house cat).

3 D. It is important to clarify that the things being compared in this sentence are prices of handbags. As written, the sentence does compare two prices; however, we know from the clause "though all handbags essentially serve the same purpose" that the two prices being compared have to do with handbags, not just any thing. Therefore, using "accessories" or "some other things" is not the best choice.

4 B. What is being compared are not the two days ("yesterday" and "today"), but rather the content displayed on the front page of each day's newspaper. Without clarifying this fact with "yesterday's cover," the sentence inappropriately compares the day "yesterday" with the front page of today's newspaper.

5 A. By removing the prepositional phrase "in a kiwifruit," it becomes clear that the sentence is comparing amounts of potassium. The phrase "that found" refers to "amount of potassium"; without it, the sentence would compare an amount of potassium with bananas themselves (as opposed to the amount of potassium in bananas).

6 B. The phrase "to make delicious sauces" describes the particular ability being compared. As written, the sentence actually compares this ability with other people (as opposed to those other people's abilities to make delicious sauces). Choice C makes a similarly erroneous comparison, while choice D compares sauce-making abilities with sauces themselves. Only by comparing "ability" with "skill" does the sentence make logical sense.

7 C. What is being compared in this sentence are not different people or different types of degrees, but rather different opportunities. It is inappropriate, therefore, to compare opportunities (of those who graduate from elite universities) to people (as choice A and B would suggest) or degrees themselves (as choice D would suggest).

8 A. In this sentence, the number of calories being consumed by different animals is being compared. Choice A clarifies this best by including the verb "do," which complements the word "consuming." The other answer choices compare the number of calories consumed to either the act of consumption, the calories "of" other animals (which is nonsensical), or the weight of other animals.

9 D. The proper way to compare the amounts of lead in different types of glassware is to refer again to the amount of lead using the phrase "what is found in." Otherwise, the sentence would suggest a comparison between the amount of lead (in crystal glassware) and actual everyday glassware itself.

10 B. While the sentence as written suggests a comparison between bagels made in different locations, the proper way to compare the two is to use the phrase "superior to" and refer to the thing being compared. Without the phrase "those made in," the sentence would compare bagels (made in New York City) with the actual city of Los Angeles or, worse yet, with Los Angeles' bagels that were made in New York City.

The Tutorverse

11   A. It is most logical to compare the capabilities of sports cars to other types of cars, rather than to compare them with other machines. Similarly, it does not make sense that sports cars can have a greater capacity "than all cars," as sports cars are themselves a type of car. In this sentence, "sports cars" cannot be compared with "other sports cars," as the capabilities of sports cars as a class are being compared with something else.

12   C. The thing that divides New Yorkers is whether one place is better than another. However, as written, the sentence compares "the West Side" with "living on the East Side." This is illogical. Comparing "living/life" on one side of New York with the other would make sense. However, this is not an option, as choices A, B, and D result in a sentence that compares the West Side itself with "living/life" on the East Side. Only C makes a congruent comparison between the two physical locations.

Frequently Confused Words

1   B. There are three homophones in this question: "you're," "your," and "yore." Homophones are words that sound like other words when spoken but are spelled differently (and mean different things). Only choice B is the proper determiner that addresses the writer's audience.

2   B. "Except" and "accept" are examples of homophones. To "accept" something means to consent or receive it, where "except" specifies that something should not be included. Neither "except" nor the words in choice C and D are appropriate in this sentence.

3   D. "Bare" and "bear" are homophones. To "bare" something means to uncover it, whereas to "bear" something means to carry, support, or endure something (unless, of course, we're talking about the large, furry mammal).

4   C. "Complement" and "Compliment" are homophones. A "compliment" is an expression of praise or admiration. A "complement" is something that completes or enhances something else.

5   A. There are three homophones in this question: "whether," "weather," and "wether." Only the former expresses doubt about the students' ability to pass the test.

6   C. "Threw" and "through" are homophones. "Threw" is the past tense of "throw"; it being impossible to throw a tunnel, only "through" works in this sentence.

7   D. The homophones "too," "two," and "to" are frequently confused. Only "too," meaning "also" or "in addition to" is appropriate in this sentence.

8   B. The homophones "their," "there," and "they're" are frequently confused. "There" denotes a place; "they're" is a contraction, shortening "they are." Only "their" is possessive, referring to people.

9   A. Only the verb "mete" appropriately describes the action that the vice principal often takes. The homophones in choices B and D are not appropriate in this sentence.

10   C. "Cites" is a verb meaning "to quote," which is nonsensical if used in this sentence. Similarly, "sighs" is nonsensical. "Sight" is a noun referring to the actual ability to see. Only the noun "sights" makes sense in this sentence, as it refers to a place of interest that can be seen, often by tourists.

11   B. To "meddle" is to interfere with something. "Medal" (an award or commendation) and "metal" (a hard, material made of certain minerals) are tangible objects; only "mettle" refers to the intangible resolve of the team. All four words are homophones.

12   C. Movie trailers give moviegoers a preview of the movie, and allow them to "peek" or glimpse parts of the movie. However, trailers do not "peek" interest (as, say, a person would "peek" around a corner). While one's interest in a movie could theoretically "peak" and reach a high point, the sentence discusses the purpose of trailers, which is not to cause interest to reach a point after which there is no further interest. Instead, trailers are designed to "pique" or stimulate the interest of something. The word "pick" would result in a nonsensical sentence.

Conventional Expression

Questions 1-5 in this section focus on examples of mondegreens, otherwise known as eggcorns. Mondegreens/eggcorns are commonly used phrases that are misheard but retain their original meaning. While there are far more examples than are included in this section, these questions illustrate examples of more common mistakes.

1   B. The phrase "an object lesson" refers to something that serves as a real-life example of an abstract idea or thought. In this sentence, falling off of a bike but eventually learning to ride a bike demonstrates the value of perseverance. The word "abject" is an adjective with a negative connotation, usually referring to something unpleasant, bad, or degrading.

2   D. The phrase "day and age" refers to an era or general period of time. In this sentence, the customer complains about the need to use an antiquated technology in a time when there are more efficient ways to accomplish the same thing. Using "in," "on," or "or" results in a nonsensical sentence.

3   A. The phrase "one and the same" refers to something that is the same as something else. In this case, the sentence suggests that some people believe that all expensive bottles of wine taste good, and that good-tasting bottles of wine

372 Explanations: Part Two – Writing & Language

must be expensive. The word "and" is often misheard as "in." Though "one in the same" may make some metaphorical sense, it is objectively incorrect when the intention of the phrase is to express equivalency between two things.

4 C. The phrase "deep-seated" refers to something (such as a belief, feeling, idea, or behavior) that is deeply ingrained in something else (such as a person, or in this case, in families). The phrase "deep-seeded" may sound like it makes sense, at least from a metaphorical point of view, but the phrase is incorrect. As with any compound adjectives, a hyphen is necessary to connect "deep" and "seated" with "hatred."

5 D. The phrase "for all intents and purposes" refers to something that is the case for all practical purposes; though something to the contrary may happen, it is highly unlikely and essentially a given. In this case, the fans knew that the game was practically over, given the large difference in points between the two teams. "Intents and" is often misheard as "intensive," making the phrase nonsensical (what is an intensive purpose?).

Questions 6-11 in this section focus on idioms, special phrases with figurative meanings that are very different from their literal meanings. While there are far more examples than are included in this section, these questions highlight some common idiomatic expressions.

6 A. The phrase "takes the cake" can mean, figuratively, that something is either especially good or especially bad (depending on the context of the sentence). In this sentence, the author compares the latest animated film based on *Macbeth* to bad movies he's seen previously, so it can be inferred that the author is using the expression's negative connotation.

7 B. The phrase "add insult to injury" means, figuratively, to make an already bad situation worse. In this sentence, it is unlikely that the government is literally insulting or injuring the homeowner. In context, the idiomatic expression is the only logical choice, as the writer describes how a bad situation becomes worse.

8 A. The phrase "back to the drawing board" means, figuratively, to rethink an idea that has proven to be unsuccessful or has otherwise failed. In this sentence, the writers and producers of a show spent a significant amount of time working on an idea, but upon learning that the show did not test well, needed to rethink the concept of the show.

9 D. The phrase "under the weather" means, figuratively, that someone is not feeling well. In this sentence, the meaning of the expression can be inferred through the use of the word "though" at the beginning of the sentence and the mother's knowledge of Avery's actual symptoms (fever; lack of appetite).

10 C. The phrase "the ball is in your/their court" means, figuratively, the person or persons being referred to (the subject of the "your" or "their" reference) must make the next move or take action next. In this sentence, the attorney has established that there is nothing further his team can do. He emphasizes this by using the idiomatic expression, suggesting that they must await action from someone else. There is no literal ball in a literal court (though the statement does discuss a legal matter).

11 B. The phrase "beat around the bush" means, figuratively, to avoid or delay some unpleasant or difficult task. In this sentence, Jill, who presumably knows Valentine well, was surprised by Valentine's apparent reticence. Because she knew Valentine to be very open and unreserved, she was surprised when he delayed and apparently avoided the subject at hand.

12 D. This question requires that students choose between various idiomatic expressions, which can be difficult without prior understanding of the expressions, as context is often of little help in determining the correct answer. Choice A refers to the fact that someone heard something from an authoritative source, which we can rule out as incorrect based on context; the sentence suggests that Swarup was "about" to share news but that he was interrupted by his mother. Choice B refers to a situation where one leaves a problem alone, or deliberately ignores it. This would also be nonsensical in context. To pull the wool over someone's eyes would be to deceive that person. Again, this is nonsensical. To let the cat out of the bag is to divulge a secret or something previously unknown. This makes sense in context, as it explains that Swarup was interrupted by his mother.

End-of-Sentence Punctuation

1 B. The sentence is an interrogative sentence (that asks a question) and should be punctuated with a question mark. Many interrogative sentences begin with similar phrases that use words such as: "who, what, where, when, why, how, do." Exclamation points are used to punctuate exclamatory sentences (that express strong emotion. Periods are used to punctuate declarative sentences (that make a statement) or imperative sentences (that give commands). Ellipses are used to show that something in a sentence has been omitted.

2 D. The sentence is a declarative sentence and should be punctuated with a period. A question mark is used to punctuate an interrogative sentence. Commas and dashes are never used to end a sentence.

3 A. The sentence is not a question and should not be punctuated with a question mark. A colon and semicolon are never used to punctuate the end of a sentence.

The Tutorverse

4   A. Though the students were excited, the sentence itself is a statement of fact – a declarative sentence. Thus, a question mark is inappropriate. The ellipses and dash are incorrectly used in this context.

5   C. The sentence is an imperative sentence and should be punctuated with a period and not with a question mark. Commas and colons are never used to punctuate the end of a sentence.

6   C. While declarative and imperative sentences (punctuated with a period) are always included before the closing quotation marks, question marks and exclamation points can either be included before or after the closing quotation marks, depending on the content being quoted. If the quoted material asks a question or is itself exclamatory, the question mark and exclamation point go before the closing quotation marks. If the sentence itself (not the quoted material) is a question or an exclamation, the punctuation goes after the closing quotation marks. In this case, the quoted material is a question – the sentence itself is not a question. When concluding a sentence with a question mark or exclamation point, no other punctuation is necessary.

7   B. This sentence is actually a question, quoting a statement made by Ashley. Because of this, the question mark does not go inside the quotation marks, but after it. No other punctuation is necessary.

8   A. The sentence is declarative, quoting Bill's emotionally charged yell. Therefore, the exclamation point goes inside the quotation marks. No other punctuation is necessary.

9   B. Based on the context of the sentence, we can infer that the writer intended to convey a strong sense of emotion – most likely one of pride and a sense of accomplishment. Therefore, this sentence is most likely an exclamatory sentence and should be punctuated with an exclamation point and not a question mark or ellipses. While a period may be correct, a sentence that ends with a quotation mark and is punctuated with a period is also included within the quotation marks (before the closing quotation mark).

10   B. Periods always go inside quotation marks.

11   A. When punctuating a quotation, periods always go before the closing quotation marks. However, the sentence is not a statement, so a period would not be used to end the sentence in this case. Walt directs a (rhetorical) question at Jessie, so a question mark is most appropriate. Because the question itself is being quoted, the question mark goes before the closing quotation marks, not after them. While an exclamation point would also be appropriate here, since the sentence conveys strong emotion, the exclamation point would go before the closing quotation marks as well, after them.

12   D. When more than one sentence is quoted from the same speaker, it is unnecessary to close the quotation marks after each sentence and to open them again at the beginning of the following sentence. Semicolons and colons are used as within-sentence punctuation marks and are not the best choice in this case.

Within-Sentence Punctuation

1   B. Commas are used to separate a series of items, to separate adjectives, to help conjunctions join two independent clauses, to signal quoted material (along with quotation marks), and to otherwise set apart clauses and phrases. Colons do not function like commas, and are used to signal a list. A semicolon is used to join two logically connected independent clauses together. In this case, "friends and family" is not an independent clause (it is incapable of standing alone as a sentence), so a semicolon is inappropriate. The sentence indicates that there are two things needed for Jordan to be happy, and a colon is best used to signal that a list of these things follows.

2   A. There is no list of items, so a colon is inappropriate. "If she could get a ride" is not an independent clause, so neither the semicolon nor the period are appropriate. The dash is used to introduce an interruption to the original thought, to emphasize a previously mentioned thought, or to expand further on something mentioned in the sentence. The main purpose of the sentence is to tell about how eager Sarah is to go home; the dash is used to provide additional information that complements the main purpose of the sentence – namely, a condition that must be met.

3   C. There are two independent and logically related clauses in this sentence: "The influential restaurant critic was famously ill-tempered" and "the restaurant staff worked diligently to make him happy." Though this sentence could be split into two sentences separated by a period, the best option of the choices offered uses a semicolon (and the conjunctive adverb "therefore") to combine the two thoughts into a single complementary sentence. Using a comma results in a run-on sentence (a comma splice). Both the dash and the colon are incorrect.

4   B. Commas are used at the end of an introductory adverb clause, in this case "Because she had recently moved to a new city." Adverb clauses are a group of words with their own subject and verb that together act like an adverb, describing a verb, adjective, or another adverb. A semicolon is inappropriate, as the adverb clause cannot stand alone as a sentence. Neither is a colon appropriate, since the phrase after it is not a list of items.

5   D. There are two independent but illogically related clauses in this sentence. Droughts in California have little to do with umbrellas in London. Because these ideas are unrelated, they cannot be joined with a semicolon. Using a comma results in a comma splice. A dash is also inappropriate to use given the content of the two clauses.

The Tutorverse

6   B. "Forgetting to set her alarm clock" is an introductory verbal. Commas are used after introductory verbals or verb phrases (words that look like verbs but are actually other parts of speech). This verbal cannot stand alone as a sentence, so a semicolon is inappropriate. The dash and colon are not appropriately used in this sentence.

7   D. There are two independent and logically related clauses in this sentence. If a period were to be used to separate the two clauses, a semicolon following the conjunctive adverb "thus" would be inappropriate. Instead, the conjunctive adverb should be preceded with a semicolon and followed with a comma.

8   A. The other answer choices use commas unnecessarily to set apart clauses that should not be set apart. If the parts of a sentence set apart by commas are removed, and the sentence still retains its original meaning, then it's a safe bet that those commas are appropriately included in the sentence. If, however, the parts of a sentence set apart by commas are removed, and the sentence no longer retains its original meaning, then it's a safe bet that those commas are inappropriately included in the sentence (more on this in the *Parenthetical Expressions* category).

9   C. Commas are used to separate two or more adjectives that describe the same noun. In this case, "sleek" and "stealthy" describe the cat and should be separated by a comma.

10   C. The statement is describing something the narrator exclaimed, so the exclamation point belongs inside the quotation marks. No further punctuation is necessary.

11   A. Hyphens are not needed in this sentence. One of the ways a hyphen is used is to denote a compound adjective, which is a situation where two or more adjectives form a single image or thought that describes a noun. In this case, the "sixteenth century" is a noun. If it were used as a compound adjective, such as in the sentence "Galileo Galilei was a famous sixteenth-century scientist," then a hyphen would be necessary.

12   A. A colon is used to indicate a list or series of items that generally cannot stand alone as sentences. The independent clause "brushing with…enamel" states examples or items supporting the preceding independent clause, but is written in such a way that it can stand alone; thus, a colon is inappropriate. Inserting a comma would result in a comma splice. A dash is used to provide more information or details about something being discussed. In this case, the consequences of not observing proper technique are discussed, but in such a way that they two clauses stand alone. Thus, a semicolon is most appropriate.

Punctuating a Series

1   A. The various clauses in this sentence are already separated effectively by commas and the use of a conjunction ("and"). Removing the comma as suggested in choice B would result in the fusing of two independent clauses. Using a dash is inappropriate, as no interruptions or emphasis is used in this sentence. A colon is used to signal to the reader that a list, separated by commas or semicolons, follows. In this sentence, there is no list, as the sentence is made up of multiple independent clauses.

2   B. In this sentence, the items in a series are part of the dependent clause. The word "because" signals that the rest of the sentence after it relies upon the preceding part of the sentence. "Many…foods" could stand alone as a sentence, but "because…cholesterol" could not. Used correctly, the commas here separate fat, salt, and cholesterol into three distinct items. Used incorrectly (or not at all) as suggested in the other answer choices, and the sentence becomes confusing (what is "fat salt" anyway?). A semicolon would incorrectly break up the sentence such that "salt and cholesterol" would stand alone, as if it was an independent clause.

3   C. In this sentence, a colon is used to signal that a list of items follows. By itself, the list would be grammatically incorrect ("Sunscreen, money for lunch, and a pen.") and meaningless. Thus, a period or a semicolon would be incorrect. Using a comma would incorrectly signal that there are actually four items, with the field trip itself being an item (as opposed to the field trip being a reason to bring items).

4   B. Semicolons are often used to separate items in a list (as signaled by the use of a colon in "cities: Phoenix") that are already punctuated with commas. By leaving a comma between "Arizona" and "New York City," it would be unclear if the author meant that he or she lived in four places as opposed to three. By using a semicolon after each location, it becomes clear that the author had lived in three places only.

5   A. A dash can be used to describe more about part of a sentence. In this case, Cheryl, Blake, and Daniel are themselves the three coworkers who argue with one another. If, instead of dashes, commas were used, the sentence would be confusing: are the three coworkers who argue Cheryl, Blake, and Daniel, or are Cheryl, Blake, and Daniel arguing with three other (unnamed) coworkers? The answer choices that use a semicolon do so incorrectly and result in fragmented sentences.

6   B. We know from the sentence that there is a three-way race around the world. As written, it is unclear whether the Kingfisher is a yacht and sailboat that competed in a race or if the Kingfisher competed with a yacht and sailboat in a race (or, if the Kingfisher yacht competed with a sailboat in a race). Separating each of these items with a comma shows that three boats were involved in a race. Choice C incorrectly uses semicolons, and choice D suggests that the Kingfisher is a yacht and sailboat, which also contradicts the information in the sentence.

The Tutorverse

7   A. The items in this series relate to the reasons why cooking is a favorite pastime. The colon in this case signals that what follows are reasons for why cooking is a favorite pastime of the author. Since each reason is complicated, and sometimes contains more than one verb (as in the case of the first reason), a semicolon is best used to separate each reason, since additional commas would be confusing.

8   A. While benefits of gardening are listed, the structure of the sentence is such that a semicolon, colon, and hyphen are not necessary. The sentence is a compound sentence and no colon is necessary.

9   C. A semicolon is needed to separate the complex items in this series. At its most basic, the items in the list describe how the holidays are an opportunity for people to spend time with loved ones, give donations, and relax. Because the item related to donations is complex, and already punctuated with commas and other semicolons, it is helpful to separate it from the other items in the list with a semicolon.

10   B. Though the first part of this sentence is an independent clause that could stand alone should a period separate it from the rest of the sentence ("When…factors."), the rest of the sentence would not be able to stand alone. Velocity, acceleration, and the impact of gravity are all items in a series that describe the factors important to determining the path of a projectile. Thus, a colon is needed; and because the factors described are complicated and already separated by commas, semicolons are used to separate each factor.

11   C. As it is written, the only acceptable choice uses a comma. A semicolon or period results in a fragmented second-half of the sentence. A colon is not used appropriately since the items in a series are already denoted as such with the use of the phrase "such as the."

12   C. As written, the sentence incorrectly employs dashes, offsetting "set the alarm" as a parenthetical when it is in fact an important part of the sentence. Choice D results in the over use of semicolons to punctuate the list. Choice B results in a sentence where the list is punctuated with a colon in the wrong place, before the infinitive phrase "to close," which itself marks the beginning of the list. By dissecting the compound sentence, we know that "remember to" applies to "close," "set," and "lock."

Parenthetical Expressions & Nonrestrictive Clauses

1   A. In this sentence, the clause "almost as much as a cat hates getting wet" is nonrestrictive. A nonrestrictive clause (also known as a parenthetical expression) can be removed from the sentence without changing the sentence's basic meaning. A parenthetical expression can be offset by commas, parentheses, or dashes, depending on the sentence's construction. In this sentence, the meaning of the sentence does not change if the parenthetical is removed. Using a parenthesis with a comma or using a dash with a comma is, in this case, incorrect. Parentheses must always be both opened and closed, and a comma must usually precede and follow a parenthetical.

2   A. In this sentence, the nonrestrictive clause provides more information about the word "routine." The meaning of the sentence would be unchanged should the clause be removed. Because a dash is used at the beginning of the clause, a dash must also be used at the end to properly offset the clause.

3   A. The sentence's meaning would remain unchanged if the parenthetical enclosed in parenthesis were to be omitted. In this case, the extra information provided by the parenthetical helps to inform the reader in case he or she does not know how *carbonara* is made. There is no need to further offset the parenthetical with a comma. Because a parenthesis is used at the end of the parenthetical, a parenthesis must also be used at the beginning of the parenthetical. In such a case, there is no need for a comma to precede the clause enclosed in parenthesis. Alternatively, "*carbonara*, which is a traditional" would work (without the closing parenthesis).

4   B. The nonrestrictive clause "which is sometimes known as 'mini golf'" should be punctuated with commas before it and after it. Generally, the word "which," when used to precede an explanation or provide more information about something already mentioned (in this case, telling us another name for "miniature golf") should be preceded by a comma. The clause should generally also end with a comma (when included as an interruption within a sentence). In this case, reading the sentence aloud can help determine where commas are necessary.

5   D. The phrase "that was docked at the end of the pier" is restrictive, as without it the sentence is unclear (To which boat are residents referring? Where is the boat?) and the meaning lost. In general, a comma does not precede the word "that," as the phrase that follows "that" generally restricts or limits the thing that it modifies. In such a case, the clause is restrictive and does not need to be punctuated with commas, parenthesis, or dashes.

6   C. If the phrase "which confuse patients the most" were nonrestrictive, a comma preceding "which" would be appropriate. However, because the phrase is actually restrictive, limiting "questions" to a subgroup (those questions confusing to patients), the word "that" is the best choice, though no dash is required since there is no closing dash elsewhere in the sentence that would complete the offsetting of the nonrestrictive clause.

7   C. The phrase "in the days and weeks to come" provides more information about when the residents of the town will face challenges. As such, commas are appropriate before and after the phrase.

The Tutorverse

8   A. The restrictive clause in this sentence is properly offset with dashes and would be erroneous if a comma replaced the first dash. The core meaning of the sentence is that Frank realized that he was mistaken, with the parenthetical providing more detail about why this happened. In choices C and D, the dash following the parenthetical would be included erroneously.

9   B. The phrase "who…offenders" is a nonrestrictive clause. Without it, we still know that Judge Jamie surprised the media with an uncharacteristic sentence. The nonrestrictive clause says something similar, albeit in a different way.

10   D. The phrase "who…manifesto" is a restrictive clause because it clarifies further the types of politicians who were put under surveillance without it, we would only know that "politicians" were put under surveillance. Because this clause restricts or limits the modified thing (politicians) into a further subgroup, it is essential to the sentence and should not have commas or other parenthesis around it. The word "who" can sometimes precede a restrictive or nonrestrictive clause. Choices C and D introduce parenthesis when no closing marks are found.

11   A. The extra information provided within the parenthesis are not necessary to the basic meaning of the sentence – they simply provide more detail. As such, punctuation is necessary to indicate the nonessential information. Note that a comma is necessary after the closing parenthesis, as the introductory clause (which in this case happens to include a parenthetical expression) must be followed by a comma before the independent clause that follows it.

12   A. The information about the trunk – that it crossed the Atlantic on the Mayflower – is unnecessary to the main idea of the sentence, which is that the family was amazed that a trunk survived a fire. Thus this information should be enclosed by commas to properly offset the nonrestrictive clause. A period or semicolon result in a fragment in the rest of the sentence.

Unnecessary Punctuation

1   D. The subordinated clause "possessing both stealth and speed" must be separated from the independent clause by a comma.

2   A. A comma is necessary to indicate that someone or something is being addressed directly. Without the comma, the sentence's meaning is confusing. With too many, the commas are distracting. Cindy is likely not addressing a "rock Brenda."

3   A. An introductory adverbial clause such as "eventually undergoing a vibrant rejuvenation" must be followed by a comma. "Vibrant," the adjective describing the noun "rejuvenation," should not be separated by a comma. Only separate adjectives when more than one adjective is being used to describe a single noun.

4   B. Multiple adjectives describing the same noun should be separated by a comma. In this case, "cold" and "rainy" both describe "season." No comma is necessary after the last adjective.

5   C. Many sentences do not require a comma to separate the subject and the predicate. The simple subject in this sentence is "multinational corporations," which is modified by the phrase "often very large and bureaucratic." Together these two form the complete subject of the sentence. While no comma is needed to separate it from the predicate (the rest of the sentence), the fact that the phrase is not enclosed by commas is a problem.

6   A. A compound adjective such as "out-of-the-way" must be separated with hyphens.

7   B. The introductory clause must be followed by a comma.

8   A. The "experts on all sides of the political spectrum" is the complete subject and requires no comma. Choices C and D incorrectly separate parts of the sentence, while choice B adds punctuation that is unnecessary. Generally, if the sentence's meaning can survive without the items enclosed by commas, then the items should be enclosed by commas. In this sentence, the meaning is entirely different if "on all sides of the political spectrum" were to be removed, and thus should not be enclosed by commas.

9   D. As written, this sentence separates the subject and the predicate with a comma. Choice C also separates the subject and predicate. Choice B incorrectly encloses the phrase "the rise of 24-hour-a-day news stations," which are crucial to the meaning of the sentence and thus do not need to be enclosed in commas; it also includes a separate comma after "rise" that interrupts the sentence.

10   A. Don't let the complexity of the sentence confuse you; the introductory clause "though…philosophy" must be followed by a comma and cannot survive alone as an independent clause as the semicolon or period would suggest.

11   C. By stripping away all of the "extra" information, it's clear that the sentence is about how it's possible to see South America from Aruba: "It's possible to see all the way to the South American continent." By adding an introductory clause in front of "Aruba" to tell the reader where this possibility might happen, the writer must include a comma. By describing that it can only happen under certain weather conditions, additional commas are necessary. A comma is necessary to separate the two adjectives that describe "day" ("clear" and "sunny").

The Tutorverse

12 A. A compound adjective must be hyphenated, as it is in choice B. The commas in choices C and D are used inappropriately and interrupt the flow of the sentence, since they are unnecessary. The entire phrase modifies "shelf" and is therefore treated as a single adjective modifying "shelf."

Guided Practice – Improving Expression
The Gambler's Fallacy

1 *Style/Tone.* B. The beginning of the passage is framed as a conversation between the author and the reader. The author uses the second person to help illustrate a point about statistics and rational thought, helping to establish his point prior to the discussion of cognitive biases and a famous example of such a bias. The contraction of "let us" is most appropriate, as the other choices result in an imperative, a formal tone, or an uncertain tone.

2 *Syntax.* A. The two sentences address the reader and as such can be combined into a compound sentence. Since "you" is the subject of both sentences, the coordinating conjunction "and" can be used to combine the actions of both sentences ("you are told" and "you are then asked"). The most economical way to do this is without repeating "you" again. Choice B includes "by someone," which is superfluous.

3 *Support.* D. The previous and following sentences are both concerned with real-world examples of The Fallacy. The proposed sentence discusses controlled experiments and studies, not real-world examples.

4 *Precision.* B. The scenario described above asks the reader how he or she would act given a particular circumstance. In this case, the word "decision" best describes the action a person would take – to either choose if the tails-side up result will be more or less likely than a heads-side up result. While the other answer choices describe different types and degrees of beliefs, they are not quite appropriate in context.

5 *Proposition.* A. The paragraph is concerned with explaining a specific type of cognitive bias, and how it arises. The sentence as written is the best summary of how The Gambler's Fallacy arises when people rely too heavily on intuition and not enough on math and logic.

6 *Concision.* A. The sentence is primarily concerned with describing the appearance of a roulette wheel. The most economical way to do so is to indicate that the numbers are non-sequential, meaning that no consecutive numbers are next to each other. The other answer choices do not convey this meaning.

7 *Focus.* B. The paragraph is concerned with explaining how a game of roulette can be won in order that the reader can understand the high improbability of the events that took place in 1913 Monte Carlo. One of the ways the game can be won is to choose a color: red, black, or green. Without proper understanding of the different possible outcomes, the reader may miss the author's point.

8 *Organization.* D. Though paragraph 6 is primarily concerned with explaining the game of roulette, it must only do so in context of the rest of the passage. The author provides just enough information about the game so that the reader can understand the rest of the 1913 Monte Carlo example, which is the subject of paragraph 7. The last choice transitions between the explanation of the game and the events of 1913.

9 *Quantitative Information.* C. The table shows the probability of the events that transpired in 1913 Monte Carlo. The probability of the ball landing on black 15 times in a row is very small, but the best answer uses data in the table to support that assertion. Looking at the table, we can see that there is a 0.00002% chance of that happening, or roughly 1 in 50,000 (or 2 in 100,000).

10 *Logical Sequence.* B. The passage first discusses rational thinking in terms of statistical laws, then goes on to explain deviations from that rational thinking, providing a famous example. Paragraph 4 serves as an introduction to the example, and should not precede the explanation of a deviation from rational thinking (i.e. a cognitive bias). Similarly, the introduction should not be placed before the rational thinking is even explained, or after the example has already been discussed.

Stranger in a Brave New Land

1 *Concision.* D. It offers a clear idea with a focused sentence structure. The other choices do not contain clear, focused wording.

2 *Support.* A. It offers a clear example of the connection to important issues of the time. The other answer choices are too general, and they do not offer a close connection to the themes and ideas in the previous or subsequent statements.

3 *Proposition.* A. It serves as a transition to subsequent paragraphs and connects to the main ideas of the passage. The other choices offer only general statements that do not effectively provide a link between paragraphs, or they directly contradict preceding sentences.

4 *Syntax.* B. The comma and coordinating conjunction "and" effectively combine the two related ideas. The other choices are inappropriate because they are incorrectly punctuated or introduce redundant information into the paragraph.

The Tutorverse

5 *Quantitative Information.* D. The graphic illustrates the relationship between when a technology is first referenced in science-fiction literature and when it is actually created in the real world. From the graphic, it is apparent that several authors have predicted inventions and innovations. The graphic is silent as to the actual source of new inventions, and is silent on the scientific training of the writers.

6 *Style/Tone.* A. The use and placement of the appositive phrase "a professor of biochemistry" mirrors the use and placement of appositive phrases used to describe Clarke and Heinlein in the preceding paragraphs. In addition, the appositive provides extra information that, if removed, would not significantly change the meaning of the sentence – that Asimov focused on themes of human society and the human condition.

7 *Focus.* D. It focuses the statement on the idea that Asimov's story looks at ideas of chaos and turmoil, an idea expressed in the paragraph's topic sentence. The other choices are inappropriate because they hint at, rather than refer directly to, the main idea of the paragraph: humanity's reaction to an apocalyptic event.

8 *Precision.* C. Huxley's world was not an actual reality, but a work of fiction. Though he conveyed his ideas through his writing, they were nevertheless imaginings.

9 *Organization.* A. The author's intention is to show that *Brave New World* is still relevant much later after the book was initially published. The author is writing in the present ("is still read widely"), and "today" best transitions the sentence in the same vein.

10 *Logical Sequence.* B. Sentence 3 serves as a topic sentence that introduces a main idea. Once moved before sentence 1, the order of ideas progresses from more general to more specific.

Can You Hear Me?

1 *Logical Sequence.* D. The paragraph flows most logically from sentence 3, to 5, to 4. Placing this sentence at the end of the paragraph also creates a strong transition into the next paragraph, which further develops the central idea of the passage, that telecommuting is good for employers and employees.

2 *Concision.* D. This is the most concise way of expressing the central idea of the sentence, that taking the commute out of the job makes telecommuters feel less stress than their commuting counterparts.

3 *Organization.* B. The paragraph goes on to explain a couple of the different stressors associated with commuting. It would be incorrect to state that the stressors are the same for everyone. Neither is it appropriate to say that office workers must accept stress on the job. Boss-related stress is off-topic and not mentioned in this passage.

4 *Style/Tone.* A. The other choices don't match the tone of the passage. Choice B uses hyperbole, exaggerating the author's opinion more so than other claims made throughout the passage. Choices C and D are less formal than the rest of the passage.

5 *Syntax.* A. Combining these sentences would result in a long sentence that would be difficult to read. These two sentences have connected themes, in that they are both about how telecommuters tend to make better use of their time, which the word *also* in the second sentence helps show. Choices B and D are contradictory. Choice C is grammatically incorrect.

6 *Precision.* A. An office's overhead costs are those costs associated with maintaining the office. The sentence explains that overhead costs include furniture, electricity, heating, and cooling. The other choices interpret these costs to be extraneous or unnecessary, when in fact such costs are typically necessary in running a business.

7 *Focus.* D. The idea introduced in the sentence (relating telecommuting to environmental benefits) is irrelevant and distracts from the central idea of the paragraph, which discusses reasons why telecommuting is good for employers.

8 *Support.* C. Although this sentence supports the central idea of the passage, this paragraph is about the drawbacks of telecommuting. Including a benefit contradicts the central idea of the paragraph.

9 *Quantitative Information.* B. The graph shows that over time, a survey of 100 people demonstrates that more people are interested in telecommuting – the opposite of telecommuting losing its appeal. "Many" and "virtually all" are subjective, and cannot be reasonably inferred from the graph.

10 *Proposition.* C. As written, the sentence is broad and sweeping, and does not accurately capture the nuance in the author's argument. Choice C represents a succinct summary of the author's arguments. Choice B states an overly specific fact more suitable for the body of the passage, while choice D makes a claim unsupported by the passage.

Table For 118, Please

1 *Concision.* B. The paragraph is primarily concerned with illustrating how the periodic table of elements has changed over time. The most concise way to express this idea is choice B, as the other choices are more wordy and do not capture the fact that the table has changed over time – merely that there has existed multiple types of formats.

2 *Support.* D. The paragraph proceeds to describe, in chronological order, some of the seminal moments in the advancement of the periodic table. Other answer choices are related to chemistry, but not to the period table itself. In addition, some of the answer choices would not follow chronological order.

The Tutorverse

3 *Style/Tone.* C. The preceding sentence describing Alexandre de Chancourtois is structured such that the independent clause is split, after the subject, by a dependent clause. Choice C mirrors this pattern, stating the subject ("John Newlands"), introducing a dependent clause ("in his 1864 table"), and completing the sentence with the rest of the independent clause. The other answer choices do not follow this pattern, or use the passive voice in a paragraph that is otherwise filled with the active voice.

4 *Syntax.* D. The two sentences are related, as they both describe the periodic table of elements published by Mendeleev. As such, the two sentences can be combined without a period or, indeed, any other punctuation. The other answer choices result in grammatically incorrect sentences.

5 *Quantitative Information.* D. The graph shows the cumulative number of elements discovered, by decade. The primary purpose of the paragraph, and the sentence preceding this question, relates to the durability of Mendeleev's theories and table. While interesting, the information presented on the graphic does not pertain to the main idea of the paragraph.

6 *Precision.* A. The paragraph is primarily concerned with Mendeleev's table of elements and how his theories and tables have remained unchanged over time. The author does not express surprise at the fact that Mendeleev's table remains unchanged, nor does he suggest that the table is unchanged on the surface only or that an officiating organization has commented on the table's format.

7 *Logical Sequence.* B. Sentence 4 is the most logical transition sentence between the preceding paragraph, which discusses Mendeleev's table of elements, and the current paragraph, which discusses in more detail Mendeleev's contributions. The rest of the paragraph flows logically from this sentence, discussing in even more detail the specific types of theories Mendeleev proposed, and detailing how and why his periodic table remains popular even today.

8 *Proposition.* A. The paragraph is primarily concerned with illustrating how Mendeleev's periodic table of elements is useful to modern science, citing examples from the 20th and 21st centuries. Details about Mendeleev's other contributions are not discussed in this paragraph, nor is there a claim made by the author about the need to study Mendeleev's creative process.

9 *Organization.* C. The passage follows a chronological order. The paragraph mentions how Mendeleev's table "paved the way for future chemists" and goes on to mention Moseley and Seaborg, as well as work being conducted in the 21st century. Since we know that Mendeleev predates the 21st century, it makes sense to use the word "subsequently," which conveys the idea that Moseley et. al. follow from Mendeleev's contributions. There is no support in the passage to suggests that the author fees Mendeleev's contributions to be regrettable. Using "previously" would be nonsensical.

10 *Focus.* D. The paragraph is primarily concerned with demonstrating how Mendeleev's periodic table will continue to change in the future, as it has done since its inception. It is the previous paragraph that describes Mendeleev's contributions. Though the sentence does show that Mendeleev's periodic table is widespread, such a fact is not relevant to the paragraph (nor does it answer any questions posed by the author).

Passage-Based Practice – Improving Expression
Junior!

1 *Precision.* B. The sentence hints that the word in question must modify "ill-tempered thugs." While "rafts," "societies," and "blocs" all describe groups of people, only cadres implies that the people are specially trained thugs, not just any run-of-the-mill amateur thugs. The other answer choices merely describe exclusive or cohesive groups of people.

2 *Precision.* A. The sentence suggests that the word in question must describe the few people who have actually lived lives as action-packed as Indiana Jones. The other answer choices would be more appropriate to describe some of the treasures recovered by Jones, not the people themselves. While "precious" could also describe treasure, it also conveys the sense that it is very rare for people to live lives like Jones.

3 *Concision.* C. As written, the sentence is too vague. The primary focus of the paragraph is to distinguish Bingham as an accomplished academic; listing the degrees obtained from prestigious universities helps to accomplish this goal. The other answer choices repeat "Harvard" unnecessarily, or else use commas excessively.

4 *Style/Tone.* D. The author here lists the various positions held by Bingham with title first, followed by subject and years held. This choice represents parallel construction, where consistency in style is applied throughout the different parts of the sentence. Though all are grammatically correct, the best stylistic choice is to structure each part of the sentence similarly.

The Tutorverse

5 *Focus*. B. The sentence discusses the rationale for the expedition, as well as steps taken to prepare for the excursion. That Bingham would suggest someone else to lead the expedition, take an extended vacation, or that he would stop further research is contrary to information presented in the passage.

6 *Logical Sequence*. D. The paragraph progresses chronologically, detailing the first trip to Cuzco and subsequent preparations for the 1911 expedition. The sentence also serves to transition to the next paragraph.

7 *Focus*. A. Without this anecdote, the rest of the paragraph would be confusing. The information shows that Bingham's discovery was due in large part to a chance meeting with a local.

8 *Syntax*. A. The most economical way to explain the answer to Bingham's question is choice A. The other answer choices result in awkward construction or redundancy.

9 *Organization*. A. The sentence as written is an idiom describing how something has been consigned to history and is generally regarded as common knowledge. In the final paragraph, the author describes the subsequent fame of Machu Picchu almost offhandedly, skipping over interceding events in the meantime. The other answer choices do not fit the tone or content of the passage. Each are also idioms, though they describe the finality of something, the bare truth of something, or the last in a series of unpleasant events, respectively.

10 *Proposition*. C. The passage is primarily concerned with illustrating Bingham's contributions. The descendants aren't the focus of the passage, neither is Bingham's credibility or the creative basis for Indiana Jones' character. The author makes reference to the comparison between Jones and Bingham first used in the introduction of the passage. However, drawing comparisons between Jones and Bingham is not the focus of the passage; highlighting Bingham's lasting contributions is the primary concern of the passage.

Living Shorelines

1 *Organization*. A. The author takes a strong stance in this passage, arguing that climate change has a detrimental impact on the environment and can be mitigated by human intervention.

2 *Precision*. B. Protected and stabilized are more precise verbs than *made* and give a better picture of exactly what the living shorelines do.

3 *Logical Sequence*. B. Sentence 2 introduces the argument that people must do something to manage climate change, so it is best placed at the beginning of the paragraph. The solution – managing carbon dioxide through the use of living shorelines, according to this author – most logically follows this introduction.

4 *Concision*. A. The sentence is already clear and concise. Choices B, C, and D make the sentence wordy and possibly confusing.

5 *Syntax*. C. Since the second clause supports and clarifies the first, using "that" is the best way to combine the sentences. The second sentence supports the first, so A and C can be ruled out as contradictory. Choice B is not grammatically correct and uses a colon inappropriately.

6 *Style/Tone*. D. The tone of the passage is formal. Choices A and B are more informal and are inconsistent with the passage. Choice C includes more descriptive words and adjectives than most of the other sentences in the paragraph.

7 *Quantitative Information*. B. This choice provides additional supporting information based on the graphic, following logically from the preceding sentence. This is evidenced by the fact that seagrass biomass is made up almost entirely of sequestered carbon. Choices C and D are not accurate based on the graphical representation of carbon sequestered either as a percentage of total biomass or total carbon sequestration.

8 *Support*. D. The ideas introduced in this sentence are irrelevant and distract from the central idea of the paragraph, which is centered on arguing that people must protect coastal environments with living shorelines because they are beneficial and help combat against climate change.

9 *Focus*. C. Improved water, air, and food quality may be a beneficial side-effect of using living shorelines to protect coastal environments, but the primary focus of the paragraph is to argue that coastal environments capture carbon dioxide and should be protected using living shorelines. While it is true that building a natural wall would prevent erosion, this fact does not follow logically from the preceding clause.

10 *Proposition*. C. It is specific to the passage, which argues that living shorelines are an effective way to combat the dangerous effects of carbon dioxide in the atmosphere.

Rosebud

1 *Support*. D. To rank a movie as one of the top movies ever produced, one would likely need to admire it. It is possible to conceive of something even if one does not like it, as it is possible for there to be a furor over something without liking it. To have a reservation about something would be the opposite of liking something enough to rank it highly.

2 *Logical Sequence*. A. Sentence 4 includes the phrase "on the other hand," indicating that it means to contradict a previously made statement. Therefore, it would be illogical to place sentence 4 as the first sentence in the paragraph.

The Tutorverse

Similarly, to compare the preferences of "regular moviegoers" to "Rosebud" or to specific information about *Citizen Kane* would be illogical.

3   *Proposition.* C. The movie is groundbreaking and impresses critics because of its innovations. Though, according to the paragraph, *Citizen Kane* was revolutionary and impressed critics, the main idea is that the movie impressed critics *because* of new techniques. Choice C conveys this sentiment by calling *Citizen Kane* a "landmark" and setting up the rest of the information that follows in the paragraph.

4   *Concision.* C. It offers a clear and concise wording (congruent with "pushing the boundaries of the art form") without redundancy. "Groundbreaking" and "progressive" are synonyms of "revolutionary" (as used in this context) and are redundant. And while something that is revolutionary does lead to dramatic change (or, can be dangerous), using the definition of the word is not economical and changes the meaning of the sentence.

5   *Organization.* A. The preceding paragraph describes how *Citizen Kane* was groundbreaking. The current paragraph offers one example: the chronology of the movie. The sentence transitions most effectively when a nod to this pattern is mentioned in choice A. The other choices suggest the opposite of what the author mentioned in the preceding paragraph.

6   *Focus.* C. The paragraph is primarily about the chronological order of the film. While the reliability of the narrators may indeed be questionable ("forgetful associates"), the primary focus of the paragraph is to describe how the film broke with traditional storytelling.

7   *Precision.* B. The sentence compares a center of interest against other images in a scene. It is implied that these other images are not as important to the scene, since they are not the "center of interest." The words "substantive" and "essential" would imply the opposite – that these images are important to the scene. "Peripheral" is the best choice, as the word implies that the other images are not central to the scene; "ancillary" suggests that the other images support the center of interest.

8   *Syntax.* A. The two sentences should remain separated, as the first discusses the impact deep focus had on the art of direction in the film, and the second discusses the result of that impact. Though the two are related, they are best left in separate sentences; the other answer choices create run-on sentences and grammatical errors.

9   *Style/Tone.* A. The style mirrors that which was done in the previous sentence – two sentences joined by a semicolon. While choice B does this as well, the resulting second sentence becomes a fragment. Choice C adds an unnecessary word, while choice D does not fit the style noted in the preceding sentence.

10 *Quantitative Information.* C. The graphic shows only the box office performance in 1941, making no connection between box office success and cinematic innovations. Orson Welles' creativity, and the popularity of the director, studio, and actors has little to do with the cinematic innovations in *Citizen Kane*. There is little data in this chart to support the passage's primary concern.

Keys to the Kingdom

1   *Style/Tone.* D. Earlier in the paragraph, the author uses a series of questions and answers to drive home the point that apps are ubiquitous and have an impact on daily life. While the other choices drive home this same point, only choices A and D do so in question and answer format. D most closely matches the sentence structure of the preceding sentences, beginning the question with the word "need" and answering the question with "there's an app…".

2   *Concision.* A. The author describes how cell phones and apps have created new industries, not how new industries have created smartphone and app opportunities. The most economical way to indicate this idea is to use the phrase "sprung up around." Because "sprung up" and "surfaced" are interchangeable here, and because "near the vicinity of" is a more indirect way of saying "around," choices C and D are inappropriate.

3   *Support.* C. The sentence describes how there are other benefits that are not typically found in a workplace. Salaries, bonuses, overtime, parking, health insurance, copies, and office supplies can typically be found in most workplaces. At the very least, one would not expect them at a country club. The opposite can be said of the items listed in choice C, making it the best choice.

4   *Logical Sequence.* D. The paragraph discusses how the smartphone and app industry has created demand for engineering talent, the result of which is high salaries and attractive benefits. Sentence 4 uses the phrase "on top of this monetary compensation" while sentence 3 discusses how in-demand software engineers can be. The most logical place to discuss engineering salaries, then, is between the two sentences.

5   *Organization.* B. The paragraph deals primarily with discussing the reasons why engineers are so valued. The paragraph does not discuss the persons most suited for the line of work, or how to become an engineer, or the timeline leading up to the profession's popularity.

6   *Syntax.* C. The two ideas in each of the sentences are related – that potential for business is huge is underscored by the idea that a popular app can generate a lot of money. The best way to show this relationship is by using a

The Tutorverse

semicolon. The two sentences are independent clauses, however, and are not best joined with "and" or with a comma. A colon is used incorrectly here, as a list of reasons is not presented.

7   *Precision.* B. The author describes consumers as fickle, stating also that there are many apps that compete for the consumer's attention. The consumer is not described then as uninterested, but rather choosy and discriminating. Choice A (which refers to a level of understanding) and choice D are not supported by the descriptions in the paragraph.

8   *Quantitative Information.* C. The two charts show that the percentage of students pursuing software engineering has increased over the course of a decade. Because the charts do not describe the sample size, we cannot know if the absolute number of software engineering majors is more or less in 2015 vs. 2005. We also do not know the author's opinion on this trend, though he is unlikely – based on the rest of the passage – to call the trend disheartening or inappropriate.

9   *Focus.* A. In the previous sentence, the author suggests that there might be a time where it might be difficult for engineers to find a job because there are too many engineers, not because the profession itself will become obsolete. The underlined sentence describes how software engineering might become obsolete, like the profession of telephone line operators who manually connected phone calls. This does not follow from the previous sentence, and is off-topic; the author does not suggest that software engineering will become obsolete altogether – just that it might be harder for some engineers to find jobs.

10 *Proposition.* B. The only choice which alludes to the changing popularity of professions is B, since it points out that the concept of an app (and, by extension, the people needed to work on those apps) did not always exist. The other choices either state or imply that software engineering will always be necessary, essentially supporting the notion that at least this profession will not change.

Determination: The Stuff of Stars

1   *Precision.* C. "Prowess" is the most contextually appropriate way to indicate that Hubble succeeded "despite little effort." "Determination" and "energy" suggest the opposite of what the sentence tells us (i.e. that Hubble did not put in much effort in school). "Indications" results in a nonsensical sentence.

2   *Organization.* A. The sentence describes how Hubble could not keep his word to his father. Therefore, "though" is the most appropriate choice, as it is used to contrast one thing against another (in this case Hubble's actions against his promise).

3   *Concision.* D. The sentence is primarily concerned with describing one of Hubble's primary responsibilities while working at the Wilson Observatory. Using phrases such as "new construction" or "due to" introduces redundancy.

4   *Focus.* A. The sentence provides a transition to the information that follows, introducing the idea that, beginning with the Hooker Telescope, Hubble's work resonated on the entire field of astronomy.

5   *Logical sequence.* D. Placing sentence 5 before sentence 4 makes the paragraph most cohesive. Sentence 5 describes a statement of fact, while sentence 4 describes a reaction to that statement of fact.

6   *Style/Tone.* A. The other options are hyperbolic or awkward, and do not fit the academic and conservative tone established in the passage.

7   *Syntax.* B. It combines the sentences logically and efficiently, with the original second sentence becoming the second part of a compound complex sentence. Choice A lacks a subordinating conjunction and results in a grammatically incorrect sentence. Choices C and D, though grammatically correct, result in wordiness and redundancy.

8   *Quantitative Information.* D. The graph shows that the speed of galaxies relative to the Milky Way is proportional to their distance from the Milky Way, which illustrates graphically the theory described in the preceding sentence.

9   *Support.* C. In paragraphs four and five, Hubble is portrayed as curious. It is his curiosity which pushes him to unlock mysteries in astronomy. Apathy and loyalty would have likely precluded him from pursuing astronomy. Though patience was likely a factor, the passage does not describe the amount of time or effort it took for Hubble to make his discoveries.

10 *Proposition.* D. The groundbreaking astronomical discoveries are the most important aspect of the passage. The passage briefly describes Hubble's life, background, and career, though primarily in context of how those factors ultimately led to important discoveries.

New York's Beanstalks

1   *Logical Sequence.* C. The sentence describing studying in France most logically belongs after the explanation that Van Alen studied at the École des Beaux-Arts in Paris. Otherwise, the description of Van Alen's design background is broken up by the statement that he partnered with Severance when he moved back to New York.

2   *Proposition.* A. The other choices are all details that support the main idea that Van Alen and Severance were each involved in—and helped forward—the race to build the world's tallest building.

3   *Organization.* A. The preceding sentence describes a competition and a challenge – something that Van Alen and Severance participated in and aspired to win, as indicated in the last sentence of the paragraph. The other answer choices reflect the opposite of this intention and interest, or else are irrelevant.

4   *Focus.* C. The detail is interesting, but doesn't add much to support the main idea of the paragraph, which is mostly about innovations the developers made when planning construction.

5   *Syntax.* B. The use of "though" creates a contrast between the building being brick but mostly supported by steel. The other answer choices lack this comparison, are grammatically incorrect, or are otherwise illogical in context.

6   *Concision.* C. It eliminates the wordiness in the sentence to make it cleaner and more concise.

7   *Precision.* B. While many of the other choices may be true, in context the word that makes the most sense has to do with the height of the building.

8   *Support.* C. This sentence contains support for the main idea of the passage that the Chrysler Building was significant in the history of architecture by explaining that, in addition to being taller than 40 Wall Street, it was the first man-made structure taller than 1,000 feet.

9   *Quantitative Information.* Explanation: A. The Empire State Building stands about 200 feet taller than the Chrysler Building, according to the chart, and remained the tallest building in the world until the World Trade Center was completed 41 years later.

10   *Style/Tone.* C. This sentence most closely mirrors the tone of the passage, which is serious and mostly formal. Choice A is over-the-top in its description and not consistent with the tone in the rest of the passage. Choice B is far less formal than the rest of the passage. Choice D introduces new information, which is inappropriate for a concluding sentence.

Masters of the Universe

1   *Quantitative Information.* C. The graph shows that over the period mentioned earlier in the sentence, real GDP declined from about $14.9 trillion to about $14.4 trillion, which is approximately half a trillion dollars, or $500 billion.

2   *Proposition.* A. The passage is concerned with explaining the human aspect of how the financial crisis came to be, stating that the essence of the crisis was rooted in greed and risk taking. "Notwithstanding" and "In spite of" are used interchangeably with "despite," and indicates that the greed and risk taking are unrelated to the housing crisis. Choice C downplays the importance of risk taking and greed contrary to the rest of the passage.

3   *Logical Sequence.* D. The sentence refers to other companies and how they were rescued. The paragraph discusses the role that financial companies played in the crisis, and it is not until the end of the paragraph that there is enough context to support the sentence in question. That some companies were rescued by taxpayers makes logical sense only after knowing that some institutions were bankrupted.

4   *Organization.* A. The preceding paragraph discusses the events of the crisis and involvement of the companies. The current paragraph introduces the reasons why the events transpired. Choice A asks a logical question that extends from the discussion of companies and the events in which they were involved and the underlying causes of those events. The rest of the current paragraph does not discuss the other answer choices, nor does the rest of the passage.

5   *Style/Tone.* B. If the author's goal is to blame the decision makers for their bad decisions, only the adverb "deliberately" properly conveys the author's feelings toward the subject. The adverbs "unwittingly, mistakenly," and "reluctantly" produce the opposite effect, instead partially exculpating the decision makers.

6   *Focus.* C. The paragraph is primarily concerned with describing the reason that people made bad decisions; certain professionals, such as asset managers and traders make commission and do not risk their own money. Therefore, it is important to know how asset managers and traders are paid in order to understand the broader argument: that their pay structure was part of the reason why they made bad decisions.

7   *Syntax.* B. The two sentences share the same subject: asset managers and traders. Therefore, it is possible to combine the sentences into a compound sentence, joining two clauses with the conjunction "but." When using a semicolon, it would not be necessary to repeat the same subject. Using "those" is grammatically incorrect and also unclear.

8   *Support.* D. The other answer choices describe incentives. Only answer D presents another way in which asset managers and traders' risks were mitigated. The sentence suggests that a lack of legal and political action set a precedent that irresponsibility would go unpunished.

9   *Precision.* D. The paragraph discusses how some people were able to avoid responsibility for their actions. To abdicate or to relinquish suggest that such people once bore responsibility – shirk instead implies that they intended to avoid responsibility in the first place. To bear a responsibility would be to accept it – the opposite of the intended meaning.

The Tutorverse

10   *Concision.* B. The last sentence summarizes the author's opinion about what steps can be taken to address the perceived issues. A more concise way to convey the meaning – that the real problems to be addressed are a person's motivation and responsibility – is to use the word "incentive." This echoes earlier phrasing and word choice in the passage.

Money Matters

1   *Concision.* C. The subject of both sentences is "economic policy," so it is possible to combine both sentences. The phrase "such as" introduces a dependent clause, which must be preceded by a comma, and is only appropriate to use when there is a shared subject (as is the case in this sentence). In this case, a semicolon results in a fragment. The other answer choices result in wordiness that can be eliminated without changing the meaning of the sentences.

2   *Precision.* B. Imperative, which means that something is a priority, is needed in order to note the importance of having knowledge about the topic at hand. The other answer choices do not reflect the idea that this knowledge is very important.

3   *Proposition.* D. It connects to the ideas previously mentioned (that demand is a key economic driver) and serves as a logical transition to the next sentence. The other choices do not connect to the main idea, nor do they logically follow from the first part of the sentence.

4   *Syntax.* D. The comma and the pronoun "who" effectively combine the two phrases that share a similar idea. The other choices do not work because of the repetition of "Friedman" and the unnecessary or incorrect use of punctuation.

5   *Style/Tone.* C. It clearly states that this is a part of supply-side philosophy and it reflects the idea of a debate between the two economic philosophies. The other choices do not fit within the context of the debate between the two economic philosophies.

6   *Support.* C. It offers a complete definition of inflation, its connection to the control of the money supply, and impact on the broader economy. The other answer choices give partial, incomplete, or incorrect explanations of what inflation is and the effects it has. For example, choice A contradicts the statements made earlier in the paragraph.

7   *Logical Sequence.* C. The statement introduces the idea of government spending, which is more fully developed by the ideas in sentence three. The other choices do not work because they do not show a clear sequence of thoughts or ideas.

8   *Organization.* A. The supply-side economists disagree with demand-side economists. Therefore, "conversely" is the best choice to show that the two schools of thought differ. "Similarly" and "analogously" suggest the opposite (that the two philosophies agree). "Ultimately" is a neutral term typically describing the last part of a step, which is inappropriate in this context.

9   *Quantitative Information.* D. The graph does not show a strong correlation between tax rates and GDP growth and does not support the statements made by the supply-siders.

10   *Focus.* C. It focuses on the main idea of the passage, which is a clear understanding of different economic theories. The other choices are too general and do not directly connect to the thesis of the passage. Voting and the control of a society are indirectly related to the topic at hand, but veer in a direction unsupported by the rest of the paragraph and passage.

Cellular Breakthroughs

1   *Syntax.* B. A colon is often used to introduce a list, and in this sentence it offers a clearer sentence structure and idea. The other answer choices result in run-on sentences or sentences that incorrectly utilize punctuation.

2   *Style/Tone.* B. It provides a sentence with a clear, formal structure to express the important idea of tissue and organ repair. The other answer choices are either too general or do not reflect a formal, academic style in sentence structure and tone.

3   *Concision.* D. It offers clear wording with a focused idea. The other choices do not contain clear, focused wording, resulting in awkward construction or redundancy.

4   *Organization.* A. The second part of the sentence provides examples of two types of stem cells. A proper introduction to this sentence would not be to describe these two types as "a plethora" or "countless"; to introduce the sentence with "one stem cell" is similarly incorrect.

5   *Logical Sequence.* B. Sentence 2 best introduces the rest of the sentences in the paragraph, which discuss the types of stem cells researched. Once moved before sentence 1, the order of ideas progresses from earliest to latest. The other choices do not reflect the correct logical order of research and discovery.

6   *Proposition.* B. It serves as a clear introduction to the main ideas of the paragraph: breakthroughs and medical benefits of stem cells. The other choices offer general statements that do not effectively introduce the topics discussed in the paragraph.

The Tutorverse

7   *Support.* D. It offers a brief and clear definition of iSPCs and summarizes the preceding sentences, supporting the main topic of the paragraph.

8   *Precision.* B. The use of "malleable" highlights the flexibility of these cells in performing different applications. The other answer choices do not connect to the idea of specialization or how such flexibility can apply to the treatment of new diseases.

9   *Quantitative Information.* B. It illustrates why the graph would not be useful in this spot due to a lack of focus on the paragraph's main ideas: medical applications. The other answer choices either do not connect to the main ideas of the paragraph or they introduce a new idea not discussed in the passage.

10   *Focus.* D. It focuses the statement on the main ideas of the passage: stem cell advancements and medical applications. The other answer choices are either too general or they offer an idea separate from the main ideas of the passage.

Data-mancy

1   *Concision.* D. The sentence implies that data science can help businesses make more informed decisions. It's not necessary to repeat "without data science" as the comparison being made is implied. "Better" and "improved" decisions with "better results" is redundant.

2   *Precision.* B. The previous sentence describes how people desire to know what the future holds, which is echoed in the current sentence. The verb "divine" means to discover something, usually by guessing or some intuition (this is different from the adjective or noun "divine"). In this case, the word is most appropriate, as "contemplate" suggests that people merely think about the future, as opposed to trying to know it as "divine" would suggest. Similarly, "appreciate" and "dream about" are too vague.

3   *Syntax.* A. The first sentence in this pair discusses examples of people in different cultures and times who are believed to be able to tell the future. The second sentence in the pair goes on to list several more, but the point is to add an unexpected person (data scientist) to the list. The purposes and subjects of the sentences are different, and combining them together makes the sentence a run-on sentence, which is confusing. The two sentences are best left as separate sentences.

4   *Focus.* C. The last sentence of the paragraph explains the tools used by the data scientist to predict the future. The examples provided in the underlined portion are a useful comparison that parallels the last sentence. Used together, the examples are meaningful and contribute to the understanding of the central idea of the paragraph.

5   *Proposition.* C. The previous passage describes how different "fortune tellers" used different instruments in their craft. Choice C transitions from this idea and applies it to the data scientist. The paragraph does not discuss the creation of tools, rather merely how the data scientist uses those tools. The author does not pass judgment on the use of such tools as computers and software.

6   *Support.* B. The preceding sentence describes how data science will be important in daily life as new technologies develop. The sentence in question does not describe the speed of fitness software's development, nor does it speak to its medical soundness. Instead, the sentence in question describes how the software is widely used and personal, implying that it is part of peoples' daily lives. Because the software collects and analyzes data, we can infer that data science has a hand in the technology.

7   *Organization.* C. The paragraph discusses how there are inherent problems with data science that prevent it from being a perfect forecasting of the future. "Likewise" and "because of this" suggest that these problems originate with the preceding paragraph, which actually describe all of the positive attributes of data science. In fact, the author does not make this case, instead saying that the problems rest in "the imperfect nature of data sets." Thus, "however" is most appropriate, as it signals a shift from discussing positives (in the preceding paragraph) to discussing some concerns (in the current paragraph). "Conceivably" suggests that the faults are merely a possibility – a tone not adopted by the author.

8   *Style/Tone.* A. The earlier paragraphs were optimistic about data science's ability to forecast the future; to temper the optimism does not mean to disprove or disparage it – merely to call into question and balance that optimism. To say that data science "is the final word in" telling the future or has "upped the ante" continues the optimism found earlier. "Fails to present" does the opposite, fully disparaging or disproving the earlier optimism. Choice A presents the best neutralizing phrasing, as "may just" and "shinier" – implying that the future can never truly be known, and that data science is but the latest fad in trying to tell the future.

9   *Precision.* D. "Magnanimous" means "generous," and "juvenile" means "childish." Both words are inappropriate at describing the problem of knowing what tomorrow will bring, in context of the passage and final sentence. "Unimaginable" means that something cannot be conceived – yet this contradicts what millennia of fortune tellers would claim: that the future can be conceived of. "Insurmountable" is the best choice in context, indicating that perhaps even data science will not be able to answer a question that is simply not answerable.

10   *Logical Sequence.* B. Paragraph 1 describes what a data scientist does, where paragraph 2 introduces the idea of a data scientist. The most logical order would be to first introduce the idea of future-telling and data scientists, then explain how data scientists tell the future. It would be inappropriate to include the introductory paragraph near the end of the passage.

Soul Crisis

1   *Syntax.* C. The prepositional phrase "from the Oval Office" does not require punctuation to separate it from the rest of the sentence. The other answer choices result in awkward structure or redundancy due to unnecessary repetition.

2   *Precision.* C. In order to stress the importance of America's dependence on foreign oil, the word "paramount", which means "most important", can be added to the beginning of the sentence. The other answer choices do not reflect the idea of importance.

3   *Proposition.* B. The paragraph goes on to describe Carter's personal point of view as well as observations from letters he would receive. The idea that Carter was the first to mention this after WWII is ancillary to the paragraph, as are the thoughts of pre-WWII presidents. The paragraph does not discuss Carter's own feelings.

4   *Style/Tone.* B. It reflects the idea of a crisis that would be difficult to define and solve. The other choices do not fit within the context of concern for a crisis, or they alter the tone of the statement.

5   *Organization.* A. In the preceding sentence, Carter refers to the problem he sees as a crisis. This phrasing and idea is mirrored in the current sentence. While a crisis is a problem, the latter carries less intensity. That there is a change or revolution does not necessarily imply a crisis so dire that it "looms on the horizon."

6   *Logical Sequence.* D. "Ultimately" signals the end of a succession of ideas. The other choices are not appropriate because they do not show a clear sequence of thoughts or ideas and confuse the main idea of the paragraph.

7   *Support.* B. It offers a contrast to how the speech was viewed when it was given in 1979. The other answer choices do not reflect this contrast and do not develop an account of reactions to the speech. Choice A in particular is repetitive, conveying the same idea as in the preceding sentence and making the use of the word "nevertheless" nonsensical.

8   *Concision.* D. it is a repetitive idea stated in the phrase "are all themes that America is still dealing with today." The other choices are inappropriate because they have an unclear sentence structure or are too wordy.

9   *Quantitative Information.* C. The graph shows how American households have increased their use of credit cards, loans, and other types of debt even beyond their means, as the ratio increases. This suggests that people are taking on amounts of debt that they cannot afford to pay back – a fixation on consumption that Carter laments. The data in the graph does not suggest, one way or another, that America is peaceful, prosperous, or that Americans are saving.

10   *Focus.* A. Though it may appear that the inclusion of pundits is relevant to the main idea of the passage, the media's reaction to Carter's speech is mentioned only in passing. The central idea of the passage is concerned with explaining Carter's speech and drawing modern day parallels. Whether or not pundits are respected or not is not discussed in this passage.

Hammer, Meet Feather

1   *Organization.* C. This paragraph is primarily concerned with explaining how understanding of natural phenomena has evolved over time. The other answer choices allude to explanations during specific periods of time, or else contradict sentences in the passage.

2   Support. A. No examples, in addition to "fire" and "lightning" are necessary; adding any additional examples is extraneous and does not enhance the claims made in the rest of the paragraph.

3   *Precision.* D. Only "invaluable" conveys the sense that the experiments are very important to the understanding of gravity. That experiments are important to scientific knowledge is an extension of the main purpose of the paragraph, and is established by the preceding sentence.

4   *Concision.* B. The sentence as written, as well as the proposal in choice D, uses words that introduce redundancy. "Everyday occurrences" is the most succinct way to convey the idea that ordinary phenomena support the theory in question (regardless of whether they happen each and every day, as "daily" would imply).

5   *Focus.* A. The example is relevant to the sentence (and paragraph as a whole) in that it explains why it would make intuitive sense that a theory (disproven by experimentation) might be true.

6   *Syntax.* B. As written, the sentence is a run-on sentence. Similarly, using a colon makes the sentence grammatically incorrect. The dash and the ellipses are inappropriate, as only the period properly separates the two distinct thoughts.

7   *Quantitative Information.* A. With no air friction to slow down the feather, the feather will fall to the ground at the same time as a hammer. This demonstrates that the rate of acceleration on all objects, regardless of their mass, is the same. Mass/weight is irrelevant to the rate of freefall of an object; air friction, however, plays a large role.

The Tutorverse

8   *Logical Sequence.* B. Sentence 2 most effectively transitions between the discussion regarding air friction and Galileo's experiments and subsequent discovery. Moving the sentence elsewhere, or leaving it where it is now, disrupts the flow of the paragraph, which is primarily concerned with describing the experiment itself and the resulting discovery.

9   *Style/Tone.* A. The sentence as written also follows a similar pattern as the final sentence in the paragraph. Both sentences begin with a subordinated clause. The other sentences needlessly alter this pattern.

10   *Proposition.* D. That something has shaped modern science is a sweeping and grand statement, which aligns with the author's goals for the sentence. That theories are established or proven is helpful information, but does not carry the same weight as the last answer choice. To use the phrase "at times" is to qualify and detract from it's importance.

Mile by Mile

1   *Support.* D. The passage is concerned with the lack of sleep on drivers, so the most applicable example would be to liken the physical activity described in the paragraph to driving.

2   *Organization.* C. The paragraph discusses the negative effects of getting too little sleep, not too much. The preceding paragraph discusses the reasons why people need sleep. Thus, the best choice introduces the possibility of not getting the sleep necessary. The passage does not discuss the consequences of too much sleep, or give advice about getting more sleep. The importance of sleep is discussed in the previous paragraph.

3   *Focus.* C. The paragraph is primarily concerned with the negative effects of lack of sleep on drivers. Accident prevention classes may help reduce accidents, but would likely have little effect as a solution on the problem of drowsy drivers.

4   *Precision.* C. To indict is to formally accuse someone of something, but generally refers to people, not concepts (one does not indict drowsiness). To inculcate or to indoctrinate means to instill an idea in people, and is sometimes used with a negative connation. This too applies to people, not concepts. Thus, "implicate" is the best choice, which indicates that someone (or something) is responsible for something else (in this case, drowsiness was the primary reason for the accident).

5   *Syntax.* A. The first two sentences are rhetorical questions, addressed by the final sentence in the paragraph. The second question and final sentence should be separate sentences, as the question requires a question mark at the end of the sentence. The final sentence must suppose that the answer to the rhetorical question is "yes," since it uses the word "then." It is grammatically incorrect to use a comma or semicolon as suggested, and illogical to omit "if so."

6   *Concision.* B. The sentence discusses limits placed by the FMCSA; limits typically apply to the maximum amount of something that can be done. "Maximum" is the most efficient word used to describe this, idea, with "upper limit," "most number of hours," and "threshold of hours that cannot be exceeded" being awkward and inefficient variations.

7   *Quantitative Information.* B. The chart illustrates the percentage of fatigue-related accidents attributable to the number of hours driven since a break. It is important to clarify, in the sentence, that the accidents are due to fatigue. The trendline indicates that at the 11th hour, the number of fatigue-related accidents is proportional to the rest of the data. As a percentage, a large number of fatigue-related accidents are due to long-haul drivers (greater than 11 hours of driving since break).

8   *Style/Tone.* A. To refer to something as pejorative, absurd, or unbelievable is to take a very negative stance about that thing. To refer to something as understandable does not necessarily mean to view that thing in a positive light – it merely acknowledges the thing in question.

9   *Proposition.* D. The first part of the sentence makes the author's intent clear – that preventable accidents should be prevented even at the cost of money and profits. We can infer that, given the author's writing, sleep plays an important role in preventing accidents. Thus, we can infer that the FMCSA's ruling is one that the author would agree with. Therefore, we don't need to better understand sleep or interview more truckers or spend more time weighing pros and cons; we should follow the FMCSA's ruling.

10   *Logical Sequence.* B. The rhetorical questions used in the paragraph introduce the topic of sleep, which is a critical component of the author's passage. The appeal to the reader's own experiences serves to draw in the reader and help convince the reader of the author's argument. Such a tactic would be less effective towards the end of the passage.

There Can Be Only One

1   *Syntax.* B. In keeping with the stylistic choices made in the earlier part of the paragraph, where each branch of philosophy has its own sentence, aesthetics too should be described in its own sentence. The other answer choices result in run on and grammatically incorrect sentences.

2   *Precision.* D. The paragraph discusses the sizes of different communities, and describes how ruling communities becomes more difficult as they grow larger. "Atomic" describes the most basic, fundamental – and implicitly, strongest – communities that are made up of family and friend. The author describes that these atomic communities are easier to govern because they are stronger and more cohesive.

3   *Style*. C. The passage is filled with questions that the author deliberately poses to the reader. The following sentence is a question, beginning with "and"; this suggests that the current sentence might be a question. Similarly, stating a fact about something does not have the same rhetorical effect as asking a question, which engages the reader to question and arrive at his/her own ideas. The question in choice B fails to capture the motivation of the question.

4   *Focus*. A. The purpose of the paragraph and of the sentence is to illustrate the practical importance of political philosophy. The author provides many examples of this importance, not least of which is who must participate in war, and when it must be waged.

5   *Organization*. A. The sentence goes on to list several questions that are relevant to the real-world. This choice effectively expands on the idea that political philosophy is a framework, an idea mentioned in the preceding sentence. The passage does not suggest that philosophers have made any misinterpretations, nor that they question the practicality of political philosophy, nor confuse theory with practice.

6   *Quantitative Information*. B. The chart demonstrates that the richest fifth of the world's population controls nearly three-quarters of the world's wealth. This disproportionate ownership supports the statement made in the sentence regarding an unequal distribution of wealth.

7   *Concision*. D. This is the most economical way to convey the idea that there are many people who have grappled with political philosophy. The author does not suggest that those that tried have failed, as "in vain" would suggest. The other answer choices are redundant and result in awkwardness.

8   *Support*. C. Earlier in the passage, the author mentions the examples of the impact of political philosophy: transfer of wealth, the administration of justice, and the waging of war. All of the examples in the current sentence mirror these topics (taxes and serving in the military) except for the topic of friendship. This choice most effectively mirrors both the style of previous examples in the current sentence and the topics mentioned in an earlier paragraph. Immigration, while a valid issue that can be addressed by political philosophy, does not mirror earlier topics mentioned.

9   *Logical Sequence*. D. The paragraph provides an example of how political philosophy is more than just a series of questions that are difficult to answer. The author indicates that many people have attempted to not only answer difficult questions, but have also attempted to put their ideas to practice. The example of Karl Marx is best related after the exposition that transitions from philosophical questions (mentioned in the previous paragraph) to practical action.

10   *Proposition*. A. The author uses questions throughout the passage to great rhetorical effect, using them to prove his point that political philosophy has both theoretical and practice implications. The author does not suggest that any branch of philosophy is superior or inferior to another, nor does it directly address any other branch of philosophy specifically.

Explanations: Part Three – Math

Algebra

Guided Practice – Solving Linear Equations & Inequalities

Multiple Choice – No Calculator

1   D. If $k = 4$, then $\dfrac{x-1}{2} = 4$. Multiply both sides by 2 to get $x - 1 = 8$, so $x = 9$.

2   D. Solving the first equation yields $x = 8$, so $4(8) + 5 = 37$.

3   B. Combing like terms on each side results in $\dfrac{4}{6}x = \dfrac{12}{6}$. Multiplying all terms by 6 yields $4x = 12$, so $x = 3$.

4   C. Multiplying both sides by 4 cancels out the 4 on the left side, creating $x + 3 = 5 \cdot 4$, so $x = 20 - 3 = 17$.

5   D. If we distribute, we get $8x - 8 = ax + 3x - 8$, which we can simplify to $5x = ax$, which means $a = 5$.

Student Produced Response – No Calculator

1   0. Start by distributing: $-6x + 7.5 = -15x + 7.5$. Adding $15x$ to both sides and subtracting 7.5 from both sides results in $9x = 0$, so $x = 0$.

2   4. Since $5c - 12$ must be greater than or equal to 8, the least possible value of c is when $5c - 12$ is equal to 8. If we solve the equation $5c - 12 = 8$, we get $c = 4$.

3   22. If $3x + 7 = 22$, then $x = 5$. Therefore, $6(5) - 8 = 22$.

4   5. Combining like terms results in $\dfrac{2}{8}x = \dfrac{5}{4}$. We can cancel out the coefficient of x by multiplying both sides by its reciprocal, resulting in $x = \dfrac{5}{4} \cdot \dfrac{8}{2} = \dfrac{40}{8} = 5$.

5   1/40 or 0.025. Solve for p by first distributing the 2: $1 - 2p = \dfrac{3}{4} + 8p$, then combine like terms, resulting in $\dfrac{1}{4} = 10p$. Finally, divide both sides by 10, resulting in $\dfrac{1}{40} = p$.

6   0.7. We could distribute and solve for x, but we don't have to. The structure of this equation reveals that a quantity, $4x - 2.8$, multiplied by -3 is equal to that same quantity multiplied by -5. This is only possible if $4x - 2.8 = 0$. Therefore, $4x = 2.8$ and $x = 0.7$.

Multiple Choice – Calculator

1   D. Simplify the inequality: $2b > 10$, so $b > 5$, which means b can be any value greater than 5.

2   C. 10 more than 17 is 27; therefore $12 + 3x = 27$, which leads to $3x = 15$ and finally $x = 5$. But that's not the answer. You must find $4x$, so $4(5) = 20$.

3   A. $g = \dfrac{3}{5} \div \dfrac{1}{2} = \dfrac{3}{5} \times \dfrac{2}{1} = \dfrac{6}{5}$.

4   A. If $\dfrac{1}{4}a > -\dfrac{5}{8}$, then $a > -\dfrac{5}{8} \times \dfrac{4}{1}$, which means $a > -\dfrac{5}{2}$.

5   B. 20 more than 4 is 22, so $6 + 9x = 24$, which leads to $9x = 18$, and finally $x = 2$. But that's not the final answer because we are asked to find the value of $5x$, which is $5(2) = 10$.

6   C. Solving $7x + 3 = 38$ yields $x = 5$. But that's not the answer, because the questions asks us to find $4.5x$, which is $4.5(5) = 22.5$.

7   B. Multiplying both sides of the equation by $(x + 1)$ yields $x + 2 = 5x + 5$, which leads to $-4x = 3$, so $x = -\dfrac{3}{4}$.

The Tutorverse

8   B. Simplify the equation by applying the distributive property and combining like terms. The right side of the equation becomes $-15x + 12 - 6$, which simplifies to $-15x + 6$. Thus, $3x + 3 = -15x + 6$, and $18x = 3$, so $x = \dfrac{1}{6}$.

9   D. Isolating the variable yields $x \leq 5$ so 6 cannot be a possible solution to the inequality.

10   C. For the equation to have infinitely many solutions, both sides of the equation must be equivalent. Simplifying the left side of the equation yields $8x - 1$ and simplifying the right side yields $ax + x - 1$. So, $8x - 1 = ax + x - 1$. Combine like terms to simplify: $7x = ax$, so $a = 7$.

11   C. If $2a - 3 \geq 1$, then $2a \geq 4$ and $a \geq 2$. So the least possible value of $2a + 3$ occurs when $a = 2$: $2(2) + 3 = 7$.

12   C. Statement I is not correct because x has to be between the positive and negative values of a number, but we do not know whether x itself is positive or negative. (For example, if y and $-y$ are 5 and -5, then x could be any number in between them, including a negative number.) Statement II is incorrect because the given information states that $x < y$. Only statement III is correct, because regardless of whether x is a positive or negative number, it must be less than y.

13   C. We could solve for x, but we don't need to. If you look closely, you can notice that $-10x - 25$ is just $-2x - 5$ multiplied by 5. If we multiply the whole inequality by 5, we get $20 > -10x - 25$, which can be flipped to read $-10x - 25 < 20$.

14   D. We start by distributing: $6x + 4 < 6x - 3$. If we try to solve further, the $6x$ on both sides cancels out, leaving us with $4 < -3$, which is not true, so there is no solution.

15   A. If we combine like terms, we get $11x + 5 > 11x - 6$. This is always true, because no matter what number we plug in for x, adding 5 to a value is always greater than subtracting 6 from that value. Therefore, all real numbers satisfy the inequality.

16   B. If x is 50% more than the sum of the other two numbers (y and z), then $x = 1.5(y + z)$ or $y + z = \dfrac{x}{1.5}$.

We can rewrite $\dfrac{x}{1.5}$ as $\dfrac{2x}{3}$ and substitute it in the equation for $y + z$ such that $x + y + z = x + \dfrac{2}{3}x = 670$.

Combine terms to find $\dfrac{5x}{3} = 670$. So $x = 670 \times \dfrac{3}{5} = 402$.

17   A. We want to write each of the three averages as algebraic equations, then find the average of those three equations. First, we write $x = \dfrac{1}{2}(m + 8)$, $y = \dfrac{1}{2}(2m + 12)$, and $z = \dfrac{1}{2}(3m + 16)$. Then, to find the average of x, y, and z, we add $\dfrac{1}{2}m + 4 + m + 6 + \dfrac{3}{2}m + 8 = 3m + 18$, and then divide $3m + 18$ by 3, which yields $m + 6$.

Guided Practice – Solving Systems of Equations

Multiple Choice – No Calculator

1   A. Isolate one variable to solve. In the second equation, $-x = -6 - 2y$, so $x = 6 + 2y$. Substitute this in the first equation: $3(6 + 2y) + 2y = 2$, so $18 + 6y + 2y = 2$ and $8y = -16$. Therefore, $y = -2$. $3x + 2(-2) = 2$, so $3x = 6$ and $x = 2$.

2   B. Since the second equation has been solved for x, we can use substitution by plugging in $3(y + 1)$ for x in the first equation: $\dfrac{3(y + 1)}{y} = 4$, which can be simplified to $3y + 3 = 4y$, and finally $y = 3$.

3   C. We can use elimination to solve. If we multiply the top equation by 2, we get $2x + 2y = 6$. If we subtract this equation from the second, we are left with $x = 6$. Plugging that back into the second equation, we get $3(6) + 2y = 12$, in which case $2y = -6$ and $y = -3$.

4   C. First, find the values of x and y. One way to solve is to add the equations, yielding $5x + y = 11$, so $y = 11 - 5x$. Substitute this value of y into the first equation: $2x + 3(11 - 5x) = -6$, which simplifies to $2x + 33 - 15x = -6$ and then $33 - 13x = -6$. Therefore, $x = 3$. We can then plug 3 back into either equation.

The Tutorverse

If we use the first equation: $2(3) + 3y = -6$, which leads to $6 + 3y = -6$. Ultimately, $y = -4$. But we're not done, because we want to find the value of $x - y$, which is $3 - (-4) = 7$.

5 C. One way to solve is by using elimination. The top equation can be rewritten as $3x - 2y = 8$. If we add the two equations, we get $4x = 16$, which results in $x = 4$. Plugging that into the second equation gives us $4 + 2y = 8$, which turns into $2y = 4$, so $y = 2$. But we're not done, because we are asked to find the product of xy, which is $4(2) = 8$.

Multiple Choice – Calculator

1 B. Linear functions have 0 solutions if the slopes are equal (because that means the lines are parallel), 1 solution if they intersect at 1 point, and infinite solutions if the equations are equivalent (meaning the lines overlap). Solving the first equation in terms of y yields $y = \frac{1}{2}x$. This means the two functions have different slopes, so the lines must intersect at exactly one point, meaning there is one solution.

2 C. The system has no solutions when the lines are parallel, meaning they will have the same slope. Multiplying the first equation by 2 yields $6x + 4y = -4$, which shows a different y-intercept but the same slope as the second equation, so a must be equal to 4.

3 B. The number of solutions is equal to the number of times the lines that represent these equations intersect. If we solve the second equation for y, we get $y = 0.5x - 0.5b$. Since the two equations do not have the same slope (indicated by the x coefficient), they are not parallel and do not overlap, which eliminates choices A and D. The equations represent lines that only intersect at one point, so B.

4 B. If we solve the top equation for x, we get $x = b + 5$. If we solve the bottom equation for y, we get $y = c + 5$. Since we've been told that $b = c + \frac{1}{2}$, we can substitute and get $x = c + \frac{1}{2} + 5$, or $x = c + 5 + \frac{1}{2}$. Now we can substitute y in for $c + 5$ and get $x = y + \frac{1}{2}$, which is answer choice B.

5 A. We can use substitution by first solving the top equation for x. If we divide both sides by -3, we get $x = -2y - 4$. We can then plug that into the second equation: $2(2y + 3) - 3(-2y - 4) = 2$, which simplifies to $4y + 6 = -6y - 14$. Solving for y results in $y = -2$. If we plug that back into the top equation, we get $-3x = 6(-2) + 12$, so $-3x = 0$, and $x = 0$. Thus, the solution is $(0, -2)$.

6 A. A system with infinite solutions will overlap, so the value of a that makes this true can be found by finding the value of a that makes both lines have the same graphs, meaning both lines have the same slope and y intercept. In this case, multiplying both sides of the first equation by 2 yields $6x + 10y = -4$, so the value of a that makes the second equation equivalent is -10.

7 B. Linear functions have 0 solutions if the slopes are equal (because that means the lines are parallel), 1 solution if they intersect at 1 point, and infinite solutions if the equations are equivalent (meaning the lines overlap). We can solve both equations for y so that they are in the same $y = mx + b$ format. In the top equation, we can subtract 15 from both sides and then divide the equation by -5, which gives us $y = 2x + 3$. In the bottom equation, we can subtract 3 from both sides, and then divide by 4, which gives us $y = 3x - 2$. Since the lines have different slopes, they must intersect at exactly one point, meaning there is one solution.

8 A. The system will have no solutions when the lines are parallel, meaning the lines will have the same slope. To determine the slope, rewrite the equations in the format $y = mx + b$, where m is the slope. If $-2x = 6y + 8$, then $-6y = 2x + 8$ and $y = \frac{2x + 8}{-6}$ and $y = -\frac{1}{3}x - \frac{4}{3}$. In the second equation, $3ay + 15 = 4x - 3$, so $3ay = 4x - 18$. Thus, $y = \frac{4x - 18}{3a}$ or $y = \frac{4}{3a}x - \frac{6}{a}$. If these equations have the same slope, then $-\frac{1}{3} = \frac{4}{3a}$. Solve for a by multiplying both sides of the equation by 3: $-1 = \frac{4}{a}$. Multiplying both sides by a yields $-a = 4$, so $a = -4$.

The Tutorverse

Student Produced Response – Calculator

1   3/4 or 0.75: The two equations must be equivalent. Multiplying both sides of the first equation by 2 yields $2ax + 2by = 20$. Since both equations now equal 20, equating the coefficients gives $2a = 3$ and $2b = 4$.

Therefore, $a = \dfrac{3}{2}$ and $b = 2$. $\dfrac{a}{b} = \dfrac{3}{2} \div 2 = \dfrac{3}{4}$.

2   9. The graphs of these inequalities are represented by the given half-planes and include the boundary lines $y = -15x + 54$ and $y = 3x$, respectively. The solution set of the system of inequalities will be the intersection of these half-planes, including the boundary lines, and the solution (a,b) with the greatest possible value of b being the point of intersection of the boundary lines. The boundary lines can be found by setting them equal to each other: $3x = -15x + 54$, which has solution $x = 3$. Thus, the x coordinate at the point of intersection is 3. Therefore, the y coordinate of the point of intersection of the boundary lines is $3(3) = -15(3) + 54 = 9$. This is the maximum possible value of b in the solution set of the system of inequalities.

3   1. The number of solutions of a system of equations is equal to the number of times the system intersects on the xy-plane. A system has zero solutions if the lines are parallel, or if they have the same slope. Find the slope by rewriting both equations in the form $y = mx + b$, where m is the slope. The first equation can be rewritten as $2y = -3x - 4$ or $y = -\dfrac{3}{2}x - 2$. The second equation can be rewritten as $2x - 8 = 3y$ or $y = \dfrac{2}{3}x - \dfrac{8}{3}$. The equations do not have the same slope, and they are lines, so they will intersect at only one point on the xy-plane, and thus have only one solution.

Guided Practice – Linear Equations, Inequalities, & Systems in Word Problems

Multiple Choice – No Calculator

1   C. The number of emails Jack and Amy each sent can be represented by the number of message per hour multiplied by the number of hours, and then Jack's ($3m$) and Amy's ($4a$) messages should be added together to find the total number of emails sent ($3m + 4a$).

2   D. The coefficient 4.5 can be interpreted as the rate of change in this equation, so the kitten's weight will increase by 4.5 ounces each week.

3   D. If x represents the number of 4-person tables, then $15 - x$ represents the number of 6-person tables. The number of people at each 4-person table is $4x$, and the number of people at each 6-person table is $6(15 - x)$. The total number of people can be represented by $4x + 6(15 - x) = 86$. Solving for x yields 2, which is the number of 4-person tables. Therefore, the number of 6-person tables must be 13.

4   B. To solve, find the number of weeks after delivery when $a = s$ by solving for x, so $1 + 0.2x = 0.4 + 0.4x$. Simplifying yields $0.6 = 0.2x$, so $x = 3$. The price of aluminum 3 weeks after delivery is $1 + 0.2(3)$, so the price is \$1.60.

5   C. Toby must increase his swim distance by 600 meters over the course of 12 weeks, which is equal to 50 meters per week. That is not an answer choice, but it is equal to 100 meters every 2 weeks, which is choice C.

6   C. Each volunteer has 3 hours to set up 6 tables per hour, so each volunteer will set up 18 tables. Therefore, if s is equal to the number of set-up volunteers, $18s = 180$. So the organization needs 10 set-up volunteers. If a volunteer hands out 20 flyers each hour for 3 hours, each volunteer will hand out 60 flyers. Therefore, if f is equal to the number of volunteers handing out flyers, $60f = 300$. So the organization needs 5 volunteers to hand out flyers. The total number of volunteers is equal to $s + f = 10 + 5 = 15$.

7   D. To solve, find the number of days after Labor Day when $d = p$ by solving for x, so $145 + 0.1x = 75 + 0.2x$. Simplifying yields $70 = 0.1x$, so $x = 700$. The price of both coats 700 days after Labor Day is $145 + 0.1(700) = 145 + 70 = 215$.

8   D. Let p represent the cost of a paperback, in dollars, and h represent the cost of a hardcover, in dollars. The question is asking for the sum of $h + p$. From the problem, we know that: $\begin{array}{l} 4p + 2h = 36 \\ 3p + 5h = 69 \end{array}$. One way to

solve this equation is to add both equations to yield $7p + 7h = 105$. Dividing both sides of the equation by 7 yields $p + h = 15$.

9   C. A 10% commission could be expressed as $0.10p$, where p is equal to the total price of the items she sold, because $10\% = 0.10$.

10   C. This shows that the total number of cookies and brownies the class will sell will be less than or equal to 400, because the students can sell less than they have, but they can't sell more than they have. It also shows that the earnings from the bake sale will be more than or equal to $500.

11   B. The question is asking for the number of years after release when $b = f$. Solve for x in $6.5 + 0.5x = 4.5 + 0.7x$, which simplifies to $2 = 0.2x$. So $x = 10$.

12   B. This system of inequalities shows that the sum of the number of baseballs and tennis balls is greater than or equal to 50, meaning the teacher wants to buy at least 50 total, and the sum of the prices is less than or equal to the $150 budget. A, C, and D show the less than or greater than signs applying to the incorrect values.

13   C. Write a system of equations to solve. If c is equal to the number of boxes of cupcakes sold and m is equal to the number of boxes of muffins sold, then: $\begin{array}{l} c + m = 30 \\ 6c + 4m = 140 \end{array}$. Solving for m will yield the number of boxes of muffins. We know from the first equation that $c = 30 - m$. This can be substituted in the second equation to find that $6(30 - m) + 4m = 140$, which simplifies to $m = 20$.

14   C. If she sold 26 shirts on Friday and twice as many on Thursday, then $x = (26)(2)$. Written another way, $\dfrac{x}{2} = 26$.

Student Produced Response – No Calculator

1   30. Determine the value of m when $a - b$, so $10 + 0.1m - 5.5 + 0.25m$. This simplifies to $4.5 - 0.15m$, so $m = 30$. Therefore, the Wi-Fi plans will cost the same at 30 minutes of use.

2   10. If c represents the number of pounds of chicken sold and p represents the number of pounds of pork sold, then: $\begin{array}{l} c + p = 15 \\ 3c + 4p = 50 \end{array}$. Isolate a variable and substitute. $p = 15 - c$, so $3c + 4(15 - c) = 50$. This simplifies to $-c = -10$, so $c = 10$.

3   1.6 or 8/5. A change in depth of 500 meters results in a temperature change of 8°C. Dividing both values by 5 gives us a temperature change of 1.6°C for every 100 meters.

4   0.6 or 6/10 or 3/5. Determine the price of both when $t = l$: $2.6 - 0.5x = 1.8 - 0.3x$. This simplifies to $0.8 = 0.2x$, so $x = 4$. After 4 weeks, the price of tile is equal to $2.6 - 0.5(4) = 0.6$, or $0.60 in dollars.

5   16. The maximum number of yoga classes requires spending as much as possible on instructors. If instructors are paid $40 per hour for a 1.5-hour class, they earn $60 per class. Since we are looking for the maximum number of classes, we will assign that number a variable, x. The cost for all the classes will be $60x$. Since the total cost cannot exceed $1,000, we have the inequality $60x \leq 1,000$, in which case $x \leq 16.67$. Since Tamara cannot offer part of a yoga class, she can offer a maximum of 16 classes per week.

Multiple Choice – Calculator

1   C. It shows the rate of online subscriptions multiplied by the number of online subscriptions, added to the rate of print subscriptions multiplied by the number of print subscriptions.

2   C. Sam's bill can be represented by the equation $9.98 + 2.5x = 17.48$, where x is the number of on-demand programs he watched. Solving for x results in $x = 3$.

3   B. It's easiest to assign the variable to the smaller value. Let $x = $ Rafael's hours. Then Joanna's hours will be $x + 12$, and their total hours can be represented as $x + x + 12 = 64$. Solving for x results in $x = 26$, meaning Rafael worked 26 hours. If Joanna worked 12 more hours than Rafael, then $26 + 12 = 38$.

4   C. If x is the number of adults and y is the number of students, then $x + y$ equals the total number of people who went to the theme park, and $12.5x + 6.75y$ represents the total admission fee of $2,118.

The Tutorverse

5   D. It shows the total books in January, plus 95 books per month. When this number is greater than or equal to 15,000, the library will be at or above capacity.

6   A. It shows that $x + y$ is equal to the total number of slots. We don't see 60 or 30 in the answer choices, so we should conclude that the numbers in the equations are not in seconds. Since most of the second equations have coefficients of 0.5 and 1, we can conclude that the numbers represent minutes. In an 18-hour period, there are 216 minutes of ads (6 minutes per 30-minute program, $(6)(2)(18)$ equals the total number of minutes of ads), so the number of 1-minute ads plus the number of 0.5-minute ads is equal to the total number of minutes.

7   A. This system of equations shows that the total weight of the boxes is less than or equal to 96 ounces and the total number of boxes is less than or equal to 12.

8   B. Adding 2.5 to the cost of a six-inch sandwich yields the cost of a foot-long, and the total cost of 2 foot-long sandwiches and 4 six-inch sandwiches is $37.70, so these equations can be used to find the value of a foot-long sandwich. A and D use multiplication instead of addition to find the price of a foot-long sandwich. C uses subtraction instead of addition to find the total cost.

9   A. If t is equal to the number of one-way trips the plane can take: $2,000t \le 5,300$ and $190t \le 400$. A round trip is equal to $2t$, since it is 2 one-way trips, so the pilot can only make 1 round trip, which will use 4,000 gallons of fuel and last 380 minutes. In both inequalities $2 \le t \le 3$, so the plane only has the fuel capacity and allotted flying time to make 1 round trip.

10   D. This system of equations shows that the total weight in a truck is less than or equal to 2,000 pounds and the total number of crates is less than or equal to 30.

11   B. Based on the information in the equation, if c is the price of one cup and p is the price of one plate, then: $\begin{aligned} p - c &= 6.5 \\ 5c + 3p &= 55.5 \end{aligned}$. Therefore, $p = 6.5 + c$, which you can substitute into the second equation: $5c + 3(6.5 + c) = 55.5$, which simplifies to $8c = 36$, so c is equal to 4.5.

12   A. To solve, find the value of p when $s = d$. So, $\frac{1}{2}p + 65 = 200 - p$. This simplifies to $1\frac{1}{2}p = 135$. So $p = \$90$.

13   C. This scenario can be represented by the equation $k - 5q = p$, where q is equal to the number of incorrectly answered questions and p is equal to the number of points the player has. Therefore, $k - 5(30) = 50$. So, $k = 200$.

14   A. The total distance is 6 miles, so $b + w = 6$. The other three choices are all incorrect because none of the second equations have $b + w = 6$. Additionally, Sharon bikes b miles at 9 miles per hour, which takes $\frac{b}{9}$ hours. Similarly, she walks $\frac{w}{3}$ hours. The sum of these is less than 1 hour. Therefore, $\frac{b}{9} + \frac{w}{3} < 1$.

15   B. These inequalities separate time and sheets of paper into two separate inequalities. The first inequality shows that the sum of each 90-minute writing assignment and each 20-minute math assignment is greater than 300 minutes (thereby eliminating choices A and D because they do not show less than or equal to 300 minutes) and that the number of sheets of paper used is less than or equal to the greatest amount of paper that can be used, which is 20 sheets (eliminating choice C for showing the amount of paper must be less than 20 sheets instead of less than or equal to 20).

16   D. If the total dinner sales at the restaurant were $785, then the tips earned by all servers is shown by $t = 0.15(785) = 117.75$. So, during an 8 hour shift, the server earns $s = 5.5(8) + \frac{117.75}{6} = 44 + 19.625 = 63.625$.

17   A. If x and y are the length and width of the playground, this system of inequalities shows that the difference between the length and width is greater than or equal to 20 (eliminate choices B and D). Since the perimeter cannot be greater than 2,000 feet, the sum of 2 lengths and 2 widths ($2x + 2y$) must be less than or equal to 2,000 (eliminate choice C).

The Tutorverse

18   C. If a is the cost of an adult ticket and c is the cost of a child ticket, the information in the problem can be represented as: $\begin{array}{c} 4a + 8c = 116 \\ 6a + 2c = 89 \end{array}$. Isolate one of the variables and use substitution to solve. One way is to add both equations together to find that $10a + 10c = 205$. This yields $c = 20.5 - a$, which can be substitute back into one of the original equations to solve for a. The child ticket costs $8.50 and the adult tickets costs $12.00.

19   B. x student tickets at $12 each can be represented as $12x$. 2 adult tickets at $15 each is $30. Since the total amount of money must be between $90 and $105, we can create the compound inequality $90 \le 15(2) + 12x \le 105$. Taking 30 away from all sides simplifies the equation to $60 \le 12x \le 75$, or $5 \le x \le 6.25$. The only integer values that make this inequality true are 5 and 6, so the only possible answer is B.

20   C. If s is equal to the number of superhero comics sold and g is equal to the number of graphic novels sold, then: $\begin{array}{c} s - g = 40 \\ 3.5s + 12.5g = 700 \end{array}$. Therefore, $g = s - 40$. Substitute this in the second equation: $3.5s + 12.5(s - 40) = 700$. This simplifies to $16s = 1,200$, or $s = 75$. So the comic book store sold 75 superhero comics.

21   C. If n is the number of copies made and there is a fee of $0.10 per page, then the cost for the copies is $0.10n$. Adding the base fee of $1.00 to use the machine results in a total cost of $t = 1.00 + 0.10n$.

22   C. The expression shows the number of miles traveled per day divided by the number of miles per gallon of gas to find the number of gallons of gas used per day. This amount is then multiplied by x days to find the total number of gallons of gas needed for the trip, which is then multiplied by 2.19 to find the total cost, in dollars.

23   C. If 4 times x plus 10 is equal to 6, then $4x + 10 = x$, and $x = -1$. In that case, 2 times x plus 5 feet can be written as $2(-1) + 5$, which equals 3.

24   C. For Store A, $y = 500 + (25 + 70)x$. For Store B, $y = 450 + (20 + 80)x$. These two equations simplify to $y = 500 + 95x$ and $y = 450 + 100x$. To find when Store B is less than or equal to Store A, solve the inequality $450 + 100x \le 500 + 95x$. Solving for x results in $x \le 10$.

25   C. The number of boxes of cereal in each carton (18) is irrelevant to the question asked. The machine fills c cartons in 60 minutes, and the question asks how many cartons the machine fills in 5 minutes, so $\dfrac{c}{60} = \dfrac{x}{5}$, where x is equal to the number of cartons the machine fills in 5 minutes. This can be simplified as $\dfrac{5c}{60}$.

26   C. Since we are looking for the number of players, we will assign that value a variable, x. In the first situation, each player gets 8 ounces, which is a total of $8x$ ounces, plus the 76 extra ounces. In the second situation, each player gets 10 ounces, or a total of $10x$ ounces, but they are 30 ounces short. The total amount of water can be represented as both $8x + 76$ and $10x - 30$, in which case $8x + 76 = 10x - 30$. Solving for x results in $x = 53$.

Student Produced Response – Calculator

1   15. To solve, write an equation. $36 = 2.4y$ where y is equal to the number of years. $y = 36 \div 2.4 = 15$ years.

2   45. If r represents the number of bouquets of roses and d represents the number of bouquets of daisies sold by the florist, then from the problem we know: $\begin{array}{c} r - d = 30 \\ 25r + 15d = 1,350 \end{array}$. You can use substitution to solve. $d = r - 30$, so $25r + 15(r - 30) = 1,350$. This simplifies to $40r = 1,800$, so $r = 45$. So the florist sold 45 bouquets of roses.

The Tutorverse

3   65. If b is equal to the cost of a bush and t is equal to the cost of a tree, then: $\begin{array}{c}13b+4t=485\\6b+2t=230\end{array}$. Multiplying

both sides of the second equation by –2 yields $\begin{array}{c}13b+4t=485\\-12b-4t=-460\end{array}$. Adding these equations yields $b=25$.

Plug this into one of the equations solve for t: $6(25) + 2t = 230$. This simplifies to $t = 40$. So $b+t=25+40=65$.

4   1,925 (entered into bubble sheet as 1925). We assign the smaller value the variable, so Damon drove x hours, Geoff drove $x + 15$ hours, and they drove a total of $x + x + 15 = 55$, resulting in $x = 20$. Damon therefore drove 20 hours and Geoff drove 35 hours. At an average speed of 55 mph, Geoff drove $(35)(55) = 1,925$ miles.

5   38. Write a system of equations to solve. If p is equal to the price of the pants and b is equal to the price of the backpack, this system represents the problem: $\begin{array}{c}p+b=78\\p+1.06b=80.40\end{array}$. Subtracting the first equation from

the second yields $(p + 1.06b) – (p + b) = 80.4 – 78$, which simplifies to $0.06b = 2.4$. This gives $b = 40$. So the backpack cost \$40 before tax. Substituting in the first equation yields $p + 40 = 78$ so $p = 38$. Thus, the cost of the pants is \$38.

Guided Practice – Linear Equations, Inequalities, & Systems on the Coordinate Grid

Multiple Choice – No Calculator

1   D. If the x-axis represents time t, and the y-axis represents the amount of money in the account, then at the beginning (time zero) when money is first deposited into the account, the y-value should be 500. Only choice D represents this. The equation of the line is $V = 150x + 500$, where 500 represents the initial deposit (the y-intercept) and 150 represents the amount of change over a particular period t.

2   C. If Jake starts each week with 95 computers and can repair 12 per day, then the number of computers to be repaired that week minus the number of days he worked multiplied by the number of computers he can fix in a day will leave the number of computers still left to repair.

3   C. If $3y-x=12$, then $x=-12+3y$. Plugging into the first equation: $2(-12+3y)+5y=-2$ and $-24+6y+5y=-2$ and $11y=22$, resulting in $y=2$. Thus, $2x+5(2)=-2$, so $2x=-12$ and $x=-6$.

4   A. A line parallel to the line of the given equation will have the same slope. Choice A can be rewritten as $y=4x+12$, where the coefficient of x is the slope of the line. This is the same as the slope in the given equation.

5   B. If the first equation has an x intercept at $(1, 0)$, then we can plug those (x,y) values into the equation: $0=a(1)+1$, then $a=-1$. If a system of equations has no solutions, the linear equations must be parallel lines. Therefore, they both have the same coefficient of -1.

6   B. A line with the slope $\dfrac{1}{5}$ will have an equation $y=\dfrac{1}{5}x$. Therefore, the value of x will be 5 times the value of y. This is only true for choice B.

7   C. The equation is written in the form of $y = mx + b$, where (x,y) is a point on the line. In this case, $(3,26)$ is a point on the line $c = 7h + b$, so $26 = 7(3) + b$, which simplifies to $b = 5$.

8   D. A line with slope m has a perpendicular line with slope $-\dfrac{1}{m}$. The given equation is written in the form $y = mx + b$, so the slope is –6. Therefore, the slope of the perpendicular line will be $\dfrac{1}{6}$. This is only true of

choice D, which can be rewritten as $y=\dfrac{x-18}{6}=\dfrac{1}{6}x-3$.

Student Produced Response – No Calculator

1   2. The equation is written in the form $y = mx + b$ and $(8,26)$ is a point on the line of this equation. Therefore, $26 = a(8) + 10$, which simplifies to $a = 2$. The hourly rate is \$2 per hour.

The Tutorverse

2   5. Since the slope of the first line is 3, an equation of this line can be written in the form $y = 3x + c$, where c is the y-intercept of the line. Since the line contains the point (1,9), one can substitute 1 for x and 9 for y, which gives $9 = 3(1) + c$, so $c = 6$. Thus, an equation for the first line is $y = 3x + 6$. The slope of the second line is equal to $\frac{1-3}{4-2} = -1$. Thus, an equation of the second line can be written in the form of $y = -x + d$, where d is the y-intercept of the line. Substituting 2 for x and 3 for y gives $3 = -2 + d$, so $d = 5$, so an equation for the second line is $y = -x + 5$. Since a is the x-coordinate and b is the y coordinate of the intersection point of the two lines, one can substitute a for x and b for y in the two equations, giving the system $b = 3a + 6$ and $b = -a + 5$. Use substitution to find the values of a and b: $3a + 6 = -a + 5$, so $a = -\frac{1}{4}$ and $b = \frac{1}{4} + 5$. So the value of $a + b = 5$.

Multiple Choice – Calculator

1   C. This equation can be written as $y = mx$, where m is the slope of the line. In the context of the problem, the slope represents the daily rental fee, because multiplying the fee by the number of days, x, yields the total cost, y.

2   B. If the system has infinite solutions, then both lines overlap on the xy-plane and must have the exact same equation. Therefore, a must be equal to b.

3   B. The only points both graphs have in common are solutions to the system. If $y = 2x - 3$, then $2x - 3 = x - 3$, so $x = 0$. $y = 2(0) - 3 = -3$. The graphs intersect at $(0,-3)$.

4   A. The second equation can be rewritten as $y = 3x - 5$. Both equations have the form $y = mx + b$, where m is equal to the slope and b is equal to the y-intercept. Since both equations have the same slope but different y-intercepts, the lines must be parallel. Only the points where both graphs have in common are solutions to the system. Since the lines are parallel, they will never intersect, so there are no solutions.

5   B. Since the inequalities show that y values are greater than or equal to (or greater than) a value, the solutions for both inequalities will be all possible values above the lines on the xy-plane. Both lines have negative slopes and intercept the y-axis at 1, so no solutions will be in Quadrant III.

6   C. A line with points Quadrants I, II, and III is a line with a positive slope that intercepts the y-axis at a point above the x-axis. It cannot have a slope of zero, because it would be a horizontal line, and so would only pass through two quadrants.

7   D. To find the point where any two straight lines intersect, find the solutions (x,y) for both. At this point, $2x - 4 = -3x + 6$, so $5x = 10$, so $x = 2$. Thus, $2(2) - 4 = y$, and $y = 0$. So, the two lines intersect at $(2,0)$.

8   C. A line that is perpendicular to a line with slope m will have a slope equal to $\frac{-1}{m}$. The line above intercepts the y-axis at $(0,3)$ and a point at $(-1,1)$. You can find the slope by substituting into $y = mx + b$, where m is the slope and b is the y-intercept: $1 = m(-1) + 3$, so $m = 2$. The slope of the perpendicular line will be $-\frac{1}{2}$. That rules out choices A and B. Rewriting choice C in terms of y yields $y = -\frac{1}{2}x + 3$. Rewriting choice D in terms of y yields $y = \frac{1}{2}x + 2$. C is the perpendicular line.

9   A. B is the amount of water, so the B-intercept is the initial amount of water in the bucket.

10   C. The equation of a line can be expressed as $y = mx + b$, where m is the slope and b is the y-intercept. Since the line is decreasing, it has a negative slope, which rules out choice A and B. Since the line intercepts the B-axis at 10, the equation will be $B = -2d + 10$.

11   D. The graph shows the increase in the number of loaves of bread the bakery baked, so the L-intercept shows the number of loaves of bread the bakery had when they started tracking how many they baked.

12   B. The equation of a line can be expressed as $y = mx + b$, where m is the slope, or rate of change, and b is the y-intercept. Since the line is increasing, it has a positive slope, which rules out choice D. According to the graph, the bakery bakes 8 loaves per hour, so 8 is the slope. Since the line intercepts the L-axis at 3, the equation will be $L = 8h + 3$.

The Tutorverse

Student Produced Response – Calculator

1 4. If the system has one solution, then both lines intercept at the point $(1,1)$. Therefore, $1 = -b(1) + 5$, so $b = 4$. Since b is a constant, this is also true for the second equation.

2 2. The cost, c, will be the same for both companies for the same number of hours at the point (h,c) where the graphs overlap. In this case, $30 + 12(3)h = 42 + 10(3)h$. This simplifies to $h = 2$. Plugging 2 in for h in the equation would give you the cost, but the question only asks for after how many hours the jobs are the same price, so the answer is 2.

Guided Practice – Absolute Value

Multiple Choice – No Calculator

1 A. Solve by isolating the absolute value part of the equation: $|x + 4| = 4$. This equation has two possible solutions: $8 - 4 = 4$ and $0 - 4 = -$, so the value of x could be 8 or 0. Since 8 is not an option, 0 is the correct answer.

2 A. $|x - 2| - 2$ will equal 0 if $|x - 2| = 2$. So x could be equal to 4 or 0. The other three choices cannot be the correct answer because any value of x substituted into the absolute value part of the expression will yield a positive number, so adding 2 will yield a sum greater than 0.

3 D. When isolating $|5x + 4|$ on one side of the equation, you'll find that $|5x + 4| = -8$. An absolute value cannot be negative, so this equation has no solution.

4 A. $|2 - 4(-4)| = 18$, which is greater than 10. For choice B, $|2 - 4(-1)| = 6$. For choice C, $|2 - 4(2)| = 6$. For choice D, $|2 - 4(3)| = 10$. You can also solve the absolute value inequality by rewriting it as a compound inequality: $-10 > 2 - 4x > 10$. We isolate x by subtracting 2 from all three sides and then dividing by -4, which gives us $3 < x < -2$. (Don't forget that multiplying or dividing an inequality by a negative number makes the inequality change direction!) Therefore, x must be greater than 3 or less than -2. Choice A is the only number that works.

5 C. This states that the difference between dancers' heights and 70 must be less than or equal to 4.

6 D. The easiest way to answer this question is to try all four answer choices. $f(2) = |5 - 4(2)| = 3$.

$f\left(\dfrac{1}{2}\right) = \left|5 - 4\left(\dfrac{1}{2}\right)\right| = 3$. None of the other choices are equal to 3.

7 A. If a is a negative number, then the absolute value of a is the opposite of a, or $-a$. So the absolute value of a plus the absolute value of b is equal to $-a + b$.

Student Produced Response – No Calculator

1 1. There are two possible solutions to x. First, isolate the part of the equation within the negative value signs: $|x - 3| = 2$, therefore $x - 3 = \pm 2$. Solving for x in both equations yields possible values of x of 5 and 1, respectively. Since 1 is the least value, it is the correct answer.

2 13. Solving the first equation results in $8 - k = 5$ and $8 - k = -5$, in which case k could be equal to 3 or 13. Solving the second equation results in $k - 2 = 11$ and $k - 2 = -11$, in which case k could be equal to 13 or -9. 13 is the only value that works for both equations.

3 2,000. If $t = 1$, $s = -2|1 - 20| + 40$, which simplifies to $s = -2(19) + 40 = -38 + 40 = 2$. Since s is the weekly sales in thousands, the maximum sales the band will have in one week is 2,000.

Multiple Choice – Calculator

1 D. If $|n - 2| + 2 = 0$, then $|n - 2| = -2$. However, the absolute value can never be a negative number. Therefore, there is no value for which $|n - 2| + 2 = 0$.

2 B. For each point, find the value of $|x| - |y|$. For point B, $|-5| - |-2| = 3$. For choice A, the equation will be $2 - 4 = -2$. For choice C, $2 - 3 = -1$. For choice D, $3 - 3 = 0$.

The Tutorverse

3 B. Set up an absolute value inequality to solve. $|x - 2.5| \leq 0.05$, which is solved with the compound inequality $-0.05 \leq x - 2.5 \leq 0.05$. This gives a possible range of values of $2.45 \leq x \leq 2.55$. The only choice in this range is B.

4 C. In the given inequality, $-y < y$, so y must be positive, and statement II is true. If $-y < x < y$, the value of x is either between y and 0 or $-y$ and 0, so statement III is true. It is possible for x to be either positive or negative, so statement I is not necessarily true. Therefore, only II and III must be true.

5 A. This scenario can be represented by the inequality $|x - 12.25| \leq 0.06$, in which the difference between the diameter of the gear x and 12.25 is less than 0.06, so the range of possible diameters can be represented by $2.19 \leq x \leq 12.31$.

6 B. This expression can be simplified as $-|-1| + |-11| = -1 + 11 = 10$.

7 C. To find the range, find the values for which $t - 75 = \pm 145$. When $t = -70$, $t - 75 = -145$. When $t = 220$, $t - 75 = 145$. So the range is $-70 \leq t \leq 220$.

8 D. This expression shows that the low or high temperature subtracted from 34 will yield 7, which gives a range of $27 \leq t \leq 41$, which shows a high temperature of 41° and a low of 27°. You can check by putting these values back into the equation. $34 - 27 = 7$ and $34 - 41 = -7$.

9 A. If $|26x| = 13$, then $26x = \pm 13$. So $x = \pm\frac{13}{26}$ or $\pm\frac{1}{2}$. So x can only be equal to $\frac{1}{2}$ and $-\frac{1}{2}$.

10 B. This equation shows that the absolute value of the difference between the weight and 16 is 0.5, which means that the range of acceptable weights is $15.5 \leq x \leq 16.5$.

11 C. The difference between the actual temperature of the oven and 180° cannot exceed 5°. Answer choice B says the difference between the actual temperature and 5° cannot exceed 180°. Answer choice A says the difference between the actual temperature and 180° must be at least 180°. Answer choice D says the difference between the actual temperature and 5° must be at least 180°. Only answer choice C says the difference between the actual temperature and 180° cannot exceed 5°.

12 B. It takes Jane $30 \leq m \leq 40$ minutes to get to her friend's house, but the question asks for this in miles per hour. The distance is 25 miles, so to solve, determine Jane's speed to travel 25 miles per hour in 30 minutes and Jane's speed to travel 25 miles per hour in 40 minutes. This is equal to $37.5 \leq m \leq 50$. To find the correct inequality, find the midpoint (or average) of the two values, which is 43.75, then find the difference between that midpoint and the two values, which is ±6.25.

13 A. If $x < 0$, x is a negative number, so the absolute value will be positive; in other words, it will be $-x$. You can check by substituting a few negative values for x. For example, if $x = -2$, then $|-(-2)| = 2$.

Student Produced Response – Calculator

1 61. If $|x - 72| = 10.8$, the low score will be $x = 72 - 10.8$, so x will be equal to 61.2 or 61 rounded to the nearest whole number.

2 93.5. If $|x - 110| \leq 16.5$, there is a range of possible prices from $93.5 \leq x \leq 126.5$. So, the lowest possible price for a painting is $93.50.

3 2. If $|s - 30| \leq 5$, $30 \pm 5 = 7.5p + 3.75 + 2.25$, where p is equal to the number of people Tom buys tickets for. Since the question asks for the maximum number of people Tom can buy tickets for while staying within his preferred budget, you want to find how many tickets he can purchase within the $35 budget. So, $35 = 7.5p + 3.75 + 2.25$. Isolating the variable yields $29 = 7.5p$. So $p \approx 3.87$, but since Tom can't bring a partial person to the movies, he can bring himself and 2 friends with him to the movies.

Mixed Practice – Algebra
Multiple Choice – No Calculator

1 Solving Linear Equations & Inequalities: D. If $3x = 27$, then $x = 9$, so $6x + 5 = 6(9) + 5 = 59$.

2 Linear Equations, Inequalities, & Systems in Word Problems: C. If a peanut butter bar has 40 more calories than a fruit bar, then the fruit bar can have x calories and the peanut butter bar can have $x + 40$

The Tutorverse

calories, in which case 3 peanut butter bars and 4 fruit bars having a total of 750 calories can be represented as $3(x + 40) + 4x = 750$. Solving for x yields $x = 90$, to which we must add 40 to arrive at 130.

3 Absolute Value: C. Julio's score must be between 80 and 100. To create the correct inequality, take the midpoint (or average) of the high and low values, which is 90. Now, notice that he must score within 10 points of that midpoint. The difference between Julio's score and 90 must be no more than 10. Only choice C shows this relationship.

4 Linear Equations, Inequalities, & Systems on the Coordinate Grid: D. The slope of a line that passes through two points is $m = \dfrac{y_2 - y_1}{x_2 - x_1}$, so the slope of the line through the given points is $\dfrac{3-6}{-1-0} = 3$. The diagonals of a square are perpendicular, and so the line that passes through A and C must have a perpendicular slope. Perpendicular slopes are negative reciprocals of each other. If the given line has a slope of 3, the perpendicular line will have a slope of $-\dfrac{1}{3}$. Choice D is the only one with that slope.

5 Solving Systems of Equations: B. If we solve the top equation for x, we get $x = b + 7$. If we solve the bottom equation for y, we get $y = c + 7$. Since we're told that $b = c + \dfrac{1}{2}$ we can use substitution and get $x = c + \dfrac{1}{2} + 7$, or $x = c + 7 + \dfrac{1}{2}$. Now we can substitute y into the equation, getting $x = y + \dfrac{1}{2}$, which is answer choice B.

Student Produced Response – No Calculator

1 Linear Equations, Inequalities, & Systems on the Coordinate Grid: 4. Since we are solving for b, we only need to work with the second equation. If $(1,-1)$ is a point in both lines, then $-1 = b(1) - 5$, so $b = 4$.

2 Solving Linear Equations & Inequalities: 11. If $3a - 5 \geq 1$, then $3a \geq 6$ and $a \geq 2$. Since a must be greater than or equal to 2, the least possible value of a is 2. Therefore, the least possible value of $3a + 5$ occurs when $a = 2$: $3(2) + 5 = 11$.

Multiple Choice – Calculator

1 Solving Linear Equations & Inequalities: C. The given information states that $9 + 3x = 3$, so $x = -2$. The question asks to find the value of $15 + 2x$, which is $15 + 2(-2) = 11$.

2 Linear Equations, Inequalities, & Systems in Word Problems: C. If we assign Lisa's dinner the variable x, then the price of Stacey's dinner is $x + 3$, and the total cost of the meal is $2x + 3$ dollars. If this is split evenly, Lisa and Stacey each paid $\dfrac{2x+3}{2} = x + 1.5$ dollars, plus an 18% tip. After adding the tip, each of them paid $(x + 1.5) + 0.18(x + 1.5) = 1.18(x + 1.5) = 1.18x + 0.27$ dollars.

3 Solving Linear Equations & Inequalities: D. Isolating the variable yields $b \leq -4$, meaning the greatest possible value of b is -4, so -3 cannot be a possible solution to the inequality.

4 Linear Equations, Inequalities, & Systems in Word Problems: A. Let s represent the number of songs and p represent the number of podcasts. Based on the data in the problem: $\begin{aligned} s + p &= 25 \\ 3.5s + 20p &\leq 300 \end{aligned}$. So, $s = 25 - p$ and $3.5(25 - p) + 20p \leq 300$. This simplifies to $16.5p \leq 212.5$. Dividing both sides of the inequality by 16.5 yields approximately $p \leq 12.878787$. Any value less than this is a possible answer for p. The other choices will either require more than 300 megabytes of data.

5 Absolute Value: D. In the first equation, m could be equal to 9 or -1. In the second equation, k could be equal to 5 or -15. Since both m and k are less than 0, $m = -1$ and $k = -15$. So, $m - k = -1 - (-15) = 14$.

Student Produced Response – Calculator

1 Linear Equations, Inequalities, & Systems in Word Problems: 38. Determine the price of both when $a = b$: $26 + 0.3x = 18 + 0.5x$. This simplifies to $8 = 0.2x$, so $x = 40$. This means that their houses had the same price per square foot after 40 weeks. At that time, the price of both of their houses is equal to $26 + 0.3(40) = 38$, or \$38.

The Tutorverse

Data Analysis
Guided Practice – Ratios & Proportions
Multiple Choice – Calculator

1   B. Since $y = kx$ and $y = 42$ when $x = 7$, then we can plug in 42 and 7, giving us $42 = k(7)$. Solving for k results in $k = 6$. Substitute 6 into the equation yields 6 times 9, which is 54.

2   B. To find the unit price of the cupcakes sold by the dozen, divide 21 by 12, which equals $1.75. This is $1.00 cheaper than the individual price of $2.75.

3   B. If Rover started at 20 kg and now weighs 46 kg, his weight gain was 26 kg. Rover's weight gain was 30% more than Spot's, meaning Rover's weight gain was 1.3 times Spot's weight gain. If we call Spot's weight gain x, we can create an equation $1.3x = 26$. Solving for x results in $x = 20$. This is how much weight Spot gained; the question asks for Spot's current weight, which is $20 + 20 = 40$.

4   B. Though it may seem intuitive that the area would remain the same, the best way to tackle this problem is to calculate the new dimensions and area. A change of 10% to a side with length 20 meters would be a change of 2 meters (either increasing or decreasing, depending on the side). $20 + 2 = 22$, and $20 - 2 = 18$; $18 \times 22 = 396$. Alternatively, $20 \times 0.9 = 18$ and $20 \times 1.1 = 22$ (a decrease and increase of 10 percent, respectively).

5   C. Calculate the old area and the new and use the formula $\dfrac{new - old}{old}$ to determine the percentage change. The old area of the rectangle is equal to the length times the width: $50 \times 40 = 2,000$. To find the area of the new rectangle, find the length and width after the 20% decrease and increase, respectively. $20\% = 0.2$. A 20% decrease means 80% remains, and so can be determined by multiplying 0.8 by the length; in this case, $50 \times 0.8 = 40$. A 20% increase can be determined by multiplying 1.2 by the width; in this case, $40 \times 1.2 = 48$. The new area is $40 \times 48 = 1,920$. Substituting into the percentage change formula: $\dfrac{2,000 - 1,920}{1,920} = 0.04$ or 4%.

6   C. Since 1 hour = 60 minutes, there are $\dfrac{60}{15} = 4$ periods of 15 minutes per hour. The total number of hours the messenger worked is $5 + 4 = 9$ hours. $9 \cdot 4 = 36$ periods. At $5 per delivery, the messenger made $180 for the nine hours of work.

7   D. Let y be the amount of money earned for selling 180 items. Set up the proportion $\dfrac{40}{1500} = \dfrac{180}{y}$. Cross multiplying produces $40y = (180)(1,500)$. Solving for y results in $y = \$6,750$.

8   A. 67% of $1,500 is $1,005. Using that much for living expenses leaves $495 for his savings account.

9   B. You must take note of any word or information written in italicized, bold, or underlined font. The question asks how many juniors were *not* wearing the school colors that day. If 48% are wearing the school colors, then 52% are *not* wearing the school colors. To find a percent of any value, multiply the percent (in decimal form) by the value: $0.52(650) = 338$.

10   C. To get the total number of hours for a 9.5-year trip, multiply 9.5 years $\times$ 365 days $\times$ 24 hours per day to arrive at 83,220 hours. To find the average miles per hour for the trip, divide the total miles 4,670,000,000 by 83,220 hours $\approx$ 56,116 miles per hour, which can be written in scientific notation as approximately 5.61×10^4.

11   B. 30% of 200 can be found by multiplying $(0.30)(200) = 60$. Subtracting 60 from 200 results in 140.

12   B. We are looking for the number of pages reviewed on Wednesday, which we will call x. The number of pages reviewed on Thursday was 125% of the pages on Wednesday, so Thursday was $1.25x$. Since we know she reviewed 40 pages on Thursday, $1.25x = 40$. Solving for x results in 32.

13   C. If a $600 phone is on sale for 40% off, then the customer still has to pay 60% of the original price, so the sale price is $0.6(600) = \$360$. The question asks what the discount is, which is the same as asking for the percent change. We find percent change by dividing the difference of the two values $(360 - 252 = 108)$ by the sale price (360). This gives us 0.3, which is 30%.

The Tutorverse

14 D. A formula is described in the first sentence: $D = \dfrac{m}{V}$. All we have to do is plug in the values and solve.

If density is 2.7 and volume is 8, and we are looking for mass, then $2.7 = \dfrac{m}{8}$. Solving for m results in 21.6.

15 B. To solve, we set up the proportion $\dfrac{7}{200} = \dfrac{x}{35,000}$, where x is the number of widgets the analyst will inspect. Cross multiplying produces $200x = (7)(35,000)$, which results in $x = 1,225$.

16 B. 3 miles is equal to 15,840 feet, found by multiplying 5,280 by 3. 15,840 feet is equal to 24 furlongs, found by dividing 15,840 by 660.

17 C. 3.5 acres = 3.5(43,560) square feet, which is 152,460 square feet. If there are 9 square feet in 1 square yard, then we can find the number of square yards by dividing 152,460 by 9, which gives us 16,940.

18 A. 11.9 stone is equal to 166.6 pounds (found by multiplying 11.9 by 14), and 166.6 pounds is equal to 2,665.6 ounces (found by multiplying 166.6 by 16).

19 D. We are trying to find Ms. Martinez's original salary, so we will call that value x. If her salary increases by the constant amount of 5% of her starting salary, then 10 years later, her salary is $x + 0.05(10)x$, which is $1.5x$. Since her current salary is $72,000, we can solve for x by setting up and solving $1.5x = 72,000$, which results in $x = 48,000$.

20 C. 0.1 pounds = 1.6 ounces (found by multiplying 0.1 by 16), which equals 45.36 grams (found by multiplying 1.6 by 28.35). If he is paying 20% less than $40 per gram, he is paying $32 per gram. 45.36 grams $\times$ $32 = 1,451$.

21 C. To find the total percentage, we set up a proportion using the total values from the two years:
$\dfrac{x}{100} = \dfrac{240 + 144}{300 + 240}$, where x is the percentage. Cross multiplying results in $540x = 38,400$. Solving for x gives us $x \approx 71.11$, which is the percentage of students who passed over the last two years.

22 B. One way to solve this question is to set up a proportion. The ratio of clothing percentage to dollar amount is $\dfrac{3}{1,920}$. This should be equal to the ratio of rent percentage to dollar amount: $\dfrac{26}{x}$. Setting them equal to each other creates a proportion, $\dfrac{3}{1,920} = \dfrac{26}{x}$, we can solve by cross multiplying:
$3x = 26(1,920)$. Solving for x results in $x = 16,640$. The question asks for the approximate amount in thousands. Rounding 16,640 to the nearest thousand results in 17 thousands.

23 B. Write the given rate as a ratio, $\dfrac{300,000,000 \text{ m}}{1 \text{ sec}}$, and multiply by identity fractions in order to cancel out unwanted units and replace with the units that the question is asking for:
$\dfrac{300,000,000 \text{ m}}{1 \text{ sec}} \cdot \dfrac{60 \text{ sec}}{1 \text{ min}} \cdot \dfrac{1 \text{ km}}{1,000 \text{ m}} = \dfrac{18,000,000,000 \text{ km}}{1,000 \text{ m}}$. This simplifies to $\dfrac{18,000,000 \text{ km}}{\text{min}}$.

24 A. To convert units, start by writing the given rate as a ratio. Here, it would be $\dfrac{30 \text{ miles}}{1 \text{ hour}}$. Then multiply by identity fractions (fractions that are equal to 1) that will cancel out unwanted units and leave you with your desired units. Here, our desired unit ratio is feet per minute, or $\dfrac{\text{feet}}{\text{minute}}$. That means multiplying $\dfrac{30 \text{ miles}}{1 \text{ hour}} \cdot \dfrac{5,280 \text{ feet}}{1 \text{ mile}} \cdot \dfrac{1 \text{ hour}}{60 \text{ minutes}}$. The miles cancel each other out and the hours cancel each other out, leaving you with feet per minute.

25 C. If there are 3 boys for every 7 kids in the school, then there must be 4 girls for every 3 boys, so the ratio of boys to girls is $\frac{3}{4}$. If there are 1,200 girls in the school, then we can set up the proportion $\frac{3}{4} = \frac{x}{1,200}$. Cross multiplying gives us $4x = 3,600$, which simplifies to $x = 900$.

26 C. You can set up a proportion to solve. The ratio of aluminum to steel is 330:2400. This is proportional to the total number of pounds used in one full day. However, since we need the units to match, so we must turn 200 tons into pounds by multiplying by 2,000, which gives us 400,000 pounds. Therefore, the proportion is $\frac{330}{2,400} = \frac{400,000}{x}$. Cross multiplying gives us $330x = 960,000,000$, which simplifies to $x = 2,909,090$. This is closest to answer choice C.

27 C. You can set up a proportion to solve. The ratio of cars to minutes is 10:12. This is proportional to the number of cars made in 12 hours. However, we need the units to match, so we must turn 12 hours in minutes by multiplying by 60, which gives us 720 minutes. Therefore, the proportion is $\frac{10}{12} = \frac{x}{720}$. Cross multiplying gives us $12x = 7,200$, which simplifies to $x = 600$.

28 D. When a ratio is given as a single number, we can rewrite it was a fraction over 1. Here, the given ratio is $\frac{1.618}{1}$, which is equal to the ratio of the length to the height of the wall, which is $\frac{x}{20}$. We can create the proportion $\frac{1.618}{1} = \frac{x}{13}$. Cross multiplying gives us $x = 21.034$.

29 A. If one hour uses 16% of a tank of gas, we want to find out how many times 16% fits into a full tank, or 100%. Dividing 100 by 16 results in 6.25, which is the number of hours she'll be able to drive on a full tank. However, the question asks how many _more_ hours will she be able to drive after having driven that first hour, which is 5.25.

30 A. To find percent decrease, divide the positive change in values by the original number. The percent decrease in carbon monoxide is $(197 - 89) \div 197$, which equals a 54.8% decrease. The percent decrease in sulfur dioxide is $(31 - 15) \div 31$, which equals a 51.6% decrease. Carbon monoxide had the greater percent decrease.

31 D. To find a percentage divide the part by the whole. However, we're not going to divide 1,312,960 by 4,594,539 because we are asked to find the percent _outside_ the U.S., which means we must subtract 1,312,960 from 4,594,539 first, giving us 3,281,579. Dividing $3,281,579 \div 4,594,539 \approx 0.714$, which equals 71.4%.

Student Produced Response – Calculator

1 393. Write the given rate as a ratio, $\frac{2m}{1sec}$, and multiply by identity fractions in order to cancel out unwanted units and replace with the units that the question is asking for: $\frac{2\,m}{1\,sec} \cdot \frac{60\,sec}{1\,min} \cdot \frac{1\,ft}{0.305\,m} = \frac{120\,ft}{0.305\,sec}$. This simplifies to approximately $393.44\,\frac{ft}{sec}$, which rounds to 393.

2 60. First, we need to know how large the actual park is. The map shows that 1 in = 10 m. Since we are looking for square units, we should square both sides of that equation, giving us $1\,in^2 = 100\,m^2$. Since the park takes up 120 in^2 on the blueprint, the actual park is $100(120) = 12,000\,m^2$. To find how many tons of concrete are needed, we divide the total area of 12,000 m^2 by 200 m^2, which gives us 60.

3 89. To find the average of a set of numbers, we take the sum of all the numbers and divide that sum by the number of values in the set. Here, we need to find the total sum of all of Susan's test scores and divide that sum by 8. To find the total of the first three test scores, multiply the average by the number of tests, or $84 \times 3 = 252$. Do the same to find the total of the last five test scores, or $92 \times 5 = 460$. The total of all 8 scores is $252 + 460 = 712$. Divide that sum by 8 to get the final average, which is 89.

4   11.1. If 935.8 is equal to 8.4% of a total amount, we can call the total amount x, in which case $0.084x = 935.8$. Dividing both sides by 0.084 results in $x \approx 11,140$. However, that number is in millions, but the question asks for the number to be provided in billions, so we must divide that number by 1,000 (because there are 1,000 millions in a billion), giving us 11.14, which is rounded to 11.1.

Guided Practice – Linear & Exponential Growth

Multiple Choice – Calculator

1   C. The formula for compound interest is $A = P(1+\frac{r}{n})^{nt}$, where P is the principal, r is the annual interest rate expressed as a decimal, t is the number of years the deposit is held, and n is the number of times the interest is compounded per year. Substituting the provided information into the formula for compound interest yields $A = \$10,000\left(1+\frac{0.15}{1}\right)^{(1)(t)} = \$10,000(1+0.15)^t$.

2   D. Choice A is incorrect because the amount of interest earned depends on how much the interest from the previous year increases the principle. Choice B is incorrect because this also describes a situation where the principle increases as a result of the interest rate being added to it. Choice C is incorrect because it describes a situation where interest increases based on the interest earned the previous year. Choice D is correct because it describes a situation where a constant amount is added and is therefore linear growth, not exponential.

3   C. Choice A is incorrect because each succeeding term is found by adding $\frac{2}{2}$ to the term before it, a constant increase. Choice B is incorrect because each succeeding term is less than the term before it and is exponential decay. Choice D is incorrect because each succeeding term is found by adding 4 to each term before it. Choice C is exponential growth because each term is found by raising the common ratio $\frac{3}{2}$ to increasing integer exponents. $\left(\frac{3}{2}\right)^1 = \frac{3}{2}, \left(\frac{3}{2}\right)^2 = \frac{9}{4}, \left(\frac{3}{2}\right)^3 = \frac{27}{8}, \left(\frac{3}{2}\right)^4 = \frac{81}{16}, \left(\frac{3}{2}\right)^5 = \frac{243}{32}$. The sequence is exponential growth, not exponential decay because the common ratio is greater than 1.

4   B. The number of lizards observed decreases at a constant rate of 30 every three weeks. This is a linear decrease.

5   C. Since $\$480/\$240 = 2$, we are trying to find the number of years required to double the amount $240. Following the rule, we divide 72 by the fixed annual rate of 6 to get 12.

6   C. The pattern of exponential growth can be found by dividing each number after the first by its preceding number: $150,000 \div 100,000 = 1.5$; $225,000 \div 150,000 = 1.5$. This means the values are growing by 50% at each interval. The next value should be $225,000 \times 1.5 = 337,500$. However, that is only at 3:30PM. We are looking for 4PM, so we need to add 50% one more time: $337,500 \times 1.5 = 506,250$.

7   B. This problem may look confusing, but it is nothing more than simple plug-in algebra. You are given a formula. You are given the values of every variable except one. Plug everything in and then solve for the last remaining variable. Here, you will plug in 10,000 for every instance of N_{NOW} and 50,000 for every instance of K, then solve for the variable N_{NOW+20}. $N_{NOW+20} = 10,000 + .07(10,000)\left(1-\frac{10,000}{50,000}\right) = 10,000 + 0.7(10,000)(0.8) = 10,000 + 5,600 = 15,600$.

8   A. Plug 14,200 in for N_{NOW+20} and 10,000 in for N_{NOW} then solve for K. $14,200 = 10,000 + 0.7(10,000)\left(1-\frac{10,000}{K}\right)$. First, subtract 10,000 from both sides: $4,200 =$

The Tutorverse

$0.7(10,000)\left(1-\dfrac{10,000}{K}\right)$. Then divide both sides by $0.7(10,000)$: $0.6 = 1 - \dfrac{10,000}{K}$. Subtracting 1 from

both sides and multiplying by -1 yields $0.4 = \dfrac{10,000}{K}$. K then equals 25,000.

9 A. When thinking about percent problems, it can be helpful to use 100 as your starting number. If an investor invests $100 and earns 100% on that investment, then she earns $100 and now has $200, effectively doubling her money. If she reinvests her profit (meaning she now has $200 invested) and again earns 100%, she then earns an additional $200, for a total of $400, again doubling her money. Choice B is incorrect because growing by 100% is not the same as multiplying by 100. Choice C is incorrect because her investment is growing, not remaining unchanged. Choice D is incorrect because the amount is not growing by a constant $100 each year.

10 B. Answer A is incorrect because it can be simplified to $A = P(0.8)^t$. Since the expression in the parentheses is less than 1, this would lead to an exponential decay, not an exponential growth equation. The amount described in the problem would still be undergoing exponential growth, just at a lower rate. Answer C is incorrect because the amount in the parentheses reflects an increase in the rate to 20%. Answer D is incorrect because it is the simplified version of answer A. Answer B is correct because it results from the amount of interest added to the account at 9% minus the amount of interest added at 7%.

11 D. Percent increase is a form of percent change, which is found by (amount of change) ÷ (original amount). Trying each pair of consecutive numbers, we get $\dfrac{20,000-16,000}{16,000} = 0.25$, $\dfrac{25,000-20,000}{20,000} = 0.25$, and

$\dfrac{31,250-25,000}{25,000} = 0.25$. Each time, the change is 25%.

12 D. The formula for compound interest is $A = P\left(1+\dfrac{r}{n}\right)^{nt}$, where P is the principal, r is the annual interest rate, t is the number of years the deposit is held, and n is the number of times the interest is compounded per year. For annual compounding, $n = 1$, so the formula becomes $A = P(1+r)^t$. For semiannual compounding, $n = 2$, so the formula becomes $A = P\left(1+\dfrac{r}{2}\right)^{2t}$. The difference between semiannual compounding and annual compounding is found by subtracting the two amounts and factoring out P.

13 D. The formula for interest is $A = P\left(1+\dfrac{r}{n}\right)^{nt}$, where r = rate, and n = number of times per year interest is compounded. If $r = n$, the formula can be rewritten as $A = P\left(1+\dfrac{n}{100n}\right)^{nt}$, (where $\dfrac{n}{100}$ represents the percentage interest rate) which can be rewritten as to $A = P\left(\dfrac{100n}{100n}+\dfrac{n}{100n}\right)^{nt}$, which equals $A = P\left(\dfrac{101n}{100n}\right)^{nt}$, and finally simplifies to $A = P(1.01)^{nt}$. Answer A is incorrect because it does not include division of the rate by 100 to account for r being a percent.

Student Produced Response – Calculator

1 $\dfrac{5}{3}$ or 1.66. Each successive term is found by raising the common ratio by the next integer power. The common ratio can be found by dividing any term in the sequence by the term before it.
$\dfrac{125}{27} \div \dfrac{25}{9} = \dfrac{125}{27} \times \dfrac{9}{25} = \dfrac{5}{3}$

2 7. This is essentially a simple interest problem where the number of perch increase exponentially based on the original 4,290 fish. The percent change in the number of perch can be found by subtracting the

The Tutorverse

observed number of perch in any year from the number of perch observed during the previous year and then dividing the difference by the number in that previous year. Percent change =

$$\frac{4{,}590 - 4{,}290}{4{,}290}(100) = 7\%.$$

3   96. Percent problems like this can be solved by starting with 100%. If the panda's weight increases by 40% of the original weight, it is now 140%. If it increases by 40% again, we must find 40% of 140%, which is 56%, and add that to the total, giving us 196%. This represents an increase of 96% from the original weight.

4   3,125. Percent change can be found by subtracting any year's observed number of rabbits minus the number of rabbits from the previous year and dividing by the number of rabbits from the previous year: $\frac{2{,}000 - 1{,}600}{1{,}600} = 0.25$. This means there is 25% growth each year. Adding 25% to 2,500 results in 3,125.

5   8. The percentage rate can be found from: $\frac{\$43{,}200 - \$40{,}000}{\$40{,}000} = \frac{3{,}200}{40{,}000} = 0.08 = 8\%$.

6   10.5. We must figure out the number of grams of the two samples separately. The oxygen-exposed element will decrease by 0.4g per second for 60 seconds: $48 - 0.6(60) = 12$. Since there are five 12-second intervals in one minute, the hydrogen-exposed element will decrease by half five times: $48(0.5)^5 = 1.5$. The difference between the two is $12 - 1.5 = 10.5$.

7   3,795. We must find how many stars each astrophysicist found on the 10th day. Since the first astrophysicist doubles each day, we can use $10(2)^{10-1}$, which gives us 5,120. For the second astrophysicist, we can use $200 + 125(10 - 1)$, which gives us 1,325. The difference is 3,795.

Guided Practice – Interpreting Graphs & Tables

Multiple Choice – Calculator

1   C. On the graph, a line segment with a positive slope represents an interval over which the target heart rate is strictly increasing as time passes. A line segment with a negative slope represents an interval over which the target heart rate is strictly decreasing. The only interval in which the slope strictly increases and then strictly decreases is between 30 and 50 minutes.

2   B. A graph with a strong negative association between x and y would have the points on the graph closely aligned with a line that has a negative slope. Graph B most closely shows such a line.

3   B. If Jennifer writes 70 words per minute and the assignment is 7,500 words long, it will take her approximately 107.14 minutes to type the information, or 1.79 hours. She also needs to complete 3 hours of research. Therefore, she needs about 5 hours to complete the assignment. If she works 2 hours a day, it will take her 3 days to complete the assignment.

4   C. The question is simply asking us to find the point on the given line that aligns with 6,500 on the y-axis, and find what number on the x-axis it matches with. If a horizontal line is traced from 6,500 on the y-axis to the line of best fit, and then drop a line straight down from the point where they intersect, it will go to 2010.

5   B. There is a 30-minute period in which Joe did not move further from home, which shows the time when he stopped to take photos. The graph begins increasing again at 2:00 to show he is traveling further from home, so that is when his break ended. The rest of the choices indicate times when Joe resumed biking, but after a break other than 30 minutes in length.

6   A. There were 5 adult dramas put on at the theater, out of a total of 35 productions, so the fraction of adult drama productions is $\frac{5}{35} = \frac{1}{7}$.

7   A. To find the average decrease, first take note of the unit of measure in each axis. Each gridline represents 5 degrees on the vertical axis, and 4 days on the horizontal axis. The line does not pass through intersecting gridline points, and is in fact less steep than the 5/4 slope that a line passing through each intersecting gridline point would have. A slope of 3, 5, and 20 would be very steep on this graph.

8   B. The line of best fit shows a decrease in temperature.

The Tutorverse

9 C. If a line of best fit were drawn, one could tell that the most likely length of an eruption after an 80-minute interval would be 4 minutes.

10 A. About 60% of people in this age group voted for Candidate B, compared with 51% for the 30–44 age group, 40% for the 45–64 age group, and 55% for the 65 or over age group.

11 A. For a data point to be above the line $y = x$, the value of y must be greater than the value of x. Here, that means years during which homes built after 2000 have a higher value than homes built before 2000. That occurs 1 time in this bar graph.

12 C. The amount of energy consumed by most appliances has gone down since 2000, but the number of appliances per household has gone up. Therefore, the decrease in energy consumption leads to an increase in appliances.

13 A. Since the number of bacteria in the dish doubles each hour, it increases exponentially over time. Only graph A shows an exponential increase.

14 C. The line of best fit shows, from a data set, what expected values are. In this case, these values are the number of books sold at different price points. Thus, the line of best fit shows the expected number of books sold at any given price point. There are five data points that lie above the line of best fit, which mean that at these points (for a given price), more books were sold than expected.

15 D. The x-intercept represents a situation where the number of books sold is almost zero. The actual data shows that there were about 10 books sold at $10. However, the question does not ask how many books were sold at a price point of $10, but what the x-intercept of the line of best fit means. Since, where the line of best fit crosses the x-axis, the number of books sold is 0, and since the crossing happens around $10, we can expect that there would be no books sold at that price point.

16 D. The x-axis represents the number of bathrooms, so if we follow the midpoint of 3 and 4 up to the line of best fit, we can trace it over to $60. However, $60 is the price per night per bathroom, so the approximate cost of the entire vacation home would be $60 \times 3.5 - \$210$. A better way to solve this question would be to plug 3.5 into the equation for the line of best fit: $y - 90 - 9(3.5) = 58.5$. If we multiply 58.5×3.5, we get 204.75, which rounds to 205.

17 B. The slope of the line is –9, so for every integer increase in bathroom, the average price per night per bathroom drops $9.

18 C. Interest compounded annually will lead to exponential growth, so the amount in Tanisha's account after t years is equal to the initial deposit multiplied by the interest rate expressed as a decimal plus 1, to the power of the number of years.

19 B. Grace's top speed is 5 miles per hour, which occurs from the 25-minute mark to the 30 minute mark. We need only properly interpret the graph to know that we are looking for coordinates where the y value is highest.

20 D. The graph tells us commute time, but not distance. It is possible that the person who takes the longest to get to work lives very close to work, but takes long because he walks slowly while everyone else drives. There is no definite correlation between commute time and distance from work.

21 A. The ratios of each point are as follows: $A: \dfrac{30}{4}$, $B: \dfrac{15}{7}$, $C: \dfrac{45}{8}$, and $D: \dfrac{50}{10}$. Of these, A is the greatest.

Student Produced Response – Calculator

1 1/3 or 0.33. According to the graph, there were 400 phones sold in 2012 and 1,200 sold in 2015. The fraction of phones sold in 2012 is equal to $\dfrac{400}{1,200} = \dfrac{1}{3}$.

2 5/11 or 0.45. There were 500 shirts sold in January and 1,100 shirts sold in April, so the fraction of shirts sold in January to shirts sold in April is $\dfrac{5}{11}$.

The Tutorverse

3   1200. There were 1,600 shirts sold in May, the month with the highest number of shirts sold. The month with the fewest number of shirts sold was March, with 400 shirts having been sold. The difference is 1,200. Note the graph indicates that shirts sold is represented in hundreds.

Guided Practice – Additional Data Analysis & Statistics

Multiple Choice – Calculator

1   C. The graph shows the number of households in intervals of 1,000. In other words, if x is equal to the number of households that each unit on the y-axis represents, then $8x + 6x + 9x + 7x + 4x = 34,000$, and $x = 1,000$.

2   A. The probability of the winner being over 18 is equal to the total number of men and women out of 100 that are over 18, so: $\dfrac{75}{100}$.

3   C. The world population does not increase by a fixed amount each year, as it would under a linear growth model. Instead, the increases between periods are greater and greater, indicating exponential growth.

4   A. The lowest price per egg is in the carton of 18. 5 cartons of 18 eggs hold a total of 90 eggs and cost $29.45. An additional carton of 6 costs $3.50, and then 4 additional eggs cost a dollar each. So the lowest possible cost for exactly 100 eggs is $36.95.

5   B. The sum of the two categories is approximately $6 + 22 = 28$, which represents 28% of 100 commuters.

6   A. The confidence interval only applies to the average life of batteries manufactured that day, not to individual batteries or to all batteries the factory produces.

7   C. Illegal tickets will be detected for 50 customers, 12 of which were not illegal. So the probability that the customer did not use an illegal ticket is $\dfrac{12}{50} = 0.24$ or 24%.

8   D. The better results of these students may have been a result of being more motivated, as shown in their willingness to do extra work, and not in their attendance at the study session necessarily, so no conclusion can be drawn regarding a cause and effect relationship between the two events.

9   C. The total number of students surveyed is 260. 15% of 260 is 39, which is the number of male students taking chemistry.

10   C. The range changes from $78 - 59 = 19$ to $70 - 59 = 11$. This is a greater change than will occur for either the mean or the median. The median will not change at all. The mean will change from 65.2 to 64.5, which is a change of only 0.7.

11   B. The budget for public protection increased by $0.31 million, from $7.32 million to $7.63 million, over the course of two years, for an average rate of change of $0.155 million, which is equal to $155,000.

12   A. The recreation & culture department budget can be represented as $\dfrac{0.65}{0.85} \approx 0.76$. The closest is the budget for health: $\dfrac{6.48}{8.56} \approx 0.76$.

13   D. Each point in the scatterplot represents a house in the town and tells how many square feet it is and what its price is. The line of best fit represents expected prices for houses of different sizes, but doesn't necessarily represent any particular house. The line intersects the y-axis at $71,000 when $x = 0$, meaning a house that is 0 square feet in size would still cost $71,000. However, this is an expected cost, as there are no data points there to represent an actual house. Choice A is incorrect because the 71 represents the total price of the house in thousands, not the price per square foot. Choice B is incorrect because we don't know how much the cheapest house in town costs. Choice C is incorrect because, even if there was a house that was 0 square feet, again, 71 does not represent price per square foot. Only Choice D makes sense.

14   A. The sample size is so small, it is difficult for the researcher to draw a conclusion that represents the entire population of the city.

15   D. Calculate the mean by adding the values together and dividing by the number of values. $32 + 27 + 54 + 43 + 35 + 48 + 32 + 29 = 300$, which divided by 8 results in 37.5.

The Tutorverse

16   C. To solve, set up a proportion: $\dfrac{150}{159.6} = \dfrac{175}{x}$. Cross multiply to get $150x = 27{,}930$, so $x = 186.2$.

17   B. We can solve using a proportion: $\dfrac{150}{354.6} = \dfrac{100}{x}$, so $150x = 35{,}460$ and $x = 236.4$. We can also logically eliminate all the incorrect choices because we are looking for a planet where objects weigh more than twice what they do on Earth. Looking at the chart, the only planet that even comes close is Jupiter.

18   D. The sample for this study is well defined, so it is reasonable to conclude that, if conditions are the same – that is, if this model of car is given the new engines – that gas mileage would improve for this model of car produced by this factory. Choices B and C are not supported by the given data because other conditions were not tested. Choice A is too strong a conclusion and not supported by the given data.

19   C. Let x be the number of female students who do not play sports and y be the number of male students who do not play sports. Given the data in the problem, we know that $x + y$ must equal 45. We also know that $2x$ represents the number of female students who play sports and $3y$ represents the number of male students who play sports, giving us the system of equations:

$x + y = 45$

$2x + 3y = 110$

Solving this system yields $x = 25$ and $y = 20$, in which case 50 of the students who play sports are female. Therefore, the probability that a randomly selected student who plays sports will be female is $\dfrac{50}{110}$, or about 0.45.

20   A. The standard deviation is a measure of how far the data set values are from the mean. In the data set for City B, the vast majority of the data are in the middle three of the five possible values, which are the three values closest to the mean. In the data set for City A, the data are more spread out, with many values at the minimum and maximum values. Therefore, by observation, the data for City A have a larger standard deviation.

21   B. If the team scores an average of 11 points per game, their total for 4 games is 44 points. $44 - (7 + 18 + 6) = 13$, so the team must have scored 13 points at the 4th game.

22   A. In order to answer a probability question, we need to know the total. Here, the total of all students is $8{,}221 + 5{,}243 + 4{,}723 + 4{,}916 = 23{,}103$. The probability of a student chosen at random from the entire population being a junior from the Midwest is equal to $\dfrac{1{,}212}{23{,}103} \approx 0.0525$.

23   C. The average of Wendy's times is 2.5 minutes. However, that is the average time it took her to run one lap at the track, which is 0.25 mile. Since there are 24 blocks of 2.5 minutes in every hour (60 minutes ÷ 2.5 minutes = 24), Wendy could on average run a total of 6 miles in that hour (24 × 0.25 miles). Thus, Wendy's average speed is 6 miles per hour.

24   C. If Amar's average is 134 points, then the sum of all 3 rounds was $134 \times = 402$. Subtract the known scores to find the missing one: $402 - (116 + 148) = 138$.

25   B. The range will remain the same (a change of 0) and the mean only changes slightly. Putting the numbers in order – 5, 8, 13, 36, 43 – we see that the median of the original data set is 13, but with the addition of a chapter with 25 recipes, the new list becomes 5, 8, 13, 25, 36, 43, in which case the median number of recipes per category becomes 19.

26   C. Statement I is true because adding 5 to every score will increase the mean by 5. Statement II is also true, because increasing every score by 5 will also increase the median by 5. But statement III is false, because increasing every score by the same amount will result in the same spread of scores as the original, so the standard deviation will remain the same.

27   C. The vertical axis of the chart shows us the number of values in the data set (for example, there are 5 people who work between 10-20 hours). The best way to question of median is to approximate the vertical values: 5, 12, 23, 8, and 2 would be reasonable. There are, then, approximately 50 values in the data set. The median will occur in the middle of that data set, so approximately 25 values in from either the lowest

The Tutorverse

or highest ends of the data set. Starting from either side, we can see that the median must occur in the bucket of 23 employees working from 30-40 hours. This means either choices B or C are correct. The mean, in this case, can be visually determined to be in the same bucket, since there are so many values in the data set corresponding to 30-40, which happens to be in the middle of the data set.

28 C. If 12 people are taking both classes, then there are 42 people taking only martial arts, 11 people taking only yoga, and 12 people taking both, or a total of 65 people enrolled in these classes. $121 - 65 = 56$.

Student Produced Response – Calculator

1 64. The sum of the temperatures for the first days is 396. Adding 52 yields a sum of 448. Divided by 7, the new average is 64°F.

2 7.5. To find the range of a data set, subtract the greatest value from the lowest value. In this case, 9.5 is the greatest and 8.3 is the lowest. To find the least possible value, subtract the range of 2 from the highest number, meaning x is equal to 7.5.

3 633. Find the mean by adding all of the home runs together: 7,059. Then divide by the number of players (11): 641.72. The average age, rounded to the nearest whole number, is 642.

4 5. If the mean is 7, the sum of the first 5 ratings is 35. In order for the mean to be 8 for the first 10 ratings, the sum of the first 10 ratings should be $8 \times 10 = 80$. So, the sum of the second ten ratings is equal to $80 - 35 = 45$. The maximum rating is 10, so the maximum possible value of the sum for the 7th through the 10th rating is $4 \times 10 = 40$. Therefore, for the product to be able to have an average of at least 8 for the first 10 ratings, the least possible value for the 6th rating is $45 - 40 = 5$.

5 81.4. If the average for 18 students is 82, then the sum of their scores is $18 \times 82 = 1,476$. The sum of the scores of the additional students is $2 \times 76 = 152$. Therefore, the sum of the scores of all 20 students is equal to 1,628. Dividing by 20 yields an average score of 81.4.

6 0.13. If the winner is chosen from the entire pool of customers, then the odds of the winner being someone who purchased a CD after the show would be $\frac{44}{342} \approx 0.1286$, so the probability rounded to the nearest hundredth is 0.13.

7 99. If 20 students scored an average of 80, then the sum of the scores is 1,600. If 19 students averaged 79 points, then the sum of their scores was 1,501. The 20th score is the difference between these two sums: 99 points.

Mixed Practice – Data Analysis

Multiple Choice –Calculator

1 Additional Data Analysis & Statistics: A. One way to solve this is to try each answer choice. Looking at choice A, if there were 2 athletes who each scored 40 points, then there were 15 athletes in all, making the eighth number from the left (i.e. from lowest to highest) the median. The eighth number is 20, so that works. Looking at choice B, if 3 athletes each scored 40 points, then there were 16 athletes, making the average of the 8th and 9th numbers the median. The 8th and 9th numbers are 20 and 30, making the median 25, which does not work. That means that C and D won't work either.

2 Linear & Exponential Growth: B. The acceleration of gravity is given at 9.8m/s², which acts on an object continuously as it falls. This means that the speed of the object (for example, in meters per second) that falls does not stay constant. Instead, the object's speed is constantly increasing, or accelerating.

3 Ratios & Proportions: C. This problem asks about percent change, which is found by dividing the difference of the two values by the original value. Tom's percent change is $\frac{|8-9|}{9}$, which equals a 11.1% change. Everett's percent change is $\frac{|10-12|}{12}$, which equals a 16.7% change.

4 Ratios & Proportions: C. An efficient way to solve this problem is just to find the price per square foot of each house, which we can find simply by dividing the price of each house by its square footage. The Howell Boulevard house results in the lowest cost per square foot, of approximately $321 per square foot.

The Tutorverse

5   Interpreting Graphs & Tables: D. Since age is on the vertical axis, the oldest sprinter is represented by the data point that is highest in the graph. Here, if we follow that point down to the time axis, it lands just past 9.95. Choice D is the only choice that satisfies that value, as all others are below 9.95.

6   Additional Data Analysis & Statistics: C. The histogram shows that there are 23 parks in total, meaning the median is the 12th park from the left. That places the 12th park in the 600-699 bar, and only 602 falls within that range.

Student Produced Response – Calculator

1   Linear & Exponential Growth: 2,500. This problem may look confusing, but it is nothing more than simple plug-in algebra. You are given a formula. You are given the values of every variable except one. Plug everything in and then solve for the last remaining variable. Here, you will plug in 580 for

"$N_{next\ month}$" and 500 for "$N_{this\ month}$", then solve for the variable K: $580 = 500 + (0.2)(500)\left(1 - \dfrac{1}{K} \cdot 500\right) =$

$500 + (100)\left(1 - \dfrac{500}{K}\right)$. Then subtract 500 from both sides and divide by 100, giving you $0.8 = 1 - \dfrac{500}{K}$.

Solving for K results in $K = 2,500$.

2   Interpreting Graphs & Tables: 3. If Jason can get 36 miles per gallon and his gas tank can hold 18 gallons of gas, he can travel 648 miles on each tank of gas. The total mileage (2,522 miles) divided by 648 means he will need approximately 3.89 tanks of gas to make the trip. Since he starts with a full tank, he will need to refill 3 times.

3   Ratios & Proportions: 450. If 60% of the penguins are female, then 40% are male. The 300 male penguins therefore represent 40% of the total. We can solve most percent problems using a proportion: $\dfrac{40}{100} = \dfrac{300}{x}$, where x is the total number of penguins. Cross multiplying results in $40x = 30,000$, in which case $x = 750$. That is the total number of penguins, so there must be 450 female penguins.

Advanced Math

Guided Practice – Working with Polynomials

Multiple Choice – No Calculator

1   B. Add together like terms. $7x^2 + 3x^2 = 10x^2$ and $(-4x) + (-x) = -5x$ and $8 + 7 = 15$.

2   C. Multiply by FOIL method. $(4x + 3)(5x - 10) = 20x^2 - 40x + 15x - 30 = 20x^2 - 25x - 30$.

3   D. Multiply by FOIL method, then distribute the 5. $5(3x + 1)(2x + 1) = 5(6x^2 + 3x + 2x + 1)$. This simplifies to $30x^2 + 25x + 5$.

4   B. Multiply by FOIL method, then distribute the $\dfrac{1}{2}$.

$$\frac{1}{2}(2x + 4)(x + 1) = \frac{1}{2}(2x^2 + 2x + 4x + 4) = \frac{1}{2}(2x^2 + 6x + 4) = x^2 + 3x + 2$$

5   C. Since both $7x$ and 3 are multiplied with $(2x + 1)$, the given expression is equivalent to $(7x + 3)(2x + 1)$. By expanding this expression out, you get $14x^2 + 13x + 3$. Therefore, both I and II are equivalent to the given expression.

6   C. Since $\dfrac{20}{ab} = 10$, it follows that $ab = 2$, so $a^2b^2 = 2^2 = 4$. Plugging this into the second expression, we get $\dfrac{32}{a^2b^2} = \dfrac{32}{4} = 8$.

7   B. Since $\dfrac{x}{y} = 3$, it follows that $\dfrac{y}{x} = \dfrac{1}{3}$, so $\dfrac{6y}{x} = 6 \cdot \dfrac{1}{3} = 2$.

8 D. $\dfrac{\dfrac{1}{x+4}+1}{\dfrac{2}{x-2}}=\dfrac{\dfrac{1}{x+4}+\dfrac{x+4}{x+4}}{\dfrac{2}{x-2}}=\dfrac{\dfrac{x+5}{x+4}}{\dfrac{2}{x-2}}=\dfrac{x+5}{x+4}\cdot\dfrac{x-2}{2}=\dfrac{x^2+2x-10}{2x+8}$

9 A. $\dfrac{\dfrac{x+5}{x+4}}{\dfrac{x-7}{2x+8}}=\dfrac{\dfrac{x+5}{x+4}}{\dfrac{x-7}{2(x+4)}}$ By multiplying the numerator and denominator by $2(x+4)$, we can make

cancellations and get $\dfrac{2(x+5)}{x-7}$ which equals $\dfrac{2x+10}{x-7}$.

10 D. Multiplying with the FOIL method, choice D gives us
$(2a^2+5b^2)(2a^2+5b^2)=4a^4+10a^2b^2+10a^2b^2+25b^4$ which simplifies to $4a^4+20a^2b^2+25b^4$.

11 C. $\dfrac{a+3}{x}+\dfrac{b-5}{2x}=\dfrac{2(a+3)}{2x}+\dfrac{b-5}{2x}=\dfrac{2a+6+b-5}{2x}=\dfrac{2a+b+1}{2x}$

12 C. $(3x-6)^3=(3x-6)^2(3x-6)$ and becomes $(9x^2-36x+36)(3x-6)$. This equals
$27x^3-54x^2-108x^2+216x+108x-216$, which simplifies to $27x^3-162x^2+324x-216$.

13 D. The expression in the question will have different values depending on the value of x. Therefore,
choice A and B must be incorrect because they are constant. Simplifying choice D into a single fraction,

we get $6-\dfrac{25}{x+4}=\dfrac{6(x+4)}{x+4}-\dfrac{25}{x+4}=\dfrac{6x+24-25}{x+4}=\dfrac{6x-1}{x+4}$, so D is the correct answer.

14 A. $\dfrac{3}{x+2}-\dfrac{2}{x^2+4x+4}=\dfrac{3}{x+2}-\dfrac{2}{(x+2)^2}=\dfrac{3(x+2)}{(x+2)^2}-\dfrac{2}{(x+2)^2}=\dfrac{3x+6-2}{(x+2)^2}=\dfrac{3x+4}{x^2+4x+4}$

15 B. All the answer choices start with $\dfrac{y}{x}=$, which means that we have to solve for $\dfrac{y}{x}$. Breaking the fraction

on the left side of the equation into two fractions, we get $\dfrac{y}{x}+\dfrac{1}{x}=\dfrac{6}{7}$. Subtracting $\dfrac{1}{x}$ to both sides, we get

$\dfrac{y}{x}=\dfrac{6}{7}-\dfrac{1}{x}$. Combining the fractions on the right, we get $\dfrac{y}{x}=\dfrac{6x}{7x}-\dfrac{7}{7x}=\dfrac{6x-7}{7x}$.

16 D. Expanding out the original function and converting it to standard form, we get $f(x)=x^2-10x+24$.
However, this does not give us the roots, so we much convert it again into factored form, which is
$f(x)=(x-4)(x-6)$. This indicate that both roots are positive (4 and 6). Negating each factor, we get the
equivalent function $f(x)=(4-x)(6-x)$ which has constants 4 and 6.

Student Produced Response – No Calculator

1 32. We get this by manipulating $4x(2x+3)+5(4x+1)=8x^2+12x+20x+5$, which simplifies to
$8x^2+32x+5$, so $b=32$.

2 3. The left side of the equation is a square, so we get $(x^2-9)^2=0$. Factoring this further, we get
$[(x+3)(x-3)]^2=0$, so $x=\pm3$. However, the question asks for a positive answer, so it is 3.

3 7. Factoring the equation by grouping, we get $x^2(x-7)+3(x-7)=0$ and then $(x^2+3)(x-7)=0$, so the
only real solution to the equation is $x=7$.

4 1. Dividing both sides of the equation by 6 we get $x^4(x^4-2)=-1$. Expanding out the left side we get
$x^8-2x^4=-1$ or equivalently $x^8-2x^4+1=0$ which is a square polynomial, $(x^4-1)=0$. This has real
solutions $x=\pm1$, and the problem specifies to take the positive answer.

The Tutorverse

Multiple Choice – Calculator

1 D. The given expression is a difference of squares. It can be rewritten as $(8w^3)^2 - (v^3)^2$. Using the difference of squares formula, we get choice D.

2 B. Expanding the function using FOIL, we get $f(x) = x^2 - 4x - 21$. The minimum will occur at the vertex when $x = -\dfrac{b}{2a} = -\dfrac{-4}{2(1)} = 2$. By completing the square, we can rewrite the function as $f(x) = (x-2)^2 - 25$ which shows that when $x = 2$, the value of the function is –25. B is the correct choice because it includes the minimum value (–25) and it is equivalent to the original function.

3 C. $f(x)$ is an upturned parabola with vertex at the origin, so its minimum value is zero. $g(x)$ has its minimum at its vertex, where $x = -\dfrac{b}{2a} = -\dfrac{-6}{2(1)} = 3$. Plugging 3 in for x, we get $g(3) = 3^2 - 6(3) + 19 = 10$ so the minimum value of $g(x)$ is 10. Thus, the difference in the minimum values is $10 - 0 = 10$.

Student Produced Response – Calculator

1 17. Distribute the –5 to get $7x^2 + 2x - 4 - 5x^2 + 15x - 10$. Then combine like terms to get $2x^2 + 17x - 14$. The value of b is 17.

2 25. The first part of the expression factors as $3x(y - 5)$. Since the first part of the expression is divisible by $y - 5$, the second part of the expression, $y^2 - c$, must also be divisible by $y - 5$ in order for the entire expression to be divisible by $y - 5$. The expression $y^2 - c$ resembles a difference of squares. Using the factor $y - 5$, we get $(y - 5)(y + 5) = y^2 - 25$. Therefore, $c = 25$. Another way to solve this problem is to plug in 5 for y, and see what value of c will make the expression equal to 0.

3 6. Apply the distributive property to get $x^3 = 48x - 2x^2$, which can equivalently be written as $x^3 + 2x^2 - 48x = 0$. Factoring this, we get $x(x + 8)(x - 6) = 0$ so the solutions are $x = -8, 0, 6$. The question is asking for the greatest of the solutions, which is 6.

Guided Practice – Working with Polynomial Factors in Expressions & Equations

Multiple Choice – No Calculator

1 D. The value of t cannot be 3 because that would make the fraction undefined. Multiply both sides of the equation by $t - 3$ and we get $t + 3 = 6t - 18$. Subtract t from both sides and add 18 to both sides. It becomes $21 = 5t$, so $t = \dfrac{21}{5}$.

2 B. The value of the function is 0 when $x = 1$. Therefore, 1 is a root of the polynomial, so $x - 1$ must be a factor of the polynomial.

3 D. The value of the function is 0 when $x = 3$. Therefore, –3 is a root of the polynomial, so $x - (-3)$ or, equivalently, $x + 3$ must be a factor of the polynomial. $x - 1$ is also a factor, though it is not an answer choice.

4 A. The value of the function is 0 when $x = 6$. Therefore, 6 is a root of the polynomial, so $x - 6$ must be a factor of the polynomial.

5 B. If we were to use either long division or synthetic division, we would find that the quotient is $4x + 2$ with a remainder of 11. However, the SAT will NOT require students to perform long division of polynomials. Instead, this question tests students on their knowledge of the Polynomial Remainder Theorem, which states that any polynomial $p(x)$ is equal to the product of its quotient times its divisor $(x - a)$, plus its remainder. Here, that means $4x^2 - 2x + 9 = (4x + 2)(x - 1) + 11$. The trick to remember is that when you plug a (from the divisor) into $p(x)$, the resulting value is the remainder. Here, we see that plugging 1 into the polynomial results in 11.

6 D. The Polynomial Remainder Theorem (see question #5 above) states that when any polynomial $p(x)$ is divided by $(x - a)$, the remainder is equal to $p(a)$. Here, the value of a is –3. Plugging that into the original polynomial, we get $9(-3)2 + 5(-3) - 2$, which equals 64.

The Tutorverse

7 C. Remembering the Polynomial Remainder Theorem, we know that for any divisor $(x - a)$, when you plug a into the polynomial dividend, the result will be the remainder. Here, we are told that when a is -3 (meaning the divisor is $x + 3$) the remainder is 0, and when a is 2 (meaning the divisor is $x - 2$) the remainder is 4.

8 B. Cross-multiply the original equation. It becomes $2(x + 24) = 10x$, which multiplies out to $2x + 48 = 10x$. Subtract $2x$ from both sides to get $48 = 8x$. Then divide both sides by 8 to get $6 = x$. The question asks for the value of $\dfrac{x}{2}$ which is $\dfrac{6}{2}$ and simplifies to 3.

9 D. Cross-multiply the original equation. It becomes $4x = 1(x + 6)$ or simply $4x = x + 6$. Subtract x from both sides to get $3x = 6$. Then divide both sides by 3 to get $x = 2$. The question asks for the value of $\dfrac{1}{x + 6}$, which is $\dfrac{1}{2 + 6}$ and simplifies to $\dfrac{1}{8}$.

Student Produced Response – No Calculator

1 28. Working backwards from the given information, we can see that the result, multiplied by $4x - 6$, will give us the original polynomial. As an equation, this becomes $8x^2 - 20x + 40 = (4x - 6)\left(2x - 2 + \dfrac{R}{4x - 6} \right)$.

The right side can equivalently be written as $(4x - 6)(2x - 2) + R$, which expands to $8x^2 - 20x + 12 + R$. So our new equation becomes $8x^2 - 20x + 40 = 8x^2 - 20x + 12 + R$. Cancelling terms and solving for R gives us 28.

2 6. We can clear the denominators in this equation by multiplying through by $(t + 2)(t + 10)(4)$. The new equation becomes $1(4)(t + 10) = -2(4)(t + 2) + 1(t + 2)(t + 10)$. This becomes $4t + 40 = (-8 - 16) + (t^2 + 12t + 20)$. If we collect all of these terms on the right side of the equation, we get $0 = t^2 - 36$. This factors as $(t + 6)(t - 6)$, so $t = \pm 6$. Because the problem states that t must be positive, the answer is 6.

Multiple Choice – Calculator

1 B. Multiply both sides of the equation by $t - 5$ and we get $t - 3 = 7t - 35$. Subtract t from both sides and add 35 to both sides. It becomes $32 = 6t$, so $t = \dfrac{32}{6}$. This simplifies to $\dfrac{16}{3}$.

2 C. Cross-multiply and we get $(3t)(10) = (t + 6)(1)$, which becomes $30t = t + 6$. Subtract t from both sides. It becomes $29t = 6$, so $t = \dfrac{6}{29}$.

3 A. The expression can be factored as $(x - 3)(x - 4)$, which means that $(x - 3)$ is a factor of $x^2 - 7x + 12$. When we divided by a factor, the remainder will be zero.

4 D. Remembering the Polynomial Remainder Theorem, we know that for any divisor $(x - a)$, when you plug a into the polynomial dividend, the result will be the remainder. Here, since we are plugging in 4, the divisor must be $(x - 4)$ and the resulting value of -1 is the remainder. This matches choice D.

5 C. Since $y \neq 0$ we can cancel y from the numerator and denominator of the right side. Next, cross-multiply the equation. It becomes $5(x + 2) = 2(x + 11)$, which multiplies out to $5x + 10 = 2x + 22$. Subtract $2x$ and 10 from both sides to get $3x = 12$. Then divide both sides by 3 to get $x = 4$. The question asks for the value of $x + 11$ which is $4 + 11$ and simplifies to 15.

6 A. To eliminate the denominator, multiply both sides by $ax - 6$. The equation becomes $30x^2 - 26x - 19 = (6x + 2)(ax - 6) - 7$. The coefficient of x^2 on the left side is 30 and on the right side it will be $6a$. Therefore, $30 = 6a$, so the value of a is 5.

7 B. To eliminate the denominators, multiply through by $2x + b$. The equation becomes $8x^2 - 22x - 9 = (4x + 3)(2x + b) + 12$. The constant term on the left side of the equation is -9 and on the

The Tutorverse

right side it will be $3b + 12$. Therefore, $-9 = 3b + 12$. Subtract 12 from both sides and then divide by 3. We get -7 as the solution for b.

Student Produced Response – Calculator

1 4. We can clear denominators in this equation by multiplying through by $(6)(t-1)(t+2)$. The new equation becomes $2(6)(t+2) + 1(t-1)(t+2) = 5(6)(t-1)$. This simplifies to

$(12t + 24) + (t^2 + t - 2) = 30t - 30$. If we collect all of these terms on the left side of the equation, we get $t^2 - 17t + 52 = 0$. This factors as $(t - 13)(t - 4) = 0$ so the solutions are 13 and 4. Since the problem states that $t < 12$, the answer is 4.

2 112. Working backwards from the given information, we can see that the result, multiplied by $7x + 4$, will give us the original polynomial. As an equation this becomes $7x^2 - 38x + 88 = (7x + 4)\left(x - 6\dfrac{R}{7x + 4}\right)$.

The right side can equivalently be written as $(7x + 4)(x - 6) + R$, which expands to $7x^2 - 38x - 24 + R$. So our new equation becomes $7x^2 - 38x + 88 = 7x^2 - 38x - 24 + R$. Cancelling terms and solving for R gives us 112.

3 74. Multiplying both sides by $5x + 8$, we get $10x^2 - 34x - 6 = (5x + 8)(2x - 10) + R$. The right side can equivalently be written as $10x^2 - 34x - 80 + R$. So our new equation becomes $10x^2 - 34x - 6 = 10x^2 - 34x - 80 + R$. Cancelling terms and solving for R gives us 74.

Guided Practice – Quadratic Functions & Equations

Multiple Choice – No Calculator

1 B. All of the answer choices have the factors $(x - 4)$ and $(x + 5)$, except for choice B which has the factors $(x + 4)$ and $(x - 5)$. This means that the solutions to equation B are -4 and 5, whereas all the other equations have the solutions 4 and -5.

2 A. This equation factors as $(x + 7)(x - 5) = 0$ so x is -7 or 5.

3 D. This equation factors as $(x + 1)(2x + 1) = 0$ so x is -1 or $-\dfrac{1}{2}$.

4 B. The quadratic formula says $x = \dfrac{-b + \sqrt{b^2 - 4ac}}{2a}$. Plugging in $a = 1$, $b = 5$, $c = 2$, we arrive at

$x = \dfrac{-5 \pm \sqrt{25 - 8}}{2}$ which simplifies to answer choice B.

5 B. Before using the quadratic formula, we must determine the equation in standard form by adding $4x$ to both sides. This gives $x^2 + 4x + 1 = 0$. Using the quadratic formula, we arrive at $x = \dfrac{-4 \pm \sqrt{16 - 4}}{2}$, which simplifies to answer choice B.

6 B. The equation factors as $(x - 4)(x - 4) = 0$. Since both factors are the same, the equation has only one real solution, $x = 4$.

7 D. Before using the quadratic formula, we must represent the equation in standard form by using the distributive property on the left side and then subtracting 1 from both sides. This gives $3x^2 + 6x - 1 = 0$. Using the quadratic formula, we arrive at $x = \dfrac{-6 \pm \sqrt{36 + 12}}{6}$ which simplifies to answer choice D.

8 D. From the original equation, we see that $ab = 6$. Since $a + b = 5$, the values of a and b must be 2 and 3, but we don't know which is which. Trying both possibilities, we arrive at $(2x + 4)(3x + 5) = 6x^2 + 22x + 20$ or $(3x + 4)(2x + 5) = 6x^2 + 23x + 20$, so c is either 22 or 23.

The Tutorverse

9 C. From the last term in the equation, we see that $ab = -7$, so the values of a and b are either -1 and 7, or -7 and 1. Trying both possibilities, we arrive at $(x-1)(x+7) = x^2 + 6x - 7$ or $(x+1)(x-7) = x^2 - 6x - 7$, so c is either 6 or -6.

10 C. The value of ab will be whatever we arrive at for the constant term on the right side of the equation when we put it in standard form. $(x+3)^2 + 11 = (x^2 + 6x + 9) + 11 = x^2 + 6x + 20$. Therefore, the value of ab is 20.

11 D. To determine the value of a, plug in 0 for $f(x)$. $0 = x^2 - 10x + 25 = (x-5)(x-5)$, so $x = 5$ when $f(x) = 0$. This tells us that the function passes through the point $(5, 0)$, so the value of a is 5. To determine the value of b, plug in 0 for x. You arrive at $f(x) = 0^2 - 10 \cdot 0 + 25 = 25$, so $f(x) = 25$ when $x = 0$. This means that the function passes through the point $(0, 25)$, so the value of b is 25. Therefore, $a + b = 5 + 25 = 30$.

12 A. This question is asking when the function has a value of 0, so you have to solve the equation $25x^2 - 9 = 0$. This factors as $(5x+3)(5x-3) = 0$, so the solutions are $\pm\dfrac{3}{5}$ which yields $k = \dfrac{3}{5}$.

13 D. Notice that the right side of the equation has no x term. This means that the factor $(ax+b)$ must be $(3x-2)$ or some multiple thereof, because that is the only way to determine the x term to cancel out when we multiply $(ax+b)$ with $(3x+2)$. With any multiple of $(3x-2)$, the two constants a and b must have different signs (one positive, one negative). Using basic rules of positive and negative integers, we know their product ab must be negative. The example $ax + b = 3x - 2$ shows that choices A and C are false. The example $ax + b = -3x + 2$ shows that choice B is false.

14 B. To find the intersection points of two functions, you must find when they are equal. Setting these two functions equal to each other, we arrive at $-x^2 + 8x - 7 = x^2 - 8x + 17$. Bringing all terms to the same side of the equation, we arrive at $2x - 16x + 24 = 0$. This factors as $2(x-6)(x-2) = 0$ so the solutions are $x = 6$ and $x = 2$. These numbers give us the x-coordinates of the two intersection points. By plugging either of these values into either of the two functions, you arrive at 5 as the y-coordinate of both intersection points, so $k = 5$.

15 C. To find the intersection points of two functions, you must find when they are equal. Setting these two functions equal to each other, we arrive at $16 - x^2 = x^2$. Bringing the x^2 terms to the same side of the equation, we arrive at $2x^2 = 16$ and dividing both sides by 2 we arrive at $x^2 = 8$, so $x = \pm\sqrt{8} = \pm 2\sqrt{2}$. These are the x-coordinates of the two intersection points, so $a = 2\sqrt{2}$.

16 A. Notice that $g(x)$ will be undefined when its denominator is equal to zero. However, the equation $x^2 - 4x + 8 = 0$ has no real solutions, because when you perform the quadratic formula, you get a negative number under the square root: $\sqrt{b^2 - 4ac} = \sqrt{(-4)^2 - 4 \cdot 1 \cdot 8} = \sqrt{-12}$. This means there are no values of x for which the function is undefined.

17 C. $Volume = Depth \times Width \times Length = 60$. If x represents the width, then the length is $(2x + 4)$. This gives us $3x(2x + 4) = 60$. Using the distributive property, we arrive at $6x^2 + 12x = 60$. Then, subtracting 60 from both sides and dividing both sides by 6, we arrive at $x^2 + 2x - 10 = 0$.

Student Produced Response – No Calculator

1 15. First, put the equation in standard form by expanding the left side to get $x^2 + 8x + 16 = 1$ and then subtracting 1 from both sides to arrive at $x^2 + 8x + 15 = 0$. This factors as $(x+3)(x+5) = 0$ so the solutions are -3 and -5, which have a product of 15. Another way to figure this out is by using the following rule:

For any equation $ax^2 + bx + c = 0$, the product of the solutions is $\dfrac{c}{a}$. In this case, $\dfrac{c}{a} = \dfrac{15}{1} = 15$.

The Tutorverse

2 7. Notice that $f(x)$ will be undefined when its denominator is equal to zero. The expression $x^2 - 5x - 14$ factors as $(x - 7)(x + 2)$ and this is equal to zero when x is 7 or –2. Since the problem only asks for positive values, the answer is 7.

Multiple Choice – Calculator

1 C. You can figure out how many solutions a quadratic will have by calculating the number under the square root in the quadratic formula. This number, $b^2 - 4ac$, is called the determinant. If the determinant is positive, the equation will have two real solutions. If the determinant is 0, there will be one solution, and if the determinant is negative, there will be no real solution. The determinants of equations I, II, and III are 61, 0, and –16 respectively, so equation III is the only one with no real solutions. (Since this is a calculator problem, you could also graph the three equations and see which one does not touch the x-axis).

2 A. The equation factors as $3(r + 3)(r + 4) = 0$, so the possible values of r are –3 and –4, which have a sum of –7. Another way to figure this out is by using the following rule: For any equation $ax^2 + bx + c = 0$, the sum of the solutions is $-\dfrac{b}{a}$. In this case, $-\dfrac{b}{a} = \dfrac{21}{3} = -7$.

3 B. A function is undefined when its denominator is zero. You can calculate the zeros for each denominator, but in this case, the question only asks about $x = 2$. Therefore, you can just plug 2 into the denominator of each function. For the denominator of $f(x)$, you get $(2 - 2)^2 + (2 - 4)^2 = 4$. For the denominator of $g(x)$, you get $2^2 - 6 \times 8 - 0$. For the denominator of $h(x)$, you get $2^7 + 10 \times 2 + 16 - 40$. Since $g(x)$ is the only one with 0 in the denominator, the answer is g only.

4 D. Since the problem gives us the total distance, we can make an equation involving distance. Remember that *distance = rate * time*. For the first part of the hike, the hiker's rate is $\dfrac{x}{2}$ and his time is $x + 2$, so his distance is $\dfrac{x}{2}(x + 2)$. For the second part of the hike, his rate is the half of the original rate, which gives us $\dfrac{1}{2} \cdot \dfrac{x}{2} = \dfrac{x}{4}$. His time for the second part is 3, so his distance is $\dfrac{x}{4} \cdot 3$. The problem tells us that the total distance is 15. By adding up the distances from the two parts of the hike we arrive at $\dfrac{x}{2}(x + 2) + \dfrac{x}{4} \cdot 3 = 15$. If we multiply both sides of the equation by 4, we arrive at $2x(x + 2) + 3x = 60$. Rearranging this into standard form gives us choice D.

5 C. Since the problem gives us the final distance for her trip, we can make an equation involving distance. Remember that *distance = rate * time*. For the first part of the trip, the driver's rate is $\dfrac{2x}{3}$ and her time is $3x$, so her distance is $\dfrac{2x}{3}(3x)$. For the second part of the drive, her rate is still $\dfrac{2x}{3}$ and her time is 30 minutes, but we need to convert this to hours, so the time is $\dfrac{1}{2}$ an hour. Therefore, the distance for the second part of her trip is $\dfrac{2x}{3} \cdot \dfrac{1}{2}$. After both parts of the trip, she was 50 miles from home. Since she reversed direction, we must subtract the distances so we arrive at $\dfrac{2x}{3}(3x) - \dfrac{2x}{3} \cdot \dfrac{1}{2} = 50$. If we multiply both sides of the equation by 3, we arrive at $2x(3x) - 2x \cdot \dfrac{1}{2} = 150$. Rearranging this into standard form gives us choice C.

The Tutorverse

Student Produced Response – Calculator

1 1/3 or 0.33. This equation factors as $(3x - 1)(x + 5) = 0$, so x is $\frac{1}{3}$ or –5. However, the question asks for a positive solution, so the answer is $\frac{1}{3}$, or its decimal equivalent, 0.33.

2 17/2 or 8.5. First put the equation in standard form: $2x^2 - 17x + 35 = 0$. The equation factors as $(2x - 7)(x - 5) = 0$, so the possible values of x are $\frac{7}{2}$ and 5, which have a sum of $\frac{17}{2}$. Another way to figure this out is by using the following rule: For any equation $ax^2 + bx + c = 0$, the sum of the solutions is $-\frac{b}{a}$. In this case, $-\frac{b}{a} = \frac{-17}{2} = \frac{17}{2}$.

3 6. Notice that $h(x)$ will be undefined when its denominator is equal to zero. First, put the denominator in standard form. $(x - 7)^2 + 2(x - 7) + 1 = (x^2 - 14x + 49) + (2x - 14) + 1 = x^2 - 12x + 36$. This expression factors as $(x - 6)(x - 6)$, so the denominator is equal to zero when $x = 6$.

<u>Guided Practice – Exponents & Radicals</u>

Multiple Choice – No Calculator

1 D. By definition, $a^{\frac{m}{n}} = \sqrt[n]{a^m}$. It follows, therefore, that $a^{\frac{4}{5}} = \sqrt[5]{a^4}$.

2 B. $4 = 2^2$, so 4^x can be written as 2^{2x}. Since both the numerator and denominator have a common base, $\frac{4^x}{2^y} = 2^{2x-y}$. Since we know that $2x - y = 18$, the value of the original expression is 2^{18}.

3 C. If $\sqrt{3k^2 + 9} - x = 0$ and $x = 6$, then $\sqrt{3k^2 + 9} = 6$. Square both sides to get $3k^2 + 9 = 36$. This yields $k^2 = 9$, or $k = 3$.

4 A. If there are 4 million subscribers at the start of 2014, and that number increases by 3% each year, then after 1 year, the website has 1.03 times more subscribers. It has 1.03 times more subscribers in each subsequent year, so multiplying 4 by 1.03 to the power of the number of years will yield the number of subscribers after t years.

5 A. $\frac{x^a}{x^b} = x$ can be rewritten as $x^{(a-b)} = x^1$. Therefore, $a - b = 1$. We now know that a and b must be consecutive whole numbers, so $b - a$ is equal to –1.

6 B. Since $10^3 = 1,000$, if $b = 1$, $a = 3$. None of the other responses are mathematically possible.

7 C. This function shows the initial amount multiplied by the percent of the substance that remains to the power of the time, in days.

8 D. Squaring each side yields $(x - 6)^2 = (\sqrt{x + 42})^2$ or $x^2 - 12x + 36 = x - 6$. To find the solutions, subtract the right side from the left side of the equation: $x^2 - 13x + 42 = 0$. This quadratic equation can be factored: $(x - 7)(x - 6)$. So $x = 7$ and $x = 6$.

9 C. Keep in mind that $k^{-1} = \frac{1}{k}$. Simplifying $m^2k^{-1} = 10m$ yields $10k = m$, so $\frac{1}{m} = \frac{1}{10k}$.

Student Produced Response – No Calculator

1 20. If $5x^2 = 20$, $x^2 = 4$. If $4y = 20$, $y = 5$. So, $x^2y = 20$.

2 9. Since the numerator and denominator have a common base, the expression can be rewritten using the law of exponents as $x^{a^2 - b^2}$. Since this expression is also equal to x^{36}, $a^2 - b^2 = 36$. This can be factored as $(a + b)(a - b) = 36$. Since it is given that $a + b = 4$, substituting gives $4(a - b) = 36$. Dividing both sides by 4 yields $a - b = 9$.

The Tutorverse

3 36. If $a = 3\sqrt{3}$, $2a = 6\sqrt{3}$. Therefore, $6\sqrt{3} = \sqrt{3x}$. Squaring each side yields $(6^2)(\sqrt{3})^2 = (\sqrt{3x})^2$, which simplifies to $108 = 3x$, so $x = 36$.

Multiple Choice – Calculator

1 B. When $t = 2$, $P(t) = 4,000$. When $t = 4$, $P(t) = 8,000$, so the population increased by 4,000 organisms.

2 B. $64 = 2^6$, so $a + b + c = 6$. Since they are different integers, 1, 2, and 3 are the only possible values. $2^1 + 2^2 + 2^3 = 2 + 4 + 8 = 14$.

3 C. Squaring both sides yields $x + 16 = x^2 - 8x + 16$. Subtracting 16 from both sides yields $x = x^2 - 8x$.

4 C. One fast and simple way to solve this is to just try each answer choice by plugging them in for n in the equation. $20,000(0.8)^3$ is the only value that gives 10,240. If you are comfortable working with logarithms, you could also solve algebraically with the equation $10,240 = 20,000(0.8)^n$. Dividing both sides by 20,000 gives you $0.512 = 0.8^n$. You can solve for n with $n = log_{0.8}0.512$, which equals 3.

5 C. Substituting 4 or 5 into the expression do not yield integers, but 20 does: $\sqrt{\dfrac{5 \times 20}{4}} = \sqrt{\dfrac{100}{4}} = \sqrt{25} = 5$.

6 B. The perimeter of the triangle is $6 + 10 + 12 = 28$, so s is 14. Therefore, the area of the triangle can be represented by the formula as $A = \sqrt{14(14-6)(14-10)(14-12)} = \sqrt{14(8)(4)(2)} = \sqrt{896}$. If you're calculator does not put radicals into simplest form, just try each answer choice. $\sqrt{896} \approx 29.93$ so we're looking for the answer choice that equals the same value, which is choice B.

7 A. Squaring both sides of the equation yields $4x^2 + 1 = 4x^2 + 4x + 1$. Subtracting $4x^2$ and 1 from both sides leaves you with $0 = 4x$, so x must equal 0.

8 D. A decrease of 10% means the population will be 90% of the initial amount after 4 years. Since this decrease happens every 4 years, the decrease must be calculated for every 4-year period of time that elapses. Since t represents a number of years, dividing by 4 will yield the correct model.

9 C. The problem can be represented by the expression $500,000(0.95)^t$. So, after ten years, the bee population will be $500,000(0.95)^{10} \approx 299,368.47$. So 300,000 is the closest approximation of the possible answers.

Student Produced Response – Calculator

1 2. In this equation, $r = 0.76$, because the value of the stock will be 76% of its total value if it decreases by 24%. If the stock decreases by $114, its value is $156. So, $156 = 270(0.76)^t$. The easiest way to solve might be to substitute possible values for t, since this model only works for 3 weeks. If $t = 1$, $V = 270 \times 0.76$ which is not true because $156 \neq 205.2$. If $t = 2$, $V = 270 \times 0.76^2$, so $V = 155.95$, which rounds to $156.

2 7. To solve, substitute a few values for t. Since, after 3 weeks, $V \approx 118.52$, less than half its original value, it is reasonable to expect that it would only take a few more weeks for the value to be less than $1. Plugging the numbers into the original equation, when $t = 4$, $V = 90.08$. When $t = 5$, $V = 68.46$, when $t = 6$, $V = 52.03$, and when $t = 7$, $V = 39.54$. So the value for the stock will be < $50 after 7 weeks.

3 5/4 or 1.25. We want to solve for $\dfrac{x}{t}$. First, squaring both sides yields $x^2 - t^2 = 4t^2 - 4tx + x^2$. Subtracting x^2 from both sides and adding t^2 to both sides gives us $0 = 5t^2 - 4tx$. Dividing everything by t leaves us with $0 = 5t - 4x$, or $5t = 4x$. The last steps are to divide both sides by t and then divide both sides by 4, finally leaving us with $\dfrac{x}{t} = \dfrac{5}{4}$, or the decimal equivalent 1.25.

Guided Practice – Systems of Equations

Multiple Choice – No Calculator

1 D. We have two expressions for y, which we can set equal to each other. We get the equation $2x - 3 = x^2 + 6x$. In standard form, this is $x^2 + 4x + 3 = 0$, which has the solutions $x = -1$ or $x = -3$. Since

The Tutorverse

none of the answer choices have an x value of -3, we can plug -1 back into either equation and get $y = -5$, so the answer is D. Another method would be to simply test every answer choice. Choice A satisfies the first equation, but D is the only ordered pair that satisfies both equations.

2   D. The second equation represents a vertical line. The first equation represents a function. Since a vertical line can only intersect a function once, the system has only one solution. Another way of solving this problem is to replace x with -3 in the first equation. You get $y = 9 - 3a + b$. No matter what constants you choose for a and b, there is only one possible value for y (and -3 is the only possible value for x). Therefore, the system has only one solution.

3   B. The first equation is a circle centered at the origin. The second equation is an upward opening V shape with its vertex at the origin. This is true for any non-zero value of r. Therefore, the two graphs will intersect in quadrants I and II.

4   C. In answer choices A and B, we have the equations of two lines, which will only intersect at one point. These cannot be the answer, because the problem says there are exactly two solutions. Answer choice C has a circle crossed by a horizontal line, so there will be two solutions with the same y-coordinate (this is what the problem asks for). Answer choice D has a circle crossed by a vertical line, so there will be two solutions, but they will have the same x-coordinate and different y-coordinates, so D is incorrect. Another method would be to solve each system. Choice A has solution $(5,0)$. Choice B has solution $(0,5)$. Choice C has solutions $(3,0)$ and $(-3,0)$. Choice D has solutions $(0,3)$ and $(0,-3)$.

5   C. Take the expression for x that is given in the second equation, and substitute it for x in the first equation. The new equation is $y = 2(y^2 - 2y) - 10$ which simplifies to $y = 2y^2 - 4y - 10$. In standard form, this becomes $0 = 2y^2 - 5y - 10$. The discriminant is $b^2 - 4ac = (-5)^2 - 4(2)(-10) = 105$. Because the discriminant is positive, there are two real solutions for y (which would yield two distinct ordered pairs if we plugged y back in to find x). If you didn't remember the discriminant rule, you could also use the quadratic formula to see that there are two real solutions for y.

6   A. A system of quadratic equations has no solution when the parabolas never intersect. One way to solve is to draw a rough sketch of the first equation $y = x^2 + 4$. The second equation must either fit inside it (meaning have a higher y-intercept and steeper slope) or it must fit outside of it (meaning a lower y-intercept and a wider slope). A is the correct choice because the y-intercept is 2 and the slope is 1/2.

7   C. Take the expressions for y in each equation and set them equal to each other. The new equation is $x^3 + 15x = cx^2$, which is $x^3 + 15x - cx^2 = 0$ in standard form. This factors as $x(x^2 - cx + 15) = 0$. This equation has $x = 0$ as a solution, so the system will have three solutions if the equation $x^2 - cx + 15 = 0$ has two solutions. That will occur for $c = 8$. It will not occur for $c = -5$ or $c = 3$, because in both of those cases, the equation $x^2 - cx + 15 = 0$ would have no real solutions, so the entire system would have only one solution.

8   A. Solve the first equation for x. You get $x = -\frac{4}{3}y$. Substitute this for x in the second equation. You get

$$y = \frac{9}{4}\left(-\frac{4}{3}y\right)^2 - 6\left(-\frac{4}{3}y\right) + 3.$$ This simplifies to $y = 4y^2 + 8y + 3$. In standard form, this becomes

$4y^2 + 7y + 3 = 0$, which factors as $(4x + 3)(x + 1) = 0$ so $x = -\frac{3}{4}$ or $x = -1$. The only solution that appears in the answer choices is A.

Student Produced Response – No Calculator

1   7. Replace y with x in the first equation. It becomes $x = x^2 - x - 35$. In standard form, this becomes $x^2 - 2x - 35 = 0$, which factors as $(x - 7)(x + 5) = 0$, so the solutions are 7 and -5. The problem states that $x > 0$, so 7 is the correct answer.

2   202. The problem tells us that x is negative, which means that $|x - 2| = -(x - 2) = -x + 2$, so we get $y + 4 = -x + 2$. Solve this equation for x and it becomes $x = -y - 2$. Substitute this for x in the second equation and we get $(-y - 2) + 2y = 200$. Finally, we can solve this equation for y and we get $y = 202$.

The Tutorverse

Multiple Choice – Calculator

1   B. This choice does not match with the others. The solution to the system is (1,4), so choice B has the x and y coordinate reversed. The other three choices all represent the same system of equations.

2   C. Take the expression that is given for y in the first equation, and substitute it for y in the second equation. The new equation is $4x + (x-3)(x-7) = 13$. This simplifies to $4x + x^2 - 10x + 21 = 13$. In standard form this becomes $x^2 - 6x + 8 = 0$ which has the solutions $x = 2$ or $x = 4$. None of the answer choices have an x value of 4, so we can plug in 2 for x in either equation and get $y = 5$. This problem can also be solved by testing each answer choice.

3   D. If we put both equations in standard form, we can see that they are both equivalent to $y = x^2 + 10x - 24$. Since the equations are equivalent, there are infinitely many solutions.

4   A. Set the two y expressions equal to each other. The new equation is $5x^2 + x + 8 = 3x^2 + 4$. In standard form, this becomes $2x^2 + x + 4 = 0$. The discriminant is $b^2 - 4ac = (1)^2 - 4(2)(4) = -15$. Because the discriminant is negative, there is no real solution. If you didn't remember the discriminant rule, you could also use the quadratic formula to see that there is no real solution to the equation $2x^2 + x + 4 = 0$.

5   B. Take the expression for y in the second equation and substitute it into the first equation. The new equation is $4x + mx^2 + n = 0$, which we write in standard form as $mx^2 + 4x + n = 0$. This equation will have exactly one real solution when its discriminant is equal to zero. The discriminant is $b^2 - 4ac = (4)^2 - 4(m)(n) = 16 - 4mn$. If we test each answer choice by plugging in the values of a and b, the only choice that yields a negative discriminant is B.

Student Produced Response – Calculator

1   236. Replace x with -4 in the second equation. We get $y = (-4)^3 + 300 = 236$.

2   3/2 or 7/2 or 1.5 or 3.5. Set the two expressions for y equal to each other. The new equation is $5(x^2 - 4x + 4) = x^2 - 1$. Distribute the 5 to get $5x^2 - 20x + 20 = x^2 - 1$. When we collect all terms on the left side, this becomes $4x^2 - 20x + 21$. This factors as $(2x - 7)(2x - 3) = 0$, so $x = \dfrac{7}{2}$ or $x = \dfrac{3}{2}$. Since a calculator is allowed for this problem, you could also graph both functions on the calculator and find the x-coordinates of their intersection points.

Guided Practice – Function Notation

Multiple Choice – No Calculator

1   D. Calculate $g(4)$ and plug it into the $f(x)$ equation. $f(4) = 5g(4) = 5[2(4) + 1] = 5[9] = 45$.

2   C. We know that $g(6) = 7$. Therefore, $f(g(6)) = f(7) = 6$.

3   A. From the table, $f(10) = 10,000$ and $f(10,000) = 1$. It follows that $f(f(10)) = 1$.

4   B. Check the answers by substituting $2x + 7$ for x in each of the answer choices. For answer choice B, you get $\sqrt{(2x+7) - 4}$ which simplifies to $\sqrt{2x + 3}$ so this is the correct answer.

5   C. Plug 2 into the equation for x. We get $g(2) = a(2)^2 - 2a(2) + 6 = 4a - 4a + 6$. The terms $4a$ and $-4a$ cancel out, and we are left with $g(2) = 6$.

6   A. We know that $f(a) = b$. Therefore, $g(f(a)) = g(b) = a$.

7   C. Replace the variable x in the $f(x)$ equation with the function $g(x)$. We get $f(g(x)) = (x+5)^2 - 9$. This simplifies to $x^2 + 10x + 25 - 9$, which becomes $x^2 + 10x + 16$.

8   B. This is the only option that makes all of the possible values of n true for $f(n)$.

9   C. This is the only option that makes all of the possible values of n true for $f(n)$.

10 C. Test each answer choice by replacing x in the original equation with the expression given by the answer choice. Choice C becomes $f(2x + 2) = 2(2x + 2) + 4 = 4x + 4 + 4 = 4x + 8$. None of the other answer choices result in $4x + 8$.

11 D. To calculate $f(g(x))$, replace x in the $f(x)$ equation with $5x$. We get $f(g(x)) = (5x)^2 + 2 = 25x^2 + 2$. To calculate $g(f(x))$, replace x in the $g(x)$ equation with $x^2 + 2$. We get $g(f(x)) = 5(x^2 + 2) = 5x^2 + 10$. Finally, we subtract these two expressions and get $f(g(x)) - g(f(x)) = (25x^2 + 2) - (5x^2 + 10) = 20x^2 - 8$.

12 C. Substitute $\sqrt{x^2 - 6}$ for x in the original equation. You get $\sqrt{\sqrt{x^2-6}^2 - 6}$. This simplifies to $\sqrt{x^2 - 6 - 6}$ which equals $\sqrt{x^2 - 12}$.

13 B. When any point or function is reflected over the y-axis, its x-values negate and its y-values stay the same. In function notation, the x inside the parentheses should negate and the value of the function, or g, should stay the same.

14 D. Based on the transformations described, we can write the equations $q(x) = -p(x) - 4$ and $r(x) = -p(x) + 4$. It follows that $q(x) = r(x) - 8$.

Student Produced Response – No Calculator

1 23. Calculate $g(3)$ and plug it into the $f(x)$ equation. $f(3) = g(3) + 10 = [3(3) + 4] + 10 = 13 + 10 = 23$.

2 13. The value of the function at 0 is $f(0) = (0)^2 - 13(0) + 40 = 40$. To find the value of a, we must find the other point at which the function has a value of 40. This means solving the equation $40 = x^2 - 13x + 40$ which simplifies to $x^2 - 13x = 0$. The solutions to this quadratic equation are 0 and 13. Since the problem says that $a > 0$, the answer must be 13.

Multiple Choice – Calculator

1 A. Since we know that $g(2) = 6$, we can plug in 2 for x and 6 for $g(x)$. This gives the equation $6 = c(2)^2 - 6$. Solving this equation, we get $c = 3$, so the function becomes $g(x) = 3x^2 - 6$. When we plug in -2 for x, we get $g(-2) = 6$. There is also a shortcut. Notice that the variable x only appears as x^2. Since the value of 2^2 is the same as the value of -2^2, the values of $g(2)$ and $g(-2)$ will also be equal to each other, so $g(-2) = 6$.

2 A. Since we know that $f(2) = 16$, we can plug in 2 for x and 16 for $f(x)$. This gives the equation $16 = a(2) - 4$. Solving this equation, we get $a = 10$, so the function becomes $f(x) = 10x - 4$. When we plug in 3 for x, we get $f(3) = 26$.

3 B. Choice B is true because $f(-x) = (-x)^2 - 3 = x^2 - 3 = f(x)$ for all values of x. All of the other choices will be false for most values of x. For example, if you plug in 2 for x, the equations in choices A, C, and D will all be false.

4 B. First calculate the value of $g(3)$, the inner function. $g(3) = 2(3) + 2 = 8$. Next, plug this into the outer function. $f(g(3)) = f(8) = 3(8) - 4 = 20$.

5 A. The graph of $y = 2f(-x)$ is equivalent to the graph of $y = f(x)$ reflected across the y-axis and then stretched vertically by a factor of 2. This is shown in answer choice A. Choice B is incorrect because the graph is translate up two units, not stretched. Choices C and D are incorrect because they show the original function reflected over the x-axis instead of the y-axis.

6 B. Replace x in the original equation with $-5x$. We get $f(-5x) = 4(-5x) + 6 = -20x + 6$.

Student Produced Response – Calculator

1 108. Calculate $f(20)$ and plug it into the $g(x)$ equation. $g(20) = 3f(20) = 3[2(20) - 4] = 3[36] = 108$.

2 22. Calculate $f(2)$ and $g(2)$ and add them together. $h(2) = f(2) + g(2) = [2(2) + 5] + [3(2) + 7] = 9 + 13 = 22$.

3 9. The graph has a y-value of 1 when the x-value is 3. This means that $f((3) + 6) = 1$. It follows that $f(9) = 1$, so the answer is 9. Another approach is to recognize that the graph $y = f(x + 6)$ is equivalent to $y = f(x)$ translated 6 units left. If we translate it 6 units back to the right, the point $(3,1)$ maps to $(9,1)$ which means that $f(9) = 1$.

The Tutorverse

Guided Practice – Graphs of Functions

Multiple Choice – No Calculator

1   A. The x-intercepts of the graph of a function correspond to the zeroes of the function. If a function has x-intercepts at –3 and 2, then the values of the function at –3 and 2 are each 0. The function in choice A is in factored form and shows that $f(x) = 0$ if and only if $x + 3 = 0$ or $x - 2 = 0$, so this function has x-intercepts at –3 and 2.

2   C. Choices A, B, and D all intercept the y-axis at –1, so there is at least one value less than 0 in each of these graphs. If we expand $y = (x - 1)^2$ we get $y = x^2 - 2x + 1$, which is a parabola that opens upward and has a minimum at $(1,0)$, so every point on this function will have a y-value of at least 0.

3   A. The line at $y = 4$ intercepts with the parabola when $(x - 5)2 = 4$. Taking the square root of both sides, we get $x - 5 = 2$ or $x - 5 = -2$, so x could be equal to 7 or 3. The line intersects the parabola at $(3,4)$ and $(7,4)$. The length of AB is therefore equal to the difference between 7 and 3, which is 4.

4   C. Since a negative square root yields an imaginary number, $2x - 8 \geq 0$. This can be simplified to $x \geq 4$.

5   C. The range of a function is the set of all possible y values. Since x^2 is positive, we know the graph of the function will be a parabola that opens upward. You can either graph the function on a graphing calculator or find the vertex of the parabola, which will show the lowest value of y, by solving $x = -b/2a$, which equals –1, and then plugging that into the function, which gives you $f(-1) = (-1)^2 + 2(-1) + 2 = 1$. The vertex of the parabola is located at $(-1,1)$. Since the domain of this function is all real numbers, and substituting any real number for x would yield a y-value greater than 1, the range of this function is $y \geq 1$.

6   D. The equation $f(x) = k$ will have 4 solutions if and only if the graph of the horizontal line with equation $y = k$ intersects the graph of f at 4 points. The graph shows that of the given choices, only for –1 will the graph of $y = -1$ intersect the graph of f at 4 points.

7   D. This parabola intersects the x-axis at 2 and –6. The x-coordinate of the vertex of the parabola is halfway between these points (because a parabola is symmetrical): $\dfrac{-6+2}{2} = -2$, which is the value of c.

     To find the y coordinate of the vertex, substitute –2 for x in the equation: $y = a(-2 - 2)(-2 + 6) = -16a$.

8   C. One can find the intersection points of the two graphs by setting the functions $f(x)$ and $g(x)$ equal to one another and then solving for x. Thus, $3x^2 - 3 = -3x^2 + 3$. This can be simplified to $6x^2 = 6$, so $x^2 = 1$ and $x = \pm 1$. Choice C is the only value that matches.

9   C. Since the graph shows two straight lines that form a "V", it is an absolute value function. The absolute value by itself would show all values greater than 0, but since this graph has values for $-2 \leq x \leq 0$, this graph shows a transformation. For a graph of a function f, a change in the form of $f(x) - 2$ will result in a vertical shift of 2 units down, and a change in the form of $f(x - 2)$ will result in a horizontal shift of 2 units, so $f(x) = |x - 2| - 2$ is the only possible answer.

Student Produced Response – No Calculator

1   3. In this function $f(1) = 5$, so $5 = b(1) + 2$. So $b = 3$.

2   10. The line at $y = 25$ intercepts with the parabola when $(x - 4)^2 = 25$. Taking the square root of both sides, we get $x - 4 = 5$ or $x - 4 = -5$, so x could be equal to 9 or –1. The line intersects the parabola at $(-1,25)$ and $(9,25)$. Therefore, the length of AB is equal to the difference between –1 and 9, which is 10.

3   2. If the vertex is located at $(1,-8)$, it is a point on the graph of the function. Therefore, $-8 = a(1 + 1)(1 - 3)$, so $-8 = -4a$ and $a = 2$.

Student Produced Response – Calculator

1   6. If $f(x) = 2x^2 - bx + 2$, then $2 = 2(3)^2 - b(3) + 2$, so $2 = 20 - 3b$ and $3b = 18$. So $b = 6$.

2   2. Substituting 1 for x and 0 for y yields: $0 = (1)^3 + 3(1)^2 + k(1) - 6 = 1 + 3 + 1k - 6 = k - 2$. So, $k = 2$.

3   26. The equation for $g(x)$ is $g(x) = (x + 2)^2 + 1$. So, $g(3) = (3 + 2)^2 + 1 = 26$.

Multiple Choice – Calculator

1   D. The x-intercepts of the parabola are the values of x for which y is equal to 0. The factored form of the equation shows that y equals 0 if and only if $x = 3$ or $x = 4$. Thus, the factored form shows the x-intercepts of the parabola as the constants 3 and 4.

The Tutorverse

2   D. The graph of a function f on the xy-plane is the set of all points $(x, f(x))$. In this function, the value of $f(a)$ is 1 if and only if the unique point on the graph of f with the x-coordinate a has a y-coordinate equal to 1. This is true for the x-coordinates –3, 1, and 2. Therefore, I, II, and III are all equal to 1.

3   D. To find the vertex, we can plug into the formula $x = \dfrac{-b}{2a}$ to find the axis of symmetry, which results in 4, and then plug that value back into the original function to find the y-value, which gives us –4. The vertex is therefore (4,–4), which are values found only in choice D.

because, when $y = 0$, the possible values of x, and thus, the x intercepts, are 2 and 6.

4   C. Since $f(-x) = f(x)$, $f(-1) = f(1) = 4$, so point (–1,4) will also be on the graph of $f(x)$.

5   C. If (–1,0) is a point on the function, we can substitute –1 for x and 0 for y:

$0 = 2(-1)^3 + (-1)^2 + k(-1) + 4$, which simplifies to $0 = 1 - 2 - k + 4$, so $k = 3$.

6   D. The x-intercepts of the parabola are the values of x for which y is equal to 0. The factored form of the equation shows that y equals 0 if and only if $x = -3$. Thus, the factored form shows the x-intercept of the parabola as the constant –3. (The vertex of the parabola is located at (–3,0).)

7   A. In a rational function, the asymptote is equal to the value of x that makes the denominator equal to zero. In this case a is equal to the value of x when $x + 2 = 0$. So a is equal to –2.

8   C. The smallest value of the function would be equal to $f(x)$ when $|x - 4|$ is equal to 0, because the absolute value indicates all other values will be positive numbers greater than 0. In this case, when $|x - 4| = 0$, $f(x) = 2$, so 2 is the smallest value in the range. (In the graph of this function, the vertex is at (4,2), making 2 the smallest value of y.)

9   D. We can see that the vertex is at point (2,–16). Choice D is the only one that has these two numbers. (It is in the form of $f(x) = a(x - h)^2 + k$ where a, h, and k are constants and (h, k) is the vertex of the parabola.)

10   C. All of the given choices are polynomials. If the graph of a polynomial function f on the xy-plane has an x-intercept at b, then $(x - b)$ must be a factor of $f(x)$. Since $-2, -1$, and 2 are each x-intercepts of the graph of f, it follows that $(x + 2)$, $(x + 1)$, and $(x - 2)$ must each be a factor of $f(x)$.

11   B. When the graph of a quadratic function is translated, we use $f(x) = a(x - h)^2 + k$, where h represents the translation along the x-axis and k represents the translation along the y-axis. The equation for $g(x)$ is therefore $g(x) = -(x + 3)^2 + 1$. We then plug –2 into the function: $g(-2) = -(-2 + 3)^2 + 1 = 0$.

12   D. The graph only has one x-intercept, so it has 1 real solution. Therefore, II is not true. The graph has two turning points, the second of which is at (1,6). Therefore, the graph is increasing for $x \geq 1$ and $f(x) \geq 6$ for all $x \geq 0$, so I and III are true.

13   B. Note that the question asks for the range, so we need to solve in terms of y. First, solve for x in terms of y: $y = \dfrac{1}{x} - 2$, so $y + 2 = \dfrac{1}{x}$. Therefore, $x = \dfrac{1}{y + 2}$, meaning that there is an x value for all y values except –2 (since there cannot be a 0 in the denominator). You can also check this by graphing the equation; there is a horizontal asymptote at $y = -2$.

14   B. The graph of this function has vertical asymptotes when the denominator of the fraction is equal to 0. Factoring the denominator yields $0 = (x + 5)(x - 2)$, so –5 and 2 cannot be possible values of x.

15   B. For any value of x, say $x = a$, the point $(a, f(a))$ lies on the graph of f and $(a, g(a))$ lies on the graph of g. Thus, for any value of x the values of $f(a) + g(a)$ is equal to the sum of the y coordinates of the points on the graph with an x coordinate equal to a. Therefore, the value of x for which $f(x) + g(x) = 0$ will occur when the y-coordinates of the points representing $f(x)$ and $g(x)$ at the same value of x are equidistant from the x-axis and are on opposite sides of the x-axis. On this graph, this occurs at $x = -1$. The point (–1,3) lies on $f(x)$ and (–1,–3) on $g(x)$. Thus, at $x = -1$, $f(x) + g(x) = 3 + -3 = 0$.

16   B. One way to solve is to isolate y so that the equation is in $y = mx + b$ format. First, we distribute k: $y + x = kx - ky$. Then we move ky to the left side of the equation and x to the left side of the equation so that both y's and both x's are together: $ky + y = kx - x$. We can factor out the common terms: $y(k + 1) = x(k - 1)$. Finally, we isolate y by dividing both sides by $k + 1$:

The Tutorverse

$y = \left(\dfrac{1-k}{1+k}\right)x$. Since this equation does not have a y-intercept, the graph must be a line that passes through the origin.

<u>Guided Practice – More Word Problems</u>
Multiple Choice – No Calculator

1   B. Solve the equation for m. First, subtract 40 from both sides to get $b - 40 = 0.45m$. Then divide both sides by 0.45 to get $m = \dfrac{b - 40}{0.45}$.

2   A. Solve the equation for y. First, add 24 to both sides. We get $c + 24 = 12y$. Next, divide both sides by 12. We get $\dfrac{c + 24}{12} = y$ or, equivalently, $\dfrac{c}{12} + 2 = y$.

3   C. Solve for a. First, subtract b from both sides and add $0.5y^2$ to both sides. The result is $w - b + 0.5y^2 = ay$ Next, divide both sides by y to get $\dfrac{w - b + 0.5y^2}{y} = a$ or, equivalently, $\dfrac{w - b}{y} + 0.5y = a$.

4   C. The rate of change for the function $L(t)$ is the coefficient of t, which is 2. The rate of change is positive, so the temperature will increase at a rate of 2 degrees per minute. Therefore, in ten minutes, the temperature will increase 20 degrees. 33 represents the starting temperature.

5   B. The function $L(t)$ increases at a rate of 2 degrees per minute. The problem tells us that the temperature of the lemonade increased by 10 degrees, which means that 5 minutes passed. Now examine the equation for $C(t)$. The coefficient of t is -1, which means that the coffee temperature is decreasing at a rate of 1 degree per minute. Therefore, in a period of 5 minutes, the temperature of the coffee with decrease by 5 degrees.

6   D. Begin with the equation $R = \dfrac{\sqrt{P}}{2}$. To solve for P, the first step is to multiply both sides by 2. The equation becomes $2R = \sqrt{P}$. The next step is to square both sides. We get $4R^2 = P$.

7   A. The simplest way to solve this problem is to pick numbers for Anna and Brenda. We know that Anna completed 9 times as many projects as Brenda. Let's say that Anna completed 9 projects and Brenda completed 1. Then Anna's rating is $\dfrac{\sqrt{9}}{2} = \dfrac{3}{2}$ and Brenda's rating is $\dfrac{\sqrt{1}}{2} = \dfrac{1}{2}$. Brenda's rating is $\dfrac{1}{3}$ of Anna's rating because $\dfrac{\text{Anna Rating}}{\text{Brenda Rating}} = \dfrac{\frac{1}{2}}{\frac{3}{2}} = \dfrac{1}{3}$.

8   A. The rate of change in this function is the coefficient of m, which is $\dfrac{1}{6}$. This means that the animal grows $\dfrac{1}{6}$ inch per month. Therefore, in one year (12 months) the animal will grow $\dfrac{1}{6} \cdot 12 = 2$ inches.

9   B. Begin with the equation $h = \dfrac{w}{5r^2}$. Get r^2 out of the denominator by taking the reciprocal of both sides. The new equation is $\dfrac{1}{h} = \dfrac{5r^2}{w}$. To get r^2 by itself, we must multiply both sides by w and divide both sides by 5. The final equation is $\dfrac{w}{5h} = r^2$.

10   A. Let h represent the amount of time that it takes for Field A to absorb the water. Then Field B absorbs the water in the time $4h$. Using the rearranged formula from the previous problem we see that for Field A,

The Tutorverse

$r^2 = \dfrac{w}{5h}$, so $r = \sqrt{\dfrac{w}{5h}}$. Similarly, for Field B, $r = \sqrt{\dfrac{w}{5(4h)}} = \sqrt{\dfrac{1}{4} \cdot \dfrac{w}{5h}} = \dfrac{1}{2}\sqrt{\dfrac{w}{5h}}$. This demonstrates that the radius of Field B is half of the radius of Field A. Another approach to this problem would be to plug in numbers (e.g. Let $w = 5$ for both fields and let h be equal to 1 for Field A but 4 for Field B).

11   C. The old mass was $6ds^2$. The new mass is $6(2d)\left(\dfrac{s}{2}\right)^2 = 6(2d)\left(\dfrac{s^2}{4}\right) = 3ds^2$. This is half of the original mass because 3 is half of 6 and ds^2 remains the same.

12   A. When the rock hits the bottom of the lake, the height will be 0, so the question is really asking for the time when $h = 0$, so we solve the equation $-3t^2 - 3t + 60 = 0$. If we divide by -3, we get $t^2 + t - 20 = 0$, which factors as $(t + 5)(t - 4) = 0$. The solutions are -5 and 4, but time cannot be negative, so the only acceptable answer is 4.

13   B. The straightforward way to figure out the answer to this question is to look at the units associated with each variable. The cost, c, is measured in dollars, the distance, d, is measured in miles and the price, p, is measured in dollars per gallon or $\dfrac{dollars}{gallons}$. If we replace each variable with its unit, we get

$$\dfrac{dollars}{1} = \dfrac{miles}{1} \cdot \dfrac{dollars}{gallons} \cdot k$$. In order to get the proper cancelation of units on the right side of the

equation, the unit for k must be $\dfrac{gallons}{miles}$, which is shown in choice B.

Student Produced Response – No Calculator

1   15. Based on the information described in the problem, the left side of the equation has been multiplied by 2 (because V was doubled) and the right side of the equation has been multiplied by $1.5 \times 20 = 30$ (because T was multiplied by 1.5, and n was multiplied by 20). In order for the two sides to balance, we need the left side to be multiplied by 15, so the pressure must be multiplied by 15.

2 $\dfrac{4}{9}$ or 0.44. Let l_A represent the length of the thicker rod and l_B represent the length of the thinner rod. We

know their masses are equal, so $m = 12\left(\dfrac{3}{2}t\right)^2 l_A$ for the thicker rod and $m = 12t^2 l_B$ for the thinner rod. We

can put these equations together to get $12\left(\dfrac{3}{2}t\right)^2 l_A = 12t^2 l_B$. We want to find the ratio of the length of the

thicker rod to the length of the thinner rod, so we should solve for $\dfrac{l_A}{l_B}$. We get

$$\dfrac{l_A}{l_B} = \dfrac{12t^2}{12\left(\dfrac{3}{2}t\right)^2} = \dfrac{1}{\left(\dfrac{3}{2}\right)^2} = \dfrac{4}{9}$$, or 0.44.

Multiple Choice – Calculator

1   C. Changing the material with which the bricks are made would change the weight per brick. It would not change the number of bricks (n), number of boxes (b), or weight of an empty box (w), so it must be K by process of elimination. Another way to see this is that the expression $n(bK + w)$ represents the total weight and n represents the number of boxes, so the expression $(bK + w)$ must represent the weight per box. Since w is the weight of an empty box, bK must represent the weight of all the bricks in each box. Since b is the number of bricks in each box, K must be the weight of each brick. That is the quantity that changes in this scenario.

2   B. We want to find the time when the ball hits the ground, which occurs when the height is 0. Therefore,

The Tutorverse

we want to solve the equation $-16t^2 + 65t = 0$. This factors as $t(-16t + 65) = 0$, so the solutions are $t = 0$ and $-16t + 65 = 0$. The first solution represents when the ball is launched and the second represents when it lands. Solving for the second solution, we get $t = \dfrac{65}{16} \approx 4.0$.

3   A. Whenever a problem asks for an equation that shows the minimum/maximum and where it occurs, you should put the equation in vertex form. This means it should look like $y = a(x - h)^2 + k$. The only equation in this form is answer choice A. To get the equation in this form, you need to complete the square. $t(s) = s^2 - 16s + 75 = s^2 - 16s + 64 - 64 + 75 = s^2 - 16s + 64 + 11 = (s - 8)^2 + 11$. Another approach would be to calculate the coordinates of the vertex and see which equation contains those numbers. To find the coordinates of the vertex, use the equation $x = -\dfrac{b}{2a} = -\dfrac{(-16)}{2(1)} = 8$. If we plug 8 into the original equation for s, we get $t(8) = 11$. The only answer choice with 8 and 11 in the equation is Choice A.

4   D. Solve for w. First, square both sides to get $\dfrac{\pi^2 d^2}{16} = \dfrac{w}{p}$. Then multiply both sides by p to get

$$\dfrac{\pi^2 d^2 p}{16} = w.$$

5   C. One option is to test the answer choices. By looking at the equation $D = \dfrac{2r}{2r + b}$, we can see that D is not equal to P or $2P$, so we only need to test the last two answer choices. For answer choice C, we get

$$\dfrac{2P}{P + 1} = \dfrac{2\left(\dfrac{r}{r + b}\right)}{\dfrac{r}{r + b} + 1}, \text{ which simplifies to } \dfrac{2r}{2r + b}. \text{ However, with answer choice D, we get } \dfrac{2P}{2P + 1} = \dfrac{\dfrac{2r}{r + b}}{\dfrac{2r}{r + b} + 1}$$

which simplifies to $\dfrac{2r}{3r + b}$. Alternatively, the quantity D results when r is doubled, so $D = \dfrac{2r}{2r + b}$. We want to rearrange this expression to get it in terms of P. A good first step is to divide the numerator and denominator by $r + b$ so that they look more like P. We get $\dfrac{2r}{2r + b} = \dfrac{\dfrac{2r}{r + b}}{\dfrac{2r + b}{r + b}} = \dfrac{2\left(\dfrac{r}{r + b}\right)}{\dfrac{r}{r + b} + \dfrac{r + b}{r + b}} = \dfrac{2P}{P + 1}$.

6   D. Whenever a problem asks for an equation that shows the minimum/maximum and where it occurs, you should put the equation in vertex form. This means it should look like $y = a(x - h)^2 + k$. The only equation in this form is answer choice D. To get the equation in this form, start by factoring out the leading coefficient. The new equation becomes $m(v) = -\dfrac{1}{10}(v - 40v)$. Next, complete the square. This gives you $m(v) = -\dfrac{1}{10}(v^2 - 40v + 400 - 400) = -\dfrac{1}{10}(v^2 - 40v + 400) + 40 = -\dfrac{1}{10}(v - 20)^2 + 40$. Another way to solve this problem is to calculate the coordinates of the vertex and see which equation contains those numbers.

7   D. If we replace r with $2r$ we get $c = ke^{2rt} = ke^{rt + rt} = ke^{rt}e^{rt}$. Therefore, the original value of c is multiplied by e^{rt}.

Student Produced Response – Calculator

1   0.88. The value of r is the number by which V will be multiplied each day. Since the volume is decreasing, we must subtract 12% from 100%, so $r = 1 - 0.12 = 0.88$.

2   184. To calculate this, we must plug in 0.88 for r and 3 for t. The answer is $270(0.88)^3 = 183.99744$, which rounds to 184.

The Tutorverse

3   0.81. The taller person's body mass index is $\dfrac{m}{h^2}$. The shorter person's body mass index is $\dfrac{m}{(0.9h)^2}$.

Therefore, the ratio is $\dfrac{m}{h^2} \div \dfrac{m}{(0.9h)^2} = \dfrac{m}{h^2} \cdot \dfrac{(0.9h)^2}{m} = (0.9)^2 = 0.81$.

Mixed Practice – Advanced Math

Multiple Choice – No Calculator

1   Exponents & Radicals: C. Since three of the answer choices start with $x^3 =$, we can start by isolating x^3.
First, subtract 3 from both sides, giving you $9\sqrt{x^3} = x - 9$. Then divide both sides by 9, giving you
$\sqrt{x^3} = \dfrac{x-9}{9}$. Finally, square both sides, which gives you $x^3 = \left(\dfrac{x-9}{9}\right)^2 = \dfrac{x^2 - 18x + 81}{81}$. Answer choice
B is incorrect because you cannot cancel out the 81's from the top and bottom of the fraction. Answer
choice D is incorrect because solving for x requires finding the cube root of both sides ($\sqrt[3]{}$), not the
square root.

2   More Word Problems: D. Solve for k. First, subtract $20x + b$ from both sides to get $c - 20x - b = kx^2$ or,
equivalently, $c - b - 20x = kx^2$. Next, divide both sides by x^2 to get $\dfrac{c-b-20x}{x^2} = k$, or equivalently,
$\dfrac{c-b}{x^2} - \dfrac{20}{x} = k$.

3   Systems of Equations: D. Take the expressions that are equal to y in each equation and set them equal to
each other. The new equation is $3x^2 - 8x + 36 = 2x^2 + 2x + 11$. In standard form, this becomes
$x^2 - 10x + 25 = 0$ which factors as $(x - 5)(x - 5) = 0$, so the only solution is $x = 5$. Plug this back into either
equation to find the value of y. We get $y = 71$. This means that $x + y = 5 + 71 = 76$.

4   More Word Problems: D. The original energy was $E = kdr^3$. The new energy is
$k(2d)(2r)^3 = k(2d)(8r^3) = 16kdr^3$. This is 16 times the original energy.

5   Function Notation: D. We know that $f(0) = -1$. Therefore, $g(f(0)) = g(-1) = 2$.

6   Working with Polynomials: B. Equation I factors as $(x - 3)(x - 3) = 0$ so it only has the solution $x = 3$.
Equation II factors as $x(x^2 + 5) = 0$ where $x^2 + 5$ is not factorable, so the only real solution is $x = 0$.
Equation III factors as $(x + 2)(x - 2) = 0$, so it has two real solutions, $x = 2$ and $x = -2$. Thus, I & II have
exactly one real solution.

7   Graphs of Functions: B. If the graph of a polynomial function f on the xy-plane has an x-intercept at b,
then $(x - b)$ must be a factor of $f(x)$. In this case, the vertex of the parabola is at $(0,-2)$, so this is the only
x-intercept.

Multiple Choice – Calculator

1   Working with Polynomial Factors in Expressions & Equations: D. To add fractions, we need them all to
have the same denominator. Factoring $t^2 - 6t + 8$ gives us $(t - 2)(t - 4)$. All three fractions will have the
same denominator if we multiply the first fraction by $\dfrac{t-4}{t-4}$ and the second fraction by $\dfrac{t-2}{t-2}$. This gives
us $\dfrac{t^2 - 4t}{(t-2)(t-4)} + \dfrac{t-2}{(t-2)(t-4)} = \dfrac{2}{(t-2)(t-4)}$. Therefore, $t^2 - 4t + t - 2 = 2$, or $t^2 - 3t - 4 = 0$, which we
can solve by factoring: $(t - 4)(t + 1) = 0$. Finally, t can equal -1 or 4. However, 4 cannot be a solution
because plugging 4 into the original equation results in a denominator of 0, so the only solution is -1.

2   Working with Polynomial Factors in Expressions & Equations: C. Since this equation shows two fractions
equal to each other, we can solve by cross multiplying. $4(x + 8) = 7(x - 1)$, which gives us
$4x + 32 = 7x - 7$. This produces $3x = 39$, or $x = 13$.

3   Function Notation: A. Replace x in the original equation with $(x + 4)$. We get
$f(x + 4) = 2(x + 4) - 7 = 2x + 8 - 7 = 2x + 1$.

The Tutorverse

4   Quadratic Functions & Equations: A. The problem talks about two sets of books. The first set of books had x books costing 10 dollars each for a total cost of $10x$. The second set of books was the rest of the books, which is $30 - x$ and they cost $\frac{x}{2}$ dollars each, so the cost for the second set of books was $\frac{x}{2}(30 - x)$. Adding up the cost of the first and second set of books, we arrive at $10x + \frac{x}{2}(30 - x) = 200$. If we multiply both sides by 2 we arrive at $20x + x(30 - x) = 400$. When you rearrange that into standard form you arrive at choice A.

5   Systems of Equations: B. The second equation can be rearranged to get $y = 3 - 2x$. If we substitute this expression for y in the first equation, we get $(3 - 2x) - 6 = -(x + 2)^2$ which simplifies to $-3 - 2x = -x^2 - 4x - 4$. In standard form, this becomes $x^2 + 2x + 1 = 0$. This equation has only one solution, $x = -1$, and if we plugged that solution into either equation, we would get only one possible value for y. Therefore, only one ordered pair satisfies the equations.

6   Working with Polynomials: B. Answer choice A factors as $(x^4 + 17)(x - 8)$. Answer choice C factors as $x(x - 5)(x - 8)$. Answer choice D factors as $y(x + 8)(x - 8)$, so all of those are divisible by $x - 8$. In choice B, $x - 8$ is a factor in first part of the expression, but there is a 6 at the end, which is not divisible by $x - 8$.

Student Produced Response – Calculator

1   Exponents & Radicals: 1,200. The amount of money in Joe's account can be represented by the equation $A = d(r)^t$, where d is the initial deposit, r is the interest rate plus 1, and t is the time in years. We know the current balance (A) but not the value of d. Substitute into the equation: $1,325 = d(1.02)^5$. Solving for d yields approximately \$1,200.

2   Graphs of Functions: 127. The formula for a parabola is $y = (x - h)^2 + k$, where h is the horizontal shift and k is the vertical shift. For this function, shifting 3 units to the left and 2 units up gives us $g(x) = (x + 3)^3 + 2$. We can then plug in 2 for x: $g(2) = (2 + 3)^3 + 2 = 127$.

Additional Math Topics

Guided Practice – Geometry

Multiple Choice – No Calculator

1   B. Since AB and DE are parallel, $\angle EDC$ and $\angle DBA$ are congruent because they are alternate interior angles. $\angle BAC$ and $\angle DEC$ are congruent for the same reason. Finally, $\angle DCE$ and $\angle ACB$ are congruent because they are vertical angles. Thus, the triangles are similar. AB corresponds to ED in the ratio 3:1, meaning the top triangle is three times the size of the bottom triangle. DC is 5 meters long, so BC must be 15 meters long.

2   B. The formula for a cylinder is given on the reference sheet at the beginning of each math section: $V = \pi r^2 h$. Since the diameter is 20 m, the radius is 10 m. We simply plug 10 in for r and 8 in for h: $V = \pi(10)^2(8) = 800\pi$.

3   B. Since lines j, k, and l are parallel, $\angle 1$ is congruent to the acute angle between line l and line n. Since lines m and n are parallel, $\angle 1$ and $\angle 2$ are congruent because they are formed by the intersection of parallel transversals to parallel lines. Basically, all the acute angles are congruent and all the obtuse angles are congruent.

4   A. $\angle ADC$ is congruent to $\angle 1$ because they are vertical angles so it must be 78°. If we focus on the angles we know the measures of, we see that we have two angles in triangle ADC. Therefore, $\angle ACB$ must equal $180° - (33° + 78°) = 69°$. Note that lines m and p are unnecessary to solving this question.

5   C. Since $\angle ACB$ is supplemental to $\angle DCA$, their measures must add up to 180°. Therefore, $\angle ACB = 180° - 105° = 75°$. Since the internal angles in triangle ABC must add up to 180°, then $\angle ABC = 180° - (75° + 35°) = 70°$.

6   C. The diagonal of a square effectively creates a 45°–45°–90° triangle. Using the reference sheet at the beginning of each math section, we can figure out that each side of the square should have a length of 4, meaning each side of the hexagon is 4. If we connect all of the opposite vertices, we can see that a hexagon is composed of 6 congruent equilateral triangles, each of which can be split into two 30°–60°–

90° triangles with base 4 and height = $2\sqrt{3}$. This leads to the area of each equilateral triangle:

$A = \frac{1}{2}bh = \frac{1}{2}(4)(2\sqrt{3}) = 4\sqrt{3}$. Since the area of the regular hexagon is 6 times the area of the triangle, $4\sqrt{3} \cdot 6 = 24\sqrt{3}$.

7   C. An important rule to know is that the central angle subtended by two points on a circle is twice the inscribed angle subtended by those points. Here, that means angle AOC is twice the size of angle ABC. Since angle $AOC = 60°$, angle ABC must equal 30°.

8   B. If angle $AOC = 56°$, then angle $AOB = 180° - 56° = 124°$ because the two angles form a straight line. Triangle AOB is isosceles because two of its sides are radii of the circle. Thus, angle

$OAB = \frac{1}{2}(180° - 124°) = 28°$.

9   C. An important rule to know is that the angle formed by the intersection of two tangents (in this case, angle M) equals half the central angle formed by the radii to the tangent points. Therefore, the central

angle here is 60°. Since $60° = \frac{1}{6}(360°)$, and the entire circumference is 720, then the major arc is

$\frac{5}{6}(720) = 600$.

10   D. I is true because $B + C + D$ and $A + F + B$ both add up to 180° because both sums are half-circles. II is true because $A + B = C + D$ and $A = D$ because they are vertical angles leaving $B = C$ and $E = B$ because they are vertical angles. Thus, $E = C$. III is true because A and D are vertical angles. Thus, all three statements must be true.

11   B. From the hash marks on the sides, we can see that both triangles are isosceles. That means $w = 180° - 2v = 180° - 2(40°) = 100°$. Since $w = 2x$, x must be 50°, and so the other two angles in that triangle $= (180° - 50°)/2 = 65°$. Finally, $y = 180° - 65° = 115°$.

12   B. Since the diameter of the circle = 20, the area of the semicircle = $\frac{\pi \cdot 10^2}{2} = 50\pi$. Since the triangle is inscribed in a semicircle, it must be a right triangle and angle $BAC = 30°$ because it subtends an arc of 60° from a point on the circle. Therefore, the triangle is a 30°– 60°– 90° triangle and has an area = $\frac{1}{2}(base)(height) = \frac{1}{2}(10)(10\sqrt{3}) = 50\sqrt{3}$. The area of the shaded region is the difference between the areas of the semicircle and the triangle. This yields $50\pi - 50\sqrt{3}$.

13   C. One way to solve this is to plug in values for each choice. The volumes of a right circular cylinder and a right circular cone are $\pi r^2 h$ and $\frac{1}{3}\pi r^2 h$, respectively. The only difference in the formulas is the $\frac{1}{3}$. That means that, if the radius and the height are the same, the volume of the cone will be one-third the volume of the cylinder. Statement I is wrong. The radius gets squared, so if the cone's base radius is one third the cylinder's, the volume will be multiplied by $\frac{1}{9}$, making the final volume $\frac{1}{27}$ that of the cylinder. The height of the cone would have to be 27 times that of the cylinder to balance out the volumes, not nine times. Since answer choices A, B, and D all have Statement I, they must all be eliminated, leaving only choice C. Statement II is correct because doubling the radius of the cylinder would result in a base area 4 times the base area of the cone and to compensate, the cone would have to have height $3 \times 4 = 12$ times as high as the cylinder. Statement III is correct because if the cone and cylinder have the same base areas, then the cylinder needs to have one third the height of the cone for their volumes to be equal.

The Tutorverse

Student Produced Response – No Calculator

1   86. In a circle, the degree measure of an inscribed angle is half the measure of the arc it intercepts. If angle BAC is 43°, then arc BC must be 86°. The degree measure of an arc is equal to the measure of the central angle that intercepts the arc. Therefore, if arc BC is 86°, then central angle BOC must also be 86°.

2   50. Segment BD is divided into parts in the same proportions as AB. The three parts of segment $AB = x$, $3x$, and $5x$, which add to $9x$. $BF = \dfrac{1}{9}$ of the length of $BD = 10$. Therefore, $DE = 5(10) = 50$.

3   16. Since the circumference is 8π, the length of AC (the diameter) must be 8. Since the triangle is inscribed in a semicircle, it must be a right triangle, and since it is isosceles, it must be a 45°– 45°– 90° triangle. From here, we can solve in one of two ways: We either use the reference information at the beginning of each math section to figure out that sides AB and BC must each be $\dfrac{8}{\sqrt{2}} = 4\sqrt{2}$ and then plug into the formula for area of a triangle: $\dfrac{1}{2}(base)(altitude) = \dfrac{1}{2}(4\sqrt{2})(4\sqrt{2}) = 16$. Or, we can draw a line from point O to point B, splitting the triangle into two smaller right triangles, each with base 4 and altitude 4 (since OA, OB, and OC are all radii), giving us: $2\left(\dfrac{1}{2}(base)(altitude)\right) = 2\left(\dfrac{1}{2}(4)(4)\right) = 16$.

Multiple Choice – Calculator

1   D. The slant heights in the structure proportional to the vertical heights, so $4x + 3x + x = 8x = 32$ feet. Therefore, x must equal 4. The height of the first floor is $4x$, which is $4(4) = 16$ feet.

2   B. Any problem involving the lengths of shadows of multiple objects in the same vicinity can usually be solved using a simple proportion because the sun's rays form the same angle with both objects, creating similar triangles. Here, the ratio of the bush's shadow to the tree's shadow is $\dfrac{2}{15}$, so we can set up and solve the following proportion: $\dfrac{2}{15} = \dfrac{0.7}{x}$. Cross multiplying gives us $2x = 10.5$, which means x must equal 5.25.

3   D. If angle x is 8°, it represents $\dfrac{8}{360}$, or $\dfrac{1}{45}$, of the circle, which means minor arc AB represents $\dfrac{1}{45}$ the circumference of the circle. The circumference must be $1.58 \times 45 = 71.1$. Since circumference = $2\pi r$, we get $71.1 = 2\pi r$. Solving for r gets us approximately 11.32.

4   C. We are given that segment AD has a length of 3. Using the reference information at the beginning of each math section, we can figure out that side $BD = \dfrac{3}{\sqrt{3}}$. Side BC is then $\dfrac{3}{\sqrt{3}} \cdot \sqrt{2}$, which we can then simplify: $\dfrac{3\sqrt{2}}{\sqrt{3}} \cdot \dfrac{\sqrt{3}}{\sqrt{3}} = \dfrac{3\sqrt{6}}{3} = \sqrt{6}$.

5   B. If the radius is 12, then the circumference is 24π, or approximately 75.4. If the arc length is between 23 and 24, then it represents a fractional part of the circumference that is between $\dfrac{23}{75.4}$ and $\dfrac{24}{75.4}$, or 0.305 and 0.318. Angle x represents the same fractional part of the total number of degrees in a circle (360), which would be greater than $0.305(360) = 109.8$ and less than $0.318(360) = 114.48$. Therefore, the integer values could be 110, 111, 112, 113, or 114.

6   C. This problem is describing a right triangle. It has given the lengths of two sides and is asking you to find the third side. Using the reference information at the beginning of each math section, we can use the formula $a^2 + b^2 = c^2$, where c is the hypotenuse, to find the missing side: $a^2 + 25^2 = 57^2$. Solving for a results in approximately 51.225, which is nearest to choice C.

The Tutorverse

7   D. The altitude, radius, and slant height form a 30°– 60°– 90° triangle with hypotenuse 12. Using the reference information at the beginning of each math section, we can figure out that the radius is 6 and the height is $6\sqrt{3}$. We then plug values for r and h into the formula:

$$V = \frac{1}{3}\pi r^2 h = \frac{1}{3}\pi(6)^2(6\sqrt{3}) = 72\sqrt{3}\pi \approx 391.8 \text{ cubic centimeters.}$$

8   C. The reference information at the beginning of each section gives the volume of rectangular solids and rectangular pyramids. The volume of a right pyramid with square base $= \frac{1}{3}lwh$, and the volume a rectangular solid = lwh. Try each answer choice. Choice A has a pyramid with volume 48 and rectangular solid with volume 54. Choice B has a pyramid with volume 12 and rectangular solid with volume 18. Choice D has a pyramid with volume 96 and rectangular solid with volume 72. Choice C is correct: a pyramid and rectangular solid, both with volume 81.

9   A. As given in the reference information at the beginning of each section, the volume of the sphere is $V = \frac{4}{3}\pi r^3$. Plugging in 4 for r results in $V = \frac{4}{3}\pi(4)^3 = \frac{85}{3}\pi$. Since the question is asking for the closest of four values, we can estimate to 268.08. The volume of the cylinder: $V = \pi r^2 h = \pi(12)^2 h = 144\pi h \approx 452.39h$. The only variable left is h for height, which is what we're trying to find. Set the two equations equal to each other and solve: $268.08 = 452.39h$, which results in $h = 0.593$.

Student Produced Response – Calculator

1   320. Since $\angle ABC$ has its vertex on the circle, the angle of subtends an arc twice as large, so arc AC must be 40°. For the same reason, $\angle BAC$ subtends an arc of 160°. The remaining arc $AB = 360° - (40° + 160°) = 160°$. The ratio of the arc length to the circumference of the circle = the ratio of the arc angles 160° to 360°. $\frac{160}{360} = \frac{AB}{720}$. Therefore, arc AB must be 320.

2   12. As given in the reference information at the beginning of each math section, the volume of a sphere is $V = \frac{4}{3}\pi r^3$. Plugging in 288π for V gives us $288\pi = \frac{4}{3}\pi r^3$. The only variable left is r, which we can solve for by dividing both sides by $\frac{4}{3}\pi$, giving us $r^3 = 216$, and then finding the cube root of both sides, giving us $r = 6$. Since the radius is 6, the diameter must be 12.

Guided Practice – Equations of Circles

Multiple Choice – Calculator

1   A. Remember that the equation of a circle is $(x - h)^2 + (y - k)^2 = r^2$, where (h,k) is the coordinate center of the circle and r is the radius. This means that the center of the circle must be at $(6,-8)$ and the radius must be the square root of 16, or 4.

2   D. To answer this question, you must remember the equation of a circle, which is $(x - h)^2 + (y - k)^2 = r^2$, where (h,k) is the coordinate center of the circle and r is the radius. Note that the equation negates both h and k. Since the coordinates of the center are $(5,-4)$, the equation must say $(x - 5)^2$ and $(y + 4)^2$. Squaring the radius gives an r^2 value of 64.

3   C. The equation of a circle is $(x - h)^2 + (y - k)^2 = r^2$, where (h,k) is the coordinate center of the circle and r is the radius. Since the equation negates both h and k, the equation should say $(x + 3.6)^2 + (y + 13.4)^2$ which, when squaring the radius, should equal 8.

4   B. The equation of a circle is $(x - h)^2 + (y - k)^2 = r^2$, where (h,k) is the coordinate center of the circle and r is the radius. Since the equation negates both h and k, the equation should say $(x - \frac{1}{6})^2 + (y - \frac{5}{7})^2$ which, when squaring the radius, should equal $\frac{4}{9}$.

5   D. The equation of a circle in standard form is $(x - h)^2 + (y - k)^2 = r^2$ where the center of the circle is located at (h,k) and r is the radius. Since this circle has its center at $(4,2)$ and a radius of 2, the equation

The Tutorverse

would be $(x - 4)^2 + (x - 3)^2 = 4$, which is choice D. Choices A and B are incorrect because the equations equal 2, which is the radius, instead of 4, which is the radius squared. Choice C is incorrect because the coordinates of the center are supposed to be negated.

6   C. We know that the equation of a circle is $(x - h)^2 + (y - k)^2 = r^2$, where (h,k) is the coordinate center of the circle and r is the radius. Since the two given points have the same y-value, they must lie on a horizontal line and their distance from each other is exactly 12, giving an r^2 value of 144. The equation negates h and k, so the equation must be $(x + 8)^2 + (y - 11)^2 = 144$.

7   C. The original circle has its center at $(0,-3)$ and radius of 4. If the center of the circle is translated 1 unit up and the radius is increased by 1, then the new center will be at $(0,-2)$ and the radius will be 5, giving us the equation $x^2 + (y + 2)^2 = 25$.

8   C. The graph of this equation is a circle with the center $(0,0)$ and a radius 5. If the center is translated 2 units up, the new center of the circle will be $(0,2)$. If the radius is decreased by 1, the radius of the new circle will be 4. Therefore, the equation is $x^2 + (y - 2)^2 = 36$.

9   A. The equation for a circle is $(x - h)^2 + (y - k)^2 = r^2$ in which the center of the circle is at the point (h,k). In this circle, since the x coordinate in the radius is the same as the x coordinate of the endpoint, this is a vertical line, so the radius can be calculated by subtracting the y coordinates: $5 - 2 = 3$, so the radius of the circle is 3. Substitute within the equation to get $(x - 2)^2 + (y - 5)^2 = 9$.

10   A. The equation for a circle is $(x - h)^2 + (y - k)^2 = r^2$ in which the center of the circle is at the point (h,k). In this circle, the diameter is a horizontal line with a length of 12, meaning the radius has a length of 6. r^2 must equal 36, allowing us to eliminate choices C and D. The center of the circle is halfway between -4 and 8, so the coordinates of the center are $(2,-2)$. Thus the equation: $(x - 2)^2 + (y + 2)^2 = 36$.

11   D. The equation of a circle in standard form is $(x - h)^2 + (y - k)^2 = r^2$ where the center of the circle is located at (h,k) and r is the radius. This circle would have a center at $(4,5)$ and a radius of 6. This is only true for choice D.

12   C. The standard form of an equation of a circle is $(x - h)^2 + (y - k)^2 = r^2$ where the center of the circle is located at (h,k) and r is the radius. The center of this circle is located at $(-4,2)$ and the radius is equal to 7, so the equation is $(x + 4)^2 + (y - 2)^2 = 49$.

13   D. The graph of this equation is a circle with the center $(0, 7)$ and a radius 3. If the center is translated 2 units to the left, the new center of the circle will be $(-2, 7)$. If the radius is increased by 7, the radius of the new circle will be 10. Therefore, the equation is $(x + 2)^2 + (y - 7)^2 = 100$.

14   A. The equation for a circle is $(x - h)^2 + (y - k)^2 = r^2$ in which the center of the circle is at the point (h,k). Since the length of the diameter is 14, the radius must be 7, and r^2 must be 49. We can thus eliminate choices C and D. Choice A has a center at $(-1,-6)$ and choice B has a center of $(-6,1)$. Only choice A has a center that is 7 units away from the given endpoint.

15   A. The given circle has a center at $(3,-2)$ with radius 5. The radius was increased by 3; thus, the radius was 2 prior to the changes, and $r^2 = 4$, allowing us to eliminate choices B and D. To undo a translation of 3 units to the right, we decrease the value of the x-coordinate by 3. Thus the center was at $(0,-2)$.

Student Produced Response – Calculator

1   5. The radius will be a diagonal line. To find the length of any diagonal line on a coordinate grid, use the distance formula: $d = \sqrt{(x_2 - x_1)^2 + (y_2 - y_1)^2} = \sqrt{(4 - 7)^2 + (0 - 4)^2} = \sqrt{(-3)^2 + (-4)^2} = \sqrt{9 + 16} = 5$.

2   18. The given equation is not in the standard form for a circle, $(x - h)^2 + (y - k)^2 = r^2$. You can put it in standard form by completing the square. Since the coefficient of x is 4 and the coefficient of y is -12, write the equation in terms of x and y by first adding 4 and 36 to both sides of the equation: $(x^2 + 4x + 4) + (y^2 - 12y + 36) = 41 + 4 + 36$. Next, rewrite each trinomial as a square, and combine the constants on the other side: $(x + 2)^2 + (y - 6)^2 = 81$. 81 is the same as 9^2, so the radius of the circle is 9. The diameter of a circle is $d = 2r$, so the diameter is 18.

3   20. The given equation is not in the standard form for a circle. You can put it into standard form by completing the square. Since the coefficient of x is -6 and the coefficient of y is -16, you can write the equation in terms of x and y by first adding 9 and 64 to both sides of the equation:

$(x^2 - 6x + 9) + (y^2 - 16y + 64) = 27 + 9 + 64$. Next, rewrite each trinomial as a square, and combine the constants on the other side: $(x - 3)^2 + (y - 8)^2 = 100$. 100 is the same as 10^2, so the radius of the circle is 10. The diameter of a circle is $d = 2r$, so the diameter is 20.

Guided Practice – Trigonometry

Multiple Choice – No Calculator

1   D. The two acute angles in a right triangle are always complementary (add up to 90 degrees). Therefore, the sine of one is equal to the cosine of the other. Therefore, we get $\sin(m) = \cos(n) = 0.8$.

2   A. The two acute angles in a right triangle are always complementary (add up to 90 degrees). Therefore, the sine of one is equal to the cosine of the other. The 75 degree angle is R, so we get $\sin(R) = \cos(T)$

3   C. Whenever we have two acute angles and the sine of one is equal to the cosine of the other, it means that the angles are complementary (add to 90 degrees). Therefore, $a + b = 90$ which means that $(k + 6) + (3k + 4) = 90$. Combining like terms, we get $4k + 10 = 90$ and if we solve this for k, the answer is 20.

4   A. The question asks for the length of AD, which is a leg of triangle ADB, so we need to use either angle BAD or angle ABD. The measure of angle BAD is 20 degrees, so the measure of angle ABD must be $90 - 20 = 70$ degrees. If we try to find side AD using angle ABD, we must use the identity

$\tan(70°) = \dfrac{AD}{10}$. If we solve this for AD, we get $AD = 10\tan(70°)$. (We could try to use angle BAD to

find the length of AD, but we would end up with $AD = \dfrac{10}{\tan(20°)}$ which is not one of the answer choices).

5   B. First look at the answer choices. They all involve either AD or DC, which are legs of right triangles, and we are trying to find BD, which is also a leg. Therefore, we should be using the tangent function (eliminate choice C). Since all the answer choices all involve $x°$, we should be looking at either angle DCB or angle DBA, since those are the only angles measuring $x°$. Using this second angle, we see that

$\tan(x°) = \dfrac{AD}{BD}$. If we solve for line segment BD, we get $BD = \dfrac{1}{\tan(x°)} AD$. (You can try using angle

DCB, but you would end up with $BD = \tan(x°)DC$, which is not an answer choice.)

Student Produced Response – No Calculator

1   30. Based on the given numbers, ABD is a 30-60-90 right triangle with $\angle ACB$ having measure 30 degrees. Because the figure is a rectangle, we know the two triangles are congruent, so and $\angle CAD$ is also 30 degrees.

Multiple Choice – Calculator

1   C. Because the triangles are similar, angles A and D are congruent, so they have the same sine.

2   D. The question gives us the length of CB and asks for the length of AC. In relation to $\angle BCA$, the segments CB and AC are the adjacent leg and hypotenuse, respectively. This suggests that we should use

cosine. We get $\cos(65°) = \dfrac{3}{AC}$, which we can solve for AC to get $AC = \dfrac{3}{\cos(65°)}$. If we plug in the

given cosine value, we get 7.14.

3   C. This is a 45-45-90 right triangle (45-45-90 right triangles have legs of length x and a hypotenuse with length $x\sqrt{2}$). Therefore, $\angle PRQ$ has measure 45°. The drawing is clearly not of a 45-45-90 triangle, which is why it is important to read the note that the triangle is not drawn to scale. If you didn't remember the

rule for 45-45-90 right triangles, you could use the formula $\cos(PRQ) = \dfrac{3}{3\sqrt{2}}$. By taking the inverse

cosine of the right side of the equation, you would get the measure of $\angle PRQ$.

The Tutorverse

4 B. The sine of x is equal to the sine of angle BCA, which is equal to $\dfrac{3}{AC}$. To calculate the length of AC, use the Pythagorean Theorem on triangle ABC. $3^2 + 4^2 = AC^2$. It follows that $AC = 5$. Therefore, the sine is $\dfrac{3}{5}$, which is between 0.5 and 0.7.

Student Produced Response – Calculator

1 4/5 or 0.8. The cosine of x is $\dfrac{20}{25}$, which simplifies to $\dfrac{4}{5}$ or 0.8.

2 $\dfrac{5}{13}$ or 0.38. Since the opposite side equals 12 m., the adjacent side equals 5 m.

$Cos\ A = \dfrac{adjacent}{hypotenuse} = \dfrac{5}{13}$.

3 38. The length of EG is equal to $EH + HG$. First figure out EH: Triangle EHF is a 30-60-90 right triangle, which means that $EH = \sqrt{3}FH \approx 1.73 \cdot 14 = 24.22$. Next, figure out HG: Triangle FHG is a 45-45-90 right triangle, so $HG = FH = 14$. Finally, we add together $EH + HG = 24.22 + 14 = 38.22$, which is just 38 when rounded to the nearest inch.

4 12/5 or 2.4. The tangent of x is equal to $\dfrac{YZ}{XY}$. We already know YZ and we can calculate XY using the Pythagorean Theorem. $XY^2 + 12^2 = 13^2$. Solving this for XY, we get $XY = 5$. Therefore, the tangent of x is $\dfrac{YZ}{XY} = \dfrac{12}{5}$.

Guided Practice – Radians

Multiple Choice – No Calculator

1 B. Because the x and y coordinates of point A are the same, the segment AO is halfway between the x-axis and y-axis. Since B is on the y-axis, this creates a 45 degree angle, which is $\dfrac{\pi}{4}$ radians (to convert from degrees to radians, multiply by $\dfrac{\pi}{180}$).

2 A. The sine and cosine of an angle are equal when the angle is 45 degrees or $\dfrac{\pi}{4}$ (to convert from degrees to radians, multiply by $\dfrac{\pi}{180}$). To see why it is 45 degrees, think about a right triangle. If the sine and cosine of an angle are equal, that means that the opposite side and adjacent side are equal. If the two legs of a right triangle are equal, then its angles are 45-45-90.

3 C. When you have two complementary angles, the sine of one is equal to the cosine of the other. This statement can be expressed in all of the following equivalent ways:

$$\sin(x) = \cos(90 - x), \cos(x) = \sin(90 - x), \sin(x) = \cos\left(\dfrac{\pi}{2} - x\right), \cos(x) = \sin\left(\dfrac{\pi}{2} - x\right).$$

4 A. This is a 30-60-90 right triangle because the hypotenuse is twice the shorter leg. It is worth remembering (and it also is provided in the reference information at the beginning of each math section) that a 30-60-90 right triangle has sides with lengths $x, \sqrt{3}x, 2x$ for some number x. Since $\angle A$ is the smallest angle, it is 30 degrees or $\dfrac{\pi}{6}$ radians (to convert from degrees to radians, multiply by $\dfrac{\pi}{180}$).

The Tutorverse

5   C. Points A and B are each equidistant between the x-axis and y-axis, so they each make and angle of 45 degrees with the x-axis. Adding these together, we get 90 degrees or $\dfrac{\pi}{2}$ radians (to convert from degrees to radians, multiply by $\dfrac{\pi}{180}$).

6   D. The formula for converting degrees into radians is *degree measure* $\dfrac{\pi}{180}$. Therefore,

$210° \cdot \dfrac{\pi}{180°} = \dfrac{210\pi}{180} = \dfrac{7\pi}{6}$. You can also remember that one full circle, or 360°, is equivalent to 2π radians and that 180° is therefore equal to π radians. A 210° measure is slightly larger than 180°, so the radian measure would be slightly larger than π. Choice D is the only answer with a value larger than π.

Student Produced Response – No Calculator

1   4. Because the x and y coordinates of point B are the same, the segment BO is halfway between the x-axis and y-axis. Since A is on the x-axis, this creates a 45 degree angle, which is $\dfrac{\pi}{4}$ radians(to convert from degrees to radians, multiply by $\dfrac{\pi}{180}$).

2   7/16 or 0.44. The question asks, "the area of the sector… is what fraction of the area of the circle?" However, we would get the same ratio if we asked, "the central angle is what fraction of the full circle?"

The central angle is $\dfrac{7\pi}{8}$ out of a total of 2π. This becomes the fraction $\dfrac{\frac{7\pi}{8}}{2\pi} = \dfrac{7}{16}$.

Multiple Choice – Calculator

1   B. The angles shown in the figure are supplementary, so they must add up to 180 degrees or π radians. In other words, $\angle BOA + \angle COB = \pi$. This becomes $\dfrac{\pi}{6} + COB = \pi$. Solving this, we get $\angle COB = \dfrac{5\pi}{6}$.

2   B. The coordinates of B could represent the legs of a 30-60-90 right triangle whose hypotenuse is OB. This means that the angle between OB and the negative x-axis is 60 degrees or $\dfrac{\pi}{3}$ radians (to convert from degrees to radians, multiply by $\dfrac{\pi}{180}$). That angle is supplementary to $\angle AOB$, so we must subtract it from π. We get $\pi - \dfrac{\pi}{3} = \dfrac{2\pi}{3}$.

3   C. The coordinates of A could represent the legs of a 30-60-90 right triangle whose hypotenuse is OA. This means that the angle between OA and the y-axis is 30 degrees or $\dfrac{\pi}{6}$ radians (to convert from degrees to radians, multiply by $\dfrac{\pi}{180}$). Similarly, OB makes an angle of $\dfrac{\pi}{6}$ radians to the other side of the y-axis. Together, they make $\dfrac{\pi}{6} + \dfrac{\pi}{6} = \dfrac{\pi}{3}$.

4   D. The sector for pizza is 45% of the circle so that is $\dfrac{45}{100} \cdot 2\pi$ which simplifies to $\dfrac{9\pi}{10}$. If we remember that a full circle is 2π and half a circle is π, then we can see that we are looking at an angle that is a little less than π. Choices A, B, and C are all far too small.

The Tutorverse

5   A. We can represent the measures of angles A and B as $2x$ and x respectively. Since they are supplementary, they must add up to 180 degrees or π radians. We get the equation $2x + x = \pi$, which simplifies to $3x = \pi$. Dividing by 3, we get $x = \dfrac{\pi}{3}$. This is the measure of angle B.

Student Produced Response – Calculator

1   3/10 or 0.3. The question asks, "the length of the arc… is what fraction of the circumference of the circle?" However, we would get the same ratio if we asked, "the central angle is what fraction of the full circle?" The central angle is $\dfrac{3\pi}{5}$ out of a total of 2π. This becomes the fraction $\dfrac{\frac{3\pi}{5}}{2\pi} = \dfrac{3}{10}$.

Guided Practice – Imaginary & Complex Numbers
Multiple Choice – No Calculator

1   D. Since $i = \sqrt{-1}$, we can determine that $i^2 = \sqrt{-1}^2 = -1$. Therefore, $i^2 + i^2 = (-1) + (-1) = -2$.

2   B. Complex numbers are added by combining the real parts and the imaginary parts separately. Essentially, just combine like terms: $(3 + 4i) + (7 + 6i) = (3 + 7) + (4i + 6i) = 10 + 10i$.

3   C. Complex numbers are subtracted by combining the real parts and the imaginary parts separately and distributing the negative through the second set of parentheses. $(4 + 2i) - (7 - 2i) = (4 - 7) + (2i - (-2i)) = -3 + 4i$.

4   B. Multiply by distributing: $-6i(3 - 2i) = -18i + 12i^2$. Since $i^2 = -1$, we can determine that $-18i + 12i^2 = -18i + 12(-1) = -18i - 12$, or in complex number form, $-12 - 18i$.

5   B. Multiply by distributing and recognizing that $i^2 = -1$. $12i(4 + 3i) = 48i + 36i^2 = -36 + 48i$.

6   C. Dividing a complex number by a real number is done by dividing each part of the complex number by the real number: $\dfrac{12 + 8i}{2} = \dfrac{12}{2} + \dfrac{8i}{2} = 6 + 4i$.

7   D. Since $i = \sqrt{-1}$, we can determine that $i^2 = \sqrt{-1}^2 = -1$, and that $i^4 = (i^2)(i^2) = 1$. Therefore, $5i^4 - 5i^2 - 5 = 5(1) - 5(-1) - 5 = 5$.

8   A. Complex numbers are subtracted by combining the real parts and the imaginary parts separately and distributing the negative through the second set of parentheses. Here, $(-5i^2) - (-3 - 7i^2) = -5i^2 - (-7i^2) - (-3) = -5(-1) - (7) + 3 = 1$.

9   D. Multiply by distributing: $5i^3(4 - 2i^2) = 5i^3(4) - 5i^3(2i^2) = 20i^3 - 10i^5 = -20i - 10i = -30i$.

10   B. Distributing $8i$ through the parentheses yields $56i - 24i^2 = 24 + 56i$ after substituting $i^2 = -1$.

11   A. Multiply by distributing: $(4 - i)(4 - i) = 16 - 8i + i^2$. Since $i^2 = -1$, the equation simplifies to $15 - 8i$.

12   A. To multiply two binomials, distribute (i.e. FOIL): $(5 - 5i)(4 + 4i) = 20 + 20i - 20i - 20i^2 = 20 - 20i^2$. Since $i^2 = -1$, we arrive at $20 - 20(-1) = 20 + 20 = 40$.

13   C. Since $i^1 = i$, we can determine that $i^2 = -1$, $i^3 = -i$, and $i^4 = -i^2 = -(-1) = 1$. Every fourth power of i is equal to 1, so $i^{32} = (i^4)^8 = 1$.

14   B. Since every fourth power of $i = 1$, we can determine that $i^{47} = i^{44} \times i^3 = 1 \times i^3$. Since $i^3 = -i$, $1 \times i^3 = -i$.

15   D. Multiplication of binomials is done by distributing: $(4 + 2i)(3 - 7i) = 12 - 28i + 6i - 14i^2$. This equals $12 - 22i - 14i^2$. Since $i^2 = -1$, we arrive at $12 - 22i - 14(-1) = 26 - 22i$.

16   D. Whenever we FOIL a binomial by its conjugate, the two middle terms cancel each other out and we're left with the difference of squares. When we multiply a complex number by its complex conjugate, we always arrive at a real number answer: $(8 - 3i)(8 + 3i) = 64 + 24i - 24i - 9i^2 = 64 - 9i^2 = 64 + 9 = 73$.

17   D. Multiplying the two binomials written in reverse order yields $(i + 1)(i - 1) = i^2 - i + i - 1 = -1 - 1 = -2$.

The Tutorverse

18 D. Denominators must always be rational numbers, so answers may not be left with an imaginary number in the denominator. Multiply both numerator and denominator by i: $\left(\dfrac{7}{2i}\right)\left(\dfrac{i}{i}\right) = \left(\dfrac{7i}{2i^2}\right) = \dfrac{7i}{2(-1)} = \dfrac{-7i}{2}$.

19 B. Denominators must always be rational numbers, so answers may not be left with an imaginary number in the denominator. Simplify by multiplying the denominator and numerator by the complex conjugate of

the denominator: $\left(\dfrac{9i}{1+8i}\right)\left(\dfrac{1-8i}{1-8i}\right) = \dfrac{9i - 72i^2}{1 - 64i^2} = \dfrac{9i - 72(-1)}{1 - 64(-1)} = \dfrac{72 + 9i}{65}$.

20 A. Denominators must always be rational numbers, so answers may not be left with an imaginary number in the denominator. Multiply both the numerator and denominator by i:

$\left(\dfrac{9-4i}{-5i}\right)\left(\dfrac{i}{i}\right) = \dfrac{9i - 4i^2}{-5i^2} = \dfrac{9i - 4(-1)}{-5(-1)} = \dfrac{9i + 4}{5}$.

21 A. Since $i = \sqrt{-1}$, we can determine that $i^2 = \sqrt{-1}^2 = -1$, that $i^3 = (i^2)(i) = -i$, and that $i^4 = (i^2)(i^2) = 1$. Therefore, $i + i^2 + i^3 + i^4 = i + (-1) + (-i) + 1 = 0$.

22 B. Simplify by multiplying the denominator and numerator by the complex conjugate of the denominator: $\left(\dfrac{4}{2+3i}\right)\left(\dfrac{2-3i}{2-3i}\right) = \dfrac{8 - 12i}{4 - 9i^2} = \dfrac{8 - 12i}{4 - 9(-1)} = \dfrac{8 - 12i}{13}$.

23 A. To rewrite in $a + bi$ form, we must rationalize the denominator. Multiply the numerator and denominator by the complex conjugate of the denominator: $\dfrac{(8-3i)}{(2+i)} \cdot \dfrac{(2-i)}{(2-i)} = \dfrac{16 - 8i - 6i + 3i^2}{4 - i^2} =$

$\dfrac{16 - 8i - 6i + 3(-1)}{4 - (-1)} = \dfrac{13 - 14i}{5} = \dfrac{13}{5} - \dfrac{14}{5}i$. Therefore, $a = \dfrac{13}{5}$.

24 A. To add fractions, we need a common denominator, so we'll multiply the numerator and denominator of each fraction by the denominator of the other fraction:

$\dfrac{5}{5+i} + \dfrac{i}{5-i} = \left(\dfrac{5}{5+i}\right)\left(\dfrac{5-i}{5-i}\right) + \left(\dfrac{i}{5-i}\right)\left(\dfrac{5+i}{5+i}\right) = \dfrac{25 - 5i}{25 - 5i + 5i - i^2} + \dfrac{5i + i^2}{25 - 5i + 5i - i^2}$. Since the denominators

are now the same, we can add the fractions: $\dfrac{(25 - 5i) + (5i + i^2)}{25 - 5i + 5i - i^2} = \dfrac{25 + i^2}{25 - i^2}$. Since we know that $i^2 = -1$,

we can arrive at $\dfrac{25 + (-1)}{25 - (-1)} = \dfrac{24}{26} = \dfrac{12}{13}$.

Student Produced Response – No Calculator

1 9. Complex numbers are added by combining the real parts and the imaginary parts separately. $(5 + 4) + (6 - 6)i = 9 + 0i = 9$.

2 15. Since $i = \sqrt{-1}$, we can determine that $i^2 = -1$ and $i^4 = 1$. Therefore, $i^4 - 6i^2 + 9 = 1 - 6(-1) + 9 = 1 + 6 + 9 = 15$.

3 41. Expand the expression using FOIL: $(4 + 5i)(4 - 5i) = 16 - 20i + 20i - 25i^2 = 16 - 25i^2$. Since we know that $i^2 = -1$, we can determine that $16 - 25i^2 = 16 - 25(-1) = 41$.

4 1/5 or 0.2. Denominators must always be rational numbers, so answers may not be left with an imaginary number in the denominator. Multiply both the numerator and denominator by i:

$\left(\dfrac{i^3}{-5i}\right)\left(\dfrac{i}{i}\right) = \dfrac{i^4}{-5i^2} = \dfrac{1}{-5(-1)} = \dfrac{1}{5}$ or the decimal equivalent of 0.2. Alternatively, $\dfrac{i^3}{-5i} = \dfrac{i^2}{-5} = \dfrac{-1}{-5} = \dfrac{1}{5}$.

The Tutorverse

5 68. Expand the expression using FOIL: $(-2-8i)(-2+8i) = 4-16i+16i-64i^2 = 4-64i^2$. Since we know that $i^2 = -1$, we can determine that $4-64i^2 = 4-64(-1) = 4+64 = 68$.

6 1. One way to solve this is to use rules of exponents: $\dfrac{i^7}{-i} = -i^{7-1} = -i^6$. Since $i^6 = i^2 = -1$, we can determine that $i^6 = -(-1) = 1$. Another way to solve is to divide by multiplying both the denominator and numerator by the complex conjugate of the denominator: $\left(\dfrac{i^7}{-i}\right)\left(\dfrac{i}{i}\right) = \dfrac{i^8}{-i^2} = \dfrac{(i^4)^2}{-(-1)} = \dfrac{1}{1} = 1$.

7 6/5 or 1.2. To add fractions, we need a common denominator, so we'll multiply the numerator and denominator of each fraction by the denominator of the other fraction:

$\dfrac{2-i}{2+i} + \dfrac{2+i}{2-i} = \left(\dfrac{2-i}{2+i}\right)\left(\dfrac{2-i}{2-i}\right) + \left(\dfrac{2+i}{2-i}\right)\left(\dfrac{2+i}{2+i}\right) = \dfrac{4-2i-2i+i^2}{4-2i+2i-i^2} + \dfrac{4+2i+2i+i^2}{4+2i-2i-i^2}$. Since the denominators are now the same, we can add the fractions: $\dfrac{(4-2i-2i+i^2)+(4+2i+2i+i^2)}{4-2i+2i-i^2} = \dfrac{8+2i^2}{4-i^2}$. Since we know that $i^2 = -1$, we can arrive at $\dfrac{8+2(-1)}{4-(-1)} = \dfrac{8-2}{4+1} = \dfrac{6}{5}$ or the decimal equivalent of 1.2.

Mixed Practice – Additional Math Topics

Multiple Choice – No Calculator

1 Trigonometry: B Whenever we have two acute angles and the sine of one is equal to the cosine of the other, it means that the angles are complementary (add to 90 degrees). If angles A and C add to 90 degrees, then the remaining angle, B, must also be 90 degrees in order for the triangle to have the required angle sum of 180.

2 Imaginary & Complex Numbers: D. Expand the expression as multiplication of two binomials: $(12+2i)^2 = (12+2i)(12+2i) = 144+24i+24i+4i^2 = 144+48i-4 = 140+48i$.

3 Equations of Circles: C. The equation for a circle is $(x-h)^2 + (y-k)^2 = r^2$ in which the center of the circle is at the point (h,k). You can use the distance formula to find the radius, or the distance between (2,-4) and (8,-4): $d = \sqrt{(x_2-x_1)^2 + (y_2-y_1)^2} = \sqrt{(8-2)^2 + (-4-4)^2} = \sqrt{6^2 + (-8)^2} = \sqrt{100} = 10$. Therefore, the radius is 10. Plugging these back into the formula yields $(x-2)^2 + (y-4)^2 = 100$.

4 Radians: D. The coordinates of point B, $(-2,2)$, indicate that segment OB bisects the 4th quadrant, forming an angle of 45 degrees or $\dfrac{\pi}{4}$ with the positive y-axis and with the negative x-axis (to convert from degrees to radians, multiply by $\dfrac{\pi}{180}$). If we start at A, on the positive x-axis, we must travel counterclockwise by $\dfrac{\pi}{2}$ to get from the x-axis to the y-axis and then an additional $\dfrac{\pi}{4}$ to get from the y-axis to point B.

5 Imaginary & Complex Numbers: B. To rewrite in $a + bi$ form, we must rationalize the denominator. Multiply the numerator and denominator by the complex conjugate of the denominator:

$\dfrac{(10+40i)}{(-3+5i)} \cdot \dfrac{(-3-5i)}{(-3-5i)} = \dfrac{-30-50i-120i-200i^2}{9-25i^2} = \dfrac{-30-170i-200(-1)}{9-25(-1)} = \dfrac{170-170i}{34} = 5-5i$.

Therefore, $b = -5$.

6 Equations of Circles: D. The equation of a circle in standard form is $(x-h)^2 + (y-k)^2 = r^2$ where the center of the circle is located at (h,k) and r is the radius. So this circle would have a center at (4,2) and a radius of 7. This is only true for choice D.

7 Geometry: B. Since lines m and n are parallel, angle 1 and angle ADB must be congruent because they are alternate interior angles, meaning angle $ADB = 98°$. Focusing on triangle ADB, we see that we have two of the interior angles, so angle $DBA = 180 - (98 + 12) = 70$.

Multiple Choice – Calculator

1 Geometry: A. The volume of the rocket engine is the sum of the volumes of the right circular cylinder and the right circular cone, both of which are given on the reference sheet at the beginning of each math section: $\pi r^2 h + \frac{1}{3}\pi^2 h = \pi(1)^2(30) + \frac{1}{3}\pi(1)^2(3) = 30\pi + \pi = 31\pi$.

Explanations: Part Five – Practice Test

Reading

1 *Text Structure.* C. The passage describes Northup's first-person accounting of a fight he had while escaping slavery. The passage switches between the telling of events/actions and Northup's own thoughts on the matter. The passage is not purely driven by plot, and there is no external dialogue between Northup and his assailant. The events related are through Northup's point of view, and would likely not be considered to be purely objective. The passage is not written as an argumentative piece, with opinions and evidence used to convince the reader of a point.

2 *Summarizing.* D. Northup, a free man kidnapped and sold into slavery, fights to free himself. In the process, he is faced with choices – whether to simply give up (paragraph 5) or whether to kill his assailant (paragraph 7). These represent inner demons – the voices that tell him to do what he knows to be wrong. Northup does not consider the future until the very end of the passage. Northup has done nothing to justify his circumstances, and has nothing to redeem through his fight – he seeks only to regain freedom.

3 *Arguments.* A. Northup describes how there were only three courses of action: run, stand still and do nothing, or rush into a fight. He describes how if he were to run, the hatchet would fly from his assailant's hand and strike him in his back (lines 3-6). Northup does not describe how he is stronger or better at hand-to-hand combat than his assailant, and dismisses standing still from the very beginning.

4 *Words/Phrases in Context.* B. "Course" has many meanings, but from context the reader knows that Northup is attempting to decide how best to act. Each type of action – each course – represents an option. "Course" can also refer to a class, or a schedule or sequence, but in this case those meanings are illogical and not supported by the context of the paragraph.

5 *Word Choice.* A. Northup likens death to "the king of terrors," referring to the fact that his life-or-death situation is tantamount to standing "in the presence of" it. In context, the reader sees how Northup's views on death changed: he had previously viewed it as a release and escape; in "the hour of peril," he sees it as something to fight against – that "no man, in his full strength, can stand undismayed" by death; ultimately, even worms will "struggle for" life. Northup would likely agree with choices B and C, the phrase in question best illustrates the idea that one must fight against death.

6 *Main Ideas.* A. Northup's views on life and death changed when he was faced with mortal danger. Though Northup would likely agree that life can be difficult and peace hard to come by, the bigger picture of the paragraph describes how he – like all living things – is willing to fight for his life.

7 *Point of View.* D. By this point in the passage, Northup has the upper hand. Northup indicates that his assailant had, previously, been hateful and angry such that his eyes "spat such venom," but that now they were "full of horror." The reader can infer that Northup's assailant is afraid for his life, and that the fear has replaced the hate. The assailant is not described as unstable, and certainly would not be happy to be in his present circumstances.

8 *Word Choice.* C. The "lurking devil" Northup refers to is the desire to kill his assailant "to retain…gone." This is a base, primal feeling of bloodlust that he ultimately pushes away, in part due to his moral conscience but also in part due to practical concerns for his own safety. Faced with this predicament, Northup suppresses the primal urge to kill.

9 *Relationships.* A. Northup indicates that he was caught between a rock and a hard place "If I…vengeance" (lines 63-65). Though there was a voice that whispered to him to run away, there's no suggestion that this was religious in nature – in fact, it was likely due to the fact that he had no other choice. The reader knows that he had won the fight with the assailant from the previous paragraph, and that he was nervous about his life as a fugitive from the following paragraph.

10 *Close Reading.* D. Northup is glad to be alive, but is concerned about his future, asking a series of questions at the end of the passage. Northup does not indicate that he feels badly about injuring his assailant, or that he has last a part of himself or done something questionable during the fight. His primary concern is surviving and getting through life as a fugitive slave.

The Tutorverse

11 *Text Structure.* C. The author suggests that it is not easy being a scientist, and explores historical examples (Mendel; Galileo) supporting that idea. The author doesn't debate the topic, instead presenting on the view that supports this suggestion in the passage. The author focuses only on this concept.

12 *Words/Phrases in Context.* C. In this sentence, the author describes how scientists today are at the very least tolerated, suggesting in fact that scientists are more than just tolerated – they are respected, a synonym for "venerated." Choices A and D are synonyms for tolerated, and would be illogical to replace "venerated" in the sentence.

13 *Summarizing.* B. The second paragraph describes Mendel's accomplishments, the fact that his work was not respected by his peers, and that his legacy vindicated only after his death. The focus of the paragraph is more than just describing the concept Mendel discovered, and is more specific than simply discussing a historical matter.

14 *Arguments.* A. The author, in comparing Mendel and Galileo, indicates that the latter suffered more for his craft than the former. This is primarily due to the fact that Galileo was subject to the Inquisition, where Mendel was work was merely underappreciated or misunderstood. The author clearly indicates that being a scientist is "not always" easy, citing these scientists' lives as examples.

15 *Textual Evidence.* C. Here, the author compares the two scientists directly, referring to Mendel's situation as "mere rejection" which "pales" when compared to Galileo's suffering due to the Inquisition. The other answer choices support incorrect answer choices to the previous question.

16 *Relationships.* C. The passage indicates that Lorini submitted Galileo's work to the Inquisition because the former believed the latter's work reinterpreted the Bible (lines 29-36). The passage does not imply that Galileo actually reinterpreted the Bible, nor that the Council of Trent ordered Galileo's persecution directly. The Galileo encountered the Grand Duchess of Florence before 1615.

17 *Word Choice.* D. The phrase is used to describe a difficult task – in this case, that Galileo desired to stand by his ideas and believed in them, yet could not do so without angering the Church. The phrase does not explain why Galileo was sentenced to house arrest, nor does it explain a charge of heresy. While the Church did disapprove of Galileo's ideas, this phrase is not used to emphasize it, instead drawing attention the need for Galileo to choose between two obligations.

18 *Close Reading.* B. The passage indicates that in the end, Galileo was "sentenced to house arrest" and managed to avoid a "far more horrible fate" than others found guilty by the Inquisition. The passage does not suggest that the Pope had a hand in determining the punishment, nor does the author draw a parallel between house arrest and Mendel's rejection.

19 *Purpose.* C. In both Mendel and Galileo's case, the author does not simply describe the difficulty each scientist had during their lives. Instead, the author describes also how, after each scientist's death, the world eventually recognized the magnitude of their contributions. This helps the author to connect both scientists in yet another way.

20 *Point of View.* D. The author's perspective throughout the passage does not suggest that Mendel and Galileo deserved what they got, nor does the author write with disregard for the plight of the scientists. Instead, the author appears to feel deeply that Mendel and Galileo suffered or went unrecognized for their contributions.

21 *Summarizing.* A. The first paragraph in Passage 1 suggest that people do not enjoy memorizing, and that tools have helped people to accomplish the difficult task of memorizing. However, the second paragraph discusses how memorizing is nonetheless a necessity, despite the creation of those tools. The only answer choice to capture this nuance is choice A.

22 *Close Reading.* B. The author cites multiple examples of how knowledge is affected by the order in which things are learned – the pedagogy of learning. The author suggests that without memorizing fundamentals (such as the meanings of words), then more advanced tasks (like putting words together in sentences) would be much more difficult or even impossible. The author does not mention any of the other answer choices in the passage.

23 *Textual Evidence.* B. The author explicitly states that memorizing allows people to "tackle more difficult problems." This aligns with the answer to the previous question. The other answer choices do not address the fact that basics must be mastered before more advanced tasks are attempted.

24 *Arguments.* D. Though the author spends much of Passage 1 describing why memorization is helpful and necessary in learning, the last paragraph cautions that memorization is not everything. Instead, the author calls it "a tool to be used" in learning. The author goes on to say that the ability to memorize is not the same as intelligence, and offers the last sentence as an example of that idea.

25 *Main Ideas.* D. The author's fundamental claim is that rote memorization is a disservice to students, citing examples of a misplaced focus on memorizing. The author's claim is most evident in the last two paragraphs, where he appeals for more focus on conceptual understanding and critical thinking.

The Tutorverse

26   *Word Choice.* B. Based on the passage, we can infer that the author has a low opinion of memorization. By starting off the passage with this phrase, the author likens it to an unmentionable word to immediately let the reader know his position on the matter. There is no evidence to suggest that this is how teachers refer to memorization, nor does this in and of itself explain why students dislike memorization.

27   *Purpose.* A. The example of a student knowing what a specific fact is yet failing to be able to explain the reasoning behind that fact underscores the author's primary point – that memorization does not lead to understanding, and that critical thinking should instead be emphasized. The role of standardized testing in promoting memorization is described later in the passage. The author's aim is not to show how poor the state of education is, or to suggest that memorization is necessary in math.

28   *Words/Phrases in Context.* D. The author argues against memorization of information that can be learned through reasoning and critical thinking. The word "tidbit" implies that the information being memorized are small, and isolated – out of context. Of the answer choices, the best choice describes how these tidbits are out of context – meaningless without a deeper level of understanding.

29   *Relationships.* A. The author of Passage 1 argues that memorization is expeditious and can help people to learn more advanced concepts. The author does not argue that memorized information is the same thing as true understanding (lines 35-40), nor does he suggest that it is pointless because of technology that can recall or process that information more quickly.

30   *Point of View.* B. The author of Passage 1 believes that memorization is important to learning, but that does not define intelligence. While the author does not define intelligence, we can infer from the last sentence that he believes that "knowing why" something is or is not is different and more meaningful than simply "knowing that" something is or is not; the "knowing why" is understanding. The author of Passage 2 argues that memorization is overemphasized and that it should be replaced by developing critical thinking skills; to be better able to understand and solve problems.

31   *Quantitative Information.* C. The graph shows that there is an optimal amount of time to spend memorizing information. It also shows that neglecting memorization results in a poor cumulative GPA, as does spending too much time memorizing. It is therefore untrue to say that spending more time memorizing always increases GPAs, nor is it true to say that spending more time always decreases GPA – it matters where on the graph one looks. Neither passage discusses the right amount of time to spend memorizing, but both graphs could be used to advance either passage's argument. The author of Passage 1 would likely use information from the 10-30% of time spent memorizing part of the graph, while the author of Passage 2 would likely use information from the 40-100% of time spent memorizing part of the graph.

32   *Main Ideas.* C. Roosevelt's chat describes the steps that have been taken to address the banking crisis described in the third paragraph. The passage does not offer a debate of or alternatives to actions taken. The future is not explicitly addressed here; rather, events that have already transpired are explained to listeners/readers.

33   *Text Structure.* B. In the first two paragraphs, Roosevelt describes context for the passage, alluding to and clarifying the confusing and complicated nature of the banking system. He then proceeds to explain the specific problem: a run on the banks in the third paragraph. Subsequently, Roosevelt describes actions taken to address the problem.

34   *Words/Phrases in Context.* A. "Temper" has many meanings. In context, however, the word is used as a noun (the adjective "good" modifies "temper"). As a noun used in context of describing the quality of a person (Roosevelt is describing everybody's "fortitude and good temper"), temper refers to mood, spirit, or temperament. Here, Roosevelt praises people's good disposition – that they have not reacted poorly given the "inconvenience and hardships."

35   *Purpose.* C. The paragraph provides the reader/listener with a basic understanding of the banking system. Without it, it would be difficult to explain the problem at hand, as described in the third paragraph. The reasons why the problem occurred, and the actions taken to address that problem, are addressed after the third paragraph.

36   *Point of View.* C. Roosevelt indicates that it is due to "undermined confidence on the part of the public" that the banking crisis took place. This suggests that the public had a low level of trust in the banking system.

37   *Arguments.* C. Roosevelt explains, in the second paragraph, that a relatively "small part of the money" deposited in a bank is kept as currency; the rest is invested to "keep the…turning" (lines 26-31). In the third paragraph, Roosevelt explains that it was "impossible to sell perfectly sound assets of a bank and convert them into cash." Thus, banks were unable to give deposits to people because most of the cash had been converted into other investments and could not be converted back into enough money. The passage does not support the suggestion that banks wasted money, or that the government had seized deposits. That the banks are funding payrolls and food distribution takes place only after the bank holiday.

38   *Textual Evidence.* A. Based on the previous question, we know that it was due to a large number of people demanding their deposits and the fact that money was invested and not kept as cash that there was an inability on the

The Tutorverse

part of banks to pay back deposits. The other answer choices support incorrect explanations or pertain to actions after the crisis, not leading up to it.

39   *Word Choice.* D. Roosevelt's choice words – calling the closure of banks a "bank holiday" – not only makes it clear what is happening (i.e. the banks are closed), but also makes it clear that this closure is just temporary (as holidays typically are) and not permanent. The words do not ridicule the seriousness of the crisis, nor do they imply that the public should go on holiday. Roosevelt praises Congress for their speedy action, not their lack of it.

40   *Close Reading.* D. Roosevelt mentions that Congress worked with him to pass legislation and grant him necessary authority to act (lines 62-76). The passage does not suggest that Congress acted slowly or refused to act altogether.

41   *Relationships.* A. Roosevelt mentions that "legislation promptly" passed by Congress "gave authority to develop a program of rehabilitation." The passage does not mention a decree, vote, or referendum.

42   *Arguments.* D. Will Hunting's achievements surprise the math community; so too do Zhang's. The author does not show how both fiction and reality differ from the other, but how, in this case, the two are similar.

43   *Summarizing.* A. The author provides mathematical background knowledge in these paragraphs to ensure that the reader can understand later paragraphs discussing Zhang's accomplishments. Such concepts include the notion of primes, prime pairs, prime gaps, and twin primes. The author builds on these concepts and raises the question of prime gaps. The anecdote about Zhang's discovery is told in context of the concepts and question, but not until later in the passage. The author does not make comparisons with other concepts or discus answers (instead saying that the question "remains unanswered").

44   *Words/Phrases in Context.* B. The author suggests that without a rule or proof, it will be impossible to know how many twin primes there are. The key here is that mathematics seek to know, not simply to guess or approximate. Thus, "estimate" is inappropriate. The author does not suggest that solving the twin prime conjecture is difficult to understand. Instead, the very act of solving it – of ascertaining the solution – is difficult.

45   *Text Structure.* D. The author uses the first four paragraphs to describe information necessary to the main point of the story that follows: that there are real life examples of "miraculous events"; that in real life, the example centers around a difficult question in math. The story that follows, about Zhang, is really only understandable in context of the first four paragraphs. Otherwise, the author's point would be lost.

46   *Word Choice.* A. Zhang's story is interesting, like Hunting's, because of the otherwise humble origins of the protagonist. Part of the reason why both stories are impressive and interesting is because a significant accomplishment came from an unexpected place. By highlight the fact that Zhang worked as an accountant and in fast food, the author indirectly builds up Zhang's accomplishments, which are described later in the passage.

47   *Purpose.* C. The GPY paper intrigued Zhang. The paper mentions that Zhang modified a process described in the GPY paper, which ultimately led to Zhang's discovery (lines 59-63). The passage does not suggest that the GPY disproved Zhang's theory, or that it was useless to Zhang.

48   *Relationships.* B. The author writes that it was on a "break from his [Zhang's] work" that an "idea suddenly hit him." The passage does not suggest that Zhang's discovery was spurred on by a conversation or another unknown paper. In fact, the passage suggests that Zhang worked alone. The GPY paper was the basis for Zhang's work, but until his time away from work, he was unable to use the GPY methodology to solve the problem.

49   *Textual Evidence.* C. From the previous question, we know that Zhang's breakthrough was catalyzed by his vacation, or break from work. This is encapsulated in choice C. The other answer choices suggest that incorrect answers to the previous question are, in fact, correct.

50   *Close Reading.* C. The author indicates that after *Annals of Mathematics* published his work, Harvard reached out to him for a speaking engagement. The passage does not state that the speaking engagement was organized while the work was still in draft, or that it was first tested by the entire math community. Zhang earned his doctorate many years before the events of his discovery.

51   *Point of View.* B. The passage repeated refers to how the mathematics community was shocked by Zhang's accomplishments, how there was "great fanfare" after his publication, and how his work would "shake the theoretical mathematics community to its core." These reactions are positive; "esteem" is the only word with a positive connotation.

52   *Quantitative Information.* D. The graph shows prime gaps and the number of pairs forming those gaps for prime numbers less than 100. Zhang's theory deals with infinity, and does not suggest that analyzing prime numbers less than 100 will yield a proof or theory that can be applied to the infinite.

Writing & Language

1   *Style/Tone.* C. The preceding sentence begins with an independent clause containing the quality that answers the first sentence's question. That clause is followed by a dependent clause, which describes more about the independent clause (i.e. intelligence is demonstrated by capacity to learn new things). The only choice that matches this style is C, which introduces an independent clause containing the quality answering the first sentence's question (curiosity) and is followed by a dependent clause explaining why this is the case (i.e. many scientists' lives).

2   *Frequently Confused Words.* B. The sentence compares two groups of people: scientists and gamblers. However, the best choice is to use the word "to" as a preposition, which identifies the thing being compared (gambler with scientist). "Too" is an adverb and would be incorrect to use as a preposition.

3   *Conventional Expression.* D. The sentence describes how scientists sometimes make discoveries by accident and offers radioactivity as an unknown concept that Becquerel unwittingly discovered. The best expression to use here is "after all," which means here "besides"; how could Becquerel have had an intention of discovering something that was unknown?

4   *Focus.* A. The paragraph – and passage in general – is concerned with explaining how some scientific discoveries are accidents. The facts that Becquerel's discovery was very important and that the unit of measurement of radiation is named after Becquerel are interesting, but blur the focus of the paragraph and do not support the paragraph's main idea.

5   *Precision.* D. From context, we can infer that the sentence describes Becquerel's early experiences in science – the things that intrigued Becquerel and the work that he was involved with (light and phosphorescence). A "foray" describes an attempt to become involved in something new, but can also refer to an attack or incursion into enemy territory. The latter does not make sense in context, nor does it make sense to use "excursion" or "expedition," which refer more to actual, physical trips.

6   *Shifting Tenses, Mood, Voice, and Number.* B. The entire paragraph is written in the simple past tense, describing Becquerel's work. It is inappropriate to shift the tense to the simple present (finds), future present (will find), and past perfect progressive (had been finding).

7   *Logical Sequence.* D. The paragraph describes the steps Becquerel took to conduct his experiment. Sentence 1 describes the repeating of these steps, but refers to things like "paper" and "phosphorescent substance" and "impression on the film." All of these elements are described only after sentence 5, so it would not be logical to include this sentence before these elements are explained.

8   *Syntax.* B. Because "days" is the topic of discussion in both sentences, it is possible to combine both sentences together. By doing so, the combined sentence would read "very cloudy days that did not provide…" This is more fluid and less choppy than separating the sentences with a period or semicolon, as the second sentence describes the impact of the days on Becquerel's experiment – the subject of the first sentence. Using "which" would only be appropriate if preceded by a comma.

9   *Modifier Placement.* C. The sentence describes Becquerel's surprise when he expected to find a weak image on the film but instead found a clear image on the film. The adverb "clearly" should be used to modify the appearance of the image. As written, the modifier is squinting and ambiguous. The other choices emphasize the wrong part of the sentence, changing the meaning entirely.

10 *Quantitative Information.* B. The graph shows that despite changing intensity of ambient light, the intensity of the image on photographic film remained relatively constant. This does not show any correlation or dependency of the image on the ambient light levels.

11 *Unnecessary Punctuation.* A. No commas are necessary in this sentence. The sentence is a single, independent clause and does not contain clauses, phrases, or appositives that would require the use of clarifying commas.

12 *Coordination.* B. The first two sentences are related in that they refer to the reasons why choosing a career can be confusing. However, because they are related, a coordinating conjunction that logically suggests the opposite – such as although – should not be used. Such conjunctions contradict the logic of the two sentences, especially the "after all" at the end of the second sentence, which provides a clue that the two sentences are logically related.

13 *Pronoun Clarity.* B. As written, "them" is unclear (a job that is too easy for whom?) and also disagrees in number to the noun "job" (which is singular). The only correct choice to ensure that the pronoun is both clear and agrees in number with the noun "job" is "a person." "Him," though singular, refers to an unknown entity, and "people" is plural.

14 *Precision.* D. Though the patients are technically the customers of RNs, the paragraph here discusses how RNs care for other people – patients and their families. The RNs "provide emotional support" to those that they care for – their wards. They are custodians of other people, not the other way around. The passage does not suggest that the RNs work with their friends.

15 *Support.* B. The sentence develops the point that RNs can also work in uncommon places in addition to places one would expect nurses to work. The only example here that supports this point is an insurance company. The other

answer choices provide examples of health-related locations where nurses can reasonably be expected to be employed.

16 *Logical Comparison.* B. As written, the sentence compares the "high rate of growth" of the RN occupation directly with "other occupations." Instead, the sentence should compare the rate of growth of the RN occupation with the rate of growth of other occupations. The only choice that accomplishes this goal is choice B.

17 *Possessive Nouns & Pronouns.* C. The sentence describes how the world population will continue to grow. In this sentence, the population is "belonging" to the world, not multiple worlds. Without an apostrophe, there is no possession indicated. "Worlds' population" suggests that the population of multiple worlds are being discussed. "World population's" suggests that the entire population of the world possesses something.

18 *Concision.* C. The sentence suggests that a growing population will result in higher demand for RNs, which is a different way of saying that people will need more RNs. To say that the demand is going to increase along with the number of people who need RNs is redundant, since they describe the same thing.

19 *Syntax.* A. The sentence is made up of two independent clauses separated by a semicolon because the two clauses discuss related topics: the RN satisfaction. The first clause makes a claim, and the second clause supports it. Using the word "however" would signal that the two clauses make opposing statements about the related topic, which is not the case here. Using a comma results in a run-on sentence. Using "and" is incorrect in this context because the two clauses remain independent.

20 *Organization.* A. The paragraph describes the requirements to becoming an RN and the steps one would need to take to do so. Preceding paragraphs discuss why people might consider becoming an RN and who might be interested in becoming an RN. The passage does not describe when it would be appropriate to become an RN.

21 *Items in a Series.* C. The two items in the series denoted by the preceding colon relate to two options to become an RN. Because there are only two options, and because the use of commas does not confuse the sentence, the comma is the most appropriate punctuation. Using a period or semicolon results in a fragment of the second option (diploma from nursing program), and the use of a dash is not appropriate. A comma (and the use of the conjunction "or") sufficiently separates the two options.

22 *Proposition.* D. The passage is primarily concerned with explaining both the pros and cons of becoming an RN. The final paragraph discusses the steps needed to become an RN, which involves education and licensure. The author does not seek to dissuade people from becoming RNs; rather, the author seeks to have the reader make up his or her own mind by evaluating information presented in the passage.

23 *Possessive Determiners.* D. Without an apostrophe, the word "its" is possessive. With the apostrophe, the word "it's" is a contraction for "it is." There is no such word as "It'" or "its'."

24 *Focus.* C. The paragraph raises a number of questions in order to demonstrate the wide breadth and depth of the field of linguistics, which is the subject of the entire passage. The question about a dog is relevant to the paragraph and passage, as it relates to the topic of morphology discussed in the fourth paragraph. The sentence does not make contradictions or make opposing arguments.

25 *Subject-verb Agreement.* C. The subject in this sentence is "question" which is a plural noun. Thus, the verb "are" – the plural form of "be/is" – is most appropriate.

26 *End-of-Sentence Punctuation.* A. When punctuating the end of a quotation, ending punctuation generally goes inside the quotation mark. However, placement of question marks and exclamation points depend on what is being quoted. In neither case is "double punctuation" used (as in choices C and D). The difference between choices A and B is subtle; the former implies that the question itself is being quoted, where the latter implies that a quoted statement is being questioned.

27 *Concision.* B. While the sentence as written and choice B are grammatically correct, "nuanced" is a more economical way of saying "subtly different" without changing the meaning of the sentence. Using words precisely and economically is preferable to using more words that accomplish the same goal. Similarly, choice C means something similar, but uses many words – some of which are confusing since they are repeated later in the sentence.

28 *Precision.* B. The sentence uses the word "though" to contrast the field of linguistics with the fact that it can be thought of more simply. Thus, the best word here is to use "broad," since a topic that is broad is one that covers many things and can be difficult to think of. It would not be appropriate to contrast a "narrow" or "inexact" field with the fact that it is possible to think of that field in two ways. Similarly, the author does not suggest that the two ways of thinking about linguistics are duplicative – in fact, the author argues that they are different.

29 *Parallel Structure.* C. The order of words here is important, though many choices are technically grammatically correct. Stylistically, the best way to ensure parallelism in writing is to ensure consistent structure. Only the second choice mirrors the earlier part of this series: "the first has to do with" and "the second has to do with."

The Tutorverse

30   *Style/Tone.* A. The second sentence in the paragraph and the last sentence in the paragraph are constructed in such a way that the different fields of study (morphology, syntax, phonology, etc) are introduced first, defined, then explained in more detail. Only choice D follows this pattern, with the other choices offering a different (but not grammatically incorrect) sequence.

31   *Proposition.* D. The paragraph enumerates different parts of the linguistics field, and how those fields relate to language itself. By first enumerating these different parts, then ending the paragraph by saying "the study of language is divided into several disciplines," the only word that makes sense is "thus" – "nevertheless" and "instead" imply that this statement is the opposite of what was shown in the paragraph. The author does not suggest that the study of language is straightforward.

32   *Organization.* A. The preceding paragraph discusses the study of the structure of the language, which is simply different from the study of language uses. The author had previously, in the third paragraph, explained that the field of linguistics is thought of in two parts that deal with different aspects of language. The two parts are different; it would be incorrect to use the words "similar" or "despite" or "in spite of" to signal the difference, as they imply more of a contrast.

33   *Parenthetical Expressions & Nonrestrictive Clauses.* B. By using a comma after "factors" followed by "which," the meaning of the sentence changes to suggest that it is the study of psycholinguistics itself that develops linguistic skills. This is contrary to the meaning of the sentence, which is to define psycholinguistics and explain what the field does. The best way to accomplish this is to omit the comma, and use "that" or "which." However, the tense of "allow" matters, as "the psychological and neurological factors" are treated as singular, requiring the use of the word "allow" instead of "allows."

34   *Parenthetical Expressions & Nonrestrictive Clauses.* D. Using a phrase that begins with "which" or "that" between two commas is a sign of a nonrestrictive clause – something that can be removed from the sentence without changing the basic meaning. In this case, both choices that suggest creating a nonrestrictive clause are incorrect, as taking the clause out would fundamentally alter the meaning of the sentence. Choice B results in a grammatically incorrect sentence, splitting "which" into a parenthetical expression.

35   *Noun Agreement.* B. The sentence provides examples of different administrators, as it speaks generally about all administrators, not a specific administrator of a specific government. Thus, the number of the noun "administrator" must match the number of the nouns in "the prime…statesmen." To do so, the noun must be plural, but not possessive, as in choices C and D.

36   *Support.* A. The paragraph is concerned with explaining how a government by rule of law differs from a government based on different forms of power. The author attempts to clarify the differences with examples and by how each type of government works. The sentence would improve the clarification of these differences. The sentence does not support the notion that power is greater than rule of law, and does in fact flow logically from the preceding sentence.

37   *Focus.* A. The primary focus of the paragraph is to describe how many ancient societies were organized and to provide an example of such organizations. The paragraph does not concern itself with describing the histories of these societies. Therefore, the sentence is irrelevant, blurs the focus of the paragraph, and should be deleted.

38   *Concision.* B. The author implies that societies governed by legal principles are more stable, unlike some regimes that can do whatever it is they want. The author writes "changing whims and feelings" is embodied by "caprices," which means "sudden and unaccountable changes in mood or behavior." This is a more succinct way to convey this point than the other answer choices.

39   *Complete Sentences.* D. As written "often…law" is a fragment, with no subject. Though choice B corrects this, it ignores the rest of the sentence which becomes illogical in the absence of further edits. A semicolon effectively serves the same purpose of a period in this case, and strands "often…law" as a fragmented dependent clause.

40   *Precision.* C. The author intends to show how Aristotle supported the rule of law, stating that he was "fervent" and an "advocate." The author does not provide evidence supporting the notion that Aristotle was flexible on the matter, as "pliant" would suggest; nor does the author suggest that Aristotle was "authoritarian" in his support. Rather, the author suggests that Aristotle was a strong supporter of the rule of law, as "outspoken" suggests.

41   *Noun Agreement.* A. The core of the sentence is "rumblings surfaced" ("similar" modifies "rumblings," and "in ancient China" modifies "surfaced"). However, "rumblings" is also modified by the rest of the sentence "form of…thought." In this sentence, "rumblings" is treated like a unit of measurement to express the quantity and proliferation of the rule of law (how much "rule of law" is in the ancient world? "Rumblings of it.") As such, the noun (though plural) is treated as singular for purposes of matching noun number. It is unnecessary to use "forms" or "schools." "Thought," in any case, should not be pluralized, since it is part of "school of thought."

42   *Style/Tone.* D. The author previously likens the rule of law to a seed being sown, but also indicates that for a long time there were no practicing societies that followed the rule of law (paragraph four). In paragraph five, the author

The Tutorverse

describes how the Magna Carta served as a framework allowing powerful countries to develop around the rule of law. The comparison to a seed helps to draw the two paragraphs together and is a metaphor for the role the Magna Carta played in terms of developing the rule of law; a seed takes root after it is sown/planted.

43 *Within-Sentence Punctuation*. D. No commas are necessary in this sentence. All of the information in the sentence is important to the meaning of the sentence (i.e. a contrast between what was once obscure becoming prevalent) so there is no parenthetical expression here (so no bookended commas are needed). The sentence does not have any subordinated clauses that would require the use of a single comma.

44 *Logical Sequence*. B. The paragraph serves to introduce the notion of the rule of law and belongs at the beginning of the passage. Paragraphs 2 and 4 discuss historical societies and their forms of government; paragraph 3 interrupts this flow, as it would if placed before paragraph 5. Paragraph 1 expands upon the idea of the rule of law, and would benefit if there was an introduction before it – in this case, paragraph 3.

Math – No Calculator

1   Solving Linear Equations & Inequalities: D. $w = \dfrac{5}{4} \div \dfrac{2}{3} = \dfrac{5}{4} \times \dfrac{3}{2} = \dfrac{15}{8}$.

2   Relationships Between Algebraic & Graphical Representations of Functions: A. This parabola intersects the x-axis at –2 and 4. So the x-coordinate of the vertex of the parabola is halfway between these points: $\dfrac{-2+4}{2} = 1$. So this is the value of c. To find the y coordinate of the vertex, substitute 1 for x in the equation: $y = a(1+2)(1-4) = -9a$.

3   Linear Equations, Inequalities, & Systems in Word Problems: B. Substituting $\dfrac{5}{9}(F-32)$ for C in the equation yields $K = \dfrac{5}{9}(F-32)+273$.

4   Linear Equations, Inequalities, & Systems in Word Problems: B. If x is the number of years since 2000, then 12 is the amount the population increases each year.

5   Linear Equations, Inequalities, & Systems in Word Problems: B. Substituting the point into the equation yields $-2 = 5(-1)+b$. This simplifies to $b = 3$.

6   Exponential & Radicals: A. One way to solve is to plug $x^2 - 3$ into each answer choice and see which results in $\sqrt{x^2 - 6}$. Choice A works because then $f(g(x)) = \sqrt{(x^2-3)-3} = \sqrt{x^2 - 6}$. Choice D is a commonly chosen incorrect answer that results from mistakenly plugging $x^2 - 3$ in for x in the expression $\sqrt{x^2 - 6}$.

7   Working with Polynomials: C. Distribute the negative sign to the second set of parentheses: $6x^2 + 2x - 3 - 10x^2 + 2x - 5$. Combine like terms: $6x^2 - 10x^2 = -4x^2$, for $2x + 2x = 4x$, and $-3 - 5 = -8$.

8   Quadratic Functions & Equations: A. Factoring the equation gives $(5m + 2)(5m - 2) = 0$. The solutions are $\dfrac{2}{5}$ and $-\dfrac{2}{5}$ which have a sum of 0.

9   Exponential & Radicals: A. This shows the initial population multiplied by the rate of growth plus 1 to the power of the number of years. This will show an increase of 6% in the population each year.

10   Working with Polynomial Factors in Expressions & Equations: A. Remembering the Polynomial Remainder Theorem (see page 413), we know that for any divisor $(x - a)$, when you plug a into the polynomial dividend, the result will be the remainder. Here, since we are plugging in –2, the divisor must be $(x + 2)$ and the remainder must be 6. This matches choice A.

11   More Word Problems: D. We want to solve the equation $R = \dfrac{T}{T + L}$ for the variable T. First, get rid of the fraction by multiplying both sides by $T + L$. The equation becomes $RT + RL = T$. Now we can subtract RT to get both T terms on the same side. The equation becomes $RL = T - RT$, which factors as $RL = T(1 - R)$. Finally, we can divide both sides by $1 - R$ to get $T = \dfrac{RL}{R-1}$.

12   Absolute Value: D. Absolute value can never be negative, so the value of the function could never be less than –6, –4, or 0, leaving only choice D. You could also try plugging in each answer choice. For choice A, $f(-6) = |3(-6) - 15| = |-18 - 15| = 33$, so in this case, $f(a) > a$. For choice B, $f(-4) = |-12 - 15| = 27$, so $f(a) > a$. For choice C, $f(0) = 15$, so $f(a) > a$. But for choice D, $f(6) = |18 - 15| = 3$, so $f(a) < a$.

13   Function Notation: B. Replace the variable x in the $f(x)$ equation with the function $g(x)$. We get $f(g(x)) = (3x)^2 + 1 = 9x^2 + 1$.

The Tutorverse

14 Working with Polynomials: A. Cross-multiply the original equation and we get $7a + 7b = 9a - 9b$.

Gathering like terms, we get $16b = 2a$. Dividing both sides by 2 and by b, we get $\dfrac{a}{b} = \dfrac{16}{2} = 8$.

15 Imaginary & Complex Numbers: B. To rewrite in $a + bi$ form, we must rationalize the denominator. Multiply the numerator and denominator by the complex conjugate of the denominator:

$\dfrac{(-16 + 4i)}{(5 + 3i)} \cdot \dfrac{(5 - 3i)}{(5 - 3i)} = \dfrac{-80 + 48i + 20i - 12i^2}{25 - 9i^2} = \dfrac{-80 + 68i - 12(-1)}{25 - 9(-1)} = \dfrac{-68 + 68i}{34} = -2 + 2i$. Therefore, $a = -2$.

16 Solving Systems of Equations: 5/18 or 0.28: The two equations must be equivalent. Multiplying the first equation by 6 yields $6ax + 6by = 72$. Since both equations now equal 72, equating the coefficients gives

$6a = 2$ and $6b = 5$. Therefore, $a = \dfrac{1}{3}$ and $b = \dfrac{5}{6}$. $ab = \dfrac{1}{3} \times \dfrac{5}{6} = \dfrac{5}{18}$.

17 Linear Equations, Inequalities, & Systems in Word Problems: 18. To maximize the amount of paint Steve can buy, we must buy the smallest amount of lumber possible, which is 1 bundle. If he buys 1 bundle of lumber for $100, he has $900 left for paint, so $50x = 900$, where x is equal to the number of cans of paint Steve can buy if cans of paint are $50 each. Solving for x results in $x = 18$.

18 Working with Polynomials: 4. Factoring the equation by grouping, we get $x^2(x - 4) + 9(x - 4) = 0$ and then $(x^2 + 9)(x - 4) = 0$. Setting $x^2 + 9 = 0$ results in an imaginary value of x; the only real solution is $x = 4$.

19 Trigonometry: (3/5 or 0.6) It is worth remembering the identities $\sin(x°) = \cos(90° - x°)$ and $\cos(x°) = \sin(90° - x°)$. Therefore, the answer to this problem is the same as the given value.

20 Geometry: 57. In a circle, the degree measure of an arc is equal to the measure of the central angle that intercepts the arc. If central angle BOC is 114°, then arc BC must be 114° as well. The degree measure of an inscribed angle is half the measure of the arc it intercepts. Therefore, if arc BC is 114°, then angle BAC must be 57°.

Math – Calculator

1 Solving Linear Equations & Inequalities: B. We could try to solve for a variable, but there are two, and we don't need to anyway. Take note of the relationship between $2 + 3mx$ and $6 + 9mx$. $2 + 3mx$ is $6 + 9mx$ divided by 3. If we divide the whole inequality by 3 (which is also the greatest common factor of all the terms in the inequality), we get
$4 < 2 + 3mx$, which can be flipped to say $2 + 3mx > 4$.

2 Graphs of Functions: C. We can choose either of the given coordinate points and plug the xy-coordinates into the function. If we choose the first point, substituting –2 for x and 0 for y yields:
$0 = (-2)^3 + 2(-2)^2 + k(-2) + 2$. This gives us $0 = -8 + 8 - 2k + 2$, which simplifies to $0 = -2k + 2$, and finally $k = 1$.

3 Geometry: B. As given on the reference sheet at the beginning of each math section, the volume of each conical cup is $V = \dfrac{1}{3}\pi r^2 h = \dfrac{1}{3}\pi(3)^2(6) \approx 56.55$ cubic centimeters. 1000 cubic centimeters divided by 56.55 cubic centimeters ≈ 17.68 cups. Since only full cups count, the answer is 17 cups.

4 Graphs of Functions: D. Any quadratic function q can be written in the form $q(x) = a(x - h)^2 + k$, where a, h, and k are constants and (h,k) is the vertex of the parabola when q is graphed in the coordinate plane. The vertex is at $(2,-1)$, which gives the value of h and k. This can be checked: $(x - 2)^2 - 1 = x^2 - 4x + 3$.

5 Trigonometry & Radians: A. The angles of a triangle add up to 180 degrees or π radians. Therefore, $\dfrac{\pi}{4} + \dfrac{\pi}{3} + C = \pi$. Simplifying this, we get $\dfrac{7\pi}{12} + C = \pi$ so $C = \dfrac{5\pi}{12}$. Remembering that a full circle (360°) is equal to 2π radians, we can also remember that π radians is equal to 180°, in which case we can figure out that one fourth of that is 45° and one third is 60°.

6   Linear Equations, Inequalities, & Systems in Word Problems: C. If m is the number of comic books Mike owns, then Dylan owns $m + 14$ and their total is represented as $m + m + 14 = 128$. Solving for m yields 57, so Dylan owns 71 comic books.

7   Ratios & Proportions: B. Let x be the number of expected red peas in the 210,000 sample. Set up the proportion $\dfrac{12}{700} = \dfrac{x}{210,000}$. Cross multiplying produces $700x = (12)(210,000)$. Solving for x results in $x = 3,600$.

8   Systems of Equations: A. Replace x in the second equation with the expression that is equal to x in the first equation. The new equation is $y = (2y + 4)^2 + \dfrac{1}{2}(2y + 4) - 2$ which simplifies to

$y = (4y^2 + 16y + 16) + (y + 2) - 2$. After canceling terms, we get $0 = 4y^2 + 16y + 16$. This is equivalent to $4(y + 2)(y + 2) = 0$, so we get $y = -2$.

9   Linear Equations, Inequalities, & Systems in Word Problems: B. If $F = kx$, then plugging in values for force and distance gives us
$2,450 = k(1.5)$. Solving for x results in $x = 1,633.3$.

10   Ratios & Proportions: B. The question asks us to find the percentage change between two numbers. We can use the formula $\dfrac{new - old}{old}$ to determine this. The old price is \$30. To find the new price, there are two calculations to perform. A 20% decrease can be determined by multiplying 0.8 by the price; in this case, $30 \times 0.8 = 24$. From 24, the price was increased 30%, which can be determined by multiplying 1.3 by the price; in this case, $24 \times 1.3 = 31.2$. Substituting into the percentage change formula: $\dfrac{31.2 - 30}{30} = 0.04$ or 4%.

11   Linear Equations, Inequalities, & Systems in Word Problems: A. There are 60 minutes in an hour, so 0.15×60 is equal to the hourly rate for the Wi-Fi. Multiplying by h to determine the total cost for a certain number of hours will yield a value for c that is equal to $0.15(60h)$.

12   Graphs of Functions: A. A parallel line would have the same slope. The above equation intercepts the y-axis at $(5,0)$ and there's a point on this graph at $(1,2)$. One way to find the slope is to use substitution in $y = mx + b$, where m is equal to the slope and b is equal to the y-intercept. So, $2 = m(1) + 5$ and $m = -3$. So the parallel equation would have the same slope, which rules out choice C and D. Choice A rewritten in terms of y is equal to $y = -3x + 4$ and choice B is equal to $y = 3x + 4$, so only choice A is parallel.

13   Ratios & Proportions: C. 2 hours is equal to 120 minutes. After 120 minutes, 28,800 cubic meters have been drained (found by multiplying 120 by 240), leaving 391,200 cubic meters left.

14   Graphs of Functions: B. Since both models are linear equations, the year they had the same average number of students per classroom can be determined by solving for x when $0.45x + 22.5 = 0.55x + 22.1$, which simplifies to $x = 4$. So the year both schools had the same average number of students per classroom was 2004.

15   Solving Linear Equations & Inequalities: C. If we translate the first sentence into an algebraic equation, we get
$7 + 5x = -13$, so $x = -4$. But that's not the answer, because the questions asks us to find $25 + 3x$, which is $25 + 3(-4) = 13$.

16   More Word Problems: C. Since t is measured in days, and the problem refers to one week, we should plug in $t = 7$ days. We get $S = B(0.95)^7 = 0.6983B \approx 0.70B$. This means that 70% of the bananas are fresh enough to sell, so 30% are no longer fresh enough to sell.

17   More Word Problems: B. Last year the value of S was $B(0.95)^d$. This year it is $B(0.95)^{2d}$, which is equivalent to $B(0.95)^{d+d}$, which is also $B(0.95)^d \times B(0.95)^d$. Therefore, the value from last year has been multiplied by 0.95^d.

The Tutorverse

18 Equations of Circles: A. Since we see that all the answer choices look almost the same except for the signs, we know this will be a process-of-elimination problem. Since the center of the circle is (7,1), we know the equation must start with $(x-7)^2 + (y-1)^2$. If we distribute both sets of parentheses, we get $x^2 - 14x + 49 + y^2 - 2y + 1$. Answer choice A is the only one that has the terms $-14x$ and $-2y$. We can eliminate all other answer choices and not even worry about the radius.

19 Function Notation: B. Observe that $f(x) = 14x - 7 = 7(2x-1)$ so $f(x)$ is divisible by $2x - 1$. Therefore, choice A is wrong. Similarly, $g(x) = 10x - 5 = 5(2x-1)$ so $g(x)$ is divisible by $2x - 1$. Since both $f(x)$ and $g(x)$ are divisible by $2x - 1$, it follows that their sum and product (choices D and C) must be divisible by $2x - 1$. The only remaining choice is B. This is not divisible by $2x - 1$ because $f(g(x)) = 14(10x - 5) - 7 = 70(2x-1) - 7$. Thus, $f(g(x))$ has a remainder of -7 when divided by $2x - 1$.

20 Additional Data Analysis & Statistics: D. According to the table there were $82 + 33$ students who passed the exam. Of those, 33 did not attend the review session. Therefore, the probability that the person chosen did *not* attend the review session is 33 out of 115.

21 Additional Data Analysis & Statistics: B. There are a total of 400 data points provided, so the median will be the average of the 200th and 201st data points. When the data points are sorted in order, there will be one hundred forty 0's, and ninety 1's. Therefore, the 200th and 201st values are 1, so the median is 1.

22 Additional Data Analysis & Statistics: B. When survey participants are selected at random from a larger population, the sample statistics calculated from the survey can be generalized to the larger population. Since 25 out of 200 students (or 1/8) surveyed at each school have 4 pets, one can estimate that this ratio holds for all students. So, to estimate the number of students with 4 pets at Pembroke school: $\frac{1}{8} \times 1,800 = 225$ and Elkwood School: $\frac{1}{8} \times 2,000 = 250$. Since $250 - 225 = 25$, the researcher can estimate that there are 25 more students at Elkwood School with 4 pets than at Pembroke school.

23 Working with Polynomials: D. $(2x + 5)^3 = (2x+5)^2 (2x+5) = (4x^2 + 20x + 25)(2x+5)$. This equals $8x^3 + 20x^2 + 40x^2 + 100x + 50x + 125 = 8x^3 + 60x^2 + 150x + 125$.

24 Additional Data Analysis & Statistics: D. It should be clear that the numbers are decreasing, so we can eliminate choices A and C. The problem says that subscribership is decreasing by 25% each year. Whenever growth or decay is by a percentage, that is an exponential change, not a linear one, since a linear change occurs when the data changes by a fixed number at each interval. We can also see in the chart that the decrease in subscribership is by a smaller amount every year, not a consistent amount, so the decrease, or decay, in subscribership is exponential, not linear.

25 Linear Equations, Inequalities, & Systems in Word Problems: C. To solve, find the number of weeks after delivery when $g = q$ by solving for x, so $60 + 0.3x = 62.25 + 0.15x$. Simplifying yields $0.15x = 2.25$, so $x = 15$. The price of granite 15 weeks after delivery is $60 + 0.3(15) = 64.5$, so the price is $64.50/sq. ft.

26 Interpreting Graphs & Tables: B. The substance decays by a constant amount, so that eliminates choices C and D. In the table, the weight decreases by 1.15 ounces every 5 days, so the weight will decrease 0.23 ounces each day. Therefore, the weight of the sample can be shown by a function of t as the original weight minus 0.23 multiplied by the number of days, t.

27 Linear & Exponential Growth: C. Answer A is incorrect because it results in a constant amount of annual pay. Answer B is incorrect because it results in a fixed amount of increased annual pay. Answer D is incorrect because the number of employees increases by a fixed amount each year. Answer C is correct because the amount of increase in pay depends on the amount of increase from the previous day, so it is compounding.

28 Interpreting Graphs & Tables: D. Even though the recorded temperatures are different, the data points for both thermometers go up and down by roughly the same amount.

29 Interpreting Graphs & Tables: C. One way to solve is to use the equation for the line of best: Since x is equal to the customer rating, when $x = 4.5$, $y = 75 - 10(4.5) = 30$. We can also find 4.5 on the horizontal axis of the graph, follow it up to the line of best fit, then over to the vertical axis. 30 is the closest approximation.

The Tutorverse

30 Interpreting Graphs & Tables: C. Count how many data points are above the line of best fit. Choice A provides the number of data points on the line, while choice B provides the amount below and choice D the total number of data points.

31 Ratios & Proportions: 160. If $y = 128$ and $x = 16$, then we just plug those values into the equation to find k: $128 = k(16)$, which results in $k = 8$. Now that we know what the value of k is, we want to find the value of y when x is increased by 25% (which means it is increased from 16 to 20). $y = 8(20) = 160$.

32 Linear Equations, Inequalities, & Systems in Word Problems: 47. Set up an inequality to solve: $240x \leq 12{,}000 \leq 260x$, where x is equal to the number of pages. The least number of pages would require the most words per page, so $12{,}000 \leq 260x$, giving us $46.15 \leq x$. Since whole pages would be necessary to complete the document, 47 is the smallest number of pages needed.

33 More Word Problems: 9/16. The taller person's body mass index is $\dfrac{m}{h^2}$. The shorter person's body mass index is $\dfrac{m}{\left(\frac{3}{4}h\right)^2}$. Therefore, the ratio is $\dfrac{m}{h^2} \div \dfrac{m}{\left(\frac{3}{4}h\right)^2} = \dfrac{m}{h^2} \cdot \dfrac{\left(\frac{3}{4}h\right)^2}{m} = \left(\dfrac{3}{4}\right)^2 = \dfrac{9}{16}$.

34 Additional Data Analysis & Statistics: 4. If $\dfrac{3}{4}$ of the distance Sadie ran on Monday was in the park, and she ran 3 miles in the park Tuesday, then she ran a total of 4 miles on Monday. ($3 \div \dfrac{3}{4} = 4$). If she ran 10 miles over the course of both days, then she ran 6 miles Tuesday. If 2 of those miles were on the street, then 4 were in the park.

35 Geometry: 9.9. This problem is describing a right triangle. It has given the lengths of two sides and is asking you to find the third side. Using the reference information at the beginning of each math section, we can use the formula $a^2 + b^2 = c^2$, where c is the hypotenuse, to find the missing side: $a^2 + 13^2 = 29^2$. Solving for a results in approximately 25.923. The problem is asking how many MORE miles the detour is, so we add the two legs of his detour and subtract the sum from his normal commute: $29 - (13 + 25.9) = 9.9$.

36 Ratios & Proportions: 4.5. Write the given rate as a ratio, $\dfrac{90 \text{ yards}}{1 \text{ min}}$, and multiply by identity fractions in order to cancel out unwanted units and replace with the units that the question is asking for: $\dfrac{90 \text{ yards}}{1 \text{ min}} \cdot \dfrac{1 \text{ min}}{60 \text{ sec}} \cdot \dfrac{3 \text{ ft}}{1 \text{ yard}} = \dfrac{270 \text{ ft}}{60 \text{ sec}}$. This simplifies to $4.5 \dfrac{\text{ft}}{\text{sec}}$.

37 Linear & Exponential Growth: 7,639. University A grew by 3% per year for 35 years, so its 2015 student body is $10{,}000(1.03)^{35} \approx 28{,}138.6 \approx 28{,}139$. University B grew by 300 students per year for 35 years, so their 2015 student body is $10{,}000 + 300(35) = 20{,}500$. The difference is $28{,}139 - 20{,}500 = 7{,}639$.

38 Exponents & Radicals: 1296. If $y = 6$, then $36 = \sqrt{x}$. Squaring both sides of the equation yields $1{,}296 = x$.

Made in the USA
Charleston, SC
11 February 2017